My Beloved World

Sonia Sotomayor

LARGE PRINT PRESS
A part of Gale, Cengage Learning

GALE
CENGAGE Learning·

Detroit • New York • San Francisco • New Haven, Conn • Waterville, Maine • London

GALE
CENGAGE Learning·

LIBRARY OF CONGRESS CATALOGING-IN-PUBLICATION DATA

Sotomayor, Sonia, 1954–
    My beloved world / By Sonia Sotomayor.
    pages cm
    ISBN 978-1-4104-5939-8 (hardcover) — ISBN 1-4104-5939-X (hardcover)
    1. Sotomayor, Sonia, 1954– 2. Hispanic American judges—Biography.
    3. Hispanic American women—Biography. 4. Judges—United States—
    Biography. 5. United States. Supreme Court—Officials and employees—
    Biography. 6. Large type books. I. Title.
    KF8745.S67A31 2013
    347.73'2634092—dc23
    [B]   2013013267

ISBN 13: 978-1-59413-703-7 (pbk. : alk. paper)
ISBN 10: 1-59413-703-X (pbk. : alk. paper)

Published in 2014 by arrangement with Alfred A. Knopf, Inc., a division of Random House, Inc.

Perdonadle al desterrado
ese dulce frenesí:
vuelvo a mi mundo adorado,
y yo estoy enamorado
de la tierra en que nací.

Forgive the exile
this sweet frenzy:
I return to my beloved world,
in love with the land where I was born.

— from "To Puerto Rico (I Return),"
by José Gautier Benítez

PREFACE

Since my appointment to the Supreme Court, I have spoken to a wide variety of groups in different settings, answering all sorts of questions. Many people, predictably, have asked about the law, the Court, and my journey as a judge. But many more, to my surprise, have asked about my personal story, curious to know how I had managed and been shaped by various circumstances in my early life, especially the ones that didn't naturally promise success.

At a conference on juvenile diabetes, a six-year-old asked plaintively if living with the disease ever gets easier. Elsewhere, a child who had recently lost a parent asked how I had coped with losing my father at an early age. Minority students have asked what it is like to live between two worlds: How do I stay connected to my community? Have I ever experienced discrimination? Many young lawyers, men as well as women, have

7

asked how I balance my personal life with the demands of career. Most perplexing of all was the question that inspired this book: How much did I owe to having had a happy childhood? I struggled with that one; until this book I have not spoken publicly about some of my darker experiences growing up, and I would not have considered myself unqualifiedly happy as a child. Ultimately, though, I realized I did have sources of deep happiness, and these bred in me an optimism that proved stronger than any adversity.

Underlying all these questions was a sense that my life's story touches people because it resonates with their own circumstances. The challenges I have faced — among them material poverty, chronic illness, and being raised by a single mother — are not uncommon, but neither have they kept me from uncommon achievements. For many it is a source of hope to see someone realize her dreams while bearing such burdens. Having caught people's attention in this way, I've thought long and hard about what lessons my life might hold for others, young people especially. How is it that adversity has spurred me on instead of knocking me down? What are the sources of my own hope and optimism? Most essentially, my purpose in writing is to make my hopeful example accessible. People who live in difficult circumstances need to know that happy endings are possible.

A student recently posed another question that gave me pause: "Given that there are only nine Supreme Court Justices, each with life tenure, can anyone realistically aspire to such a goal? How do we hold on to dreams that, statistically, are almost impossible?" As I tell in these pages, the dream I first followed was to become a judge, which itself seemed far-fetched until it actually happened. The idea of my becoming a Supreme Court Justice — which, indeed, as a goal would inevitably elude the vast majority of aspirants — never occurred to me except as the remotest of fantasies. But experience has taught me that you cannot value dreams according to the odds of their coming true. Their real value is in stirring within us the will to aspire. That will, wherever it finally leads, does at least move you forward. And after a time you may recognize that the proper measure of success is not how much you've closed the distance to some far-off goal but the quality of what you've done today.

I have ventured to write more intimately about my personal life than is customary for a member of the Supreme Court, and with that candor comes a measure of vulnerability. I will be judged as a human being by what readers find here. There are hazards to openness, but they seem minor compared with the possibility that some readers may find comfort, perhaps even inspiration, from a close examination of how an ordinary person, with strengths and weaknesses like anyone else, has managed an extraordinary journey.

My law clerks will no doubt be aghast to see how often I've broken my own very strict rules about formal writing, which include injunctions against the use of contractions and split infinitives. Every rule, however, is bound by context, and a personal memoir requires a different style than a legal opinion.

Neither is a memoir the same as a biography, which aims for the most objective, factual account of a life. A memoir, as I understand it, makes no pretense of denying its subjectivity. Its matter is one person's memory, and memory by nature is selective and colored by emotion. Others who participated in the events I describe will no doubt remember some details differently, though I hope we would agree on the essential truths. I have taken no liberties with the past as I remember it, used no fictional devices beyond reconstructing conversations from memory. I have not blended characters, or bent chronology to convenience. And yet I have tried to tell a good story. If particular friends or family members find themselves not mentioned, or are disappointed to see their roles rendered as less prominent than they might have expected, I hope they will understand that the needs of a clear and focused telling must outweigh even an abundance of feeling.

Some readers may be disappointed that I have chosen to end this story twenty years ago, when I first became a judge. I've made this choice because of the personal nature of what I wish to tell. For though I believe my personal growth has continued since that time, it was by then that the person I remain was essentially formed. On the other hand, I have no such perspective or sense of completion regarding my judicial career. Each stage of it — first on the district court, then on the court of appeals, and now on the Supreme Court — has been unique; and I can't say with any certainty how any part will inform what I may yet accomplish as a Justice. In the meanwhile, it seems inappropriate to reflect on a course still taking shape, let alone on the political drama attending my nomination to the High Court, however curious some may be about that.

A final, more private, motive for writing this book bears mention. This new phase of my career has brought with it a profoundly disconcerting shift in my life. The experience of living in the public eye was impossible to anticipate fully and has, at times, been overwhelming. The psychological hazards of such a life are notorious, and it seems wise to pause and reflect on the path that has brought me to this juncture and to count the blessings that have made me who I am, taking care not to lose sight of them, or of my best self, as I move forward.

PROLOGUE

I was barely awake, and my mother was already screaming. I knew Papi would start yelling in a second. That much was routine, but the substance of their argument was new, and it etched that morning into my memory.

"You have to learn how to give it to her, Juli. I can't be here all the time!"

"I'm afraid to hurt her. My hands are trembling." It was true. When my father made his first attempt at giving me the insulin shot the day before, his hands were shaking so much I was afraid he would miss my arm entirely and stab me in the face. He had to jab hard just to steady his aim.

"Whose fault is it your hands tremble?"

Uh-oh, here we go.

"You're the nurse, Celina! You know how to do these things."

Actually, when Mami gave me the shot my first morning home from the hospital, she was so nervous that she jabbed me even harder, and hurt me even worse, than Papi would the next day.

"That's right, I'm the nurse. I have to work and help support this family. I have to do everything! But I can't be here all the time, Juli, and she's going to need this for the rest of her life. So you better figure it out."

The needles hurt, but the screaming was worse. It made me feel tired, carrying around the weight of their sadness. It was bad enough when they were fighting about the milk, or the housework, or the money, or the drinking. The last thing I wanted was for them to fight about me.

"I swear, Juli, you'll kill that child if you don't learn how to do this!"

As usual, she walked away and slammed the door behind her, so she had to scream even louder to continue the fight.

If my parents couldn't pick up the syringe without panicking, an even darker prospect loomed: my grandmother wouldn't be up to the job either. That would be the end of my weekly sleepovers at her apartment and my only escape from the gloom at home. It then dawned on me: if I needed to have these shots every day for the rest of my life, the only way I'd survive was to do it myself.

14

The first step, I knew, was to sterilize the needle and syringe. Not yet eight years old, I was barely tall enough to see the top of the stove, and I wasn't sure how to perform the tricky maneuver with match and gas to light the burner. So I dragged a chair the couple of feet from table to stove — the kitchen was tiny — and climbed up to figure it out. The two small pots for Mami's *café con leche* were sitting there, getting cold while they fought, the coffee staining its little cloth sack in one pot, *la nata* forming a wrinkled skin on top of the milk in the other.

"Sonia! What are you doing? You'll burn the building down, *nena*!"

"I'm going to give myself the shot, Mami." That silenced her for a moment.

"Do you know how?" She looked at me levelly, seriously.

"I think so. At the hospital they had me practice on an orange."

My mother showed me how to hold the match while turning the dial, to make the flame whoosh to life in a blue ring. Together we filled the pot with water, enough to cover the syringe and needle and some extra in case it boiled down. She directed me to wait for the bubbles and only then to start counting five minutes by the clock. I had learned

15

how to tell time the year before, in first grade. After the water had boiled long enough, she said, I would still need to wait for the syringe to cool. I watched the pot and the invisibly slow creep of the clock's hand until tiny, delicate chains of bubbles rose from the glass syringe and the needle, my mind racing through a hundred other things as I marked the time.

Watching water boil would try the patience of any child, but I was as physically restless as I was mentally and had well earned the family nickname Ají — hot pepper — for my eagerness to jump headlong into any mischief impelled by equal parts curiosity and rambunctiousness. But believing that my life now depended on this morning ritual, I would soon figure out how to manage the time efficiently: to get dressed, brush my teeth, and get ready for school in the intervals while the pot boiled or cooled. I probably learned more self-discipline from living with diabetes than I ever did from the Sisters of Charity.

Fainting in church was how it all started. We had just stood up to sing, and I felt as if I were suffocating. The singing seemed far away, and then the light from the stained-glass windows turned yellow. Everything turned yellow, and then it went black.

When I opened my eyes, all I could see was the principal, Sister Marita Joseph, and Sister Elizabeth Regina, their worried faces upside down and pale inside their black bonnets. I was lying on the tile floor in the sacristy, shivering cold from the water splashed all over my face. And scared. So they called my mother.

Although I went to Mass every Sunday, which was obligatory for students at Blessed Sacrament School, my parents never did. When my mother arrived, the Sisters made a big fuss. Had this ever happened before? Come to think of it, there was the time I'd fallen off the slide, the sudden dizziness as I stepped over the top of the ladder before the ground came rushing up to me in a long moment of panic . . . She had to take me to the doctor, the nuns insisted.

Dr. Fisher was already firmly established as a family hero. All of our relatives were under his care at one time or another, and his house calls did as much to ease fears and panics as they did aches and pains. A German immigrant, he was an old-fashioned country doctor who just happened to be practicing in the Bronx. Dr. Fisher asked a lot of questions, and Mami told him I was losing weight and always thirsty and that I had started wetting the

17

bed, which was so mortifying that I would try not to fall asleep.

Dr. Fisher sent us to the lab at Prospect Hospital, where my mother worked. I didn't see trouble coming, because I perceived Mr. Rivera in the lab to be a friend of mine. I thought I could trust him, unlike Mrs. Gibbs, my mother's supervisor, who had tried to hide the needle behind her back when I'd had my tonsils out. But when he tied a rubber tube around my arm, I realized this was no ordinary shot. The syringe looked almost as big as my arm, and as he got closer, I could see that the needle was sliced off at an angle with the hole gaping like a little mouth at the end of it.

As he approached, I screamed, "No!" Knocking the chair back, I ran across the hall and right out the front door. It seemed as if half the hospital were running right behind me, shouting "Catch her!" but I didn't turn around to look. I just dove under a parked car.

I could see their shoes. One of them bent down and stuck his nose into the shadow of the undercarriage. Shoes all around now, and hands reaching under the car. But I scrunched up like a turtle, until someone caught me by the foot. I was hollering so loud as they dragged me back to the lab that I couldn't have hollered any louder when the needle went in.

When we went back to Dr. Fisher after they took my blood, it was the first time I'd ever seen my mother cry. I was outside in the waiting room, but his office door was open a crack. I could hear her voice break and see her shoulders quaking. The nurse closed the door when she noticed I was watching, but I'd seen enough to understand that something was seriously wrong. Then Dr. Fisher opened the door and called me in. He explained that there was sugar in my blood, that it's called diabetes, and that I would have to change the way I ate. He reassured me that the bed-wetting would end when we had things under control: it was just the body's way of getting rid of excess blood sugar. He even told me that he also had diabetes, although I understood later that he had the more common type 2, while I had the rarer juvenile diabetes, or type 1, in which the pancreas stops producing insulin, making daily injections of insulin necessary.

Then he took a bottle of soda from the cupboard behind him and popped the top off. "Taste it. It's called No-Cal. Just like soda but without sugar."

I took a sip. "I don't really think so." Poor

19

Dr. Fisher. My mother insisted that we always be polite even if that meant softening a strong opinion, a lesson that stuck with me. Perhaps my eventual enjoyment of being a litigator owes something to the license it gave me to disagree more openly with people.

"Well, there are lots of other flavors. Even chocolate."

I thought to myself: This doesn't add up. He's making it sound as if it's no big deal. Just skip dessert and drink a different soda. Why is my mother so upset?

We went straight from Dr. Fisher's office to my grandmother's home. Abuelita tucked me into her bed, even though it was the middle of the afternoon and I had long outgrown naps. She closed the curtains, and I lay there in the half dark listening as the front door kept opening and voices filled the living room. I could hear my father's sisters, Titi Carmen and Titi Gloria. My cousin Charlie was there too, and Gallego, my step-grandfather. Abuelita sounded terribly upset. She was talking about my mother as if she weren't there, and since I didn't hear Mami's voice at all, it was clear that she had left.

"It runs in families, *como una maldición.*"

"This curse is from Celina's side, for sure,

not ours."

There was speculation about whether Mami's own mother had died of this terrible affliction and talk of a special herb that might cure it. Abuelita knew all about healing with herbs. The least sniffle or stomachache had her brewing noxious potions that would leave me with a lifelong aversion to tea of any sort. Now she was scheming with my aunts to get word to her brother in Puerto Rico. She would tell him where to find the plant, which he was to pick at dawn before boarding a flight from San Juan the same day so she could prepare it at the peak of potency. He actually pulled it off, but sadly Abuelita's herbal remedy would prove ineffective, and this failure of her skill in a case so close to her heart would disturb her deeply.

Abuelita's obvious anxiety that afternoon, and the talk of my other grandmother's death, did achieve one thing: it made me realize how serious this situation was. Now my mother's crying made sense to me, and I was shaken. I was even more shaken when I learned that I had to be hospitalized to stabilize my blood sugar levels, which was routine in those days.

In 1962, when I was first diagnosed, the

treatment of juvenile diabetes was primitive by today's standards, and life expectancy was much shorter. Nevertheless, Dr. Fisher had managed to locate the best care for the disease in New York City, and possibly in the entire country. He discovered that the Albert Einstein College of Medicine, a leader in juvenile diabetes research, ran a clinic at Jacobi Medical Center, a public hospital, which by luck happened to be located in the Bronx. The vastness of Jacobi Medical Center awed me. It made Prospect Hospital seem like a dollhouse.

Every morning, starting at eight o'clock, they would draw my blood repeatedly for testing. Hourly, they used the thick needle with the rubber tube on my arm, and every half hour they would slice my finger with a lance for a smaller sample. It continued until noon, and the next day they did the same thing over again. This went on for an entire week and part of the next. I didn't holler and I didn't run, but I have never forgotten the pain.

Other things they did, though less painful, seemed strange. They attached electrodes to my head. They brought me to a classroom in the hospital where I sat facing rows of young doctors who stared at me as an older doctor lectured about diabetes, about the tests they had done and more they still had to do. He rattled off terms like "ketones," "acidosis," "hypo-this and hyper-that," and much else that I didn't understand, all the while feeling very much the guinea pig and terrified.

But even more than the clinical procedures, it was my absence from school for so long that set off my inner alarm. I knew I had to be seriously sick for my mother to allow it. School was just as important as work, she insisted, and she never once stayed home from work. Equally worrying, she brought me a present almost every day I was in the hospital: a coloring book, a puzzle, once even a comic book, which meant she was thinking hard about what I would like instead of what she wanted me to have.

My very last day at the hospital started again at eight o'clock with the big needle and the lances. My arm was aching, and my fingers were burning right from the very beginning. I made it through the first two hours, but just as they were lining up their instruments for the ten o'clock torture, something inside me broke. After all those days of being brave and holding it in, I started crying. And once I started, I couldn't stop. My mother must have heard me because she burst in, and I flew sobbing into her arms. "Enough!" she said, fiercer than I'd ever seen her. Fiercer even than when she fought with my father. "We stop now. She's done." She said it in a way that nobody — not the lab technician standing there with the syringe in his hand, not any doctor in Jacobi Medical Center — was going to argue with her.

"Do you know how much to give, Sonia?"

"Up to this line here."

"That's right. But do it carefully. You can't give too little and you can't give too much. And you have to be careful, Sonia, not to let any bubbles get into the needle. That's dangerous."

"I know how to do this part. But it doesn't make sense to say I'm *giving* it, Mami. I'm the one who's *getting* the shot."

"Whatever you say, Sonia."

"I'm doing both."

And I did. I held my breath, and I gave myself the shot.

ONE

I was not yet eight years old when I was diagnosed with diabetes. To my family, the disease was a deadly curse. To me, it was more a threat to the already fragile world of my childhood, a state of constant tension punctuated by explosive discord, all of it caused by my father's alcoholism and my mother's response to it, whether family fight or emotional flight. But the disease also inspired in me a kind of precocious self-reliance that is not uncommon in children who feel the adults around them to be unreliable.

There are uses to adversity, and they don't reveal themselves until tested. Whether it's serious illness, financial hardship, or the simple constraint of parents who speak limited English, difficulty can tap unsuspected strengths. It doesn't always, of course: I've seen life beat people down until they can't get up. But I have never had to face anything that could overwhelm the native optimism and stubborn perseverance I was blessed with.

At the same time, I would never claim to be self-made — quite the contrary: at every stage of my life, I have always felt that the support I've drawn from those closest to me has made the decisive difference between success and failure. And this was true from the beginning. Whatever their limitations and frailties, those who raised me loved me and did the best they knew how. Of that I am sure.

The world that I was born into was a tiny microcosm of Hispanic New York City. A tight few blocks in the South Bronx bounded the lives of my extended family: my grandmother, matriarch of the tribe, and her second husband, Gallego, her daughters and sons. My playmates were my cousins. We spoke Spanish at home, and many in my family spoke virtually no English. My parents had both come to New York from Puerto Rico in 1944, my mother in the Women's Army Corps, my father with his family in search of work as part of a huge migration from the island, driven by economic hardship.

My brother, now Juan Luis Sotomayor Jr., M.D., but to me forever Junior, was born three years after I was. I found him a nuisance as only a little brother can be, following me everywhere, mimicking my every gesture, eavesdropping on every conversation. In retrospect, he was actually a quiet child who made few demands on anyone's attention. My mother always said that compared with me, caring for Junior was like taking a vacation. Once, when he was still tiny and I wasn't much bigger, my exasperation with him inspired me to lead him into the hallway outside the apartment and shut the door. I don't know how much later it was that my mother found him, sitting right where I'd left him, sucking his thumb. But I do know I got walloped that day.

But that was just domestic politics. On the playground, or once he started school at Blessed Sacrament with me, I watched out for him, and any bully thinking of messing with him would have to mix it up with me first. If I got beat up on Junior's account, I would settle things with him later, but no one was going to lay a hand on him except me.

Around the time that Junior was born, we moved to a newly constructed public housing project in Soundview, just a ten-minute drive from our old neighborhood. The

27

Bronxdale Houses sprawled over three large city blocks: twenty-eight buildings, each seven stories tall with eight apartments to a floor. My mother saw the projects as a safer, cleaner, brighter alternative to the decaying tenement where we had lived. My grandmother Abuelita, however, saw this move as a venture into far and alien territory, *el jurutungo viejo* for all practical purposes. My mother should never have made us move, she said, because in the old neighborhood there was life on the streets and family nearby; in the projects we were isolated.

I knew well enough that we were isolated, but that condition had more to do with my father's drinking and the shame attached to it. It constrained our lives as far back as my memory reaches. We almost never had visitors. My cousins never spent the night at our home as I did at theirs. Even Ana, my mother's best friend, never came over, though she lived in the projects too, in the building kitty-corner from ours, and took care of my brother, Junior, and me after school. We always went to her place, never the other way around.

The only exception to this rule was Alfred. Alfred was my first cousin — the son of my mother's sister, Titi Aurora. And just as Titi Aurora was much older than Mami, and more of a mother to her than a sister, Alfred, being sixteen years older than I, acted more as an uncle to me than a cousin. Sometimes my father would ask Alfred to bring him a bottle from the liquor store. We counted on Alfred a lot, in part because my father avoided driving. This annoyed me, as it clearly contributed to our isolation — and what's the point of having a car if you never drive it? I didn't understand until I was older that his drinking was probably the reason.

My father would cook dinner when he got home from work; he was an excellent cook and could re-create from memory any new dish he encountered as well as the Puerto Rican standards he no doubt picked up in Abuelita's kitchen. I loved every dish he made without exception, even his liver and onions, which Junior hated and shoveled over to me when Papi's back was turned. But as soon as dinner was over, the dishes still piled in the sink, he would shut himself in the bedroom. We wouldn't see him again until he came out to tell us to get ready for bed. It was just Junior and I every night, doing homework and not much else. Junior wasn't much of a conversationalist yet. Eventually, we got a television, which helped to fill the silence.

My mother's way of coping was to avoid being at home with my father. She worked the night shift as a practical nurse at Prospect Hospital and often on weekends too. When she wasn't working, she would drop us off at Abuelita's or sometimes at her sister Aurora's apartment and then disappear for hours with another of my aunts. Even though my mother and I shared the same bed every night (Junior slept in the other room with Papi), she might as well have been a log, lying there with her back to me. My father's neglect made me sad, but I intuitively understood that he could not help himself; my mother's neglect made me angry at her. She was beautiful, always elegantly dressed, seemingly strong and decisive. She was the one who moved us to the projects. Unlike my aunts, she chose to work. She was the one who insisted we go to Catholic school. Unfairly perhaps, because I knew nothing then of my mother's own story, I expected more from her.

However much was said at home, and loudly, much also went unsaid, and in that atmosphere I was a watchful child constantly scanning the adults for cues and listening in on their conversations. My sense of security depended on what information I could glean, any clue dropped inadvertently

30

when they didn't realize a child was paying attention. My aunts and my mother would gather in Abuelita's kitchen, drinking coffee and gossiping. "*¡No me molestes!* Go play in the other room now," an aunt would say, shooing me away, but I overheard much regardless: how my father had broken the lock on Titi Gloria's liquor cabinet, ruining her favorite piece of furniture; how whenever Junior and I slept over with our cousins, my father would phone every fifteen minutes all night long, asking, "Did you feed them? Did you give them a bath?" I knew well enough that my aunts and my grandmother were all prone to exaggeration. It wasn't really every fifteen minutes, but Papi did call a lot, as I gathered from my aunts' exasperated and mechanically reassuring side of the conversations.

The gossip would then take a familiar turn, my grandmother saying something like "Maybe if Celina ever came home, he wouldn't be drinking every night. If those kids had a mother who ever cooked a meal, Juli wouldn't be worrying about them all night." As much as I adored Abuelita — and no one resented my mother's absence more than I did — I couldn't bear this constant blaming. Abuelita was unconditionally loyal to blood kin. Her sons' wives were not

31

outside the ambit of her protection, but they didn't enjoy the same immunity from prosecution. And often my mother's efforts to please Abuelita — whether a generously chosen gift or her ready services as a nurse — went dimly acknowledged. Even being Abuelita's favorite, I felt exposed and unmoored when she criticized my mother, whom I struggled to understand and forgive myself. In fact, she and I wouldn't achieve a final reconciliation before working on it for many years.

My surveillance activities became family legend the Christmas that Little Miss Echo arrived. I had seen the doll with its concealed tape recorder advertised on television and begged for it. It was the hottest gift of the season, and Titi Aurora had searched far and wide for a store that still had one in stock. I sent my cousin Miriam into the kitchen with the doll to bug the adults' conversation, knowing that I would have been immediately suspect. But before anything could be recorded, Miriam cracked and gave me up at the first question, and I got walloped anyway.

One overheard conversation had a lasting effect, though I now remember it only dimly. My father was sick: he had passed out, and Mami took him to the hospital.

Tío Vitín and Tío Benny came to get Junior and me, and they were talking in the elevator about how our home was a pigsty, with dishes in the sink and no toilet paper. They spoke as if we weren't there. When I realized what they were saying, my stomach lurched with shame. After that I washed the dishes every night, even the pots and pans, as soon as we finished dinner. I also dusted the living room once a week. Even though no one ever came over, the house was always clean. And when I went shopping with Papi on Fridays, I made sure we bought toilet paper. And milk. More than enough milk.

The biggest fight my parents ever had was because of the milk. At dinnertime, Papi was pouring a glass for me, and his hands were shaking so badly the milk spilled all over the table. I cleaned up the mess, and he tried again with the same result. "Papi, please don't!" I kept repeating. It was all I could do to keep myself from crying; I was utterly powerless to stop him. "Papi, I don't want any milk!" But he didn't stop until the carton was empty. When my mother got home from work later and there was no milk for her coffee, all hell broke loose. Papi was the one who had spilled the milk, but I was the one who felt guilty.

Two

Abuelita was going to cook for a party, and she wanted me to come with her to buy the chickens. I was the only one who ever went with her to the *vivero.*

I loved Abuelita, totally and without reservation, and her apartment on Southern Boulevard was a safe haven from my parents' storms at home. Since those years, I have come to believe that in order to thrive, a child must have at least one adult in her life who shows her unconditional love, respect, and confidence. For me it was Abuelita. I was determined to grow up to be just like her, to age with the same ungraying, exuberant grace. Not that we looked much alike: she had very dark eyes, darker than mine, and a long face with a pointed nose, framed by long straight hair — nothing like my pudgy nose and short, curly mop. But otherwise we recognized in each other a twin spirit and enjoyed a bond beyond explanation, a deep emotional resonance that sometimes seemed telepathic. We were so much alike, in fact, that people called me Mercedita — little Mercedes — which was a source of great pride for me.

Nelson, who among my many cousins was closest to me in age as well as my inseparable co-conspirator in every adventure, also had a special connection with Abuelita. But even Nelson never wanted to go with Abuelita to the *vivero* on Saturday mornings because of the smell. It wasn't just the chickens that smelled. They had baby goats in pens and pigeons and ducks and rabbits in cages stacked up against a long wall. The cages were stacked so high that Abuelita would climb up a ladder on wheels to see into the top rows. The birds would all be squawking and clucking and flapping and screeching. There were feathers in the air and sticking to the wet floor, which was slippery when they hosed it down, and there were turkeys with mean eyes watching you. Abuelita inspected all the chickens to find a plump and lively one.

"*Mira,* Sonia, see that one in the corner just sitting there with droopy eyes?"

"He looks like he's falling asleep."

"That's a bad sign. But this one, see how

he's ready to fight the others when they come close? He's feisty and fat, and I promise you he's tasty."

After Abuelita picked out the very best chicken, it was my job to watch them butcher it while she waited in line for eggs. In a room all closed up in glass, a man stood breaking necks, one after another, and a machine plucked the feathers. Another man cleaned the birds, and another weighed each one and wrapped it up in paper. It was a fast-moving line, as in a factory. I had to watch carefully to make sure that the chicken we'd chosen was the one we got in the end. I was supposed to tell Abuelita if they mixed them up, but it never happened.

We would walk back under the criss-crossed shadows of the train tracks overhead, up Westchester Avenue toward Southern Boulevard and home — which is what Abuelita's house felt like to me. Of course Abuelita's house wasn't a real house like the one her daughter Titi Gloria lived in, in the far northern part of the Bronx, with a front porch and rosebushes. Abuelita lived in a five-story tenement, three apartments to a floor, with a fire escape that zigzagged up the front, like our old building on Kelly Street, where we lived before moving to the projects.

As we walked back, Abuelita would stop to choose vegetables from the crates that were lined up on the sidewalk. For almost every meal she fried *tostones,* so we'd buy green plantains, and also peppers, some green ones and some little sweet ones, and onions, tomatoes, *recao,* and garlic to make *sofrito.* She would always haggle, and though she made it sound as if she were complaining about the quality and how expensive everything was, by the end she'd be laughing with the *vendedor.* All these years later, an open market still stirs in me the urge to haggle the way I learned from Abuelita.

"*¿Sonia, quieres una china?*"

Abuelita loved oranges, but they were expensive most of the year, so we would buy just one to share as a treat, and she'd ask me to choose. My father taught me how to choose fruit — how to make sure it's ripe by smelling its sweetness. My father had shown me how to choose good meat too, with enough fat for flavor, and how to recognize if it's not fresh. I went grocery shopping with Papi on Fridays, which was payday. Those shopping trips were the best times of the week for me, not counting my days at Abuelita's. Papi and I would walk to the new Pathmark that was built on the empty lot near our projects and come home with our cart filled. I'd pull the cart while Papi toted the extra bags that didn't fit.

I could tell we were almost back at Abuelita's when I saw the marquee across the street, though we never went to see movies there because of the prostitutes standing around. When my cousin Miriam — Nelson's sister and Titi Carmen's daughter — asked me what "prostitute" meant, I wasn't sure either, but I knew it was bad and that they wore very short skirts and very high heels and lots of makeup. We would figure out more of what the occupation entailed by the time the look came into fashion in the late 1960s, distressing our mothers deeply. When Titi Gloria did take us to the movies, it was at a different theater, farther down Southern Boulevard, and usually to see Cantinflas, the brilliant Mexican comic actor whose humor was as deft verbally as Charlie Chaplin's was physically.

Our shopping trip would conclude with a final stop to pick up bread and milk at the bodega a few doors down from Abuelita's. The bodega, a tiny grocery store, is the heart of every Hispanic neighborhood and a lifeline in areas with no supermarkets in walking distance. In those days, the bread they sold was so fresh that its warm smell filled the store. Abuelita would give me *la tetita,* the crunchy end, even though she liked it too, I knew. The bodega was always crowded with the same guys having their daily party. They sat in the corner, reading *El Diario* and arguing about the news. Sometimes one of them would read the *Daily News* and explain to the others in Spanish what it said. I could tell when he was improvising or embellishing the story; I knew what news sounded like in English. Usually, they only read the *Daily News* for the horse-racing results, although they didn't actually follow the horses. The last three digits of the total bets taken at the track became the winning number for the illegal lottery they played.

Before Abuelita moved, when she still lived on Kelly Street, there was a bodega right downstairs from her apartment. Sometimes she would send me downstairs by myself with a dollar bill wrapped up in a napkin that had numbers written on it. I had to tell the man whether she wanted to play them straight or in combination, or fifty cents each way. My grandmother counted extraordinary luck among her many gifts. Sometimes she saw the winning numbers in her dreams. I've never dreamed of numbers, but I've inherited more than my share of luck at games of chance, winning many a stuffed animal, and I'm even better at games like poker, where skill mediates luck. Sometimes Abuelita would see bad luck coming too, and that brought fear to my family. Too often in the past she had been right.

The stairs up to the third-floor apartment were narrow and dark, and Abuelita didn't have an elevator to rely on as we did. But in the projects, the elevator was more than a convenience: Junior and I were absolutely forbidden to take the stairs, where my mother had once been mugged and where addicts regularly shot up, littering the scene with needles and other paraphernalia. I can still hear Mami's warning that we should never, but never, touch those needles or take that junk: if we did, we would surely die.

Mami and my aunts would often be at Abuelita's when we got back, crowded into the kitchen for coffee and gossip. Abuelita would join them while I joined Nelson and my other cousins at the bedroom window to make faces at the passengers zipping by on the elevated train that ran just at the height of Abuelita's apartment. Gallego, my step-grandfather, would be busy with his own preparations for the party, choosing the dance music. His hands trembled slightly with Parkinson's disease, still in its early stages then, as he lined up the record albums.

Once a month, my mother and aunts would help Abuelita make *sofrito,* the Puerto Rican vegetable and spice base that enhances the flavors in any dish. Abuelita's kitchen would turn into a factory, with all of the women cleaning and peeling, slicing and chopping. They would fill up jars and jars of the stuff, enough for a month's worth of dinners in each of their homes, and enough for the Saturday parties too. On the table, waiting for their turn in the blender, were big piles of chopped peppers, onions, tomatoes: my target.

"Sonia, get your hands out of there!"

"Give me that! *¡Te vas a enfermar!* You'll get sick; you can't eat it raw!" Oh yes I can. I inherited adventurous taste buds from Papi and Abuelita, and I'll still happily eat many things more timid palates won't venture.

When we went to Abuelita's for the parties that happened most Saturdays, Mami made the hopeless effort to have me get dressed up. My dress would get wrinkled or stained almost immediately, and ribbons never stayed put in my hair, which Abuelita blamed on the electrodes the doctors had applied to my head. It's true that my curls disappeared about that time, but my hair had always been too thin for ribbons. Miriam by contrast always looked like a princess doll in a glass case, no matter the occasion. It would take me most of my life to feel remotely put together, and it's still an effort.

As soon as the door opened, I would catapult into Abuelita's arms. Wherever in the apartment she was, I would find her first.

"Sonia, careful!" Mami would say to me. "We just got here and already you're a mess." And then, to Abuelita, "Too much energy, too much talking, too much running around. I'm sorry, Mercedes, I don't know what to do with her."

"*Para,* Celina. Let the child be. There's nothing wrong with her except too much energy." Abuelita was on my side, always, and Mami was always apologizing to Abuelita. Sometimes even I wanted to say *"¡Para, Mami!"*

Next I would run to find Nelson, who would invariably be lying on the bed reading a comic book while waiting for me. Nelson was a genius, and my best friend on top of being my cousin. I never got bored talking to him. He could figure out how anything worked, and together we pondered mysteries of the natural world, like gravity. He was up for any game I could devise, including jousting knights, which involved charging at each other across the living room, each carrying on his or her back a younger brother armed with a broom or a mop. Miriam tried to stop us, but it didn't prevent Eddie, her little brother, from falling off Nelson and breaking a leg. When the screams of pain brought my aunt running, the blame was assigned, as usual, before any facts were established: "Sonia! What did you do now?" Another walloping for that one.

Tío Benny, who was Nelson, Miriam, and Eddie's dad, was determined that Nelson would grow up to be a doctor. In my eyes, Tío Benny was the ideal father. He spent time with his kids and took them on outings, which occasionally included me too. He spoke English, which meant he could go to parent-teacher conferences. Best of all, he didn't drink. I would have traded fathers with Nelson in a heartbeat. But sadly, for all his brilliance, Nelson wouldn't live up to Tío Benny's dreams, and I would do well despite a less than perfect father.

Abuelita's apartment was small enough that wherever we settled down to play, the warm smells of her feast would find us, beckoning like cartoon ribbons in the air. Garlic and onions calling, still the happiest smells I know.

"Mercedes, you should open your own restaurant."

"Don't be shy, there's plenty."

The dominoes never stopped for dinner. The game was serious. Someone would have to lose the whole match and give up the seat before even thinking about food. "*¿Tu estás ciego?* It's right in front of your eyes!" They'd yell a lot and pretend to be angry.

"Benny, wake up and look at what you have!" Mami counters. She was good at this and could keep track of every bone played.

"Hey, no cheating! How many times are you going to cough? Somebody get this man a drink, he's choking!"

"Don't look at me, I'm honest. Mercedes is the one who cheats."

"I know you have that *ficha,* so play it!"

"Nice one, Celina."

Gallego's out of the game, calling foul as he goes. He picks up his *güiro* and strums a ratchety rhythm on the gourd, playing along with the record, as if he wishes someone would show up with a guitar. Instead, sooner or later someone would lift the needle off the record, cutting off Los Panchos mid-song. The voices in the living room would settle to a hush, and all eyes would turn to Abuelita, resting on the couch, having cleaned up and taken a turn at dominoes. When the music stopped, that was the cue for those in the kitchen to crowd in the doorway of the living room. Nelson and I would scramble to a spot under the table where we could see. It was time for poetry.

Abuelita stands up, closes her eyes, and takes a deep breath. When she opens them and begins to recite, her voice is different. Deeper, and vibrant in a way that makes you hold your breath to listen.

Por fin, corazón, por fin,
alienta con la esperanza . . .

I couldn't understand the words exactly, but that didn't matter. The feeling of the poem came through clearly in the music of Abuelita's voice and in the look of faraway longing in the faces of her listeners.

Her long black hair is tied back simply and her dress is plain, but to my eyes she looks more glamorous than anyone trying to be fancy. Now her arms stretch wide and her skirt swirls as she turns, reaching for the whole horizon. You can almost see green mountains, the sea and the sky unfolding,

45

the whole world being born as she lifts her hand. As it turns, her fingers spread open like a flower blooming in the sun.

. . . y va la tierra brotando
como Venus de la espuma.

I look around. She has the whole room mesmerized. Titi Carmen wipes a tear.

Para poder conocerla
es preciso compararla,
de lejos en sueños verla;
y para saber quererla
es necesario dejarla.

¡Oh! no envidie tu belleza,
de otra inmensa población
el poder y la riqueza,
que allí vive la cabeza,
y aquí vive el corazón.

Y si vivir es sentir,
y si vivir es pensar . . .

The poems that Abuelita and her listeners loved were often in the key of nostalgia and drenched in rosy, sunset hues that obscured the poverty, disease, and natural disasters that they had left behind. Not that their yearnings were unfounded. As the poet says,

"To know it, you need to see it in dreams from afar. To learn how to love it, you need to leave it." Even those of the generations following who were born here, who have settled decisively into a mainland existence and rarely have reason to visit the island — even we have corners of our hearts where such a nostalgia lingers. All it takes to spark it is a poem, or a song like "En Mi Viejo San Juan."

The parties always wound down late. The stragglers had to be fed; Charlie and Tony, Titi Gloria's sons, might stop by after their Saturday night dates. Most others would say their good-byes and go home, like Tío Vitín and Titi Judy, who typically left carrying their kids, my cousins Lillian and Elaine, fast asleep, drooped over a shoulder.

But for those who remained, what often happened next was the climax of the evening. The *velada* was something that no one ever talked about; adults would change the subject casually if a kid asked a question. The kitchen table would be cleared and moved into the living room. A couple of neighbors from downstairs would appear, joining the party quietly. My mother and Titi Gloria would retire to the kitchen. Mami thought the whole business was silly and didn't want any part of it. Titi Gloria

47

was actually scared of the spirits.

The remaining kids — Nelson, Miriam, Eddie, Junior, and I — would be corralled in the bedroom and ordered to sleep. We knew that nothing would happen until the adults believed we were snoozing, and they were dead serious about this. Somehow they failed to reckon with the power of my curiosity, or how easily I could impose my will on the other kids. We all lay on the bed in watchful silence, perfectly still, waiting.

There was just enough light coming from the street and through the curtains on the glazed doors separating the bedroom from the living room to make the atmosphere cozy or spooky, depending on your mood. I could hear the fading rumble of the El train going by. I could hear by their breathing when Junior and Eddie both conked out.

As we lay there, my mind would rehearse what Charlie had told us: how Abuelita and Gallego call the spirits to ask them questions; how they were not evil but they were powerful, and you had to develop your own powers if you wanted their help; how Abuelita's spirit guide was called Madamita Sandorí and spoke with a Jamaican accent. His eyes got wide just talking about it. Charlie and Tony were Alfred's age, an in-between generation much older than the rest of the cousins. Charlie was adult enough that they let him sit at the table for the *velada*. Gallego, who was as skilled an *espiritista* as Abuelita, wanted to teach Charlie, but Charlie did not want that responsibility. It was one thing to have the gift, quite another to dedicate yourself and study it.

As strange as they were, Charlie's reports of the supernatural made sense. They weren't like Alfred's unbelievable stories, about the ghosts of dead *jíbaros* riding horses around San Germán, intended only to scare us. I knew that Abuelita used her magic on the side of good. She used it for healing and for protecting the people she loved. Of course I understood that a person with a talent for engaging the spirit world could equally put it to work for darker ends — *brujería,* or witchcraft. In Abuelita's own building one of the neighbors was known to put curses on people. I was forbidden to go near her door on penalty of getting smacked, which was something Abuelita had never done, so I knew she meant it.

Finally, the little bell would ring very softly. That was the cue. Nelson, Miriam, and I would climb off the bed and sneak up to the glazed doors. We'd stick our noses to the panes, peering through the tiny gaps at the edge of the curtain stretched and pinned over the glass. All I could see was the backs of chairs, the backs of heads, shoulders hunched by candlelight in a tight circle around the table. The bell would tinkle again, but except for that one clear note it was impossible to make out any sounds through the door.

I would carefully open the door a tiny crack, and we would huddle to listen. It was good to be close together, just in case. Gallego would always be the first to talk, and not in his usual voice. It didn't sound like Spanish, but it wasn't English either. It sounded like someone chewing words and swallowing them. Choking on them. Then the voice coming out of Gallego would moan louder until the table moved, seeming to rise off the floor, signaling the spirits' arrival. Miriam, trembling, would scoot back into bed fast. I wouldn't give up so easily. But no matter how hard I tried, I couldn't decipher the garbled words. After Nelson and I got tired of trying, we'd join Miriam in bed. Nelson would pull the blanket over his head and whisper in mock exasperation, "How do they expect us to sleep with a house full of spirits?" We'd all lie still for a minute. Then Nelson would pretend to snore very softly, and Miriam and I would start giggling.

■ ■ ■ ■

Except for my very earliest memories, when we still lived on Kelly Street in the same tenement as Abuelita, my father hardly ever came along to the parties. It was easier that way. On the rare occasions when he did come — on Mother's Day or Thanksgiving — I was nervous, watching and waiting for the inevitable signs of trouble. Even in the midst of the wildest mayhem that Nelson and I could concoct, even sinking my teeth into Abuelita's irresistible crispy chicken, even when everyone else was lost in music and laughter, I would be watching my father from the corner of my eye. It would start almost imperceptibly. His fingers would slowly curl up into claws. Then his face gradually scrunched up, just slightly at first, until finally it was frozen into a contorted grimace.

I usually noticed the early signs before my mother did, and for an agonizing interval I watched them both, waiting for her to notice. As soon as she did, there would be sharp words. It was time to go home, while he could still walk. I didn't have a name for what was happening, didn't understand what alcoholic neuropathy was. I only knew that I saw my father receding from us, disappearing behind that twisted mask. It was like being trapped in a horror film, complete with his lumbering Frankenstein walk as he made his exit and the looming certainty that there would be screaming when we got home.

Best were the times when I didn't have to go home. Most Saturday nights I stayed over at Abuelita's. When there was a party, Mami would take Junior home; Tío Benny and Titi Carmen somehow managed to get Nelson, Miriam, and Eddie down the street and into their own beds.

When I woke up in the morning, I would have Abuelita all to myself. She would stand at the stove in the housecoat she always wore for an apron, her pockets full of cigarettes and tissues, making the thick, fluffy pancakes she knew I loved. Those mornings were heaven. When Mami came to take me home later, I would kiss Abuelita good-bye. *"Bendición, Abuelita."* She would hug me and say without fail every time we parted, *"Que Dios te bendiga, te favorezca y te libre de todo mal y peligro."* May God bless you, favor you, and deliver you from all evil and danger. Just her saying it made it so.

THREE

With the exception of my cousin Nelson, who was in a category of his own, Gilmar was my best friend in elementary school. To tell the truth, he was my only real friend who wasn't a cousin. He lived in the Bronxdale projects too, in the building across from ours, and we played together outside almost every day.

We were lying down in the concrete pipes next to the far playground, our favorite hiding place, when he told me the news. His parents — Gilbert and Margaret, who'd each given him a bit of their names — had decided to move to California. They had palm trees in California, he told me, and the weather was always sunny. I had seen palm trees when I visited Puerto Rico, but beyond that I had no mental picture of California. Still, I could imagine what having to leave must have felt like to Gilmar: not seeing our corner of the world and all the people in it anymore, maybe ever.

"Gilmar, you have to say good-bye to everybody. Everybody! Come on, I'll do it with you."

The good-bye tour on which I accompanied Gilmar that day was a snapshot of our life in the projects. Pops was the first person we both thought of. We scrambled out of the pipe and ran to the gray truck he kept parked on the service road off Bruckner Boulevard. Every day when my father got home from work, he would give us each a penny, and we would run over to Pops's truck to buy candy. On Fridays we got a dime, because it was payday.

Pops was surprised to see us so early that day; Gilmar explained that he was moving to California. Pops said he was sad to see Gilmar go, and they shook hands. Then he let us each choose a candy and said we didn't have to pay.

We went to Louie's building next and knocked on his door. Louie lived with his grandmother because his parents had died in a car accident. It was a story that I'd only heard in neighbors' whispers, but it seemed to be confirmed by the fact that his grandmother always wore black. She was Jewish, but I surmised that they had the same custom we did, of wearing black for *el luto* when people die. Louie attended Hebrew school and didn't play much with the other kids in the projects, but Gilmar and I played with him because I liked his grandmother. She invited us in that day, but we only stayed for a minute, because we also had to say good-bye to another grandmother in the next building over.

Mrs. Beverly also had a grandson living with her, in this case because his mother had problems. Jimmy might have had something wrong with him too; it was hard to say. Maybe he was just different, or a little slow; anyway, it was clear to me that he was more than the typical burden an elderly woman might bear caring for a young boy, and that gave Mrs. Beverly a heroic aura in my eyes, especially since she also held down an office job. Sometimes my mother and I would run into her on the street and stop to chat. She always wore a fur coat even when the weather was mild, and I thought she was very elegant. Mami explained to me that her coat was probably the only precious thing she owned and that's why it was important to her. I could see that it gave her pleasure to wear it.

Mrs. Beverly wasn't expecting Gilmar and me at the door, of course, and when he explained about California and said good-bye, she almost cried. I've always thought grandmothers who take care of kids are special.

In the building kitty-corner from ours was Ana, my mother's best friend, who kept an eye on Junior and me after school until Papi got home. Ana's husband, Moncho, and her daughter, Chiqui, were both home. Junior was there, too. That was no surprise. He worshipped Moncho and followed him everywhere, even to take out the garbage. Ana called Junior Moncho's *rabo de conejo,* his rabbit tail. Ana's next-door neighbors, Irma and Gilbert, heard the commotion, so of course they came over to see what they were missing. It became almost a party as Gilmar said good-bye to everyone.

We decided to walk over to Blessed Sacrament next, to say good-bye to the nuns. Junior wanted to come with us, but Moncho asked him to stay and help him cook an octopus, which he had in a bucket. He showed it to us, all slimy arms and suckers. Junior's eyes widened, his mouth was hanging. "Mami doesn't cook *that,*" he said. Moncho was a merchant marine who brought his kids exotic souvenirs from far-off lands. I imagined he knew all about the depths of the ocean, as well as how to cook things we'd never even heard of. He certainly knew how to keep Junior occupied, and we continued our good-bye tour unencumbered.

When we reached Blessed Sacrament, the school yard was empty and silent, abandoned for summer vacation, but the office door was open. Sister Marita Joseph and Sister Elizabeth Regina both looked up.

"Hello, Sonia. Hello, Gilmar. Is everything all right? What brings you here on a Saturday?" Sister Marita Joseph looked apprehensive. When Gilmar explained that he was moving to California and saying good-bye to everyone, she asked, "And you, Sonia? Are you accompanying Gilmar on his good-byes?" I just nodded. I might have been a compulsive talker at home, but at school I spoke when spoken to. "That's very unusual," she said, looking at me strangely. I thought she approved, but I was not 100 percent sure. Why would it be unusual to keep a friend company? It had practically been my idea, even if it was Gilmar who was leaving.

Sister Elizabeth was our teacher that year. The best I could say about third grade was that it was a more or less continuous state of dread. As hard as I tried to keep a low profile, trouble seemed to find me. At Christmas, for instance, all the students brought presents for their teachers. That year my father had chosen my present for Sister Elizabeth. He'd never once come to school, had never even met her, but he chose the present, which he proudly handed to me in a long box, already gift wrapped by him. He wouldn't even tell me what it was.

Sister Elizabeth opened her presents in front of the class; there was soap, candy, a zippered prayer book, a box of stationery, and then there was Papi's present. Inside the box was a ruler. And not an ordinary wooden or plastic ruler, but a ruler made of some indestructible metal alloy no doubt invented to build rocket ships or bank safes — the Ruler of the Future, likely fabricated at the factory where Papi worked.

The sight of it was like a punch in the stomach, and actual ones came my way at recess, as I had predicted from the daggers of hatred being shot from every pair of eyes in the class. Pleading ignorance won me no mercy, and I cried all the way home. Fortunately, the hatred eventually died down, because the ruler was never to reappear, either for measurement or for punishment. Sister Elizabeth had her merciful side, too.

Discipline was what made Catholic school a good investment in my mother's eyes, worth the heavy burden of the tuition fees. The Bronx public schools of the 1960s were not yet as severely troubled as they would become, though they struggled with de facto segregation and a chronic lack of funding and offered a rough environment compared with the parochial alternative. Still, none of my uncles and aunts chose the sacrifice of sending my cousins to Catholic schools.

Among the black-bonneted nuns who managed classrooms of forty or fifty kids in my school, discipline was virtually an eighth sacrament. It might mean my copying a prayer in my clumsy cursive however many times it took to get every loop perfect or submitting to slaps and blows for some infraction. I often stewed with righteous anger over physical punishments — my own or others' — especially when they seemed disproportionate to the crime. I accepted what the Sisters taught in religion class: that God is loving, merciful, charitable, forgiving. That message didn't jibe with adults smacking kids. I remember watching as Sister continued to slap one boy who'd disrupted class even after the braces in his mouth drew blood that ran down his chin. Many of my classmates have happier memories of Blessed Sacrament, and in time I would find my own satisfaction in the classroom. My first years there, however, I met with little warmth. In part, it was that the nuns were critical of working mothers, and their disapproval was felt by latchkey kids. The irony of course was that my mother wouldn't have been working such long hours if not to pay for that education she believed was the key to any aspirations for a better life.

After we'd finished saying good-bye to everyone we could think of, Gilmar and I went back to say our good-byes to the concrete pipe and to each other. Lying inside, all we could see was the circle of bright sky. Our voices bounced around in the hollow of the concrete. We shouted and stretched the words out long and loud to get a really good echo.
"Good-bye, Gilmar!"
"Good-bye, Sonia!"
"I'll miss you!"
"Write me a letter!"
"Write me a letter, too!"
"From the palm trees?"
"From the palm trees!"

I wouldn't get to see California until my second summer at law school. I remember driving the freeways with palm trees in view and thinking of Gilmar, among other friends I've lost touch with who may never know what memories they've left behind in my keeping.

FOUR

"This is my mother, Sonia, your *bisabuela,*" said Abuelita. "Give her a kiss." The cheek that was my target was wrinkled and translucent, so fragile that I feared my lips would bruise it. Her eyes were blank. As I leaned in to kiss her, she seemed to pull away, but it was just the rocking chair easing back from my weight. There was no spark of awareness or curiosity. I don't know if I was more disturbed by this absence that gave no hint of how I should relate to her or by the shadow of Abuelita's features that I could see arranged inanimately on her mother's face.

Bisabuela Ciriata was in her nineties, though she looked two hundred years old to me. Her rocking chair of carved wood and woven cane tilted between this world and another that was beyond imagining, wafting scents of talcum and medicinal tea, auras of lace-edged *santos* whose eyes rolled up to a heaven too close for comfort.

We were in an area of San Juan called San-turce. Abuelita visited with her sisters and brothers while I played on the balcony or in half-hidden gardens. There had been ten of them all together, she said (Diezilita, Piatrina, Angelina, Eloys . . .), but I couldn't keep track or tell sisters and brothers from cousins and uncles and aunts. We were in a city, but it seemed to teeter on the edge of dissolving into nature. Vines snaked under iron fences and up balustrades. Chickens scrabbled under hibiscus bushes and bright yellow canario flowers. I watched the afternoon rains pour down like a curtain enclosing the balcony, rutting the street below with muddy streams, pounding on the corrugated roofs and wooden walls until Abuelita called me inside to a treat for *merienda* — maybe a *tembleque,* a gelatin made of coconut milk and sweet condensed milk, or fruits that I'd never seen in New York: guavas with their sharp perfume, *quenepas* with pits as big as grapes and a thin layer of featherlight flesh that puckered your mouth when you sucked on it, and mangoes of a melting sweetness unlike any I had tasted back home. At night, I slept with Abuelita in a room crowded with sisters and cousins, and the mosquito nets transformed our bed into a cozy hideaway among gauzy clouds. The traffic noise gave way to the rickety rhythm of the ceiling fan and *coquís* — the tiny musical frogs that are a symbol of the island — chirping in the shadows as I drifted to sleep.

On my earliest trips to Puerto Rico, when I was small — including my first as a toddler — it was just Abuelita and I. My mother was determined that she would never, ever go back to the island, but then she changed her mind. Some of the best summer vacations I remember were traveling with my mother and Junior to Mayagüez to visit her family.

Traveling with Mami to Puerto Rico was a little like being around Rip van Winkle on the day he woke up. She wore an expression of constant wonderment: everything surprised her by how much it had changed, except for the things that surprised her because they were just as she remembered them.

Barely out of the airport, we would stop at the food stands on the roadside, joining the traffic jam of people returning who couldn't wait another minute for a first taste of home. The coconuts were big and green, not like the shriveled hairy brown things in boxes on the sidewalks of the Bronx. We would shake them and listen to find one that had a lot of liquid swishing around inside. The vendor would hack a piece off the top with a single swipe of a long machete and stick a straw in the hole. We would sip the almost-sweet nectar as the cars passed by on the highway, and I would listen to my cousin Papo and Titi Aurora, my mother's elder sister, filling my mother in on the news she needed to know before we saw the rest of the family: who'd married whom, who'd had whose baby, who'd been sick . . . Though Titi Aurora lived in New York, she went often to Puerto Rico to visit friends and sort out family problems. Before she finished her briefing, I'd hand the empty coconut back to the vendor with the machete, and he would hack it in two so I could use the little top piece that he'd cut off first to scoop out the creamy flesh, which to me was the best part of all.

Another day, my mother stopped a perfect stranger with his cow in a field beside the road and asked him for a glass of milk. He looked at her as if thinking: crazy American. Even in Puerto Rico people were drinking their milk pasteurized by then, not straight from the cow. But memories of the old ways must have overwhelmed her. She pushed the tin cup at me, but I wouldn't touch it. I just watched as she drank, a look of heavenly bliss spreading over her face.

In Mayagüez, we usually stayed at Titi Maria's house. She was the first wife of Tío Mayo, my mother's eldest brother. Titi Maria helped to look after my mother when she was small, and their family bond outlasted the marriage. My mother is close to Tío Mayo's later families too; she has a talent for not taking sides, which is handy in a complicated extended family. It is a trait I've adopted, trying never to lose contact with cousins and second cousins whose parents have separated or divorced. We visit with everybody. There were family members whom I'd never even heard of before; my mother was set on showing Junior and me off to every single one of them over a cup of coffee. At first, people would laugh because our Spanish was clumsy and limited, but within days I could hear myself improving, and people would compliment me on it. Junior would have improved too if he'd have just opened his mouth and said something once in a while. It took me years to appreciate how hard it must have been for him to be always in the company of two chatty and strong-willed women.

At Titi Maria's house, my cousin Papo

always prepared a special welcome. Waiting for me under the sink would be two whole shopping bags of mangoes that he'd gathered from under the trees up the hill in anticipation of our arrival. I ate them all day long, in spite of constant warnings that I would get sick. Looking back, I suspect I was getting a higher dosage of insulin than I needed — not uncommon for juvenile diabetics in that day — making the added sugar manageable. In any case, I hated the sluggish feeling that high blood sugar brought on, and I didn't need reminding. I might have had to eat less of something else, but I could indulge my lust for mangoes.

At lunchtime, the whole family came home from work, and Titi Maria cooked a big meal for all her kids — my adult cousins — and some of their kids too. Even those who lived elsewhere would often come for that meal. After lunch we settled down for a siesta. I would read a book — sleep wouldn't come to me easily — but I loved this time when everyone was gathered at home and quietly connected.

Papo had a job designing window displays for a number of big stores on the island. He claimed to be the first person doing this work as a professional designer in Puerto Rico, and he often traveled to New York to gather ideas. Charo was a high school teacher. Minita was the senior executive secretary for the newspaper *El Mundo*. Evita worked in a government office. It was clear to me even then that the people I knew on the island had better jobs than the Puerto Ricans I knew in New York. When we walked down the street in Mayagüez, it gave me a proud thrill to read the little signs above the doors, of the doctors, the lawyers, and the other professionals who were Puerto Rican. It was not something I had often seen in New York. At the hospital where my mother worked, there were Puerto Rican nurses but only one Puerto Rican doctor. At the larger shops and businesses in the Bronx, there were Puerto Rican workers but rarely managers or owners.

Tío Mayo's *panadería* was my favorite place to visit. They called it a *panadería*, but it was much more than a bakery. There were loaves of bread and rolls that Tío Mayo started making while it was still dark outside, kept warm in a special case with a heat lamp. There were cases full of cakes and pastries filled with cream, homemade cheese, and guava jam. My uncle's then wife, Titi Elisa, also got up early to make lunch and snacks to sell to the workers who sewed in the factory across the street. She fried the chicken and roasted the pork, made stews and meat pies and pots of rice and beans. The smells of her cooking mixed with the yeasty smell of the bread, and the coffee, and the whole amazing cloud of flavors spread down the street and up into the balconies.

When the noon whistle blew at the factory, the bakery would fill up in minutes. I helped with serving, and I loved the two-handed challenge of the lunch hour rush. I knew the price of every item, and I knew how to make change — I was discovering that I had a facility with numbers, which I inherited from Papi — and Titi Elisa would let me work the cash register when my uncle wasn't around. Although he had seen me in action, he couldn't quite believe it. He wasn't comfortable with the idea of girls handling money.

When I wasn't busy helping, I played with my cousin Tito in the alleyway behind the bakery, reenacting scenes from the Three Stooges. Tito was Moe and I was Curly. We could usually convince Junior or someone else to be Larry, the third *chiflado,* but only Tito and I knew all the moves and the right sound effects: a twang for a fake eye poke, a ratchety sound for an ear twist, and the all-purpose "Nyuk! Nyuk! Nyuk!"

Before she left Puerto Rico, my mother had lived in Lajas and San Germán and had seen very little of the island beyond the neighborhoods of her childhood. She was eager to show us places that she'd heard about but had never seen herself. We went to the beach at Luquillo. It was nothing like Orchard Beach in the Bronx, which was the only beach I knew. There were no traffic jams in Puerto Rico, no waiting for hours packed in a hot car to get there, no dirty sand, no standing in line for the bathroom. Progress has caught up with the island since my childhood, and it has its share of traffic jams, but the water is still warm and clear, and the sand is perfectly white. When you look down into the water, you can see the bottom, and it rolls out blue until it meets the blue of the sky.

The Parque de Bombas in Ponce fascinated me, a fantasia of red and black stripes that wouldn't go away even when you closed your eyes. The fire truck looked like a giant toy with its ding-dong bell, and I couldn't imagine it in action. How did they ever put out a real fire? *"Mi'ja,"* said Mami, "all those little wooden houses burned down anyway. But they did the best they could." She would say that about a lot of things: they did the best they could.

Of all the sights, the art museum in Ponce left the deepest impression. I had never been to a museum before. The building is beautiful and seemed to me then as grand as a castle with its staircase that sweeps in a big circle on two sides. It was so magnificent that I just had to run up and down the stairs to see what it felt like. It felt horrible when the guard yelled at me. So I walked slowly and looked at the paintings one by one.

I figured out that portraits were pictures in which a person from olden times just stood there or sat, wearing fancy clothes and staring very seriously. I wondered who these people were. Why did an artist choose *them* to be in a picture? How much work was it to paint this? How long did he have to stand there like that? Other paintings were more like stories, though I didn't know what the story was. Why did she cut off his head? I could tell that dove was not just an ordinary dove that happened to be flying by. I could see that it had a meaning, even though I didn't know what the meaning was. When I got tired of not understanding the stories, I noticed other things: Sometimes you could see the brushstrokes and the thickness of the paint; other times it was smooth, without texture. Sometimes things in the distance were smaller, and it felt as if you could reach into the space; other times it was flat like a map. I wondered, were these the things I *should* be noticing? I could tell that there was more going on than I could describe or understand.

Does it seem strange that a child should be so conscious of the workings of her own mind? I have clear memories of many such moments, often turning on a recognition of something I didn't know, an awareness of a gap in my knowledge. A framed reproduction of a painting that mesmerized me hung for years on the wall in Abuelita's living room. Who knows how it got there, but it was a scene, I'm assuming in hindsight, from the French Revolution, a broad staircase leading from a public square up into a stately building, with a balcony where several elegant figures formed a cluster, including a woman — Marie Antoinette? — with a pale blue dress and imposing hair. In the street below, many other people approached, more poorly dressed, but my eye was drawn to an old man on the lower steps, shabbily clad, leaning one-legged on a cane, his back to the viewer. I knew nothing of the history, the social and political background that informed the painting, but I understood that a message was somehow intended when the artist contrived to place this man front and center. I spent a lot of time wondering about him and trying to imagine his face. But that was as far as I could get.

"Sonia, we're going to visit your grandfather. My father." This got my attention. My mother had never so much as mentioned his existence before. When I questioned her, she answered in a voice that sounded as if she were reading aloud from the small print on the back of a package of medicine. "I don't know the man. He left when I was born. I haven't seen him since then. But Tío Mayo and Titi Aurora want me to come with them to the hospital to see him, and they say you should come too." The unknown grandfather was not the whole mystery. I usually knew what Mami was thinking from the flash in her voice, the speed of her smile, as rare as it was then, the telltale arch of her brows. This woman speaking with such flat indifference was not the mother I knew.

Tío Mayo led us to the bed at the far end of the room, by the window. As we walked the length of the ward, I hardly saw the patients in the other beds, so intently was I focused on my mother and our looming destination. Nothing was going to slip by me, though I had no idea what to expect or even what I should be wondering about. Would she greet him with a kiss? How do you relate to a father you don't know?

He had Mami's light eyes. Framed by the white of his hair, the white mustache, the white of the sheets, their sea-green color seemed even lighter, bluer, more startling. He was a handsome man but gaunt. His arms were just sticks poking from the sleeves of the hospital gown. A thousand questions ran through my head, but I didn't dare speak any of them out loud: Why did you leave Mami behind? Who are you? Do you have a wife? Do you have other kids? Where have you been living?

I climbed onto the chair and watched. My mother walked up to the bed and stood looking down at the old man. In an ice-cold voice she said, *"Yo soy Celina."* That was it. He didn't say anything to her. He didn't ask how her life had been, what it was now. There were no tears, no revelations.

Titi Aurora led me by the hand to the bedside and introduced me. I got barely a nod from him. I retreated, climbed back onto the chair, and watched as Titi Aurora chattered about nothing and fluffed his pillows. Tío Mayo was there and not there, talking to the nurses, taking care of business. But in all this nothing, I understood something: that my mother had been wounded as deeply as a human being could be.

I have carried the memory of that day as a grave caution. There was a terrible permanence to the state that my mother and her father had reached. My mother's pain would never heal, the ice between them would never thaw, because they would never find a way to acknowledge it. Without acknowledgment and communication, forgiveness was beyond reach. Eventually, I would recognize the long shadow of this abandonment in my own feelings toward my mother, and I would determine not to repeat what I had seen. The closeness that I share now with my mother is deeply felt, but we learned it slowly and with effort, and for fear of the alternative.

FIVE

It was in April of the year that I turned nine. I was heading straight home after school that day because Papi had stayed home sick from work. Usually, Junior and I would go to Ana's first and then play outside till Papi got home. I didn't need to check in with Ana, because she would know that Papi was home. My mother had coffee with Ana every day before she went to work; there was nothing about each other's lives that they didn't know instantly.

When we came round the corner, I could see Moncho, Ana's husband, hanging out the window on the third floor of their building, washing the windows but also looking intently at passersby. That was odd, I thought. When he saw me, he waved at me. He didn't stop. He kept on waving furiously, signaling to me, and then he yelled "Sonia! Junior! Come upstairs!" in a voice that meant business. Junior bounced ahead of me, happy to see Moncho.

But when Ana opened the door, something was terribly wrong. Her eyes were puffy from crying, and her face was pale. This wasn't some everyday fuss that just happened to reach the level of tears; something had shaken her deeply. She wouldn't explain, but she started to cry and made us wait while she phoned Mami, saying to Moncho, "Celina should tell them." Moncho was quieter than I'd ever seen him. This was all so strange that I was scared but also riveted as I watched to see what would happen next. Ana said, "Let's go," and we walked downstairs and across the way to our building. It was the shortest of walks, but it took forever. It was hard to move my legs, as if dread were weighing them down.

Alfred opened the door to our apartment. His eyes, too, were red. Tío Vitín was there, and I could hear other voices. I looked into the living room and saw many faces looking back at me with the same teary gaze. Mami was sitting in the chair by the telephone in the hallway, staring into space, her eyes wide and wet. Junior said to her, "Where's Papi?"

"Dios se lo llevó."

God took him. I could see that Junior didn't understand. I did. She meant that Papi had died. But what did *that* mean? Had he become a spirit? I didn't know what I was supposed to feel, or say, or do. As if from a far distance, I could hear my own voice joining all the other voices crying. I ran down the hall and threw myself on the bed. I was sobbing, pounding my fists, when Ana entered the room.

"Sonia, you have to be a big girl now. Your mother's very upset; you can't cry anymore. You have to be strong for your *mami.*"

So that's what I'm supposed to do? I stopped crying. "I'm okay, Ana." She left me alone. The stillness in the room was louder than the noise down the hall. I remembered that morning how Papi had called out from the bathroom, saying that since he wasn't going to work, he wanted to make us a Sunday breakfast, even though it was a weekday. Mami had yelled: "Go back to bed if you're sick, the kids don't have time, they have to get to school, and why are you taking so long shaving?"

We had been at the funeral home for hours. It felt like forever, but my mother and Abuelita and my aunts had been there even longer, for days. It was important not to leave the body alone, and they all had to keep each other company. Mami didn't want Junior and me to come, but Titi

Aurora insisted, because the nuns and Monsignor Hart were coming from Blessed Sacrament. It wouldn't be respectful if Junior and I weren't there when they showed up.

The room smelled of flowers, cologne, and perfume masking a mustiness. People were speaking in whispers, looking at the floor, shaking their heads. There was talk of premonitions, a greeting or casual word exchanged with my father over the last few days that now took on greater significance; the way he had shaved and dressed up that morning, even though he was home sick. As if he had known. Everyone agreed that he was a good man, a family man, and that forty-two was a tragically young age to go. And Celina so young too, a widow at thirty-six with two young kids!

My aunts took turns crying. Abuelita never stopped. I sat down next to her on the couch and held her hand. Abuelita's crying was unbearably painful to me. I couldn't even tell if I had any sadness of my own, because I was so full of Abuelita's sadness. I worried that her spirit had been torn apart so painfully by Papi's death that she might never be happy again. What would happen to me if she died too?

The nuns and Monsignor Hart came and

went. Dr. Fisher came too, and some people from the factory where Papi worked. All the while, Mami just sat there. Her eyes were open, but she was not really present, not even answering when people talked to her. Titi Aurora had to tell her to say thank you to Monsignor Hart.

What happens next is that I'm supposed to say good-bye to Papi, Titi Aurora says. She wants me to kiss him. I want to scream "No!" but I swallow it because I don't want to upset Abuelita any more than she's upset already. "*No tengas miedo,* Sonia. Touch his hand." I'm not afraid, but I'm not okay either. This thing with a powdery white face resembles my father, but it's not him, and it's certainly not something I want to touch. But I close my eyes and get it over with.

A part of me was not surprised by what happened then. A knot that had been tied tight inside me for longer than I can remember began to come loose. Deep down, I'd known for a while that this was where Papi was heading. Looking at this thing that was not Papi, I realized that he was not coming back. From here, Mami, Junior, and I would be going along without him. Maybe it would be easier this way.

. . . Santa María, Madre de Dios, ruega por

80

nosotros pecadores, ahora y en la hora de nuestra muerte.

We did the *rosario* for Papi for seven straight nights at Abuelita's, and every night I thought it would never end. Abuelita cried. Mami cried. My aunts cried. The prayers went on and on, along with that horrible week. The final night should have been better because the end was in sight, and friends brought dinner instead of just pastries, but the bad news was that we had to do three . . . whole . . . rosaries . . .

Dios te salve, María, llena eres de gracia: El Señor es contigo. Bendita tú eres entre todas las mujeres, y bendito es el fruto de tu vientre: Jesús . . .

I must have fallen asleep at some point, because I woke up with my mother standing next to me, pulling my arm out of its socket, gripping my hand so tightly it hurt. Her whole body was shaking with anger, and her voice trembled as she spoke to Abuelita: "Mercedes, you can't do this! I won't let you!" The room was silent. Everyone's eyes were on Mami, standing there with the tears running down her face. "I swear, I will take her away from you and you will never see us again. Never!"

She dragged me to the bedroom and cried all night. I had no idea what had so upset

81

her that she would turn on Abuelita, and she wouldn't tell me. Much later I learned the story. As I nodded off in the midst of the prayers, I apparently spoke in a strange voice — one that sounded like Abuelita's long-dead sister to those who remembered her, a voice my grandmother might summon during one of her séances. The message I delivered was that my father was safely in her company; there was no need to worry. *"Confórmate,"* I said. Accept it.

I can't explain it. Nothing like that had happened to me before, and it hasn't happened since. Everyone there was as exhausted as I was, and it's hard to separate what they heard from what they wanted to hear. I know that I wanted more than anything to make Abuelita feel better; it's very possible I was talking in my sleep or as I drifted off. In any case, it didn't matter. Any desire my grandmother might have had to develop what she believed to be my "gift" was trumped by my mother's threat to remove me from the influence of what she saw as superstition and *brujería.*

We had been sleeping at Abuelita's every night since Papi died, because my mother couldn't bear to go back to our apartment. That meant getting up very early in the morning so Mami could get us to school on time, after which she would go to Ana's. They would drink coffee and talk and cry together until school was out, and then she would take us back to Abuelita's. Fortunately, the building manager at Bronxdale Houses let us move into a different apartment very quickly. It was over on Watson Avenue on the second floor — much better than the seventh floor if you'd rather not see what happens in the stairwells. It was much closer to Blessed Sacrament, too. Best of all, my mother was able to change her schedule at the hospital. She didn't have to work nights anymore, so she could be at home after school.

Tío Vitín and my cousin Alfred helped us with the move. They cleaned out Papi's room and carried out a big bag of clanking empty bottles. They found those flat, half-pint bottles, drained of Seagram's Seven, under the mattress, in the closet, behind the drawers, in his coat pockets, his trousers, his shirts, in every jacket. There was even one hidden inside the lining of a coat.

It occurred to me that every day when he came home from work and sent us off with pennies for candy and fifteen minutes more to play, my father was keeping us outside just long enough to have a drink before starting dinner. Junior, who had slept in the same room with Papi, in the other twin bed, and sometimes only pretended to be asleep, now confessed that he had known all along about the bottles under the mattress. I always slept with my mother in the other room, and nothing ever woke me up once I fell asleep. I wondered what else I had missed.

I do know that my father loved us. But as much as he loved us, it wasn't enough to stop him from drinking. To the end, Abuelita and my aunts blamed my mother for Papi's drinking. It's true that Mami could say all the wrong things; neither of them knew how to stop an argument once they started. But I knew too that my mother didn't make him drink any more than she could make him stop. I knew he did this to himself; even as a child, I knew he was the only one responsible.

All those hours that he sat by the window looking out . . . I treasured those times when I stood beside him, inhaling the scent of Old Spice up close and of rice and beans bubbling in the background, and he told me what he imagined the future would be: all the different stores they would build on the empty lots around us, or how one day a rocket ship would carry a man to the full moon that was rising, low and yellow, over the South Bronx. The truth is, though, that for each of those moments, there were so many more long hours of sadness, when he stared in silence at the vacant lots, at the highway and the brick walls, at a city and a life that slowly strangled him.

On the day we moved in, it smelled of fresh paint. The view from the new apartment on Watson Avenue was different. You could see the school yard at Blessed Sacrament from our window. The kids had left for the day, but there were still two guys practicing shots on the basketball court. Farther back, one of the nuns was walking along by the buildings, but I couldn't tell who it was under the black bonnet . . . As I looked out the window, a memory came to me of something that happened the day Papi died, which I'd almost forgotten in all the commotion that followed. I was down in the school yard at recess, standing by the fence, looking this way toward the projects — and I thought about him. It wasn't a normal thought that pops into your head or one that's connected to the thought that came before it. More of a feeling than a thought, but almost not even a feeling: like the barest shadow of a mood passing over, or a breeze so perfectly soft that nothing moves. I didn't know yet what had hap-

pened, but maybe that was Papi himself,
saying good-bye.

Six

In the days and weeks following the funeral, the release and relief I felt from the end of the fighting gave way to anxious puzzlement. At nine, I was equipped to understand loss, even sadness, but not grief, not someone else's and certainly not my own. I couldn't figure out what was wrong with Mami, and it scared me.

Every day Junior and I came home from school to find the apartment quiet and dark, with the curtains drawn. Mami would come out just long enough to cook dinner, leaving the back bedroom, where she passed hour after hour with the door closed and the lights out. (Junior and I shared the front bedroom in the new apartment on Watson Avenue, using the twin beds that had been in Papi's room in the old place.) After serving dinner like a zombie, hardly saying a word, she would go right back into her room. So even though she was working the early shift now and getting home in the afternoon before us, we saw no more of her than when she'd been working late. We did homework. We watched TV. We did homework and watched TV.

On weekends, I was able to rouse Mami to go grocery shopping, retracing my father's steps. I remembered what Papi used to buy, and that's what I put in the basket, though I wasn't sure Mami would know what to do with everything. I missed Papi's cooking. I missed Papi. Somehow, when he died, I had taken it for granted that our lives would be better. I hadn't counted on this gloom.

I wasn't the only one who was worried about my mother. I overheard some of her friends talking to Ana, and they decided one of them would pay a call at Blessed Sacrament to ask Father Dolan to come visit Celina. His refusal, as reported over coffee at Ana's, enraged me, all the more so because of the reason: my mother didn't go to church on Sunday.

It was true, but she did send her kids to church and always with money for the offering basket. And she worked long hours at the hospital so we could go to school at Blessed Sacrament. Shouldn't Father Dolan be forgiving if she needed help? Even if he thought she wasn't Christian enough, I reasoned, shouldn't he be more Christian? My reaction was of a piece with the frustration I felt when he stood there at the altar during the Mass, with his back turned to us, as priests did in those days before Vatican II. Show us what you're doing up there! I always thought. Now when he turned his back on us, it felt like just what it appeared to be: rejection. I was delighted when, a few years later under Pope Paul VI, the Church turned its priests around to face the congregants.

Another week passed in darkness and silence. Another friend of my mother's, Cristina, asked the pastor at her church to visit Mami. He'd never even met her before, and of course she'd never been to his church, which was Baptist. But that didn't stop him from coming. They talked quietly together for hours. I was impressed that he spoke Spanish; whether or not he had anything to say that could help, at least he cared enough to try. That I respected.

As spring turned to summer, Mami stayed shut in her darkened room, and I found myself on summer vacation longing for school to start. I didn't feel like playing outside. I couldn't articulate exactly what I feared, but I knew I should stay close by and keep an eye on things.

My solace and only distraction that summer was reading. I discovered the pleasure of chapter books and devoured a big stack of them. The Parkchester Library was my haven. To thumb through the card catalog was to touch an infinite bounty, more books than I could ever possibly exhaust. My choices were more or less random. There was no one in my family who could point me toward children's classics, no teacher who took an interest, and it never occurred to me to ask the librarian for guidance. My mother had subscribed to *Highlights* for Junior and me, and *Reader's Digest* for herself, but by now I was reading whole issues of the *Digest* myself, cover to cover. "Laughter, the Best Medicine," was what I sorely needed then. Sometimes when a story caught my imagination, I would search the library for the original book — I understood that these were excerpts or abridgments — but I never had any luck, and that mystified me. Now I realize that a tiny public library in a poor neighborhood would be unlikely to receive new releases.

My favorite book was one that Dr. Fisher had lent me. I had seen it, bound in burgundy red leather, on the shelf in his office and asked about it. He pulled the heavy volume down and said I could keep it as long as I liked. Those stories of Greek gods and heroes sustained me that summer and beyond. I imagined the gods of classical antiquity as versions of Abuelita's familiar spirits, who interfered in human affairs and kept open lines of communication to the Bronx. The heroes were admirable if flawed, as compelling as any comic book superhero to a kid who was hungry for escape, and there was grandeur in their struggles that the Flash could not match. Riven by conflicting impulses, these immortals seemed more realistic, more accessible, than the singular, all-forgiving, unchanging God of my Church. It was in that book of Dr. Fisher's, too, that I learned that my own name is a version of Sophia, meaning wisdom. I glowed with that discovery. And I never did return the book.

Usually, when I didn't understand what was going on with someone, I could listen carefully and observe until I figured things out. But with my mother, still sitting alone in darkness behind her closed door, there were no clues. As far as I knew, when Papi was alive, they did nothing but fight. If they weren't screaming, they were putting up a stone wall of bitter silence between them. I

91

couldn't remember ever having seen them happy together. And so her sadness, if that's what it was, seemed irrational to me.

Abuelita's terrible pain seemed less mysterious, if only because I was so attuned to her feelings. The parties ended. There was no more music and dancing, no more shopping for chickens, no more calling the spirits. Abuelita didn't dream the winning numbers anymore. "My son died and my luck died too," she said. She was angry at the spirits, it seemed, for not warning her that something bad would happen to her son, for not even giving her a chance to protect him. The week after Papi died, she forgot, in her distress, to place her usual bet, only to find out later that the winning number had been the number of his gravestone. It was as if the spirits were mocking her.

And yet it had been years since I'd seen her talking to Papi as her beloved firstborn, with that glow of adoration that lit up her face. On holidays when he came with us to Abuelita's house, he would sit silently, looking out the window, the same way he did at home. He might warm up if there was a ball game on TV. Before we got our own set, he might even come just to watch the game, then one of his few real pleasures. Those

92

baseball games, with some good shouting for a change, were such a rare semblance of normal family life that on those nights I would fall asleep with a smile that wouldn't go away.

But still, looking at it rationally — and I was a very rational child — why should the parties stop when Papi hardly ever came anyway? Why would his not being there make a difference now when it hadn't before? Why was even Titi Carmen so overcome with grief at the funeral that she tried to jump into the grave and had to be dragged out? I never once saw her eager to spend time with Papi when he was alive.

What was all this adult misery about? I had my theory. They must all feel guilty. If Papi slowly poisoned himself to death, then of course it must be Mami's fault (as had long been the theory), or maybe Abuelita now blamed herself and the failure of her spirit powers. Titi Carmen too might have faulted herself for not interceding. And how many times had I heard Titi Judy criticized for Tío Vitín's failure to visit the family more often — even though Tío Vitín was Abuelita's son and Titi Judy was just his wife? That was how their minds worked: if a man did something wrong, there was a woman to blame, whether wife, mother, sister, or sister-in-law. I recognized that it must be horribly painful to imagine you could have stopped him but didn't. But I also knew all that was nonsense. There was no saving Papi from himself.

It is a day like any other, and the door is still closed. My rational self hasn't yet noticed it, but I can't take another minute of this. Before I know what's happening, I'm pounding with both fists on that stupid, blank, faceless door, and when she opens it, I'm screaming in her face, "Enough! You've got to stop this! You're miserable and you're making us miserable."

Such screaming hasn't been heard in the house in months. She's just standing there, blinking at me. I can't help myself, I'm still screaming. "What's wrong with you? Papi died. Are you going to die too? Then what happens to me and Junior? Stop already, Mami, stop it!"

I turn around and march up the hall to the front bedroom, slamming the door behind me as hard as I can. I grab a book and lie down on the bed. But with my hands trembling and my eyes full of tears, there's no way I can read. I close the book and sob for a very long time. I haven't done that in ages. Crying like a stupid baby.

SEVEN

It wasn't until I began to write this book, nearly fifty years after the events of that sad year, that I came to a truer understanding of my mother's grief. For most of my life, my sense of my father, and of my parents' relationship, was confined by the narrow aperture through which I watched them as a child. That sense was frozen in time when my father died. My theory of guilt-induced grief was hardly more sophisticated than Lucy's psychiatric help at five cents a pop. The vague shame overhanging my father's alcoholism silenced any conversation among the adults that might have caused me to question what I thought. As we grew, Junior and I would speak more openly to each other, but he could add nothing to my analysis. Although he was six when Papi died, he has virtually no memories of our father or of the time before his death. And so, with the vocabulary of hindsight, I came to assume that the intensity of my mother's grief implied some form of clinical depression that was never treated but that somehow resolved itself eventually.

I had never before in all these years asked that very intelligent and perceptive woman for her own version of events. I would be startled by what I uncovered and grateful even at this remove to meet a happier version of my father — and my mother — than I ever knew. My parents' relationship was richer and more complex than a child could imagine, and the stories that have come to light are all the more precious to me for having been captured as my mother's memory is fading fast with age.

Sometimes the people closest to us are those we know the least.

"Where should I begin, Sonia?"

"Begin at the beginning, Mami."

My mother's birth, in 1927, was bad news. It was the reason, or at least the occasion, as she understood it, for her father's abandonment of the family. Her own mother was sick, an invalid, as far back as she could remember. She believed her father was somehow to blame for that, but the story was never clear, since nobody spoke about him in their home. Toward the end, the sickness afflicted her mother's mind as well as her body, and she would wander off. Celina would wake up at night alone in the bed they shared, the door open. She would find her mother by moonlight in the sugarcane field, take her by the hand, and lead her back to bed.

Home was a little wooden shack of a house near Lajas, in the middle of the fields, with a dirt floor in the kitchen and an outhouse. There was no running water. It was the child Celina's job to draw water for cooking from the hand pump at her uncle's house by the road and carry the pail back carefully, without spilling. For washing they collected rainwater in drums.

The farm had belonged to her mother, but she had sold it to raise bail when her husband landed in some drunken trouble. A brother, he of the water pump, provided some help for the bedridden mother of six, but grudgingly. There had been a prouder time, and traces of it were still visible in the way that Celina's grandmother carried herself, in her long crinoline skirts and high lace collars in the Spanish style. "Raise your head!" she demanded if she caught Celina hunching over. "You don't have to be ashamed of anything." She was strict and insisted on manners. Even Celina's brothers, rough as they were and country people, knew how to be polite.

Celina was the youngest, and her siblings raised her, their mother helpless. Aurora found work sewing. When Celina was still a toddler, Aurora, sixteen years older, was the first to marry. That's when she left for San Germán, though she never really left behind the responsibilities that had cut short her childhood. She would come back every two weeks to collect piecework from women who sewed handkerchiefs, and to pay them; she was always in a bad mood, always a dark cloud hanging over her. She taught Celina to sew too. Celina had to make two dozen handkerchiefs a week, stitching the little hems and ironing them. She didn't get paid, of course. That work was her contribution to the household. Aurora made the clothes and paid for shoes, one pair every year.

Mario Baez, the eldest brother, who was nicknamed Mayo, fed the family. He went fishing in the mornings at La Parguera before reporting to his job loading the sugarcane wagons at the train station. When he got married, he built another little house for himself, closer to the road, and his wife, Maria, did the cooking. But Celina ate mostly fruits that fell off the trees: poking around in the grass like a little bird, looking for mangoes, *grosellas, tamarindos* . . . She didn't like fish.

In the absence of a father, discipline was in Mayo's hands, and he was rough about it. Celina got the belt for climbing a tree, for coming home late from school, having stopped to wade in the stream. For standing outside Tío Foro's store, where the men were drinking, so she could listen to the jukebox. For buying candy with the three cents they gave her to mail a letter. That was a bad one; she never did that again. Her mother would get up to put *sebo de flande* on the welts, Celina crying from the pain and her mother crying too as she rubbed the sticky salve into the child's skin. Pedro, the brother closest to her in age, never got the belt. Pedro was the dear little one, the light of Mayo's eye. Celina was only trouble.

She hated Mayo for those beatings, hated him with such a passion that she swore she would never go back to Puerto Rico after she left. But of course she did, and now my mother tempers her judgment with forgiveness: he was doing the best that he knew how; a girl gone wrong would have been a terrible load to carry. With their mother helpless and their father missing, it was kids raising kids and just her bad luck to have been the youngest. At least they sent her to school. She was grateful for that, and in her warm remembrances of school I sense the stirrings of her passion for education.

When she was very small, she went to a tiny little school nearby, and later all the way to Lajas, about an hour away if she had to walk. Walking was hard because her shoes were always too small, so she'd wind up carrying them, barefoot. But often a farmer's cart would pass and she'd thumb a ride, with the bullocks swaying ahead of her and the sugarcane behind. When she wandered home afterward, there was the temptation of streams and the house where an old woman would wave to her to come have a snack.

School was a pleasure because it got her out of the house, but it was not easy. The kids were cruel in a thousand small ways. They would attempt any kind of silly *burla* — making faces or doing a little dance behind the back of the teacher as she wrote on the board — just to make Celina laugh her nervous laugh. Then she would be the one to be punished. Whack! It was just the way she would then punish her own pupils. When she got home and there was no one to play with or talk to, she taught her lessons to the trees: "Children, repeat after me!" And when they didn't get it right, she would swat them with a stick. It helped her remember the lessons, and she liked being surrounded by the trees. Nature was a solace and a kind of freedom.

The best part of school was the library and carrying home a book. She loved to read, hoarded magazines and pamphlets, any scrap of writing she could find. When the sewing was finished, she read stories into the evening, by the light of the *quinqué* with the moths dancing around the kerosene flame.

It was an evening like that when her mother died, when she was nine, the same age I was when Papi died. People came to the house that very same night for the wake, drinking and talking until dawn, with the *quinqué* burning all night long. They brought ice to put on top of the box and under it, since there was no embalming, nothing to slow the ravages of the hot days and nights. They buried Doña Francisca Toro Torres in the morning.

After her mother died, what little re-mained of the household was broken up. Pedro moved in with Mayo, and Celina was sent to live with Aurora in San Germán. Her brother Abraham had already left for

Mayagüez. He was young still, but old enough to run off with a woman and old enough to step into the ring. He loved boxing, but he didn't know how and he lost every bout.

The house in Barrio Bosque where Aurora lived with her husband was just one street over from the train station. From the little room by the kitchen where Celina slept, she could hear the sound of the train escaping down the tracks. It was the last link to Lajas, to so many people who vanished from her life. Pedro came to visit a couple of times but gradually lost touch. He got married, joined the army. She never saw her grandmother again. That was just the way it was. There was never any choice, so there was not much room for feelings. But it could have been worse: usually orphans got sent to work in rich people's houses. Aurora had saved her from that fate.

Aurora was busy with the handkerchiefs, working long hours and traveling to collect piecework from other women who sewed. Celina still made her two dozen handkerchiefs every week. She cleaned the house on Saturdays and did small things to make it nice, picking flowers to put beside the photographs in frames. They had electricity, though the toilet was still outside. Aurora's husband, Emmanuel, was an old man and crazy in his own way. He was a blacksmith, but he spent more time fussing over his son Alfred than he spent working. Alfred was just a baby but the center of his universe, and people talked about how Emmanuel seemed weirdly obsessed with the child.

In school Celina was lonely all the time and so quiet that practically no one knew she was there. She lived in the library and often read so long that there was no time left to study. Her grades suffered, but she knew a wealth of words from those precious books, words that nobody would ever guess she knew.

Walking between school and home, or during the break at lunchtime, she had the freedom of the town. San Germán is like a cap on the dome of a hill, with a sky that's bigger than you'd expect in a place where the forest closes in tightly around. She would wander and look at the fine houses that seemed to be dressed in lace, with colored windows and filigreed gates and porches that wrapped around like shawls. She used to go to the post office just to watch the girls come from the college to mail their letters, with their chaperones waiting outside, lined up on the bench: nannies for young women, really. Only the rich girls or the very intelligent ones went to college. What would happen to a girl who thought herself neither?

She didn't know then how to make friends. If she had any at all, they were just the neighbors, people who recognized the same raggedy girl passing by every day. There was a lonely old lady who lived down the street in Barrio Bosque. Her granddaughter had become a prostitute and didn't visit anymore. So Celina went to sit with the grandmother in the afternoons.

Aurora was very strict, very religious, and fearful of anything fun, but she did have a few friends who came to visit. Celina would listen to the stories they told over coffee: about who was promenading in the plaza, the ladies on the left and the men on the right; about tea dances at the Hotel Parador Oasis. Walking home from school, she would peek into the entrance and catch a glimpse of shadowy pink archways, but she would never set foot inside. When she woke in the middle of the night to singing and guitars in the street, she could guess who was being serenaded: the same girl who sat there on the balcony in the afternoon, dressed like a princess with her fingernails painted.

One morning, a group of young soldiers were leaving for Fort Buchanan, and some of Celina's classmates decided to go wave good-bye to them at the train station. Ever since Pearl Harbor, Puerto Rico was in shock, and the boys were joining up as soon as they were old enough, if not sooner. She didn't even know the ones who were leaving from San Germán that day, but she liked the idea of a *despedida* to send them off. Maybe she still missed Pedro. The girls stood on the platform at the train station and waved till the caboose disappeared into the forest. When they got to school, they were all punished for being late.

Maybe a seed was planted that day. Later she saw an ad in the newspaper: Join the Women's Army Corps! She knew the instant she saw it: this was her chance. She mailed in her name and address and said she was nineteen. Celina was only seventeen. They wrote back and told her to present herself in San Juan. Celina showed the letter to Aurora.

"You're crazy," Aurora said.

"No, it's an order from the army. I have to present myself! I can't disobey. I *have* to go."

It took six or seven hours by train to get to San Juan, and that trip was the best adventure of her short life. The conductor punching the tickets looked like a general in his smart uniform. Passengers came from who knows where, all over the island, with their bags and bundles and boxes, their *fiambreras* stacked up with what they'd brought to eat. The world zipped past the windows. A car raced alongside the tracks, the driver honking and waving. The train pulled in at little flag stops, not even stations, where kids ran on the platform to sell fruits through the windows. At one crossing, a chain beside the tracks cordoned off a road leading elsewhere, a crimson tunnel carpeted with petals dropped by a *flamboyán* tree in full bloom.

Aurora's husband had a sister in San Juan, and they had called her on the telephone. She met Celina at the train station and took her to the camp the next day. High on adrenaline, Celina took a whole battery of tests and passed every one of them, mental and physical. Then they asked for her birth certificate. Panic. They said, you leave for Miami in four days. Go home and get your birth certificate. Come back in time to ship out.

She took the train back to San Germán, another whole day traveling and plenty of time to fret. At home she told Aurora what had happened: "You have to find a birth certificate, and it has to say I'm nineteen.

Or else they'll put you in jail!"

"*¡Estás loca!* You're the one who's going to jail, not me." Well, *somebody* would be going to jail if the U.S. Army went to all that trouble to recruit a WAC and then found out she had lied. Aurora went to Lajas and found Mayo. Mayo found a lawyer. Somehow they did what they did, and Aurora came back with a birth certificate that said Celina Baez was born in 1925.

All of this my mother managed on impulse, without any real thought about where she was headed. She would never have much patience with the spirit world, always keeping a safe distance from such things, but in this particular turn of events, so unforeseen and ultimately so fortuitous, she still credits the guiding hand of her mother, who, she believes, continues to watch over her.

My mother boarded the flight to Miami with an incredulous excitement that would never completely fade. The stories of her army days were among the few memories of youth that she shared with friends and family when I was growing up. It was a coming of age, a sudden and sometimes comical meeting with the modern world, and, for all the military discipline, a time of unthinkable, giddy new freedom. It was also an extraordinary moment in history. My mother was recruited into one of the first Puerto Rican units of the Women's Army Corps. Over twenty thousand Puerto Rican men had already served in the U.S. armed forces before the women were included. And although the first units were kept segregated because of their limited English, it was for many of these women, as for so many of the men who served, how they came to see themselves as rightfully American.

Landing in Miami, the new recruits were transferred from the airport to the train station, where, shivering on the platform in their cotton dresses, they waited for the Pullman. It was December, but none of the girls from Puerto Rico had coats or stockings. A kindly black conductor found blankets for them to use until they got to Georgia, where they were headed for basic training.

At Fort Oglethorpe, the sergeant took the whole band to the PX and let them choose nylons and garter belts and brassieres to wear with their new uniforms. They were screaming with laughter, showing each other what to do with them. Many of that ragtag bunch had joined up wearing homemade underwear and had never touched such fancy things in their lives. And when they learned how to march, the stockings fell down, causing my mother to laugh so hard she got KP duty as a penalty.

The basic training was difficult, because there was so much to learn: not just the military life and duties, but simply functioning in a world that was new to her. Never having used a telephone on her own, she didn't know not to hang up when she went to find the officer someone was calling for. All the instructions were in English, which to her had been just another class in high school until then. Her schoolbooks had said nothing about KP duty, about how to light a chimney stove, how to peel a potato.

Though the war seemed far away, the WACs understood that every task given them would have required an able-bodied man. For every woman in the force, a man was freed to fight the war. After basic training, my mother's group was assigned to New York, and that was the real beginning of her new life. They lived in the Broadway Central Hotel and worked at the post office on Forty-Second Street, sorting letters and packages for the troops in Europe. They practiced their English, learned their way around the streets and the subways, learned how to be on their own. For Celina, there was also a lesson that others already knew: learning how to have a friend.

Carmin was the first real friend Celina had, and emotionally it was like learning to walk. Together the two of them explored the mesmerizing town. In those days Forty-Second Street was a beautiful place. It was classy, not yet the seedy peep-show district it would become in the 1970s or the garish tourist zone it is today. Just walking down the street you felt liberated. The restaurants and the shows — they saw Frank Sinatra and Tommy Dorsey — and so many other things were free because they were in uniform. Celina and Carmin were in a movie theater when the reel stopped and the lights came up for the announcement: the Germans had surrendered. They went out in the street, and then came the scene that my mother would describe so many times, always with the same look of wonder. "Beautiful pandemonium," she called it. Thousands of people, all the soldiers and all the girls, everybody kissing and hugging, yelling their heads off, embracing strangers, everyone so jubilant. It was magic; it was electric. Like nothing she'd ever seen.

Carmin had friends in the Bronx, and one day they braved the long subway ride to go to a party, getting up at every station so as not to miss the stop at Intervale. They had never taken the subway anywhere except back and forth between the hotel and the post office.

That was the day she met Juan Luis Sotomayor. The family called him Juli (*Juu-li*), in the typically creative Puerto Rican approach to nicknames. He saw that Celina was shy, and he was very gentle. And fine looking, *guapísimo.* She liked the way he paid attention. No one had ever paid attention to her. He talked to her about things he read in the newspaper; they both read the whole of *El Diario* every day. No one had ever talked to her about reading before either. Afterward, he would write letters, just to tell her about his day — and to ask when she was coming back. There was always a reason to come back, always another party. Even after the WACs were reassigned to Camp Shanks, somehow Celina and Carmin would find their way down to the Bronx, to 940 Kelly Street.

And at the same time as Celina fell in love with Juli, she fell in love with his mother too. "Don't call me Doña," she said, introducing herself that first day. "Call me Mercedes. Doña is for old ladies." Mercedes loved people, drew them around her, and was the life of the party. She *was* the party.

She always found something to laugh at, something to argue about, news to share. Coming into that family, for Celina, was an awakening to life and energy, to the joy of being with people. She could forget about being an orphan.

Mercedes and her son were two of a kind, both of them *embusteros,* spinning tall tales that swept you along, right up to that moment when it dawned: That can't be true! And the poetry that followed after the room went quiet and each looked to the other, mother and son, to see who would begin — the pleasure of that moment of anticipation.

¿Qué cómo fue, señora?
Como son las cosas cuando son del
    alma.

As it is with matters of the heart . . . *Y entre canto y canto colgaba una lágrima . . .* * Celina had always loved poems, as far back as Lajas, copying them onto little slips of paper so that she could learn them. But she

* You ask how it was, Madam?
    As it is with matters of the heart . . .
    And between each song hung a tear . . .
                (from "El Duelo en la Cañada," or
        "Duel in the Canefield," by Manuel Mur Oti)

had never heard anyone recite them so they came alive.

When she was coming up for discharge, she decided she didn't want to go back to Puerto Rico. Juli said: Stay in New York; we'll get married as soon as you're out of the service. They did, at city hall, with no more ceremony than a couple of signatures and a kiss. When she moved in, it was she and Juli, his brother Vitín and his sister, Carmen, all living with Mercedes and Gallego, the whole family piled into two bedrooms, girls in one, boys in the other. Until the newlyweds got their own place downstairs. The building was an old tenement, with dark and narrow rooms, but their kitchen was big and Juli made it beautiful. He put up curtains and pretty tiles. He raised a scaffold and mixed different colors and painted the old plaster molding on the wall. It was glorious, bouquets of flowers on her kitchen wall. Juli had such flair.

When friends came over, he always had something to offer them, knew how to make them at home. He taught his bride to dance. Bolero. Cha-cha-cha. Merengue. She was clumsy, apologetic. "You'll do okay, Celina," he said. "You'll do okay." She was learning to be like him, and that was all she wanted.

On her birthday, she went into the bedroom, and there on the bed was a new dress, the skirt spread wide, with roses scattered around it. Juli did everything with creative exuberance; in his heart of hearts he was an artist. He'd taught himself to sculpt and made busts of Roosevelt, Truman, and MacArthur, with nothing but newspaper photographs to go by. One day he made Celina's face. It was a strange feeling to see how he saw her, with arched eyebrows, wearing a turban. That face was stunning, and yes, somehow it looked like her, even though she had never imagined herself to be beautiful. It was stranger still when she saw how they used it as a model at the mannequin factory where he worked. There they were, a whole crowd of Celinas with those eyebrows and turbans, headed for shop windows, who knew where.

My father's education was minimal, though he had demonstrated a prodigious numerical aptitude early. Sixth grade was as far as he'd got before he joined other members of the family working full-time in a button factory in Santurce. His father got sick with tuberculosis, which was endemic on the island then, with no treatment available, so Juli had to help support the family. At one point, however, something extraordinary happened. Some professors from the university in San Juan had somehow heard about his math talent and came to watch him doing calculations in his head. They wanted to give him a scholarship to go away to school, but his mother — my *abuelita* — couldn't bear to let him go. He would stay by her side until he was twenty-two, when Abuelita decided to move the entire family, which by then included Gallego, to New York in search of work. My father arrived on the U. S. Army Transport *George S. Simonds,* which then ferried workers from the Caribbean, just days before Christmas of 1944 — within days of my mother's arrival.

When he worked at the mannequin factory, they recognized his talent. He loved that job, but the factory closed, and he went on to work at a radiator factory. There they realized he was good with numbers, and they took him off the shop floor to do their bookkeeping. People could see his intelligence, but with no education the opportunities were limited.

Despite having lost his own chance for an education, my father never resented my mother's ambitions. On the contrary, he encouraged her. She managed to finish high school, do a secretarial course, and study to qualify as a practical nurse in the first years of their marriage. In many ways, he defied

115

the macho stereotype of a Latin male. It took my mother seven years to get pregnant, and though she felt the pressure of Abuelita's impatience and comparisons with others, it was never my father who gave her a hard time. When I was finally born, he was overjoyed. She was the one, not he, who doubted her ability to be a good parent.

The family has always told stories about how difficult I was as a baby, and what a terror as a toddler. They say I learned to walk at seven months and to run the very same day, ever after the hot pepper — *¡Ají!* — a menace to myself and everyone else. How many times had they rushed me to the hospital in a panic? Once a fireman neighbor had to rescue me when I got my head stuck in a bucket, trying to see what my voice sounded like in the enclosed space.

Only lately has my mother told me that my father was the one who walked me through endless colicky nights, even drove me around in the car when he found that would settle me; who was calm and patient while she felt panicked and incompetent.

So how did it all fall apart? When did the drinking become a problem? The move from the tenement on Kelly Street to the Bronxdale Houses was a turning point, and it happened around the time the mannequin factory closed, another displacement. My mother saw the new projects as a place that was cleaner and safer to raise a family. But for my father, it was exile in a wilderness of concrete and vacant lots, far from the enfolding life of family and the give-and-take of friends, far from the whole noisy, boisterous business of the streets where everyone knew everyone, watched out for everyone, and spoke Papi's own language. In the long run, the whole family would follow us, and the Bronxdale Houses would borrow a little of the old neighborhood's warmth, but when my mother insisted on making the move, we were pioneers.

He was drinking before that, she realized, but so was everyone else. In those days it was harder to tell a bit of excess from a serious problem. The beginning of the story went back much further. When his father died of tuberculosis, in the little cottage he had built to quarantine himself from the family, Juli was just thirteen. As the eldest son, and now the breadwinner too, he was the man of the house, child or no. Then, a couple of years later, Gallego came along in his *guagua* bus and swept Mercedes off her feet. Juli didn't deal with it very well. He never completely accepted Gallego, even after they all came to New York; years later you could still see the uneasiness between them in subtle ways. It was when Gallego appeared that my father first learned to drink. But it would be a long time before his drinking became the catalyst for daily fights, before my mother realized that she not only didn't know what to do but didn't know what not to do to avoid making it worse. And still she insists: whatever else her husband did, he always worked, and he always cared about Junior and me. Just not enough, because how much could you care if you're killing yourself? If you're drinking every extra penny there is?

My mother could not have even afforded to pay for Papi's burial if Dr. Fisher hadn't insisted that my father take out a life insurance policy: twenty-five hundred dollars. When my mother balked at the payments, Dr. Fisher said he would cover it himself if my parents couldn't, which was enough to shame Mami into scraping it together each month. What kind of a doctor pays for his patients' life insurance? The man was a saint. And he knew that Papi couldn't last.

A doctor could see it coming, but for everybody else it was a shock. Even as a nurse, my mother couldn't see it as it was happening right in front of her. The day they took the bus to the hospital, she was still filling out the forms as they wheeled him away. A minute later they announce a code blue over the loudspeaker. She stops and listens out of habit: someone's in trouble. But no, this is Jacobi Medical Center, not Prospect Hospital. She's not on duty, and the moment passes. It never occurred to her that they were calling the code for Juli, that he was dying then.

In the months she sat in darkness behind her closed door, it was not just the sad waste of a man with so much talent, so much charm, so much life, that she was mourning. The death of the marriage too finally had to be mourned, a recognition so long forestalled by all the tricks the mind plays in the shadows of denial and shame. And mixed in with the mourning was fear — the practical dread of raising two kids as a single mother on a tiny income, but even more the fear that echoed a much older one, of loneliness, of being cast out. A widow, an orphan — what's the difference?

No, it was not guilt that she felt at all. It was sadness and fear. "And it was no clinical depression, Sonia. I'm a nurse, I would recognize that. It was simply *el luto,* the grief that was fitting to the time."

EIGHT

When I woke up the morning after I'd screamed at my mother, she had already left for work as usual. Ana fixed breakfast for Junior and me and got us off to school as on any other day. But when we came home that afternoon, I could feel a change as soon as I opened the door. The window shades were up for the first time in many months, and Radio WADO was playing. "We're home, Mami!" Junior shouted, and then she appeared. She had on a black dress with white polka dots, and it seemed so vivacious I didn't then register that she was still technically wearing black. She also had on makeup and perfume. I felt my smile spreading, my whole body filling up with relief.

When I look back on my childhood, most of my memories are mapped on either side of certain fault lines that split my world. Opposites coexisted without ever being reconciled: the grim claustrophobia of being home with my parents versus the expansive joy at Abuelita's; a mundane New York existence and a parallel universe on a tropical island. But the starkest contrast is between the before and the after of my father's death.

The silence of mourning was over finally, but more important, the constant, bitter conflict that had filled our lives was over too. Of course Junior and I still found plenty of reasons to yell at each other, provoking my mother's familiar warning call — her *la la la la* that rose ominously in tone, step-by-step, until we got the message that we had gone too far and that justice would be swift if we didn't immediately make ourselves scarce. We were still not like a family on television, but the screaming fights that had worn me down with sadness were no more.

My mother still often worked six days a week, but she was no longer trying to escape from us. Home was now a good place to be, and so she worked the early shift at Prospect Hospital, leaving at six in the morning in order to be home by the time we finished at Blessed Sacrament. Ana came over in the mornings to fix breakfast and get us off to school. I could have managed by myself, but Junior was such a sleepyhead that we'd never have gotten to school on time without help.

The apartment was always immaculate, but it was no longer my doing. I quit my compulsive cleaning and left it to my mother, who cared about the place now. With the bit of insurance money left over after Papi's burial, she even bought a mirror that covered one wall of the living room, making it seem bright and spacious.

I didn't entirely trust this new reality, my mother's transformation included. Once in a while, not often, she would date: a friend's brother, or someone's divorced son. I wondered what would happen to Junior and me if she got married again. Would she leave us behind? Would the fighting resume with a new combatant? My anger still lingered at what I had perceived for so long as her abandonment and her coldness toward us. It would take me many years to let go of that anger completely, and just as long for her to lose the last of her chill. It just wasn't in my mother's nature at that time to show affection, give you a hug, or get down on the floor to engage with a kid. She had been deprived of the formative security that nurtures such impulses. Besides, they would have mussed up her outfit.

My mother always dressed with effortless

style, which seemed almost magical given her modest means. Even now in her eighties, she still looks flawless, camera ready, perfectly put together at all times. She would never understand why I lacked this talent that came so naturally to her. There was always some fault in my appearance that was glaring to her and invisible to me, and she badgered me constantly for being sloppy. Ana's daughter, Chiqui, who was a few years older than I and idolized my mother, would say, "Celina looks like a movie star and acts like Florence Nightingale."

Chiqui cared about fashion, about looking good and dressing up; I was convinced that deep down my mother would have gladly swapped daughters with Ana. But about Florence Nightingale, too, Chiqui was right. However undemonstrative, Mami cared about people, and she served as the unofficial visiting nurse on twenty-four-hour call for family, friends, and neighbors throughout Bronxdale and beyond. She took temperatures, gave shots, changed dressings, and called the doctor with any questions she couldn't answer herself. She grumbled only when people took advantage — "Titi Celina! I need some suppositories for my hemorrhoids!" Perhaps they assumed she could pick up supplies for free at the hospital. The staff there would often help themselves, but my mother wouldn't dream of it. "Mayo beat me over a three-cent postage stamp!" she would remind us. "You think I'm going to steal a bottle of aspirin or a box of disposable needles, even for you, Sonia?" She hardly had extra money to pay for them, but it scared her to see my needles, reused to the point of bending when I tried to inject myself.

The healing wasn't limited to physical aches and pains. Some of her best medicine involved listening to people's troubles, which she could do with full attention and sympathy, while reserving judgment. I remember my mother's friend Cristina in tears over her son, who was struggling with drugs. That was a common theme, especially with the sons returning from Vietnam. Sometimes, even if there was no useful advice to give, I saw that listening still helped.

There was also John, the Korean War vet, who sat in his wheelchair in front of our building, the only spot of shade in the new projects, where the trees had barely grown. Every day, two neighbors, older men but still strong, would carry his chair down the four steps on their way to work. The kindness left him stranded until they returned, and so John spent his days watching people come and go. My mother always stopped. She'd ask him how he was, whether he'd heard from his family or needed anything. I never had the courage to stop and chat with John when I wasn't with Mami, but her compassion impressed me, and I would never neglect to smile at him or wave when I passed. The role of confidante to friends has come naturally to me, and I credit the example of my mother, who, left on a park bench, could probably get a tree to tell her its woes.

One memory of my mother's comforting sneaks up on me in the night sometimes. The bedroom I shared with Junior on Watson Avenue, with its one little window, was not just tiny but unbearably hot in summer. We had a little electric fan propped up on a chair, but it didn't help much. Sometimes I would wake up miserable in the middle of the night, with the pillow and sheets drenched in sweat, my hair dripping wet. Mami would come change the bed, whispering to me quietly in the dark so as not to wake Junior. Then she'd sit beside me with a pot of cold water and a washcloth and sponge me down until I fell asleep. The cool damp was so delicious, and her hands so firmly gentle — expert nurse's hands, I thought — that a part of me always tried to stay awake, to prolong this blissful taken-care-of feeling just a bit longer.

While my mother seemed to find new confidence and strength after the loss of my father, Abuelita would never emerge from her *luto* at all. She had always dressed simply, but now it was simply black, as if all color had vanished from her life. The parties were over for good; the dominoes and dancing would exist only as memories. I still went to see her often, especially after she moved to the projects, just a block away from us. But her eyesight was beginning to fail, and she didn't go out unless it was absolutely necessary. Our visits became more sedate, just the two of us talking, spending time together comfortably. I would bring my homework or read a book while she cooked; it was always quieter at her house.

That year of my father's death had been incredibly hard on her. Her mother, my *bisabuela,* would die very soon after Papi. Abuelita didn't even go to Puerto Rico for the funeral, she was so overwhelmed with grief for her son. She never spoke about my father after he died, at least not in my hearing, but my aunts and uncles understood the transformation that came over her: Juli was the firstborn, the protected one. If he could be taken away from her, then nothing in the world was safe. Something in the fabric of her universe was torn beyond repair.

Her husband's Parkinson's disease had been steadily claiming more and more of him for a long time. By the time my father died, Gallego's speech was fading, and within a few months he was completely bedridden, another reason Abuelita rarely left the house. My mother went every week on her day off from the hospital to bathe him and help change the sheets. Perhaps my grandmother was mourning prospectively for her husband too, the sadness heaving back and forth between Papi and Gallego like a trapped wave. When Gallego died a few years later, she would move to the seniors' home at Castle Hill within days. In the same way that my mother refused to go back into the old apartment after my father died, Abuelita couldn't bear to be in that space where memories and emptiness collided. And so we did the *rosario* for Gallego in a brand-new, subsidized senior citizens' home.

Things had changed at school, too. My fourth-grade teacher, Sister Maria Rosalie, made an effort to be kinder, and I enjoyed an unofficial respite from reprimand from April, when Papi died, until summer vacation. Not coincidentally, by the time fifth grade started, school had become for the first time something to look forward to. Until then, I had been struggling to figure out what was going on, especially since my return from being in the hospital. Now suddenly lessons seemed easier. It certainly didn't hurt that I had spent the entire summer vacation with my nose in a book, hiding from my mother's gloom, but there was another reason too. It was around that time that my mother made an effort to speak some English at home.

As early as kindergarten, Mami once told me, a teacher had sent a letter home saying that we should speak English in the house. But that was easier said than done. My mother's English was accented and sometimes faltering, though she could manage well enough at the hospital, even working an occasional weekend shift on the telephone switchboard. At home, however, she felt awkward speaking in front of Papi in a language that he didn't know well.

I don't know if my father spoke any English at all. Perhaps he was too shy to speak it badly in front of us. I'm guessing he would have picked up a few phrases to get through his days at the factory, though I never actually heard him say a word. I know that Abuelita couldn't manage in English, because my mother interpreted for her whenever she had to deal with officialdom. I doubt her daughters knew more than a few words, or else they would have been helping Abuelita themselves. I can't even begin to imagine Titi Gloria carrying on in English the way she does in Spanish. Some things just don't translate. In any case, our family life was conducted entirely in Spanish.

It sounded odd when my mother first started speaking English at home, addressing Junior and me as if she were talking to a doctor at the hospital. But as soon as she found the words to scold us, it began to seem natural enough. In time I hardly noticed which language we were speaking. Still, as easily as Junior and I shifted gears into English with the flexibility of youth, at the age of thirty-six my mother could not have steered that change without a mighty effort. Only her devotion to our education could have supplied such a force of will. "You've got to get your education! It's the only way to get ahead in the world." That was her constant refrain, and I could no more get it out of my head than a commercial I'd heard a thousand times.

One day the doorbell rang, and my mother opened the door to a man carrying two big briefcases. It wasn't the man who made the rounds of the projects selling insurance. It wasn't the old man who came to collect two dollars every Saturday for the drapes he'd sold us months before. My mother sat down with the salesman at the kitchen table, and they talked for a very long time, looking at books, adding up numbers. I was in the other room, overhearing bits and pieces: "priceless gift of knowledge . . . like a library of a thousand books . . . easy monthly payments . . ."

When the two big boxes labeled *Encyclopaedia Britannica* arrived, it was Christmas come early. Junior and I sat on the floor surrounded by piles of books like explorers at the base of Everest. Each of the twenty-four volumes was a doorstop, the kind of book you'd expect to see in a library, never in someone's home and certainly not twenty-four of them, including a whole separate book just for the index! As I turned the densely set onionskin pages at random, I found myself wandering the world's geography, pondering molecules like daisy chains, marveling at the physiology of the eye. I was introduced to flora and fauna, to the microscopic structures of cells, to mitosis, meiosis, and Mendel's garden of peas. The world branched out before me in a thousand new directions, pretty much as the salesman had promised, and when it became overwhelming, all I had to do was close the book. It would wait for me to return.

Not all of my mother's efforts to expand our horizons were as welcome as the encyclopedias. Ballet class was a brief torture that I managed to whine my way out of. I was too gangly and uncoordinated; end of story. Piano wasn't much better, and just as brief. I still can't hold a beat, even though the metronome mesmerized me. Guitar lessons, which Junior and I took together, were the worst of all. The real problem was getting there and back through a neighborhood on White Plains Road where a gang of taunting bullies made clear Puerto Rican kids were not welcome. I got smacked by one of them and tried to fight back, but eventually we just made a run for it: no way I could actually beat them.

My cousin Alfred had an answer for this menace: he would teach us self-defense, just the way he learned in the army reserves. We had to do push-ups with him shouting orders like a crazed drill sergeant. He slapped me. Again and again. He counted the slaps, fifty in all. This would build up my courage and resistance, he said. I didn't have the heart to tell him no amount of basic training was going to toughen me enough to take on a gang of much bigger kids just for the sake of playing guitar badly. Sometimes you have to cut your losses.

There was one more reason, beyond the pleasure of reading, the influence of English, and my mother's various interventions, that I finally started to thrive at school. Mrs. Reilly, our fifth-grade teacher, unleashed my competitive spirit. She would put a gold star up on the blackboard each time a student did something really well, and was I a sucker for those gold stars! I was determined to collect as many as I could. After the first As began appearing on my report card, I made a solemn vow that from then on, every report card would have at least one more A than the last one.

A vow on its own wasn't enough; I had to figure out how to make it happen. Study skills were not something that our teachers at Blessed Sacrament had ever addressed explicitly. Obviously, some kids were smarter than others; some kids worked harder than others. But as I also noticed, a handful of kids, the same ones every time, routinely got the top marks. That was the camp I wanted to join. But how did they do it?

It was then, in Mrs. Reilly's class, under the allure of those gold stars, that I did something very unusual for a child, though it seemed like common sense to me at the time. I decided to approach one of the smartest girls in the class and ask her how to study. Donna Renella looked surprised, maybe even flattered. In any case, she generously divulged her technique: how, while she was reading, she underlined important facts and took notes to condense information into smaller bits that were easier to remember; how, the night before a test, she would reread the relevant chapter. Obvious things once you've learned them, but at the time deriving them on my own would have been like trying to invent the wheel. I'd like to believe that even schools in poor neighborhoods have made some progress in teaching basic study skills since I was in the fifth grade. But the more critical lesson I learned that day is still one too many kids

133

never figure out: don't be shy about making a teacher of any willing party who knows what he or she is doing. In retrospect, I can see how important that pattern would become for me: how readily I've sought out mentors, asking guidance from professors or colleagues, and in every friendship soaking up eagerly whatever that friend could teach me.

At the time, all I knew was that my strategy worked. Soon Mrs. Reilly had moved me to the row next to the window, which was reserved for the top students. My pleasure was diluted, however, when I found out that Junior's teacher had assigned him to the farthest row from the window, where the slowest kids sat. Naturally, Junior was upset, and the unfairness irked me too. It's true that I called him stupid, but that was a big sister's prerogative, and I knew that he wasn't really. He studied almost as hard as I did. He was quiet, but he listened and paid attention; nothing slipped by him.

"He's a boy," said Mami. "He'll get there when he does." The Sisters of Charity held a pessimistic view of male children: they were trouble for the most part, often in need of a good thrashing, and unlikely to amount to much. There was more wisdom in my mother's open-ended encouragement. She would never push Junior and me to get better grades, never crack the whip regarding homework or lecture us about setting our goals high, the way Tío Benny did with my cousin Nelson. When I brought my report card home for her to sign, I could tell she was delighted to see that I was getting As. That same proud smile greeted the news in later years that I'd made valedictorian or was graduating summa cum laude. It didn't matter that she didn't understand exactly what I'd accomplished to earn her pride. She trusted me, and Junior too. "Just study," she would say. "I don't care what grade you get, just study. *No me importa si trabajan lavando baños. Lo importante es hacerlo bien.*" I don't care if you clean toilets, just do it well. Achievement was all very well, but it was the process, not the goal, that was most important.

On that first Christmas without Papi, Alfred helped me carry the tree home. He held the base and I supported the top as we walked it all the way, retracing the expeditions my father had led in years past. People always used to stop him to ask where he found such a perfect tree. No one stopped Alfred and me, but it wasn't until we got that sorry specimen up the elevator and into the apartment that we noticed how much it leaned to one side. It was a lesson I'd always remember, if only seasonally: make sure the trunk is straight.

I was in charge of decorating now. I did remember how Papi always said you couldn't have two lights of the same color next to each other, or two identical ornaments side by side, and you had to drape each icicle of silver tinsel separately over a branch. No tossing clumpy handfuls, which disqualified Junior from helping, since he just didn't have the patience to do it right. But what I couldn't figure out was how Papi always managed to string the lights so cunningly that the wires were invisible. I spent hours at it without success. He'd always fussed over it a long time too. So I knew it wasn't easy, but obviously it involved some particular trick that he had never let me in on. I was reminded of another Christmas when I was very young — young enough that family still came to our house for holidays, before Papi's drinking was out of control. I had gone into the kitchen, and there was a *lechón asado* occupying the entire table, with golden, crackly skin and an apple in its mouth. I was mystified: the pig was clearly too big to have fit in our oven, and I couldn't imagine how my father had cooked it. Had he carefully cut it up, roasted it in sections, and put it back together afterward? Stare as I might, I couldn't see any seams.

As the string of lights turned into a hopeless cat's cradle in my hands, Mami walked in and I gave her a desperate look of distress, but she just shook her head and said, "Juli always did the tree. I don't know how."

No good ever did come of trying to unravel Papi's sleight of hand. One year, I had been especially zealous about snooping for presents and discovered the mother lode in the back of one closet, very artfully camouflaged. A little ripping revealed an unimaginable treasure: our own TV! Before that, we used to go to Abuelita's when there was a ball game, and to watch cartoons or the Three Stooges, I went to Nelson's house. I was so excited at what I'd found I thought I would bust. I ran straight to Papi to ask if we could watch it right away. The startled look, and then the total deflation in his face — it was heartbreaking. I had ruined his surprise. That feeling of excitement crumpling into shame would ensure I was never again tempted to peek, even when, years later, my mother had me wrap gifts that I knew, from the absence of a name card, were destined for me.

I'd always taken that part of Christmas seriously. For years when I was small, I bought presents for everyone with money I saved from the penny deposits on bottles. I collected the bottles and washed them and carried them back to the store. I recruited Abuelita and my aunts to save their bottles for me too. Abuelita would even take her empties to the bodega and then just give me the money. I earned a bit more by picking up the little winged sycamore pods from Tío Tonio's backyard: five cents for each shopping bag full. Nelson labored alongside me, but everyone else thought the work was too boring. By the end of the year, I'd have a couple of dollars stashed away, and with that I went shopping at the five-and-dime: a little mirror for Abuelita, a handkerchief for Titi Gloria, some candy for Titi Aurora . . . None of my cousins did that. I was the only one desperate to do right, to be liked, to be invited over.

Finally, one way or another, the tree was finished. The cotton skirting around the base became a snowy setting for the *Nacimiento* with its tiny manger. The picture was complete, soft sparkle and twinkling color, lights peeping shyly from behind the veil of tinsel, the crowning star aglow.

A hug from Papi would have been nice

just then. I couldn't deny that our life was so much better now, but I did miss him. For all the misery he caused, I knew with certainty that he loved us. Those aren't things you can measure or weigh. You can't say: This much love is worth this much misery. They're not opposites that cancel each other out; they're both true at the same time.

NINE

Dr. Elsa Paulsen intrigued me. She was tall and very polished, even regal, in her white coat. She spoke with a hint of an accent that was not from New York, but not foreign either. When she walked into the pediatric diabetes clinic at Jacobi Medical Center, everybody — interns, residents, nurses — came to attention. You could tell that they wanted to please her, that she was the boss, though she was also warm and friendly. When she checked in on me, she actually talked to me, not just to my mother.

Dr. Paulsen was the first woman in a position of real-world authority I'd encountered. At Prospect Hospital, where my mother worked, all the doctors were men. The nursing supervisors were women, but that's as far as it went. Even at Blessed Sacrament, the nuns wielded power only over kids. To Monsignor Hart and Father Dolan the Sisters deferred.

At the clinic, the nurse would weigh me and take urine samples. If I was lucky, she took my blood too. If I was unlucky, I'd have to face one of the interns doing this for the first time. Feeling now and then like a guinea pig was in retrospect a small price to pay for the benefit of the cutting-edge treatment being developed there by the Albert Einstein College of Medicine. They had a research program on juvenile diabetes, and considering how rare the disease was then, it was amazing good fortune that the clinic happened to be located in the Bronx, even though we still had to take a long subway ride and then a bus to get there.

With a strong focus on patient education, the clinic was pioneering much that is now standard practice: child-friendly lessons on how to live with diabetes, on nutrition, and on what's going on in your body. Since I'd first begun treatment, my disease had progressed to the point where my pancreas was producing no insulin at all. Without my shots, I'd have been dead within days, if not sooner. The insulin available then was long acting, a single dose given in the morning, but there were sometimes unexpected fluctuations in blood sugar throughout the day. So you had to eat on a rigid schedule and keep snacks or juice at hand in case of a sudden drop. It wasn't true that I couldn't eat sweets, or that mangoes would kill me, as my aunts warned. Fortunately, my mother had a better understanding, and we celebrated after each visit to the clinic by sharing a piece of cherry cheesecake from the hospital cafeteria. It wasn't so much a lesson in moderation; she already knew she could trust me to eat right. Nor was it really my reward: my mother was always fonder of sweets than I was, and there was maternal guilt to be fed.

For the most part, moderation with sweets came naturally to me because I so disliked the sensation caused by a spike in blood sugar. I could recognize the first hints of that slow-motion heaviness, that feeling of trying to get out of the chair with a thousand-pound barbell on my lap. Low blood sugar felt just as bad but in a different way. I would start to sweat and get dizzy; I would lose patience, and my thinking became fuzzy. Complicating matters, there was then no easy, accurate way to test your own blood sugar, no glucose meter, only urine strips that reflected what your levels had been hours earlier. So to keep track of my blood sugar, I cultivated a constant mindfulness of how my body felt. Even now, with much more precise technology at hand,

I still find myself mentally checking physical sensations every minute of the day. Along with discipline, that habit of internal awareness was perhaps another accidental gift from my disease. It is linked, I believe, to the ease with which I can recall the emotions attached to memories and to a fine-tuned sensitivity to others' emotional states, which has served me well in the courtroom.

But even if I took the shots like clockwork and watched my diet carefully, there was the grim reality of the disease then: I would still probably die sooner rather than later from complications. Given the advances in treatment since I was a child, a shortened life span is no longer as likely as it was. But that was the reality at the time, and it explains why my family had received my diagnosis as a catastrophe of tragic dimensions. My mother's biggest fear was the threat of amputations, blindness, and a panoply of other complications that were then typical. As collected and professionally cool as she was in the emergency room, as confident and reassuring when helping a sick neighbor, she would fall apart when I was the patient. If I stubbed my toe, she'd be yelling about gangrene. Sometimes I would vent my annoyance through reckless antics on the playground, just to scare her.

And always, since that first day, I had asserted my independence by giving myself my own shots.

It could have been worse, I realized. My cousin Elaine had one arm that was paralyzed and stunted since birth, encased in a brace. My diabetes, being invisible, seemed the lesser evil. And Elaine got even more grief from Titi Judy than I did from my mother. As soon as Elaine would muster the courage to venture the simplest move on the playground, Titi Judy would panic. Her mother's fear was contagious and I thought might be holding Elaine back from much that she was perfectly capable of doing.

My cousin Alfred was the only one who refused to believe that diabetes was a terrible disability. Perhaps that explained his drill sergeant's determination to toughen me up. It was Alfred who would get me up on a pair of skis and even put me on a horse two or three times. When he took Junior and me to the Statue of Liberty, he made us climb all the way to the crown. I was spent by the time we had scaled the pedestal, but no: "Onward and upward! All the way to the top!" The last flights were torture, my legs in such pain that I couldn't stop tears from coming. But no way was I going

144

to let Alfred see me cry, which meant I had to stay ahead of him, and that's how I made it to the top.

Eventually, I would translate my family's fatalism into an outlook that better suited my temperament: I probably wasn't going to live as long as most people, I figured. So I couldn't afford to waste time. Once in school, I would never contemplate taking a semester or year off. Later might never come, so I'd better get to work right now. That urgency has always stayed with me, even as the threat has receded.

Sitting in the waiting room at the clinic, I wondered, did it never occur to anyone at the Albert Einstein College of Medicine that kids who might not have long to live shouldn't have to wait endless hours with nothing to read but stacks of old *Highlights*? I should have brought my Nancy Drew book, I grumbled.

But when my turn came, they gave me something else to read — a pamphlet about choosing a profession. I am ten years old, I thought. Isn't it a little early to be worrying about this? *You can be a famous actress,* the pamphlet assured me, *like Mary Tyler Moore. You can be a professional athlete. You can be:*

a doctor
a lawyer
an architect
an engineer
a nurse
a teacher . . .

The list of possibilities for a diabetic didn't seem very long. And then, more darkly, there was a list of professions that were out-of-bounds. You couldn't be an airline pilot or a bus driver. Fair enough, I thought: you don't want someone flying a plane who might pass out. You couldn't serve in the military. Fine: I'd had enough of boot camp for a lifetime thanks to Alfred. And you couldn't be a police officer . . . uh-oh. That one stopped me like a slap in the face.

You couldn't be a police officer? That meant you couldn't be a detective. This was a catastrophe! It's true that Nancy Drew manages without being a police officer, but she is an exception. She was also fictional. I knew enough about the real world to know that detectives are normally cops and not eighteen-year-old girls with charmed lives. And yet Nancy Drew had a powerful hold on my imagination. Every night, when I'd finished reading and got into bed and closed my eyes, I would continue the story, with me in Nancy's shoes until I fell asleep.

The young sleuth tools around in her little blue roadster with the top down. She is an incurable optimist who cleverly turns obstacles to her own advantage. Nancy Drew's father is a lawyer. He talks to her about his cases and gives her tips that help her solve crimes. They are like partners, father and daughter.

The world they live in is a kind of fairy tale, where people own houses on winding, tree-shaded driveways; visit summer homes at the lake; and attend charity balls at the country club. Nancy travels, too. She's even been to Paris. What I wouldn't have given to see the Eiffel Tower one day! But even though Nancy Drew is rich, she isn't a snob. And even though it is fiction, I knew such a world did exist. It wasn't Cinderella and pumpkins turning into carriages. It was real, and I was hungry to learn about it.

I was convinced I would make an excellent detective. My mind worked in ways very similar to Nancy Drew's, I told myself: I was a keen observer and listener. I picked up on clues. I figured things out logically, and I enjoyed puzzles. I loved the clear, focused feeling that came when I concentrated on solving a problem and everything else faded out. And I could be brave when I needed to be.

I could be a great detective, if only I weren't diabetic.

"Junior, change the channel! *Perry Mason*'s on." Okay, so I couldn't be a police officer or a detective, but it occurred to me that the solution to my quandary appeared on that small black-and-white screen every Thursday night.

Perry Mason was a lawyer, a defense attorney. He worked alongside a detective, Paul Drake, but even so it was Perry Mason who untangled the real story behind the crime, which was never what it seemed. And it was once the trial started that things got really interesting. You assume, of course, that Perry Mason is the hero. He's the one the show is named after, the one who gets the close-up shots, who wins the case almost every time and gets the hugs and tears of gratitude at the end. But my sympathies were not entirely monopolized by Perry Mason. I was fond of Burger, the prosecutor, too. I liked that he was a good loser, that he was more committed to finding the truth than to winning his case. If the defendant was truly innocent, he once explained, and the case was dismissed, then he had done his job, because justice had been served.

Most of all it was the judge who fascinated me. A minimal but vital presence, he was more of an abstraction than a character: a personification of justice. At the end of the hour, when Perry Mason said, "Your Honor, I move to dismiss the charges against my client and release him," it was the judge who made the final decision — "case dismissed" or "motion granted" — that wrapped up the episode. You had to watch carefully because it was over in a flash, but I knew that was the most important moment in the show. And even before that final decision, it was the judge who called the shots, who decided whether it was "overruled" or "sustained" when a lawyer said, "Objection!"

There was a whole new vocabulary here. And though I wasn't sure what every detail meant, I followed the gist of it. It was like the puzzles I enjoyed, a complex game with its own rules, and one that intersected with grand themes of right and wrong. I was intrigued and determined to figure it out.

I could be a great lawyer, I decided. But a part of me, I knew, would have preferred to be the judge rather than Perry Mason. At the time, with no knowledge of what either aspiration might entail, the one didn't seem any more outlandish than the other.

TEN

I was doing my homework in front of the TV one night when my mother and her friends piled in to watch *The Ed Sullivan Show*. Ana, Cristina, and Irma were all there, chattering away. They used to give my mother a hard time for letting Junior and me do homework with the TV on, but she always answered them: "Those kids are a lot more intelligent than I am. They study four, five hours every night, and they bring home good grades. Who am I to tell them how to study?" They couldn't argue with that logic. Still, they were not alone in their anxieties. The nuns at Blessed Sacrament had their own theories about the dangers television posed to impressionable minds. They could tolerate Ed Sullivan but not *The Man from U.N.C.L.E.,* a godless Russian spy in the role of a good guy being too great a threat to the received cold-war narrative. It seemed lost on everyone that television helped broaden our horizons beyond the Bronx, where I was unlikely to have encountered a lawyer in action, or much else I could aspire to.

In any case, it wasn't as if I was actually watching the TV most of the time. It had now become just background noise, where once it had been a talisman to ward off the suffocation of an engulfing silence in the house. I'd long since learned how to concentrate with other things going on around me. Sometimes a bomb could have dropped on Bruckner Boulevard, and it wouldn't have distracted me. So Mami and her friends probably thought I had totally tuned them out that night in 1965 when Tom Jones was grinding his hips and growling, "It's not unusual . . ."

"¡Qué guapo!" Ana said, whistling under her breath.

"If he asked me for a date, I wouldn't say no." My ears perked up. Did my mother just say that? Okay, maybe it's not true that nothing could distract me.

Cristina topped them both: "I wouldn't mind finding his slippers under my bed." I must have turned beet red.

Not that I was innocent. I knew that my new friend Carmelo and his girlfriend did more than kiss in our bedroom when they

152

came over; it was one of the reasons they liked visiting our house. Kids gossiped. Donna showed off her hickeys. Stuff happened. Stuff happened all the time, whether you wanted it to or not. But I, for one, wasn't there yet.

I was beginning to find my own role in the social scene of middle school, and Carmelo had a lot to do with it, especially his nickname for me: Computer-Head, or Compy for short. He meant it as a compliment: I was rational and methodical. When my mind went to work, he imagined, lights blinked and tapes whirred, men in white coats with clipboards feeding me punch cards for breakfast. Carmelo saw the benefit of being friends with a nerd and would always sit beside me for every quiz and test, even though I didn't make it easy for him. He must have pulled his share of neck muscles trying to get decent grades. But he was still grateful: in turn, he looked out for me and wouldn't let me be bullied by anyone.

Carmelo was one of the most popular kids at school. He had the special ease of a cute boy: tall, with close-cropped curly hair and a dimple on one side when he smiled. He and Eileen, another one of the cool kids, were both good friends of mine, which did wonders for my social standing. Both lived in the Rosedale Mitchell-Lama co-op on the other side of the highway, a notch up from the Bronxdale Houses. (Or several notches, if you listened to Titi Judy and Tío Vitín, who lived there too.)

The gang liked to hang out at my place because my mother, happy to have her kids nearby and under her surveillance, made everyone feel at home. There was never a hint of disapproval about anyone I might choose to invite: all were welcome, with plenty of rice and beans to go around. Often, Eileen's stepsisters, Solangela and Myra, came too, even though they were older, in high school. They were Mami's friends as much as mine, endlessly discussing their love lives with her.

"Mami, if I invite some kids over tomorrow, can you make your *chuletas*?" I stuck my nose in the refrigerator, taking stock of what we had, what we needed to buy. My mother gave me a look as if I'd just asked her to address the United Nations General Assembly in five minutes. For all her willingness to welcome my friends, she remained convinced that she was a lousy cook, ever since the Thanksgiving after Papi died, when she roasted her first turkey with the paper packet of giblets left inside. It was a

154

mystery how someone who never enjoyed cooking made such heavenly pork chops.

I was more than happy to handle the shopping and the rest of the preparations. Hosting a party came naturally to me. I loved it when the apartment was full of talk and laughter, music and cooking smells. It reminded me of Abuelita's parties, even if it was just a bunch of middle school kids. I tried to remember how Abuelita had made it happen and translate that for seventh graders. No rum but plenty of Coke and heaps of rice and beans and Mami's pork chops.

Junior stuck his head in the kitchen door and chanted a whiny taunt, "Sonia's in love with Ringo, nyeah, nyeah, nyeah . . ."

Junior was still my cross to bear, perpetual pest of an unshakable little sibling. When my friends came over, he listened to every word we said, pretending to be doing homework or watching TV. Sooner or later anything I said, even a confession of my favorite Beatle, would be used against me.

At that age, we fought routinely, and our fights were physical. At least that's how it worked at home. Outside, at school or on the street, I was still Junior's protector, and I took it as a grave responsibility, suffering lots of bumps and bruises on his behalf. For these I would settle with him later, privately. We continued in that manner until the day I recognized the beginning of a growth spurt I knew I could never match. He would always be three years younger, but he was a boy, with all that entailed hormonally, and a boy who spent hours every day on the basketball court. The time had come for war by other means: "Junior, we're too old for this. Let's be civilized, we can talk things out and" — though I don't remember saying this last bit in so many words — "we can always blackmail each other." Henceforth that was the form our hostilities took. We tracked each other's trespasses, we snitched to Mami, or threatened to, whichever availed the greater advantage. Our snitching often entailed phone calls to the hospital that must have driven my mother nuts, not to mention her supervisors, bless their forbearance. I've always believed phone calls from kids must be allowed if mothers are to feel welcome in the workplace, as anyone who has worked in my chambers can attest. Eventually, in high school, Junior and I outgrew our warring ways, and over time we've become very close. We don't talk all that often, but when something really matters, each of us naturally reaches out to the other before anyone else. Still, to this day my brother claims a deep resentment that he spent his childhood waiting to get big enough to beat me up and on the threshold of his triumph I changed the rules.

When Pope Paul VI came to New York in the fall of 1965, Monsignor Hart arranged for a group of students from Blessed Sacrament to go see him. I wanted more than anything to be included. This wasn't just a field trip — not that we ever went on field trips at Blessed Sacrament. It was history in the making, the first time a pope had visited the United States. And Paul VI wasn't just any pope. He was elected the summer after my father died, when I had spent so much time reading. Everything I'd read about him inspired me, and now once again there were magazine and newspaper articles appearing almost daily, describing the plans for his visit and the ideas he had — about ending the war in Vietnam and using the money from disarmament to help poor countries, about dialogue between religions, and about continuing the work of Vatican II to make the Church more responsive and open to ordinary people.

I was often moved and excited by books, but how often does a newspaper article give you chills? I had to look up unfamiliar words — "ecumenism," "vernacular" — but all his impulses resonated deeply with me. I loved this pope!

So I was especially upset and disappointed at not being allowed to see him — though not surprised: only kids who had attended church regularly were included. Ever since Father Dolan had refused to pay a call on my mother in her misery, my Sunday attendance at Blessed Sacrament Church had faltered. I often went to St. Athanasius with Titi Aurora instead. That didn't count at Blessed Sacrament, though. And so I would conclude that I had to figure out for myself what really counted.

"So what was it like? Did you shake hands? Did he talk to you?" I interrogated my classmates. Despite the bitterness of exclusion, I was hungry for details. It was a relief to learn that I hadn't missed much. The kids from Blessed Sacrament were among a crowd of thousands, and they saw less than I did on television. The cameras had followed the pope through the thronged streets of Manhattan, into St. Patrick's, to a meeting with President Johnson, and to a Mass at Yankee Stadium. Best of all, they had captured his address to the UN General Assembly: "No more war, never again war.

Peace, it is peace that must guide the destinies of people and of all mankind." All in one amazing day.

It occurred to me that if I was going to be a lawyer — or, who knows, a judge — I had to learn to speak persuasively and confidently in front of an audience. I couldn't be a quivering mess of nerves. So when they asked for volunteers to do the Bible reading in church on Sunday, I spied an opportunity to test myself. Girls reading was a new thing, a small ripple from Vatican II along with the tidal wave that had changed the Mass from Latin to English. We couldn't be altar servers, though; that was still for boys only.

Doing the Bible reading was not the same as giving a speech, of course, because you didn't need to worry about what you would say or even memorize it. It was a long way from arguing a case in a trial, but a small step in the right direction. And I had to start somewhere.

As I walked up the few stone stairs to the pulpit, my knees were buckling. I watched my hand tremble as it came to rest on the banister, as if it belonged to someone else. If I couldn't even keep my hands still, what would happen when I opened my mouth to

159

speak? Every pew was packed, rows and rows of faces looking at me, waiting, it now seemed, for me to make a fool of myself. I could feel a faint gagging reflex. Suppose I threw up right there, all over the Bible? I had practiced the night before, read the passage aloud so many times — would it all be for nothing?

Wobbly at first, my voice soon steadied, and so did my knees. The words started to flow. I knew it was important to look up at the end of each sentence, but I didn't dare. The faces terrified me. If I looked in their eyes, I'd be lost, maybe even turn into a pillar of salt. So at the end of each sentence I looked at the ceiling instead: the wooden beams marking off rectangular coffers, gold spiral edges, lamps hanging from black metal rings. But soon the weirdness of looking up made me even more self-conscious, and I began to worry how this was coming across: "Does this kid think she's reading to God?" Fortunately, after the next verse or two came inspiration: to avoid the trap of their eyes, I would focus on their foreheads . . .

Before I knew it, I made it down the stairs and back to my seat. I had done it, and I knew I could do it again.

■ ■ ■ ■

I spent eight years at Blessed Sacrament School, far more than half my life by the time the last bell of eighth grade rang. Ted Shaw, a high school friend who later became the legal director of the NAACP Legal Defense and Educational Fund, describes Catholic school as his salvation and damnation: it shaped his future and terrified his heart. I identify with this depiction. The Sisters of Charity helped to shape who I am, but there was much that I wouldn't be sad to leave behind.

In the mimeographed pamphlet that was our eighth-grade yearbook, each child wrote a "last will and testament" to the life being left behind at Blessed Sacrament; the Sisters responded in turn with a few words of "prophecy" about each child. Looking over those pages, I am struck by how low were their expectations for their young charges. Of one girl, for instance, it is written that she had "hopes of becoming a fashion designer but we think she'd make a better mother with six children." Sadly, such discouragement, directed even at the many girls who aspired to more traditional occupations like secretaries, was not unusual. And yet for a tiny school with very limited resources, in a poor neighborhood where many young lives were fatally seduced by drugs and alcohol or cut short by violence, Blessed Sacrament launched so many of my classmates toward a productive and meaningful existence, success often well beyond those mimeographed prophecies. There is no denying that credit is due to the Sisters of Charity and the discipline they instilled, however roughly.

My own yearbook entry surprises me with its self-assurance. I was confident by then of my own intellect:

I, Sonia Sotomayor, being of sound mind and body, do hereby leave my brains, to be divided evenly, to the incoming class of 8-1, so they will never have to know the wrath of Sister Mary Regina because of lack of knowledge.

And here, less confident but still hopeful, is what Sister Mary Regina wrote:

This girl's ambitions, odd as they may seem, are to become an attorney and someday marry. Hopefully, she wishes to be successful in both fields. We predict a new life of challenges in Cardinal Spellman, where she will be attending High School, we hope she will be able to meet these new challenges.

I recently returned to Blessed Sacrament for a visit. It has many fewer students and much smaller classes than when I attended. It is also clear that the teachers, now more laypeople as well as nuns, subscribe to a more nurturing approach since abandonment of the rod. Every generation has its own way of showing it cares.

ELEVEN

Cardinal Spellman High School was a good hour's ride from the Bronxdale Houses, assuming the trains and buses were running on time. The school building was divided right down the middle by a crack in the wall, girls on one side and boys on the other. On each floor, a nun stood guard at the crack to make sure that neither sex crossed over into the other's side without a teacher's permission slip. The nuns were Sisters of Charity, the same as at Blessed Sacrament, but by the time I entered high school in 1968, many had shed the black bonnets and long black habits, looking a lot less menacing than they used to.

Girls and boys were allowed to mix in the lunchroom, but we had separate classes, except for religion and a very few upper-level courses, mostly Advanced Placement. Another exception was freshman Spanish. All the kids who spoke Spanish at home were in one accelerated class, taught by a nun recently arrived from Spain. It was her plan, she told us, to condense three years of high school Spanish into one month of "review" and then start teaching us literature.

We were only a week into the semester when the class was on the verge of mutiny. A desperate mob surrounded Eddie Irizarry and me — the two biggest mouths — asking us to plead the class's case.

"Tell her we aren't Spanish, we're American."

"Forty-five minutes and nobody understood a word that she said!"

Our teacher was totally unaware that Puerto Rican kids raised in the Bronx would have had no formal instruction in their native language. As for the acquired tongue, many of us had struggled in earlier years through a sink-or-swim transition in schools that had provided no support for kids who'd first enrolled speaking little or no English. And so I started high school having never studied Spanish grammar, conjugated a verb, or read more than a few sentences at a time: an advertisement, or a newspaper headline, maybe a very short article. I had certainly never read a book in Spanish. None of us could understand the teacher's proper Castilian accent or her elegant diction. We looked on blankly, unable even to follow her instructions, let alone do the assignments.

My Spanish was so deficient that I wasn't even pronouncing my own name properly. She called me on it. "You have the most regal of Spanish names," she said. "Don't you ever let anybody mispronounce it. You are *Sonia Sotomayor — Soh-toh-mah-yor —* and anything less is disgraceful. Say it correctly, and wear it with pride."

I could tell that her heart was in the right place. And sure enough, when Eddie and I explained the situation, she was very understanding and accommodating. The very next day she came back with a gentle apology and a new plan that was much more realistic: we would still go twice as fast as the regular Spanish class, but we'd cover the basics and learn grammar first, then start Spanish literature the second year. It was a good lesson in the value of learning to express your basic needs and trusting you will be heard. Teachers, I was finally realizing, were not the enemy.

Not most of them, anyway. There was the geometry teacher nicknamed Rigor Mortis. Word had it she'd been at Cardinal Spellman since before the invention of the triangle, standing before eons of freshman classes, like a prehistoric scarecrow, skinny and wrinkled with a bright thatch of red hair.

I was shocked when she called me into her office and accused me of cheating. The basis for her accusation was my perfect score on the Regents geometry exam. No one in all her centuries of experience had ever scored a hundred on the Regents.

"So who did I cheat from?" I asked indignantly. "Who else got a hundred that I could have copied from?"

She looked flummoxed for a moment. "But you've never scored higher than eighties or low nineties on the practice tests. How could you get a hundred?"

The truth, as I explained, was that I'd never once got an answer wrong on the practice tests; points had been deducted only because I hadn't followed the steps she had prescribed. I had reasoned out my own steps, which made sense to me, and she had never explained what was wrong with them. On the Regents exam we only had to give the answer; no one was checking the steps.

What happened next truly amazed me. She dug out my old tests and reviewed them. Acknowledging the validity of my proofs, she changed my grades. Even Rigor

Mortis, it turned out, wasn't quite as rigid as all that.

Perhaps the most improbable turn of events in those first months: my cousin Miriam and I signed up to be maritime cadets. On Friday nights, we went to P.S. 75 at Hunts Point and marched around the gym. We wore uniforms. We memorized nautical terms and learned how to tie knots. We would never actually set foot on a boat, but we did march in the Puerto Rican Day Parade.

Our ulterior motive for joining the cadets was to chaperone her brother Nelson, who played trumpet in their marching band. Nelson, my childhood accomplice, my genius sidekick, had grown into a girl magnet. He was incredibly handsome, as smart as ever, with a wicked sense of humor. He'd also become an impressively talented musician. In fact, he was desperate to pursue this love, even though Tío Benny had always wanted him to be a doctor. He'd only agreed to let Nelson join the marching band because he thought the discipline was good for him and it would keep him off the street.

The seductions of girls and music weren't the only reasons Tío Benny felt someone had to keep an eye on Nelson. Nelson had started at Bronx Science the same year I entered Cardinal Spellman, and already he was struggling. There was no question of his scientific aptitude. By the time he got to high school, he'd won several prestigious awards for his science fair projects, and his teachers had recognized him as a prodigy, equally talented at science and music. No, Nelson's real difficulties were not intellectual but emotional: Tío Benny and Titi Carmen were breaking up.

I myself couldn't bear to hear people gossiping about it. I'd cover my ears against any talk of who had wronged whom. And I certainly didn't subscribe to the theory of Abuelita and my other aunts, who were convinced that a hex put on the couple by means of some chicken guts left on their doorstep had caused the breakup. It was heartbreaking enough whatever the reason, and I couldn't imagine what it was doing to Nelson, Miriam, and little Eddie, too.

Especially Nelson.

When we were little, Miriam always found a thousand reasons to say no to any new game or plan that I suggested. Eventually, she would agree, but it was such an effort cajoling her. We would have a lot of fun together in high school, but she'd been one prissy little kid growing up. Nelson, on the other hand, never said no to me. He was game for anything, sticking his neck out for a friend without thinking twice. Those were qualities that I loved in him when we were little, but those same qualities would leave him vulnerable to the worst temptations, especially in a neighborhood that was drowning in drugs.

Sometimes when I watched Nelson practice for the band, I'd imagine him standing on the bow of a boat, blowing his trumpet with all his heart, only for that boat to drift slowly out to sea and leave me standing on the dock.

The summer vacation between freshman and sophomore years, I was working my way through the summer reading list when *Lord of the Flies* brought me to a halt. I wasn't ready to start another book when I finished that one. I'd never read anything so layered with meaning: it haunted me, and I needed to think about it some more. But I didn't want to spend the whole break doing nothing but reading and watching TV. Junior was happy shooting baskets all the daylight hours, but there wasn't much else going on around the projects if you were too old for the playground and not into drugs. Orchard

Beach still beckoned, roasting traffic and all, but getting there was a trek you couldn't make every day. Besides, without Abuelita's laugh and the anticipation of her overgenerous picnic in the trunk, without Gallego gunning the engine of a car packed with squirming kids, somehow it just wasn't the same.

So I decided to get a job. Mami and Titi Carmen were sitting in Abuelita's kitchen over coffee when I announced my plan. There were no shops or businesses in the projects, but maybe I could find someone to hire me in Abuelita's old neighborhood. Titi Carmen still lived on Southern Boulevard and worked nearby at United Bargains. The mom-and-pop stores under the El wouldn't hire kids — leaning on family labor rather than paying a stranger — but the bigger retailers along Southern Boulevard might. I proposed to walk down the street and inquire in each one. "Don't do that," said Titi Carmen. "Let me ask Angie." Angie was Titi Carmen's boss.

My mother meanwhile looked stricken and bit her lip. She didn't say anything until Titi had gone home. Then, for the first time, she told me a little bit about her own childhood: about sewing and ironing handkerchiefs for Titi Aurora since before she could remember, for hours every day. "I resented it, Sonia. I don't want you to grow up feeling like I did." She went on to apologize for being unable to buy us more things but still insisted it would be even worse if I blamed her one day for depriving me of a childhood.

I didn't see that coming. Nobody was forcing me to work. Sure, a little pocket money would be nice, but that wasn't the main motivation. "Mami, I *want* to work," I told her. She'd worked too hard all her life to appreciate that leisure could mean boredom, but that's what I knew I'd be facing if I sat home all summer. I promised never to blame her. In that moment, I began to understand how hard my mother's life had been.

Titi Carmen reported back that Angie was willing to hire me for a dollar an hour. That was less than minimum wage, but since I wasn't old enough to work legally anyway, they would just pay me off the books. I would take the bus, meet Titi Carmen at her place, and then we'd walk over to United Bargains together. That became our routine. It wasn't a neighborhood where you walked alone.

United Bargains sold women's clothing. I pitched in wherever needed: restocking, tidying up, monitoring the dressing rooms. I was supposed to watch for the telltale signs of a shoplifter trying to disappear behind the racks, rolling up merchandise to stuff in a purse.

Junkies were especially suspect. They were easy to spot by the shadow in their eyes, though the tracks on their arms were hidden under long sleeves even in summer. There was never an argument, never a scene. Once in a while I had to say, "Take it out." Most of the time I didn't need to utter a word. She would pull the garment out of her bag, put it back on the hanger, or maybe hand it to me, our eyes never meeting as she slinked out. We always let them go. There wasn't much choice: in a precinct that had come to be known as Fort Apache, the Wild West, the cops had their hands full dealing with the gangs. Besides, the management understood that the shame and pity were punishment enough, and I naturally agreed. I abhorred feeling pitied, that degrading secondhand sadness I would always associate with my family's reaction to the news I had diabetes. To pity someone else feels no better. When someone's dignity shatters in front of you, it leaves a hole that any feeling heart naturally wants to fill, if only with its own sadness.

173

On Saturday nights the store was open late, and it was dark by the time we rolled down the gates. Two patrol officers would meet us at the door and escort us home. I don't know how this was arranged, whether it was true that one of the saleswomen was sleeping with one of these cops, but I was glad of it anyway. As we walked, we could see the SWAT team on the roofs all along Southern Boulevard, their silhouettes bulging with body armor, assault rifles bristling. One by one the shops would darken, and we could hear the clatter of the graffiti-covered gates being rolled down, trucks driving off, until we were the only ones walking. Even the prostitutes had vanished. You might trip on tourniquets and empty glassine packets when you got into the courtyard area at Titi Carmen's, but you wouldn't run into any neighbors. I would spend the night there, talking the night away with Miriam. I wished Nelson were there too, but he was never home anymore.

I remember falling asleep thinking again about *Lord of the Flies.* It was as if the fly-crusted sow's head on a stick were planted in a crack of the sidewalk on Southern Boulevard. The junkies haunting the alley were little boys smeared with war paint, abandoned on a hostile island, and the eyes of the hunters cruising slowly down the street glowed with primitive appetites. The cops in their armor were only a fiercer tribe. Where was the conch?

The next morning, in daylight, Southern Boulevard was less threatening. The street vendors were out, shop fronts were open, people were coming and going. On the way home I stopped at a makeshift fruit cart to buy a banana for a snack. I was standing there peeling my purchase when a police car rolled up to the curb. The cop got out and pointed here and there to what he wanted — there was a language barrier — and the vendor loaded two large shopping bags with fruit. The cop made as if to reach for his wallet, but it was only a gesture, and the vendor waved it off. When the cop drove away, I asked the man why he didn't take the money.

"*Es el precio de hacer negocios.* If I don't give the fruit, I can't sell the fruit."

My heart sank. I told him I was sorry it was like that.

"We all have to make a living," he said with a shrug. He looked more ashamed than aggrieved.

Why was I so upset? Without cops our neighborhood would be even more of a war zone than it was. They worked hard at a dangerous job with little thanks from the people they protected. We needed them. Was I angry because I held the police to a higher standard, the same way I did Father Dolan and the nuns? There was something more to it, beyond the betrayal of trust, beyond the corruption of someone whose uniform is a symbol of the civic order.

How do things break down? In *Lord of the Flies,* the more mature of those lost boys start off with every intention of building a moral, functional society on their island, drawing on what they remember — looking after the "littluns," building the shelters, keeping the signal fire burning. Their little community gradually breaks down all the same, battered by those who are more self-indulgent, those who are driven by ego and fear.

Which side was the cop on?

The boys need rules, law, order, to keep their worst instincts in check. The conch they blow to call a meeting or hold for the right to speak stands for order, but it holds no power in itself. Its only power is what they agree to honor. It is a beautiful thing, but fragile.

When I was much younger, on summer days I would sometimes go along with Titi Aurora to the place where she worked as a seamstress. Those must have been days when Mami was working the day shift and, for some reason, I couldn't go to Abuelita's. That room with the sewing machines whirring was a vision of hell to me: steaming hot, dark, and airless, with the windows painted black and the door shut tight. I was too young to be useful, but I tried to help anyway, to pass the time. Titi Aurora would give me a box of zippers to untangle, or I'd stack up hangers, sort scraps by color, or fetch things for the women sewing. All day long I'd keep an eye out for anyone heading toward the door. As soon as it opened, I'd race over and stick my head out for a breath of air, until Titi saw me and shooed me back in. I asked her why they didn't just keep the door open. "They just can't," she would say.

Behind the closed door and the blackened windows, all those women were breaking the law. But they weren't criminals. They were just women toiling long hours under miserable conditions to support their families. They were doing what they had to do to survive. It was my first inkling of what a tough life Titi Aurora had had. Titi never got the schooling that Mami got, and she'd borne the brunt of the father Mami was spared from knowing. Her married life would have many challenges and few rewards. Work was the only way she knew to keep going, and she never missed a day. And though Titi was also the most honest person I knew — if she found a dime in a pay phone, she'd dial the operator to ask where she should mail it — she broke the law every day she went to work.

One evening at United Bargains, the women were making crank calls, dialing random numbers out of the phone book. If a woman's voice answered, they acted as if they were having an affair with her husband, then howled with laughter at their poor gull's response. Titi Carmen would join in, taking her turn on the phone and laughing as long and hard as any of them. I couldn't understand how anyone could be so cruel — so arbitrarily, pointlessly cruel. What was the pleasure in it? Walking home, I asked her, "Titi, can't you imagine the pain you're causing in that house?"

"It was just a joke, Sonia. Nobody meant any harm."

How could she not imagine? How could the cop not imagine what two large shopping bags full of fruit might measure in a poor vendor's life, maybe a whole day's earnings? Was it so hard to see himself in the other man's shoes?

I was fifteen years old when I understood

how it is that things break down: people can't imagine someone else's point of view.

Twelve

Three days before Christmas and midway through my freshman year at Cardinal Spellman High School, we moved to a new apartment in Co-op City. Once again, my mother had led us to what seemed like the edge of nowhere. Co-op City was swampland, home to nothing but a desolate amusement park called Freedomland, until the cement mixers and dump trucks arrived barely a year before we did. We moved into one of the first of thirty buildings planned for a development designed to house fifty-five thousand. To get home from school, I had to hike a mile — down Baychester Avenue, across the freeway overpass, and through the vast construction site of half-built towers and bare, bulldozed mud — before reaching human habitation. An icy wind that could lift you off your feet blew from the Hutchinson River. Flurries of snow blurred the construction cranes against an opaque sky of what seemed like Siberia in the Bronx.

At least now we lived close enough for me to walk to school, and I was glad of that. The hour-long trek by bus and train from Watson Avenue had been tedious. Poor Junior, who was only in sixth grade when we moved, would make the commute in reverse from Co-op City to Blessed Sacrament for another two and a half years. No one we knew had ever heard of Co-op City. My mother learned about it from some newspaper article on the city's plans for building affordable housing. The cost of living there was pegged to income, and at the same time you were buying inexpensive shares in a cooperative, so in theory there was a tax break.

My mother was eager to get us into a safer place because the Bronxdale projects were headed downhill fast. Gangs were carving up the territory and each other, adding the threat of gratuitous violence to the scourges of drugs and poverty. A plague of arson was spreading through the surrounding neighborhoods as landlords of crumbling buildings chased insurance. Home was starting to look like a war zone.

It was Dr. Fisher who made the move possible. When he died, he left my mother five thousand dollars in his will, the final and least expected of the countless kindnesses that we could never repay, although we tried. When Dr. Fisher was hospitalized after his wife died, Abuelita made Gallego stop on the way to work every morning to pick up Dr. Fisher's laundry and deliver clean pajamas to him.

Yes, Co-op City was the end of the earth, but once I saw the apartment, it made sense. It had parquet floors and a big window in the living room with a long view. All the rooms were twice the size of those cubbyholes in the projects, and the kitchen was big enough to sit and eat in. Best of all, my mother's friend Willy, a musician who did handiwork too, was able to partition the master bedroom into two little chambers, each big enough for a twin bed and a tiny bureau, so Junior and I could finally have separate rooms. Each had its own door, and Willy even let us each choose our own wallpaper. Junior chose something neutral, in a restrained shade of beige. Mine had constellations, planets, and signs of the zodiac in an antique style, as if a Renaissance cartographer had drawn a map for space travel.

I was reading a lot of science fiction and fantasizing about travel to other worlds or slipping through a time warp. It had been only the summer before, in July 1969, that two astronauts had walked on the moon, and I was awestruck that it had happened in my own lifetime, especially when I remembered how Papi had predicted this. From the earth's leaders, Neil Armstrong and Buzz Aldrin carried messages etched in microscopically tiny print on a silicon disk, messages that could fit on the head of a pin, to be deposited on the surface of the moon. Pope Paul's was from Psalm 8: "I look up at your heavens, made by your fingers, at the moon and stars you set in place. Ah, what is man that you should spare a thought for him? Or the son of man that you should care for him? You have made him a little less than an angel, you have crowned him with glory and splendor, and you have made him lord over the work of your hand."

I started a new job at Zaro's Bakery, in the small shopping center right across the street from our building in Co-op City. On the days that I worked the morning shift, I would open the shop along with the manager and her assistant. I'd fire up the machine that boiled the bagels and fill the display cases with the pastries and breads. Then, while waiting to open, we all settled down together for coffee and a snack, always a chocolate-covered French cruller for me, offset by a low-starch lunch, of course. I loved those few minutes every day, laughing over the stories amid the smells of fresh bread and coffee. It carried me back to Tío Mayo's bakery in Mayagüez.

Soon the customers would be lining up for the familiar ritual of making change and small talk. I would shake my head when they tried to engage me in Yiddish. "What, no Yiddish? A nice Jewish girl like you?" I heard that so often that I knew the routine: my boss would explain with a bit of Yiddish I did recognize. "Shiksa" was technically derogative, but she said it so affectionately that I couldn't fault it. At least it wasn't "spic" — elsewhere I'd get that often enough too.

Co-op City gradually transformed from a construction site to a community. When the harshest days of winter had passed, you could see young couples strolling, little kids playing, senior citizens watching from the benches. A fair portion of the residents were Jewish, as the bakery's clientele indicated, but you saw people of every imaginable background, drawn from across the five boroughs, a slightly more prosperous population than we were used to in the projects:

teachers, police officers, firefighters, and nurses like my mother. The buildings were pristine and flawless then, the shoddiness of their construction not yet apparent. The grounds were landscaped with trees and flowers, and the whole place was lit up at night.

Once Mami planted the flag in Co-op City, it started to look like a good idea to everyone else. Alfred, married and with kids by then, ended up in a building not far from us. Eventually, Titi Carmen arrived with Miriam and Eddie; Charlie with his new wife, Ruth; and finally Titi Gloria and Tío Tonio came too. Titi Aurora had beaten them all to the punch: as soon as we were settled, my mother's sister moved in with us.

As fond as I'd always been of Titi Aurora, this was not good news. No sooner had we finally acquired enough space to breathe than we were overcrowded once again. Titi slept on a daybed in the foyer. She was an early riser and grumbled if Junior and I stayed out past ten. If we had friends over, she would retire to my mother's bedroom. Titi was also a bit of a pack rat. I couldn't open a closet to grab a towel without triggering an avalanche on my head. And to say Titi Aurora was frugal would be an understatement. I don't think she ever spent a penny on her own pleasure or bought anything that wasn't strictly necessary. She wore the same clothes year after year and mended them expertly until mending was a lost cause. The very idea of eating out in a restaurant, of spending a dollar for eggs and toast, was deeply upsetting to her. Titi's frugality, in turn, was deeply upsetting to my mother, who took pride in dressing well and delighted in splurging on small pleasures. Mami never saved, never put money away, and she would overextend herself for something that really mattered — like the encyclopedias or keeping us in Catholic school. She often had to go into debt, but she worked long and hard to pay off those commitments.

They were an odd couple, those two sisters. Neither of them showed affection, and Titi especially could be austere and forbidding, but it was also clear that they were bound to each other in a way that I didn't entirely understand. They were like two trees with buried roots so tangled that they inevitably leaned on each other, and also strangled each other a bit. The sixteen-year difference between them made them more like mother and daughter, which was how they'd begun and how they would remain. Junior and I both suspected that one of Mami's motivations for inviting Titi Aurora to move in was to enlist her as a spy or at least as a deterrent. Surveillance was maintained, and Mami ducked the blame. They did have an understanding, however, that Titi was not permitted to discipline us directly. She had to report to Mami whatever terrible thing we had done — or rather, Mami, who wasn't eager to hear bad news, would reluctantly extract a report from Titi's pointedly sullen mumbling — and then it was up to our mother to decide what punishment was warranted. This often worked in our favor. When Titi phoned the hospital in a panic to report that Junior had committed an unspeakable offense, how could Mami be anything but relieved to learn that no, he hadn't committed a crime, or turned to drugs, or landed in jail? Catching him with a girlfriend in the bedroom was almost good news if you framed it like that.

Just as in the projects, our home was still my friends' favorite hangout. And even with Titi grumbling, the party continued, my mother coming in for a cup of coffee at regular intervals, just to remind us of her presence. If we got too noisy, though, one of the neighbors was bound to call Co-op City security. The first time that happened and a uniformed guard was banging at the door, we scrambled, looking for somewhere to hide two whole six-packs of beer. But the next thing I knew, Mami came bounding out of her bedroom like a tigress, fire in her eyes. She threw open the door and yelled into the hallway, "You tell those neighbors that these are young kids having fun in my house! That's why kids get into trouble, because people don't let them have fun at home!" Then louder still, "If anyone has a problem with that, they can come talk to me! Not call security!" When she was done shouting, she invited the guard in for coffee and told the kids already gathering their stuff that they could stay, but just keep the volume down, please.

And so, thanks to Mami, our home became party central as well as campaign headquarters for student council elections. We threw poster-making parties, painting slogans on banners stretched all the way down the halls. We threw victory parties when we won and consolation parties when we lost. Throughout my high school years, apartment 5G, 100 Dreiser Loop, was the place to be.

Marguerite Gudewicz and I both had a crush on Joe. He was messing around with both of us, being straight with neither. What did he think, that girls don't talk? When he dumped us both for someone else, Marguerite and I became best friends.

There was something about going to Marguerite's house that stirred memories of Abuelita's when I was small. The place was like a village, with grandparents living downstairs, Marguerite and her brother and parents upstairs, and Uncle Walter in the basement apartment. I felt right at home.

Marguerite's father, John Gudewicz, was not one to censor himself, but at least he made an effort to tone down his remarks when I was in earshot. He still had his views on "those Puerto Ricans," but his kindly laugh made it impossible to take offense. In 1971, when Archie Bunker first appeared on *All in the Family,* we all joked that Mr. Gudewicz could sue CBS for copyright infringement. Still, when push came to shove, he stood up for me. One night at a party, his brother asked pointedly, "Who's the spic?"

"She's a guest of ours, and if you don't

like it, you can get the hell out," he said. And he wasn't just being a good host. I learned that when Marguerite's parents married, in their communities a match between a German and a Pole was virtually miscegenation. What's more, Marguerite's mother, Margaret, a modest woman who never talked about herself, had hidden Jews in wartime Germany. The Gudewiczes were not people who needed any lessons on the evils of prejudice.

Beyond the very circumscribed world of my family and our few blocks of the South Bronx, a much wider world was opening up to me, if only in a New York sort of way. If you grow up on salsa and merengue, then polkas and jitterbugs look as if they jumped off the pages of *National Geographic*. To Puerto Rican taste buds, the blandness of German, Polish, and Irish food left something to be desired, but it did seem we had a lot to learn about preparing vegetables. I noticed too that the *mishigas* on display in the hallways of Co-op City or at Zaro's more than matched the volubility of Puerto Rican family life, but if we'd slung the kinds of insults that our Jewish neighbors regularly did, the dishonor and acrimony would have stuck for generations. I was always amazed to hear them laughing together again within minutes of a flare-up.

The differences were plain enough, and yet I saw that they were as nothing compared with what we had in common. As I lay in bed at night, the sky outside my window reflecting the city's dim glow, I thought about Abuelita's fierce loyalty to blood. But what really binds people as family? The way they shore themselves up with stories; the way siblings can feud bitterly but still come through for each other; how an untimely death, a child gone before a parent, shakes the very foundations; how the weaker ones, the ones with invisible wounds, are sheltered; how a constant din is medicine against loneliness; and how celebrating the same occasions year after year steels us to the changes they herald. And always food at the center of it all.

Just as my emotional world was growing in Co-op City, my intellectual horizons were beginning to expand at school. Miss Katz, who taught us history my junior year, was different from any teacher I'd had before, different, in fact, from anyone I had ever known. Compared with the nuns, she seemed young and vibrant. She warned us against getting stuck in rote learning, about how we needed to master abstract, conceptual thinking. The meaning of all this would be revealed once we'd written our first essays. Our first what? There we sat, rows of blank faces in our regulation navy skirts, white blouses, and sweater vests. Eleven years of memorization had molded our minds to be no less uniform. Essay? Somehow we had reached junior year in high school without having written anything beyond book reports. The nuns had always fed us facts, and we had always parroted them back. I was very good at it. I prided myself on being able to soak up vast oceans of facts. No teacher had ever asked anything more in exchange for an A.

Miss Katz asked something more. Her pronouncements and challenges intrigued me. What would it mean to think critically about history? How do you analyze facts? At least I'd learned by then the value of asking for help. If I went to talk to her after class, she wouldn't slam the door on me.

In fact, the door was wide open, and we had several long and fascinating conversations. She told me about her boyfriend, a Brazilian she described as a freedom fighter working on behalf of the poor and oppressed under the military dictatorship. I asked how, being Jewish, she'd come to work at a Catholic school, and she told me she was inspired by the nuns and priests she'd encountered in Latin America. They put their lives at risk for the sake of helping the poor. She talked in a similar way about Father Gigante, too, which took me by surprise, but it made sense.

Father Gigante was our priest at St. Athanasius, where I'd attended Mass with Titi Aurora before the move to Co-op City. I would only gradually become aware that the familiar figure at the altar was a larger-than-life presence beyond the sanctuary, an activist for tenants' rights who famously walked the mean streets with a baseball bat as he negotiated with gangs and landlords. In the same parish where Abuelita and all my family had lived until my mother led the exodus, Father Gigante was working to reclaim buildings that were abandoned or gutted by arson and renovate them as low-cost housing. It wouldn't have occurred to me to call him a freedom fighter, but why not?

Miss Katz was the first progressive I'd ever encountered up close. There certainly weren't many others at Cardinal Spellman High School in those days, and she would last there only one year. I remember wondering what made her so intriguing. How could one become an interesting person? It wasn't just having a boyfriend you could describe as a hero, though that certainly got my attention. It had more to do with her questioning the meaning of her existence, thinking in terms of a purpose in life. She was a teacher but still educating herself, learning about the world and actively engaged in it. I began to have an intimation that education could be for something other than opening the doors of job opportunity, in the sense of my mother's constant refrain.

I wish I could say that the same kind of reflection that lit up my conversations with Miss Katz had thrown some light on the problem of writing a history essay. Somehow her prescription for critical thinking and analysis remained abstract, if tantalizing. Though I did well enough in her class, I would have to wait till college before I could really understand what she meant.

It had been established that Sonia Sotomayor was not much to look at. I had a pudgy nose. I was gawky and ungraceful. I barreled down the halls of Cardinal Spellman, headfirst, unlike those who knew how to amble with a sexy sashay. My own mother told me that I had terrible taste in clothes.

I did get asked out occasionally. Usually, a friend's boyfriend had a friend, and they were looking for a fourth to double-date.

Sometimes he would ask me again, and sometimes it would last for a while but never as long as going steady. Once I was the one to put an end to it: as his contribution to a meal that some friends were making at my house, my date decided to shoplift the bacon for the BLTs. Making matters worse, it wouldn't have happened except that Mami didn't have enough money to put together a meal for us that day. She was terribly ashamed, but she would have been horrified to learn about the shoplifting. I wanted nothing more to do with that guy.

Mostly, I felt like everybody's second choice, which is why a compliment could catch me off guard, especially an unconventional one. For instance, according to Chiqui, I had "baseball bat legs." Thanks a lot, Chiqui.

"No, that's good! You see how your ankles are small and the calves curve? You've got good legs."

I would hear worse: Kevin told me that Scully's dad said I was "built like a brick shit-house."

"It's a compliment, Sonia."

"What kind of compliment is that?"

"It's just an expression," Kevin insisted. "It means you're well built. Not like some flimsy wooden job." I couldn't believe my ears. Was that what they meant by Irish wit?

Apart from dubious flattery, the truth was that Kevin Noonan made me feel attractive in a way that was new to me and not unwelcome. I, in turn, was entranced by his blue-gray eyes. I found myself scanning the hallway on the far side of Cardinal Spellman's divisive crack to catch a glimpse of that frizzy halo of sandy curls that made his slight figure stand out in the uniformed crowd.

On our first date, we took the train down to Manhattan. We walked the entire city, walked for hours, talking as he showed me his favorite spots. The first place he took me was a tiny park on East Fifty-Third Street where a curtain of water still runs down a stone wall. The sound of the fountain makes the city seem far away and turns the vest-pocket park into a private cove.

From that first date, we were inseparable. For the first month that I knew Kevin, he brought me a rose every single day. One time after school I was walking with him to the stop where he caught the bus home to Yonkers. We passed by Titi Gloria's house, and I dragged Kevin in to meet her and Tío Tonio. Really, I just wanted to postpone our parting, but as soon as we got there, Kevin turned pale and clammed up. I thought maybe he was put off because Titi Gloria and Tío Tonio kept switching to Spanish, even though they were making quite an effort, welcoming us with cake and cookies and sodas. But Kevin remained stony, and I was more than a little upset by this.

The next day when I got to school, there was no rose. I was getting seriously worried that things were over between us. But finally Kevin confessed: he had been stealing my daily roses from Tío Tonio's garden! He looked at me with a hangdog expression that didn't go with his sparkling eyes and said, "There's a lot of them, Sonia." It was true: Tío Tonio's rosebushes were magnificent. I laughed so hard I almost choked. I was happy to accept that the rose-colored phase of our romance was over. Now we were just a couple.

Kevin practically moved in with us except, of course, that my mother made him go home at night. We couldn't afford much dating beyond the local pizzeria. Instead, we hung out at home, studying together or watching TV. He loved reading as much as I did, and we might silently turn the pages side by side for hours at a time. We went for walks, or visited my family, or worked on Kevin's car. And we talked constantly about everything imaginable.

We didn't go over to his house much, because his mother had a hard time accepting me. She wouldn't say it to my face, but the message came through with a tightening of the lips, a slant of the eyebrow, a slam of the door. She would have been happier if I were Irish, or at least not Puerto Rican. I'd seen this before. One guy I'd dated before Kevin had ducked a teacup thrown at his head when his mother found out I was Puerto Rican. Kevin's mom was not so kinetic about her distress, seeking the counsel of her priest. He either shared her opinion of my people or else lacked the backbone to tell her that it was not a very Christian view. Kevin defended him. The parish in Yonkers was 100 percent Irish, he rationalized, and the priest had no choice but to affirm his community's values. I disagreed. Bigotry is not a value.

At some point I introduced Kevin to Abuelita, which made the relationship official. From then on it was taken for granted that we would get married. Whatever the differences between Puerto Ricans and Irish, among our friends and families a common expectation prevailed: you married your first sweetheart. The only question was whether we would do it right after high school or wait till we finished college.

■ ■ ■ ■

I remember standing at the bedroom window. Beyond the parking structure, at the corner of the empty lot where junk was strewn among the weeds, I could see Kevin's Dodge, his skinny legs stretching from under the chassis. An assortment of parts and tools were laid out carefully on the sidewalk beside him. The engine had recently taken its last gasp, and he was swapping it out for one that he'd bought at a salvage shop. Much closer, on the basketball court below, there was Junior alone with the ball, doing his endless private dance.

Mami came into the room and stood beside me. She saw what I saw and laid a hand gently on my shoulder. "My two sons," she said.

Thirteen

Cerveza Schaefer es la mejor cuando se toma más de una . . . ★

   Kenny Moy was sitting next to Titi Aurora in front of the TV, belting out the beer jingle. That was pretty much the extent of his Spanish, but it didn't prevent him from bonding with Titi Aurora. They conducted bizarrely bilingual conversations while watching pro wrestling together. Titi would be bobbing up and down, screaming at the referee, cheering on her favorite of the day. I loved to watch her: wrestling was the only thing that made her loosen up and enjoy herself. It reminded me of Papi's periodic emergence from his mournful silence to root for the Yankees on Abuelita's little black-and-white TV. But the Sheik? The Crusher? Killer Kowalski? Gorilla Mon-

★ "Schaefer is the one beer to have when you're having more than one"

200

soon? How could Titi believe this was for real?

Ken Moy was the student coach of the girls' team of the Forensics Club at Cardinal Spellman. I signed up as part of my self-imposed preprofessional program in public speaking, which advanced whenever an opportunity presented itself. The dozen or so girls on the team were an especially interesting bunch of self-selected high-functioning nerds, and Kenny coached us in debate and extemporaneous speech. He was brilliant at debate. His mind was an analytic machine that could dismantle an opponent's position, step by inexorable step. His affirmative arguments would make a concrete bunker look like a house of cards. And he was utterly untainted by emotion. I aspired to Ken's unflappable, rational cool, though I feared that I came across more like Titi Gloria in the usual nervous tizzy that accompanied her every mundane decision — red dress or blue?

"Sonia, I don't care if you have to cut off your hands, get that gesture out of your goddamn repertoire!" That was Kenny ringside. Tell a Puerto Rican not to talk with her hands? Ask a bird not to fly.

Ken should have gone to Bronx Science, but his mother made him come to Cardinal

Spellman to keep an eye on his sister. Janet was a radical individualist with a completely uncensored approach to the world, a ticking time bomb in a Catholic school. She even cursed the principal to his face in the cafeteria when he caught her holding hands with her boyfriend. Ken had to tax his mighty rhetorical powers to win her a reprieve. But the truth was that if Janet had been expelled, Ken would have left too, and the school would have lost a star pupil.

They lived in East Harlem, where their parents ran a Chinese hand laundry. I never visited Ken's home or met his parents. His dad was trouble three ways, he said — heroin, gambling, and a violent temper — and since they lived almost an hour away by subway, we hung out at my place. Ken claimed they were the only Chinese family in the barrio, and he was a barrio kid through and through, slamming down dominoes with the best of them. He was skinny as a knife blade, but he could eat more of Mami's rice and beans and *chuletas* in one sitting than the rest of us together.

In philosophy class, we were studying logic. I'm not sure what I expected of philosophy, but formal logic took me by surprise. I loved it. I perceived beauty in it, the idea of an order that held under any circumstances. What excited me most was how I could immediately apply it down the hall in debate practice. I was amazed that something so mathematically pure and abstract could transform into human persuasion, into words with the power to change people's minds.

Forensics Club was good training for a lawyer in ways that I barely understood at the time. You got handed a topic, as well as the side you had to argue, pro or con. It didn't matter what you believed about the issue; what mattered was how well you argued. You not only had to see both sides; you had to prepare as if you were arguing both in order to anticipate your opponent's moves. In your allotted five minutes, you had to use language carefully to paint a picture for those who would decide the match. Then you had to listen. "Half a debate is listening to what the other person says," Ken advised. It was easy to present your own points, much harder to listen well enough to respond effectively to your opponent.

Listening was second nature to me. My friends confided in me, unloaded their problems, and leaned on me for advice, the same way my mother's friends leaned on her. When I was little, listening and watching for cues had seemed like the key to survival in a precarious world. I notice when people hesitate or get defensive, when they care more about what they're saying than they'll admit, or when they're too quick about brushing something off. So much is communicated in tone of voice, in subtleties of expression, and in body language.

What Ken taught us was a different way of listening, more formal than my own intuitive skill. He taught us to pay attention for the vulnerable links in a chain of logic, the faulty assumptions and the supposed facts that you know you can challenge when your turn comes. But even as I absorbed Ken's logical strategies, I knew instinctively that emotion doesn't disappear. Much as you had to keep your own in check, there was still that of your listeners to consider. A line of reasoning could persuade, but so could a sequence of feelings. Constructing a chain of logic was one thing; building a chain of emotions required a different understanding.

I've made it to the finals of the extemporaneous speech competition. The timer starts, and I pick a slip of paper blindly. Three topics based on current events: choose one. I have fifteen minutes to brainstorm and organize a five- to seven-minute speech. Two of the three are so loud with the din of the nightly news — outrage at My Lai, the killings at Kent State, the war spreading across borders, the protests spreading across campuses — that it's hard to hear myself think. The third topic catches my eye: the cold-blooded murder of Kitty Genovese and the neighbors who witnessed it but did nothing. Closer to home — Queens instead of Cambodia — and it touches a nerve.

The clock is running. What can I recall of the news reports? Where do I want to take this? What's my purpose? What's the best point of entry? I'll start by painting a picture . . . and remember to keep my hands still.

"On a cold night in early spring, six years ago, a young woman drove home from the bar where she was working to her apartment in Queens. It was around 3:00 a.m. She parked her car in a nearby parking lot and was walking up the alley toward her building when a stranger appeared out of the shadows and approached her. Frightened, she ran, but he caught up with her. He stabbed her in the back. She screamed and cried for help. Several neighbors heard her cries and the struggle that ensued as Winston Moseley assaulted Kitty Genovese."

I look out and observe a rapt stillness in the room. I've got them.

"But the night was cold, and windows were closed. Those who heard thought it was probably just a lovers' quarrel or a couple of drunks getting rowdy. Kitty Genovese screamed and screamed for help as her assailant punched her and beat her over the head, stabbed her repeatedly, and bruised her all over her body. Finally, he raped her as she lay dying. When it was all over, one of the neighbors called the police. They arrived within minutes, but Kitty Genovese died in the ambulance on the way to the hospital.

"Winston Moseley got away that night. He was apprehended later on a burglary charge and confessed to the murder. He's locked up for life. That's not what I'm concerned with today. No, what concerns me is this: Thirty-eight neighbors also confessed. Each one of them heard or witnessed some part of the attack, which lasted over half an hour. Thirty-eight neighbors did nothing to intervene. They looked on and let this young woman die a horrible death."

When I pause to look at the faces before me, I see an opening: These are the bystanders, I imagine, sitting right here in the auditorium. How do I get past whatever it is that paralyzes them? How do I get them to step up and take responsibility?

"Thirty-eight neighbors did nothing. How does this happen? It happens when we become apathetic about our roles in society. It happens when we forget that we are a community, that we are connected to one another and have an obligation to engage with other human beings." Okay, I have to unpack this a bit, cover the bases, then circle back. "A crime like what happened to Kitty Genovese may be the act of a deranged individual. Other crimes may be different in their causes, pointing to broader failures of society. But in the moment of opportunity, when a criminal grabs his chance and a victim is suffering, our own responsibility is the same. When the criminal finds his victim in a dark alley, an observer too has a moment of opportunity. Will you see the victim not as a stranger or a statistic but as another human being like yourself? Will you be fully human in that moment and feel the obligation to care, to act, to get involved? Will you be fully a citizen and rise to the responsibility?"

They're still with me, every one of them. So I start to sum up and come in for a landing . . . "There was a young woman at the threshold of her life, a budding flower ready to open." And there's my hand, almost as if it doesn't belong to me, the fingers cupped and opening in bloom, then closing to a hard fist: "We destroyed that flower."

The applause carries me down the steps. Ken is grinning broadly, proudly. They announce that I've won first prize! A little cocky, I tell Ken that sometimes talking with your hands is fine. It's who I am, where I come from.

I was doing my homework at the kitchen table and Junior was doing his, as usual, in front of the TV, when the door opened. Mami made a dramatic entrance, slamming the stack of books in her arms straight down on the floor.

"I'm not going back!" she announced, her voice trembling. "It's too much for me. I'm sorry, I can't do it."

"Junior, get in here!" I yelled. He appeared in the doorway instantly. "If you can't do it, Mami, then we can't either. Take a break, Junior, no more school for us." With both hands I snapped shut the textbook I was reading — a very satisfying sound. I did glance at the page number first, though.

This mutiny was incited only a few months

after my mother had sat Junior and me down at that same kitchen table and asked whether we would be willing to make some sacrifices so that she could study to qualify as a registered nurse. She had wanted years before to continue her schooling, but that hope was dashed when Papi died. Over time, the salary she earned as a practical nurse lagged further and further behind what registered nurses were earning. She was worried that with her Social Security survivors' benefits ending when Junior and I finished school, she wouldn't be able to manage on her own. She certainly didn't want to lean on us to support her. We would have to tighten our belts for a while, while she took leave from the hospital to attend school.

The money was not an insurmountable problem. My mother took a Saturday shift at a methadone clinic to make up a bit of lost income. I had worked the previous summer in the business office at Prospect Hospital, and they let me continue on weekends during the school year. Junior was working at Prospect too, in reception, and he had a second job as a sacristan at St. Patrick's Cathedral. All the little pieces added up.

No, the problem was not money. The

problem was that my mother was scared out of her wits. Never mind that she was one very intelligent and ambitious woman. Never mind that Hostos Community College, where she enrolled, was specially created to serve the South Bronx Latino community with a bilingual program for students like my mother. Never mind that she had done the work of a registered nurse unofficially for years, if only because Prospect Hospital was so tiny, and she was so well trusted there. Never mind even that she had nursed half the residents of Hunts Point, Bronxdale, and Co-op City at one point or another. Do I exaggerate? Not much.

My mother was tortured by lack of confidence in her own mental ability. She was especially terrified as soon as anything could be labeled a math problem, instead of just a matter of calculating a dosage. The word "quiz" was to her a stun gun. Most of the time, she beat back her fear with furious effort. She would crack the books as soon as she walked in the door, and midnight would find her still studying. Occasionally, though, anxiety got the better of her, and it was then that a bit of reverse psychology — some might say emotional blackmail — was in order. The idea that Junior and I might quit too, however improbable, was far more ter-rifying than any quiz.

Seeing my mother get back to her studies was all the proof I needed that a chain of emotion can persuade when one forged of logic won't hold. But more important was her example that a surplus of effort could overcome a deficit of confidence. It was something I would remember often in years ahead, whenever faced with fears that I wasn't smart enough to succeed.

FOURTEEN

As much as I aspired to Kenny's cool, dispassionate rationality, *Love Story* succeeded in sucking me in, along with every other high school girl in America. But there was something on the screen that mesmerized me even more than the heart-tugging story of Ali MacGraw's sickness or Ryan O'Neal's blue eyes. The college campus where the movie was set, supposedly Harvard, seemed a wonderland. Set among pristine snowy fields, here was a cathedral of learning whose denizens lived out what seemed like an antiquarian fantasy, debating under pointy arches, scaling book-lined walls, and lounging on leather couches. Apart from Camden, New Jersey, and the alternate reality of Puerto Rico, I had never traveled far from the Bronx, and I had certainly never seen anything like this. If I had known then that many scenes of *Love Story* were actually filmed at Fordham

212

University in the borough where we lived, my future might have turned out very differently.

Until those darkened hours in a movie theater, I hadn't given much thought to what life at college might be like or how it might be different from high school. Then, in the fall of my senior year, the phone rang. It was Kenny, the familiar deep, steady voice calling long-distance from Princeton, where he was a freshman. As he fed coins into the box every few minutes, he described the strange new world he was navigating. He advised me that it was time for me too to be thinking about applying to college, and one thing he said sticks clearly in my memory, because I had no idea what he meant: "Try for the Ivy League." Ken was the first student we knew from Spellman ever to have crossed into that world, and it wasn't a term that had ever come up in conversation. He explained that this was the finest college education available and that it would open every door, which sounded oddly like a more knowing version of Mami's claim for higher education generally. I jotted down the names of the colleges as he rattled them off, tossing in Stanford for good measure.

The next day the guidance counselor had

only one question as she was thumbing through the thick catalog she'd taken down from the shelf: "Have you thought about Fordham?" A couple of pages of the book were devoted to each college: a mission statement in blandly aspirational code, a few statistics, generic black-and-white photographs of students looking earnestly engaged. When I said no to Fordham, she offered the names of several more Catholic colleges.

I told her that I wasn't really interested in parochial colleges; I wanted to apply to Harvard, Yale, Princeton, Columbia, Stanford . . .

She looked at me. "Okay." And that was the extent of her guidance. This was an occasion when it would never have occurred to me to ask for advice. At a Catholic high school that served the kids of Irish and Italian immigrants, a focus on parochial colleges made perfect sense: just getting into college was already more than most students' parents had accomplished. I happened to be graduating on the cusp of a change that would soon see many of Spellman's students going on to the most highly competitive schools. But that fall, Kenny Moy at Princeton was pretty much the first Spellman student to walk on the moon.

I got the application forms and wrote my essays, scribbling in the dark with not a clue as to what might be a worthy subject or how to shape such a thing. I tackled the SAT in much the same way. The brochure that came with the registration form was the only hint I had of what to expect on the test. Anyway, I could not have afforded a prep course, even if I'd known there was such a thing.

It is hard for students today to imagine the void before the Internet and how common my naïveté was at the time. If you attended an elite prep school, no doubt there was valuable information swirling in the air, impossible not to inhale. And obviously, those applicants whose parents had attended the same college had access to insider knowledge, to say nothing of eligibility for legacy admissions. If your own parents had gone to college at all, they still had some firsthand experience to draw on. The rest of us, for the most part, just blundered into it.

Qualifying for financial aid was the easiest part. With my mother enrolled at Hostos Community College at the time, we were living mainly on the Social Security survivors' benefits, supplemented slightly by Mami's part-time work at the methadone clinic, her summer pay at Prospect Hospital, and the little that Junior and I contributed from our part-time and summer jobs. There were no assets to report. None of us even had a bank account. On paydays I would walk five blocks from Prospect Hospital to the check-cashing place near the train station to cash my paycheck, just as my mother had always done, just as the rest of the staff at the hospital did. To pay the phone bill, you could get a money order there too. Cash was good enough for everything else.

It's just as well I had no idea how selective the colleges I was applying to were. If I had known, I might have hesitated. I did understand enough to hedge my bets, though: CUNY could serve as my safety school, since it was public admission. Among the alternatives, I figured it likeliest I would end up at the state university at Stony Brook, at which Kevin was aiming. I had quickly given up on Stanford as being too far away. Flying cross-country to have a look would have already cost more than I could afford, never mind coming home for Christmas.

Come November, a postcard arrived from Princeton with three boxes, a cryptic message beside each — "likely," "possible," and "unlikely." On my card, the first was marked

with an *X*. This seemed more like communication from a Magic 8 Ball than from
a university. I wasn't sure what I was expected to do with this occult clue, so I
trooped off once again to the guidance
counselor's office.

Behind the look of utter surprise that
completely rearranged her features, the ora-
cle pronounced: " 'Likely' means just what
it says. There's a very good chance you'll
get in." I thought to myself, really?

I was still getting my head around this
when a couple of days later I happened to
walk by the school nurse's office. "I heard
you got a 'likely' from Princeton," she called
out to me as I passed.

I stopped in my tracks. "Yes, I did."

"Well, can you explain to me how you got
a 'likely' and the two top-ranking girls in
the school only got a 'possible'?"

I just looked at her. What did she mean by
that? Not to mention that accusatory tone.
My perplexed discomfort under her baleful
gaze was clearly not enough; shame was the
response she seemed to want from me.

Sometimes in such situations, an apt
answer only occurs to you hours later:
"Because of what I've accomplished on the
forensics team and in student government.
Because I work part-time during the school

year and full-time during the summers. I may be ranked below them, but I'm still in the top ten, and I *do* much more than the others do." But even that undelivered comeback was far from complete. Her question would hang over me not just that day but for the next several years, while I lived the day-to-day reality of affirmative action. At the time I was applying to college, I had little understanding of how the admissions process functioned generally, let alone how affirmative action might affect it in particular. Barely a decade had passed since affirmative action had been implemented in government contracting. It was still experimental in Ivy League college admissions, and few of the first minority students to benefit from it had even managed to graduate yet.

Soon, those fat envelopes I came to recognize as acceptance packages stuffed the mailbox almost daily. Now that the choice was real and imminent, I sat down to more serious deliberation. Columbia, I realized, a mere subway ride away, was too close for comfort: I'd have no choice but to live at home, unable to justify the extra expense of a dorm room. That left Radcliffe (Harvard's sister school), Yale, and Princeton, each worth a visit.

With *Love Story* still lodged in my mind, I scheduled Radcliffe first. I was told that after an interview at the admissions office, a student group would show me around. But first I had to find my way to Massachusetts. As close as we had lived to Manhattan my whole life, I had only been there on special occasions — that first date with Kevin; the Christmas and Easter shows at Radio City Music Hall; Alfred's death march to the summit of Lady Liberty. On the miserable rainy day that my visit was scheduled, the cavernous hall of Grand Central seemed cold shelter, its vault dark with decades of grime. The railways then were staggering back following a long decline, only recently rescued by the establishment of Amtrak and, in New York, the long reconstruction of Penn Station as Madison Square Garden. My nine dollars and ninety cents bought me a seat in a tattered car carpeted in cigarette butts.

A sooty rain fell uninterrupted from New York to Boston, and by the time I had navigated the Boston subway and walked the last few blocks to the admissions office, I was dripping like a sewer rat. I was also feeling a shade of disappointment. There was neo-Gothic architecture aplenty, but the campus was no idyllic haven set apart from the world. Harvard and Radcliffe were fused with Cambridge, densely urban, tangled with honking traffic.

Inside the waiting room, when the inner door finally opened, I found myself face-to-face with a creature such as I had never encountered: a woman with a hairdo — no, "coiffure" would be the word — of sculpted silver, in a perfectly tailored black dress, a pearl necklace and earrings, beautiful little pumps. This is different! I thought.

I followed this apparition into her office and was stunned again by what met my eyes. I had never before seen an Oriental rug, its intricate pattern the most gorgeous of puzzles meandering across the floor. And I had never before seen a white couch. To be honest, I had probably never seen a couch that wasn't covered in plastic. I was ushered into an elegant, high-backed, winged throne of a chair, in which I felt as small as Lily Tomlin's Edith Ann, surprised to feel my feet touch the floor. I had never seen such a room with my own eyes, but I knew: This was good taste. And this was money.

That's when the yapping dogs shattered my trance. They must have been barking since I'd walked in, but now they were jumping up at me, all bare teeth and bony claws. They were just lapdogs, really, one black and one white, but they scared me. She called to them, and they scrambled onto the white couch and sat beside her, and there the three of them completed a surreal tableau, three pairs of eyes gazing at me, a vision in black and white.

That may have been the shortest interview of my life, perhaps all of fifteen minutes. The flow of words that always came to me naturally, and still does whenever I meet a stranger, mostly dried up. When I found myself back in the waiting room, too early for the students who were to meet me, the numbness dissolved into a suffocating panic: I don't belong here! For the first and, so far, the last time in my life, I did the unthinkable: I fled. Asking the receptionist to leave word for the students who were coming to get me, I said, "I'm sorry, but I have to leave."

It was early evening by the time I retraced my journey in reverse. My mother looked up from her homework at the kitchen table. "What's wrong? You were supposed to be away for a couple of days."

"Mami, I don't belong there."

Her gaze seemed inclined to question this conclusion, but after a moment's thought she said, "You know best, Sonia." She would say it often hereafter, to confess the limits of her judgment in the world I was entering and acknowledge my having reached the stage of adult self-determination. And that was the last we would speak of Radcliffe. I was convinced they would retract their offer. They didn't, but my list was now shorter by one.

My visit to Yale was a very different story. When I arrived at the station in New Haven, an old hand at Amtrak by now, the two Latino students sent to pick me up said they were coming from a campus protest. Eager to jump back into the fray, they apologized, saying that they would just be dropping me off for now. They would give me the tour later . . . unless, perhaps, I'd like to come along to the protest?

My experience of the antiwar protests was limited to the television screen. Though friends worried plenty about their luck in the draft lottery and Vietnam would come up as a topic in Forensics Club, debates weren't boiling up spontaneously in the lunchroom. Cardinal Spellman, the archbishop of New York for whom my school was named, was also vicar to the armed forces and a fervent supporter of the war, spending Christmases in Vietnam with the troops. As the bombings escalated and spilled over into Cambodia and Laos, the protesters on the steps of St. Patrick's Cathedral called it Spelly's war. But the closest we had ever come to protesting at Cardinal Spellman High School was to lobby for a smoking room and the occasional no-uniform Friday.

That's not to say I didn't understand the reasons underlying the cause, but raising voice and fist against Yale's involvement in the war effort didn't seem a smart way to prepare for an interview there. Instead, I went for a walk. The inner city of New Haven was impoverished then, depressed and threatening, no better than the South Bronx and a lot less lively. Actually, it made Co-op City seem idyllic.

When my guides found me again, they were buzzing from the protest and eager for a rap session. We joined up with a larger group of Hispanic kids, some from New York, others from the Southwest, all of them more radical than anyone I had ever known before. For two days I camped in the dorm and scouted the campus in their company, listening to talk of revolution, Cuba, and Che Guevara and feeling generally uninformed. At least Fidel Castro was a familiar name, and news of the Cuban missile crisis had penetrated even the cocoon of my

Catholic school childhood, where communism was deemed a godless threat, more cosmic than political. I could tell purgatory from limbo better than I could recognize the distinctions between socialism and communism that spurred the arguments during those two days at Yale. So embarrassed was I by my innocence that I would go to the library and read up on Che Guevara after I got home.

I was embarrassed, too, by all the "down with whitey" talk. It wasn't an attitude I shared, nor one I was eager to adopt. Many of my friends, most of my classmates, and virtually all of my teachers were white. Whether it was due to the indeterminate color of my skin or my very determined personality, I moved easily between different worlds without assuming disguises. Yes, I'd experienced prejudice aimed straight at me, from the blatant taunts of my street-fighting days to the cold shoulder of Kevin's mom, to the subtler barb from the school nurse more recently. Of course I knew that the painful consequences of bigotry — then so common, even endemic — went far beyond the sting of being called a spic, as I had often been. But I couldn't see such narrow-mindedness as the workings of systemic forces of history and certainly not as fitting neatly into a master narrative of perpetual class struggle, the way these Yale kids did. This stuff simply didn't define me in any meaningful way: if somebody called me a spic, it told me a lot about them, but nothing about myself. And how could it help the situation to hurl a slur in reply?

It was difficult to picture myself spending four years in this environment, especially with Kevin coming to visit on weekends. I left Yale thinking: not here — though I didn't feel the same panicked urge to flee that I had felt at Radcliffe. Even if I didn't share their attitudes, I knew where these kids were coming from, and when they talked of family and home, I recognized how much we did share.

By the time I went to see Princeton, I was down to gathering loose change for bus fare, Amtrak now beyond my budget. When Kenny met me at the bus station, I was surprised to see his hair grown very long, an expression of his new freedom. We dropped my bag at his dorm before heading out to tour the campus.

As we entered the main gates from Nassau Street, the sunlight on that balmy spring day danced magically on the sandy Collegiate Gothic architecture and the emerald lawns and the surrounding woodlands, a prospect that has enchanted generations of Princeton students but that took me completely unprepared. Even the bronze tigers flanking the entrance to ivy-covered Nassau Hall, while reminding me of the stone lions that guard the New York Public Library, seemed more pensive and more elegant.

Kenny had gathered a very small group of friends. Like him, they were exceptionally bright but slightly offbeat inner-city kids, radical in their politics, though quietly so, who conducted their lives at arm's length from Princeton's preppy mainstream. We sat up late together in a dorm room that night, talking easily. "Socially, it's a wasteland here," Kenny said, his judgment affirmed by solemn nods from the other freshmen. "It's a bunch of very strange, privileged human beings, and you're not going to understand any of them. But intellectually, you can deal with these people. They're not *that* smart." Nobody seemed to mind, or even notice, that I didn't join in when the pipe was passed. I didn't feel a need to make excuses or explain about being diabetic. This group was mellow through and through.

At my interview the next morning I felt just as comfortable chatting with the admissions officer in his tiny corner office. He was professorially tweedy, down to his leather elbow patches and little horn-rimmed glasses, but he was open and easy to talk to.

Before the weekend was over, my decision was firm. A full scholarship capped it.

I didn't begin to understand the power of those Ivy names Kenny had first disclosed to me until I saw the reactions of people when they learned that I was headed to Princeton. Prospect Hospital was abuzz with the news, and all day long the staff — not just the nurses and orderlies, but the doctors too — were popping into the business office: "Congratulations! Sonia, how wonderful! We're so proud of you!" All those women I had spent long summer lunch hours with in the cafeteria over card games and surprisingly good roast chicken as soap operas droned in the background and the women shared their own incrementally unfolding family dramas — they all came to give me a hug. Mr. Reuben, the comptroller, who had never been thrilled to have a kid working in the office, softened his habitual scowl. Even Dr. Freedman, who owned the hospital and who had overridden Mr. Reuben's objections when I asked for a job more challenging than candy striper, stopped by just to join the well-wishers. All this left me a little shaken. Other kids had gotten into college too. I had certainly expected to. Was Princeton really so special?

When, at the end of summer, it finally came time to say good-bye, the women at the hospital had taken up a collection. "Sonia, go buy yourself some new shoes for college. Please!"

"But these shoes are comfortable," I said, my usual line. It wasn't the first time they had begged me to upgrade my footwear. My feet blistered easily in new shoes, so once I had broken in a pair, I would never give them up. Everyone in the office had heard me on the phone defending my raggedy shoes to my grandmother. "Buy some new shoes already! Make your grandmother happy" was an old story. New shoes for college was just the latest twist.

On Kenny's advice, I planned to get a bicycle once I got to Princeton. The only other purchase he advised was a raincoat. Mami offered to buy it and came shopping with me. We searched up and down Fordham Road without finding anything I liked. We even stepped into Loehmann's, my first time there. Though it was a discount house, and popular in Co-op City, the

prices, to us, were a shock. So we went —
where else? — to La Tercera, the Latino
shopping heart of the South Bronx on Third
Avenue.

No luck at Alexander's. I wasn't being
fussy; I was just having a hard time pictur-
ing myself in that magical land of archways
and manicured lawns wearing anything I
saw on these racks. On the other side of the
street, which was divided by the elevated
train line rumbling overhead, were the
slightly more upscale dress shops, places
where you might shop for a wedding or
some other very special occasion. In this
case, a last resort.

There it was: glowing white with toggle
buttons and a subtle flair of fake fur trim
up the front and around the hood. As
improbably white as a white couch, white as
a blanket of snow on a college lawn.

"You like it, Sonia?"

"I love it, Mami." This was another first.
Unlike my mother, or Chiqui, or my cousin
Miriam, or many of my friends, I'd never
cared enough to fall in love with a garment.
But wrapped in this, I knew I wouldn't feel
so odd. Unfortunately, it was a size too
small. I tried on a couple of other coats, but
my heart had been claimed, and Mami
knew it.

I was ready to leave and try elsewhere, but she said, "*Espera* . . . Sonia, wait, maybe they can order it." She went to the counter and waited in silence as the saleswoman helped another customer. And then another and another. My mother is a very patient woman, so I knew what it took for her to finally say, "Miss, I need help."

"What do you want?" she snapped without turning.

"Do you have this in a twelve?"

"If it's not on the rack, we don't have it."

"Do you have another store? Can you order it?"

The woman finally turned and looked at her. "Well, that would be a lot of trouble, wouldn't it?"

I was halfway to the door, fully expecting my mother to give up, but she stood her ground. "I know it's a lot of trouble, but my daughter's going away to college and she likes this coat. I want to give it to her as a gift. So would you please look to see if you can find this coat for my daughter."

Her silent shrug spoke loudly enough: You're a pain in the ass. But as she turned away, she asked indifferently, "So where's she going to college?"

"To Princeton."

I saw the saleswoman's head swing round

as in a cartoon double take. The transformation was remarkable. She was suddenly all courtesy and respect, full of praise for Princeton, and more than happy to make a phone call in search of my coat, which, as it turned out, would arrive in a week. Mami thanked her profusely and left a deposit. It was a lot of money, but that coat would last me all four years of college. It had to.

As we were walking back to the station, I commented on the saleswoman's change of attitude. My mother stopped in the shadow of the elevated track and said to me, "I have to tell you, Sonia, at the hospital I'm being treated like a queen right now. Doctors who have never once had a nice word for me, who have never spoken to me at all, have come up to congratulate me."

Overhead, the train rumbled loudly, and I had to pause for a long moment before I admitted that I had never dreamed what a difference Princeton would make to people.

She looked at me steadily. "What you got yourself into, daughter, I don't know. But we're going to find out."

FIFTEEN

In the week since Alfred drove off with Mami waving good-bye out the window, a look of doom overcoming her firm-set jaw, the collegiate fairy tale in my mind was becoming something more akin to science fiction. In part it was the record-breaking heat that summer of 1972, which silvered Princeton's leafy vistas, endowing everything with a more unearthly aura than I had remembered. But I was also finding that many of my classmates seemed to come from another planet and that that impression was reciprocated.

Waiting outside Dillon Gym, where we were to meet our advisers, I struck up a conversation with another freshman sitting beside me. She was from Alabama, she said. I had never before heard an accent like that in real life. I listened spellbound as she explained how her father, her grandfather, and her elder brother were all Princeton alums. She couldn't have been more delighted to be there representing her generation. "And it really is just the friendliest, most welcoming place you'll find," she gushed. "I mean, look at all the unusual people that come here!" She was indicating an approaching pair, their heads together, laughing loudly.

I recognized my roommate, Dolores, and our friend Teresa. Dolores was vaguely Mexican looking, with light brown skin and Indian-black hair. Teresa was barely a shade darker than I am, hardly dark at all, but her features were distinctively Latina. They both looked pretty normal to me. Without premeditation, I greeted them exuberantly in rapid-fire Spanish, though we usually spoke English together. I meant no malice toward the girl from Alabama, but my pulse was speeding with a sense of purpose. Nothing more needed to be said.

Dolores Chavez was from New Mexico. We must have been assigned to room together because someone had assumed two Hispanics would have a lot in common. But all Dolores knew of Puerto Ricans came from *West Side Story,* and I suspect that initially she was half afraid I'd knife her in her sleep. I knew even less of New Mexico than she knew of New York. Dolores seemed to me a country girl, sweet-tempered, shy, and very far from home. One night soon after we'd arrived, she got her guitar out and sang softly for a while before we went to sleep, such deep longing in her voice.

As social as I am, I was quiet in those early days, trying to make sense of the conversations flowing around me. One evening, I found myself with a group of girls sitting in our resident adviser's dorm room. One of them mentioned being invited to a wedding and that she'd decided just to choose a gift from the bridal registry. What the hell is a bridal registry? I wondered. Our adviser, a senior, allowed that her father sometimes received wedding invitations from people whose names he didn't even recognize, probably strangers hoping he would blame his memory and send a gift anyway, she figured. Who invites strangers to their wedding? For that matter, who sends them gifts? Where I came from, you handed the couple an envelope with money at the reception. Were people here so rich they could afford a wedding without gifts of cash?

Whenever I felt out of place or homesick, I took refuge at Firestone Library. Books had seen me through an earlier time of trouble, and their presence all around me was both a comfort and an answer to the question of why I had come here. From my first day on campus, I'd enviously eyed the carrels in Firestone, which were reserved for upperclassmen. One day, one of those would be mine! Meanwhile, I reveled in the vastness of the main catalog room, riffling through the drawers full of cards, rows and rows of cabinets running almost the full length of the ground floor. And above them, like cathedral spires, rose the stacks, shelf after shelf, carrying a book for every card below, books ranging in subject from the majestic to the comically arcane. Here, in one of the world's great libraries, was my first exposure to the true breadth of human knowledge, the humbling immensity of what was known and thought, of which my days spent pawing the *Encyclopaedia Britannica* had offered only a foretaste.

My grazing in Firestone that first week was not at random, however. The course offerings at Princeton seemed a bewildering buffet: so many unfamiliar subjects that whet my appetite. I dug into the library catalog to get a taste of each subject that tempted me before committing to a whole meal. At the same time, I was already well aware that in our freshman class, some, like me, were far fresher than others. Many from across the United States and abroad had gone to high schools that sounded more like mini-colleges, with library buildings of their own and sophisticated electives. I had made it into Princeton but, in this way too, with far more meager resources than most. I was under no illusions about how much remedial education could be accomplished skimming a few books in the stacks.

That there was no official pre-law curriculum turned out to be a blessing of sorts. I had to decide for myself what would be the most useful way to fill in the wide blank areas in my understanding. Having negligible prior knowledge of practically everything, I planned with each course to gulp down as much as I could. And so introductory surveys seemed ideal. I was drawn to psychology and sociology, having always been interested in the patterns of individual behavior, as well as the structure of communities; history, especially American, seemed essential and promised to reveal how a larger scheme of things had developed over time. Moral philosophy sounded a lot like what I imagined legal reasoning to involve. And just from reading the newspaper since entering Spellman, I knew that one day I would need to grapple with economics. An art history survey seemed like just the way to answer the many questions that had lapped at my mind since my childhood visit to the Ponce museum. But I would err on the side of practicality for now, saving that one for a sophomore treat.

My adviser approved my course load without question, and I felt I was on my way. But back at the dorm, deflation awaited. Everyone had returned from taking care of the same business, and the freshman floor was abuzz with talk of exotic upper-level courses my classmates were taking thanks to their Advanced Placement work in high school, which had allowed them to leapfrog ahead. By comparison, my course selections sounded boring, even lazy. Was I squandering an opportunity to really challenge myself? Maybe I just wasn't as smart as they were?

That tide of insecurity would come in and out over the years, sometimes stranding me for a while but occasionally lifting me just beyond what I thought I could accomplish. Either way, it would wash over the same bedrock certainty: ultimately, I know myself. At each stage of my life, I've had a pretty clear notion of my needs and of what I was ready for. There would be time enough in those four years at Princeton to sample Chinese Politics and Roman Law, to delve into Social Disorganization, Crime, and

Deviant Behavior. Meanwhile, the introductory surveys would involve just as much work, given their broad scope, as more specialized advanced courses and would allow me for the first time to cultivate the critical faculties that Miss Katz had tried to instill: understanding the world by engaging with its big questions rather than just absorbing the factual particulars. This was the way to be a student of anything, and learning it has served me ever since. As a lawyer and even more as a judge, I would often be called upon to make myself a temporary expert in some field for the duration of a case. From the sciences to technology to the arts, the variety of industries and other endeavors that come before the courts is vast, and often there is no determining how the law applies without a working knowledge of the field in question.

I still had to choose a science lab course to meet a core requirement. Those in the natural sciences were known to be backbreakers, requiring a share of one's waking hours more appropriate for a pre-med or a budding scientist than an aspiring lawyer. I did notice, however, that Introductory Psychology included a lab that met the need. An introduction to Freud and other schools of thought, as well as an overview of brain function, seemed as if it might prove very handy over time. There was only one challenge to overcome, but one far more daunting than any rigors of organic chemistry or molecular biology labs: rats.

I have always had a deathly fear of anything that scurries or crawls: bugs, rodents, what have you. It isn't just the stereotypical fear of a lady standing on a chair, though I've done that. The special revulsion I feel goes back to childhood. The giant cockroaches that infested the projects one year — we called them water bugs — brought me to hysteria. How many times had I seen my mother take the whole place apart trying to locate the nest? The very thought of their proximity would keep me awake all night. And so when I realized that the psych lab would oblige me to handle rodents while I studied their reactions, I decided, a little perversely, to make the most of it. Undertaking a course of what psychologists call exposure therapy, I devised an experiment that required me not only to hold the rats but to implant electrodes in their brains.

It was going surprisingly well at first. I had steeled myself to picking the rats up by the tail and holding their furry bodies as I gave them a sedative injection. Once they were drugged, implanting the electrodes wasn't so bad. Tracking their behavior was no fun: it meant watching them continuously, without turning away in disgust. But I was doing it. It wasn't until the final weeks of the semester that everything went awry. I came into the lab one day to find all my rats milling around the same spot in the cage in an oddly intent way. I couldn't see what the attraction was, but the sight of their frenzied huddle was enough to stir the old revulsion: I certainly wasn't going to stick a hand in that cage. I found a stick and poked one of them off the pile. He turned to look at me, and in the gap that opened up, I saw the rat they were gnawing at, its abdomen already half devoured.

The grad student overseeing my efforts intercepted me as I ran out of the room screaming. Trying to contain my hysterics, he explained that cannibalism is normal rat behavior, that it had evolved as a way to control disease in the population and, as such, was a widely recognized sign of plague. Somehow that didn't help. He suggested I calm down and come back tomorrow.

The next day my state of mind was no better: the trauma had done its damage. It was horrifying even to imagine handling a rat as I had been doing for months, and no less so to think I had botched a whole semester's work. Fortunately, my professor took a philosophical view when I explained why I was utterly incapable of seeing my project through. As a psychologist he credited the motive of trying to cure my phobia by means of this experiment, and as a teacher he could see I had been at it diligently from the start. My grade wouldn't suffer much because of this fiasco. "Your plan was perfectly suited to what the course was intended to teach," he allowed. "Not every experiment is a success. That's the nature of doing science." The nature of doing many things, I might add: success is its own reward, but failure is a great teacher too, and not to be feared.

Part of my financial-aid package committed me to weekly hours in the work-study program. At the start of freshman year, I was assigned to food service at the commons, but a lingering case of mononucleosis took me off the cafeteria line. I needed a desk job where I couldn't cause an epidemic. I was eager, too, to explore something new. The food service job was standard student fare in a predictable environment. But when I saw a posting for a keypunch operator at the Computer

Center, I was intrigued.

Computers were a brave new world when I started work there in 1972, and access to their powers was confined to cavernous campus centers. Judith Rowe, head of the center's social sciences division, was a pioneer; among the first to envision the potential of quantitative analysis in the social sciences, she saw that computers would be the key to realizing it. To advance that vision, she encouraged graduate students to use the computer in analyzing their research data, an effort she facilitated by hiring work-study students like me to do the data entry. One project I worked on was with the historian Vernon Burton, who had discovered a treasure trove of old census records near his hometown in South Carolina. (There is such serendipity in historical research: Vernon had stopped on a back road to buy a soda when he spotted the stacks of ledgers holding up a shelf; he offered to build the shopkeeper some proper shelves in exchange for the ledgers.) My job was to key all the census data onto punch cards and help Vernon run the analysis.

I'd taken a typing class in high school, figuring that I could always get a job that way if necessary. That was qualification enough to start, as no one beyond the programmers themselves had any computer skills. Under Judith's guidance I learned a bit about programming and became skilled at keypunching. Because the work was specialized, I earned double what I had been making in the cafeteria. There were other perks too: we could set our own hours and come as we were, in jeans and T-shirts. It was a student's dream job, and I kept it all four years at Princeton, working there ten or fifteen hours a week on top of other jobs that came and went.

The mainframe computer housed in the center gave off so much heat that its room was cooled to frigid temperatures, and I wore a jacket and gloves whenever I went down into the basement to feed my stacks of punch cards into the machine. If the program crashed, I had to inspect each card individually to find the error. Often that meant perusing hundreds or even thousands of punch cards for a single mistaken keystroke, a maddening effort. Next to the monitor that showed the jobs queuing to run on the computer was a metal post that seemed to serve no purpose. It was a while before someone explained it to me: after repeatedly replastering the wall, the administration had decided to install the post for the convenience of frustrated students, who invariably needed something to kick when their code crashed.

Later, in my senior year, I was taking a break from writing my thesis to catch up on a couple of hours of keypunch work when an idea occurred to me: Why not enter the text of my thesis on the same types of punch cards that we were using for data analysis? That way, I could make changes as needed to individual cards without having to retype all the subsequent pages. Judith was intrigued. She thought it was a worthwhile experiment, and she assigned another operator to do the data entry for me. It's hard to be certain, but I might have submitted the very first word-processed senior thesis in Princeton's history, and I didn't even have to type it myself.

In my freshman year, however, I had cause to doubt that I would be able to write a senior thesis eventually. My very first midterm paper, for American history class, came back with a C, a grade I couldn't remember getting since the fourth grade. I was flattened, but even worse I had no idea where I had gone wrong. I'd fallen in love with the subject — the Great Depression and Roosevelt's New Deal — pursuing it with everything I had. And the professor had been so inspiring that I wanted to

244

impress her. Nancy Weiss was chair of the department, one of the first women in the whole country to hold such a post; later, as Nancy Malkiel, she would become the longest-serving dean of the college.

Professor Weiss told a familiar tale: although my paper was chock-full of information and even interesting ideas, there was no argumentative structure, no thesis that my litany of facts had been marshaled to support. "That's what analysis is — the framework of cause and effect," she said. Her point was a variation of what Miss Katz had been getting at, though now it was coming across more clearly and consequentially. Obviously, I was still regurgitating information. It was dawning on me that in all my classes I was so concerned with absorbing the facts in the reading that I wasn't marshaling them into a larger argument. By now, several people had pointed out where I needed to go, but none could show me the way. I began to despair of ever learning how to succeed at my assignments when quite unexpectedly it occurred to me: I already knew how.

Running into Kenny Moy outside Firestone one day got me thinking about my days in Forensics Club. Suddenly I realized that what had made me a winner on his team was precisely what I needed to do in my papers. I would not have dreamed of opening my mouth in a debate without first mapping out a position, anticipating and addressing objections, considering how best to persuade my listeners. Seeing the task in the context of another I already performed well largely demystified the problem. In my next few papers I would start doing in prose what I learned how to do in spoken words. But before I could do that really well, I'd have to face up to another obstacle: the general deficiency of my written English.

Whether it is a pregnant pause or even talking with her hands, a debater has many expressive tricks in her repertoire, some of which may cover a multitude of sins against the language. In writing, however, one's words stand naked on the page. Professor Weiss had minced none of her own informing me that my English was weak: my sentences were often fragments; my tenses erratic; and my grammar often just not grammatical. If I could have seen it myself, I would have fixed it, but what was wrong sounded right to me. It wasn't until the following year, when I took Peter Winn's course in contemporary Latin American history, that the roots of my problem were uncovered: my English was riddled with

Spanish constructions and usage. I'd say "authority of dictatorship" instead of "dictatorial authority," or "tell it to him" instead of "tell him." Peter's corrections in red ink were an epiphany: I had no idea that I sounded so much like my mother! But my English wouldn't be as easy to fix as the lack of an argument in my essays. I bought some grammar handbooks and, as part of the same effort, a stack of vocabulary booklets. Over summer vacations spent working at Prospect Hospital, or later at the Department of Consumer Affairs in Spanish Harlem, I'd devote each day's lunch hour to grammar exercises and to learning ten new words, which I would later test out on Junior, trying to make them my own. Junior was unfazed by my semantic challenges. He was just happy to be out of my shadow in his final years at Cardinal Spellman.

I came to accept during my freshman year that many of the gaps in my knowledge and understanding were simply limits of class and cultural background, not lack of aptitude or application as I'd feared. That acceptance, though, didn't make me feel less self-conscious and unschooled in the company of classmates who'd had the benefit of much more worldly experience. Until I arrived at Princeton, I had no idea how circumscribed my life had been, confined to a community that was essentially a village in the shadow of a great metropolis with so much to offer, of which I'd tasted almost nothing. I was enough of a realist not to fret about having missed summer camp, or travel abroad, or a casual familiarity with the language of wealth. I honestly felt no envy or resentment, only astonishment at how much of a world there was out there and how much of it others already knew. The agenda for self-cultivation that had been set for my classmates by their teachers and parents was something I'd have to develop for myself. And meanwhile, there could come at any moment the chagrin of discovering something else I was supposed to know. Once, I was trying to explain to my friend and later roommate Mary Cadette how out of place I sometimes felt at Princeton.

"It must be like Alice in Wonderland," she said sympathetically.

"Alice who?"

She was kind enough to salvage the moment with a quick grace: "It's a wonderful book, Sonia, you must read it!" In fact, she would guide me thoughtfully toward a long list of classics she had read while I'd been perusing *Reader's Digest.* What did my mother know of *Huckleberry Finn* or *Pride and Prejudice?*

Later, at the Computer Center, I would enter data for a project that Judith Rowe described as a study of how people paid for college. My fingers froze on the keys as I read what I was typing: financial figures of the most well-off at Princeton. This was my first glimpse of trust funds; tax write-offs and loopholes; summer jobs at Daddy's firm that paid the equivalent of a year's tuition; incomes in the millions, disbursed a half million here, a few hundred thousand for that poor guy there. Between her own salary from Prospect Hospital and her survivors' benefits, which would end very soon, my mother's income was never more than five thousand dollars a year. Nothing could have clarified as starkly where I stood in relation to some of the people among whom I was now living and learning.

I never deluded myself that I could fill in everything I had missed growing up. Nor did I fail to appreciate that I'd had experiences of my own to prize or that I'd seen some aspects of life of which my classmates were sometimes naively unaware. Suffice it to say that Princeton made me feel that long after those summers spent first discovering the world's great books, I'd have to remain a student for life. It has been my pleasure to be one, actually, long after the virtue has ceased to be such a necessity.

SIXTEEN

Every week, like clockwork, a small, square envelope arrived in the mail, addressed in a familiar, scratchy hand. Inside the envelope was a paper napkin and inside that a dollar bill. Abuelita wasn't much of a correspondent. She might sign the napkin, or not, but the loving gesture was reliable and steadfast. It meant a lot to know she was thinking of me, and a dollar was no small thing, for her or for me. Once in a rare while she would send a five-dollar bill, and I could see her smiling from seventy miles away.

Kevin came to visit with an equally reliable regularity. Driving down to Princeton from SUNY at Stony Brook every single weekend, he would make a detour through Co-op City to pick up a care package of fruits and juice from my mother. He would arrive around midnight frazzled and exhausted, still not accustomed to freeway driving, but as the weeks passed, he became more confident at the wheel.

When I asked my roommate, Dolores, if she would mind Kevin sleeping on our floor, she offered to spend weekends in a friend's room. I thought that was so generous of her, so graciously thoughtful. She meanwhile was thinking I was incorrigibly wild. She never let on, but later, after we'd gradually warmed to each other and become good friends, we'd have occasion to laugh about our first impressions of each other.

Actually, I wasn't wild at all: Kevin and I spent our wild weekends studying side by side. Stony Brook was a party scene, and he was glad of the chance to catch up on work. I offered many a time to come visit him there and save him the drive, but I don't think he wanted me to see just what a party scene it was. Only once did he accept, and that was on a holiday weekend when the campus was deserted. I could see why he preferred Princeton to the institutional, nondescript concrete of Stony Brook. He fell in love with the environment the same way that I had; later he would find his way back there for graduate school.

My mother came to visit me on campus once or twice each year. The first time, my cousin Charlie drove her and Junior down, along with Charlie's girlfriend. Kevin came too, of course. Nassau Inn, where many of my classmates' families would stay, was unimaginably expensive, so we had a slumber party. I gave Mami my bed and borrowed sleeping bags, mattresses, blankets, and pillows to make the rest of us comfortable on the floor. Charlie had a moment of profound shock in the bathroom, having forgotten that this was a girls' dorm. I sent him over to the male dorm next door, but their informal policy of sharing the showers with girlfriends was even more shocking to him. He's talked about it ever since.

If you happened to visit Princeton on a weekend, the cafeteria food in the commons was a crapshoot. Most of the regular staff was off duty, and students cooked. They laid on steak when there was a football game, but there was no game when my family first came to visit. My mother was aghast at what was on her plate, afraid that I might starve to death, a very bland death, before I could graduate. "I have to take you out tonight, Sonia," she said grimly after her first bite. I didn't know what to suggest. The hoagie shop on Nassau Street was the only place in town I could routinely afford. Advice from friends sent us ten miles out on Route 27, to the A-Kitchen and the beginning of a tradition. Just reading the menu downwind from the kitchen, I was jumping out of my skin with excitement, my mouth watering at descriptions of ginger, garlic, and chilies. The prices were right, and judging by the crowd, the fare was authentic. Chinese food of that quality and spiciness was new to me, a far cry from the spareribs and egg foo yong of the Bronx.

When I came home from Princeton for a midterm break in my first year, Mami was panicking. She was in the final stretch of getting her nursing degree. The bilingual program at Hostos Community College included an English writing requirement. It wasn't as terrifying to her as the math, but it was onerous and she was struggling with it. She conceived the insane plan that I should write her paper for her.

"No way! That's cheating!" Facing dire threats that she would quit, I compromised. I agreed to look at what she had written and give her advice. We spent untold hours of my brief vacation at the kitchen table poring over her sentences. "There's no structure here, Mami. It wanders."

"I don't know, Sonia, I'm not good at embellishing."

"Forget about embellishing. What's the story you're trying to tell? What's your theme?"

"Ay, Sonia, please just write it for me!"

I didn't say it out loud, but I thought: Please, Mami, I don't have time for your insecurities. I have my own to deal with.

Her final exams were a torture worse than the English papers. Studying was not the problem. She had been doing that relentlessly for two years; she was used to it. But when exams loomed, the tension rose to a pitch higher than human ears could bear, the whips and chains came out, and the self-flagellation began in earnest. "I'm never going to pass," she moaned. I reassured her. She knew the material inside out. She had been doing these same procedures at Prospect Hospital for years.

"No, Sonia. I must have had some brain damage when I was small. Nothing stays in my memory."

"Don't be ridiculous! You're going to pass. Do you want to bet on it?"

"Yeah, I bet I'll fail."

We wagered a trip to Puerto Rico and shook hands on the stupidest wager I'd ever heard of: The winner would be the bigger loser. If she passed the exams, she would buy me a plane ticket. If she failed, I would pay for her trip.

I don't know if the bet was reverse psychology or a perverse good luck charm, but it seemed to steady her resolve. In the end, of course, I won: my mother passed all five of her qualifying exams on the first try, which doesn't happen very often.

Late in the fall semester of my sophomore year, I sensed that something wasn't right. For two weeks in a row, no envelope had arrived in the mail. I was worried and phoned my mother: "Where's Abuelita? Why haven't I heard from her?"

There was a long silence before Mami finally spoke. A tone of blustering hesitation in her voice told me that I was the last to hear the news. No one had the courage to tell me. Abuelita was in the hospital, at Flower–Fifth Avenue. She had ovarian cancer. Like so many older women, she had stopped seeing a gynecologist long before. She thought — and she was sadly wrong, I want to stress — that routine checkups were pointless since she was past having children. And so the cancer was far advanced when they found it. I was ready to get on the next bus, but Mami said, "No, wait till you come for Christmas. Hopefully, she'll be home by then."

That was a few weeks away. I had no experience with cancer of any kind then, no point of reference, no way to guess at how serious it might be. All I knew was that winter had set in and the sky hung lower with each passing day.

By the time I got there, Abuelita was delirious and hallucinating. I spent the days at her side, just being there, studying while she slept. Aunts and uncles and cousins squeezed into her hospital room, and then at some point on Christmas Eve the crowd vanished. People were anxious because the oil embargo meant hour-long lines at every gas station and they needed to fill up before the pumps closed for the holiday. Titi Gloria said, "Come, you'll get stuck here." My cousin Charlie and I looked at each other: no way were we leaving.

We decided to go get a Christmas tree for Abuelita; Charlie was the one who always decorated her apartment for the holidays, just as I had done our tree ever since Papi died. It started to snow as we walked down Lexington Avenue in the fading light. We'd gone all the way to Ninety-Sixth Street before finding a florist that was open. We picked out a small tabletop tree that was beautifully decorated and took turns carrying it back, our hands freezing. The snow was already sticking; it was that cold.

"Do you remember . . . ?" The whole way

there and back, Charlie talked. His voice is gentle, musical; just the sound of it was a comfort. He had so many memories of Abuelita, many from before I was even born. He was very close to Gallego too and had stories to tell from when they all lived in Puerto Rico, some he'd heard others tell. When Abuelita was just twelve years old, the parish priest in Manatí recognized that she could heal people who were suffering mentally. He used to bring her to the asylum to exorcise their demons. She couldn't help with physical ailments, but if an unclean spirit possessed someone's mind, she could order it to leave. Even the patients she couldn't cure found a sense of peace in her presence.

Charlie has always had complete faith in Abuelita's spiritual powers. I'm too rational for that. You don't need to credit any superstition to feel how Abuelita protected the people she loved. Charlie confided in me a particular experience, his eyes getting bigger and bigger as he told the tale: One time, he had walked his girlfriend home to her place in Brooklyn, only to fall asleep on the train back up to the Bronx. Suddenly he woke, the sound of Abuelita's voice calling to him urgently, and he jumped off at the next station, just in time for the doors to close on three men who were about to mug him. The next day he saw Abuelita in person, and without any prompt the first thing she said was that he'd better give up that girl in Brooklyn!

Her fierce protectiveness also showed itself in ways that had nothing to do with spirits. She was wildly jealous of Gallego. Once at a party, he was dancing a slow merengue with the wrong woman. Abuelita grabbed the record from the Victrola and smashed it on the floor; then she kicked off her shoes and chased the woman down the stairs screaming. That was before my time, but I can imagine it easily. Mercedes was famously impulsive: joyrides at midnight, picnics on the highway median . . .

At her bedside, Charlie was trying to feed Abuelita a few spoonfuls of Jell-O, but she wouldn't take any. She kept asking for her clothes, as if she were going home. I was sitting in the chair by the door, and she looked right through me, talking to someone who wasn't there. "Angelina," she said. A chill went down my spine. I recognized the name: her sister, who'd passed away years ago. Charlie left the room for some reason, and then Abuelita said to me, *"Sonia, dame un cigarrillo."*

It was the first time she'd said my name

since I'd arrived from Princeton. "Abuelita, this is a hospital," I said gently, hating to deny her. "You can't smoke in here."

She said it again, imperiously: "Sonia, give me a cigarette!" The voice of the matriarch. I found my purse, pulled out a cigarette, lit it. I held it to her lips. She took a puff and gave a little cough. Then, as I watched, the life left her face.

I gave her a hug. *"Bendición, Abuelita."* And then I yelled for the nurse. People came running, shooed me out of the room. It was just as well. I didn't go back in. I needed to be alone.

At the funeral, Charlie in his grief assumed an irrational added burden of guilt. He remembered Abuelita's having told him the year before that she wouldn't live to see another Christmas. "We should never have bought that tree, Sonia," he said, shaking his head. "We should have kept Christmas out of that room." My own sorrow flared into rage when I saw Nelson appear briefly, a spectral presence on the fringe of the mourners. I hadn't set eyes on him for three years, and now here he was, nodding in a doped-up daze. It was disrespectful of him to show up in that state, I fumed in silence. And it was desperately sad, sadder than I could bear just then. Nelson had got himself addicted to heroin while he was still in high school and then flunked out of half a dozen colleges while his father refused to accept the reality right before his eyes. His test scores were stellar, off the charts, so he'd get in the door easily enough, but he couldn't bring himself to show up for class or do the work. He slipped away from the funeral before we could say anything to each other, and I wouldn't see him again for several more years.

In the weeks that followed, I understood for the first time Abuelita's devastation when Papi died, how it had cut into her spirit. Her death did the same to me. A piece of me perilously close to my heart had been amputated. The sense of loss was startling, physically disorienting. It occurs to me that Flower–Fifth Avenue is the same hospital where I was born. "Full circle" is the phrase that pops into my mind, as if we were one person. *"Mercedes chiquita."* I can still hear her voice sometimes, all these years later. "Don't worry, *mi'jita,*" she says, and I feel her protection.

SEVENTEEN

I met Margarita Rosa a few weeks after arriving at Princeton, and we soon became fast friends. Coming from a poor neighborhood of Brooklyn and a traditionally conservative Puerto Rican family herself, Margarita understood instinctively the path I had traveled to Princeton. We rarely needed to talk about the incongruities of our being there, and so our rapport progressed quickly to more urgent matters.

"Three guys for every girl, and I can't get a date! What's wrong with this picture?"

"Don't take it personally," I'd say. "They didn't want to let women in the door, and now that we're here, they don't know what to do with us." Princeton had turned coed just three years before, and the presence of women on campus was still a thorn in the side of many old-school diehards.

"Not true, Sonia. If you're a blue-eyed blonde, they know what to do with you. If you're black, there's at least a handful of brothers ready to stand up and say you're as beautiful as they are. But a *café-con-leche* Latina with a 'fro? That they don't know what to do with."

Margarita's tough luck with men mystified me. To my eyes, she was indeed attractive, petite, and lively, as well as being eloquent and passionate about making the world a better place. She was a junior when I was a freshman, and I could only hope to become like her.

"At least you don't have a pudgy nose," I offered.

"At least you've got Kevin," she returned.

We often studied at Firestone Library until closing time, when we would walk back to the dorms together. About once a week, before going home, we would stop off at the pub to continue the conversation over a glass of sangria and a slice of pizza. Margarita was pushing me to join Acción Puertorriqueña, the Latino student group that she was involved in, and I was pushing back. It was no reflection on the group; nor was I being standoffish. I just wasn't inclined to join anything until I'd gathered my bearings and felt more comfortable with my course load.

I've since come to recognize a personal

tendency. In high school, I hadn't tried anything like student government or the Forensics Club until my second year, and it would be the same at Princeton and again at law school. The first year that I face the challenges of any new environment has always been a time of fevered insecurity, a reflexive terror that I'll fall flat on my face. In this self-imposed probationary period, I work with compulsive intensity and single-mindedness until I gradually feel more confident. Some of the looming panic is no doubt congenital; I often see in my reactions something of my mother's irrational fear of being unequipped for nursing school. I have gone through this same kind of transition since becoming a judge, first on the federal district court, then on the appeals court, and finally on the Supreme Court.

Sure enough, I would join Acción Puertorriqueña during my sophomore year. I would bicycle out to the far edge of campus, where the architecture descended from Gothic Revival heights to the more human scale of colonial, and then on to the less-than-human industrial modern of graduate student housing. Just before the campus dissolved into suburban New Jersey, you reached the modest redbrick building of the Third World Center: headquarters and party central not just for Acción Puertorriqueña but for all the minority student groups on campus. I knew the area well: across the avenue were the Computer Center and Stevenson Hall, a relatively new dining facility that offered alternatives to the exclusive Princeton eating clubs. I'd embarrassed myself once in Stevenson asking for a glass of milk with my meal in the kosher canteen there, but after that I felt right at home. In fact, that part of campus became my neighborhood.

A space where one had a natural sense of belonging, a circle of friends who shared the same feeling of being a stranger in a strange land, who understood without need for explanation: it amounted to a subtle but necessary psychic refuge in an environment where an undercurrent of hostility often belied the idyllic surface. *The Daily Princetonian* routinely published letters to the editor lamenting the presence on campus of "affirmative action students," each one of whom had presumably displaced a far more deserving affluent white male and could rightly be expected to crash into the gutter built of her own unrealistic aspirations. There were vultures circling, ready to dive when we stumbled. The pressure to succeed was relentless, even if self-imposed out of fear and insecurity. For we all felt that if we did fail, we would be proving the critics right, and the doors that had opened just a crack to let us in would be slammed shut again.

We were different: not only from the generations of Princetonians who had walked through Nassau Gate before us, but, increasingly, from the friends and classmates we had left behind. I couldn't shake the feeling of having been admitted because of some clerical oversight. Margarita felt it too, Ken said the same thing, and the sentiment has been expressed countless times by minority students everywhere: by some accident of fate, we few among the great many had won the lottery. As the winners we stood in for all those not so lucky — some truly brilliant kids like Nelson, who slipped up, or others who'd never crossed paths with someone who could point the way, or who'd never even heard there was a way. Many of us experienced our election as survivor's guilt. I tried to frame it more optimistically: when she'd won a big pot, Abuelita used to say it was important to share the luck with others. Still, the sense of arbitrariness — unfathomable and irreducibly unsettling — would linger so that even in the best of times you could never be entirely sure that you were home safe.

It was because of this uneasy climate that so much of the work of Acción Puertorriqueña and other such groups focused on freshman admissions. In those early days of affirmative action — again, the practice was so new to Ivy League admissions that the first Latino students had yet to graduate when I arrived — many factors that complicate the cost-benefit analysis a generation later were at the time nonexistent.

Until we would raise kids of our own, no minority students had alumni for parents, and rare indeed were those who had not come from poor communities. The typical undergraduate had been guided to Princeton by relatives, by prep school guidance counselors, or else by teachers savvy about the system. Minority kids, however, had no one but their few immediate predecessors: the first to scale the ivy-covered wall against the odds, just one step ahead ourselves, we would hold the ladder steady for the next kid with more talent than opportunity. The blacks, Latinos, and Asians at Princeton went back to their respective high schools, met with guidance counselors, and recruited promising students they knew personally. Then, every time a minority application landed in the pile of potential admissions, they'd reach out to make the applicant feel welcome or at least a little less intimidated.

This outreach was vital because disadvantaged students often had no idea that they stood a chance at a place like Princeton, assuming they'd even heard the name. In high school, I was vaguely aware that affirmative action existed, but I had no idea how or to what extent it worked in practical terms. When the two Hispanic students met me at the station in New Haven to show me around Yale, I was inclined to see their ethnicity as more a matter of pleasant coincidence than a programmatic effort. At most, I figured, they were being nice to one of their own kind, rather in the way Ken had encouraged me to consider Princeton and the other Ivy League colleges, not out of any political agenda. My innocence was the result of being unaware of just how few Latinas there would be in a place like Princeton, or for that matter that my being one could have figured so much in my admission.

Beyond freshman recruiting, Acción Puertorriqueña and similar groups were vocal in campus protests relating to national issues. It was an honorable tradition, most recently involving resistance to the Vietnam War and Princeton's entanglement with the military, but the war was over, and being a rabble-rouser did not appeal to me. Not that I didn't care passionately about the group's causes; rather, I had my doubts that linking arms, chanting slogans, hanging effigies, and shouting at passersby were always the most effective tactics. I could see that troubling the waters was occasionally necessary to bring attention to the urgency of some problem. But this style of political expression sometimes becomes an end in itself and can lose potency if used routinely. If you shout too loudly and too often, people tend to cover their ears. Take it too far and you risk that nothing will be heard over the report of rifles and hoofbeats.

Quiet pragmatism, of course, lacks the romance of vocal militancy. But I felt myself more a mediator than a crusader. My strengths were reasoning, crafting compromises, finding the good and the good faith on both sides of an argument, and using that to build a bridge. Always, my first question was, what's the goal? And then, who must be persuaded if it is to be accomplished? A respectful dialogue with one's opponent almost invariably goes further than a harangue outside his or her window. If you want to change someone's mind, you must understand what need shapes his or her opinion. To prevail, you must first listen — that eternal lesson of Forensics Club!

One of our most pressing objectives was to convince the administration to honor its commitment to increase the hiring of qualified Hispanics. There were almost sixty of us enrolled as students, a huge increase over just a few years ago, thanks mostly to the efforts of groups like ours. But there was not one Hispanic on the faculty or the administrative staff. It was hard, they said, to find qualified scholars, but could they not locate even one Latino janitor? You would never have known that Puerto Ricans made up 12 percent of the population of New Jersey. Quotas had not been declared illegal by the Supreme Court then, but we were not arguing in their favor. We were arguing only for some good faith effort to correct historical imbalances.

There were no actual villains, just inertia. The administration genuinely wanted more diversity for reasons of its image as well as fairness, notwithstanding the cranky alumni letters in *The Daily Princetonian*. The university's long-standing reputation as the northernmost school for southern gentlemen, which had bred resistance to desegregation, eventually gave way to some healthy soul-searching. Consequently, efforts to recruit black students were earnest and energetic. Faculty and administrative hiring of blacks still lagged, but it was going well compared with efforts among Puerto Ricans and Chicanos. Hiring committees had not a clue where to look for or how to attract suitable candidates. And so, though a high-level recruitment plan existed on paper, there was only foot-dragging and defensive excuse making. The administration wouldn't even respond to our letters.

It was not until we filed a formal complaint with the Department of Health, Education, and Welfare that we got President William Bowen's attention and a dialogue opened. Within a month, the Office of Civil Rights at the Department of Education had sent someone to meet with us in the provost's office. Before you knew it, Princeton had hired its very first Hispanic administrator — and not just any administrator: the assistant dean of student affairs, whose role was to advocate for students like us.

When I first joined Acción Puertorriqueña, the Mexican-Americans had their own separate group, the Chicano Organization of Princeton. Clearly, numbers as small as ours were better not divided, so we often joined forces on issues of mutual concern, and the two groups almost always partied together. (They outnumbered us, so tortillas and *refritos* were more typically the fare than *arroz con gandules,* but our salsa dancing was more than a match for their *rancheras.*) There were a handful of nonaligned minority students — Filipinos, Native Americans, and other Latinos — so we at Acción Puertorriqueña invited them in, tacking "y Amigos" onto the end of our name. I liked the indiscriminate amiability of how that sounded, but even more the inclusiveness in practice. As much solace and strength as we gathered from group identity, it mattered greatly to have an open door. After all, the failure to include was our raison d'être.

All of the different minority student groups at Princeton shared the Third World Center, and together they elected a governance board to run the facility. To assure balance, equal numbers of seats were allotted to African-American, Hispanic, and Asian students. In addition, there was an "open" section usually filled by African-Americans, by far the largest minority on campus. I took the risk of running outside the Hispanic category, becoming the first nonblack to win one of the open seats. I was proud of that victory, seeing it as a tribute to how well I listened and brokered compromises between factions.

For all the sense of accomplishment and the embrace I felt at the Third World Center, I had no wish to confine myself to a minority subculture and its concerns. The Latino community anchored me, but I didn't want it to isolate me from the full extent of what Princeton had to offer, including engagement with the larger community. I would warn any minority student today against the temptations of self-segregation: take support and comfort from your own group as you can, but don't hide within it.

My opportunity to venture out came with the chance to serve on the student-faculty Discipline Committee. The body typically dealt with the predictable lows of student behavior: stolen library books, dorm rule infractions, intoxicated rowdiness. Sometimes I wanted to cringe, as when a pair of our "amigos," Native Americans, had had a few too many and started tossing furniture out the window at the Third World Center. I shook my head in despair: drunken Indians? Talk about making it easy for the cranky old letter writers! A more serious incident involved a brilliant student wrongly accused of hacking into the university's computer system. Getting to the bottom of that one proved a challenge more technical than any other we would face, but I was able to draw on my experience at the Computer Center for clarity, in what was arguably my first judicial role.

There are few places in this country where institutional history overlaps the national narrative as self-consciously as it does at Princeton. The cannon in the center of the green saw action in the Revolutionary War. Among the über-alumni: James Madison, class of 1771, author of the Constitution. The Continental Congress of 1783 sat in Nassau Hall to receive news of the Treaty of Paris. Those self-assured people surrounding me, who had traveled the world confident of having an influential role in it one day, were no less certain of themselves as the rightful inheritors of this history. It was not something on which I could ever hope to have the same purchase. I needed a history in which I could anchor my own sense of self. I found it when I began to explore the history of Puerto Rico.

I had studied American, European, Soviet, and Chinese history and politics, but I knew next to nothing about the history of my own people. Every people has a past, but the dignity of a history comes when a community of scholars devotes itself to chronicling and studying that past. In the course offerings in Latin American history and politics, however, Puerto Rico was barely mentioned. Fortunately, it was possible for students to initiate courses. Years before, I discovered, a Princeton student had put together a course on Puerto Rican history, and now, under the guidance of Professor Winn, I set out to revive it, bringing the syllabus up to date and recruiting the necessary quorum of students. I didn't make it easy on those who might be interested: my reading list was ambitious, to say the least.

The history that emerged from our reading was not a happy one. Under Spain, Puerto Rico suffered colonial neglect and the burden of policies designed to enrich distant parties at heavy cost to the island. Little effort was made to develop the natural resources or agriculture beyond what was needed to provision and mount the conquistadores on their way to Mexico and South America. Poor governance was compounded by bad luck — hurricanes and epidemics — as well as state-sponsored piracy by the British, French, and Dutch. For the Spanish settlers, as for the enslaved indigenous tribes and those from elsewhere in the Caribbean who took refuge on the island, it was a precarious existence that would not begin to improve until well into the nineteenth century. There was negligible civic life and minimal economic activity beyond smuggling. Any liberties the Spanish crown granted were often quickly revoked.

When Spain ceded Puerto Rico to the United States in 1898, along with Cuba and the Philippines as the spoils of the Spanish-American War, Puerto Ricans held an optimistic faith in American ideals of liberty, democracy, and justice. But that optimism would yield to a sense of betrayal for many. Governed without representation, exploited economically, some islanders came to feel they had merely exchanged one colonial master for another.

It was clear that the idea of Puerto Rico as the "rich port" was never anything but a fantasy. The island had always been poor. At the same time, it was tied to an old culture and several continents. One didn't have to romanticize the past or succumb to mythology to appreciate its thread in the fabric of history.

One of the books on our reading list to make a profound impression on me was Oscar Lewis's *La Vida*. It was a contentious inclusion, an anthropological study of one family that stretched from the slums of San Juan to those of New York. Many Puerto Ricans have been offended by its airing of dirty laundry: the granular view of prostitution and a culture that seems preoccupied with sex. But there was much else going on in the lives Lewis described and in his argument about how the culture of poverty persists by virtue of being adaptive, a set of strategies to cope with difficult circumstances. I couldn't deny that the book triggered powerful moments of recognition, often painful but nonetheless fascinating, as I saw my own family reflected in its pages. I was beginning to understand my family lore in a cultural framework, to spot sociological patterns in what had seemed mere idiosyncrasies, and dark ones at that.

What *La Vida* was lacking, I realized, was an appreciation of the good, the richness of our culture, however long overshadowed by poverty. There are strengths in our collective psyche that account for our resilience and that equally hold the potential for our renewal, if properly nourished and cultivated. I could see it in my own mother's reverence for education, her faith in community, her infinite capacity for hard work and perseverance; in Abuelita's joyful generosity, her passion for life and poetry, her power to heal. Such strong women are no rarity in our culture. I could see resilient strength, too, in the way that Spiritism and the Catholic faith have accommodated each other rather than clashing.

The classroom discussions were heated and often loud. We hadn't resisted our colonial masters in any meaningful way, some would claim. Others responded: El Grito de Lares had rallied rebels against Spain. And in the 1950s members of the militant Puerto Rico Nationalist movement, who pursued armed revolution against the United States, went as far as an attempt on the life of President Truman and a deadly shoot-out in the U.S. Congress. And yet others retorted: These moments of resistance were fleeting and never led to the kind of sustained struggle that had won independence for Cuba or the Philippines. If identity arises from struggle, and trauma spurs growth and change, did not the frailty of our opposition threaten to define us historically? Cuba's revolution, like the wars of independence fought in the Philippines, had forged those national identities in a crucible of violence. Many in the class would ask what it was in our character that had led us to a more peaceable accommodation with colonial power.

Again and again, the conversation returned to the island's political status. Did we want to remain a commonwealth, with some self-rule and a preferential trade relationship with the mainland? Half the class believed that was no better than being a colony of the United States, living as second-class citizens. But if we should aspire to statehood, the full rights of citizenship would come at the price of the full obligations, including a tax burden that, arguably, might have crippled our economy at the time. Some proposed, with passionate conviction, that full independence was the only way to preserve our culture and the proper dignity of self-determination. The economic repercussions of each position were as inscrutably complex as they were critical to the arguments. And for those who are eager to discern my own present views on the status question, I can only advise not to give too much weight to whatever ideas vied for prominence in a young student's mind.

When my mother made good on our wager of a plane ticket and I found myself in Puerto Rico for two weeks, I had my first chance to view the island through adult eyes and with an evolving new consciousness of my identity. Some things hadn't changed since childhood visits. We still made the ritual stop for a coconut on the road from the airport, but now the vendor would add a bit of rum to my libation from a bottle he kept out of sight. I still began the trip with a round of visits to every family member in order of seniority, still feasted on mangoes fresh off the tree. But instead of playing the Three Stooges, my cousins and I enjoyed dominoes, dancing, and the ubiquitous bottle of rum. The kindness of strangers was still striking: a flat tire fixed, cups of coffee offered while we waited.

Much of what I saw was familiar but now made more sense. The poverty documented in *La Vida* was visible to me now in the slums of San Juan. Compared with my family in New York, my family in Puerto Rico was modestly prosperous; they had shielded me as a child from realities that I could now reckon with, though certain aspects of the island's social stratification would remain hidden from me until very recently. San Juan also has its gracious homes, its old money, and its high culture.

The stunning natural beauty of the island, which I had barely registered as a child, also made a deep impression on that trip as I played tourist. In the rain forest at El

Yunque, waterfalls trick the eye, holding movement suspended in lacy veils. Wet stone gleams, fog tumbles from peaks to valleys, mists filter the forest in pale layers receding into mystery. On the beach at Luquillo, when the sun appears under clouds massed offshore and catches the coconut palms at a low angle, the leafy crowns explode like fireworks of silver light. At night there is liquid stardust swirling in the dark waters of the phosphorescent bay. Almost every evening there are sunsets of white gold where the sky meets the sea.

At Cabo Rojo, a little motorboat came puttering to shore after a long wait and ferried a handful of people across the lagoon to La Isla de los Ratones. There was nothing there — no food stalls, no vendors, no "amenities" — nothing but the skirt of pure white sand and a coral shelf that let you walk chest-deep in crystal translucence for what seemed like miles before the floor dropped into the ocean. I looked down into water so clear that it was invisible, except for the rocks and sand and sea fronds rippling on the floor as at the beginning of a dream sequence in a movie.

As a New Yorker of profoundly urban sensibilities, I was never very attuned to nature. During my first week on campus, a

281

cricket had me tearing the dorm room apart, searching for the source of the chirp until Kevin explained that it lived in the tree outside my window. I've been known to confuse cows for horses. The ocean was always the one grand exception. Even in the chaos of Orchard Beach, the circus of family picnics, crowded surf, and traffic jams, I could find in the rhythm of the waves a transcendent serenity. And anyone who could find peace in the beaches of the Bronx would find heaven in Puerto Rico.

Another revelation of my adult trips to the island was how much the political questions broached in my course, especially about the island's status, infused everyday life. You'd see party symbols everywhere, the straw hat for the faction supporting commonwealth, the palm tree for those supporting statehood, the green flag with the white cross for those who favored independence. Everyone pored over the newspapers, dissected the candidates' positions on economic development, education, health care, corruption . . . During one election season, in the plaza of Mayagüez — and in many other towns too, I'm sure — traffic jams proliferated as cars honking horns and flying one party's flags refused to give way to other cars honking horns and flying the other party's flags. It was chaos, but at least people cared. I learned that 85 percent of the island's population had gone to the polls in recent elections.

This manic enthusiasm that gripped the island in election years, and still does, was a marked contrast to the political despondency felt by Puerto Ricans on the mainland in those years. The summer that I won the bet with my mother, I worked as usual in the business office at Prospect Hospital before going to Puerto Rico. For a couple of weeks, however, Dr. Freedman, as part of his community outreach efforts, lent me out as an intern to Herman Badillo's ultimately unsuccessful campaign for mayor of New York City. Badillo was our congressman, the first Puerto Rican ever elected to the House of Representatives. It was then I first saw how difficult it was to energize a community that felt marginal and voiceless in the larger discourse of a democracy.

Puerto Ricans in New York then felt their votes didn't count. And so why should they take the trouble even to register? Having experienced discrimination intimately, they knew they were seen as second-class citizens, as people who didn't belong, with no path to success in mainland society. Their chances of escaping from the underclass, from the vicious cycle of poverty, were no better than those of their similarly alienated black neighbors and probably worse for those who didn't speak English.

Puerto Ricans on the island, by contrast, didn't have full consciousness of being a minority because they'd never had to live as one. There were inequalities in their world, but no one's dignity suffered merely on account of his being Puerto Rican. Whether content with commonwealth status or aspiring to statehood, or even independence, they took it for granted that they were fully American: American citizens born to American parents on American territory. To be mistaken for foreigners — aliens, legal or otherwise — would have been a shock.

It was dawning on me that if the Puerto Rican community in New York ever hoped to escape poverty and recover its self-respect, there were lessons to be learned from the island. The two communities — islanders and those on the mainland — needed to work together for their mutual benefit.

For the final paper in the Puerto Rican history course, Peter Winn suggested a marvelous project, a family oral history. It was a challenge befitting any serious student of history: going mano a mano with primary sources, my cassette recorder planted on the kitchen table. Not everyone warmed to it: "You're wasting your time! Nothing interesting ever happened to me." For some, it was a grudging surrender to interrogation, slow and halting; others, the natural storytellers, proved surprisingly eager and voluble.

I was amazed by how many of these stories I'd never heard before. People had left their past behind when they came to New York. Memories of hardship and extreme poverty were of no use starting a new life on the mainland. With so much to deal with in the present, who had the luxury of dwelling on the past? My mother had told me very little about her childhood. Now it unfolded, hesitantly at first — her mother's death, her orphan loneliness — and then, with more confidence, she recounted joining the army, coming to New York, falling into a new family at Abuelita's. She said very little about my father. Those stories, as I've said, came out only recently.

The experience of hearing my Princeton reading echoed in family recollections had the effect of both making the history more vivid and endowing life as lived with the dignity of something worth studying. When, for instance, I had read that "a woman who takes ten hours to finish two dozen handkerchiefs earns 24 cents for them," I could picture Titi Aurora holding the needle, my mother leaning over the iron. Nor were these lives lived beyond a broader scheme of historical cause and effect. It was America's wars that would transform us into real Americans, not only by reason of my mother's decision to enlist, but even earlier, with the granting of American citizenship to Puerto Ricans in 1917 — after two decades of limbo — just in time for Abuelita's first husband, my grandfather, to be drafted into World War I with a wave of young Puerto Rican men. After the war, that same grandfather rolled tobacco in a factory in Manatí, listening all day as a reader read from novels and newspaper stories to keep the rollers entertained. From my reading I knew that a tobacco factory worker made between forty cents and a dollar a day and that tuberculosis, from which my grandfather died, was the most common cause of death on the island, and particularly lethal to those who worked long hours in air heavy with tobacco dust.

Everyone agrees what a shame it is to have lost the chance to gather the stories of Abuelita's mother. Bisabuela's memories of

Manatí, the town where Abuelita grew up, vividly recalled Puerto Rico when the island still belonged to Spain. Still older stories survive in hand-me-down recollection beyond any living soul's direct experience: The Sotomayors, I heard, might be descendants of Puerto Rican pioneers. On my mother's side, once upon a time, there had been property too. I heard rumors of family ties to the Spanish nobility. Somehow there was a reversal of fortune. Was it a gambling debt that had cost them the farm? Disinheritance? The tatters of old stories are tangled, weathered, muted by long-held silences that succeeded loud feuds, and sometimes no doubt re-dyed a more flattering color.

My family's shifting fortunes followed the island's economic currents: coffee plantations sold off piecemeal until yesterday's landowners took to laboring in cane fields that belonged to someone else. Child labor and illiteracy were normal; girls were married at thirteen or fourteen. We moved from mountainside farms to small towns like San Germán, Lajas, Manatí, Arecibo, Barceloneta; and after a time, on to what were then the slums of Santurce in San Juan; from there the mainland beckoned, and we answered, boarding the venerable USAT *George S. Simonds,* the army transport that carried so many Puerto Ricans to New York, until Pan Am offered the first cheap airfares and we rode *la guagua aérea,* the aerial bus, between mainland and island. We were not immigrants. We went freely back and forth. We became New Yorkers, but we did not lose our links to the island.

Of all the links, language remains strong, a code of the soul that unlocks for us the music and poetry, the history and literature of Spain and all of Latin America. But it is also a prison. Alfred talked about moving from Puerto Rico to the South Bronx in third grade. His experience was common: no help in the transition, no remedy for his deficiency but to be held back. After that, teachers just shrugged and passed him from one grade to the next, indifferent to whether he'd understood a word all year. The sharpest kids would eventually pick up the language on their own and come out only a few years behind. Still, Alfred said, "the white kids were always the most advanced. The black kids were behind them, and the Puerto Ricans were last."

My cousin Miriam was listening in on our recording session, nodding in recognition. At the time, she was studying for a degree in bilingual education at Hunter College, and today she is no less passionate about that calling with decades of teaching experience behind her. "I want to become the kind of teacher that I wish I'd had," she told me. She'd had it rough in the public schools, where the teachers knew so little of Latino culture they didn't realize that kids who looked down when scolded were doing so out of respect, as they'd been taught. Their gesture only invited a further scolding: "Look at me when I speak to you!"

I felt my own shiver of recognition too, remembering my early misery as a C student at Blessed Sacrament, in terror of the black-bonneted nuns wielding rulers, a misery that didn't abate until after Papi died and Mami made an effort to speak English at home. It seems obvious now: the child who spends school days in a fog of semi-comprehension has no way to know her problem is not that she is slow-witted. What if my father hadn't died, if I hadn't spent that sad summer reading, if my mother's English had been no better than my aunts'? Would I have made it to Princeton?

Recently, those recordings I made have resurfaced. As I listen to them now, too often I hear my own voice. There I go again, inserting opinions and jumping on the faintest hint of racism in their comments. It was my campus conditioning: I found it unfathomable that people who'd themselves been subject to so much prejudice on the mainland still clung to ideas about color as a gauge of status, as the way to keep score of how many of your ancestors had come from Spain, how many from Africa. I also cringe to hear myself lecturing Ana and Chiqui about how women's roles are culturally constructed and therefore changeable. "Read Margaret Mead!" I yell at them. "In certain tribes in Papua New Guinea, it's completely reversed. What you consider male, the women do. And what women do here, the men do over there."

"That's over there. It's different over here," Chiqui says with finality. She wasn't taking guff from a college know-it-all. It's embarrassing, sad, and amusing, all at the same time. My own biases were exposed every bit as much as those of my informants. In those moments when arguments flared on the tape, the distance I'd traveled at Princeton was revealed, but it could also be erased in a moment when someone pushed my buttons. I could be yanked for a time into one world or the other, but mostly now I would be living suspended between the two.

For the topic of my senior thesis I chose

Luis Muñoz Marín — the island's first governor to be elected rather than appointed by a U.S. president — whose efforts at industrialization brought Puerto Rico into the modern world. I was inspired by his work in marshaling the *jíbaros,* politically marginalized peasants, into a force that could win elections. Some part of me needed to believe that our community could give birth to leaders. I needed a beacon. Of course I knew better than to let such emotion surface in the language and logic of my thesis; that's not what historians do. But it kept me going through the long hours of work, and it counterbalanced the fact that Muñoz Marín's story had no happy ending, as initial success generated other economic challenges. How could this have happened? It was hard to imagine a more fruitful area for study.

One morning, a small headline in the local paper caught my eye. A Hispanic man who spoke no English had been on a flight that was diverted to Newark airport. No one there knew enough Spanish to explain to him where he was or what had happened, and in his frustration and confusion he made a scene. He was taken to Trenton Psychiatric Hospital and held there for days before a Spanish-speaking staff member showed up and helped him reach his family. This, I fumed, is not acceptable.

When I called the hospital and asked some questions, I found that there were a number of long-term patients who spoke no English and had only intermittent access to Spanish-speaking staff. I could imagine nothing crueler than the anguish of mental illness compounded by mundane confusion and being unable to communicate with one's keepers.

The Trenton Psychiatric Hospital was beyond any influence of Acción Puertorriqueña. There was no way we could pressure the administrators to hire more Hispanics as we had the university. So I resolved to take a different approach, organizing a volunteer program under which our members spent time at the hospital on a continuous rotation so that there was always someone who could interpret for the patients and intercede with the staff if necessary. We also ran bingo nights and sing-alongs, finding that some very uneasy minds were nonetheless able to dredge their memories for the comfort of old songs their parents had sung. And before heading home for Thanksgiving and Christmas, we threw holiday parties for the patients, recruiting our mothers and aunts to prepare the traditional foods that were too complicated to attempt in dorm kitchens.

The program in Trenton was my first real experience of direct community service, and I was surprised by how satisfying I found the work. Modest as the effort was, I could envision it working on a grand scale — service to millions. But the operations of major philanthropy being then beyond my imagination, government seemed the likely provider. And so it was I began to think that public service was where I was likely to find the greatest professional satisfaction.

Under a banner reading *"Feliz Navidad,"* we had set out the stacking chairs for the patients, and on the folding tables we'd arranged a bounty of *pasteles* and *arroz con gandules.* This was not an audience you could expect to settle down and listen attentively, but when Dolores strummed the strings of her guitar, the harsh fluorescent light seemed somehow to soften. We mustered some Spanish carols, Nuyorican *aguinaldos.* But it was when she turned to old Mexican favorites that Dolores's voice truly shone as she serenaded those broken souls on a silent winter night in New Jersey:

Dicen que por las noches
*no más se le iba en puro llorar . . .**

They say he survived the nights on tears alone, unable to eat . . . Dolores sings the Mexican ballad of a lover so bereft that after he dies, his soul, in the form of a dove, continues to visit the cottage of his beloved. Even my heart, as yet untouched by such passion, is captured, and I am transfixed as Dolores coos the song of the lonesome dove: *cucurrucucú . . .*

In the audience, an elderly woman is staring into space, her face as devoid of expression as ever. She is always the unresponsive one, who has not spoken a single word since we've been coming to Trenton. Tonight, even she is tapping her foot gently as Dolores sings.

* They say that all those nights
All he could do was cry . . .
(from "Cucurrucucú Paloma,"
a popular Mexican song)

Me, age one, between Papi
and Mami

First birthday. The photo
was given to Abuelita as
a memento years later
when it was inscribed
"For Grandma, from your
granddaughter who never
forgets you. Sonia."

Para abuelita
de tu nieta que
no te olvida
Sonia

6/25/5

Celina *(right)* with her "adoptive"
family by marriage: Mercedes *(center)*
and her daughter Gloria *(left)*

Abuelita and her second husband,
Gallego, in Puerto Rico

Juli as a young man, soon after
first arriving in New York

Celina in the Women's Army Corps, age nineteen

"To my beloved grandmother, I dedicate this humble remembrance in proof of my love for you. Your little grandson, Juan Luis Sotomayor" (translated from the Spanish inscription)

Juan Luis (Juli) Sotomayor, age two, in a photograph he gave to Celina early in their courtship, with an earlier dedication to his grandmother written on the back

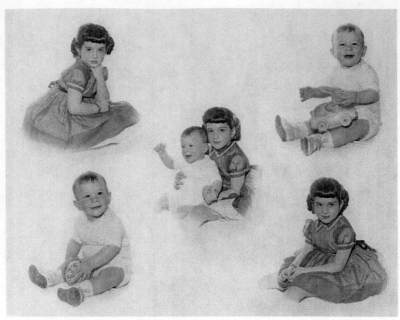

With Junior on his first birthday: Papi's handwritten notes on the backing paper were discovered for the first time fifty-four years later while writing this book.

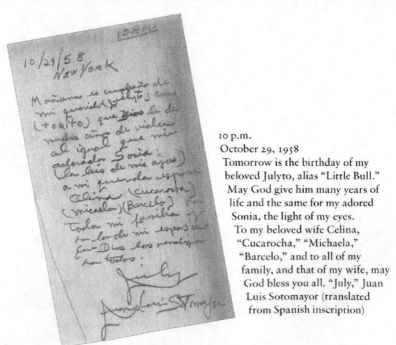

10 p.m.
October 29, 1958
Tomorrow is the birthday of my beloved Julyto, alias "Little Bull." May God give him many years of life and the same for my adored Sonia, the light of my eyes.
To my beloved wife Celina, "Cucarocha," "Michaela," "Barcelo," and to all of my family, and that of my wife, may God bless you all. "July," Juan Luis Sotomayor (translated from Spanish inscription)

Juli *(above, at left)* at the radiator factory

Juli's playful spirit would later recede.

I preferred boys' toys, like guns, to dolls. With Papi, Junior, and Mami, beside the Christmas tree decorated by Papi.

Birthday girl with *(left to right)* my godmother, Carmin; Mom, Celina; and maternal aunt Aurora

Celina *(center)* was the Jackie O of Bronxdale, but Carmen *(right)* was a beauty, too. Abuelita is second from top left, flanked by her sisters. Gloria is behind Carmen, and in the front-row peanut gallery, from left, are Junior, Nelson, me, Eddie, and Miriam.

With cousins: *(from left)* Eddie, Miriam, Nelson, and Lillian. Miriam and I often dressed like twins.

¡Vámonos de parranda!: Abuelita loved a picnic.

Trying very hard at age four to match Mami's glamour, both of us dressed in new hats for Easter

Senior year at Cardinal Spellman High School

At Blessed Sacrament, I first discovered love of learning and a lust for gold stars.

SONIA MARIA SOTOMAYOR

I am not a champion of lost causes, but of causes
not yet won.
— Norman Thomas

My Princeton experience has been the people I've met.
To them, for their lessons of life, I remain
eternally indebted and appreciative.
To them and to that extra-special person in my life

Thank You — For all that I am and am not.
The sum total of my life here, has been made-up
of little parts from all of you.

In the Princeton yearbook, class of 1976

The Bronx comes to Princeton for the weekend: Kevin on the left, standing next to me; Mami on far right, followed by Ken Moy and Junior. Kneeling, front left, is Felice Shea.

Beside one of the bronze tigers outside Nassau Hall

In the kitchen with Titi Aurora and Mami on a visit home from Yale

I whip up some homemade Chinese food for the gang at Yale.

High school sweethearts just after the wedding in the Lady Chapel at St. Patrick's Cathedral. Mami's friend Elisa helped design the dress, and Kevin rented the tuxedo.

The wedding shower, with maid of honor Marguerite Butler *(right)* and college roommate Mary Cadette *(left)*

With Kevin in the Rocky Mountains on our road trip out West, second summer at Yale

Discovering the grandeur of America's wide open spaces for the first time, while struggling to figure out a career plan

Visiting with Dolores Chavez at her parents' home in Albuquerque. She and her father did a beautiful rendition of the ballad "Cucurrucucú Paloma."

Sonia Sotomayor, Assistant District Attorney,
representing the people of the County of
New York

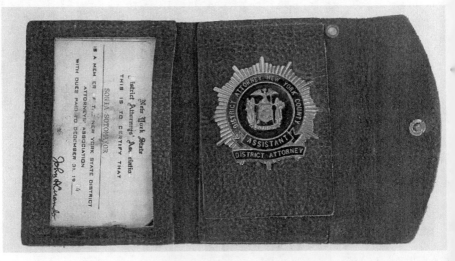

. . . and the badge to prove it

Partners and associates of
Pavia & Harcourt gathered to
celebrate a wedding of one of
their own soon after I became
a judge. David Botwinik is at
bottom left and George Pavia
is beside him.

With Alessandro Saracino-
Fendi, the client who
became like a brother

The annual courthouse
follies: After much
rehearsal, I make a
serviceable singing
hobo alongside U.S.
District Court Judges
Charles S. Haight, Jr.,
and Jed S. Rakoff

Three generations of Sotomayor
women: my niece Kiley, Mami, and me

With Robert M. Morgenthau
("The Boss") on the day I was sworn in

My Yale mentor, now Circuit Court Judge, José Cabranes administered the
oath of office at my induction to the U.S. District Court for the Southern
District of New York.

The bride Celina and her groom Omar, with Junior, now Dr. Sotomayor. As my first official act, I performed the marriage of the couple on the night of my induction to the Second Circuit Court of Appeals.

At the White House: Mami, Kiley, Conner, and Corey as President Obama announces my nomination to the Supreme Court

Justices of the Supreme Court of the United States are required to take multiple oaths. Here I take the Judicial Oath, administered by Chief Justice Roberts in the Justices' conference room, with my mother holding the Bible and Junior looking on.

EIGHTEEN

Felice Shea was sitting at my desk, waiting for me to walk over to the commons with her for dinner. She was that very fair-skinned Irish type, blushing at the slightest discomfort, and I had gotten pretty good at reading her reactions. Seeing at this moment a virtual red tide, I asked her what was up.

"I really hope you don't think I was snooping, Sonia, but I couldn't help noticing that letter in your wastebasket . . ."

"It's just junk mail from some club. They want you to pay for membership, and then they want more money for some trinket engraved with your name. What a scam!"

Felice now looked more embarrassed than ever as she tried to explain that Phi Beta Kappa was totally legitimate. More than legitimate, in fact: an honor of such prestige that she insisted I had to accept the membership even if she had to pay for it. Felice was not only exceptionally kind and generous; as the daughter of two college professors, she knew all the ins and outs of academia and had guided me through many such blind spots. After four years at Princeton, I thought I knew the terrain pretty well, but every once in a while, even as a senior, I'd hear about something that made me feel like a freshman. I wasn't going to take Felice's money, but I did take her advice.

Something similar had happened not long before. I was asleep when the phone rang; the voice on the other end said it was Adele Simmons, dean of student affairs, calling to congratulate me on having won the Pyne Prize. You'd have thought it was Publishers Clearing House from the excitement in her voice describing this honor I'd never heard of, obviously not paying attention to it in *The Daily Princetonian,* but inferring it was important from her tone, I found the presence of mind to express how astonished and grateful I was. It wasn't until after I hung up and dialed Felice's number that I got a full briefing on the Moses Taylor Pyne Honor Prize. It seemed I would have to give a speech at an alumni luncheon where the award was presented. Felice and I were already into a discussion of appropriate attire, and planning a shopping trip, when she let drop the most important detail: "It's the highest award that a graduating senior can receive."

I had not shopped for clothes seriously since the day I acquired my going-to-Princeton raincoat, which was now eligible for retirement. My complete wardrobe fit in one laundry bag, easy to carry home on the bus. It consisted of three pairs of dungarees, one pair of period plaid pants, and an assortment of interchangeable tops. When my summer job demanded a more professional look, I managed to avoid the problem by wearing a hospital uniform. Felice and her mother took me to Macy's and helped me pick out a gorgeous suit for fifty dollars. It was the most expensive outfit I'd ever worn, but to judge by how I felt wearing it, it was a good investment.

The gymnasium was transformed by tables dressed in white linen, flatware, and flowers. The crowd was vast — alumni, professors, and deans, all abuzz with greetings and congratulations, their hands extended, smiling broadly, glasses raised. A part of me still felt uncertainty — or was it disbelief? — about all this fanfare and how to take it, but there was no denying that whatever it meant, it felt great. I had worked hard, and the work paid off. I had not disappointed.

Among the recent graduates were those who, as women or as other minorities, had already altered that old image of a Princeton alumnus long cherished by some. There were friends who had graduated a year or two ahead of me, like Margarita Rosa, who came down from Harvard Law School for the occasion. Others were only names to me until that day. Nearly every living Hispanic who had ever graduated from Princeton showed up, overflowing with pride and camaraderie, for what amounted to a triumphant reunion. My family, of course, was there en masse, Mami sitting there with a dazed smile that burst into beams of happy recognition with each friend or acquaintance who came over to congratulate her. My own face was sore from all the grinning.

The vault of the gymnasium and the blank scoreboard were a distant frame, filled with the upturned faces of many hundreds of strangers. This was the view as I took to the podium to give my speech, stricken with the usual bout of nerves. With the exception of our small cluster of "Third World" friends and family, the faces were uniformly white. It was a fitting reminder of what I was doing up there. The Pyne Prize, often shared by two students, recognizes excellent scholarship but also leadership that provides "effective support of the best interests of Princeton University." My efforts on the Discipline Committee had been a significant factor in my award, but so had my work with Acción Puertorriqueña and the Third World Center, which Princeton recognized as a benefit not merely to the few dozen student members of those organizations but to the broader community as well. The dynamism of any diverse community depends not only on the diversity itself but on promoting a sense of belonging among those who formerly would have been considered and felt themselves outsiders. The greater purpose of these groups had not been self-exile or special pleading. It had been to foster a connection between the old Princeton and the new, a mutual acceptance without which the body as a whole could not thrive or evolve.

This was the work not of one person but of a community: y Amigos. And in my speech I wanted to acknowledge that collaboration, as well as bow to those among the newest alumni, like Margarita Rosa, who, walking in shoes very much like my own, had cleared a path for me to follow in.

"The people I represent are diverse in their opinions, cultures, and experiences.

However, we are united by a common bond. We are attempting to exist distinctly within the rich Princeton tradition, without the tension of having our identities constantly challenged and without the frustrations of isolation. In different ways and in different styles, some loudly and others quietly, Princeton's minorities have created a milieu in which I could act and see the efforts accepted. In this way, today's award belongs to those with whom I have worked to make Princeton realize that it contains groups which are distinct and honorable in their own traditions.

"However, Princeton's acceptance of our existence and thoughts is only a first step. The challenge to both myself and Princeton is to go beyond a simple recognition. I hope today marks the beginning of a new era for all of us: a new era in which Princeton's traditions can be further enriched by being broadened to accommodate and harmonize with the beat of those of us who march to different drummers."

Looking out at that crowd, I imagined those who had not yet arrived, minority students who, in years to come, would make this multitude of faces, the view from where I now stood, a little more various. If they could have heard me, I would have confided in them: As you discover what strength you can draw from your community in this world from which it stands apart, look outward as well as inward. Build bridges instead of walls.

Spring eased into summer, exams and final papers were wrapped up, my thesis review completed. Graduation brought one last unfamiliar laurel when Peter Winn called me into his office to tell me that I would graduate summa cum laude. Once again, facing the pleasure with which this news was delivered, I didn't have the heart to inquire what it meant; for now it was enough that I should act very glad and honored. When I'd finally looked up the translation of the Latin phrase, the irony of my needing to do so was not lost on me. It was perhaps then I made a measure of peace with my unease: the uncertainty I'd always felt at Princeton was something I'd never shake entirely. For all the As and honors that could be bestowed, there would still lurk such moments of estrangement to remind me that my being there was not typical but an exception.

I marched out of Nassau Gate with my classmates in a final ritual of return to the real world, knowing that I was headed back to the Ivy League for law school at Yale in the fall. Meanwhile, a summer job doing research in the Office of Social Responsibility at the Equitable Life Assurance Society in Manhattan would provide my first glimpse inside corporate America. It was, to say the least, a letdown: I was shocked at how much time presumably productive people were capable of wasting. It was similar to what I'd observed the summer before, working in New York City's Department of Consumer Affairs, only stranger perhaps, considering it was a business with the aim of making money.

Junior by then had graduated from Cardinal Spellman and completed the first year of a program at NYU that would lead to medical school. He hadn't grown up with dreams of becoming a doctor. His ambition at that stage of life was only to do something different from whatever I was doing, to find his own path out from under my shadow. Though our constant bickering had mellowed by then, and mutual respect prevailed, each of us was too involved in his or her own life to pay much attention to the other's. But in a bind we would always turn to each other first, and given the experience that we alone shared, not much would need to be said. Family was family.

The big event for ours that summer was the wedding. That Kevin and I would eventually marry had been a given ever since the day I introduced him to Abuelita. With hindsight I can see how unexamined that certainty was. I had long mapped out a hypothetical route to marriage at the age of twenty-eight, which had less to do with the reality of my relationship with Kevin than with a desire to avoid the mistakes of others. My aunts had married at fourteen or fifteen, my cousins at eighteen. I was going to do things in the right order and finish my education first. But with the prospect of my beginning law school at Yale, and Kevin's own plans for grad school still up in the air, it seemed sensible that he should move to New Haven with me. In our world that couldn't have happened without our getting married.

My mother and I had radically different views of what the wedding would be like. My vision was frugal, modest, and practical. Hers was extravagant. Her own wedding had consisted of a visit to city hall and dinner at Abuelita's. She had not walked down the aisle, and therefore I had to. We battled over every detail, and she wasn't above playing dirty. If I crossed someone's name off the list in an effort to trim the numbers, she'd find an opportunity for us to run into that person and mention, to my well-masked dismay, that the invitation was in the mail.

Once I recognized that this whole production had more to do with her needs than mine, I resigned myself to simply getting it done as painlessly as possible. I scoured the city for the cheapest ways to furnish the essential elements. The prices horrified me, each piece of the fairy tale seeming a bigger rip-off than the last.

"I'm not spending hundreds of dollars on a dress that I'll only wear once. I'm just not doing it!"

"So what are you going to wear, Sonia?"

How many times could we repeat that exchange? Elisa was my savior. She was an old friend and neighbor of my mother's from the Bronxdale Houses and also a seamstress. It had been a while since I'd gone back to the projects after our move to Co-op City, and I was stunned by how tiny and cramped the rooms seemed when we visited Elisa. I drew a diagram, a simple A-line dress. "That's all I want." I could see the horror rising in Mami's eyes like water in a sinking boat.

"It's too plain. You have to make it fancier!"

"It's my wedding! You've decided everything else!" I couldn't believe we were fighting so shamelessly in front of Elisa, but she handled it with a skill that hinted at plenty of prior mother-daughter experience.

"Sonia, we can keep it simple and still make it elegant with a little beadwork here and here . . ."

And so, with help from friends and family, gradually the plans came together. Junior was still working as a sacristan at St. Patrick's, and it was one of the privileges allowed employees that they could arrange to have wedding masses for family celebrated at the cathedral. Through his job selling insurance, Alfred had a client with a limousine rental service who gave him a spectacular discount on three antique Rolls-Royces.

Marguerite, who had remained a close friend since high school, was my maid of honor. She graciously volunteered to host the bridal shower, but it was not such a simple proposition given that we were all New Yorkers, among whom assumptions and traditions run deep and are as varied as the places we come from. Would it be tea sandwiches and punch for ladies only on a Sunday afternoon? Or rum and real food and dancing on a Saturday night, with the men of course invited too. Somewhere equidistant from Poland, Germany, Ireland,

and Puerto Rico we negotiated a path.

"Sonia, what are we going to do about *los regalos*?" Mami looked seriously worried. The gifts she was concerned about were those rather risqué items traditionally given a bride, who is assumed to be innocent and in need of instruction about the wedding night. Along with these oddities, there are of course practical gifts: the toaster, the vacuum cleaner, and other household necessities. Typically, the women arrive early for the giving of the gifts; the men don't need to know about such things. Asking my aunts and cousins to abandon this custom was not an option. It would have been seen as disrespectful, and anyway they wouldn't have listened. The best we could do was contain the danger of Irish sensibilities being scandalized by Nuyorican humor: we would deploy a strategic seating arrangement and various other diversionary tactics as the boxes were passed around for inspection.

The Puerto Rican idea of a registry was for the bride's aunts to check in with her mother to see whether they could help to furnish anything needed for the wedding itself. Titi Gloria, for example, took me shopping for a gorgeous pair of silver shoes to match my dress. The traditions in a modest Irish family like Kevin's were not so different. At the wedding, people gave cash in substantial amounts. That was how a young couple could be expected to pay for the party, as it was their obligation to do, and also start a new life.

On the big day, I was woken and dragged out of bed by a gang of women bent on getting an early start at the beautification effort. They were yakking nonstop, also running my mother through her own preparations, just one step ahead of mine.

"Celina, get out of the shower now!"

"You want the hair first or the makeup first?"

"Ay! Who took the iron?"

I felt like a mannequin passed from hand to hand, until at the very end, when, with the cars already downstairs, their engines idling, I finally got a word in edgewise. We had forgotten one very important thing: I needed to eat something and have a shot of insulin. My mother froze in panic: whatever she had in the kitchen had disappeared in the comings and goings. So my cousin Tony ran to the diner across the street to get a turkey sandwich. I gave myself the shot and devoured the sandwich with a towel for a bib as the roomful of women screamed at me not to get mustard on the dress. With that, we were off.

At the church, Kevin was waiting, dressed in a rented but very fashionable beige tuxedo, beaming proudly. Marguerite showed me the sugar cubes she'd tucked into her bouquet, assuring me that the maid of honor would be sticking very close by in case the bride suffered any drops in blood glucose. I was especially thrilled to see my cousin Milly arriving with her husband, Jim, and her mother, Elena. They were yet another family of Mami's brother Mayo, and when they had first arrived from Puerto Rico, before I was born, they had come to live with Mami and Papi. I rarely saw them anymore, because they lived upstate, but they were very dear to me. It was Milly, a champion at dominoes, who finally taught me to play. With them beside me, my wedding felt like one of those parties from my childhood that I missed so much.

And so it would be: after the ceremony in the Lady Chapel, we danced into the wee hours at a wedding hall in Queens, along with a dozen other nuptial parties in neighboring rooms. We ended the night by tossing frugality to the wind and splurging on a room at the Hotel St. Moritz overlooking Central Park. I was happy to sign the register as Sonia Sotomayor de Noonan. Room service was closed by the time we checked in, and I was starving; the banquet fare had left much to be desired. Kevin walked several blocks in the rain on a chivalrous quest for a greasy hamburger with cold fries.

Inside the room, Kevin opened the last of the wedding gift envelopes. It was a handful of quaaludes, compliments of his buddies at Stony Brook. I gave him a look of horror and insisted he flush them down the toilet.

"I should just give them back to the guys," he demurred. "They're worth a lot of money."

But I wasn't having it. I watched as he shook the pills into the bowl, muttering, "Man, they would kill me if they could see this."

All told, having a real wedding wasn't as bad as I'd feared, although it didn't increase my taste for such extravagance. I still tell all my cousins — and every bride-to-be I know — skip the pageant and take the money instead. Nobody listens.

Nineteen

If our decision to get married was essentially unexamined — it was what couples like us were expected to do — we were hardly more reflective about the marriage once inside it. We simply set about playing house, which seemed a natural enough extension of our companionable coexistence before exchanging vows. Like me, Kevin was young when he'd lost his father. Neither of us had observed particularly inspiring models of married life, TV sitcoms providing what baseline we had. If we'd thought about it, we might have imagined ourselves among the more progressive of those exemplars, this season's new series, in which the couple share the housework and the financial burdens, taking turns supporting each other through grad school.

Kevin's own plans were still uncertain. He was applying to medical schools while also contemplating a research track in science.

Law appealed to him too; we had taken the LSAT together, he getting the higher score. He was intellectually equipped for any path he might have chosen, but the gears hadn't yet meshed to drive him forward. So in the meantime, he took a job as a laboratory assistant in the biology department, and I picked up one in the mimeograph room of the law school. A full scholarship covered my tuition, so all we needed was money to live on.

We scoured New Haven for something affordable in an unthreatening neighborhood, finally finding a small apartment in what was once a boardinghouse on Whitney Avenue, a mile from campus. Our landlord betrayed a not very high opinion of lawyers, so I let Kevin do the talking. Home was a living room with a built-in storage chest that doubled as a couch; there was a real bedroom, separate from the living room, and a tiny cubbyhole of a kitchen. We loved that place and would keep it for the three years I was at Yale. Though furnished entirely with hand-me-downs, it never lost the glow of a first home, the sweet mix of nesting and independence.

Kevin decided that we needed a dog to complete our nuclear family, and Star was the much-loved addition. He was a tiny, camel-colored greyhound mutt with steel springs for legs and a passion for chewing. The very first sacrifice to his toothy enthusiasm was my wedding shoes, that pair of gorgeous silver sandals that Titi Gloria had spent an unthinkable fortune on. Well, they were wretchedly uncomfortable the one night I wore them, anyway.

The housework, as I said, was a team effort. I handed Kevin my paychecks, and he paid the bills. I dusted and made the bed; Kevin mopped the floors. He washed the clothes; I ironed them. I did most of the shopping and cooking; he did the dishes. I learned how to boil an egg, and much more, from the *Joy of Cooking.* When in doubt, I phoned Mrs. Gudewicz, Marguerite's mother. One time I found turkey drumsticks on sale for pennies a pound, and she helped me wrangle them long-distance. Every few months, Marguerite and her boyfriend and future husband, Tom, would come for a weekend visit, always with a care package of quality meat we couldn't have afforded. Marguerite's mother was a second mother to me, and nothing says "we believe in you" like a New York sirloin.

Yale Law School was and is uniquely small among the top law schools in the country.

There were only about 180 in our class. The numbers reflect not only highly selective admissions but also a commitment to fostering a supportive environment on a human scale. Not surprisingly, I found myself surrounded by the most brilliant, dazzlingly articulate, and hard-charging people I'd ever met. Many were entering the field having already established stellar reputations doing something else. There were PhDs in philosophy, economics, math, and physics. We had writers, a doctor, a film critic, an opera singer, not to mention several Rhodes scholars in our class. It would have been even more daunting if we could have known at the time that the class of 1979 would go on to extraordinary success even by the school's extraordinary standards: so many members are now deans and professors at top law schools, federal and state judges, or otherwise in the highest echelons of government or practice. I'm told that this rarefied company made everyone feel as insecure as I did, but that would be difficult to verify.

To take a bit of the edge off this ultimate clash of academic all-stars, grading was elided into something resembling a pass-fail system. Students were not ranked. One friend believed there would have been a significant homicide rate otherwise. No one wanted to be seen trying too hard, and all affected a coolly casual demeanor. But behind closed doors they were working like maniacs, and I was no exception. I read the cases scrupulously and would never have dreamed of walking into class unprepared. But that wasn't enough to banish the threat of being humiliated at any time. Instruction proceeded by a process of interrogation, an only somewhat less terrifying version of the Socratic method at Harvard that had recently been dramatized in *The Paper Chase.* If I faced no one as sadistic as John Houseman's character, professors still sometimes relished eliciting an inadequate answer as an opportunity to dig deeper and lay fully bare the flawed understanding that had produced it. Even a correct answer could lead to further probing that might leave you looking for a hole to crawl into.

I could see there was a method to this torment. We were being conditioned to think on our feet and immunized against the emotional rough-and-tumble of an adversarial profession. Professors at Yale did not look down on us: they assumed that everyone there was smart and in many ways related to us as peers. But often I felt as if I were floundering. It wasn't merely the intense circumstantial pressure. Listening to class discussions, I could follow the reasoning, but I couldn't anticipate where it was headed. For all Princeton had taught me about academic argumentation, law school seemed to operate on a plane of its own. If history involved more than memorizing names and dates, the practice of law was even more removed from merely learning a body of rules and statutes, as I had naively assumed it would be. Instead, becoming a lawyer required mastery of a new way of thinking, and not one that followed obviously from other disciplines. What's more, there was often recourse to distinct and not necessarily concurrent frameworks of jurisprudence, theories of law that our professors had devoted whole careers to exploring and elaborating. In retrospect, it occasionally made for a rather chaotic and perhaps overly theoretical approach to the basic aim of preparing new lawyers for practice. But there is no doubt that the jurisprudential systems to which I was exposed would be put into service much later when I came to the bench.

What systems particularly? I know some readers will be inclined to sift this chapter for clues to my own jurisprudence. I regret to disappoint them, but that's not the purpose of this book. Suffice it to say, during my years there, from 1976 to 1979, Yale was on the cusp of some radical changes in the way that law was taught and understood.

But let me not overstate the influence of those innovations, which seem in hindsight more dramatic than they did at the time and which sometimes were more methodological than theoretical (Guido Calabresi's torts class, for instance, which I took in my first semester, incorporated quantitative methods from economics, an approach that appealed to me given the computer work I'd done at Princeton and that heralded further melding of law with the social sciences at Yale). For the most part, however, of necessity, we were learning the law as it had traditionally been taught. In constitutional law and other areas, the theories presented were primarily those enshrined in the particulars of Supreme Court cases, as articulated in the opinions, concurrences, and dissents of the justices. Many of my courses were taught by established giants in their field; I had Grant Gilmore for Contracts, Charles Black for Admiralty, Elias Clark for Trusts and Estates, Geoffrey Hazard for Procedure, Ralph Winter for Antitrust Law. They followed the time-honored approach to common-law development: analyzing particular cases to extract principles and then considering whether those principles applied in subsequent cases, and if not, what exceptions they created.

In fact, most of the theoretical ferment that would come to dominate the study of law, particularly constitutional law, with professors' commentaries coming to overshadow the opinions of justices, was as yet on the horizon. I did take a course on Speech, Press, and the First Amendment with Robert Bork, but arguments about judicial restraint, original intent, and strict construction had not yet entered our conversations as students, let alone the focus of our training. The Federalist Society, with its commitment to originalism, would not be founded until three years after I'd left Yale, and its liberal responders were still further in the offing. My own awareness of these debates would not gel until I'd become a judge, when, by happy coincidence, I joined three of my colleagues on the Second Circuit Court of Appeals — Guido Calabresi, Ralph Winter, and José Cabranes, former professors of mine at Yale. It was then I'd have the conversations I was not remotely equipped to have as a student.

It may seem unlikely, but even among my ultra-high-wattage classmates, and with minimal time to spare for social life or extracurriculars, I did not feel isolated at Yale. Partly, this was because "ILS" were divided into small groups for some classes. In this way, the intense pressure we all felt became a bonding experience, with competitive animus channeled outside the group while within it we made some friends for life.

There was also something of a sisterhood in my class. Although the law school had been admitting women since 1918, they were still a minority. In our class of 180, there were only 41 of us, and that was a significant increase over previous years. Naturally, we felt connected and especially supportive of one another. There was Martha Minow, now dean at Harvard; the future professors Susan Sturm and Ellen Wright Clayton; the journalist-lawyer Carol Green; and Susan Hoffman, now a leader in the California state bar. The obvious brilliance of these women often frightened me, but I realized quickly that it didn't make them any less human or companionable. And once we became friends, I learned that some of them, in their own way, felt just as insecure at Yale as I did.

My very closest friends, however, were of a different stripe.

Felix Lopez, a Puerto Rican orphan from

the tenements and projects of East Harlem, was a high school dropout who'd been clever enough to let himself get caught in a minor act of controlled arson so that he could enter the safe haven of a home for juvenile delinquents. From there, via Vietnam and the GI Bill, he would graduate at the top of his class at the University of Michigan. Early struggles wouldn't prevent Felix, a teddy bear with a huge heart, from committing himself to alleviating the suffering of others. If he hasn't yet saved the world, he's not done trying.

Born a member of the Mohawk nation, Drew Ryce, with his streety Spanish, could have passed for Latino, especially after he'd cut off his braids. He recounted tales of surviving a childhood on the streets of Chicago so close to hell that its fires burnished his accounts of that time with a sometimes unbelievable glow, or of how Yale had poached him from Harvard. He had a mind like an IBM mainframe, only much less predictable. He and Kevin would become very close, spending long hours talking music and old movies.

A Chicano from small-town New Mexico, Rudy Aragon spent six years in the air force as an intelligence officer, after which he had a very clear objective for his career in law:

he was aiming for the top of a major law firm. George Keys, who had known Rudy since their U.S. Air Force Academy days, was similarly hell-bent on corporate success, determined to attain what had been denied his father as a black man living in the segregated southern town that was this nation's capital.

These compadres, whose concern and intelligence I could always count on, were the four older brothers I'd never had. Each remained acutely aware of the parallel universe, the other America, from which he had been beamed into New Haven. Each was worldly-wise beyond any experience of mine. They all called me "kid." And that's how I felt around them. When Kevin and I played host to them, the menu consisted of stretchable specialties I had recently mastered — soups, stews, spaghetti. But when it was Felix's turn, he pulled out the stops with exotic offerings he'd picked up during his tour in Vietnam — summer rolls with peanut sauce, and a lemongrass-caramel chicken dish — and finished with a French apple galette. These guys even knew how to choose a bottle of wine and couldn't have been nicer the one time I got drunk trying to keep up with them.

They became the center of my extracurricular life, what time for it we could spare. With Rudy, I co-chaired LANA, Yale's Latino, Asian, and Native American student association. The focus was on recruitment and other issues like those I'd dealt with at Princeton. It was sometimes surprising how the support of their own kind, which had been so essential to my survival at Princeton and which in a smaller way I'd re-created among my law school friends, was not such a priority among some of the minority students at Yale. Here I found more Latinos and members of other groups who seemed determined to assimilate as quickly and thoroughly as possible, bearing any attendant challenges and psychic costs in private. I could understand the impulse, but it was never a choice I could have made myself.

Drew got me into more mainstream activity at the Graduate and Professional Student Center, better known as the GPSC — or "Gypsy." Essentially, it was a bar for grad students — the cheapest drinks in New Haven — and as vice president of operations, he hired me to work the door, taking tickets and checking IDs. I would have preferred to work behind the bar, which paid better, but I was a more than adequate bouncer. Nobody could talk their way past me, and I ejected many a townie trying to climb in through the window to avoid the cover charge. My instincts only failed me once: A group of girls wanted to have a look around inside before paying the cover, to see if they really wanted to stay. Not having been born yesterday, I told them nice try and was about to send them on their way, when Drew appeared. Getting worked up when he caught wind of the situation, he wound up apologizing to the ladies and insisting I let them in for free. The bar, he told me, was full of desperate guys with no one to dance with — a very bad situation for liquor sales.

"It's not right, Drew, the guys are paying, why should the women get in free? Can't you see that's sex discrimination?"

"Not everything is a civil rights case, Sonia!" he yelled. "I've got a band to pay and nobody's drinking." We argued some more, until finally he solved the problem by promoting me to bartender and putting someone else on the door.

With such a colorful crew, alliances could shift and tensions flare from time to time, but the gravitational pull of adoptive family always held. I invited my compadres to Co-op City to meet my mother and then for many a holiday dinner. They felt comfortable enough to critique Mami's taste in art. The Three Graces that hung in the living room, a metal bas-relief on velvet, they dubbed "a tit and three asses." But behind their bravado I could sense that they were slightly in awe of my mother's steadiness and her unassuming concern for so many people around her; it was something they in their wanderings had missed out on and would sometimes struggle to find.

It was at Yale that I met the first person I can describe as a true mentor. I had long known the good of seeking out the guidance of teachers, from Miss Katz to Nancy Weiss and Peter Winn at Princeton. And I had an even older understanding of how much friends and classmates could teach me. But I had not yet discovered the benefit of sustained dialogue with someone who epitomized the kind of achievement I aspired to, and much beyond that. It was not the comfort of handholding; rather, it was a style of learning by means of engaging a living example. Some of us are natural autodidacts; others learn best by visual representation; others still by auditory cues. For me the most agreeable and effective instruction has come from observing the nuances and complexity of live action, the complete package of knowledge, experience, and judgment that is another human being. Whenever I make a new friend, my mind goes naturally to the question, what can I learn from this person? There are very few people in the world whom you can't learn something from, but even rarer are those souls who can reveal whole worlds to you if you observe them carefully.

I first met José Cabranes through a Princeton friend who'd worked with me in Acción Puertorriqueña. Charlie Hey-Maestre had been a year behind me, and when I was in my first year at Yale, he was writing his senior thesis, which dealt with issues around U.S. citizenship for Puerto Ricans. He had come to Yale to consult José Cabranes, who was an expert on the topic. I had offered Charlie our couch for the night, and we stayed up late talking. "So who is this Cabranes guy?" I asked. Charlie explained: José Cabranes had served as special counsel to the governor of Puerto Rico and head of the commonwealth's Washington office, and he was now Yale's general counsel, the first ever named to that position. Earlier, he had been a founder of the Puerto Rican Legal Defense and Education Fund and a professor at Rutgers. He was a trailblazer and a hero to many for his work promoting civil rights for Hispanics.

Charlie insisted that I come along to the lunch meeting he had arranged. José Cabranes was gracious, warm, and brilliant. He spent the first half hour addressing Charlie's questions and then gradually drew me into the conversation. We talked about the relationship between the mainland and the island and how it affected Puerto Ricans' view of the world, our self-image, and the scope of our future. I was surprised at the way he used the term "colonial" so neutrally, as if it were a statement of fact rather than a moral condemnation, a description of present economic and political circumstances rather than a judgment on history. Our discussion turned on the tensions inherent in a circumscribed statutory citizenship, a status with more limited rights than were enjoyed by citizens on the mainland, and the consequences of living under those limitations for the better part of a century and perhaps indefinitely.

It had been three hours when José looked at his watch and said he needed to get back to work. Charlie and I thanked him and said our good-byes. As we were about to leave, José turned to me and said, "What are you doing this summer? Come work for me." I had just arrived at Yale and certainly hadn't thought that far ahead. But I didn't hesitate a moment before accepting, nor did I wait for summer before starting work for him.

My job involved research for the book he was writing on the legislative history of U.S. citizenship for Puerto Ricans, as well as minor assistance with the day-to-day legal work of the university. But what I learned came from having a front-row seat, observing his conduct of meetings or simply the traffic of people, issues, and ideas through his office. In the hothouse of very bright people that Yale was, he was one of the brightest, with an intimate knowledge of the law, a passion for history, and the skill to engage with warmth and depth whomever he encountered.

Until I met José Cabranes, I could not have imagined him. I had glimpsed Congressmen Herman Badillo and Bobby Garcia at work when I interned on Badillo's mayoral campaign. But they were dealing with their constituents, people like those I knew. José maintained similar community relations in his pro bono work as the very model of a citizen-lawyer, but he could maneuver with equal skill and self-assurance, a kind of courtly grace, in the most rarefied corridors of power. And yet he remained infinitely generous with his knowledge, time, and influence, especially with young people. He would take Felix under his wing, too, and offer Drew guidance on the confusing thickets of Indian tribal law, a different manifestation of the American empire. We tried mightily to impress him. If he doubted some of the ideas we presented to him, like so many dead mice offered up by eager kittens, he always tempered his skepticism with good humor.

When a young person, even a gifted one, grows up without proximate living examples of what she may aspire to become — whether lawyer, scientist, artist, or leader in any realm — her goal remains abstract. Such models as appear in books or on the news, however inspiring or revered, are ultimately too remote to be real, let alone influential. But a role model in the flesh provides more than an inspiration; his or her very existence is confirmation of possibilities one may have every reason to doubt, saying, "Yes, someone like me can do this." By the time I got to Yale, I had met a few successful lawyers, usually in their role as professors. José, the first I had the chance to observe up close, not only transcended the academic role but also managed to uphold his identity as a Puerto

Rican, serving vigorously in both worlds.

I knew better than to try to imitate José. I had enough self-awareness to understand that the best I could do was derive what lessons I could from his success as they might relate to my own capacities. I still consider his advice carefully — indeed, I've sought it at every crossroads in my career — though I'm more likely to translate it into my own terms than to take it up directly. José has often spoken of what an unusual protégée I've been: how I often confer with him, only then to do exactly as I please. He's only half joking.

In the absence of grades and class rank, the only clear mark of standing at Yale Law School is to get on *The Yale Law Journal*. The most straightforward way to do that is to write a piece and have it accepted for publication. It's called a "note," but it's really a very thorough paper.

"Bring me a proposal," said Bill Eskridge, who was the note and topics editor. Bill has since returned to Yale as a respected professor specializing in statutory interpretation, though in my memory his lanky form, forever in plaid shirt and jeans, is of a piece with the journal's stifling, dust-caked offices at the top of the Sterling building. He laid out the criteria: the note had to be original, significant, and logically cogent. I had to find some unresolved legal problem — one tightly focused but of real consequence — and then solve it. It sounds straightforward until you consider that countless students have ascended this temple to propose a topic and been rebuffed.

At Princeton, I had pondered the question of Puerto Rican citizenship historically, politically, and economically, but in doing research for José Cabranes's book, I had started to see it in legal terms, a different lens and perhaps a more powerful one for some purposes. But if you look too closely at what the islanders had been granted as against what other U.S. citizens enjoy by birth or naturalization, issues emerge that no one wants to grapple with. Could, for instance, the U.S. citizenship of Puerto Ricans living on the mainland be revoked were they to return to the island in the case of independence? Such unresolved questions constitute the legal morass underlying decades of political stalemate and still sway small but decisive percentages of the commonwealth's electorate. If I could find one legal knot to untangle, it might avail not only a good topic for a note but something useful for Puerto Rico.

The island couldn't afford statehood or independence, many people reasoned at the time. But having studied seabed rights, treaties, and offshore territorial sovereignty in Admiralty class, I could see a wealth of potential for the island underwater. Might the unexploited mineral and oil resources be tapped to fund development? After all, the island's poverty had always been ascribed to the dearth of natural resources. Control of those neglected rights would be vital to local prosperity, whatever the island's future, be it commonwealth, statehood, or independence. Many have since argued, however, that the economic impact of the seabed rights would be negligible, and in fact thirty years later little of their promise has been realized.

I was in the ballpark. Now I had only to narrow the topic to a single legal question I could answer. I focused on statehood for purposes of the note because that was where precedent was clearest. I combed the old case law cases relating to the so-called equal footing doctrine, which gives new states joining the Union the same constitutional rights enjoyed by existing states, even while ceding to the federal government other powers enumerated in the Constitution. There were among the precedents a variety of obstacles, strange particulars of what some states had been permitted or denied. In the end, I couldn't establish affirmatively that Puerto Rico was entitled to its seabed rights in all circumstances, but I could prove that retaining them would not violate the doctrine of equal footing in the event of statehood. It was one small step, a tiny clearing in the jungle that has grown around the status question, but I thought it unassailable.

Bill Eskridge liked the idea. Fortunately, the other members of the journal did too, despite their preference that notes address themselves to current case law. After seemingly endless rounds of drafts and revision, "Statehood and the Equal Footing Doctrine: The Case for Puerto Rican Seabed Rights" was published.

One day, we were having a perfectly civil exchange when out of the blue Rudy interrupted me: "You know what I love about you, Sonia? You argue just like a guy." Kevin, stretched out on the couch, snorted a gulpful of his soda, choking down a laugh.

"What is that supposed to mean, Rudy?"

Suddenly I was seething, and they knew it. Felix asserted his calming influence: "It's a good thing, Sonia, he means it as a compliment." I had heard compliments like that before.

Rudy forged on, explaining: I didn't hedge every statement with disclaimers, apologies, and self-doubts. He did his impression of how women raised their hands in class. " 'Excuse me, Professor, I'm sorry, this might not be important, but you may want to consider the possibility . . .' Not you, Sonia," he said. "When you ask to be called on, you just state your case plain and defy anyone to prove you wrong."

Rudy was right in that sense: I have always argued like a man, more noticeably in the context of those days, when an apologetic and tentative manner of speech was the norm among women. I don't know where I learned this style, but it has served me well, especially in the years when most of the people I was arguing with were men.

Where Rudy was wrong, however, was in suggesting that I had ever volunteered to speak in class. Having suffered the repetitive trauma of getting grilled, I was well into my third year before I'd ever raised my hand. But when I did, Rudy would be there to see it. It happened in Clark's class on Trusts and Estates; he was teaching the common-law rule against perpetuities, which limits how far into the future a will can control a line of inheritance. Professor Clark was charting a hypothetical family tree on the blackboard, a sequence of births and deaths, when it occurred to me that the fate of this inheritance was essentially a math problem. Moreover, I could see a mistake in his calculation. I raised my hand, he called on me, and I pointed out the error. He turned and stared at the blackboard for several very long, silent minutes. Finally, he turned around. "She's absolutely right," he said. "I've made a mistake." He explained to the class what I'd caught and put up another example, only to make a similar mistake. When I raised my hand this time, he paused more briefly before turning around and saying, "Why don't you come up and teach this part?"

I got a slap on the back from Rudy after class. But an even bigger confidence breakthrough was shortly to come, with my participation in the mock trials for the Barristers' Union competition. Perhaps the courtroom playacting somehow liberated my inner Perry Mason. Or maybe Forensics Club experience had come to the rescue again, or a buried memory of Abuelita mesmerizing her audience. Somehow or other, in this setting I felt for the first time I could actually be a lawyer.

As it happened, in one trial, Drew was my client, the defendant in a he-said/she-said rape case. We rehearsed the argument in great detail, but in the moment when I stood before the jury, people recruited from the community through an ad in the local paper, the analytic preparation receded into the background, and some other instinct came forward. I found my eyes automatically scanning their faces, trying to read them: Are they following me? Do I need to push harder or to pull back? There was a sweet spot where I was able to meet them halfway. Most of them, anyway.

In the jury box, one middle-aged man kept shaking his head ever so slightly and pursing his lips, again and again. But the subtle signals of antipathy didn't track my remarks; they were out of sync, as if he were responding to some other stimulus rather than what I was saying. We were encouraged to approach the jury members afterward for feedback on our performance. As people were milling around at the end of the session, I approached him and said, "I have a feeling I rubbed you the wrong way. Can you tell me why?"

He seemed startled, then shook his head. "It's nothing you did."

I told him that I was trying to learn. That

was the purpose of the exercise. Whether it was something I was doing or not doing, I wished he would let me know so that I could adjust my approach in the future.

He shut down. "It's my own thing," he said. "I can't help you." But I continued to press him politely. Finally, he blurted it out. "Look, nothing personal. I just don't like brassy Jewish women." That took me by surprise. I froze as my mind raced through the things I could possibly say to this man, when the right response occurred to me.

I looked at him. "You're right," I said. "I can't do anything about that." And I walked away.

My second summer at Yale, I landed a job as a summer associate at Paul, Weiss, Rifkind, Wharton & Garrison, one of the very top law firms in Manhattan. I was working under men known as giants in litigation, and I was given a variety of assignments, the most challenging of which was a contribution to a brief being prepared for a huge antitrust case — an auspicious opportunity if ever there was one. But when I sat down to write, my arguments seemed continually wide of the mark. True, antitrust was not an area of the law I'd studied, and I had no background in business to speak of. But

335

considering the difficulty of proving a violation of the Sherman Act, I couldn't figure out why I was failing to articulate a persuasive argument on the client's behalf, despite racking my brains on the long daily commute between New Haven and New York. I finally handed in my effort to a young associate one notch up the totem pole. Only when I saw what he eventually wrote himself and passed up to the next level did I fully realize how poor a job I had done. I obviously wasn't thinking like a lawyer yet. If this was what it meant to work in a prestigious law firm, I clearly was not ready.

The sense of failure was confirmed when I concluded my stint as a summer associate without receiving a job offer. I had never heard of such a thing happening at Yale Law School, and though I've learned since it was not so uncommon, of course no one advertised it. But anyway, in my own eyes I had officially blown it. I had worked hard — I always had and still do — but somehow that wasn't enough. And it was difficult not to conclude that I was simply not in the same league as my classmates who were pulling in job offers from firms just like this one. There were some around me encouraging me to view the rejection as an expression of bias or personal animus, but I had seen no evidence of that, while my sense of having underperformed seemed to me well enough substantiated. For this pain of failure — the first real failure since having enrolled in law school — I had only myself to blame, and knowing that, I was profoundly shaken.

The way forward was daunting if obvious. I needed to figure out what I was doing wrong and fix it. At the very least I had to learn this area of law, and so I signed up for Professor Ralph Winter's class on antitrust as well as one called Commercial Transactions. The trickier part would be mastering the skill that was at the heart of being a lawyer, my deficiency in which had been exposed: how to write a brief, not as some classroom exercise aspiring to an objective analysis of the case law, but as a piece of persuasive advocacy, advancing the interests of my client. In both kinds of remedial efforts, I would do what I'd always done: break the challenge down into smaller challenges, which I could get on with in my methodical fashion. And certainly I would need to prove myself at another kind of work in the legal profession before I could even consider joining a large commercial firm. In the meantime, the unfamiliar taste of utter failure from that summer would stay in my mouth. The memory of this trauma, which I was determined not to repeat, while not suffocating my ambitions, would overhang my every career choice until I became a judge.

One obvious good did come of my ordeal at Paul, Weiss: I made more money that summer than I had ever seen before. Now Kevin and I could actually afford a honeymoon, and a change of scene seemed in order as I licked my wounds and considered the way forward. Soon dreams of America were unfolding across our living room floor as we planned to cross the continent and head west.

Carol Green, a close friend from my study group, was a journalist from Denver visiting Yale for a yearlong program on law and journalism. She invited us on a camping tour down into New Mexico, Four Corners, the Grand Canyon ... She and her husband were old hands at this, equipped with all the right gear and experienced at roughing it. The appeal of sleeping under the stars, protected by nothing but a tarpaulin and far from the safety of civilization, eluded me then and still does. But Kevin, no less a city kid than I, was eager to try it, and so we did. There was so much that I had wanted to see for so long, so many sights that would inspire a pilgrim's awe, that I wasn't going to complain about the want of a few urban comforts.

For years I had studied American history, law, and society, but I had barely scratched the surface of the great geographical reality. What I knew of this land was a library's worth of cases, treaties, the shifting tides of politics, human migrations, and technologies. The natural wonders I recognized only from childhood picture books and the plates of our *Britannica,* but it was something else altogether to watch the vast stretches of forest and plain unfurl for hours along the highway, or to feel dwarfed by the immensity of the sky. As we headed south out of Denver, the Rocky Mountains lay to the west like bones of the continent exposed to the afternoon light. As the road ran straight and flat, my mind rambled along its own bumpy, winding course. Two-thirds of the way through law school, and everyone around me was considering job offers. I needed to figure something out.

Most of my classmates were aiming in the direction of prestigious midtown law firms, including Rudy, whose objective couldn't have been more unvarnished: make big bucks. If the shortest path to that goal was to defend corporations in massive tort cases and antitrust litigation, then so be it. He could always pursue labors of love by doing pro bono work on the side. My own ambitions were not as susceptible to the same inducements, but I did recognize a greater good in Rudy's approach. Until minorities learned how to navigate at those altitudes of the legal system, their communities would lag the rest of the country. If our experience as a group was ever to advance beyond disadvantage and grievance, we needed to move with ease where money and power move.

The splat of raindrops on the windshield interrupted my reverie. Surely we now had to find a motel. No way was I sleeping out in the rain, pitching a tent in a puddle. "Let's see if it passes," said Carol. She's got to be kidding, I thought, as a bolt of lightning cracked the sky open and electrocuted the mountains.

My ruminations continued through the days of driving, as if the white line in the road were an arrow pointing toward the future. José Cabranes had advised me to keep my sights on a major law firm in the long term, saying it was a good platform from which to launch into government or any other direction, but that first of all I should clerk. I had heard classmates mention clerking and I knew it was prestigious, but José had to explain to me that it meant working, essentially as a researcher, for a judge. Though I knew he wanted the best for me, clerking sounded tediously academic. How much longer could I live in the library? If I was wary of going to a big firm, I still felt the need to get out in the real world and earn some money.

Much later I would realize my naïveté. Especially working with my own clerks, I've come to appreciate how clerking for a judge can be the most vital mentoring relationship open to a young lawyer. It has become even more prestigious over the years since I left law school and the most direct stepping-stone to higher levels of legal practice. Many minority students and others who struggle under financial pressure sacrifice the long-term benefits of clerking for better pay in the near term. I advise them to resist that temptation and aim for the necessary grades, journal experience, and mentoring relationships with professors that can open the door to a clerkship. Part of me still regrets not having taken José's advice at face value.

When we rolled to a crunchy graveled stop and cut the engine, the silence of the desert was complete. The ruins of a Pueblo village were visible halfway up a cliff, nooks and crannies revealing themselves as we walked. You could see traces of daily life in the contours carved into the mountain, the footholds for climbing out of enemies' reach, the cistern to capture precious rain-water. I tried to populate the village in my mind and imagined myself looking out from a window of that cliff-side aerie to the desert expanse. The only moving feature in the landscape was the light itself and the slow shadow of clouds piled in the distance. The wind was a constant, and when you paid attention, it seemed like the earth's own breathing.

One possibility I'd long had in mind was the State Department. I was fascinated by Professor Michael Reisman's course Public Order of the World Community, as well as my glimpse of international law working with José on his book about the Puerto Rican status problem and citizenship, and also exploring the narrower question of maritime rights in my journal note. As tiny as Puerto Rico is, studying maritime issues had given me a taste of what it might be like to work on the exceptionally complex intellectual puzzles of international law, whose solutions have very real consequences for millions of people. And the idea of public service on a big stage appealed to me deeply.

Of course, such thoughts might all be moot: Kevin was applying to medical schools and graduate programs, and when I finished at Yale, it would be his turn to decide where we would live among the places where he was accepted. At least Washington was on his list of possibilities.

I had not forgotten my childhood dream of becoming a judge, but if law school had taught me anything, it was what pure fantasy that dream would have to remain. Even at Yale, there was no such thing as a "judge track" to prepare you specifically for the rigors of those heights of the legal profession. I could see that it was a matter of accumulating a broad range of legal experience in positions that are challenging and respected and, eventually, being visible to those who could offer a nomination. And still, luck and timing would play their inscrutable roles. The relative scarcity of women on the bench and the practical nonexistence of Latinas also gave me reason to keep this idea in the drawer with other idle wishes, any expression of which would have marked me as delusional.

Kevin and I made a detour to Albuquerque to visit Dolores, whom I hadn't seen since Princeton. She was so much more at ease on home turf. Her family's modest house reminded me of Puerto Rico, with her father, mother, and three sisters filling the small rooms with their laughter and chatter. And I discovered that Dolores hadn't been the only one their father had taught to sing and play guitar; all Mr. Chavez's daughters made music together. As half-familiar smells drifted in from the kitchen — roasting peppers and cumin, caramelizing onions, the earthy steam of beans — as well as others I couldn't identify, the guitars got passed around. For me, the most precious memory of the evening was hearing Dolores and her father's duet of "Cucurrucucú Paloma." In that gentle exchange, the handing of the melody back and forth between them, I recognized again how very far from home she had felt at Princeton.

We flew on to San Francisco for the final leg of the trip, a visit with Ken Moy, who was living in Berkeley with Patricia Kristof, with whom he'd been a couple since Princeton. There was a sense of completion in seeing a sunset on the Pacific Coast, and it felt equally fitting to close out the trip with the touchstone of very old friendship. Celebration was in order. I accompanied Ken to the market, where he chose things I'd never seen before: passion fruit and butternut and spaghetti squash. He cooked up a feast, and I marveled to see him so happy in a home, and a family, of his own creation, a long way from East Harlem.

At the all-star break in 1978, the Yankees lagged a dozen or so games behind the Red Sox, and yet there was no question but that I'd be betting on them to win the American League East. My hometown loyalties run deeper than any season's ups and downs, and while I'll root for the underdog in many other arenas, when it comes to baseball, the Yankees' knack for setting aside the day's personal dramas to get out there and win always impresses me. Felix, as a New Yorker, was with me of course, and Drew was shrewdly calculating the odds. But Rudy and George were backing the Red Sox out of sheer contrariness, and so I arranged that when the Yankees won the pennant, those guys would buy me dinner at the best restaurant in New Haven.

It was the top of the seventh in the final, tie-breaking game. The Yankees had two men on when Bucky Dent, a shortstop with no hitting power in his history, came up to bat. The bat cracks, like a sign from heaven.

He takes a new bat, and when it kisses the ball, a hand reaches down from the sky and lifts it out of the park. There's an eerie silence over Boston as Bucky Dent crosses home plate. All hell broke loose. Rudy and George were screaming in agony, Felix was crowing like the sun just rose, I was sitting there shaking my head, saying over and over, "They did it! They pulled it out again!"

My winner's dinner would have to wait till another night, however, even if we hadn't already felt stuffed to bursting on Felix's feast of *picadillo* with rice and black beans — the best I'd had since Papi died. Though nothing would have made me happier than to stay right there, basking in the glow of victory and friendship, I had to pull myself together for a recruiting dinner that same night. The host was Shaw, Pittman, Potts & Trowbridge, a well-respected, small Washington firm that did varied corporate and international work. Scott Rafferty, who had graduated summa cum laude alongside me at Princeton before also coming to Yale, had worked there as a summer associate and loved the experience. He enthusiastically encouraged me to attend the dinner.

There were eight or ten of us at a large table, and I happened to be seated facing the partner who was steering the event.

346

Scott made introductions, circling the table with a few words about each of us. "Sonia's Puerto Rican and from the South Bronx in New York. She was at Princeton before she came to Yale." Very few words, as it happened, but as students we didn't have long résumés.

As soon as the introductions were over, and before another word was spoken, the partner facing me asked whether I believed in affirmative action. "Yes," I said, somewhat guarded but hardly imagining what my answer would unleash.

"Do Princeton and Yale have affirmative action programs?" Yes, of course they do, I told him, at which the challenge only escalated: "Do you believe law firms should practice affirmative action? Don't you think it's a disservice to minorities, hiring them without the necessary credentials, knowing you'll have to fire them a few years later?"

I was stunned, as much by the bald rudeness of the interrogation as by its implications. I'd heard nothing of the kind so blatant since the school nurse caught me off guard at Cardinal Spellman. "I think that even someone who got into an institution through affirmative action could prove they were qualified by what they accomplished there."

He looked at me skeptically. "But that's the problem with affirmative action. You have to wait to see if people are qualified or not. Do you think you would have been admitted to Yale Law School if you were not Puerto Rican?"

"It probably didn't hurt," I said. "But I imagine that graduating summa cum laude and Phi Beta Kappa from Princeton had something to do with it too."

"Well, do you consider yourself culturally deprived?"

Gee, Officer Krupke, I thought, how do I explain? Shall I talk about my ancestors, the heritage of Spain? About having two languages, two ways of seeing the world? Is there only one culture that counts? I didn't even know where to begin answering that one. And an awkward silence descended upon us, before spreading like a stain to the other end of the table, where Scott was seated. Sensing the discomfort, he deftly jumped in with a new topic. My adrenaline ebbed slowly, and I did what I could to get through the rest of the dinner without making others more uncomfortable. Afterward, Scott came to me to express outrage and apologize.

"It was horrible," I admitted. "So insulting."

"It was completely out-of-bounds," he said, adding he intended to complain about it the next day. But I asked him to wait. I needed to figure out what to do.

In the cafeteria the next morning, Scott had already found Rudy, Felix, and George. The forces were marshaled, the coffee flowing.

"I would have punched him out," Rudy announced, rarely one not to verbalize a thought.

"This guy was a lot bigger than me; I don't think I could have taken him," I said.

But when we got more serious about considering a proper response, I decided to go ahead with the formal recruiting interview scheduled later that same day, at which I could engage the partner from Shaw, Pittman in a more private setting.

With my résumé in front of him, he seemed to think that we were on a cordial footing. Before I knew it, he was encouraging me to come to Washington for the next step in the hiring process. That's when I called him on what he had said at the dinner.

"That was really insulting. You presumed that I was unqualified before you had seen my résumé or taken the trouble to learn anything about me."

He seemed to be waving it off as just a conversational gambit, albeit on a sensitive topic, and he expressed admiration at how I had stood my ground.

"You didn't seem terribly upset. You didn't make a scene. You were perfectly civil."

Now I really couldn't believe my ears. What was he expecting, Hysterical Puerto Rican Syndrome?

"That was the Latina in me," I said. "We're taught to be polite." If we were going to rely on stereotypes, at least they should be accurate. I further explained that it wasn't in my nature to cause everyone at the table discomfort because of how I felt about his behavior. But neither was I simply going to accept being treated so unfairly. I've long known how to control my anger, but that doesn't mean I don't feel it.

After the interview I talked through my options with the gang. I decided to address a formal complaint to the firm through the university's career office and challenge Shaw, Pittman's right to recruit on campus in light of that partner's disregard for Yale's antidiscrimination policy.

"You're going to need counsel, Sonia," Rudy said. "You're going to need one tough lawyer."

"You're hired," I said. "Pro bono, I assume."

"I think 'jailhouse lawyer' is the correct term," said Felix. Bluster aside, Rudy was the one who came to meetings with the dean and to the ensuing formal hearings of a student-faculty tribunal.

News of the incident flared across campus and divided the school into camps — those who thought I had made too much of some off-hand comments, jeopardizing Yale's relationship with an important employer of its graduates, and those who were solidly in support of my action. The latter view spread far beyond New Haven as word reached one minority student group after another across the country. Letters and news clippings describing similar affronts elsewhere started to arrive. Clearly, I had opened a bigger can of worms than I'd intended. For while I was pleased that this type of offensive behavior was being brought to light, I had no wish for personal notoriety, as a symbol or anything else. I still wanted a career in law, not a place on every firm's blacklist.

The university, clearly uncomfortable with the attention the complaint was drawing, was eager to reach a settlement. The student-faculty tribunal impaneled to investigate the complaint negotiated a full apology from Shaw, Pittman. They were not barred from recruiting, but the firm and the offending partner did voluntarily keep a low profile at Yale for a time.

Throughout, I marveled at the courage that Scott Rafferty had shown in taking my side without hesitation. It meant giving up a plum job that he had been looking forward to. He had been very happy at Shaw, Pittman as a summer associate, but he was not eager to join a firm where a partner would behave in that way. That disillusionment did nothing to advance the start of his career, but it signaled a measure of integrity that would remain evident over a distinguished professional life in public service.

When the anger, the upset, and the agitation had passed, a certainty remained: I had no need to apologize that the look-wider, search-more affirmative action that Princeton and Yale practiced had opened doors for me. That was its purpose: to create the conditions whereby students from disadvantaged backgrounds could be brought to the starting line of a race many were unaware was even being run. I had been admitted to the Ivy League through a special door, and I had more ground than most to make up before I was competing with my classmates on an equal footing. But I worked relentlessly to reach that point, and distinctions such as the Pyne Prize, Phi Beta Kappa, summa cum laude, and a spot on *The Yale Law Journal* were not given out like so many pats on the back to encourage mediocre students. These were achievements as real as those of anyone around me.

My brother's story was similar. Junior stumbled into a program that put minority kids on a fast track to medical school, essentially free of cost. He wasn't inspired by childhood dreams of becoming a doctor; he had never considered the possibility. But once he started, he found that he loved what he was doing, loved the process of learning itself, and had excellent study habits compared with most kids in the program, 45 percent of whom would drop out. Affirmative action may have gotten him into medical school, but it was his own self-discipline, intelligence, and hard work that saw him through, where others like him had failed.

Much has changed in the thinking about affirmative action since those early days when it opened doors in my life and Junior's. But one thing has not changed: to doubt the worth of minority students' achievement when they succeed is really only to present another face of the prejudice that would deny them a chance even to try. It is the same prejudice that insists all those destined for success must be cast from the same mold as those who have succeeded before them, a view that experience has already proven a fallacy.

When my note for *The Yale Law Journal* was finally laid out and pasted up, typeset, proofed, printed, collated, and bound — in short, when it was a physical reality ready to go forth into the world — the editors took the unusual step of sending out a press release announcing it. It was an indication of their belief that my work had practical import beyond the limits of academia: that my argument might even have some influence on the outcome of the status question.

Meanwhile, acceptance of the note had come with an obligation to work on the journal in other capacities, such as checking citations. The teamwork of the job was wonderfully rewarding, and out of that camaraderie, as from my small group, would come some lifelong friendships. I so enjoyed the work that I volunteered to serve also as managing editor of another student-run journal, *Yale Studies in World Public Order,* which specialized in a rigorous quantitative policy-oriented approach to international law, as developed and taught by Professor Reisman. After editing a couple of lengthy articles by alumni working in the field, I noticed myself feeling intellectually comfortable in a way that I could not imagine when I first arrived at Yale. That, together with the enthusiastic reception of my note among those working on Puerto Rican status issues, provided a feeling of real-world validation that was moving and meaningful in ways student honors could not rival.

Maybe, I thought, I am ready to go out there.

TWENTY

Yale was one of the very first law schools in the country to admit women, and yet every point in the building seemed to be separated by miles of corridor from the nearest women's restroom. On a typical trek, of an early evening, taking a break from the library and a treatise on tax law, I passed the open door of a conference room. At the back, I spotted a bonanza — a table of cheese and crackers and cheap wine, the kind of arrangement that passes for hospitality in university budgets and a free meal in the straitened lives of graduate students. The makeshift sign on the door read, "Public Service Career Paths." A panel of public-interest lawyers were pitching alternatives to private practice to a thin scattering of third-years. Just then, the moderator was introducing the final speaker, a district attorney from New York whose name I didn't recognize. He seemed none too comfortable at the

356

podium and promised to be brief. I decided it was worth sticking around until he finished so I could make for the cheddar cubes.

My ears perked up when I heard him say that he had a couple hundred assistants who all tried cases. "Within your first year on the job," he said, "you'll be going to trial, with full responsibility for how you develop and present your own cases. You'll have more responsibility than you would have at any other job coming out of law school. At your age now, you'll be doing more in a courtroom than most lawyers do in a lifetime." I liked what I was hearing. At Paul, Weiss, I had watched an associate who was thoroughly steeped in the details and strategy of a case brief a senior partner who then did a star turn in the limelight before a judge. The associate was too diplomatic and well compensated to admit to any demoralized frustration, but clearly work in a big firm meant laboring in the shadows for years.

When the presentation was over and we descended on the food, I found myself in line next to the New York district attorney, Robert M. Morgenthau, a legend unbeknownst to me. His halting, raspy voice was no different talking face-to-face. This was not a man who relished chitchat. But being capable of talking up anybody, I proceeded to ask him to tell me a bit about his background, what he'd liked about each of his jobs. Maybe he was used to talking to ignorant students; he didn't betray any hint of annoyance. He asked me what my plans were — not sure, maybe a small firm, still exploring — and then he said, "Why don't you come by and see me? I have some openings in my schedule tomorrow."

Sure enough, the next morning at the Career Office, there were still interview slots open: among Yalies, the DA's Office was not the most sought-after place to work. But I was surprised to find my name already penciled in. In fact, Bob Morgenthau had come by, pulled my résumé, and already placed a call to José Cabranes, whom he knew well from their work together on the Puerto Rican Legal Defense and Education Fund. The interview was actually enjoyable and ran a half hour longer than scheduled. At the end he invited me to visit his office in New York.

"You're interviewing *where*?" said Rudy, aghast. Even José, who had given me a glowing recommendation, seemed disappointed that I found the DA's Office more interesting than a clerkship. "Do you have any idea what they pay?" Rudy demanded. I did, but

I had never seen money as the definitive or absolute measure of success. Sure, I wouldn't make much compared with an associate at a major firm. But my starting salary would still be more than what my mother had ever made as a nurse, which to Titi Aurora, who worked as a seamstress, had always seemed lavish.

In the end, as I usually do, I trusted my instincts, although I was a bit surprised where they were leading me. I knew I wasn't ready for a big firm, but apart from applying for a job at the State Department, I had not devoted much thought or effort to public-interest options. Nor was I encouraged to: unlike today, there were few pro bono law clinics at Yale then; I knew of one on prison disciplinary hearings, one of the few settings in which students were allowed to practice, another on landlord-tenant disputes, and a third on denial of veterans' benefits. But they were not attracting many from our hyper-ambitious cohort. Perhaps Bob Morgenthau's job stirred a memory of what had first intrigued me about being a lawyer: the chance to seek justice in a courtroom. Despite my success in the trial advocacy program and in reaching the semifinals of the Barristers' Union mock trials, Perry Mason was a vision that had been eclipsed at Yale amid the immersion in case law and theory and self-doubt. Now, it seemed, that untutored fantasy was beckoning me again, conspiring with a bit of free cheddar to decide my fate.

TWENTY-ONE

At the New York District Attorney's Office, "duckling" is the term of art for a rookie assistant DA, and in the mouth of a senior prosecutor it expresses gallows humor more than endearment. Forty of us tender, fuzzy types were about to be crunched in the jaws of a huge, complex, and fast-moving machine. Guidance of senior colleagues would add seasoning over time, but meanwhile we would need every scrap of what scant training would be provided during our first few weeks. I wasn't the only one among us with minimal background in criminal law — just the required basic course at Yale and the mock trials. But even if I had devoted all my studies to the finer points of the field, there remained essential lessons inaccessible in the classroom or from books and acquired only through the fiery baptism of the courtroom. I was about to get that baptism.

New York City in 1979 had been struck by a crime wave of tsunamic proportions. Mayor Ed Koch had been elected two years before on a promise to restore order after a summer of widespread looting, vandalism, and arson triggered by a ten-day blackout. If the immediate threat to public safety had lifted after the lights and air-conditioning came back on, New Yorkers still had reason to live in a state of diffuse chronic fear. The city's fiscal troubles summed a decade of economic doldrums nationwide, and severe budget cuts were preventing the DA's Office, as well as the police department, from adding enough staff to cope with an avalanche of criminal cases. To make matters worse, rising tensions brought a rising number of police brutality complaints.

Most of the new ADAs were assigned immediately to one of six trial bureaus, each with up to fifty prosecutors of varying levels of experience, along with support staff. We would cut our teeth on misdemeanors: petty thefts, minor assaults, prostitution, shoplifting, trespass, disorderly conduct, graffiti . . . Later we would be promoted to felonies, and we might move to one of the bureaus that investigate fraud, racketeering, public corruption, sex crimes, or other specialized crimes. There was no choice in the matter, we were told. Soldiers go where they're assigned. Ducklings, too, apparently.

First we had to get to know the procedural maze. If a defendant is arraigned on an unsworn complaint, how many days do you have to fix it? Failing that, how do you handle a preliminary probable cause hearing? We also went out on patrols to get a sense of how cops do their job, the routines and the issues we needed to be sensitive to. Every sixth day we were in the complaint room for a nine-hour shift, interviewing arresting officers and witnesses to draw up the initial charges on each case. Every street arrest in the city funneled into the system through this room, which was not unlike a hospital ER on a rough night. Decisions made quickly would have a long tail of repercussions. It looked like chaos, but there was order and discipline under the surface, and that combination appealed to me. So did the pressure to improvise, the comfort of clear rules, and the inspiration of a higher good.

The way Bob Morgenthau, the Boss, structured the office to meet extraordinary challenges was a model of efficiency and integrity for jurisdictions across the country. All of our case work, for example, was organized horizontally, with cases assigned the same prosecutor from beginning to end, rather than handed off up the hierarchy. The Boss also pioneered collaborative efforts with counterparts in other boroughs, as when the Office of the Special Narcotics Prosecutor was established to coordinate investigations citywide so that prosecutions were not restricted by boundaries that the drug rings crossed routinely. He set up units for sex crimes, Chinese gangs, consumer fraud — each a center of specialized expertise and methods of investigation.

But great ideas couldn't shift the reality that the city was strapped for cash. The physical plant creaked under the burden of incessant use, our headquarters a warren of small rooms, the larger of which had three or four metal desks squeezed into them. My first office was an anteroom, actually more of a doorway, into which a desk had somehow been implanted. Eventually, turnover would deposit me in slightly more commodious shared space, though my desk still blocked the entrance, behind which door was wedged an old couch, horsehair poking out of cracked leather. Papers were piled everywhere, stacks of files, boxes of evidence, somebody's lunch. In the summer the air-conditioning failed constantly and sweat soaked through my suit, while in winter the same rooms became drafty caverns in which I might need to keep my coat and gloves on all day. The lights were dim, the electrical cords were frayed, and the plumbing leaked — sometimes into the courtrooms.

Of all the resources in short supply, time was the shortest, and mine perhaps more than most. Kevin had been accepted into the graduate program in biochemistry at Princeton, so we had moved there from New Haven. After our cozy nest on Whitney Avenue, we found ourselves living near campus in graduate student housing that had been built during and after World War II to shelter the families of returning soldiers. I was commuting by train between Princeton and Manhattan, sometimes up to two hours each way. I left home at dawn and rarely got back before nine. Kevin cooked and we'd share a late dinner every night, though I was routinely dead on my feet until the weekend brought a brief respite. I made it through the workweek on cans of Tab and my own adrenaline.

If the long hours were straining our marriage, I was too preoccupied to notice. What I did see, in the small corner of my awareness not cluttered with cases, procedures, and the minutiae of criminal law, was Kevin finally doing work that excited him and earning recognition for it. He was thrilled to be at Princeton again, this time on his own account, and he was making new friends. He was thriving at his own thing, just as I was at mine.

In the practice hearings that were part of our training, I was cast in the role of the defense attorney. Somehow by pure instinct I realized a witness implied vaguely that she had seen something, though she avoided stating it outright. On cross-examination, I asked an apparently tangential question that led her to describe the precise conditions that would have made a direct line of sight impossible for her. The senior assistant DA leading the exercise came up to me afterward. "I've been doing this training for years. You're the first person who ever spotted a hole like that in a witness's story and then pried it open." It was fortunate that thinking on my feet in such a situation came naturally to me, because I was the first of the ducklings to have a case assignment come to trial. It happened faster than I thought possible, just weeks after I'd started in August. None of us had expected to enter a real courtroom before the new year.

The defendant was a young black man

who'd been charged with disorderly conduct for getting involved in a street fight. He was a college student, a pretty good one too, and from a solid family; at arraignment he pleaded not guilty. His counsel was Carole Abramowitz, a seasoned Legal Aid attorney, who had defended felony cases for years. I don't know why she was handling a misdemeanor that day, but she was determined to get the case thrown out, knowing full well that any plea to the least of charges could destroy a black kid's future. That was all I knew about the case, and I was learning it on the spot as the defense attorney and I stood before Judge Joan Carey in the first conference. Normally, I would have written up the complaint myself and interviewed the arresting officer, but this case had been reassigned after the departure of my predecessor, one file in a big stack of them that had been dumped on my desk and that I hadn't so much as opened yet.

"We're ready to go to trial," said Carole Abramowitz.

"We'll start Monday," said Judge Carey.

"But, but, but, but . . . ," I stammered. It was then Friday. I needed some time to prepare. I needed to find the witnesses. This was a real trial!

Judge Carey looked at me without pity.

She complained that we weren't getting dispositions fast enough. "You'll start the wah-deer on Monday or I'll dismiss the case."

At least that's what I heard. I ran upstairs to Katie Law, adviser for the ducklings in our trial bureau. Katie was a Harvard graduate who had returned to law school after raising three daughters and getting a divorce. A southern belle from a wealthy family, she certainly didn't need to be in the trenches at the DA's Office, but she was passionate about community service. And she was infinitely patient with beginners.

"Katie, what does 'wah-deer' mean?"

She shook her head in despair. "They're sending babes into the wolves' den." It wasn't my fault, she assured me: not everything could be covered in our two-week training course. It was expected the rest would be learned by example and osmosis during the months new ADAs typically worked in the complaint room covering the pretrial motions before one of their cases went to trial. It was just my bad luck getting there so fast. Katie spent the remainder of the afternoon explaining the voir dire process and jury selection, the strategies for making the most of this chance not just to disqualify unfavorable jurors but to establish

a rapport with those selected. Public awareness of voir dire is much greater these days
thanks to media coverage of high-profile trials, to say nothing of television court dramas, and the science of juror selection that
has spawned an industry of consultants. But
when I joined the DA's Office, it was all
rather arcane stuff, especially since New
York State is one of the few jurisdictions
where lawyers can get involved in the
process, which in many states, as in the
federal system, is handled by judges.

I wish I could say that my first real trial
was a triumph of spirit over experience, but
in fact Carole Abramowitz mopped the floor
with me, and then bad luck wrung me out.
The courtroom was a repurposed office
with a few rows of rickety wooden folding
chairs serving as a jury box and gallery, and
the bench was of painted plywood. In the
middle of my summation, everyone's attention suddenly turned elsewhere: the defendant's grandfather clutching his chest in a
sweat, the old man's daughter panicking
beside him. The judge called a recess; the
paramedics came trooping in. And by the
time it was clear that the poor man was all
right, an hour of confusion had intervened
before I could continue my remarks. The
jury took less time than that to find the boy

not guilty.

Although the grandfather's cardiac crisis seemed at the time the ultimate fluke, soon I would discover that among trial lawyers it was a familiar variant in the canon of mishaps that occurred so frequently as to have been enshrined in the lore and legend of the courtroom. Some view these events as rites of passage for a young lawyer, although their recurrence is likely due to a predictable degree of coincidence in the ways people react to the stress of a trial. In any case, there could not have been a better lesson in the necessity of being ready for any contingency. If anything redeemed that day, it came in the swell of pride I felt when I first introduced myself to the jury — "I am Sonia Sotomayor de Noonan, and I represent the people of the County of New York" — a moment of grace that would repeat, and ground me, at the opening of every subsequent trial I prosecuted.

If my first trial was a cartoon of chaos, my second was a mess of a very different kind. A man had got into an argument with his wife while riding the subway. He chased her screaming off the train, before beating her and then kicking her in the face when she fell to the station platform. A Good Samaritan rushed to intervene, striking the husband with an umbrella, whereupon the defendant punched the Good Samaritan in the face, leaving him with a black eye. As often happens in cases of domestic violence, the wife was unwilling to testify against her husband, but a righteous and determined young prosecutor was not going to let that stand in her way. I subpoenaed the defendant's wife.

But on the day of the trial, the wife didn't show. She had a fair excuse; she was in the hospital. But then it became clear that she had scheduled an elective procedure on that day to avoid coming to court. When I learned that she had had an abortion, I felt a terrible rush of sadness and guilt. What had I set in motion by pursuing her? My action could not have reasonably provoked the decision, but by the time violence enters a marriage, often reason has already receded.

Even without the wife's testimony, however, we got a conviction. The defense attorney was Dawn Cardi, a rookie from the Legal Aid Society in her very first trial. She fumbled as badly as I had in my own maiden voyage, and this time by comparison I seemed like an old hand — pity the poor judge and jury with the likes of us two presenting! There were moments during

371

cross-examination when Dawn seemed to be working for the other side, as when she got the Good Samaritan to repeat his story. Fortunately, there were no heart attacks, but Dawn did suffer the distraction of admission to the bar: while the jury was out for deliberations, she had to run out to attend her swearing-in ceremony. When she had raced back, the jury returned the guilty verdict. But any pleasure I might have derived from my first conviction vanished when we reconvened for sentencing.

"Ms. Cardi, I'm disposed to send your client to jail for a year," the judge said. The color drained from Dawn's face, and she began to tremble. I too was thunderstruck in that moment, realizing the terrible thing I'd accomplished.

"You can't do that!" Dawn sputtered. "He has a job. His family depends on him for support. He's never had an arrest before in his life. This will destroy him. You can't put this man in jail!" As Dawn's nervous verbal torrent flowed on, I was thinking about the abortion and the length this man's wife had gone to not to be there. And a part of me would have preferred not to have been there either. I have always believed that individuals are ultimately responsible for their own actions, and I have no tolerance for spousal abuse. But I also understood that the defendant would not be the only one bearing the hardship of his punishment. Jail might be a justifiable punishment, and the only absolute insurance against his striking his wife, but it would exact a high price on his whole family.

Dawn trailed off, and the judge looked to me. "I think Ms. Cardi is right," I heard myself saying, without premeditation, and feigning a self-assurance I wasn't feeling inside. I acknowledged that putting him in jail would have significant negative consequences for his family. I said that I would be satisfied with probation if Dawn could get him into a treatment program for domestic abuse that required regular attendance and that also checked in on his wife regularly. For a man in his thirties with no prior arrests, I thought that treatment and the imminent threat of jail would be sufficient protection for his wife.

"Find the program," the judge said to Dawn. And we both breathed a sigh of relief.

Dawn thanked me afterward. She was stunned by my concession, which seemed especially strange for a beginner, given that a prosecutor's career is built on a reputation for toughness and winning stiff sentences. I was having my own doubts by the time I reported my actions to John Fried, my bureau chief. John heard me out and responded in his typically thoughtful and deliberate way. He noted that he might have done differently himself, since the assault on the Good Samaritan suggested a danger to society, but he acknowledged my reasoning: "You did what you thought was right." I can't know if he extended the same trust to everyone who worked under him, but the freedom to exercise my judgment without fear of being disciplined promoted a confidence that helped me grow into the job more quickly.

Dawn and I would cross paths often, as her section at the Legal Aid Society was assigned to my trial bureau. Despite the unofficial rule against fraternization between prosecutors and defense attorneys, we would chat sometimes over brown-bag lunches on a park bench. We'd talk shop: the ins and outs of our cases, the temperaments and tempers of the judges we dealt with, the routine sexism that was an occupational hazard. Eventually, we became friends, and as we did, our conversations often edged into bigger themes that were written between the lines of the daily procedures: the explosion of misdemeanors that seemed more symptomatic of social ills than evidence of criminal natures; the crudeness of the tools the system wielded against complicated problems. We often started at opposite poles of an argument, recognizing that our views were conditioned by personality differences. Dawn was a born public defender, her support of the underdog grounded in a native distrust of authority. I was by nature more the prosecutor, a creature of rules. If the system is broken, my inclination is to fix it rather than to fight it. I have faith in the process of the law, and if it is carried out fairly, I can live with the results, whatever they may be. And knowing that the poor and minorities are disproportionately the victims of crimes, I'm loath to view the adversarial process of the law as class warfare by another name.

By the same token, I don't view prosecutors and defense attorneys as natural enemies, however common that view is both within and without the legal profession. The two simply have different roles to play in pursuit of the larger purpose: realizing the rule of law. Though the roles are oppositional, their very existence depends on a shared acceptance of the law's judgment no matter the passion of either side for a desired outcome. This is not to deny that the will to win drives both efforts. Nor is it to claim some simplistic equivalence between prosecution and defense. Rather, it is simply to insist that ultimately neither the accused nor society is served unless the integrity of the system is set above the expedient purposes of either side. This may sound naively idealistic, but there is a place for idealism in the practice of the law. It is what makes many of us enter the profession in the first place; it is certainly what drives some of us lawyers to become judges.

Dawn came to me in distress over another case we shared. "You've got to help me," she pleaded. It was a sad story: Her client had lived his entire life in institutions, foster care followed by twenty years in prison for killing a man in a fight. Then, released on lifetime parole, he had been given no support but a bus token. Without life skills, unable to find a job, he survived by selling copper pipes that he stripped from a derelict building, not fully aware that this was theft. The terms of his parole were such that a single violation, even a plea to a reduced charge of disorderly conduct, would have sent him back to state prison. There was something about this man that made Dawn trust him. All things considered, he wasn't doing so badly. He hadn't been dealing drugs; he hadn't robbed anyone. He wouldn't have been stealing pipes if he'd had any help finding a job. He had even met a girl and was in love . . . Dawn talked me into accepting an ACD, an adjournment in contemplation of dismissal, and she got him into a job program. If he stayed out of trouble for six months, the charge would be dismissed.

One day, two years later, he would be waiting for me outside the courtroom. He introduced himself, shook my hand. "You don't remember me," he said. "I'm the guy who was stealing the pipes." He had found a job and been promoted to supervisor. He had also married his girlfriend. By now, they had one child and were expecting another.

The quality of mercy: "It blesseth him that gives and him that takes."

The occasional merciful impulse notwithstanding, I was racking up convictions. Whatever my insecurities — and I had plenty (still do) — I was also fiercely competitive (still am). I became addicted to the thrill of verbal sparring at trial, the exhilaration of having to reinvent strategy on the spot, not knowing whether it would work, under the specter of a judge who at any moment might catch me out with a question. Fearing such humiliation, I prepared compulsively, the way I had in law school, and my reward was the chance to go out and risk it all again the next day. That I could never be sure of myself while doing it was a big reason I loved my work as a trial lawyer.

Notching up top-count prosecutions — convictions for the most serious charges — while giving up little ground in plea bargains became the adult equivalent of collecting gold stars in fifth grade. I liked the particular challenge of taking cases to trial with unsympathetic victims and unreliable witnesses, like the drug addict whose methadone was stolen by another addict, or the elderly couple with fifty felonies between them who were robbed by their young protégé, a grifter in training; or cases that were hopelessly circumstantial, like the jeweler whose half-million-dollar pouch of gems went missing after a family of Gypsies swept through his store — who could be sure the jewels even existed, until I managed to get them returned? I won quite a few of those.

Certainly, no one could accuse me of being a soft touch, but talking with Dawn always reminded me of the human costs of my success, the impact on an individual's life and his family. Her perspective allowed me to trust the voice in my own head that occasionally whispered: how about exercising a little discretion; having a little faith in human nature? It wasn't easy, with around a hundred cases on my desk at any time and constant pressure to dispose of them as quickly as possible. Cases with the same charge tended to blur together, especially since the DA's Office offered standard plea deals for certain crimes: Possession of a gun? Settle it today, and it's a class A misdemeanor. Make me wait, and tomorrow it becomes a felony. Forget about mitigating circumstances; I don't want to hear it.

Still, I wasn't willing to prosecute a case that I simply didn't believe in, my zeal as a prosecutor finally circumscribed by my impulse to always keep both sides in mind. The impulse had first developed in Forensics Club as a matter of strategy, but in this setting it sometimes produced the inescapable awareness that, though I might win, justice would not be served. I was especially lucky, therefore, to have a mentor in John Fried, who embodied just that kind of measured attitude. Under an impossible caseload, his commitment to fairness was fundamental. If I believed in a defendant's innocence or doubted a witness's story, I would knock on John's door. We'd sit down together and analyze the evidence for as long as it took. In the end he might suggest offering a very low plea bargain, but he always left me an out: "If you can't in good conscience try the case, then don't."

John's essential fairness was of a piece with the idealistic standards that Bob Morgenthau set for the DA's Office. Nevertheless, it often felt as if we were swimming upstream against muddy currents with the right answer not clearly in view. With each prosecutor handling around a hundred cases at a time, expediency and rough justice were the order of the day. We fudged, we made do with the tools at hand, we performed triage in the trenches, but we still made an effort to do it with integrity.

Maybe my prosecuting misdemeanors with a ferocity usually reserved for felonies looked to some like real fire in the belly. In reality, it was still more like butterflies and the unremitting fear of leaving anything to chance that made me prepare and argue so intensively. But for whatever reason, I was among the first in our duckling group to be moved up to more serious crimes. By the time I switched to felonies, John Fried had moved up too and was replaced as bureau chief by Warren Murray. Warren had a very different style: extremely soft-spoken but a

100 percent hard-as-nails prosecutor. I worried about how I would fare under him.

I was given a handful of low-level felony cases and a few others that were being retried. One of those cases involved a purse snatching. The defense attorney alerted me that it was flimsy, and I was dismayed to see that the facts were indeed thin to the point of being nonexistent. The young defendant had a clean record. His teachers had described him as quiet, polite, well behaved, but developmentally slow. He'd never missed a day of school. I interviewed the victim, an elderly woman. She hadn't seen the thief's face as he ran up from behind her, heading in the general direction of the subway entrance. The police grabbed a confused kid they found sitting downstairs on the platform bench, waiting for his train home from school. The woman identified him by the dark jacket he was wearing, like that of the thief, though she couldn't say what color it was. The purse was never found.

I wrote up a description of the evidence and took it to Warren. "You're right," he said. "It's weak. But we have the indictment, and it's our job to prosecute. Let the jury do theirs; they'll acquit him." I went back to my desk and pondered how to argue this to a jury. I went home to Princeton that night and thought about it some more. But I could imagine no way of standing up in court and saying with a straight face that there was sufficient evidence to convict.

By the time I marched into Warren's office in the morning, I was full of righteous indignation, fiery but totally in control. "I'm not trying this case. I can't lie to a jury. If you think you can go into that courtroom and argue that this is grounds to convict, then you'll have to do it yourself." I threw the file on his desk and walked out.

He came running after me. "Look, I just needed to make sure that you were sure."

"Why didn't you just ask?"

"Sometimes I figure I have to play devil's advocate."

I could have done without the drama. The office declined to prosecute the case.

The first time I found myself before Judge Harold Rothwax, he was in a full-throttle tantrum over the many delays that had dragged out a case before I'd caught it on reassignment. "And now, obviously," he shouted, "you're going to tell me that you're new and need a month to prepare!" I promised him that if he gave me fifteen minutes to confirm the availability of the witness, I'd be ready for trial the following week. That endeared me to him permanently. With plenty of misdemeanor trials under my belt, I had enough confidence — or the bravado of ignorance — to trust my performance under pressure. If nothing else, I knew my own standards of preparation. And sure enough, I would never once suffer the shame of his sarcastic warnings about "avoiding the dangers of over-preparation" dished out to so many other attorneys. I would, however, one time get a compliment of sorts out of him when, reading one of my motion papers, he allowed, "Misspellings are supposed to be a sign of genius. You must have plenty of it."

Judge Rothwax dealt with all felony pretrial motions for my trial bureau. He was painfully exacting and infamously unforgiving of lawyers who wasted his time, on one occasion sending defense counsel to jail for ten days for preventing the start of a trial. He was known as the Prince of Darkness, Dr. Doom, and Yahweh, among other epithets, particularly for striking terror in the heart of defendants whenever one with a weak case would decline his offer of a plea. His notorious stock line to defense counsel: "Your client has the constitutional right to go to prison for the maximum time allowable."

But it wasn't just fire and brimstone. Behind the infernal humor, a formidable clarity of mind and a keen legal acumen kept the docket moving with astonishing efficiency. A good judge must possess management skills as well as a deep understanding of the law. And there is no overstating the value of being able to keep all the facts of a case in your head. He might spend two minutes at a conference on a routine case, more on especially complicated ones, but two months later he would remember every detail.

However caustic, Judge Rothwax was no cynic, though like many a cynic he had been disillusioned, having started his career as a Legal Aid attorney and civil rights advocate before becoming a prosecutor. That early experience led him to conclude that given all the elaborate protections of the rights of the accused, any defendant whose case eventually came to trial was almost certainly guilty. In a controversial book, the judge proposed abolishing the *Miranda* warning and other rules that he believed handicapped the police and prosecutors; he also argued that a 10–2 jury verdict was close enough to unanimous for conviction. I wasn't prepared to accept his presumption of guilt, although it is borne out statistically: policemen don't normally make arrests on sheer caprice; most defendants do turn out to be guilty. But a probability of guilt doesn't seem reason enough to revise our standards of due process. These are designed to protect everyone from the human frailties of those whom we entrust to enforce the state's tremendous powers. Even if the vast majority of the law's agents exercise these powers scrupulously, it is unconscionable that anyone should pay for a crime of which he was unjustly accused. Blackstone's famous ratio ("better that ten guilty persons escape than that one innocent suffer") still speaks to a deep-seated sense of what is just.

Though I differed with some of Judge Rothwax's views of procedure, and didn't have much use for his hammy Prince of Darkness persona, the integrity and rigor of his thinking, his passion for the law, and the efficiency of his courtroom won my admiration. And he, in turn, offered me kind encouragement, even inviting Kevin and me to his home. As with José Cabranes, the deepest respect could not make me into a good enough protégée to take all his advice. Nevertheless, during those years at the DA's

Office, a long-nurtured dream finally found a living example in Harold Rothwax's black-robed presence, the first embodiment of an ideal I would be able to observe up close.

Not long after I moved to felonies, I prosecuted the same defendant in two trials back-to-back. It was two different crimes; hence the two trials: the accused had jumped bail on an older charge of burglary, the outstanding warrant discovered when he was caught for a subsequent robbery. My cases were solid, but matched against a very experienced defense attorney from Legal Aid, I lost them both. It was a hard blow to my ego, but what was even worse, I couldn't figure out where I had gone wrong.

"Okay. Tell me what you did," Warren said in his usual tones, still the quietest voice I've ever strained to hear. I walked him through my presentation of both cases. He identified the problem instantly: I was appealing to logic, not morality, and in effect letting the jury off the hook. Since it is painful to most jurors to vote "guilty" and send a human being to jail, you couldn't simply reason with them to do it; you had to make them feel the necessity. "They have to believe that they have a moral responsibility to convict," Warren said. Even the most perfectly logical argument, absent passion, would make the choice seem like one of personal discretion rather than solemn duty.

Communicating your own moral certainty didn't necessarily mean chewing the scenery. But as when I had described the Kitty Genovese murder in forensics competition, the difference between winning and losing came down to the appeal by emotion rather than fact alone. It was something Abuelita could have told me without ever having gone to law school. And it was something I apparently knew in high school, if only intuitively, before the awareness was pushed aside by years of learning to reason dispassionately at Princeton and Yale.

Granting myself permission to use my innate skills of the heart, accepting that emotion was perfectly valid in the art of persuasion, amounted to nothing less than a breakthrough. Warren would teach me much else in the way of trial skills, as had John Fried, Katie Law, and others at the DA's Office. But that was the single most powerful lesson I would learn. It changed my entire approach to jurors, from the voir dire to the structure of my summations, and the results spoke for themselves: I never lost a case again. I had hung juries a couple of times, and once or twice a conviction on fewer than all counts of the indictment, but never an acquittal.

Leveraging emotional intelligence in the courtroom, as in life, depends on being attentive; the key is always to watch and listen. You don't need to take notes with the court reporter getting down every word. Lower your eyes to your pad, and you're bound to miss that hint of a doubt that flits across the witness's face. Scribble instead of listening, and you won't notice the split second of hesitation in which a witness hedges a choice of words, avoiding the ones that would flow naturally in favor of the ones whose truth he or she is more certain of.

Such attentiveness also figures in upholding one of a litigator's paramount responsibilities: not to bore the jury. Again, the key is not rhetorical pyrotechnics. What holds a jury's attention, essentially, is the quality of one's own attention. If you are palpably present in the moment, continuously mindful of and responsive to your listeners, they will follow where you lead. If, however, you are reading from a script, droning on as though they weren't there, soon enough they won't be, irrespective of how unassailable your argument.

Often the difference is a matter of remembering what makes sense to a human being as opposed to another lawyer. For example, a prosecutor usually has no need to prove motive under the law, and yet the human mind naturally constructs its reality in terms of causes and effects, weighing any theory against the plausibility of these links and how they might operate in someone else's mind. "Why would she have done that?" is something we instinctively ask before we allow ourselves to conclude "she did it." The state's case is a narrative: the story of a crime. The defense has only to cast doubts on the coherence of that story. The "why" elements of the story must make sense — what would have motivated this person to hurt that person — before you can engage the jurors' empathy, put them in the shoes of the accused or the victim, as needed: make them feel the cold blade held against their necks, or the pang of unappreciated devotion that might drive someone to steal from a former employer. It is the particulars that make a story real. In examining witnesses, I learned to ask general questions so as to elicit details with powerful sensory associations: the colors, the sounds, the smells, that lodge an image in the mind and put the listener in the burning house.

Of course, narratives can be slippery. A story might change midway through the telling or the retelling. It wasn't enough to prepare meticulously, to anticipate every contingency, every conceivable counter-argument. Katie was the one who taught me what to do when, through no fault of your own, the story unfolding suddenly changes, throwing your case into unexpected chaos. In that eventuality, everything depends on the power to improvise, the dexterity to change tack as if doing so were part of your strategy all along. If a witness alters his testimony without warning, the savvy prosecutor simply de-emphasizes the testimony and stresses the cumulative weight of circumstantial evidence. Devising the case is always a two-step process: build the strategy out of reason and logic; then throw yourself into it, heart and soul. But if you have to revise the plan, suspend feeling and revert to logic until you can think of something you can sell with passion.

Other lessons I would figure out for myself, often contrary to conventional wisdom. Some prosecutors, for instance, would look for legitimate reasons to eliminate black and Hispanic juror candidates in the voir dire, the assumption being that minorities are biased in favor of defendants. But to me that made sense only if you saw all people of color as potential perpetrators and believed, even more implausibly, that they all saw one another that way, too. It was obvious to me that any black or Latino who held a job, or went to school, or stayed home to care for an elderly parent was likely as law-abiding as anyone in my own family and, if anything, far likelier to be the victim of a crime than to commit one. The notion that such a person would, on the basis of racial or ethnic solidarity, let anyone walk who might pose a danger to the community would have seemed laughable where I came from. And so I packed my juries with the kinds of people I'd grown up among; the results, again, spoke for themselves.

Few aspects of my work in the DA's Office were more rewarding than to see what I had learned in childhood among the Latinos of the Bronx prove to be as relevant to my success as Ivy League schooling was. It was in effect to see that mastery of the law's cold abstractions, which had taken such effort, was actually incomplete without an understanding of how they affected individual lives. Laws in this country, after all, are not handed down from on high but created by society for its own good. The nearer one was, in fact, to the realities that had inspired those laws, the more persuasively one could argue for the justice of upholding them. To be able to relate to jurors as their own sister or daughter might, with real appreciation of their concerns and the constraints upon their lives, often put me at an advantage facing an adversary from a more privileged background — a refreshing change after years of feeling the opposite. But even more important, that connection fed my sense of purpose. Each day I stood before a jury, I felt myself a part of the society I served.

It was, as I've said, not the job that most Yale Law School graduates dreamed of, but it did furnish me with the basis for an eventual judicial temperament in ways that Yale could not. It also gave me the confidence that came of recognizing my personal background as something better than a disadvantage to be overcome.

Twenty-Two

In the spring of 1980, seven months into my first year at the DA's Office, Bob Morgenthau encouraged me to join the board of an organization he had helped to found and had served for the better part of a decade. "They're on a campaign to recruit young talent, and I have given them your name," he said. In those days, few ADAs gave much time to pro bono work, or had much time to give. I already felt the combination of the daily commute and my caseload was testing my limits, which should have activated my natural tendency to avoid taking on too much too soon. But it's always hard to refuse the boss's invitations, and this was especially true of the Boss, who would become such a patron of my career. Besides, I was no stranger to the organization in question: the Puerto Rican Legal Defense and Education Fund (now LatinoJustice). I had applied for a summer internship there while I was at Yale. During the interview, they asked about my career goals. I allowed that I hadn't settled on a short-term plan, but I did know that in twenty years I wanted to be a federal district court judge. The interviewer raised an eyebrow, causing me to conclude that in the future it would be better to keep my fantasies to myself. I didn't get the job, but I remained interested in the group's mission.

The Fund, otherwise known by the acronym PRLDEF ("Pearl-def"), was founded in 1972 by a group of young Puerto Rican lawyers who drew inspiration from the NAACP's Legal Defense and Educational Fund and wanted to use their legal skills to challenge systemic discrimination against the Hispanic community. By the time I joined, PRLDEF was solidly established and had won significant reforms, its landmark *ASPIRA* suit against New York City's Board of Education proving as vital to Hispanics as *Brown v. Board of Education* had been to blacks. Until the *ASPIRA* case, Puerto Rican kids coming from the island, where Spanish was used in public schools, or from families like mine that spoke little English entered the New York City public school system with no help at all making the language transition. These kids routinely floundered and, though otherwise perfectly capable, would often find themselves in classes for the intellectually disabled. They naturally dropped out in staggering numbers, turning an imagined handicap into a real one, a temporary need for remedial help into a lifetime of minimal employment and poverty. The *ASPIRA* consent decree won by PRLDEF in 1974 established the right of students with limited English to receive bilingual education in New York City's public schools. The very next year, my cousin Miriam would enter college, eventually to graduate as one among the first wave of young teachers to earn a degree in bilingual education.

If PRLDEF seemed a natural follow-up to my work at Acción Puertorriqueña, this was no ragtag band of student activists but a committed group of highly skilled professionals with far more experience and savvy than I had, their sights set far beyond trying to get one Ivy League college to hire one Hispanic administrator. Some of the victories won by PRLDEF — for voting rights, or against discriminatory hiring practices — would open doors for hundreds or thousands of individuals. These efforts would shift the boundaries of opportunity and civic engagement for people across the nation, far beyond Puerto Rican New York. At the same time, the group was decidedly of my community, and that moved me deeply. It was the same pride I'd felt observing José Cabranes, so committed to his people and yet maneuvering so effortlessly in the wider world. On our board sat the Brahmins of Nuyorican society — as well as Puerto Ricans from the island and across the mainland — but there were also figures prominent in mainstream media or businessmen wealthy beyond what I had imagined possible in our corner of society. I was awakening to how much broader the Latino community was than I had known growing up in the Bronx.

As the youngest member of the board — even the others recruited as "young blood" were older and more established professionally — I felt honored just to be included and given the chance to learn from individuals already so accomplished and destined to achieve even more. If I could have looked into the future, I would have seen friends I made there going on to become federal judges, ambassadors, a U.S. attorney, college presidents, professors of law, partners at major law firms — every one of them upholding a lifelong dedication to public service. The women were especially inspiring, and not only for offering one another constant camaraderie and moral support, rare in any organization. At the DA's Office, I had seen very few women in positions of genuine power; the bureau chiefs were all men. But here were women — competent, authoritative, professional Hispanic women — who were leaders in their own fields as well as determined to give of themselves for the sake of others.

I worked on the litigation committee, which hired the staff lawyers and set strategy for the types of cases we would take on. I also served on the education committee, which arranged internships and found mentors for minorities, as well as developing LSAT preparation materials to help more Latinos become law students. Beyond what I was learning from all the potential role models around me, these activities gave me a grounding in the nature of organizations and how competing interests within them had to be balanced: in a word, politics. The staffing work in particular threw me square into the problem of allocating limited resources. There were those with visions of taking on ever bigger cases and more areas of advocacy, my own preference as always being for smaller, more careful steps. Sometimes personalities clashed, especially given the presence of so many lawyers who had succeeded as aggressive litigators in large corporate settings and who were now maneuvering in the close quarters of a small nonprofit where everyone involved had a deep emotional investment. Occasionally, such conflicts can tear the very fabric of an institution if they aren't handled wisely, and indeed that almost happened.

Problems at PRLDEF came to a head in a labor strike that split the organization and proved traumatic for every single member of the board and staff. The points of contention were the familiar stuff of labor-management disputes, not salaries so much — because no one signing up to work there could have expected much of one — as benefits, the formulas for calculating hours, and the compensation for extra work. My natural sympathies were with the staff lawyers, being myself employed as one in the DA's Office and never having been a manager anywhere. But as a board member I had a fiduciary obligation to the institution, a ponderous word but a real responsibility that I took seriously, appreciating as I did PRLDEF's value to the larger community.

Learning how to balance the needs of individuals with the no-less-real needs of an institution was an important lesson. It's fine to be on the side of the little guy, but he too will ultimately suffer if the health and concerns of the greater body he belongs to are neglected. That point would be driven home a year later, when my mother phoned in tears to tell me that she had lost her job. She, along with the entire staff of Prospect Hospital, had been locked out when it closed without warning. The sudden bankruptcy eliminated dozens of jobs, shattered a close-knit family that had shared their workdays for decades, put homes at risk, and destroyed an institution that had revitalized an entire neighborhood. Once again, my heart inclined to those who were locked out of their livelihood, but my head was calculating: What concessions, what better choices, might have preserved the institution and avoided this sad loss for all sides? Seeing Prospect Hospital disappear, I appreciated all the more the fine balance, the hard reckoning, and the personal sacrifices that ultimately kept PRLDEF intact through difficult times.

PRLDEF was my first real experience of pro bono work and the honorable role of a "citizen lawyer." I would continue serving there for twelve years, long after I'd left the

DA's Office and right up to becoming a judge. To use my education to help others was so gratifying that despite having no time to call my own, I would get involved with other groups as well over those years. There was, for instance, my work with SONYMA, the State of New York Mortgage Agency, which was establishing a program to make mortgages available to working-class families. We prided ourselves then on the strict criteria for qualification and the fact that most of the loans were repaid. Still, it gave me pause to realize that someone with my own mother's earning power, for all her years of hard work and spotless financial history, could not have qualified even in the category designed to capture the lowest-income applicants. It seemed wrong that there was no way to reconcile the standards of secure underwriting, and the imperative of protecting the institution, with the good of helping the most marginal but still deserving, including those like my mother who had never defaulted on any obligation and never would.

I particularly welcomed any chance to work on issues such as economic development and education that were crucial to the community in which I was raised. I not only cared deeply about those people but also understood their needs from firsthand experience. As I made my way in the world, however, I was seeing more and more that no group is an island. Even the most cohesive (or the most marginalized) consists of overlapping circles of belonging, just as every individual's identity is constituted of many elements. To do good ultimately meant seeing any particular interests in a larger civic context, a broader sense of community. The specific needs of people like those I grew up with would always tug at my heart, but increasingly the call to serve was beckoning me beyond the confines of where I'd come from.

It was somewhat in that spirit that I joined New York City's Campaign Finance Board. Unlike PRLDEF and SONYMA, the Campaign Finance Board was a relatively new organization, founded in the wake of scandals that shook New York State in the mid-1980s, when certain vast campaign contributions, undoubtedly corrupting but some perfectly legal, were exposed. The need for oversight in the financing of the electoral process was dramatic, not only to guard against graft, but to ensure access for candidates who would be excluded if money alone determined the race. But before the board's creation there were no regulations in place, no model for the disbursement of public moneys. New York was the first major American city to institute such reforms, the only other example being Tucson.

What appealed to me was the possibility of devising a structural solution to a long-entrenched problem simply by creating an appropriate set of rules. That's as elegant as ethics gets. It was also an exhilarating exercise in the art of crafting compromise between opposing interests, always my first response to political division. The fact that I had always registered independently, without a party affiliation, enhanced my credibility as a dispassionate mediator. But the board's greatest asset in laying claim to evenhandedness and procedural transparency was its chairman, Father Joseph A. O'Hare. A Jesuit priest and the president of Fordham University, Father O'Hare was a man of such unassailable integrity that fairness seemed assured, even as his irreverent sense of humor banished every trace of sanctimony. Under his leadership the board exemplified how a government agency could rise above partisanship to work for a general good.

The CFB was my introduction to the city and state political scenes. Many lawyers I met working there would go on to become power brokers whose awareness of me and eventual support would matter to my career in ways that I couldn't yet imagine. I had always thought my career would be devoted to principles that transcended politics, but the fact is there would have been no way to the federal bench except through such political channels. It would matter crucially that I was familiar to people of influence who, though recognizing I did not involve myself in partisan efforts, could see that I was at least an honest broker. The integrity I had cultivated so jealously out of personal pride would be my calling card when the time came. Or so I was later told.

Sometimes, idealistic people are put off the whole business of networking as something tainted by flattery and the pursuit of selfish advantage. But virtue in obscurity is rewarded only in heaven. To succeed in this world, you have to be known to people. Nevertheless, where politics is involved, associations and recognition can work both ways. Years after I left PRLDEF, my involvement with the organization would be raised as an issue when I was nominated to the Supreme Court. Critics charged that Latino-Justice PRLDEF (as it was known by then) was a radical organization that no acceptable candidate should ever have been associated with. To hear PRLDEF's activities so grossly distorted during the Senate hearings, with no regard for the good it had done the Hispanic community and the cause of civil rights generally, was painful to me and to everyone else who had served on the board generously and honorably. But PRLDEF did not cower from the attacks. The entire staff and board, led by Cesar Perales, a founding member who is now New York's secretary of state, worked tirelessly to rebut the charges and muster community support on my behalf, efforts for which I will be eternally grateful.

TWENTY-THREE

"This is difficult for me," my mother said. "He is like my son, Sonia. I watched him grow up. This is not easy for me."

"Please, Mami. You think it's easy for me?"

I can't deny my portion of the blame. The vortex of the District Attorney's Office was all-consuming, and I felt driven to do my utmost on every single case. How many nights had I spent poring over briefs I'd brought home, barely aware of his presence? But Kevin was also finding a new life of his own at Princeton, of which I had no part. One way or another, we had outgrown the first innocent bloom of love and its loyal attachment without having evolved new terms for being together.

On vacation together at Cape Cod in the summer of 1981, our first time there, an unseasonable chill hung in the air between us as tensions kept flaring up over nothing. It was a prelude to Kevin's cautious mention of the changes that had come over us and of how he no longer felt connected to me. Talking about our relationship, about feelings, was not something we did naturally. Even in the early days in high school, when we could talk for hours on end, it was always about some shared interest, or nothing in particular, but never ourselves. How long had it been since we talked like that, like children? Even the memory of those days seemed increasingly distant.

It was late when we got home to the apartment in Princeton after a four-hour drive in uncomfortable silence. I tripped over the mail that had piled up. Tomorrow's business. I fell into bed.

In the morning, I opened an envelope from the DMV. It had taken the whole five years we'd been married for them to send me a new driver's license with my married name on it.

"You know, Kevin, if we break up, it will probably take another five years for them to change my name back again." I was joking, sort of.

"I'm sure they do it all the time."

There are things you may know in your heart for a long while without admitting them to conscious awareness, until, unexpectedly, something triggers an inescapable realization. In that unhesitating matter-of-fact reply was a truth that I could no longer shut out: our marriage was over. When Kevin left for work, I picked up the phone. I had never complained about him to Mami, never mentioned any problems between us. To me relationships are private. In my experience when a friend unloaded about a boyfriend or spouse, the listener soaked up the complaint and remembered it long after the speaker had forgiven the offense. Unless something was really serious, my mother didn't need to know. As this was the first she had heard of any trouble, I was especially grateful that she didn't argue.

"Can I come home?"

"*Siempre,* Sonia." Always.

Kevin and I talked through the details without rancor. We agreed that I would assume our credit card debt, since I was the one bothered by it. In return I got custody of the Honda Civic. The only problem was that I didn't know how to drive a stick shift.

Never take driving lessons from someone while you're breaking up with him. Every time I popped the clutch, Kevin was apoplectic, and neither of us needed the added stress. But it was unavoidable, especially since I was running out of time. Marguerite and Tom would soon be coming to Princeton to help me move out. Though over-whelmed and sad and frustrated at still be-ing unable to drive that stupid car, I was determined to get out of the apartment that same weekend, even if they had to tow me all the way to Co-op City. I packed late into the night before finally collapsing in a troubled sleep. I had an extraordinarily vivid dream: I'm in the car, engine idling. I put it in gear, lift my foot off the clutch very gently till it engages, a little more gas, the wheels are rolling. Nice . . .

The next morning, Marguerite and Tom arrived. It was clear from her sighs and the strained conversation that this was painful for them too. We loaded up their car as well as the Civic with boxes of books and pre-cious little else. I hadn't accumulated much of a life if you measured it in stuff. Five years of marriage and barely two carloads. Marguerite, it turned out, knew how to drive a stick, and so she offered to take the wheel. But I insisted on doing it and asked her just to ride with me. As I started the car, the knowledge I possessed in the dream seemed to be real. My sleeping brain must have learned the lesson my waking mind couldn't master because of the tension between Kevin and me. In a hyperalert state, I made it onto the highway and into fourth gear. From there it was a long, clear glide with plenty of time to gather my wits before I had to face traffic in the Bronx.

Mami greeted us with grim cheer as we unloaded boxes from the elevator. The house felt strange in spite of the old familiarity, empty somehow without Junior. He had graduated from medical school and moved to Syracuse for his residency. Mami cooked us a welcome dinner of *chuletas,* and the smells from the kitchen were more comforting than I could have imagined. Soon enough she and I would start pushing each other's buttons, but that night it was a relief to be home.

After I moved out, Kevin and I began to talk in earnest. We dated intermittently for a year or so and spent the occasional weekend together. It was, in part, an unspoken effort to rekindle a spark, though as such it never took. In the end, it amounted to more of an extended attempt at understanding what had gone wrong.

One night, Kevin really opened up. "I was always proud of you," he said, "but it was hard not being able to keep up. While you were acing Princeton, I was partying at Stony Brook. But I always figured that I was smart enough to make it up. I always had an excuse, always believed I could fix things later. Now I'm working as hard as I can. I love where I am, and I like what I'm doing. It's a struggle in a couple of classes; overall, though, I'm doing okay. But it's finally sinking in: even doing the best I can, I'm not going to catch up with you."

It was a painful admission, and I was touched by his generosity in putting it like that. Many men, feeling as he did, would have lashed out to soothe their egos. Certainly, the idea of a wife outshining her husband was something neither of us had been brought up to expect in marriage. But there was more, too. "I want to be needed," he said. "I knew you loved me, but I felt you didn't need me."

He wasn't wrong about that, but it wouldn't have occurred to me as a problem. I'd never seen need as an essential part of love. Weren't caring and affection, mutual respect, and sharing a life really more the point? If anything, need seemed to make the feeling contingent, less genuine, almost as if there were an ulterior motive to loving someone. In retrospect, maybe I was looking at it too rationally. The truth is that since childhood I had cultivated an existential independence. It came from perceiving the adults around me as unreliable, and without it I felt I wouldn't have survived. I cared deeply for everyone in my family, but in the end I depended on myself. That way of being was part of the person I would become, but where once it had represented salvation, now it was alienating me from the person I had vowed to spend my life with.

It might be that if I'd been in more relationships before getting married, I would have understood a bit more of what it takes to make one last. Being with someone never seems simpler than it does when you are very young. The ease of companionship, the familiarity of knowing each other for half our lives, had been a glue between us. But as a certain lopsidedness in our natures and our degrees of success became more pronounced, with neither of us paying much attention, that glue dissolved. I have feared, at times, that my self-reliance, even more than my prominence, might prove hard for any man to take. My friends and family are incredulous, sometimes annoyingly so, that I could be as content as I appear to be without someone. But whatever security or comfort I find in being single, a happy relationship remains an alluring alternative, and I'm actually optimistic about the chances of having one.

In the spring, Kevin called to say that his

thesis adviser was moving to Chicago. There was no one else at Princeton doing the work that interested Kevin, and so he had to follow. He knew there'd be no question but that I would stay behind. My work at the DA's Office mattered to me at least as much as his research did to him. Besides, at that point I couldn't see what I'd be giving it up for even if I'd been willing to. And with that, our efforts to work things out came to an unofficial end.

Kevin's mother, Jean, was heartbroken by our breakup. As rocky as my relations with her had been initially, her prejudice had been worn down by the fact of having a daughter-in-law, and a real friendship had grown up between us over the years. She would later tell me that she realized only after I'd gone how many gestures on Kevin's part — holiday gifts or a thoughtfully timed phone call — had been prompted by me.

In the end, I sold my wedding ring to pay the lawyer who handled our divorce. Saddened though I was at seeing Kevin leave, I was no more sentimental about the formal trappings of marriage than I had been on our wedding day. When I told Judge Rothwax that I was getting divorced and wanted to revert to my maiden name, he started using it instantly and made a point of correcting anyone who still referred to me as Ms. Sotomayor de Noonan. The DMV would take longer to straighten out.

TWENTY-FOUR

My ability to compartmentalize leaves my friends incredulous and sometimes even a little frightened. But it works for me. When I'm focused on a project, nothing else intrudes. It's only when I stop on an evening or a weekend that I look down to realize I've walked off a cliff. Fortunately, those same friends are usually down there waiting to catch me.

Every weekend for almost a year, Jason Dolan, with whom I shared cramped office space, and Ted Poretz, our pal from another bureau, made plans for us three: Sunday brunch, a movie, a party. We never talked about my divorce or what prompted our regular socializing. It was simply their kind impulse to stand by a friend and minimize the possibility of loneliness.

Girlfriends, of course, had a different approach.

Nancy Gold, now Nancy Gray, had been

my friend ever since taking the seat next to mine during orientation on our very first day at the District Attorney's Office. By lunchtime we were racing over to the Citibank on Chambers Street together to take advantage of a great promotional offer she'd seen advertised. Later, when Nancy learned I was commuting from Princeton, she offered me the use of her fold-out couch whenever I had a jury sequestered overnight. And then, through the uncertain months when Kevin and I were coming apart, the haven she provided included not only that sofa but easy conversation and moral support. "It's perfectly obvious to everyone but you, Sonia," Nancy would say in her capacity as a natural practitioner of talk therapy. She drew me out, gave me the full Freudian breakdown, and even tried Kevin in absentia.

There was shopping therapy as well. "Sonia, you've got how many pairs of shoes under your desk? Every single one of them is frumpy. Buy yourself one nice pair, will you?" It was tough love, challenging my ingrained relentlessly negative physical self-image: "Who cares what your mom told you twenty years ago? What matters is how you look this Saturday night. Stop censoring yourself. You look great." No, I don't.

Maybe not quite as bad as I did then, but great I don't look. Standing beside Nancy in front of the dressing room mirror, I would say to myself: She has such great style. This would really look good on her. I wish I had my own sense of style.

When summer came around, I still hadn't figured out my next move, but I knew I needed a break from my mother. We would be at each other's throats if I couldn't get away at least for some weekends. Nancy had a summer share on Fire Island, a group house she wanted me to join, and so I went to check it out. It was quite a scene: more people than rooms, parties, and late nights.

"It's not my style, Nancy."

But she insisted it would be a great way to kick-start my social life. "Never mind the crowd," she said. "I don't know most of them myself." I wasn't sure why she thought that made it more appealing.

"Just try it."

In the end, I refused to be convinced, saying I needed something more sedate. So Nancy introduced me to a college friend who was in another group house on the island, a very different scene, as she described it: shared meals, quiet evenings playing board games and reading. I threw caution to the wind and signed up for that one sight unseen.

My first trip out, the ferry abandoned me on the dock late at night in the middle of a storm that had knocked out the power and phone lines. I got hopelessly lost on the half-mile walk through the dunes from the ferry landing. Knocking on a random door for directions, I was embarrassed to discover I had disturbed somebody's illicit love nest. When I finally found the house and burst in, Mark Serlen, a housemate who'd been dozing, looked as if he'd just seen a sea monster come through the door. But from there on it was a lovely, exquisitely peaceful summer. Every other weekend would find Valerie, her fiancé, Jack, Mark, and assorted other friends playing Trivial Pursuit and Scrabble, reading the Sunday *Times* or a good mystery, sailing the weathered little skiff, cooking marvelous meals with clams gathered from the bay, and smoking endless cigarettes. I confess that the first night I spent alone there, many things went bump in the dark and I armed myself with a kitchen knife and broomsticks. But I would eventually come to feel there was no place safer.

We repeated the house share for a few summers, each of us eventually moving on

417

to other arrangements, but the friendships that began at Fire Island continue. The kids have grown up and have their own kids. The summer rituals have given way to other traditions, like season tickets to the ballet year after year with Mark. But at least one weekend every summer I still find my way back to the beach with my Fire Island family.

"You've got to find yourself a cop," Nancy said. "Cops are sexy, believe me." I began to open up to the possibility of dating again. It was tentative at first, I'll admit, but being outgoing and enjoying the process of getting to know a person in all his curious particularity, I grew to like dating. I wouldn't exactly fall hard for anyone, but I did meet some men who renewed my faith that I might be appealing and who even caused some of that nervousness of anticipation that I hadn't really felt since high school. Even a little romance can do wonders, if you are prepared to enjoy the moment and let the moments accumulate, whatever may come of it.

Probably nothing constrained my dating life as much as living at home with my mother. To hear her screaming from the bedroom "Sonia, it's midnight. You have to work tomorrow!" did not exactly make me feel like Mary Tyler Moore. If I was out late, she panicked. If she couldn't reach me by phone, she would call all my friends looking for me. We were making each other miserable.

Dawn Cardi told me her next-door neighbor in Carroll Gardens, Brooklyn, had an apartment for rent. By train it was twenty minutes from my office at 100 Centre Street, forty minutes on foot. The neighborhood was great, she said, a kind of Mayberry-on-the-Gowanus, only Italian. Many of the families on the block had been there for generations, and they watched out for one another, which sounded something like Abuelita's neighborhood when I was little. I went to see it that same evening. The building had real character, even an original tin ceiling, and the apartment was adorable. Naturally, the landlord wanted a security deposit. I said I could bring a check the next day, not yet knowing where I would get the money. But before I committed, I told him, my mother would have to see the place, not to make the decision, but for her own peace of mind, to be sure it was safe. The landlord liked that so much, he later told me, he called the real estate agent as soon as I left to delist the apartment.

Marguerite would lend me the money for the deposit and take the opportunity to tutor me in certain basic life skills, like handling personal finances, which I hadn't yet learned. To be fair, there hadn't been much occasion. On my mother's salary, plus what Junior and I brought home working part-time, we had always lived paycheck to paycheck. In that context, I had always feared debt as something that could easily snowball, a worry that arose whenever Kevin used our credit card for small luxuries. Though I often made loans to my aunts, I was never the borrower. As for saving, I had no acquaintance with that beyond collecting bottles as a child to buy Christmas presents. So Marguerite helped me set up a plan to pay her back in regular installments. When the debt was clear, she had me putting the same amount every week into a savings account. Marguerite knew this stuff. She'd done things in the right order: college, a job, saving money, and then getting married. Dispensing practical wisdom was her low-key expression of profound emotional support.

Moving into Carroll Gardens, I began to enjoy decorating the place, getting a bit of confidence that I could develop a personal sense of style. I realized, to my surprise, that I had an intuition for how space works, how scale and dimensions affect feeling. Architecture has always had a visceral effect on me. But the affective power of Carroll Gardens had more to do with the people there. When Dawn and I became neighbors, we developed a cozy routine. Getting off the train after a ridiculously long day, often after ten, I would stop at her place most nights before going home. Her husband, Ken, who got up very early for work, had usually gone to bed, but he always left a plate of dinner for me — he's still a great cook. Dawn would pour us a drink, and we'd talk over that day in the life of New York's criminal justice system.

Actually, by then we'd found much more than work to talk about, having discovered our backgrounds had plenty in common. She was the daughter of first-generation immigrants who had weathered the sorts of challenges that can break a family, causing her to cultivate a certain self-reliance early on. And like me, she had a mother with extraordinary strength of character, one whom I would come to know and love like an extra mother of mine, just as I had Marguerite's. Over the years and many holidays, I'd get to know Dawn's entire family: her parents, her kids — Vanessa, Zachary, and Kyle, who became my unofficial godchildren — her sisters, brothers-in-law, nieces and nephews, cousins, and in-laws.

I've always turned the families of friends into family of my own. The roots of this practice are buried deep in my childhood, in the broad patterns of Puerto Rican culture, in the particular warmth of Abuelita's embrace and her charged presence at the center of my world, the village of aunts, uncles, cousins, in-laws, and compadres scattered across the Bronx. I'd observed how the tribe extended its boundaries, with each marriage adding not just a new member but a whole new clan to ours. Still, in Abuelita's family, blood ultimately came first, and she strongly favored her own. My mother, being more or less an orphan, poor in kinfolk, approached the matter less dogmatically. She treated my father's family as her own, and when he died, it was to her sister, Titi Aurora, that Mami would bind herself with an almost metaphysical intensity, not to mention filling the available space in the household. But she continued to expand the family of friends among our neighbors, whether in the projects or in Co-op City: Ana and Moncho, Irma and Gilbert, Cristina, Dinora and Tony, Julia . . . they were all family to us.

I have followed my mother's approach to family, refusing to limit myself to accidents of birth, blood, and marriage. Like any family, mine has its rituals and traditions that sustain my tie to every member, no matter how far-flung. My friend Elaine Litwer, for instance, adopted me for Passover, and though I otherwise see her family only rarely, joining her Seder nurtured our connection. Thanksgiving is Mami's and Dawn's in perpetuity. Christmas belongs to Junior and to Junior's kids, Kiley, Corey, and Conner, when they came. Travel becomes another source of tradition; friendships that might have faded with distance are preserved because every trip to a friend's city, for whatever reason of business, becomes an occasion to visit. In this way I stay meaningfully connected to old friends, like Ken Moy and his family, and establish new relationships that have sustained me, like those with Bettie Baca and Alex Rodriguez, and Paul and Debbie Berger, whom I met while traveling. We may hardly talk in the intervening years, but we pick up right where we left off.

Children elevate the art of found families to another level. I adore kids and have a special affinity with them, an ability to see the world through their eyes that most adults seem to lose. I can match any kid's stubbornness, hour for hour. I don't baby anyone; when we play games, I play to win. I treat kids as real people. Sometimes I think I love my friends' kids even more than I love my friends. Over the years, I have gathered more godchildren than anyone I know, and I take the role seriously. I was only thirteen when my cousin Adeline asked me to be godmother to her daughter. Erica was my first, and I was more than a little awed by the responsibility and the honor that the request implied. Alfred's son Michael was next, then Marguerite's Tommy. Tommy's brother John has adopted me as his surrogate godmother. I thought David, the son of my dentist and dear friend Martha Cortés, would be the last, but then Erica asked me to be her own son Dylan's godmother. Michael and his wife Lisandra have just had a baby girl, Alexia, and they have asked me to be her godmother.

Kiley is mine in a different way.

When I first set eyes on her, she was little more than a tangle of stick-thin limbs and tubes in the neonatal intensive care unit: one pound, eleven ounces. She was impossibly frail, and then very unlikely to survive, but I stood there awestruck at the sight of her drawing little breaths, a miracle of both life and science. I thought I knew everything about family before that ringing phone woke me up in the middle of the night: Junior, calling from Detroit to say that he had rushed Tracey to the hospital. I got on the next plane.

Junior had met Tracey during his residency at Syracuse, where she was a nurse. She'd followed him to Philadelphia for a fellowship, where they married before moving to Michigan. Now Junior stood beside me before the glass partition of the ICU, reciting the clinical details in his best doctor's voice. It was how he kept himself from going to pieces, but I could tell he was very scared. I felt closer to him in that moment than I ever had. It was not just the effect of seeing my little brother going through the worst experience of his life. It was also seeing what fatherly strength and devotion he had learned. Junior, who couldn't even remember Papi, had figured out for himself what it was to be a man.

Kiley's prognosis was not good, but she would be spared the seizures that can lead to complications. Tracey spent hours and hours every day sitting beside the incubator, watching, until the amazing day when she was first able to hold her daughter in her hands. Almost daily, it seemed, the doctors were intervening to solve some new problem. But slowly, very slowly, we allowed hope to take root. And then one day, sitting alone beside her, I somehow knew with absolute certainty that Kiley would make it.

It was almost a year before she first laughed, every milestone seeming to come at an excruciatingly slow pace. She'd remain a tiny child, my mother horrified at how little she ate. But I would be the one to get her to have mashed bananas laced with brown sugar and to introduce her to White Castle hamburgers, watching with delight as she actually finished her very first. But not until she was five could I persuade Junior to let her spend the day alone with me. Kiley needed no persuading. We explored the Children's Museum, ate ice cream at Serendipity, saw the Christmas show at Radio City Music Hall and the crèche at St. Patrick's — all on our first solo outing. After Junior moved the family from Michigan to Syracuse, Kiley never missed a chance to come stay with Titi Sonia.

Seeing my enthusiasm for being something of a crazy aunt — Titi Sonia might drive for hours to deliver on a promise to a child, or show up in an elf costume — many loved ones naturally asked whether I would one day have kids of my own. The question was never uncomplicated, even when my marriage seemed secure.

The prospects of my having a baby, or rather the potential for complications caused by diabetes, terrified my mother. She let Kevin know that if we had any intention of having children, she was counting on him to become a doctor first, not so as to be able to support a family, but to understand fully the risks involved. It wasn't my mother's decision, but I was not indifferent to her fears. In fact, a part of me felt them too. I knew of course that type 1 diabetics did have kids. It wasn't impossible, but the incidence of maternal complications was sobering, especially since I'd spent most of my life imagining I'd be lucky to live past forty. My projected longevity and the chance for a safe pregnancy had certainly improved alongside the methods of disease management since I'd been diagnosed, but I still feared that I wouldn't see old age. Even if that risk did not dictate my decision entirely, it seemed inarguable that having kids would be tempting fate.

Adoption was an attractive alternative. Eight years after Kiley's birth, Junior and Tracey adopted a pair of twins, Conner and

Corey. Tracey likes to point out that they are Korean boys with Irish names, a Polish mother, and a Puerto Rican father — the perfect American family. My nephews are all the proof I could have needed of how emotionally satisfying adoption might have been. Still, there remained the fear that I might not be around long enough to raise a child to adulthood. Ultimately, the satisfaction of motherhood would be sacrificed, though I wouldn't say it was sacrificed to career.

It is interesting to me how, even after all the strides of the women's movement, the question of whether we can "have it all" remains such a controversy in the media, as if the ideal can be achieved. Most women of my generation who entered professional life did not forgo motherhood, and many did succeed at both. But they paid a price, one still paid by most women who work outside the home (and men too, I believe, if they parent wholeheartedly): a life of perpetual internal compromise that leaves you always feeling torn, neglectful by turns of one or the other. Mindful of this struggle and of how often Junior and I needed to interrupt Mami's workday at Prospect Hospital with our phone calls, I have always made a point of running my chambers in such a way as to help mothers feel comfortable working there. And if in some corner of my heart I am still sulking about her absence during our childhood, I nevertheless credit the powerful example my mother set me as a working woman. But as for the possibility of "having it all," career and family, with no sacrifice to either, that is a myth we would do well to abandon, together with the pernicious notion that a woman who chooses one or the other is somehow deficient. To say that a stay-at-home mom has betrayed her potential is no less absurd than to suggest that a woman who puts career first is somehow less a woman.

During my time at the District Attorney's Office, women were only beginning to enter the legal profession in significant numbers. Fewer still were those practicing criminal law, either as prosecutors or as defense counsel. As Dawn would grimly observe, the only client happy to have a female defender was one accused of rape. Men and women got equal pay at the DA's Office, but promotions came far less easily for women, my own quick move from misdemeanors to felonies being unusual. I saw many women who were no less qualified wait much longer than men for the same advance. And they would have to work twice as hard as men to earn it, because so much of what they did was viewed in the light of casual sexism.

Nancy was doing arraignments one time, and the judge kept addressing her as "honey." She actually approached the bench and said, "Judge, I don't think it's appropriate; I'd prefer you didn't call me that." But he didn't even acknowledge her plea and went right on doing it. I've even heard a court security officer call a woman judge "sweetie" in her own courtroom.

And how many times would a defendant's lawyer enter the courtroom before a session and ask each of the male clerks and paralegals around me, "Are you the assistant in charge?" while I sat there invisible to him at the head of the table? My response was to say nothing, and my colleagues would follow suit. If it rattled him a bit when he eventually discovered his error, that didn't hurt our side, and perhaps he'd be less likely to repeat it.

Nancy and Dawn had no use for such patient strategies. They faulted my reluctance to rage vocally, just as my friends at Princeton had wanted me to be more of a firebrand. I credited their passion, and admired their brave readiness to jump into the fray of protest, but I continued to

430

believe that such wasn't necessarily the best or the only way of changing an institution. As difficult an environment as the DA's Office could be, I saw no overarching conspiracy against women. The unequal treatment was usually more a matter of old habits dying hard. A male bureau chief who'd headed a predominantly male bureau for many years would naturally have a man as his image of an exemplary prosecutor.

But this is not to deny that the culture was decidedly and often inhospitably male. I was lucky to be in Trial Part 50 under the unusually enlightened leadership of John Fried and then Warren Murray. Some of the other chiefs were disdainful of having women lawyers around, and in their bureaus a locker-room atmosphere prevailed. Sexual innuendo was used to explain everything, from the judge who was in a foul mood (obviously he wasn't "getting any") to the sensation of winning a guilty verdict. When they did win a case, they would celebrate at Forlini's, a restaurant of wood paneling and tufted red leather banquettes, where lawyers dined alongside judges in clubby conviviality. I never felt the sting of exclusion from such outings. Though I was always glad to have won my cases, somehow the idea of a person going to jail, with all the misery that entailed for a family, never quite seemed cause for celebration.

Otherwise, I could hold my own among my male colleagues, not losing my sense of humor in the face of their macho antics. It certainly helped that I could, as Rudy had observed, argue like a man and that I'd actually heard far lewder jokes in two languages than most of these guys could have dreamed up. But could I have managed to negotiate this culture as well as the crushing caseload with a child tugging at my awareness in the background of every moment? I thought not. The idea of another life utterly dependent on me, the way a child needs his mother, didn't seem compatible with the professional necessity of living at this punishing pace. As it was, I thought there was already too little time to accomplish the things I envisioned.

Having made a different choice from that of many women, I occasionally do feel a tug of regret. When her mother died, Dawn's eulogy was an expression of such feeling and care that I was shaken beyond the grief of having lost the dear friend her mother had become. I spent the following days pondering the bond between parent and child and wondering whether anyone would miss me that much when I died. Ultimately, I accept that there is no perfect substitute for the claim that a parent and child have on each other's heart. But families can be made in other ways, and I marvel at the support and inspiration I've derived from the ones I've built of interlocking circles of friends. In their constant embrace I have never felt alone.

TWENTY-FIVE

In retrospect, I've wondered how I could have devoted all my waking hours to a job without reflecting more on the kind of work I was doing. Joining the DA's Office had represented a chance to be a practicing lawyer right away and to play a tangible part in protecting the public. There was no denying the allure of the mission, or the thrill I derived from accomplishing it, but while I was working fifteen-hour days, I wasn't giving much thought to the daily experience of confronting humanity at its worst, any more than I was noticing the subtle signs of the rift developing at home. It was Kevin who had made me see what was happening between us, but eventually, when the divorce was behind me, I would have to discover for myself what my job was doing to me.

Law enforcement is a world unto itself: few outsiders can appreciate the psychic effects of inhabiting it. And so prosecutors and police socialize mainly among themselves. They do a lot of drinking together. And their divorce rates are well above average. During our many talks about what had gone wrong in the marriage, Kevin had never suggested that being a prosecutor had changed me, even though the long hours had undeniably contributed to the strain. But once I realized that my intense focus might have blinded me to certain cues at home, I couldn't help examining myself for unremarked changes as well.

There are those in law enforcement who manage to remain unaltered by the work in their private selves, but they stand out with the rarity of saints. All around me I saw personalities darkened by cynicism and despair. Trained in suspicion, skilled at cross-examining, you will look for the worst in people and you will find it. I'd felt from the beginning that these impulses were at odds with my essential optimism, my abiding faith in human nature and its enduring potential for redemption. But now I could see the signs that I too was hardening, and I didn't like what I saw. Even my sympathy for the victims, once such an inexhaustible driver of my efforts, was being depleted by the daily spectacle of misdeeds and misery. I began to ask myself whether there weren't other equally worthy jobs. Meanwhile, I would persevere at the DA's Office, convinced at least I was doing something valuable.

It was a relatively minor crime that caused me to doubt even that. I was working in the complaint room one day, my eyes, as usual, skipping over the names, when I picked up a new file, going straight to the facts of the case. Names don't appear in the arresting officer's narrative: it's always the defendant did this; the victim did that. But as I read to the bottom of the page, I said to myself, I've already seen this episode. We caught this guy. We tried him. We locked him up. I swear, it's Mr. Ortiz!

Sure enough, it was. He had served his time, but no sooner had he landed back on the street than he was caught in a carbon copy of the earlier crime. What had been a misdemeanor in the first instance became a felony now by virtue of repetition, but otherwise the cases were identical. He was, of course, not the first repeat offender I'd come across, but somehow his unremarkable case crystallized a certain sense of futility in my efforts. If this was the system, maybe I should be working to improve it rather than simply enforcing it on the front lines.

It was now that the old dream of becoming a judge seemed, if still not within reach, at least something that I might reasonably start working toward, and I was aiming for the federal bench. The federal bench was where matters of broad consequence, cases affecting far more lives than those of a victim and a defendant, were decided. I'd been aware of this since law school, when I studied with particular fascination how the landmark rulings of southern judges like the legendary Frank M. Johnson Jr. had done so much to advance civil rights and bring an end to Jim Crow. The idea that a single person could make such a difference in the cause of justice was nothing less than electrifying, and having more or less accepted the primacy of career in my life, I saw no reason to stint on ambition.

By now I had seen enough of the world to imagine what a path to such a goal might look like. Most federal judges come to the bench with one of two accomplishments behind them: partnership in a prominent law firm or an important stint, at some point in their careers, in government. There are exceptions, of course, and the only invariable requirement is a record of excellence — in academia or elsewhere — that rises to the attention of a senator's selection

437

committee or the president's staff. Nowadays many federal judges have served first as federal prosecutors, and though this was a less likely path when I was at the DA's Office, I knew that I needed a rest from criminal law. Throughout my time there I had interviewed occasionally when I spotted an opening in public service, but it became clear that I would need more varied experience if I was going to aim higher than a line attorney in a government bureaucracy.

In any case, I wanted to gain experience in civil law, a challenge I welcomed, having certainly enjoyed my courses in business law at Yale (how many people got honors in Commercial Transactions or really took an interest in tax law, anyway?). Those courses had also taught me how much of legal work involved representing corporations and economic power. To be a judge, I'd need to learn to move comfortably in that world. And so I decided that my next job would be an immersion in civil law.

When I announced my intention to jump, Bob Morgenthau tried harder than I might have expected to dissuade me. He indicated I would likely become a bureau chief if I stayed and that post could lead to a state court judgeship, unaware that my gaze was set on the federal bench. He did manage to delay my departure for well over a year by assigning me to a handful of exceptionally challenging cases that were very much in the public eye.

It was very soon after that exchange that my bureau chief called me. "Sonia, this is a very sensitive situation. The Boss wants you to be the one to handle it." The office needed to investigate an accusation of police brutality made by a church leader in Harlem. Relations between police and the black community were already severely strained. A year before, a man picked up for graffiti vandalism had gone into a coma and died in custody. Now a Harlem reverend was claiming to have been beaten after being stopped for a traffic violation. The two officers countered that he had assaulted them. "I'm not going to tell you what the outcome should be," the Boss said. "Just make sure the office doesn't look bad in the press." I would hear from him once again during the investigation, asking for a status report. Otherwise, he left me to it and kept his distance.

Vernon Mason, the well-known civil rights lawyer, was representing the minister. Visiting my alcove office, Mason lectured me at length on the alienation of the community, its anger at the police, its distrust of the prosecutor's intentions, and his own belief that justice could not and would not be done, and he declared his client's unwillingness to cooperate. I in turn lectured him back: assuming the corruption of everyone in law enforcement was a self-fulfilling prophecy, I said, whose effect was only to sabotage the system, ensuring that justice could not be done. I made an emotional plea for him to give me a chance. While I could not pledge in advance to prosecute the officers, I did promise a thorough investigation with an open mind. But he would give me neither the benefit of the doubt nor any help at all in the investigation.

Mason didn't understand where this prosecutor was coming from. As much as I respected the police and appreciated the difficulty of their job, I was never so naive as to believe that abuse didn't happen. As in any other population, some on the force had emotional problems that could dispose them to misconduct. I had seen for myself how the frustrations of a massive crime wave and a woefully underfunded response could change people who'd started out with the best of intentions. The streets had become dangerously unpredictable, a place where violence might escalate faster than anyone could reason. But if the community could have no faith in law enforcement, the job of policing would be infinitely harder, the mission ultimately doomed. If I found wrong had been done that day, I would prosecute it.

For three months I scoured the streets of Harlem daily for witnesses. I knocked on every door within blocks of where the encounter had taken place, plastering the neighborhood with my card, begging anyone who would listen to talk to me if they had seen what happened. I parked myself on a stool at Sylvia's famous soul food counter and chatted with anyone coming or going. But no one ever came forward. If anyone had seen something, no one was saying.

One thing was accomplished, however: a genuine effort was observed. Ultimately, there would be no indictment, but there would be no explosive headlines either. Tensions had been defused, at least this time. But the larger story would not end any day soon. The DA's Office would continue to make outreach a priority. It had to: activists like Mason would continue to light a fire whenever abuse was alleged. The only long-term answer was to cultivate better relations with the community, but that would take time and effort. The cops would need special training. The community would need to learn the value of helping the force recruit, instead of branding anyone of their own who joined a traitor. Looking back over decades since, you can see that those efforts have borne some fruit. Even New York's high-crime areas are nothing like they were, although suspicion still remains even when the community cooperates.

The second big assignment that Bob Morgenthau sent my way would be my first murder trial. It was a huge case, very complex, and real tabloid fodder. As a homicide novice, I couldn't have led the prosecution, but Hugh Mo, the senior assistant DA in charge, ensured that my second-seat role was far from pro forma. Hugh was a slightly built figure with a booming voice and a big personality to match; a hard-driving prosecutor, he was also a gentle family man — an all-around confounder of stereotypes. Our offices were side by side, and we developed an easy, seamless teamwork and camaraderie. He generously allowed my visible participation in the prosecution of Richard Maddicks, who was charged with being the Tarzan Murderer.

The press had so dubbed the perpetrator because his modus operandi included swinging through a victim's apartment window from a rope secured to the roof. In a marathon of armed burglaries over a few months, he had terrorized one small area of Harlem, shooting three people to death and seriously wounding seven others. He would shoot anyone he found at home, whether or not the person resisted or posed any threat. He even shot one victim's small dog. If anything prevented him from finishing a job, he might return to the same building on another day or just lurk on a nearby rooftop or in an air shaft for a few minutes until he could resume.

Maddicks's rap sheet told the tale: a twenty-five-year career in assault and robbery. He was on parole when he was arrested and supporting a two-hundred-dollar-a-day drug habit. His hauls as a thief suggested what sorts of people he preyed on: a pocketful of subway tokens, a wad of bills that had been stuffed in a shoe or a bra, the food in the kitchen. One of his big jackpots was a few thousand dollars one couple had kept at home, their life savings. His victims were barely hanging on to begin with, and their lives were usually destroyed by his visit, if they survived it.

Maddicks's signature was not perfectly consistent, but there was enough overlap in the incidents to suggest a single perpetrator. The gun was one common denominator and the acrobatics another, whether he swung from a rope, scaled an air shaft, or crawled over a ladder stretched between two buildings. There was the flowerpot, the paint can, or the bucket weighted with a rock that came crashing through a window before he did. There was the chilling absence of fear.

Hugh and I had discovered twenty-three separate incidents, eleven of which had strong enough evidence to bring to trial and which we consolidated into one indictment. We figured the only way a jury could see the big picture of Maddicks's villainy was to try all eleven together. Easier said than done: the law does not allow you to try unrelated crimes together, and it was no surprise that the defense filed a motion to sever the various counts.

When the law permits this or prohibits that, the first question to ask is why. The "why" is the essence of the principle, and once you understand it, you can structure an argument for not applying it in a particular case. Why is evidence from unrelated crimes inadmissible? Because suggesting that someone is prone to criminal activity would prejudice a jury trying to decide whether he has committed the one for which he is being tried. There are, of course, exceptions where a common element links the crimes and makes a joint trial both sensible and legally permissible, but they are carefully circumscribed and complicated by differences between state and federal law.

"It's not a conspiracy," said Hugh. "There's only one of him." I dug into the library looking for an appropriate way to frame the common elements that linked the crimes, and we requested a *Molineux* hearing, a New York State proceeding in which a judge decides whether the facts of the case justify allowing evidence that is normally inadmissible. We argued that our purpose was to show not criminal propensity but rather proof of identity: given the rare level of physical strength and agility required for the acrobatics common to all the incidents, we could reasonably claim that this element, not unlike a signature modus operandi, identified Maddicks as the perpetrator.

Judge Rothwax handled the pretrial motions. As usual, I made sure to be prepared, and he was perfectly reasonable. We would prosecute all eleven incidents in one trial. I felt the very real satisfaction of having devised an argument persuasive enough to show the facts of our case fell within the boundaries of this corner of the law. The critical faculty that had remained an abstraction to me at Yale, and eluded me at Paul, Weiss, and wasn't even necessary to prosecuting most cases was now in my sure possession: I was undeniably thinking like a lawyer.

We located forty witnesses who were willing to testify, Hugh and I each taking twenty to interview and prepare for trial. This being my first murder, much of the legwork was new to me. So was the huge volume of records — autopsy, fingerprint, and ballistic reports, multiple witness statements given to different officers — to be assimilated. But with Hugh's guidance I learned how to sift them for the crucial details to fashion our case. He instructed me too in the preparation of charts and maps and diagrams by which the evidence could be visually represented to prevent the jury from being overwhelmed by the dizzying minutiae, always a danger in complex prosecutions.

The effort also required Hugh and me to become intimately familiar with those few blocks in Harlem where Maddicks had conducted his spree. It's essential for a prosecutor to visit the scene of the crime. You have to root yourself in the space, internalize it, and absorb details that you would invariably miss in a secondhand description. You have to make the scene come to life in the minds of the jurors, and so it has to live in your mind first.

One squalid apartment I visited had been used by addicts as a shooting gallery. There were used needles and spoons all over the floor. The power had been cut, and you could barely see anything in the light coming through the windows dark with grime. A mattress already reeking of ancient urine had soaked up blood like a blotter. What could a man lying here possess that would cost him his life?

Another household reminded me sadly of Abuelita's. An extended family — a mother, three grown children and their spouses, several grandchildren — all sharing two apartments in the same building. The kids were in school; the parents had jobs — restaurant work or maintenance. Their father, long deceased, had been a security guard, and it was his old nightstick that the brothers had grabbed when Maddicks appeared at the window. They chased him to the roof, from which he spidered down the gap between two buildings as they rained blows on him from above. He seemed to disappear. Back in the apartment, the family gathered in the commotion to phone the police. His sister, brother, mother, and young niece were standing beside Steve Robinson when a bullet came through the window from the opposite building and entered his forehead.

Was Maddicks a skilled sniper too, or was it just a lucky shot? Either way, Steve Robinson's death would devastate that family, scattering them to the winds. Only one brother, broken and with few words, remained to show me what had been their home, the bloodstain still visible on the floor.

Azilee Solomon had come home from work to find her door unlocked, her home ransacked, her longtime companion — her husband, really, by common law — dead in the blood-soaked chair where he had been napping. They had both worked at the Hilton hotel for twenty years, she as a chambermaid, he as a janitor. Every last penny that they had saved for retirement was stolen. The meat and coffee from their refrigerator were gone, along with the shopping cart that Mrs. Solomon used to wheel her groceries home.

At Maddicks's girlfriend's apartment, detectives found the same meat and coffee, but that proved nothing: anyone could have bought those brands. Outside the building, however, there were six shopping carts lined up by the trash, among which Mrs. Solomon instantly recognized her own. It was true that shopping carts were also mass-produced. But only one could have had the piece of yellow tape that Mrs. Solomon had used to mend a broken rung. "Take out those old clothes," she told the detectives. "And you'll find that yellow tape underneath." At trial we staged a dramatic shopping cart lineup in Judge James Leff's court to re-create the moment of discovery.

I spent a lot of time with Mrs. Solomon in the process of preparing for her testimony. I got to know her well. She was a deeply religious woman who radiated kindness. My gift of faith was not as great as hers, but I was deeply touched to see the solace it brought her. Though the murder of her partner was senseless and had turned her life upside down, she somehow accepted it as God's will. She wanted Maddicks removed from the proximity of anyone else he might harm, but she expressed no desire for vengeance. Her tears flowed but without self-pity as she told her story in a matter-of-fact tone, first to me and then to the jury. I could tell that she had been loved.

The Tarzan Murderer himself was, by

disturbing contrast, my first real-life encounter with a human being beyond salvage. Throughout the trial, I watched him obsessively, searching his face for the least trace of feeling. Something in me badly needed to see even a glimmer of empathy or regret, as witness after witness told one more horrifying story of loss. I would be disappointed. He sat there, utterly impassive, hour after hour, and I couldn't help thinking: the devil is alive right here. I've always had a fundamental faith in rehabilitation, always believed that education and effort, if applied intelligently, could ultimately fix anything. Richard Maddicks taught me that there are exceptions, however few. What we do with them is a separate question, but after he was sentenced to sixty-seven and a half years in prison, I was glad to know that he was unlikely to be free in my lifetime.

Later, when we said good-bye after the trial, Mrs. Solomon turned back to me as she left my office and added, "Miss Sonia" — she couldn't manage my last name — "there's something very special about you. You've been blessed. I'm glad we met." She was gone before I could answer, but I thought: Mrs. Solomon, there's something very special about you too. I am humbled and honored to have known you. There are people who make me believe, in ways that I can't fully explain, that I have something important to accomplish in this life. Sometimes it's a seemingly random encounter. The inscrutable words of a stranger that somehow say to me: Sonia, you have work to do. Get on with it.

The last of the really tough cases that I perceived as Bob Morgenthau's challenge to me carried a different stench of evil. Nancy and Dawn were both concerned about how it would affect me. "Can you handle it?" they asked. I knew I could, though I would surprise even myself with the ferocity of determination this one provoked, a steelier side of me than I'd ever known.

I was working late one night when I reached my limit for the day. I turned off the projector, flipped the lights on, took a deep breath, and tried to will away the nausea. Could I show these films to a jury? Of course they were prejudicial; the defense attorneys would fight me over this. But until a person has seen this stuff, it remains abstract. You can understand that child pornography is abominable, you can appreciate the harm that's done to the children used to make it and to the morals of a society, but you can't begin to imagine the depth of revulsion you'll feel. You can't anticipate pity will be so overwhelming that you yourself feel violated. I had to get the films admitted. But there remained the question of strategy. I always remembered Warren Murray's advice about persuading the jury of the moral necessity of a conviction. Some crimes, however, are so heinous that they can't fail to stir outrage. In such cases, hammering the point can even prove counterproductive. So I decided I would let the films themselves do the emotional work and put my own energy into building the most crushing argument for guilt, a logical structure that was impervious to denial.

There were two defendants. Scott Hyman was small-fry, the retail front end who'd sold a few films to an undercover cop and was supposed to connect him with the wholesaler for the big purchase. He was young, even vulnerable looking, showing up for court every day with the same oversized sweater hanging on his scrawny frame. When I learned that his own parents had run an adult bookstore, I wondered what kind of a childhood he'd had. His partner Clemente D'Alessio cut a much less sympathetic figure, stocky with slicked-back hair and a pockmarked face, a garish gold crucifix hanging on his chest. If he wasn't the brains of a bigger operation, he was at least smart enough to stay out of sight. Everything we had on him was circumstantial and hinged on identifying his voice in a single recorded phone call. My plan was to implicate them both in the same transaction, focusing on the link between retail and wholesale.

The case had its weaknesses. The wholesale deal — selling up to three hundred films to the undercover agent — was never consummated, because the police couldn't come up with the cash fast enough. They tried to stall, but D'Alessio got spooked and backed off. Then it took them six months before they got around to arresting him. They hadn't made my job easy. In a case where police credibility was essential, where so much rested on the testimony of the undercover cop, a lot had actually been bungled. Even the crucial phone call — Hyman calling D'Alessio on tape — was arguably tainted, the call having been placed minutes after Hyman was in custody, before he'd had access to counsel. On the other hand, the sloppiness of the investigation didn't mean those guys weren't guilty, only that I would have to work that much harder. Fortunately, I got plenty of able help from my second seat, Karen Greve Milton, and it was a relief to share the emotional weight of the case as well as the workload.

The first day and opening arguments were more nerve-racking than any I had experienced in a while. I remembered how a bureau chief had advised another female ADA. "Handle it like a man," he told her. "Go to the bathroom and throw up." The laugh was sufficient to quell my stomach. I've since accepted that all trial lawyers get nervous, even some judges, and the day you find being in court routine enough that you feel relaxed will probably be a day you'll regret.

D'Alessio's attorney was a high-priced criminal defense lawyer with more than twenty years of trial experience, often on high-profile cases. A large man with surprisingly quick reflexes and a nose for publicity, he was intimidating on many levels. He poured on his rhetoric liberally and dripped condescension. Condescending to the prosecutor might be a tactic, but he was sloppy with it, and it sloshed onto the jury sometimes, which can be very damaging. I made a mental note to be extra polite to the panel and acknowledge the inconvenience we were putting them through.

The defense might have argued entrapment, but they chose not to. Instead, Hyman's attorney went for "diminished capability." Apparently, Hyman was addicted to quaaludes, and in exchange for them he supplied a pharmacist with child pornography. It was the pharmacist who, after the police had picked him up for another crime, turned informant, initially setting up Hyman with the undercover cop. The defense contended that Hyman only supplied the porn to keep the drugs flowing, and the drugs had in turn impaired his judgment.

Diminished capability is always a flimsy argument at best. It has no legal standing, and I could see maybe five different ways to knock it down. But the attorney dragged it out into an endless distraction, ordering the federal prescription records and bringing the pharmacist in to testify. As it happened, the pharmacist was under federal indictment on so many other charges that he had trouble keeping track of what his immunity covered. He couldn't say much at all. Another witness the defense had lined up was arrested on a completely separate charge while waiting outside the courtroom. It was hard to imagine a sleazier bunch of characters.

D'Alessio's attorney decided on a mistaken-identity strategy: there was another Clem who worked in the same building, and he, the defense claimed, was obviously the one Hyman was speaking to in the incriminating phone call. So D'Alessio had found a way to remain invisible, even as he sat there at the defense table. I would have to find a way of using to our advantage that cloak of secrecy he'd wrapped around himself. That he'd evidently taken such pains to keep his hands clean despite a mountain of circumstantial evidence was entirely in keeping with our view that we had netted quite a big fish.

I presented my evidence over six long, methodical, painstaking days. There was so much stuff — piles of films, tapes, documents — that we had to wheel it into the courtroom on carts. I mapped the locations in detail, painting a scene of seedy storefronts with names like Peep-In, Show Palace, the Roxy Burlesque Theatre. This wasn't just atmosphere. I needed the territory laid out clearly so as to lead the jury along the disjointed trail of evidence that came from the surveillance teams: Hyman coming and going between D'Alessio's office and the vault where the films were kept; the brown paper bag seen here, seen there, seen going in and not coming out; the locations where conversations were caught on hidden mics . . .

Was I pushing the jurors too far by subjecting them to the tedium of listening to the undercover cops' recordings? They had to suffer through long silences, incongruous music from the car radio while the clock hand swept slowly, and wait for a few damning words. But the tapes left no doubt about the nature of what was happening. You could hear Hyman boasting about other sales he'd made, about the quality of the films he was offering, and explaining how films with younger kids, "kiddie porn," were easier to come by; older kids got wise to the business and wanted their cut. He also talked about the wholesaler's concern for secrecy. And then, finally, we get the link between Hyman and D'Alessio: "Just like the last time, yeah, same guy."

The films were the very last piece of the puzzle I was helping the jury put together before I could rest my case. They were scratchy and grainy, the colors having shifted from having been copied too many times. They were silent: no sound, no dialogue, no plot. A bare bedroom was the set. The children appeared to be as young as seven or eight, no older than ten or eleven. Their little limbs were scrawny, bruised, and grimy. The lens zoomed in ruthlessly on genitals, probing and thrusting. Though you never saw or heard an adult presence, the awkward unmotivated action left no doubt about the ghost that gave orders from behind the camera.

I had thirteen films screened in all, each around ten or fifteen minutes. As the previous one rewound, the police officer would recite the litany of identification for the next one, and we all braced ourselves. Midway through the screenings, I noticed the journalist who had been sitting in the gallery every day, following the case for a book she was writing. She had taken off her glasses in a quiet refusal to see more and was staring sadly into space. The members of the jury didn't have that choice.

My summation didn't need rhetoric. The facts were damning enough. All I needed to do was to show how they were connected with relentless logic, step-by-step, leaving no piece out. I tried to put myself in the jurors' shoes and anticipate any possible misgiving or misunderstanding. Would they balk at the circumstantial nature of the evidence against D'Alessio? Words like "circumstantial" carry an exaggerated load when you consider the degree to which most of us live our lives by inference. Keep it simple, straightforward, I reminded myself. This was a panel of citizens, not legal scholars. Having exposed them to enough horror, I addressed them with a bit of humor. How did your mother know it was you whenever you raided the cookie jar? I asked them. Only one of her kids was too short to reach it without the stepladder. And say you forgot to put the stepladder away, left it out there covered with cookie crumbs — it was a pretty safe bet the culprit was you and not one of your bigger siblings.

My closing ran two and a half hours. The judge took another two hours to charge the jury, reviewing all the elements of the law. It was early evening by the time they began their deliberations. But by the end of the next day, the jury forewoman was reading the verdict, pronouncing "guilty" eighty-six times — forty-three counts for each defendant. Hyman and D'Alessio had expected this; they had bail on hand.

But there remained the matter of the sentencing. I had seen cases in which defendants found guilty on all counts had evaded the full weight of justice because a single jurist was, for one reason or another, unwilling to impose it. In the conversations we had taped, when Hyman bragged about other crimes — drug deals and credit card scams — he said he never worried about getting caught. When it came time for sentencing, he said, you just had to keep postponing until you got the right judge. I could not let that happen. When we reconvened a month later, I pressed for the maximum. And when D'Alessio's attorney offered a profoundly offensive analogy — the maximum here, he said, would be like twenty years for possession of a single joint — my answer came with a fury so controlled that I doubt it registered as fury, but I felt it.

"In those films you see children about the age of seven and eight engaged in activities which are normally reserved for an adult bedroom," I said, hoping now to make the moral case that I had the films make for me to the jury. "But it was more than that, Your Honor. There was an eight-year-old girl in one of the films, a small girl depersonalized to the extent that we don't even know her name or who she is, but she is a human being. An eight-year-old girl on a film was directed offstage to engage in acts which I am not sure she fully understood. That young girl was robbed and she was raped. She was raped of her virginity and her innocence by the individuals who produced those films. In a sense, her innocence was murdered . . . That is not the equivalent, when we request our sentence, of selling a stick of marijuana. When you sell a stick of marijuana, the buyer and the seller can make free choices. The children could not."

D'Alessio got three and a half to seven years; Hyman got two to six.

Earlier, Bob Morgenthau had offered me a promotion to head the Juvenile Office. My work on this trial had got him thinking that this might be a specialty area for me and asking himself whether the office needed a dedicated unit for child pornography. My refusal of his offer was instantaneous, an instinctive gesture of self-preservation. I knew I couldn't witness that much sorrow and depravity without drowning in it. It was time for me to move on.

When the child pornography case was wrapped up, I took a brief vacation in Puerto Rico, but my mind was back in New York, and in particular on my cousin Nelson, who had reentered my life. After disappearing for about eight years through the worst of his addiction, he had somehow managed to join the military and clean up. There would still be ups and downs, but he didn't lose touch with the family again, and so gradually we had been able to reestablish our connection. The worst had seemed long past when he married Pamela. She had a daughter that he cherished as his own. They had just learned that a second child was on the way when Nelson was diagnosed with AIDS. His was one of the very first cases linked to needle use, just before awareness of the disease exploded in the public consciousness.

Nelson, like me, had had a special connection with Abuelita, and it didn't end when she died. His old premonitions of an early death were haunting him now. He told me he could hear ghostly trumpets. "Abuelita is calling me, and I'm telling her I'm not ready. I want to live to see my child born." He would, but not much longer than that, the end coming before his thirtieth birthday. In his last weeks, we would have many talks for hours at a stretch, slipping into the transparent ease we'd had in childhood, as if making up for lost time. I hadn't understood until then that one could be addicted to drugs and yet function normally in the world, holding a job and supporting a family. Nelson wasn't robbing people to get his fix; he wasn't shooting up in stairwells. He managed his addiction like a chronic disease, not unlike my diabetes.

I told him how I had been dazzled by his brilliance and his limitless curiosity about how the world works. And how I despaired of ever matching up to him. He looked at me and shook his head. "You really don't understand, do you? I've always been in awe of you. There was nothing you couldn't learn if you set your mind to it. You would just study until you figured it out. I can't do that; I never could. That's why I couldn't finish college, why I couldn't stick with a job. I didn't have the will. That determination that you have is special. It's a different kind of intelligence."

One day after little Nelson had arrived, we talked about his happiness at his son's birth and his sadness at the prospect of not being there for his children. We talked as well about the time a couple of months earlier, before his condition had gotten really bad, when he'd asked me to give him a ride to run an errand. He could no longer get around easily, and there was someone he needed to see, just for a little while. He asked me to wait, and so I sat in the car, parked outside the run-down tenement in Hunts Point, just a few blocks from where Abuelita used to live. I figured this was an old friend to whom he wanted to say his good-byes while he still could. But as he now confessed, inside he'd been scoring heroin. I wanted to kick myself — how could anyone, let alone an assistant district attorney who'd seen everything I'd seen, be so naive? I recited that essential lesson of Papi's, simplistic but also simply true: Good people can do bad things, make bad choices. It doesn't make them bad people.

As he begged me to forgive him, there was a hint of delirium fueling the shame and sadness in his voice. But I knew forgiveness was beside the point. I myself was carrying a load of survivor's guilt. Who was going to forgive me? Why was I not lying in that hospital bed? How was it I had escaped when my soul's twin, my smarter half, once joined to me at the hip, had not? His request only made the load heavier. My God, what a waste.

July 1983, I'm at the house on Fire Island. I wake very early from a deep sleep. It's still dark out, but I'm completely alert, even though I was up late last night. The clock says four thirty. I throw on jeans and a T-shirt and walk out to the bay. I sit on the dock and watch the deep blue draining from the sky in the early dawn. The sun is still hidden behind the island. It's probably just breaking the edge of the Atlantic. Nelson is here, I can feel him. He's come to say good-bye. Morning erases the last stars and dissolves the remaining night.

I walked back to the house to find the phone ringing: Nelson's dad. "Sonia, it's Benny," he started. I knew how difficult it was for him to make this call.

"*Yo ya sé.* I already know. I'll be on the first ferry home."

TWENTY-SIX

If I try to understand in my heart how it could happen that two children so closely matched could meet such different fates, I enter a subterranean world of nightmares — the sudden panic when Nelson's hand slips from mine in the press of the crowd, the monster I evade but he cannot.

Reason seems a better defense against the pain. Let me understand in my logical way what made the difference between two children who began almost as twins, inseparable and, in our own eyes, virtually identical. Almost but not quite: he was smarter; he had the father I wished for, though we shared Abuelita's special blessing. Why did I endure, even thrive, where he failed, consumed by the same dangers that had surrounded me?

Some of it can be laid at the door of machismo, the culture that pushes boys out onto the streets while protecting girls, but there's more. Nelson had mentioned it that day at the hospital: the one thing I had that he lacked. Call it what you like: discipline, determination, perseverance, the force of will. Even apart from his saying so, I knew that it had made all the difference in my life. If only I could bottle it, I'd share it with every kid in America. But where does it come from?

Good habits and hard work matter, but they are only the expressions of it, an effect rather than the cause. What is the source? I know that my competitive spirit — my drive to win, my fear of failure, my desire constantly to outdo myself — bubbles up from very deep within my personality. It's rarely directed at others; I compete with myself. But if ambition only feeds the ego and self-regard, what does it avail? The urge to win might serve to accumulate life's material pleasures, but those pleasures can be no less ephemeral and addictive than Nelson's high and often just another way of becoming the biggest and baddest on the block.

What Nelson saw driving me arises from a different kind of aspiration: the desire to do for others, to help make things right for them. Strange ambition for a child? Some might say so, but I've been aware of it for as long as I can remember. Self-aggrandizing?

I've never felt such release from the awkward hold of ego as when helping others. Reaction to early years in a house of pain? Perhaps, but at some point I let go of my compulsion to please: it's my own standard of character that I need to meet. In any case, I'm sure of having learned it from others, my examples. And very good ones.

If I try to imagine my most immediate examples of selfless love, instinct leads me first to those who were closest: Abuelita, healer and protector, with her overflowing generosity of spirit; and my mother, visiting nurse and confidante to the whole neighborhood.

My understanding of my survival was bound up in every way with the fact of my grandmother's protection. It amounted to more than a refuge from the chaos at home: my sense of being under safekeeping, physically and metaphysically. It had given me the will to manage my illness, to overcome my insufficiencies at school, and ultimately to imagine the most improbable of possibilities for my life. And that feeling of Abuelita's protection would only grow after her death, made manifest in countless ways, from bizarrely fortuitous interventions that would save my life in diabetic crises to strange alignments of circumstances that have favored me unreasonably. Things that might easily have happened to me somehow did not; things that were not likely to happen for me somehow did. This seemed like luck with a purpose.

I was under no illusion of having been singled out, chosen for some particular destiny. But I did come to recognize in my good fortune the work of a blessing, a gift that made my life not entirely my own: I was not free to squander it if I chose. Gifts, Abuelita showed us, were for sharing with others. And though I was not given a mission, I had to find a worthy purpose, to earn this protection. The language of cause and effect would be misleading here, the implied exchange of one thing for another not relevant: suffice it to say, somehow a synergy of love and gratitude, protection and purpose, was implanted in me at a very young age. And it flowered in the determination to serve.

My childhood ambition to become a lawyer had nothing to do with middle-class respectability and comfort. I understood the lawyer's job as being to help people. I understood the law as a force for good, for protecting the community, for upholding order against the threat of chaos, and for resolving conflict. The law gives structure to most of our relationships, allowing us all to promote our interests at once, in the most harmonious way. And overseeing this noble purpose with dispassionate wisdom was the figure of the judge. All kids have action heroes: astronauts, firemen, commandos. My idea of heroism in action was a lawyer, the judge being a kind of superlawyer. The law for me was not a career but a vocation.

My earliest exposure to helping professions had been to those of medicine and teaching: Dr. Fisher, the staff at Prospect Hospital and the clinic at Jacobi, and the Sisters of Charity, who taught us at Blessed Sacrament. The law, I understood at a very young age, was different in scope. Doctors and nurses and teachers helped individuals, one by one. But through the law, you could change the very structure of society and the way communities functioned. In this way the law could help vast numbers of people at once. With so much hardship and suffering all around me, the need for change was glaring.

The spirit of the times inhabited this ideal of law as a noble purpose. The civil rights movement was the backdrop for my generation growing up. While Perry Mason's judge was an iconic glimpse of possibility to a child, the same small black-and-white screen framed the evening news stories about those courageous southern judges who unflinchingly defied mobs and the rule of the crowd. It was the same grandeur I perceived in Miss Katz's stories of nuns and priests working with the poor in Latin America, or in news reports about our own parish priest, Father Gigante, whose ministry took him into the blighted streets of the South Bronx. In those times, there seemed no higher purpose than to seek justice on behalf of those denied it.

Out of this tumultuous panorama came one heroic lawyer I would see in the flesh. Campaigning for the presidency, Robert F. Kennedy visited the Bronxdale projects in 1968. I remember pressing my face to the bars on our kitchen window, which overlooked the entrance to the community center, waiting to catch a peek of him as he passed through the crowd. I was thirteen then. Soon I would be starting high school, getting involved in student government, swept up in our own elections, our poster parties and cafeteria stump speeches. Kennedy gave thrilling voice to the cause of justice for all and to a life lived in the service of that cause. And when, soon after my

471

sighting, he was killed, the silencing of that voice, and the eloquence of those who mourned it, confirmed for me the nobility of his purpose, which I would make my own.

There are no bystanders in this life. That had been my point about Kitty Genovese's neighbors during my best showing in forensics competition. Our humanity makes us each a part of something greater than ourselves. And so my heroes were never solitaries. The figure of the lone visionary that enthralls so many young people in their own feelings of isolation never called to me. My heroes were all embedded in community. And the will to serve was first stirred by the wish to help my community.

When I got to Princeton, I saw right away that a sense of belonging would not come easily. The community was much bigger than any I had known, bound by its own traditions, some of them impenetrable to women and minorities. And so I found my place where I could, working with Acción Puertorriqueña and the Third World Center. Through those associations came my efforts at the Trenton Psychiatric Hospital and my most formative experience of doing for others. Near as it was to Princeton, Trenton could not have been farther in human terms, a world apart from the certainties of privilege. But even by the standards of that afflicted city, the patients I served were vulnerable in the extreme: confused; distanced from whatever ties of family or friendship might have once sustained them; and, for want of a common language, cut off even from those looking after them. My outrage at their abandonment made palpable an emergent awareness that my community extended well beyond the place I came from, the people I knew.

While I was at Yale, the South Bronx was in the news again. President Carter paid a visit in 1977, the news cameras framing him against a moonscape of charred buildings, piled rubble, a neighborhood shattered by unemployment and other economic ills. The motorcade pulled up within sight of where Abuelita and my parents had lived when I was born, but until I had seen the place at the remove of the television cameras, I couldn't really see it. When you live in the midst of such decay, everyday life renders it almost invisible. Somehow communities continued to function amid their own ruins, and though this was perhaps America's worst urban catastrophe, it was hardly the only scene of desolation. Civil society, though carefully ordered by its laws, had nonetheless left a huge number of its members stranded. It was to the rescue of such communities that I first felt myself summoned, believing that the law must work for all or it works for none.

There were those at Princeton and Yale who, coming from such places as I had come from, resolved never to look back. I don't judge them. A degree from an Ivy League college or a top law school is assumed to guarantee entry to a world of plenty, and nothing obliges you to look back on what you've worked hard to escape. But I didn't see good fortune as a chance to write my own ticket; my sense of it remained as something entrusted to me, not given outright; and I would have enjoyed no peace of mind until I'd found some worthy use for it. My chance encounter with Bob Morgenthau over the cheese table would have led nowhere if I hadn't been deeply primed for what he offered. It was not what most of my classmates were looking for, but I could see that it fit into the scheme I imagined. Now, having completed that part of the journey, I was only more convinced that nothing had happened by chance.

All that remained to be seen was how far along the next step would take me.

TWENTY-SEVEN

Shea Stadium, the 1986 World Series. The Mets and the still-cursed Red Sox are tied in a tense tenth inning of play that has the crowd on their feet cheering, first for one side, then the other, like kids on a wild seesaw ride.

The real drama, however, is happening in the parking lot, where I'm on the back of a motorcycle, wearing a bulletproof vest, a walkie-talkie screeching in my ear, in pursuit of a truck full of counterfeit goods. We're doing fifty, then sixty, circling the lot like a racetrack, when the truck dodges around a corner. It's a dead end, a concrete cul-de-sac, and in just a moment he's spun around and is barreling straight for us. My driver's about to bolt, but I tell him, "Stay put, he won't hit us. We'll stop him right here." This guy's not crazy, I'm thinking. But he could be, or maybe just panicked. Whatever the case, he's speeding up. Next thing I know, he's got half his wheels up on the concrete wall beside us, like a stuntman riding the wall of death — can you even do that in a truck? Before I know it, he's slipped past us, doing almost ninety in the opposite direction. Enough. Does someone have to die for a load of fake Mets caps, cheap shirts, and souvenirs?

What am I even doing here?

Good question. After I worked through the cases that Bob Morgenthau assigned me as inducement to remain at the DA's Office, it was finally time to leave. Believing that economic development was the only real cure for so many of the ills plaguing poor communities, I thought commercial law would prove useful. I was also open to something in international law, an interest since my days at Yale. One thing I knew for certain: I wanted to continue doing trial work, having learned to love my days in the courtroom.

I also knew very well what I didn't want: the life of a cubicle-encased cog in the machinery of a large firm. The practice that kept associates in the library for years, hoisting papers up the layers of organization to a partner at the apex of responsibility still appealed to me about as much as working in a coal mine. As I had when looking at opportunities after Yale, I would aim for a smaller firm where I might grow more quickly into a substantial role. But as I interviewed, I found that size was no guarantee of ethos. Small firms were often spin-offs that not only poached clients from but also reproduced the culture of the larger firms where their partners had started their careers.

One that stood out as an exception was Pavia & Harcourt, a tiny firm by New York standards, barely thirty lawyers when I was interviewing in 1984. Its founder, a Jewish refugee from Italy during World War II, had built its reputation on representing elite European business interests in the United States. Much of the firm's work related to finance and banking, to licensing of trademarks and distribution of products, and the diverse range of legal tasks attending international trade and business operations.

Arriving for my first interview, I was struck by the aura of the place — a midtown oasis of restrained elegance. George Pavia, the founder's son and now managing partner, was said to be fond of continuity, and the decorum of the offices befitted a roster of clients whose names were synonymous with European luxury and high style: Fendi, Ferrari, Bulgari . . . Conversations shifted constantly between English, Italian, and French. It was hard to imagine an atmosphere more remote from that of the DA's Office.

In spite of the old-world ambience, the firm was ahead of its time in welcoming women. There were two among the nine partners at a time when it was rare to find even one in the upper echelons of big Manhattan firms. This one was exceptional in its organization too: associates worked directly with partners in two-person teams that made mentoring natural. It was a situation where I could learn quickly and, I hoped, quickly advance.

I interviewed many times over, meeting with each of the nine partners and all of the litigation associates. The positive impressions I was forming seemed to be mutual. It was clear that my trial experience appealed greatly and would fill an immediate need. A degree from Yale didn't hurt. But at some point my progress seemed to lose momentum inexplicably, and I found myself waiting for a call that didn't come. Meanwhile, interviews with other firms only made it clearer where I really wanted to be. Pressing the headhunter who had connected us, I learned that George Pavia feared I would quickly get bored with the work of a first-year associate — the position they were hiring for — and move on.

Be diplomatic but direct, I told myself. I don't tend to bang people over the head, but some situations require a bit of boldness. I asked for another meeting and once again found myself ushered into that serene nest lined with Persian carpets and delicately etched views of old Genoa.

"Mr. Pavia, I understand that you have some hesitations about hiring me. Are you comfortable talking about it?"

"Yes, of course." He explained his concerns. They were valid, I acknowledged, and then laid out my own position: Never having practiced civil law, I had a lot to learn. As long as I was learning, there was no chance of boredom. As I became more familiar with the work, one of two things would happen. Either I'd still be struggling to keep up — still no chance of boredom, although I probably wouldn't last at the firm. Or else they would recognize what I was capable of and give me more responsibility. I didn't see how they could lose. I made clear that I had no reluctance about accepting the starting salary of a first-year associate — a fraction of what I could expect from a large firm — as long as he was willing to increase it when my work warranted it.

The bonus and raise that followed my first year-end review were huge, and by the second review my salary was up to standard.

My first cases at Pavia & Harcourt involved customer warranty disputes and problems with real estate leases. The work of a beginning associate typically involved eclectic and sometimes marginal legal work for clients the firm represented in more crucial aspects of their business. It did, however, draw on skills that were second nature to a prosecutor. Within my first couple of days on the job, a colleague who sat within earshot of my phone calls let it be known to another litigation associate, who then spread the word, that I was "one tough bitch" who could not be pushed around by an adversary.

I was shaken to hear myself so harshly categorized. Trying case after case by the seat of your pants at the DA's Office, you develop a bravado that can seem abrasive to lawyers who have no acquaintance with that world. It was a kind of culture shock in both directions. The great distance from the grimy halls of Centre Street to our genteel bower on Madison Avenue made itself known in other small ways, too. A gift from a grateful client, for instance, did not have to be returned in the presence of a witness — a nice perk I didn't expect.

"You're in private practice now, Sonia. There's no threat of corruption," counseled David Botwinik, the partner I turned to — indeed, we all turned to — for advice on any question of ethics. I called him the Rabbi. It was okay to accept a gift, he said, though allowing that "in the ten years I've had them as clients, they never gave *me* a gift."

The more I observed Dave in action, the more profoundly his sense of integrity, fairness, and professional honor impressed me. Just as I had done with John Fried at the District Attorney's Office, I turned to Dave instinctively as a guide. His presence was comforting, avuncular, and expansive in a way that suggested a hearty appetite, though his greatest interests were more of the mind than the body. Blinking owlishly behind his glasses, he stuttered slightly. The hesitation only made his words seem more thoughtfully considered.

In the practice of law, there are rules that establish a minimum standard of acceptable conduct: what the law permits. This is the floor, below which one can't go. There are other rules, not formally encoded, which set

481

the higher bar that defines what's ethical behavior, consistent with respect for the dignity of others and fairness in one's dealings with them. There is no law, for example, saying you can't serve someone court papers at five o'clock on the Friday evening of a long holiday weekend. On the other hand, it's no way to deal honorably with an adversary, who is also a human being, with family, plans, and a personal life outside business. Some lawyers might argue that you owe your client any advantage you can squeeze out of a situation. But underhanded moves invite retaliation in kind, and then both sides end up grappling in the mud. Concerning the intersection of common decency and professional honor, Dave Botwinik's instincts were flawless.

It was through his instruction, too, that I became versed in a complex and little understood area of the law. Dave had specialized for thirty years in representing foreign commodity traders who bought in the American grain markets. He had worked hard to institute more evenhanded arbitration practices that tempered the influence of the big grain houses. Observing how I prepared witnesses and conducted cross-examinations, he asked me to assist him in grain arbitrations, which, though less formally structured than a trial, involved similar strategies.

"I'm too old for this now, you can do it," he said, but I could never have managed without his vast knowledge. He could read between the lines of any contract and see immediately why it was drafted as it was, what issues were important, respectively, to the parties involved. He knew all the players in the industry, which was a man's world entirely. Having begun as the scene of actual farmers bringing grain to market in the nineteenth-century Midwest, the game had evolved into an arcane trade of financial instruments conducted by roomfuls of traders working the phones. Even with my knowledge of admiralty law, I struggled at first to grasp the logic of the business. Finally, it clicked, though it took a late-night cry for help to cut through the Gordian knot of interwoven contracts: We were not actually tracking shipments of grain. The ephemeral exchange of contract rights that began with grain futures intersected with physical reality only at the end of a long chain of transactions.

Only once did I even see the grain. Our client had sent a sample for tests, and it was clear to me that the lab results had been falsified. I knew that a sealed plastic pouch from a private laboratory is no guarantee of a chain of custody when anybody can buy a heat-sealing kit for plastic bags at the supermarket. So I did. During arbitration, at the end of my cross-examination, I asked the witness to open the supposedly inviolate sample of grain. He tore the seal off the plastic bag and found inside it a note in my handwriting: "Bags can be tampered with."

I had learned over the years never to reveal that I could type. In the days before everyone had a personal computer, it was a sure way for a young lawyer to find herself informally demoted to secretary, and I stuck to that rule rigidly. Only once, in the wee hours approaching a morning deadline, did I ask Dave Botwinik to cover his eyes so I could type a final draft. Dave I could trust. He had a deft way of turning aside other lawyers' requests for the only woman in the room to get coffee.

Fran Bernstein, on the other hand, was far above this fray in the gender wars. She could sit for unbroken hours at her Smith-Corona while it rattled like a machine gun, as if her brain were plugged directly into the machine. I was astonished by her writing process, how the pages of elegant prose in no apparent need of polishing just rolled off the typewriter. But it was only one of her remarkable qualities. When she spoke, the flow of her ideas was just as irrepressible, as was the smile that lit up her dimpled face. As a law student, Fran was one of the first women to edit the law review at Columbia, where she later became a lecturer. She had also been among the first women to clerk for a judge on the Second Circuit. Having left work for several years to raise her children, she had returned only part-time. If that had put a crimp in her career, she didn't seem to mind. Though I was at first intimidated in her presence, she would become a true friend and another of my mentors at Pavia & Harcourt.

Fran's effortless eloquence so humbled me that when she first asked me to write a brief, I was paralyzed. For all my success in the courtroom, writing still terrified me. At the DA's Office, I had often volunteered for the overspill of appeals work that the trial bureaus were obliged to help with, just for the chance to work on my writing. Working on Fran's brief, I stayed up all night, my brain contorted in uncomfortable positions, suffering flashbacks to that traumatic summer at Paul, Weiss. The draft that I managed to finish past dawn was subpar. But when I confessed how utterly incompetent I felt, Fran was more than gracious. As a professor, she noted, she had been writing prolifically her whole career. The same role furnished her an instinctive sense of how to encourage someone trying to learn.

The one corner of my life in which I resisted Fran's influence was politics. She earnestly counseled me to join the Republican Party, though not so much for reasons of ideology. Reagan was running for president. Joining the party, she said, was a matter of affiliating oneself with where power in our society was headed, a necessary qualification for the kind of advancement I ultimately sought. I was historian enough to know that the GOP was the party of Lincoln, a connection that once held real meaning. And I was enough of a fiscal conservative to appreciate what Fran admired about Republican economic policy. But I couldn't see why those ideas had to be wed to the social views the party was now espousing. New York had produced some exceptionally progressive Republican leaders, Nelson Rockefeller having enacted some of the boldest social reforms the state had seen. At any rate, I felt no need to find a label that covered all my opinions, so I registered without any party affiliation. Contrary to Fran's careful calculations, that nonalignment served me well when I later joined the

Campaign Finance Board, and in other political encounters since then too.

"What do you know about handbags?" Fran asked me one day.

"Nothing. What's to know?" I was about to become an expert. To start with, Fran explained, a Fendi bag sold for eight hundred to several thousands of dollars. That deserved a double take. My cash, keys, and cigarettes were stashed in a bag that cost all of twenty dollars. She showed me one of the legendary pocketbooks, explained the finer points of stitching technique, how to recognize the quality of the fabric and the hardware — all the details that distinguished the real thing from a knockoff.

Fran had been tracking the development of intellectual property law for several years. It was a new field, as yet barely mentioned in law schools. Although patent and copyright laws were a well-established area of practice, trademarks drew less attention in those years. Meanwhile, fake Gucci and Fendi handbags, counterfeit Rolex and Cartier watches, and gallons of faux Chanel No. 5 were an exploding business on the sidewalks of Manhattan.

Fran presciently understood that the ultimate danger of not defending a trademark was loss of the precious rights to its exclusive use. She set about educating our clients, many of whom were in the business of fashion, creating luxury products whose worth was as tightly bound to the prestige of a name as to the quality of production. Fendi was the first to appreciate the importance of what Fran was trying to do. Cheap knockoffs of Fendi handbags were being sold not only in Chinatown and at flea markets all over the country but on the shelves of a reputable retail chain. Eventually, they showed up on the sidewalk right in front of Fendi's Fifth Avenue store.

Fran decided to educate me as well, because she wanted my help in taking that big retail chain to court. She was handing me books, and we discussed cases that we read together. When the Fendi case came to trial, we were excited to learn that it was assigned to Judge Leonard Sand, who was reputed to be brilliant. He had tried a very contentious case against the City of Yonkers over desegregation — a case that would eventually stretch over decades but was then fresh in the public awareness and especially familiar to me from my work at PRLDEF.

Leading up to the trial, I was in the conference room watching Fran prepare a witness when she was called away to the phone. She asked me to continue in her stead. The Fendi fashion house was very much a family business. Candido Speroni, our expert on the intricacies of Fendi's production processes, was married to one of the five Fendi sisters, each of whom was responsible for a different aspect of the business. Candido's nephew Alessandro Saracino, a young lawyer himself, was acting as interpreter.

Preparing witnesses is an art form. As a prosecutor, you learn that you can't tell witnesses what to say or not to say: they will blurt out the damnedest things when they're put on the spot in court. Instead, the purpose of coaching is to help them understand the reason behind each question so that you're working as a team to communicate their relevant knowledge to jurors. I was deep in the process with Candido, completely focused on the task at hand, when I looked at my watch and realized that Fran had been gone for a very long time indeed. I wondered aloud what had happened to her, and she answered from the corner by the door, "I'm here. I've been watching." After suggesting that we break for lunch, she said to Alessandro, "Please talk to your uncle and ask if he'll agree . . . Sonia should be the one to take this to trial, not me. It will cost you much less, but ultimately it's not the money. She's just that good at it!"

And so began my friendship with the Fendis, and the unlikely experience of going to court in front of the esteemed judge Leonard Sand as the only young associate calling the office at the end of each day to tell a senior partner what papers I needed prepared for the next morning.

Fran's handing me the Fendi case as my first crack at civil litigation was a tribute not only to her personal generosity but to the nature of Pavia & Harcourt, where freehanded collaboration was ingrained in the culture. The people I worked with were comfortable enough in their own skin to share clients and knowledge easily. That spirit of transparent teamwork was a joy to me, and I strove to be as open and helpful to others as Fran and Dave were to me. One young associate who struggled with dyslexia was as awed by my reading speed as I was by Fran's rapid-fire writing skills. "Sonia, you just inhaled that article as fast as you could turn the pages!" he moaned. But he had a reliable knack for spotting what was likely to be most useful, and so we often worked in tandem hacking through the dense undergrowth of required reading, swapping observations and ideas.

In this comradely environment, I learned to be more attentive to how I was perceived by colleagues. That initial impression of "one tough bitch" had mostly faded with experience but would resurface now and again when someone new joined us. Theresa Bartenope was hired as a secretary for a different department on the far side of the building, but I lured her into becoming my paralegal in the intellectual property practice. That meant I was often calling over the crackly intercom, "Theresa, I need you in my office." She would appear at my door a few minutes later, panting from the sprint, hands shaking, hives spreading up her neck. What's with her? I wondered. After she'd withdrawn to her side of the building, people in the hallway burst out laughing at the spectacle. Finally, someone clued me in, and I called Theresa in again, this time more gently: "Theresa, why are you so scared of me? I don't bite."

When I'm focused intensely on work, I become oblivious to social cues, or any cues for that matter. I block out the entire universe beyond the page in front of me or the issue at hand. Colleagues who knew me well didn't take it personally. In fact, they sometimes found it convenient. Hallway conversations could be carried on right outside my door, because I was the only person impervious to distraction, completely unaware. The same tendency as a prosecutor gave me a reputation — undeserved, I believe — for ruthlessness in cross-examinations. It's not how I mean to be; when I'm concentrating hard and processing information quickly, the questions just shoot out unceremoniously.

Theresa, thank heaven, overcame her fear, and she has since accompanied me on every step of my career. She remains my right hand and protector, the dearest of friends. When I miss something, she's the one who sees it. She's the one who holds a mirror up when she notices me getting intimidating or too abrupt, an effect only amplified by the trappings of my current office. When I am too wrapped up in something, she pulls me up for air and reminds me to be kind.

As it happened, the case I argued against the big retailer was settled mid-trial, but I would continue working closely with Fran Bernstein on intellectual property cases for the Fendis, as well as other clients. Litigation, however, was not an effective remedy to the problem of counterfeit goods sold on the street and in Chinatown; there was no point bringing petty vendors to trial. Instead, trademark owners decided to join forces in applying for a court order permitting us to confiscate the goods and the records related to their production and distribution. In building the case for a seizure order, we worked with private investigators to track down the suppliers funneling knockoffs into New York from several manufacturing points in Asia as well as moonlighting craftsmen in Italy. Investigators would purchase items from vendors at different locations, and we could map connections by matching hardware or fabrics from different lots. Keeping an area under surveillance, they could often identify a warehouse by spotting the runners who moved between that location and the vendors. If we could intercept the contraband at that distribution point, we might even find customs and shipping documents that would lead further up the supply chain.

I showed Fran how to work up an affidavit. She wrote most of the briefs. I loved the investigative work, the challenge of the puzzle, and the thrill ride of the seizure operations. Together we were Cagney and Lacey.

Dempster Leech, our private investigator, had a rumpled little absentminded-professor aspect and hesitant way of speaking that belied his own love of the chase. Through the pungent streets of Chinatown, he led a posse of burly sidekicks, most of them retired or off-duty police officers from beyond the five boroughs. They had to be armed: the street trade in knockoffs was controlled by gangs who, in addition to dealing drugs and whatever else, extorted protection money from the vendors. At a seizure, lawyers for each of the trademark holders were needed on hand to monitor the operation. It was our job to examine the goods and ensure that only counterfeits were taken, that papers were served properly, and that receipts were given for inventory seized. Normally, anyone involved vanished the instant our presence was detected. At the slightest hint of trouble, the glint of a weapon, Dempster would evacuate us quickly. No one wanted heroics. But a few times we brushed too close for comfort.

I was the lead lawyer one afternoon when I saw Dempster running toward me in the hubbub of Canal Street. His lookout had spotted someone leaving a building, pushing a hand truck loaded with boxes. One had fallen off the hand truck, spilling what looked like Fendis. Dempster's men were staking out the building. No windows, but he put his nose to the ground on a loading dock and peeked under the rolling gate that was left open a crack. In the shadows of the room, strewn all over, were hundreds and hundreds of counterfeit handbags. I phoned the judge, and minutes later we had a seizure order.

The place was so full of fake Fendis that after loading up all of Dempster's jeeps, we still had to bring in a trailer truck. Each time we thought we'd cleared the whole lot, another trail of stray bags would lead like bread crumbs to a further stash. The interior of the building, like that of many in China-town, was a labyrinthine warren of rooms that connected behind several separate storefronts. What had from the outside looked to be a small stand-alone structure actually stretched across most of the block.

Typically, a few days after a seizure, I would have been back at the courthouse to file an affidavit for the inventory. But on this occasion I had to be elsewhere, and so I sent a young associate who had been with us on the raid. When Tony walked out of the subway stop at Centre Street, a circle of young Asian guys with ominous tattoos closed in around him. "Where's the black-hair lady? Tell her we're looking for her. Tell her we know who she is." Tony wasn't the only one shaken that day. The entire litigation department at Pavia & Harcourt was called to a meeting, the partners aghast. The judge, when informed, was no less horrified, and marshals were dispatched to accompany me whenever I came to the courthouse . . .

The irony was not lost on me: I was now apparently in greater danger representing luxury brands at a genteel law firm than I had ever been prosecuting armed thieves and murderers. Dave Botwinik and some of the other partners argued that we should quit the seizures entirely, and right away. I, like Tony, understood that the risks were very well managed and that the value to our clients was huge. Perhaps we were also enthralled by the excitement: I wasn't ready to retire my bulletproof vest just yet. The debate within the firm was resolved with a lawyerly compromise that made explicit the full extent of risks on any specific operation and ensured there'd be no pressure to participate on anyone who might not care to take them.

Within two years of recruiting me to the work on intellectual property, Fran suffered a recurrence of the breast cancer that she had beaten into remission a few years before. The news weighed heavily: her mother, sister, grandmother — virtually every female in her family — had succumbed to the same disease. As her treatment, and the illness itself, progressed, she was less and less present. For a time, I depended on her guidance over the phone and tried to cheer her on through that same thin connection, but she was failing rapidly.

When I was up for partner in my fourth year at the end of 1988, she came into the office for the first time in months to cast her vote. She had lost a lot of weight and was very frail, but her spark was still there. That night, she and her husband, Bob, took me to dinner at La Côte Basque. It was my first time at a restaurant of such stellar opulence, and I was thrilled by the experience, though sad to see that Fran could barely eat. The outcome of the partnership vote was still under wraps, so it wasn't obvious yet that there was reason to party, but Fran couldn't wait. "You'll have to pretend that you don't know what I'm going to tell you, but tonight we celebrate!"

Later, as we stood at the curb while Bob was getting the car, Fran looked me up and down. "If you're going to become a partner, you'll have to dress the part. Fendi is your client now. You should represent them appropriately. You need to buy a Fendi fur coat."

"Fran, I don't want a fur coat!" She sounded like my mother complaining about the way I dressed. I already had a wonderful relationship with the Fendi family, and it didn't depend on my wearing haute couture. Alessandro, the young lawyer who was apprenticing to the family business, had become a good friend over months of daily phone calls between New York and Rome, at all hours, irrespective of my time zone or his. Eventually, I helped to smooth the way for him and his wife, Fe, to move to the United States, and after some initial reluctance they would become confirmed New Yorkers, deeply in love with their adopted home and passionate in their support of its cultural life.

It was Alessandro's grandmother Adele who, with her husband, had established the Fendi name as the epitome of Italian luxury, quality, and design. It was she too who had groomed each of her five daughters to assume a different facet of the financial or creative management, their husbands in turn also drawn into the family business. Alessandro was therefore perfectly at ease working with assertive women, and I instinctively warmed to a business environment bound together by strong family ties. It was a natural collaboration.

Princeton and Yale had furnished me my first glimpses of how the extremely privileged lived. Working at Pavia & Harcourt would give me an even better look, with invitations to social events hosted by wealthy clients, where a kid from the Bronx would incredulously find herself rubbing shoulders with the likes of Raquel Welch and Luciano Pavarotti. Still, I felt much more like an observer than a participant in the splendor. The Fendis' friendship pulled back the curtain onto a more private world of luxury and exquisite taste. When I visited their place in Rome and vacationed with them across Europe, my eyes were opened not only to the finest of modern Italian design and a glorious classical legacy but to an entirely different sensibility. Spirited through celebrations of theatrical enchantment, I collected dreams to last a lifetime. Perhaps also a certain understanding, and with it the confidence that comes of having seen life from all sides.

What mattered most of all, though, was that they became family. Alessandro is a brother to me. He'll jump to my defense ferociously — I daresay he'd offer to meet you with pistols at dawn if my honor was at stake. I, in turn, wouldn't pause to draw breath before boarding the next flight to be by his side in a moment of need. Just as I never hesitated to invite his parents, Paola and Ciro, to Co-op City for Thanksgiving dinner at my mother's.

TWENTY-EIGHT

A couple of weeks after my celebratory dinner with Fran and her husband, George Pavia called me into his office so he and Dave Botwinik could tell me, this time officially, that the firm's partners had elected me to membership. The good news came with a curious proviso, words that have stuck in my mind. "It's clear that you won't stay in private practice forever," George said. "We know you're destined for the bench someday. Dave is even convinced you'll go all the way to the Supreme Court. But with this offer, we ask only that you remain with us as long as you continue in private practice."

To offer a partnership to someone not planning to stick around was unusually generous, especially in a firm so small that each partner is an integral part of the team. I accepted with enormous gratitude but also obvious mortification at Dave's fantastical prophecy. If he could have known that I'd

dreamed of becoming a judge since childhood, I might have taken it as an affectionate but overheated compliment. In fact,
though, I had long refrained from verbal-
izing the ambition, understanding that any
federal judgeship would require a rare align-
ment of political forces, as well as no small
bit of luck. Dave may have intuited the
direction of my dreams — as I would soon
see, there was at least one other thing I kept
mum about that was more obvious than I'd
imagined — but even so, his talking about
the Supreme Court like that made me
wince, the way you might when an uncle
exaggerates your accomplishments. It was
awkward to hear such a naive thought from
someone I respected so deeply, and I felt
embarrassed for my Rabbi. I also felt
strangely exposed standing there as colleagues alluded casually to my secret pipe
dream in the same breath they were marking the professional milestone of my making partner, and even more so with the
shadow of Fran's death looming.

When she finally lost her fight the following spring, the loss devastated everyone.
Each death of someone close to me has
come as a slap, reminding me again of my
own mortality, compelling me to ask: What
am I accomplishing? Is my life meaningful?

When Abuelita died, I felt spurred to study even harder in college. When it was Nelson's time, I could no longer put off thinking about life beyond the DA's Office. Fran had entrusted me with the groundbreaking work in intellectual property that would become her legacy, and when she died, I threw myself into it with my best single-mindedness. Still, to see her go at fifty-seven, only one year younger than I am now, fired my habitual sense that I might not have enough time to make a real run at my ultimate goal.

I've lived most of my life inescapably aware that it is precious and finite. The reality of diabetes always lurked in the back of my mind, and early on I accepted the probability that I would die young. There was no point fretting about it; I have never worried about what I can't control. But nor could I waste what time I had; some inner metronome has continued to set a beat I am unable to refuse. Now diabetes has become more manageable, and I no longer fear falling short in the tally of years. But the habit of living as if in the shadow of death has remained with me, and I consider that, too, a gift.

On a glorious day at the end of June, a

group of friends were celebrating my thirty-seventh birthday with a barbecue in my backyard. I was lucky to have stumbled on the apartment right down the block from my old place and Dawn's, lucky to have grabbed it at a discount before the co-op conversion was even concluded, and luckier still that Dave Botwinik helped me find an unusually affordable loan for the down payment. Best of all, the backyard was perfect for parties.

Everyone was taken care of. All their glasses were filled. Let them dance, I thought. Exhausted, I needed to lie down for a few minutes. I didn't feel right, light-headed, but once supine I couldn't get my body to move. Eventually, I managed to drag myself off the bed, opening the screen door to the backyard. But that was as far as I could get. I needed to sit down right there. Fortunately, there was a step. And there was Theresa. She was talking to me, but I couldn't make out the words. She came closer, still talking gibberish. There was something in her hand that I wanted badly. I needed it. I grabbed for it, but my aim was shaky. I smashed the piece of birthday cake into my mouth. Theresa stood there with her own mouth open in shock. I must have looked pretty disconcerting with frosting smeared all over my face.

When I recovered and we talked about what had happened, Theresa told me that although she was vaguely aware that I was diabetic, she had no knowledge of what a sugar low looked like. Friends who saw me lie down just assumed that I'd had a few too many. But I was so busy playing host that I hadn't had even one yet. The card I'd been given as a child was still in my wallet, carried around for all these years. I'd made it to my thirty-seventh birthday with no occasion for someone to pull it out. It said:

I HAVE DIABETES

I AM NOT drunk. If I am unconscious or acting strangely, I may have low blood sugar.

EMERGENCY TREATMENT

I need sugar immediately. If I am able to swallow, give me candy, soda pop, fruit juice or table sugar. If I cannot swallow or do not recover within 15 minutes, call a doctor or the closest emergency medical help and tell them I have diabetes.

Very few of my friends were aware of my

being a type 1 diabetic and completely dependent on insulin shots. Not that I was aware of hiding it. I would have said that I was being politely discreet, but the truth is my secrecy was a deeply ingrained habit. I was averse to any revelations that might have seemed a play for pity. And managing this disease all my life had been the hallmark of the self-reliance that had saved me as a child, even if it may have partly cost me a marriage. I didn't need anyone's help with it. But in truth, I was more vulnerable than I was willing to admit.

The secrecy wasn't simply in my nature. When I was young, disabilities and illnesses of all sorts were governed by a code of silence. Such things were private matters, and you didn't speak about them outside the family. I wouldn't have dreamed of giving myself a shot in public, though I rarely had to worry about that because I was only taking one shot a day, first thing in the morning. If the situation somehow arose, traveling or spending a night away from home, my mother would tell me to go do it in the bathroom.

When I was a teenager, there was nothing to be gained by advertising that I was carrying around needles and syringes in a neighborhood where so many people were using heroin. Walking to work at Prospect Hospital one day, I tripped and spilled the contents of my bag at the feet of a police officer. There on the sidewalk lay my "works"; I happened to be carrying a syringe and needle, having planned to spend the night at Abuelita's. "Oh, no, no," said the cop incredulously as I explained, scooping everything up as fast as I could with trembling hands. My explanation carried no weight; neither did my bottle of insulin. What crazy story would a junkie come up with next? I had to persuade him to walk with me to the hospital so my supervisor could vouch for me. I was completely terrified: an arrest would have dimmed any hope of college, let alone law school.

By the time I was in college, the condition had seemed to become more of a nonissue, hardly rating a mention to anyone. I continued with the same regimen — one shot a day — no longer checking in at the clinic at Jacobi Medical Center, where I would have become aware of treatment advances. As it was, I still had no more accurate way of testing my blood glucose than those practically useless, delayed-report urine strips. But so long as I continued to eat carefully and mind how I was feeling, I was able to manage. That discipline was easier than the alternative: I hated the heavy lethargy that came with a blood sugar spike; and the effects of a dip — sweats, trembling, and disorientation — were unpleasant enough that I was quick to answer them with extra sugar.

It didn't occur to me, however, that my own body might be changing. Subtle hormonal shifts, long after the turbulence of puberty, can affect blood sugar levels. Exercise can make a difference too, speeding up the absorption of the insulin recently injected. Constantly on the move at Princeton, whether bicycling around campus or racing upstairs to class, I was oblivious to how, with these factors added, blood sugar levels could drop so fast that the usual telltale symptoms had no time to register before I was too disoriented to respond.

During my junior year, I started to have trouble waking up in the morning. Once I was so groggy that I managed to take an exam without being fully conscious and even make it back to bed, only to wake up later in a panic that I had missed the test. I still haven't figured out how I could have aced it. Another time I woke up and answered the phone with so little presence of mind that Kevin's mother finally figured out we were sleeping together. And then one morning I didn't wake up at all. If my roommate hadn't circled back to the dorm at an odd time, contrary to habit, she wouldn't have found me unconscious on the bed. After she was unable to rouse me, I ended up in the infirmary for several days.

All through college, law school, and my years at the DA's Office, I would stick with essentially the same regimen I'd had as a child. It wasn't until I reached thirty and settled in Brooklyn that I decided to seek out a specialist in type 1 diabetes. The advances in treatment that had passed me by were significant. I started to catch up, using improved forms of insulin and taking shots twice a day. When my first doctor moved, she referred me to Andrew Drexler, one of the foremost diabetic endocrinologists in the country. Under Andy, now a cherished friend and confidant, my treatment is as good as it gets.

I still use the tried-and-true approach of injecting insulin, though many diabetics today have switched to convenient insulin pens or pumps with computerized controls to adjust dosages continuously during the day. Urine strips are ancient history. In the mid-1980s, I bought my first portable blood glucose meter, which cost what seemed like a fortune at the time. It was four times the size of today's versions, which provide a reading in five seconds. I test my blood sugar and give myself shots five or six times a day now. When deciding what I'm going to eat, I calculate the carbohydrate, fat, and protein contents. I ask myself a litany of questions: How much insulin do I need? When is it going to kick in? When was my last shot? Will I walk farther than usual or exert myself in a way that might accelerate the absorption rate? If I weren't good at math, this would be difficult.

This regimen certainly takes a lot more attention than I gave to the disease when I was young, but it also allows for a much more fine-tuned regulation of my blood sugar levels. The benefit adds up, since the dire complications of diabetes — heart disease, blindness, neuropathy that can lead to amputation of limbs — are mostly the effects of long-term damage caused by chronically high levels. Meticulously keeping mine within normal range gives me an excellent chance of a normal life span. No matter how careful I am, though, a fever or infection can send my sugars soaring. Trauma or extreme stress has the same effect.

Even with the most conscientious monitoring, blood sugar can swing suddenly in a way that is a threat to one's life not in the future but in the immediate present. That's what happened the day I grabbed that hunk of birthday cake from Theresa. Surprises can insinuate themselves insidiously. I knew, for instance, how much carbohydrate was in a meal at a typical Chinese restaurant, but one time my calculations were thrown perilously off by a very different style of cooking at a Szechuan place of great refinement. Jet lag or losing track of shifts in time zone probably figured in another crisis. I'd flown to Venice for the wedding of a friend, an Italian lawyer who had worked for a time at Pavia & Harcourt. Somehow, after I checked into my hotel room, my blood sugar dropped precipitously, and I passed out.

Fortunately, Alessandro and his wife, Fe, had come to Venice for the wedding too. They realized something was wrong when I didn't show up on time. After trekking across the city to my hotel, Alessandro threatened to break down my door if the concierge didn't put aside hotel policy and unlock it. Orange juice was administered, an ambulance was called, which was in fact a boat and too big to squeeze into our back-alley canal. So a Venetian stretcher, which is to say a chair on poles, was provided, and I was conveyed, variously in and out of consciousness, to a hospital that was really a nursing home in an ancient convent, with facilities to match. I tried to show the doctor how to use my fancy glucose meter, but he was having none of it. "I am the doctor; you are the patient," he insisted, as Alessandro translated with chagrin.

We laughed at the story afterward, especially as recounted with Alessandro's gloriously expressive Italian gestures, conjuring images of Fe in a stunning blue evening gown and himself in black tie preparing to batter my door down, or the ultimate indignity of having the Italian hospital staff refer to the two of them as "the Americans."

Although they stick out in my memory, such episodes didn't happen very often and have been rare in the last decade, as technology has improved and my body has settled into middle age. Still, each time I found myself in a blood sugar crisis, I couldn't help but notice that some unlikely intervention had saved my life, whether a friend just happening by or phoning out of the blue, or, one time, Dawn's little Rocky, who, finding me unconscious, barked furiously, refusing to be calmed, until he drew attention where it was needed. Contemplating such good fortune reinforced my sense that Abuelita was still watching over me. But I decided that was no basis to push my luck.

Though the Fendis and I would, for years to come, dine out mirthfully on the story of the Venetian affair, the bald truth is that if Alessandro had not been aware of my diabetes, I'd be dead. It was the final confirmation I needed that for safety's sake I had to be open about my condition. And since taking my present job these many years later, when the danger seems to have receded, I have another good reason to claim the disease publicly. I don't know whether they still give diabetic children a list of professions they can't aspire to, but I'm proud to offer living proof that big dreams are not out-of-bounds.

There is one person with whom I have deferred opening up as long as possible. The stories of those close calls suggestive of my nine lives have never been mentioned to my mother. I'll have to deal with the fallout when she reads this book. Her guilt, pity, sadness, and ultimately fear of my disease are still beyond all reason, and at times have driven me nuts. But then, any problem of mine she has discovered belatedly has resulted in the same hysteria. Junior reports she once called him to complain that I don't tell her what's happening. He answered her far better than I could have: "Sonia's never going to tell you anything, Mami, because you always overreact." Even more important, he told her, he didn't know a happier person than his sister. "Sonia lives her life fully. If she dies tomorrow, she'll die happy. If she lives the way you want her to live, she'll die miserable. So leave her alone, okay?"

I love my brother dearly. He knows me in ways the rest of the world never could. We've always watched out for each other. His kids still crack up whenever they hear me calling him Junior — he's Juan to everyone else now — but he'll always be Junior to me, even if he's no longer such a nuisance.

Mami hung up on him that time, he said. I could picture her sitting there in Co-op City, fuming in her jungle of houseplants, stems shooting up to the ceiling, the vines clinging to the corners, fringing the picture windows. That message would not go over easily, but eventually it would be received.

The story of my secrecy and the self-reliance that produced it does not begin and end with my diabetes. But I've come to see that it does begin and end with my mother, who became my most constant emotional paradigm, informing my character for good and for ill, as well as the character of my relations with her.

Many times I felt there was a wide moat separating me from the rest of the world, in spite of my being, by all accounts, a great listener to all my friends. They felt free to tell me their troubles. Like my mother, I would suspend judgment, feel their pain, perhaps even point out a fact they might have overlooked: I have a knack for translating the mysteries of other people's minds and could open their eyes to what the world looked like to their husband, their boss, or their mother. The only trick I couldn't manage was to ask the same of them.

Sharing was not my style; my problems were mine to deal with. Ever since fifth grade, ever since putting behind me the misery and isolation visited upon an alcoholic's family, ever since that cute boy, Carmelo, convinced me that being smart could be cool, I'd surrounded myself with a crowd of friends. And yet inside I remained very much alone. Perhaps even within my marriage, which, for all our mutual regard and affection, had suffered from a certain self-sufficiency of mine that frustrated Kevin. It was not until these years after the DA's Office, as I started making more purposeful strides toward the person I wanted to be professionally, that I could begin to dream of reshaping the person I was emotionally, too. My faith in my potential for self-improvement, which had been the foundation for all my academic and professional success so far, would now be tested in more inaccessible regions of the self. But I was optimistic: if I could help fix your problems, surely I can fix my own.

I'd always believed people can change; very few are carved in stone or beyond redemption. All my life I've looked around me and asked: What can I learn here? What qualities in this friend, this mentor, even this rival, are worth emulating? What in me needs to change? Even as a child, I could reflect that my anger was accomplishing nothing, hurting only myself, and that I had to learn to stop in my tracks the instant I felt its surge. Learning to be open about my illness was a first step, and it taught me how admitting your vulnerabilities can bring people closer. Friends want to help, and it's important to know how to accept help graciously, just as it's better to accept a gift with "Thank you" than "You shouldn't have."

If there's a measure of how well I've succeeded in this self-transformation, it's that very few of my friends — even those who have known me the longest — can remember the person I was before undertaking the effort. Such is the nature of familiarity and memory. They also swear that they've always known about my diabetes and claim memories of seeing me give myself shots long before I ever did so openly. But there is no better indicator of progress, or cause for pride, than the thaw in relations with my mother.

Mami gone, checked out, the empty apartment. Her back to me, just a log in the bed beside me as a child. Mami, perfectly dressed and made up, like a movie star, the Jacqueline Kennedy of the Bronxdale Houses, refusing to pick me up and wrinkle her spotless outfit. This was the cold image I'd lived with and formed myself in response to, unhappily adopting the aloofness but none of the glamour. I could not free myself from its spell until I could appreciate what formed it and, in its likeness, me.

There was so much about my mother I simply hadn't known. When she was struggling through her nursing degree at Hostos Community College, terrified of failure, facing every written exam like a firing squad, she had told me a little about her school days in Lajas and San Germán. About her fear of being ridiculed by classmates, scolded by teachers, her certainty that she was stupid. Beyond that I knew practically nothing about her childhood. Her most telling stories would trickle out slowly, in dribs and drabs, but it was only when I had the strength and purpose to talk about the cold expanse between us that she confessed her emotional limitations in a way that called me to forgiveness.

"How should I know these things, Sonia? Who ever showed me how to be warm when I was young? I was lonely; I was angry at Mayo. What else did I see?"

My anger at her would still surge from time to time, and when it did, I would call on this awareness: she had her own story, pieces that were missing in her own life. I called too on a talisman of memory, one I could grasp like the smooth beads of a rosary. I'd return to it like some childhood storybook I knew by heart but of which I never tired. It was the memory of those summer nights when I woke in a terrible sweat, and Mami would towel me down with a cool wet cloth, whispering softly, so as not to wake Junior, because this was for me, my time. The little fan whirring away; my neck turning cool as the moisture evaporated; my mother's hand on my back.

I wouldn't suffer the same lack of examples as my mother. Friends would show me how to be warm, and I would learn by allowing others a chance to do for me as they had let me do for them, until no one remembered a time when it was not that way. As I learned, I practiced on my mother — a real hug, a sincere compliment, an extra effort to let down my guard — and miraculously she softened in turn, out of instinct long dormant, even if she didn't quite know what was going on. Opening up, I came to recognize the value of vulnerability and to honor it, and soon I found that I wasn't alone even on this journey. My mother was taking every step alongside me, becoming more affectionate and demonstrative herself, the person who, given a chance, she might have been.

Kiley runs to greet me, jumps into my embrace. She throws her skinny little arms around my neck, squeezes her tiny, birdlike three-year-old body to mine in crazy disproportion. And without warning my heart bursts, tears well in my eyes. A tenderness I have no name for rushes like a drug through my veins, as I realize that the absence of human touch has been, for so long, a burden carried unwittingly.

I wrote myself a prescription for hug

therapy. I told each of the children in my life that I wasn't getting enough hugs. Tommy, Vanessa, Zachary . . . "Would you help me out by giving me a hug whenever you see me?" Kiley didn't need telling, of course, but every one of the others got it instantly. In this, the wisdom of toddlers is unassailable. The hugs came. And feeling flowed that had never come so easily before. Even as the kids grew into gangly teenagers, the hugs never stopped. Younger siblings, John and Kyle, would join the cause as the years went by.

What I've learned from children I've been able to give back to adults. The stroke on the arm that says I understand, the welcome hug, the good-bye kiss, the embrace that lingers that much longer in a time of sorrow. I've discovered the palpable difference between such acts as mere gestures and as sluices of true feeling between two people.

We were in the dressing room, and I was getting out of my jeans, ready to attack the pile of possibilities that my friend Elaine had gathered off the racks, when she dropped the armful of clothes and doubled over, hooting hysterically. I was afraid she would bring down the flimsy partition walls. A client of Pavia & Harcourt's who'd become a very close friend, Elaine Litwer was a gutsy and street-smart survivor of extreme poverty and a colorful family from the Lower East Side. She talked nonstop, was never wrong, and suffered no fools in wielding her merciless wit. Many weekends we'd prowl the shops and hang out like a pair of teenage girls.

"Sonia! My God! Who buys your underwear? Your mother?"

"As a matter of fact, in this case, yes."

"We have to fix that right away!"

Any offense I might have taken at Elaine's uncensored mockery was offset by a discreet satisfaction at the thought of Mami's having, for once, been knocked off her pedestal as a fashion authority. I was happy to let Elaine help me choose some age-appropriate undergarments.

This was part of a much bigger project. Elaine was teaching me to shop, to recognize what looks good on me, how color works with skin tone, the drape of a fabric, how the eye follows a line. Alas, it was one subject in which I was not to prove a quick study. But little by little I developed confidence in my own judgment, and Elaine, bless her, found a way to make this process fun. Until she took me in hand, I'd hated shopping and confined myself to mail-order catalogs rather than suffer the smirks of salesgirls and the taunts of full-length mirrors. And even when I did something right, my mother's idea of encouragement was scarcely encouraging. Any compliment would be immediately qualified: "That looks nice, Sonia, but now you need to paint your nails."

But to be perfectly honest, it wasn't all my mother's fault. Dressing badly has been a refuge much of my life, a way of compelling others to engage with my mind, not my physical presence. I'm competitive enough that I'll eventually withdraw from any consistently losing battle. Elaine gave me the precious gift of showing me that it didn't need to be that way. I am a woman; I do have a feminine side. Learning to enjoy it would not diminish any other part of me.

She looked at me with her wide-eyed, wicked grin. "I would never in a million years have chosen that for you, Sonia, but it looks great on you. You see? You're becoming your own person."

Not every relationship ends with such mutual respect and dignity as Kevin and I somehow salvaged from our youthful mistakes. I would discover what it is to go down in flames romantically, disappointment that shakes your foundations. The despair would pass, but until it did, friends came to my rescue, just as they had after my divorce. Being left alone in my misery was never an option. Elaine's taking me shopping every weekend was part of a campaign undertaken in the aftermath of one ill-fated romance. Alessandro and Fe, too, have been known to jump into the breach of a breakup: "Mama says you must come to Ibiza with us for vacation."

One remedy for heartache I concocted on my own was learning how to dance. I scheduled the lessons, rolled up the carpet, and committed myself to learning salsa. No longer would I sit there like a potted plant watching others on the floor. The gawky, uncoordinated Sonia would make peace with herself in motion. I may never have a natural rhythm, but I know that the knees make the hips move, and I would learn to read a partner so well that I can now follow like an expert.

I still can't sing to save my life — a slight hearing impairment doesn't help matters — but after unnatural amounts of rehearsal to memorize where each syllable falls, I can now get up onstage at a holiday party and hold my own in a musical skit.

I finally learned how to swim, too. Okay,

maybe not with athletic grace, but I can swim twenty laps without stopping. I can jump off the boat with the best of them, and no one will ever need to rescue me. I never imagined that even later in life I would learn to throw a baseball, but really you never know. During my first term on the Supreme Court, I practiced twenty minutes every afternoon for weeks so I could be ready to throw the first pitch at Yankee Stadium. Not from the mound, of course, but I did send it straight down the middle. Exercise of all kinds has been a joyous discovery, and I've even biked a century tour. It would take years, but now when I look in the mirror, what I see is really not bad. It's true, I love food too much; my weight goes up and down. But when time permits, I actually enjoy the effort of keeping it off.

One reckoning with my physical self would prove harder than all the others. I had been a smoker since high school, burning through three and a half packs a day for much of my life. I made my first serious attempt at quitting in my final year at law school: every time I felt the urge, I ran around the block, often with Kevin and Star chugging alongside in solidarity. Going cold turkey during exams may sound like a needlessly brutal rigor, but in retrospect it seems less perversely self-punishing than lighting up again two years later when Kevin and I split. There would be further attempts, using various methods, including hypnosis, but nothing worked for good until I saw little Kiley holding a pencil between two fingers, blowing imaginary smoke rings. The guilt of endangering the health of a loved one is by far the best motivation I've discovered.

I checked into a five-day residential program and even wrote a long love letter, saying farewell to what had been my most constant companion for so many years. It was another heartbreak, but I comforted myself by imagining that if I were ever to become a judge someday, I couldn't very well be calling a recess every time I needed a cigarette. And it worked. I remain a nicotine addict, a fact that inspires a certain compassion for the addictions of others, but I haven't had a cigarette since. I no longer worry about slipping, but I do fantasize that I might indulge one last smoke on my deathbed, just as Abuelita did.

Ferrari was a client of mine, and I was invited to take one of the original Testarossas for a spin. The twelve-cylinder was a marvel of technology that Ferrari had developed for the racetrack, packed into the fastest street-legal car ever built: zero to sixty miles per hour in under five seconds, and a price tag of about a quarter of a million dollars.

Negotiating hills, winding through fields and scattered woods, I was fearless, even as I thrilled to the feeling of such vast power under perfect mechanical control. As the hills rose and fell and the woods blurred past, other scenes appeared to my mind's eye like so many glimpses in the rearview mirror. I remembered our useless car in the projects, my anger that Papi wouldn't drive . . . A dozen or more of us piled into Gallego's jalopy for a picnic, like a crazy *guagua* . . . Kevin lying on his back at the curb all summer long as I read aloud to him from the manual . . . The relief I'd felt that first time when, eerily, I got the clutch to engage, and I knew I'd be able to drive my things home to Mami's in Co-op City . . . Then Abuelita calling out to everyone, *¡Vámonos de parranda!* — a joyride at midnight! It was broad daylight, but for a long moment as the road rolled under the Testarossa, her smile didn't fade.

Twenty-Nine

Sometimes, no matter how long we've carried a dream or prepared its way, we meet the prospect of its fulfillment with disbelief, startled to see it in daylight. In part that may be because, refusing to tempt fate, we have never actually allowed ourselves to expect it.

In 1990, I flew to London with Alessandro, Fe, his parents, and his sister for a Boxing Day celebration. When I got back to work after the Christmas holiday, my office looked like the office of someone who had been let go. The towers of paper that normally obscured my desktop had vanished, exposing a dark polished wood grain I'd all but forgotten about. Upon it sat only one document for my attention: an application form for the position of a federal district court judge. This was obviously Dave Botwinik's doing. I grabbed the form and charged the short distance down the hallway to his office.

"Dave, come on."

"It's from Senator Moynihan's judicial selection committee. They vet the recommendation he makes to the president. Fill it out."

"Are you crazy? I'm thirty-six years old!"

"Humor me, Sonia. They're looking for qualified Hispanics. You're not only a qualified Hispanic but eminently qualified, period." He promised to give me back my files if I filled it out, which I promised to do before counting the pages: it was endless. But Dave would not be deterred: he volunteered his assistant as well as my own, plus the help of a paralegal, whatever I needed to get the job done. I had long suspected that Dave Botwinik's ambitions on my behalf were partly a displacement of ambitions he'd once had for himself. Until then, I'd just ignored it whenever he raised the topic. But this time he was showing a whole new level of determination, and he was not the only one on the case.

A few weeks earlier, I had shared a cab with Benito Romano after a PRLDEF board meeting. Having served as interim U.S. attorney when Rudy Giuliani quit the post to run for mayor, Benito had himself been approached by a colleague on Senator

Moynihan's search committee. He had declined the offer, he said, but given them my name.

"Why not you?" I asked.

"I have a wife, Sonia. I have kids. How am I going to put them through college on a judge's salary?" It's a very real problem that has discouraged many a talented person from considering the bench. The pay cut I would suffer as a young partner wouldn't be as severe as a more experienced lawyer's, and having no children spared me the impossible choice. But this calculus didn't alter my feeling of reaching for too much too soon.

Even with help, the application took the better part of a week to complete. I had to account for every jot of my adult life, it seemed, as well as furnishing current addresses for each landlord, supervisor, judge, and legal adversary who had ever crossed my path. At least the financial information was easy; I still had little to report on that front. Beyond the summary of professional experience typical of job applications, this document would be the starting point for an investigation scouring my past for any ethical lapse. But I wasn't daunted by that. I soon realized that, perhaps more than I would ever have admitted, most of the choices I'd made over the years have anticipated this very moment.

I heard back from the senator's committee very quickly after submitting the application, the interview scheduled within a couple of weeks. If I still couldn't take the whole business quite seriously, I nevertheless prepared as if my life depended on it. When I had gone for recruiting interviews at Yale, it never occurred to me to do research in advance or rehearse the answers to likely questions. The entire culture of the law school was geared to the law firms that were the most sought-after recruiters, to answering the very sorts of questions most likely to come up in such an interview, and to knowing those one ought to ask. Years later, having waltzed into an interrogation for a very different sort of position at a federal agency in Washington, I would realize, only too late, that it was not the sort of cakewalk a Yale JD could expect interviewing with a big Manhattan firm. I would never make that mistake again.

So I prepared as thoroughly as I would have done for a criminal prosecution, reading whatever I could find and seeking out colleagues and any friends and family of theirs with the least experience of the judicial nomination process: What kinds of questions could I expect to be asked? What objections might I need to rebut? I was no longer afraid of the obvious one I myself first anticipated: "Aren't you too young to be applying for this position?" I'd certainly presumed so, but a bit of digging revealed I would not be the youngest to hold it. Becoming a judge in one's thirties was uncommon but not unheard of, and I would have the names of those exceptions at my fingertips. And also one ready truth: although wisdom is built on life experiences, the mere accumulation of years guarantees nothing.

Judah Gribetz, a childhood friend of David Botwinik's and longtime adviser to Senator Moynihan, chaired the committee, with whom I met in the conference room of a downtown law firm. I was facing some fifteen people around the table, most but not all of them men and lawyers. One of the few I recognized was Joel Motley, son of Constance Baker Motley, the first African-American woman to be appointed a U.S. district court judge. As questions flew at me from all sides, the answers were flowing easily, and I was pleased with how well I'd prepared. Then Joel asked one I'd never predicted. "Don't you think learning to be a judge will be hard for you?" I took a breath to gather my thoughts, and then the answer poured out: "I've spent my whole life learning how to do things that were hard for me. None of it has ever been easy. You have no idea how hard Princeton was for me at the beginning, but I figured out how to do well there and ended up being accepted to one of the best law schools in the country. At Yale, the DA's Office, Pavia & Harcourt — wherever I've gone, I've honestly never felt fully prepared at the outset. Yet each time I've survived, I've learned, and I've thrived. I'm not intimidated by challenges. My whole life has been one. I look forward to engaging the work and learning how to do it well."

When the discussion turned technical, my trial experience held up very well under scrutiny. As a state prosecutor, I'd tried many more cases than an attorney working in the federal system would have done. We talked at length about the child pornography and Tarzan Murderer cases, and I explained those investigations and the legal strategies employed. What about the areas where I lacked experience? There was much about criminal law at the federal level that I would need to learn, though my work at Pavia & Harcourt had included several hearings and a trial in federal court on trademark cases; I was at least familiar with the differences in the evidentiary rules. More important, I'd studied the resources that a novice judge would inevitably rely on — the readings, the seminars, the Federal Judicial Center. I might not know the procedural particulars as well as some, but I knew perfectly well where the issues lay. I cited the new Federal Sentencing Guidelines as an example. You can always look up answers to specific questions in specific situations, I said, so long as you have enough experience to know that a question exists. Learning the rules isn't hard when you're aware there's a rule to learn.

We talked about my community service, which I knew was especially important to Senator Moynihan. My work at PRLDEF was clearly a point in my favor, as was the Campaign Finance Board and my other pro bono activities. As I sat there fielding questions, I dared to believe that the interview was actually going very well. With each question, I could see the pitch coming toward me as if in slow motion. I was relaxed but also alert, centered but agile, ready to move in any direction. If I was not picked, I knew it wouldn't be because I had blown the interview. And that sense alone made the experience worth it.

But the whole process still seemed like

make-believe, even when Senator Moynihan's office phoned soon after, inviting me to meet him in Washington. He turned out to be so forthright and gregarious that I warmed to him at once. We talked about Puerto Rico and the challenges facing the Puerto Rican community in New York, our conversation ranging widely from Eddie Torres (a judge who also wrote crime novels that the senator admired), to getting out the Latino vote, to the eternal question of the island's status. Here, clearly, was a scholar as well as a politician, someone who understood the sociology as well as the policy issues while also possessing the social skills of a master diplomat. I was enjoying our talk so much I would have forgotten entirely about being on the hot seat were it not for the continual interruptions of phone calls and questions from his aides. Each time, he filled me in afterward on the issue he was dealing with, and we would continue, weaving the new theme into the conversation. There was a gracious art to this seemingly effortless chat and to the way he exerted his prodigious intellect, never to intimidate, but rather to invite you to engage him at whatever level you found comfortable.

After more than an hour of this, I sensed that we were coming to an end and prepared to thank him before going off to wait out the predictably interminable period of deliberation I'd already girded myself for. But the senator had one more surprise in store, saying, "Sonia, if you accept, I would like to nominate you as a district court judge in New York." He warned me that the confirmation process would not be easy. The Bush administration was not in the habit of smiling on recommendations from a Democrat; on principle, it would fight any candidate he proposed. "It may take some time," he said, "but I'll make you a promise: If you stay with me, I'll get you through eventually. I won't give up."

Then he asked if I was willing to hold up my side of the bargain: Was I prepared to spend a good portion of my remaining professional life as a judge? I was stunned. Until that moment, I had still not allowed myself to believe lest I awaken from this daydream. But here was Senator Moynihan looking at me, waiting for an answer. "Yes!" With all my heart, yes.

I floated out of the Russell Senate Office Building and wandered down the street in a daze. After a couple of blocks I saw a monumental flight of stairs, familiar white columns: the Supreme Court Building glowing serenely, like a temple on a hill.

There could not have been a more propitious omen. I felt blessed in that moment, blessed to be living this life, on the threshold of all I'd ever wanted. There would be plenty of time soon enough to deal with my insecurities and the hard work of learning this new job. For the moment, though, I just stood there, dazzled at the sight and glowing with gratitude — until reality intervened: Where could I find a cab to the airport?

All during the flight home my mind was racing through the practical considerations. How would all this change my life? Would I need to move to Manhattan? How much, exactly, does a judge make anyway? I was still immersed in such lofty considerations when I got off the plane and noticed all the people making a big fuss over some celebrity who had arrived on the same flight. I'd been too distracted to notice that I'd been sitting next to Spike Lee for over an hour.

My mother and Omar had been together for a few years at that point. At first she'd told me only that she was renting my old bedroom to this man. Then, meeting him a couple of times on visits home, I sensed that there was more to the story than they were saying. Arriving late one night, I surprised them kissing in the lobby. "Do you have something to tell me?" I asked. Mami was flustered, beaming, embarrassed, and clearly very happy.

"We were going to tell you, Sonia. I just didn't know how." As I got to know Omar over time, I fully approved of my mother's choice. Now they were sitting side by side on the couch in my living room in Brooklyn, and I was the one who had to figure out how to break the news.

"Mami, Omar, I'm going to tell you something, but you have to promise to keep it a secret. There won't be a public announcement for a couple of weeks, but I've been given permission to tell you." I asked if they knew who Senator Patrick Moynihan was. Tentative nods. "The senator is going to nominate me to become a U.S. district court judge in Manhattan."

"Sonia, how wonderful! That's terrific news!" As always, Mami's initial reaction was enthusiasm. She didn't always understand fully what my news meant, but as a matter of maternal principle she was a loyal cheerleader. Omar too congratulated me earnestly. Then the questions started.

"So, you're going to earn more money, right?" my mother said.

"Not exactly, Mami. A judge's salary is

much less than I'm earning now."

She paused for a long moment. "Well, I guess you'll be traveling a lot, seeing the world?"

"Not really. The courthouse is in downtown Manhattan, and I can't imagine I'll be going anywhere else. Not the way I have at Pavia."

The pauses were growing a little longer. "I'm sure you'll meet interesting people and make friends as nice as the ones you've met at the firm."

I was determined not to laugh. "Actually, the people who appear before a judge are mostly criminal defendants in serious trouble or people fighting with each other. There are ethical reasons too why I wouldn't be socializing with them."

Silence, and then: "Sonia, why on earth do you want this job?"

Omar, who knew me well by now, came to my rescue. "*Conoces tu hija.* You know your daughter, Celina. This must be very important work." The look on Mami's face carried me back to that moment under the rumbling El train when we shared our uncertainty about what lay ahead of me at Princeton: "What you got yourself into, daughter, I don't know . . ." In truth, I'd had no idea then that Princeton would be only the first stop on a magical ride that by now had already taken me farther than I could have ever foreseen.

Now all I had to do was wait for the political process to run its long and bumpy course. It's the president who appoints federal district court judges. In many states, however, including New York, the senators propose candidates, and the president accepts their suggestions as a courtesy. In a twist special to the Empire State, Senator Moynihan had long before hammered out a bipartisan agreement with his Republican counterpart, Jacob Javits, that would survive turnover in the Oval Office: for every three nominations from a senator of the president's party, a senator from the loyal opposition could offer one. There were several vacancies at the time, and it was Senator Moynihan's turn to submit names to President George H. W. Bush. But the existence of this entente between gentlemen of the Senate didn't oblige the administration to like it or even facilitate the process.

The eighteen months that it took my nomination to clear were an education in the arts of politics and patience. I knew that the delays had nothing to do with me personally. Two interviews with the Justice Department, investigations by various government agencies, and eventually the Senate confirmation hearings had all gone smoothly. No one had voiced doubt about my qualifications or otherwise objected to my appointment. But I was still just one piece on the board among many to be sacrificed or defended in the baroque, unknowable sport that was the biggest game in town and in which procedural delay was a cherished tactic. Through it all, Senator Moynihan was as good as his word, never flagging in his effort or allowing me to give up hope. I tried not to be overly disheartened, but the delay did put me in an awkward limbo at work. I was trying to make a graceful if protracted exit, wrapping up business with clients and making the appropriate handoffs to colleagues, but there was no clear end in sight. I can be patient but not idle, and I still needed to earn a living.

Meanwhile, I would become aware of a chorus of voices rising in my support. The Hispanic National Bar Association lobbied the White House steadily and rallied grassroots support from other Latino organizations. If confirmed, I would be the first Hispanic federal judge in the state's history, a milestone the community ardently wished to achieve (José Cabranes had very nearly claimed the honor in 1979 but was simultaneously nominated for a judgeship in Connecticut and chose to serve there instead, though much later he would take a New York seat on the Second Circuit Court of Appeals). Even before Senator Moynihan had settled on my name for the nomination, a veritable *This Is Your Life* cast of backers came forward: my fellow board members at PRLDEF, Bob Morgenthau and others at the DA's Office, Father O'Hare and colleagues on the Campaign Finance Board, lawyers I'd known through mutual clients. They wrote letters, made phone calls, and volunteered to make the sorts of informal appeals to colleagues that can be persuasive when echoing from many sides. I was astonished to see all the circles of my life telescoping on this one goal of mine, making it seem all the more as if everything until now had been a prelude to this moment.

Finally, on August 12, 1992, the U.S. Senate confirmed my nomination to the District Court for the Southern District of New York, the mother court, the oldest district court in the nation. The public induction ceremony followed in October. Though brief — perhaps all of five minutes — it was far from perfunctory. Every moment of it

541

moved me deeply: donning the black robe, swearing solemnly to administer justice without respect to persons, equally to the poor and the rich, and to perform my duties under the Constitution faithfully and impartially. So help me God. I took, for that occasion only, the traditional newcomer's seat between the chief judge, Charles Brieant, and Judge Constance Baker Motley, the next most senior of the estimable colleagues I was joining. Such ritual was profoundly humbling, signaling as it did the paramount importance of the judiciary as an institution, above the significance of any individual, beyond the ups and downs of history. Whatever I had accomplished to arrive at this point, the role I was about to assume was vastly more important than I was.

The sense of having vaulted into an alternative reality was compounded by no less disorienting changes in my personal life. I moved to Manhattan, because I needed to live within the area of my jurisdiction. Dawn was appalled that I would shatter our neighborhood idyll on account of some minor rule, frequently bent. I feared she would never forgive me for abandoning her in Brooklyn, but for me there was a deep sense of honor at stake. I was becoming a judge! How could I not follow the rules? I don't claim to be flawless. I'm a New Yorker, and I jaywalk with the best of them. On more than one occasion I may have broken the speed limit. But at that moment in my life, my deep and rational respect for the law as the structure upholding our civilized society was tinted with a rosy glow of irrational emotion. I felt a sense of awe for the responsibility I was assuming, and my determination to show it respect trumped even my loyalty to a wonderful neighborhood and the close company of dear friends.

My mother meanwhile had plans of her own. In what seemed a flight of wild impetuousness, more in keeping with the Celina who'd run off to join the army than the mother I'd known, she decided to move to Florida, leaving me to feel once more, perhaps irrationally for an adult and now a judge, the sting of her abandonment. She and Omar had gone there on vacation the Monday after my induction, and the next thing I knew, Mami was on the phone, telling me in a giddy voice that she'd rented an apartment.

Within days of their return to New York, the apartment in Co-op City was packed up. When the cartons were removed, I stood with Mami in the empty apartment, our voices bouncing off the scuffed walls, the hollowness echoing with so many years, amid a confluence of our tears and memories. We hugged, and then it was good-bye, Mami and Omar driving away.

Before they even reached Florida, I got a phone call from Puerto Rico: Titi Aurora had died. She had gone there to move her husband to a nursing home — the second husband, who was even crazier than the first and who'd entangled her already hard life into still further knots of sadness and exhausting labor. This was not news I could break to Mami over the phone. I needed to get on the next flight to Miami and be with her when she heard it. Titi had fought bitterly with Mami over the move to Florida. They squabbled often over all sorts of small things, but this had become a much deeper rift. To learn that death had cut off any possibility of reconciliation would, I well knew, cause Mami unbearable pain.

I marveled at how two such very different women could live so tightly bound to each other. Affection was not part of the recipe, nor was any emotional expression beyond their habit of snapping at each other. There was no confiding of secrets, no sharing of comfort visible to others. A lesson would emerge for me from their strange sisterhood: the persistence or failure of human relationships cannot be predicted by any set of objective or universal criteria. We are all limited, highly imperfect beings, worthy in some dimensions, deficient in others, and if we would understand how any of our connections survive, we would do well to look first to what is good in each of us. Titi could be disagreeable because her life had been harsh, but she lived it honorably, firmly grounded on a rock-solid foundation of personal ethics that I deeply admired. For her part, Mami, though more compassionate with strangers, brought to this relationship gratitude beyond measure for mercy shown in hardship a very long time ago. It was a gratitude time hadn't faded, and that too I deeply admired.

I rented a car at the airport and arrived at the unfamiliar apartment complex very late at night after getting lost, driving in tearful circles. My mother must have phoned Junior before I arrived; however it happened, when she opened the door, it was clear that the news had already reached her. She fell into my arms sobbing.

We traveled together to Puerto Rico to bury Titi Aurora. I didn't break down until I was handed the envelope of cash that she had set aside with my name on it. We'd kept the old ritual: whenever she was going to Puerto Rico, I would lend her the money for the plane ticket. In recent years, I desperately wanted to give her the money, considering I could now afford it and she was living on Social Security. But she wouldn't have it: if she simply accepted the cash as a gift, she could never ask for it again, as, of course, she would surely need to.

Back in New York, I helped sort out the few wisps of a material life that Titi had left behind. There was precious little for someone known to us as a pack rat. Most of what remained was a closetful of gifts that she couldn't bear to part with or to use.

"What are you so scared of?" Theresa asked. "What could possibly go wrong?" She had come with me from Pavia & Harcourt, her reassuring presence in chambers perhaps the only thing keeping me tethered to any semblance of sanity. My first month as a judge I was terrified, in keeping with the usual pattern of self-doubt and ferocious compensatory effort that has always attended any major transition in my life. I wasn't scared of the work. Twelve-hour days, seven-day weeks, were normal for me. It was my own courtroom that scared me.

The very thought of taking my seat on the bench induced a metaphysical panic. I still couldn't believe this had worked out as dreamed, and I felt myself almost an impostor meeting my fate so brazenly.

At first, I worked around my anxiety by scheduling every single conference in my chambers. Until a case actually came to trial, I could skirt the problem. Finally, there came before me a case involving the forfeiture of the Hells Angels clubhouse in Alphabet City, and the marshals in charge of security drew the line. I could not meet with this bunch except in open court.

"All rise." The trembling would pass in a minute or two, I told myself, just as it always had since the first time I'd mounted the pulpit at Blessed Sacrament. But when I sat down, I noticed that my knees were still knocking together. I could hear the sound and wondered in complete mortification whether the microphone set in front of me on the table was picking it up. I was listening to the lawyers too, of course, as the telltale tapping under the table continued, a disembodied nuisance and reproach. Then a first question for the litigants occurred to me, and as I jumped in, I forgot about my knees, finding nothing in the world more interesting than the matter before me right then. The panic had passed; I had found my way into the moment, and I could now be sure I always would. Afterward, back in the robing room, I confessed my satisfaction: "Theresa, I think this fish has found her pond."

Epilogue

Looking back today, it seems a lifetime ago that I first arrived at a place of belonging and purpose, the sense of having heard a call and answered it. When I placed my hand on the Bible, taking the oath of office to become a district court judge, the ceremony marked the culmination of one journey of growth and understanding but also the beginning of another. The second journey, made while I've been a judge, nevertheless continues in the same small, steady steps in which I'd taken the first one, those that I know to be still my own best way of moving forward. It continues, as well, in the same embrace of my many families, whose vital practical support has been bestowed as a token of something much deeper.

With each of my own small, steady steps, I have seen myself grow stronger and equal to a challenge greater than the last. When, after six years on the district court, I was nominated to the Second Circuit Court of Appeals, and to the Supreme Court twelve years after that, the confirmation hearings would be, at each step, successively more difficult, the attacks more personal, the entire process faster, more brutally intense. But at each step, too, the numbers of family and community encircling me and coming to my defense would be exponentially greater.

Over a thousand people would attend my induction ceremony for the Second Circuit. A more intimate group of over three hundred friends and family stayed on to celebrate that occasion and to witness my very first official act as a judge of the Second Circuit, performed that very night: marrying Mami and Omar. Combining the festivities not only doubled the joy, making the party even livelier, but also permitted me to honor those closest to me and acknowledge a debt to them — to Mami especially — for their part in what I'd become. My awareness of that debt would not be felt so keenly again for years, until the moment when I unexpectedly saw Junior's face on the big television screen, crying his tears of joy at my nomination to the Supreme Court; the searing tears that image drew from my own eyes in turn would leave no doubt about how much the love of family has sustained me.

Just as I had to learn to think like a lawyer, I would have to teach myself to think like a judge. In my small, steady steps I have mastered the conceptual tools of a trial judge wrestling with fact and precedent and of an appellate judge dealing with the theory of law on a more abstract level. I have been a happy sponge, soaking up whatever lessons I could learn from mentors generous with time and spirit. I have been thrilled by the learning that came from the opportunities I've had to teach and the energy drawn from interaction with my law clerks and the freewheeling exchange of ideas I have nurtured in my chambers. Now my education continues on the Supreme Court as I reckon with the particular demands of its finality of review. Almost daily, people ask me what I hope my legacy will be, as if the story were winding down, when really it has just begun. I can only reply that if I were to determine in advance the character of my jurisprudence, mine would be a far more blinkered and unworthy legacy than I hope. My highest aspiration for my work on the

Court is to grow in understanding beyond what I can foresee, beyond any borders visible from this vantage.

In this connection, one memory from high school days comes to mind. During my junior year, I was chosen to attend a conference of girls from Catholic schools all over the city. Over a weekend of discussions on religious and social issues, I found myself sparring again and again with one individual, a Hispanic girl who identified herself as a Marxist. I remember her wearing an impressive Afro of the sort I had seen before only on television; nothing so radical ever appeared in the halls of Cardinal Spellman High School.

The two of us were engaging with far more energy than anyone else at the table, a vigor that, for my part at least, derived not from the certainty of my convictions but from my love of the push and pull of ideas, the pleasure of flexing the rhetorical muscles I had been building in Forensics Club, and an eagerness to learn from the exchange. I argued, as I would so often with lawyers years later, not from a set position but by way of exploring ideas and testing them against whatever challenge might be offered. I love the heat of thoughtful conversation, and I don't judge a person's character by the outcome of a sporting verbal exchange, let alone his or her reasoned opinions. But in my opponent's responses I sensed an animosity that over the course of the weekend only grew. After the final roundup session, at which we reflected on our experience of the meeting, I told her that I had very much enjoyed our conversation, and I asked her what had inspired the hostility that I sensed from her.

"It's because you can't just take a stand," she said, looking at me with such earnest disdain that it startled me. "Everything depends on context with you. If you are always open to persuasion, how can anybody predict your position? How can they tell if you're friend or foe? The problem with people like you is you have no principles."

Surely, I thought, what she described was preferable to its opposite. If you held to principle so passionately, so inflexibly, indifferent to the particulars of circumstance — the full range of what human beings, with all their flaws and foibles, might endure or create — if you enthroned principle above even reason, weren't you then abdicating the responsibilities of a thinking person? I said something like that.

Our conversation ended on that unsettled note, but I have spent the rest of my life grappling with her accusation. I have since learned how these considerations are addressed in the more complex language of moral philosophy, but our simple exchange that day raised a point that remains essential to me. There is indeed something deeply wrong with a person who lacks principles, who has no moral core. There are, likewise, certainly values that brook no compromise, and I would count among them integrity, fairness, and the avoidance of cruelty. But I have never accepted the argument that principle is compromised by judging each situation on its own merits, with due appreciation of the idiosyncrasy of human motivation and fallibility. Concern for individuals, the imperative of treating them with dignity and respect for their ideas and needs, regardless of one's own views — these too are surely principles and as worthy as any of being deemed inviolable. To remain open to understandings — perhaps even to principles — as yet not determined is the least that learning requires, its barest threshold.

With every friend I've known, in every situation I've encountered, I have found something to learn. From a task as simple as boiling water, you can learn a worthwhile lesson. There is no experience that can't avail something useful, be it only the discipline to manage adversity. With luck, there will be plenty of time ahead for me to continue growing and learning, many more stories to tell before I can begin to say definitively who I am as a judge.

Who I am as a human being will, I hope, continue to evolve as well, but perhaps the essence is defined by now. The moment when, in accordance with tradition, I sat in Chief Justice John Marshall's chair and placed my hand on the Bible to take the oath of office for the Supreme Court, I felt as if an electric current were coursing through me, and my whole life, collapsing upon that moment, could be read in the faces of those most dear to me who filled that beautiful room. I looked out to see my mother with tears streaming down her cheeks and felt a surge of admiration for this remarkable woman who had instilled in me the values that came naturally to her — compassion, hard work, and courage to face the unknown — but who'd also grown with me as we took our small steps together to close the distance that had opened up between us in the early years. I might have been little Mercedes as a child, but now I was equally my mother's daughter. I saw Junior beaming proudly, and my family who traveled from New York and Puerto Rico to be there, and so many friends who have stood by me through the years. The moment belonged as much to them as to me.

I sensed the presence too, almost visible, of those who had recently passed: my friend Elaine, who had suffered a series of strokes but to the very end managed to leaven both her own dying and the drama surrounding my nomination with her humor; Dave Botwinik, who had set this whole dream in motion toward reality.

Then I caught the eye of the president sitting in the first row and felt gratitude bursting inside me, an overwhelming gratitude unrelated to politics or position, a gratitude alive with Abuelita's joy and with a sudden memory, an image seen through the eyes of a child: I was running back to the house in Mayagüez with a melting ice cone we called a *piragua* running sweet and sticky down my face and arms, the sun in my eyes, breaking through clouds and glinting off the rain-soaked pavement and dripping leaves. I was running with joy, an overwhelming joy that arose simply from gratitude for the fact of being alive. Along with the image, memory carried these words from a child's mind through time: I am blessed. In this life I am truly blessed.

ACKNOWLEDGMENTS

Before thanking the people who helped me with this book, I must thank the inordinately large number of friends and family, mentors and colleagues, who have made significant contributions to my life, without whom there might be no reason for a book. Even acquaintances and strangers have made lasting impressions. Just as I was unable to include in these pages many of my experiences and people who have played a part in my life, I cannot acknowledge all of you here by name. To those who have shared important parts of my life, know you are deeply valued even if you or those experiences are not mentioned.

There are many who helped me in the writing of this book by sharing memories or gathering information. If I do not acknowledge you here, it is because your importance in my life and my gratitude to you has already been made clear to the reader. Others who are vitally important to me today are not mentioned because you entered my life after I first became a judge, where this book ends.

I do want to give special thanks to a number of friends not included in the book who have been directly instrumental in the process of its creation and publication.

Given the demands of my day job, this book would not have been possible without the collaboration of Zara Houshmand. Zara, a most talented writer herself, listened to my endless stories and those of my families and friends, and helped choose those that in retelling would paint the most authentic picture of my life experiences. Zara, you are an incredible person with a special ability to help others understand and express themselves better; I am deeply indebted to your assistance. One of the most profound treasures of this process has been the gift of your friendship, which will last a lifetime.

I am truly grateful for the contributions of my editor at Alfred A. Knopf, George Andreou, in helping make my stories come alive. George's deft editorial touch added much, but he also expertly guided me through the publishing process. I am enormously grateful as well to Sonny Mehta, the publisher of Knopf, who has treated me with much kindness and attention. Everyone at Knopf with whom I have met and worked, and everyone at Random House, Inc., Knopf's parent, has extended assistance with professional skill and grace. I am appreciative of all of your efforts.

Research related to Puerto Rico, help in reviewing the manuscript, and translation of this book from English to Spanish were particularly important. I am especially indebted to three people for their tireless efforts in this part of the book's development. I can never catalogue all of the work they have volunteered in helping me with this book or the many gifts of love they have given me through the years. I can only say thank you to Xavier Romeu-Matta, a brilliant lawyer who was my law clerk during my first year as a federal district court judge; his wife, the accomplished writer Lyn Di Iorio, professor of English (and unofficial language and literature in Spanish expert) at the City College of New York and CUNY Graduate Center; and Emérida Rivera, who has traveled repeatedly throughout Puerto Rico to help in my research and proven by example that saintly hearts and souls still exist in the world. The Hunter College Center for Puerto Rican Studies also provided invaluable background materials.

559

Thanks are due also to Ligia Pesquera and Ángel Rivera, whose kind hospitality supported our research in Puerto Rico; to Sylvia Gutiérrez, who assisted with travels; and to Lourdes Pérez, who provided background on Puerto Rican poetry.

I am grateful to Amanda Tong, Colin Wright, and Kate Beddall for their help in transcribing and translating interviews, and for the reflections they offered.

Another gift in the process of producing this book has been working with and befriending my book agent, Peter Bernstein, and his wife, Amy Bernstein, of the Bernstein Literary Agency. You both have shepherded this book with consummate professional skill, sage advice, and caring. I thank John S. Siffert of Lankler Siffert & Wohl LLP, and his wife, Goldie Alfasi, for introducing me to Peter and Amy and for being such supportive friends during this process. I also thank John for introducing me to Richard Hofstetter and Mark A. Merriman of Frankfurt Kurnit Klein & Selz, PC, and for their legal and professional advice. John, I am especially grateful for the wise legal counsel you gave me in drafting the book proposal, overseeing the contract negotiations, and reviewing this book. I have three brothers: my birth brother, you, and Robert A. Katzmann. All three of you have supported me through my recent life experiences in ways that cannot be acknowledged here but are inscribed in my heart.

Some friends who are not named in the text shared memories that appear in the book or reviewed the manuscript to offer advice. Each of you is special to me and I acknowledge you here in chronological order of your appearance in my life: Peter Kougasian, with whom I shared experiences at Princeton University, Yale Law School, and the New York County District Attorney's Office; Paula DiPerna, a journalist and author whose book *Juries on Trial: Faces of American Justice* provides an account of the child pornography trial; Cynthia Fischer, the second female partner at Pavia & Harcourt, and David Glasser, an associate then at the firm; Nicole Gordon, founding Executive Director of the New York City Campaign Finance Board; Mari Carmen Aponte, now United States ambassador to El Salvador and then member of the Puerto Rican Legal Defense and Education Fund (now LatinoJustice); Robert Sack, a former colleague on the United States Court of Appeals for the Second Circuit Court; and Jennifer Callahan, documentary film producer and writer.

Lee Llambelis and Ellis Cose, you encouraged me to write this book and guided me in the initial process of thinking about having it published. I give special thanks also to Sue Anderson and Kitty Reese: you pitched in each time I needed help to get things done while I worked on the book. You are all incredible friends. Thank you.

Finally, I thank Ricki Seidman, whom I worked with during my Supreme Court confirmation process and who has become a precious friend. Ricki tirelessly reviewed multiple revisions of this book and offered thoughtful suggestions that have improved it immeasurably.

A life filled with loving and caring family and friends such as mine is truly blessed.

GLOSSARY

abuelita: grandma
aguinaldo: here, Christmas folk song
ají: pepper; hot pepper
arroz con gandules: rice and pigeon peas

Bendición, Abuelita: Bless me, Grandma;
   blessing
bisabuela: great-grandmother
brujería: witchcraft
burla: mockery

café con leche: coffee with milk
chiflado: literally, crazy, a looney, and used
   to translate for "stooge" in the title and
   show *The Three Stooges*
china: orange, as in the fruit
chuletas: pork chops
como una maldición: like a curse

Dame un cigarrillo: Give me a cigarette
despedida: farewell

Dios te salve, María, llena eres de gracia: El Señor es contigo. Bendito tú eres entre todas las mujeres y bendito es el fruto de tu vientre: Jesús. Santa María, Madre de Dios, ruega por nosotros pecadores, ahora y en la hora de nuestra muerte . . .

Hail Mary, full of grace: The Lord is with thee. Blessed art thou among all women and blessed is the fruit of your womb: Jesus. Holy Mary, mother of God, pray for us sinners, now and in the hour of our death . . .

(from the Roman Catholic
"Hail Mary" prayer)

el jurutungo viejo: the boondocks; the end of the world

el luto: mourning

embusteros: liars

"En Mi Viejo San Juan": "In My Old San Juan." A bolero written by Puerto Rican composer Noel Estrada in 1943. It is considered by many Puerto Ricans to be a kind of unofficial anthem. It enshrines the narrator's desire to go back to his longed-for city by the sea, and the melancholy realization that this will never happen.

Es el precio de hacer negocios: It's the price of doing business

espera: wait

espiritismo: Spiritism

¡Estás loca!: You're crazy!

Feliz Navidad: Merry Christmas

fiambreras: lidded, stackable dinner pails made of iron or other metal; also, the food that is made elsewhere and delivered in these pails

ficha: a playing piece; usually refers to dominoes

flamboyán: flamboyant; also known in the anglophone Caribbean as the flame tree or the Royal Poinciana

grosella: a small acidic yellow or red berry that grows in backyards, or wild, in Puerto Rico; sometimes known as an Otaheite gooseberry

guagua: bus

güiro: musical instrument made from an elongated, hollowed-out gourd with notches on one side, played by rubbing a stick with tines along the notches

jíbaro: the straw-hatted peasant farmer or laborer who plays a significant role in Puerto Rican culture and identity; the values attributed to this almost mythical figure are being traditional, hardworking,

la nata: cream; also, the skin on milk
la tetita: the tit; here, to denote the crunchy end of a loaf of Puerto Rican *criollo* bread
lechón asado: roasted pig

Mercedes chiquita: little Mercedes
merienda: midday meal; light lunch; snack
mi'jita: my dear; honey

Nacimiento: Nativity scene
nena: girl
¡No me molestes!: Don't bother me!
No tengas miedo: Don't be afraid

para: here, stop
picadillo: seasoned ground beef

Que Dios te bendiga, te favorezca, y te libre de todo mal y peligro: May God bless you, favor you, and deliver you from all evil and danger
¡Qué guapo!: He's so handsome!
¿Quieres una china?: Do you want an orange?
quinqué: country-style oil lamp
recao: an herb also known as *culantro,* or Thai parsley, which is one of the basic ingredients of the spice mixture known as

sofrito used in so many Puerto Rican recipes

rosario: rosary

santos: saints; here, statues of saints

sebo de flande: mutton tallow used as a folk remedy for bruises and cuts

sofrito: seasoning sauce made of tomatoes, chopped peppers, onions, garlic, and *recao* or *culantro*

tamarindo: tamarind

¡Te vas a enfermar!: You'll get sick!

tío: uncle

titi: a term of endearment for *tía,* or aunt

tostones: fried green plantain

¿Tú estás ciego?: Are you blind?

¡Vámonos de parranda!: Let's go out caroling!; let's party!

velada: séance (although in Puerto Rico, the connotation is more often that of vigil, as for a corpse)

vendedor: salesman

vivero: livestock market

Yo soy Celina: I am Celina

A Puerto Rico (Regreso)
To Puerto Rico (I Return)
by José Gautier Benítez
Translated By Lyn Di Iorio

Por fin, corazón, por fin,
alienta con la esperanza,
que entre nubes de carmín
del horizonte al confín,
ya la tierra a ver se alcanza.

Luce la aurora en Oriente
rompiendo pardas neblinas,
y la luz, como un torrente,
se tiende por la ancha frente
de verdísimas colinas.

Ya se va diafanizando
de la mar la espesa bruma;
el buque sigue avanzando,
y va la tierra brotando
como Venus de la espuma.

Y allá sobre el fondo oscuro
que sus montañas le dan,
bajo un cielo hermoso y puro,
cerrada en su blanco muro,
mi bellísimo San Juan.

Y aunque esa ciudad amada,
mis afecciones encierra,
con el alma entusiasmada,
yo no me acuerdo de nada
sino de ver esa tierra.

Perdonadle al desterrado
ese dulce frenesí:
vuelvo a mi mundo adorado,
y yo estoy enamorado
de la tierra en que nací.

Para poder conocerla
es preciso compararla,
de lejos en sueños verla;
y para saber quererla
es necesario dejarla.

¡Oh! no envidie tu belleza,
de otra inmensa población
el poder y la riqueza,
que allí vive la cabeza,
y aquí vive el corazón.

Y si vivir es sentir,
y si vivir es pensar,
yo puedo, patria, decir
que no he dejado vivir
al dejarte de mirar.

Que aunque es templado y suave
no vive, no, en el ambiente
el pez de las ondas nave,
ni entre las ondas el ave,
ni yo, de mi patria ausente.

¡Patria! jardín del mar,
la perla de las Antillas,
¡tengo ganas de llorar!
¡tengo ganas de besar
la arena de tus orillas!

Si entre lágrimas te canto,
patria mía, no te asombres,
porque es de amor ese llanto,
y ese amor es el más santo
de los amores del hombre.

Tuya es la vida que aliento,
es tuya mi inspiración,
es tuyo mi pensamiento,
tuyo todo sentimiento
que brote en mi corazón.

Que haya en ti vida primero,
cuanto ha de fijarse en mí,
y en todo cuanto venero,
y en todo cuanto yo quiero,
hay algo, patria, de ti.

No, nada importa la suerte
si tengo que abandonarte,
que yo sólo aspiro a verte,
a la dicha de quererte
y a la gloria de cantarte.

. . .

At last, my heart, at last,
come alive with hope,
for among crimson clouds
from the horizon end to end,
I can already see land.

Dawn rises in the East
shattering dark mists,
and a torrent of light pours
on the wide swath
of the deep green hills.

The veil of thick fog lifts
off the sea;
the ship advances,

and the land begins to rise
like Venus from the foam.

And there on the dark ground
of its mountains,
against a pure and lovely sky,
enclosed by a white wall,
my beautiful San Juan.

And as a cherished city,
it holds all my loves,
and with an enthusiastic soul,
I don't recall
anything except seeing my homeland.

Forgive the exile
this sweet frenzy:
I return to my beloved world,
in love with the land where I was born.

To know her
you must compare her,
see her distant in your dreams;
and to love her
you need to leave her.

Ah! Do not let your beauty envy
the wealth and power
of another great nation,

because there is where the head lives,
and here is where the heart lives.

And if to live is to feel,
and if to live is to think,
homeland, I can say
that I have not known how to live
since I stopped looking at you.

Though its climate be temperate and soft,
the seafaring fish cannot live in the air,
nor in waves can a bird soar,
nor can I thrive
away from my homeland.

Homeland! Garden of the sea,
pearl of the Antilles,
I feel like crying!
I feel like kissing
the sands of your shores!

If between tears I sing to you,
my land, do not be astonished,
because love is in these tears,
and this love is the holiest
of the loves of man.

Yours is the life that I breathe,
my inspiration is yours,
yours is my thought,

yours all feeling
that blooms in my heart.

My life flows from yours,
and in everything I deem worthy,
and in everything I love,
there is something, my homeland,
that belongs to you.

No, luck doesn't matter
if I have to leave you,
for I aspire only to see you,
to the good fortune of loving you
and the glory of singing to you.

ABOUT THE AUTHOR

Sonia Sotomayor graduated summa cum laude from Princeton in 1976 and from Yale Law School in 1979. She worked as assistant district attorney in New York County and then at the law firm of Pavia & Harcourt. From 1992 to 1998, she served as a judge of the U.S. District Court, Southern District of New York, and from 1998 to 2009 on the United States Court of Appeals for the Second Circuit. In May 2009, President Barack Obama nominated her as an Associate Justice of the Supreme Court; she assumed this role on August 8, 2009.

CPSIA information can be obtained
at www.ICGtesting.com
Printed in the USA
FFOW04n0600200314
4398FF

Introduction

The roots of research utilization can be traced back to the time of Florence Nightingale in the mid-1800s. Over the past 150 years, nursing research has encompassed a variety of models, settings, and foci. The following historical perspective illustrates the trajectory of nursing research.

Historical Perspective

Evolution from Nightingale to Present Time

Florence Nightingale's work on sanitation in the 1800s was one of the early efforts at linking environmental variables to clinical outcomes. In the early 1900s, the focal point of nursing research was on nursing education. In the 1940s, the concentration shifted to the availability and demand for nurses in time of war. A major milestone occurred in 1952 when the first edition of the journal *Nursing Research* was published. In the 1970s, clinical outcomes again reemerged as a focus for nursing research, and the *Nursing Studies Index* by Virginia Henderson was produced. Today, through evidence-based practice (EBP), the focus is on the application of research findings to clinical decision making in an effort to improve individual patient outcomes.

? Think Outside the Box

Explore the various approaches used to generate knowledge in your practice area. For example, which information has been used to determine the method of catheterizing a laboring mother? Which information serves as the basis for the range of blood sugars used in elderly patients who are newly diagnosed with diabetes?

Florence Nightingale's *Notes on Matters Affecting the Health, Efficiency and Hospital Administration of the British Army* (1858) was one of the first published works that outlined the clinical application of nursing research (Florence Nightingale Museum Trust, 2003; Riddle, 2005). Florence Nightingale created a polar-area diagram (or coxcomb) to display data related to the causes of mortality in the British Army during the Crimean War (**Figure 3-1**). This early pie chart used color graphics to depict deaths secondary to preventable disease, war injuries, and all other causes. Using these data, Nightingale calculated the mortality rate for contagious diseases such as cholera and typhus. Her statistical analysis demonstrated the need for sanitary reform in military hospitals.

Think Outside the Box
Students can work on these critical thinking assignments individually or in a group while reading through the text. Students can delve deeper into concepts by completing these exercises online.

Multiple Choice Questions
Review key concepts from each chapter with these questions at the end of each chapter. Questions can also be found within the text's online resources, where students can submit their answers and instantly review their results.

Multiple Choice Questions

1. When developing a nursing research project, why is it important to remember the ethical constraints?
   A. The study will not be approved by the institutional review board without these constraints.
   B. The protection of human subjects underlies all human research projects.
   C. The results will not be trustworthy and replicable.
   D. The nurse researcher will not be able to get funding for the project and, therefore, will not be able to complete the project.

2. The atrocities performed on prisoners in Nazi Germany violated which ethical principles?
   A. Value of life, justice, and respect
   B. Beneficence, nonmaleficence, and value of life
   C. Autonomy, nonmaleficence, and respect
   D. Justice, autonomy, and nonmaleficence

3. Protection of vulnerable individuals is a critical ethical component in human research studies. How did Edward Jenner fail to meet this standard when he tested swinepox on his 1-year-old son?
   A. He thought the new knowledge overrode any concern he should have for the rights of his son.
   B. He did not know any better.
   C. He ignored the point that he could not get informed consent from his son, who was particularly vulnerable.
   D. Give that smallpox was such a lethal disease at that time, it was better for Jenner to ignore his son's vulnerability so to gain new knowledge.

4. The Tuskegee Syphilis Study lasted many years, and none of the human subjects were properly informed about the study's conduct. Which ethical principle was egregiously ignored in this study?
   A. Autonomy
   B. Respect
   C. Nonmaleficence
   D. Justice

5. Why does an ethical research environment assist with ensuring scientific integrity?
   A. Within this environment, expectations for scientific integrity are laid out.
   B. Federal regulations related to ethical standards are adhered to, increasing the likelihood of integrity.
   C. The researcher always works within an ethical environment, which encourages the practice of ethical research behaviors.
   D. Scientific integrity ensures funding, which means that the study will be completed.

Discussion Questions

Students can use these assignments to apply information in the text to everyday practice. Discussion questions are included in the text's online resources.

Discussion Questions

1. You are the nurse manager of a perinatal care unit. You have read a phenomenology research report on the positive effects of music on the labor and delivery process for mothers. Consider the following: The study is one of many of this type with similar findings, there were five informants in the study, and the researcher did not provide a discussion of reliability and validity in the write-up. Will you use this study to support the practice of ensuring that all labor and delivery rooms are equipped to play music throughout the labor and delivery process? Support your answer.

2. You are the charge nurse on a medical–surgical floor. After reading several qualitative research reports on pet therapy, you approach your nurse manager about the possibility of implementing a pet therapy program on your floor. Your nurse manager states that no changes should be made based on qualitative research, because the sample sizes are always too small. What is your best response?

3. You are reading a research report about a long-term care facility. The researcher describes in detail the demographics of administration, staff, and clients. There is a lengthy discussion about how problems are solved in the facility, how various departments communicate, and how the facility values family involvement in client care. Which type of qualitative study does this represent? Support your answer.

4. A nurse on the labor and delivery unit wants to study the effects of having small children participate with the family in the delivery process on the bonding process between mother and child. For this study, the nurse has determined that a questionnaire will be mailed out to families who elect to have their toddlers in the delivery room during the delivery of a sibling. The questionnaire will include both open-ended questions and closed-ended (Likert-type) questions. Which aspects of the study should be considered to provide a rationale for selecting this mixed method strategy?

5. A researcher working within a hospital striving to gain Magnet status wants to study the barriers to use of research at the bedside. For the design of this study, the individual is considering using a mixed method format. Which pieces of the design should be considered as the researcher prepares the study?

6. A group of researchers has developed a new instrument to assess the degree of destruction noted within decubitus ulcers (pressure ulcers). As part of their study, they are planning to compare the new instrument with instruments currently used within their acute care setting. Which components of the mixed method strategies need to be carefully considered as the researchers develop the study design?

Third Edition

INTRODUCTION TO NURSING RESEARCH

Incorporating Evidence-Based Practice

Edited by

Carol Boswell, EdD, RN, CNE, ANEF
Professor
Texas Tech University
Odessa, Texas

Sharon Cannon, EdD, RN, ANEF
Regional Dean and Professor
Texas Tech University
Odessa, Texas

JONES & BARTLETT
LEARNING

World Headquarters
Jones & Bartlett Learning
5 Wall Street
Burlington, MA 01803
978-443-5000
info@jblearning.com
www.jblearning.com

Jones & Bartlett Learning books and products are available through most bookstores and online booksellers. To contact Jones & Bartlett Learning directly, call 800-832-0034, fax 978-443-8000, or visit our website, www.jblearning.com.

Substantial discounts on bulk quantities of Jones & Bartlett Learning publications are available to corporations, professional associations, and other qualified organizations. For details and specific discount information, contact the special sales department at Jones & Bartlett Learning via the above contact information or send an email to specialsales@jblearning.com.

Introduction to Nursing Research: Incorporating Evidence-Based Practice, Third Edition is an independent publication and has not been authorized, sponsored, or otherwise approved by the owners of the trademarks or service marks referenced in this product.

The authors, editors, and publisher have made every effort to provide accurate information. However, they are not responsible for errors, omissions, or for any outcomes related to the use of the contents of this book and take no responsibility for the use of the products and procedures described. Treatments and side effects described in this book may not be applicable to all people; likewise, some people may require a dose or experience a side effect that is not described herein. Drugs and medical devices are discussed that may have limited availability controlled by the Food and Drug Administration (FDA) for use only in a research study or clinical trial. Research, clinical practice, and government regulations often change the accepted standard in this field. When consideration is being given to use of any drug in the clinical setting, the health care provider or reader is responsible for determining FDA status of the drug, reading the package insert, and reviewing prescribing information for the most up-to-date recommendations on dose, precautions, and contraindications, and determining the appropriate usage for the product. This is especially important in the case of drugs that are new or seldom used.

Production Credits
Publisher: Kevin Sullivan
Acquisitions Editor: Amanda Harvey
Editorial Assistant: Rebecca Myrick
Production Manager: Carolyn Rogers Pershouse
Marketing Communications Manager: Katie Hennessy
V.P., Manufacturing and Inventory Control: Therese Connell
Composition: Circle Graphics, Inc.
Cover Design: Michael O'Donnell
Cover Image: © Joseph/ShutterStock, Inc.
Printing and Binding: Edwards Brothers Malloy
Cover Printing: Edwards Brothers Malloy

To order this product, use ISBN: 978-1-4496-9507-1

Library of Congress Cataloging-in-Publication Data
Boswell, Carol.
  Introduction to nursing research : incorporating evidence-based practice/edited by Carol Boswell, Sharon Cannon. — 3rd ed.
    p. ; cm.
  Includes bibliographical references and index.
  ISBN 978-1-4496-8196-8 (pbk.) — ISBN 978-1-4496-9507-1
  I. Boswell, Carol. II. Cannon, Sharon, 1940– III. Title.
  [DNLM: 1. Nursing Research—methods. 2. Evidence-Based Medicine. WY 20.5]
  610.72—dc23

                                     2012035427

6048
Printed in the United States of America
16 15 14 13   10 9 8 7 6 5 4 3

Contents

Preface

Evidence-based practice has matured into the decisive factor for authenticating quality health care. The concept of evidence-based practice requires the integration of clinical expertise with investigational corroboration from evidence, which includes research. Nurses integrate reliable and sensible evidential knowledge into policies and procedures utilized for the provision of holistic health care. To recognize that a skill or task completed in a particular technique without justifying the process is not sanctioned by the public or by healthcare entities.

Basic research information is presented using evidenced-based research examples. Each of the concepts associated with the research process are covered. In addition, the information concerning the interconnectedness of research, evidence-based practice, and quality improvement is discussed. Another aspect included in this text is the growth and development of understanding what makes up the scope of evidence. This undertaking strives to make the information pertinent and appropriate to nurses working in healthcare venues and who are motivated to engage in evidenced-based practice.

This text represents the challenge to communicate realistic evidence-based practice and research expectations to the nurse who is responsible for the day-to-day management of health care.

The current health arena requires care be sanctioned on a realistic, evidence-based underpinning. Consequently, the nurse must be competent and capable to evaluate and initiate care based on evidence, which includes research findings. The motivation for this edition centers on providing an understanding of preliminary research processes along with an evidence-based practice mind set. The essential techniques of planning, conducting, and reporting research data are portrayed using the context of evidence-based practice. Every facet in the provision of nursing care entails meticulous deliberation and documentation of evidence-based practice and research outcomes for the care provided.

To concentrate on these challenges, this edition was prepared to facilitate the nurse in the management of analyzing the strengths and challenges evident in research projects, quality improvement reports, and manuscripts. By developing knowledge about what reflects strong evidence, nurses can employ appropriate research findings along with other evidence while disregarding inappropriate findings. It was envisioned that this edition would function as the prevailing textbook in research and evidence-based practice courses presented at universities offering baccalaureate nursing programs. The edition also anticipates being practical and constructive for practicing nurses who are engaged in evidenced-based practice.

Acknowledgments

We would like to convey our gratitude and respect for our outstanding coalition of colleagues who so willingly and enthusiastically accepted the undertaking of designated chapters. The significance and usefulness of this book results from the expertise and proficiency of the contributing authors, to whom we are immensely grateful.

We continue to value the first edition reviewers for their conscientious and systematic scrutiny of the chapters, which provided real-life examples in clinical settings and facilitated the focus of the chapter content. From their observations, we were able to preserve the scholarly level of the book. Comments and suggestions provided by the numerous users of the textbook provided insights for inclusion into the second edition and now the third edition. The suggestions and recommendations provided by the end-users have been constructive in helping to keep the original intent of this text intact. Within the third edition, we emphasize that embracing the idea of evidence is imperative to advancing the field of evidence-based practice and nursing research. Recently, we said goodbye to our friend and colleague Mary E. Nunnally. We continue our grateful recognition of Mary, who provided her strong editorial perspective to earlier editions.

Dr. Carol Boswell and Dr. Sharon Cannon

Every once in a while, our lives are enhanced by very special people. One such person is my friend and colleague, Dr. Carol Boswell. Not only is she a kindred spirit, she is also one of my "balcony" people. Many wonderful colleagues and friends have enriched my life through their loyal support and guided me on my evidence-based journey. I have truly been blessed to know them and try each day to pay forward their many kindnesses.

Along with Carol, my family has played a significant part in the shaping of my life. So, I wish to say a special thank you to Carol; my parents G.E. and Laurine Cannon (who are always with me in spirit); my family, especially Joe and Lynn Tischner, and Ryan Ganey; my grandchildren, Kelly Tischner, Andrew Ganey, Shelby Ganey, and Shannon Ganey; and my brother and sister-in-law, Gene and Cathi Cannon.

Dr. Sharon Cannon

As this book moves into the third edition, the individuals who continue to allow me to grow and reach for the stars are Dr. Sharon Cannon—extraordinary colleague and friend; Marc E. Boswell—exceptional husband; Dwight and Wanda Miller—supportive parents; Michael and Casey Boswell, Jeremy Boswell, and Stephanie Boswell—optimistic and constructive children; Matthew Boswell, Kobe Boswell, Kayia Howard, and Caleb Boswell—busy grandchildren. In addition to these magnificent and astonishing individuals who support and challenge me to strive for each and every goal, I want to acknowledge the awesomeness of the colleagues who enter my day-to-day professional and personal life. These individuals provide encouragement and excitement to continue on a journey to expand and develop the knowledge base related to evidence-based practice and nursing research. To never accept normalcy as okay is a valuable and wonderful belief to hold. Without the encouragement and conviction of my family and friends, I would not be able to brave the insanity and foolishness of the world while embracing the reality of what is critical for a person's humanity.

Dr. Carol Boswell

Contributors

Kathaleen C. Bloom, PhD, ARNP, CNM
Associate Professor
School of Nursing
College of Health
University of North Florida
Jacksonville, Florida

James Eldridge, PhD
Associate Professor
University of Texas of the Permian Basin
Odessa, Texas

Dorothy Greene Jackson, PhD, RN, FNP
Assistant Professor
School of Nursing
University of Texas of the Permian Basin
Odessa, Texas

JoAnn Long, PhD, RN, NEA-BC
Associate Professor
Department of Nursing
Lubbock Christian University
Lubbock, Texas

Margaret Robinson, MSN, RN
Retired
Midland, Texas

Jane Sumner, PhD, RN
Associate Professor of Nursing
School of Nursing
Louisiana State University Health Sciences Center
New Orleans, Louisiana

Donna Scott Tilley, PhD, RN, CNE
Associate Professor
College of Nursing
Texas Women's University
Denton, Texas

**Lucy B. Trice, PhD, RN, ARNP,
  FNP-BC**
Professor, Director Emeritus
School of Nursing
College of Health
University of North Florida
Jacksonville, Florida

Chapter 1

Connection Between Research and Evidence-Based Practice

Carol Boswell and Sharon Cannon

Chapter Objectives

At the conclusion of this chapter, the learner will be able to

1. Identify the need for research to validate evidence-based practice
2. Define evidence-based practice
3. Discuss obstacles to evidence-based research
4. Examine the nurse's role in evidence-based practice
5. State how evidence-based practice impacts nursing practice

Key Terms

➤ Evidence-based practice (EBP)
➤ Obstacle
➤ PICOT
➤ Research process
➤ Research utilization

Introduction

Regardless of the specific healthcare setting a nurse may select for practicing the art and science of nursing care, the overarching principle for the practice is the provision of quality nursing care to all clients without consideration of social, financial, cultural, ethnic heritage, or other individual characteristics. As the nurse initiates contact with the client, the client should be confident that the care provided by that nurse is based on the most current, up-to-date health information available. Having established the currency of the health information to be utilized, the nurse and client must also agree that individualized application of this information is necessary. Thus, the need for evidence-based practice (EBP) is confirmed by our expectations related to nursing care.

The nurse who receives the assignment to care for an elderly woman, a young child, or a critically ill husband must come to the nursing practice arena with more than the latest information. The information must be tested and confirmed. To see how this works, let's consider the idea of asthma information, although any disease process could be utilized for this purpose.

Within nursing practice, certain health information concerning the management of asthma is accepted. The initial question that should be asked by a nurse would be: Is this disease management information corroborated by research results? The answer to this question is frequently a negative response. The informational basis for each aspect of the nursing care to be provided should be analyzed to determine its source. Does the information come from general usage, or is it based on information that has been established through research endeavors to be accurate? Having determined the basis for the care to be provided, the nurse must then determine the application of the information based on the individuality of the client situation. The application of the information for each client situation would depend on the specifics of the client's needs, the client's expectations concerning health, and many other aspects requiring modification of the confirmed research application. The foundation of nursing care delivery must be research-tested and research-confirmed knowledge, tempered by an awareness of the unique characteristics of the client and the situation. Although the healthcare field defines "client" and "patient" differently, for purposes of this text these terms are used interchangeably.

Pravikoff, Tanner, and Pierce (2005) describe the process of EBP as including assessing and delineating a problem through verbalization of an identifiable question, pursuing and evaluating the available facts, implementing a practice intervention as a result of the evidence, and evaluating the entire process for effectiveness. Initially, EBP requires the identification of the practice problem, followed by the utilization of tested research results to improve the care provided for the clients. According to Ciliska, Cullum, and Marks (2001), the three fundamental appraisal questions are identical, whether the clinical question concerns treatment, diagnosis, prognosis, or causation:

- Are the outcomes of the study compelling?
- Which outcomes were identified?
- Will the outcomes aid in the management of the patient's care?

It was this need to incorporate proven practices into the provision of health care that fostered the expectations and development of EBP in the current healthcare arena. Bucknall (2007) notes that cognitive approaches, intuition, and analysis of information play key roles in how research is acknowledged, evaluated, and incorporated into the clinical decision-making process that impacts patient outcomes. Clinical decisions are frequently not corroborated by unambiguous, persuasive evidence. Nurses are asked to make real-world decisions with limited information in a fast-paced environment. Time is valuable to the nurse at the bedside, so any course of action has to be both practical and rational (Cannon & Boswell, 2010). This responsibility to make knowledgeable, well-supported decisions based on sound facts emphasizes the need to become effective and efficient at evidence-based practice and research utilization.

Providing a Line of Reasoning for EBP and Evidence-Based Research

Health care is a complex system addressing multiple health-related aspects in an attempt to accomplish the anticipated outcome for the client. Throughout the healthcare arena, nursing care is provided to individuals in need of assistance related to their health status. This attention requires nurses to identify a core foundation of information that reflects quality care. Thus, the need for EBP to be developed around a research-centered foundation was envisioned.

Porter-O'Grady (2006) suggested that the management of EBP requires the use of unique clinical applications based on accessible, up-to-date research. In the quest for quality nursing care, the nurse must use both reliable clinical knowledge and high-quality clinical information. This process of establishing a core foundation of knowledge has been called many things over the years, such as *best practices, evidence-based practice,* and *quality of care.* No matter what the practice is called, the basis for the care to be provided must be grounded in research. According to Melnyk and Fineout-Overholt (2005), "When healthcare providers know how to find, critically appraise, and use the best evidence, and when patients are confident that their healthcare providers are using evidence-based care, optimal outcomes are achieved for all" (p. 3). It is this assurance that the care being provided is confirmed from a tested research foundation that inspires patient confidence in nurses' commitment to quality health care. Nurses should not rely on unsubstantiated treatment plans, but rather must endeavor to critically analyze aspects of the care to be provided to ensure that quality, tested practices are utilized in the provision of nursing care for each individual. Three new developments in health care and nursing have had an impact on the understanding of the importance of EBP and research in nursing in the United States. First, in March 2010, the Patient Protection and Affordable Care Act (PPACA), also known as the Affordable Care Act (ACA), was passed by Congress and signed by President Barack Obama (Mason, Leavitt, & Chaffee, 2012). While the ACA has a primary focus on affordable, accessible care, there is an emphasis to support research effecting safe, quality patient care. Since nurses provide patient-centered care, nurses will increasingly find themselves actively engaged in EBP and research projects.

The second development in 2010 came from the Carnegie Foundation recommendation in the report by Benner, Sutphen, Leonard, and Day (2010) calling for radical transformations of nursing education. Two of their recommendations support the need for nurses to have an education grounded in inquiry and research to provide evidence-based care.

The third development came from the Institute of Medicine (IOM, 2011) and the Robert Wood Johnson Foundation (RWJF) report regarding the future of nursing. This report urged funding for collaborative nursing projects with other healthcare professionals, so that research can involve nurses in developing models of care and solutions to improve health and health care. They identified eight research priorities for nursing practice and nursing education. The priorities for research ranged from delivery models, reimbursement, care trends, nurse residencies and funding for nurses' training.

These three new recommendations require nurses to examine their knowledge, skills and most importantly, their values about EBP and research.

? Think Outside the Box

Make a list of the tasks that are routinely done by nurses during a typical clinical day. Carefully consider what evidence could be used as the foundation for these tasks. Are the skills for the tasks based on research, personal preferences, clinical guidelines, or traditions?

The practicing nurse has to value the idea of the EBP process to facilitate its complete incorporation and implementation. Nurses must understand the value of integrating research results with personal experiences and client values when determining the treatment plan that best addresses a situation's identified challenges. According to the Oncology Nursing Society (2005), even though a healthcare provider may utilize the optimal evidence available, each encounter with an individual continues to be unique. The treatments and outcomes will change based on the uniqueness of the client's values, preferences, interests, and/or diagnoses. According to Fonteyn (2005), "A bonus of nurses' involvement in EBP activities is their improved ability to think critically and their increased understanding of and comfort with research, all of which seems to perpetuate their interest and success in subsequent EBP pursuits" (p. 439). Nurses are taught, encouraged, and expected to think critically. This process of critical thinking corresponds to the use of EBP on clinical units and in primary care settings. Critical thinking embraces the need for health care to be based on a foundation of proven research data and to include the client's perspective. The use of unconfirmed reports, hearsay, and unfounded information, combined with a lack of client input, does not fit with the provision of sound, quality nursing care at this point in time.

Fineout-Overholt and Melnyk (2005) state that "Ongoing onsite and off-site learning opportunities for all providers to hone EBP skills in asking searchable, answerable questions, finding the best available evidence, efficiently appraising research reports, and determining relevance and applicability of evidence [are] essential to cultivating an evidence-based culture" (p. 28). A key element within the effective provision of EBP is the nurse's expertise. Each nurse brings serviceable knowledge to the practice arena. During the process of providing nursing care to a group of individuals, nurses build an underpinning of knowledge on which they draw when delivering future care. This underpinning knowledge base intensifies and expands with each client encounter that the nurse has. Thus, the knowledge base is not stagnant, but rather increases throughout an individual's nursing career.

Jolley (2002) articulated the expectation that practicing nurses should "be able to access, produce, and use different sorts of evidence, including research, to determine best clinical practices" (p. 34). Even if nurses are not actively involved in an actual research project, they must understand the method for accessing published information and assessing it for applicability. Rolston-Blenman (2009) supports this idea by stating that management has "to recognize the hard truth that every system is perfectly designed to achieve exactly the results it gets" (p. 20). We all know that individuals rise to the level to which we expect them to rise: If we set low expectations, that is all they will meet. If we establish challenging expectations, they will strive to attain them. At times, a knowledge base is unconsciously incorporated, because the nurse seems to manage the nursing care without directly acknowledging the underlying foundation. This process grows as the nurse gains experience and expertise.

Research is a methodical examination that uses regimented techniques to resolve questions or decipher dilemmas. The conclusions resulting from this focused chain of examination provide a base upon which to build a practice of care that is centered on tested solutions. According to Omery and Williams (1999), "Research, as a scientific process, with its inherent ability to explain and predict, enhances a practice discipline's ability to anticipate and guide interactions" (p. 50). This anticipation and guidance are related to a discipline's ability to incorporate into practice the sound evidence derived from valid research endeavors. Although EBP goes beyond research results, the foundation for the practice is the grounded knowledge that comes from the research process. This underpinning allows for the safe and effective provision of quality health care. According to Melnyk and Fineout-Overholt (2005), "The gap between the publishing of research evidence and its translation into practice to improve patient care is a cause for concern in healthcare organizations and federal agencies" (p. 4). Moving the use of researched evidence into the actual patient care setting requires that nurses become increasingly familiar and comfortable with the process of critiquing and applying the evidence to the practice arena.

Each of these aspects—thought process, client preferences, research, and nursing expertise—is included in the EBP definition used in this textbook (**Figure 1-1**). Although all of these aspects are required, the actual situation directs the weighting of the aspects, because each situation is unique. Melnyk (2004) acknowledges that a consistent, hard-and-fast weighting of the different pieces—research, patient values, and clinician's expertise—included in EBP is not possible, because the decision-making process is contingent on the situation. In this textbook, **evidence-based practice** (**EBP**) is defined as a process of using confirmed evidence (research and quality improvement), decision making, and nursing expertise to guide the delivery of holistic patient care by nurses. Holistic nursing care encompasses the clinical expertise of the nurse, patient preferences, cultural aspects, psychosocial facets, and biological components. The research process and scientific data generated serve as the foundation on which the decision-making process for nursing care is based.

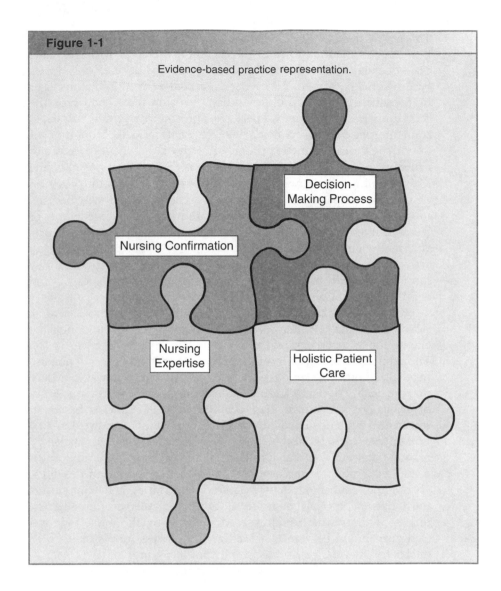

Figure 1-1

Evidence-based practice representation.

Decision-Making Process

Nursing Confirmation

Nursing Expertise

Holistic Patient Care

Assessing the Need for Research in the Practice Arena

According to Davies (2002), "The transfer of research evidence into practice is a complex process and changing provider behavior is a challenge, even when the relative advantages are strong" (p. 558). The nurse is paramount to the success of the EBP process. Each nurse, whether in the acute care, home health, community health, or other healthcare setting, regularly identifies nursing aspects of care.

Those aspects of care may seem to (1) appropriately address the care needs of the client, (2) not fit the current accepted provision of care, or (3) be better addressed via some other method of care. Most nurses have at some point in their practice identified a situation that needs to be reevaluated. Within the day-to-day provision of nursing care, the question arises about why we perform a procedure a certain way when something else seems to work better. It could also be a question of how the care can be better provided to meet the client's needs and expectations. The healthcare community is also encouraging this line of questioning in an effort to identify the best methods for the provision of care. The expectation behind EBP is that everyone will become involved in the identification, examination, and implementation of research-founded health care that can result in the provision of effective, validated client care. Nurses must accept the responsibility of being active in providing quality care to their clients. To do so effectively, they must base the provision of care on results that support the care being administered in a wide variety of healthcare settings.

Cronenwett (2002) has stated that "Evidence for practice mounts slowly over time, as scientists discover first what works in controlled environments and second what works in daily clinical practice" (p. 3). The application of research results in the everyday provision of nursing care takes both time and energy by each and every nurse to ensure that the quality of care is appropriate. All nurses have the responsibility of ensuring that the care they provide to their clients is based on sound nursing knowledge, not just "the way we have always done it." Cronenwett (2002) has further identified the need to challenge clinical community partners to become increasingly involved upfront in the recognition of the problem and the development of the intervention, which includes new research opportunities. Practicing nurses must become actively engaged at multiple levels of the different phases of the research endeavor. At each phase, the nurse's clinical expertise should be readily valued as the process moves forward to establish the evidence for use in the clinical setting.

According to the Agency for Healthcare Research and Quality (AHRQ, 2000), outcomes research is a growing expectation within health care. The provision of quality health practices requires that individuals "seek to understand the end results of particular healthcare practices and interventions" (AHRQ, 2000, para. 1). Outcomes research is viewed as a mechanism for determining which quality care is possible and how to get to that point of quality care for the patient. The linkage of outcomes experienced with the care expected empowers research to cultivate improved channels for monitoring and improving the quality of care provided within the healthcare arena. Translational research is an endeavor that seeks to move the evidence that has been collected by effective research projects into the actual provision of health care. Nurses at the bedside must become champions for the inclusion of timely, documented, substantiated results into the active provision of health care to benefit clients confronted with the health issues.

Titler, Everett, and Adams (2007) discuss the notion of implementation science as "the investigation of methods, interventions, and variables that influence adoption of evidence-based healthcare practices by individuals and organizations to improve clinical and operational decision making and including testing the effectiveness of interventions to promote and sustain use of evidence-based healthcare practices" (p. S53). It is through the use of concepts such as implementation science that research utilization, evidence-based practice, and research are coming together for the improvement of healthcare delivery. As nurses learn to appreciate the importance of investigating the different routines, interventions, and obstacles within the provision of quality care, innovative and tested systems of healthcare delivery and skills will become increasingly available and accepted. According to Malloch and Porter-O'Grady (2006), "The goal of a research course is to introduce nursing students to the basics of the scientific approach of research in the belief that they will be able to use the information produced to provide guidance to their nursing practice upon graduation" (p. 75). The idea behind clarifying the process of research is to enable practicing nurses to utilize the scientific thought process to validate and augment the nursing care provided to clients. The entire process of critiquing research articles and conducting research projects is designed to strengthen the nursing professional's critical thinking abilities, thereby allowing for the delivery of the most holistic care possible in the work environment. Malloch and Porter-O'Grady (2006) note that the critical skill required for effective EBP is the ability of nursing professionals to analytically examine research results and evidence to determine the optimal data to use in the provision of holistic health care on a day-to-day basis. Without this foundation, which enables them to methodically examine the evidence, nurses are left to vacillate among varying interpretations of healthcare information. As mentioned earlier, the ACA, IOM/RWJF and Carnegie Foundation reports of 2010 leave no room for nurses to ignore the need for research in the practice arena. Having defined research and established the need for research, an examination of EBP is in order.

? Think Outside the Box

Look at the different definitions for evidence-based practice. How do you see patient preferences meshing with research utilization?

Exploring EBP in Light of Research

Definitions of EBP

Many different definitions of EBP exist, and each definition tends to add another dimension to the concept of EBP. Each different dimension should be carefully and thoroughly considered as EBP is implemented, to ensure that actual nursing practice is comprehensive. Within each definition, however, certain aspects are consistently identified. The consistent and unique aspects can be visualized as shown in **Table 1-1**.

Melnyk and Fineout-Overholt (2005) conceptualize EBP as a method that allows healthcare providers to deliver the maximum quality of care when addressing the multifaceted requests of their patients and families. In another article by Melnyk (2003), EBP is defined as "a problem solving approach to clinical decision making that incorporates a search for the best and latest evidence, clinical expertise and assessment, and patient preference and values within a context of caring" (p. 149). Both of these definitions reflect the use of problem solving with clinical involvement and patient contribution.

Rutledge and Grant (2002) define EBP as "care that integrates best scientific evidence with clinical expertise, knowledge of pathophysiology, knowledge of psychosocial issues, and decision making preferences of patients" (p. 1). This definition incorporates the ideas of pathophysiology and psychosocial components into the mix.

According to Porter-O'Grady (2006), "Evidence-based practice is simply the integration of the best possible research to evidence with clinical expertise and with patient needs. Patient needs in this case refer specifically to the expectations, concerns, and requirements that patients bring to their clinical experience" (p. 1). This definition tends to further emphasize the importance of the patient within the entire process.

Burns and Grove (2009) define EBP as "conscientious integration of best research evidence with clinical expertise and patient values and needs in the delivery of quality, cost-effective health care" (p. 699). Consequently, these authors integrate the idea of cost-effectiveness as an additional consideration when determining the appropriate EBP components.

Magee (2005) defines evidence-based medicine as "the conscientious, explicit, and judicious use of current best evidence in making decisions about the care of individual patients" (p. 73). The entire focus of this definition is evidence-based medicine. It is directed toward physician care, not nursing care.

Another definition submitted by Pravikoff et al. (2005) for EBP is "a systematic approach to problem solving for healthcare providers, including RNs, characterized by the use of the best evidence currently

Table 1-1

Comparison of Qualities Included in Evidence-Based Practice Definitions

Author (Year)	Quality of Care	Multifaceted	Decision-Making Process	Clinical Focus	Foundation of Practice	Client Involvement	Other Aspects
Johns Hopkins Nursing (Newhouse, Dearholt, Poe, Pugh, & White, 2007)			X	X		X	
Melnyk & Fineout-Overholt (2005)	X	X					
Melnyk (2003)			X	X	Evidence, expertise, assessment	X	
Rutledge & Grant (2002)			X	X	Evidence, expertise, pathophysiology, psychosocial		
Porter-O'Grady (2006)				X	Evidence, expertise	X	
Burns & Grove (2009)	X				Research	X	Cost
Magee (2005)			X		Evidence	X	
Pravikoff, Tanner, & Pierce (2005)			X	X	Evidence	X	
Omery & Williams (1999)			X		Expertise		
DiCenso, Cullum, & Ciliska (1998)			X	X	Evidence, proficiency	X	Assets

available for clinical decision making in order to provide the most consistent and best possible care to patients" (p. 40). For their part, Omery and Williams (1999) define EBP as "a scientific process [that], with its inherent ability to explain and predict, enhances a practice discipline's ability to anticipate and guide interventions" (p. 50). Both of these definitions consolidate the idea of systematic processing with that of anticipatory consideration when providing nursing care.

DiCenso, Cullum, and Ciliska (1998) offer a model for evidence-based decision making that integrates research evidence, clinical proficiency, patient choices, and accessible assets. Within this model, each element is weighted differently based on the particular client circumstances. The evidence desired for an EBP process can be accessed via sources as diverse as bibliographical databases and a quality improvement department located within a healthcare agency. The evidence used within this process can include research, integrative reviews, practice guidelines, quality improvement data, clinical experience, expert opinion, collegial relationships, pathophysiology, common sense, community standards, published materials, and case studies. According to Ferguson and Day (2005), the forms of evidence, in descending order of credibility, include these:

1. Randomized, controlled trials
2. Single randomized, controlled trials
3. Controlled trials without randomization
4. Quasi-experimental studies
5. Nonexperimental studies
6. Descriptive studies
7. Expert consensus
8. Quality improvement data
9. Program evaluation data

While each of these forms of evidence is necessary and functional, the credibility of the evidence must be considered carefully when determining a plan of action. Each provides information to use in a decision-making process, and the support for the information (evidence) is better in those based on research than in those based on opinion.

Each of the proposed definitions supports the definition identified for this text, in which EBP is viewed as a process of using confirmed evidence (research and quality improvement), decision making, and nursing expertise to guide the delivery of holistic patient care. The four consistent aspects found within all of these definitions are (1) a decision-making process, (2) a clinical focus, (3) nursing expertise, and (4) client involvement (see Figure 1-1).

As evidence-based practice has evolved within the field of health care, the idea of what constitutes appropriate evidence has also matured

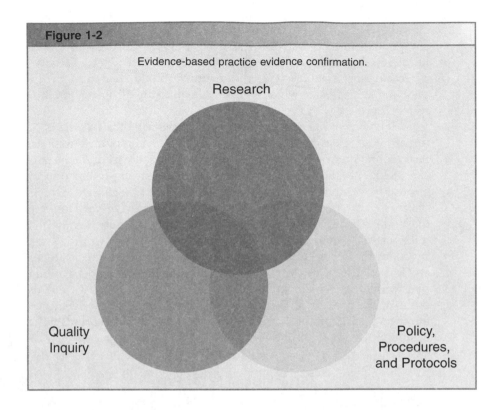

Figure 1-2

Evidence-based practice evidence confirmation.

Research

Quality
Inquiry

Policy,
Procedures,
and Protocols

(**Figure 1-2**). While research results constitute the strongest category of evidence, other evidence—such as quality improvement results, policy/procedure confirmation, and protocol guideline confirmation—is nevertheless beneficial to the provision of safe and effective health care. Within the realm of EBP, each component of the evidence must be carefully assessed in terms of the strength and applicability of the information to the unique client setting. Each agency and nurse must critically consider the results and evidence available concerning an identified healthcare problem. As the results and evidence are thoroughly examined for practicality and efficiency, nursing care practices can be modified to manage the various aspects of care.

Posing Forceful Clinical Questions

Melnyk and Fineout-Overholt (2005) have declared that "The importance of asking the 'right' question cannot be overemphasized" (p. 27). The clarification of the question focuses the search for valid evidence so that it speaks to the issue under examination. According to DiCenso, Guyatt, and Ciliska (2005), "The searchable question requires focus to avoid complicating and time-consuming searches that retrieve irrelevant materials" (p. 23). As the issue under examination is carefully considered to determine the principal focus for the investigation, two components need to be considered. First, the initial attention should be directed to answering the "what, where, when, why, and how" aspects of the issue. Second, the scrutiny should then turn to the outcome of interest, which reflects the nursing diagnosis and/or research project.

Melnyk and Fineout-Overholt (2005) describe the two types of initial questions as background questions and foreground questions. Background questions address the core knowledge within the health-care field. This type of information provides a strong foundation of knowledge related to biological, psychological, and sociological facets of care that can be located in any textbook. Obtaining answers to these questions does not require access to research databases, because the information is preparatory to the provision of basic holistic care. In contrast, foreground questions address the "scientific evidence about diagnosing, treating, or assisting patients with understanding their prognosis" (Melnyk & Fineout-Overholt, 2005, p. 28). At this point in the process of EBP, the search for answers to the identified question focuses on the combination of core knowledge and scientific evidence.

? Think Outside the Box

`www`

Within every organization, obstacles to incorporating changes such as evidence-based practice are present. Look at an institution. Which obstacles do you see? What can you do to confront and overcome these obstacles?

The use of the acronym **PICOT** is helpful in focusing the development of the foreground questions (**Table 1-2**). The PICOT acronym has the following meaning (Melnyk & Fineout-Overholt, 2005):

P Patient population of interest
I Intervention of interest
C Comparison of interest
O Outcome of interest
T Time

In considering the population aspect within the question, time is needed to determine specific information about the characteristics of the group under investigation. This description could relate to age, gender, diagnosis, or ethnicity. The process needs to be specific enough to provide direction, while not restricting the search too much. According to Dawes et al. (2005), "There is a balance to be struck

Table 1-2

Examples of Searchable Questions for Research in EBP

Example 1: Labor and Delivery

You are a staff nurse in a rural hospital that performs 120 to 150 vaginal deliveries each year. Within the past 6 months, the institution has hired a certified registered nurse anesthetist (CRNA) to help with anesthesia for the facility. The CRNA and physicians have decided to begin offering epidural anesthesia for routine vaginal deliveries. You offer to seek out studies that address the use of epidural anesthesia in the labor and delivery process.

Preliminary Question: Is epidural anesthesia appropriate for all laboring patients?

Clarification of Question: This question identifies the population and time as *all laboring patients* and the intervention as *the use of epidural anesthesia*. It fails to document any comparison with other anesthesia methods or the outcome that the hospital is interested in achieving. Here is the PICOT analysis:

   Population: All laboring patients
   Intervention: Use of epidural anesthesia
   Comparison: Versus other anesthesia methods
   Outcome: Reduction in labor complications
   Time: Individuals in labor

Revised Searchable Question: For all laboring patients, will the administration of epidural anesthesia be more effective in reducing labor complications than other forms of anesthesia administered during the labor process?

Example 2: Routine Checkup

A 50-year-old man comes to the clinic for his yearly physical examination. His blood pressure is recorded as 158/90 mm Hg. He complains of frequent headaches during stressful periods. The patient has been fired from his place of employment. When you confer about the findings with him, he asks you about the potential of having a heart attack or stroke. Because these areas are regular potential complications identified within the clinic population, you elect to search for the best evidence to use for discussion with the clinic population.

Preliminary Question: Which type of patient information needs to be included in the teaching related to hypertension and cardiovascular accidents?

Clarification of Question: The limitations of this question include the failure to stipulate the population and to supply adequate particulars about the situation. Here is the PICOT analysis:

   Population: Ambulatory clients between the ages of 30 and 60 years
   Intervention: Development of cardiovascular symptoms such as hypertension and headaches
   Comparison: Ambulatory clients without cardiovascular symptoms
   Outcome: Development of cardiovascular complications
   Time: Within the initial year following diagnosis

Revised Searchable Question: Within the initial year following diagnosis, are ambulatory clients between the ages of 30 and 60 years who have developed cardiovascular symptoms at an increased risk for developing cardiovascular complications, such as stroke and acute myocardial infarction, compared with ambulatory clients who do not exhibit cardiovascular symptoms?

Example 3: Pediatrics

You work for the pediatric unit at the local hospital. The same children keep getting readmitted for earaches, injuries, and respiratory diseases. You have been assigned to prepare and deliver parenting classes for adolescent parents who have had their child admitted to the hospital. As you are thinking about the classes to be prepared, you question whether the adolescent parents are at greater risk and if they need different information than the general community of parents. You want to provide the most recent and best practices for child rearing.

Preliminary Question: Which type of information must be included in a parenting class for adolescent parents?

Clarification of Question: Although the population has been somewhat specified, additional clarification is needed. Other limitations within the preliminary question are the lack of clarification about the interventions, comparisons, outcomes, and time component of the PICOT. Here is the PICOT analysis:

   Population: Parents who have had children admitted to the hospital for reoccurring health problems
   Intervention: Parenting classes
   Comparison: Age of parents affects the information needed in the classes
   Outcome: Reduction in the number of admissions for reoccurring health problems
   Time: Within a 6-month period

Revised Searchable Question: Does the age of the parents (adolescent versus non-adolescent) influence the number of child admissions for reoccurring health problems within a 6-month period for parents who attend a parenting class program?

(continues)

Table 1-2

Examples of Searchable Questions for Research in EBP (continued)

Example 4: Cancer-Related Illness

A 75-year-old woman who had been admitted to the hospital for cervical cancer treatment asks to talk with you about general cancer-related issues. She has three children between the ages of 40 and 55 years. She is worried about their potential for developing cancer and wants to know what she should tell them about getting routine checkups. She does tell you that her father died of colon cancer at the age of 71 years.

Preliminary Question: Which type of routine screening examinations should be performed for children who have a family history of cancer?

Clarification of Question: Within this question, the population is briefly delineated. The question does not clearly denote the intervention, the outcome, or the time aspects of a PICOT question. Here is the PICOT analysis:

  Population: Individuals with a family history of cancer
  Intervention: Scheduling of routine cancer screening examinations
  Comparison: No comparison used in this example
  Outcome: Early diagnosis of cancer
  Time: Routine cancer screening examinations

Revised Searchable Question: For individuals with a family history of cancer, what effect does the timing of routine cancer screening examinations have on the early diagnosis of cancer compared with those individuals who do not have an identified family history of cancer?

Example 5: Staffing

As a new nurse manager on a medical-surgical unit in a large acute care setting, the unit has a turnover rate of 25% during the last 6 months. The patient satisfaction scores do not reflect good nursing care being provided. The unit is staffed with 4 BSN prepared nurses, 4 AD prepared nurses, 3 LVNs, and 8 CNAs.

Preliminary Question: What type of nursing model should be used to improve the staff retention on this unit?

Clarification of Question: The question does not adequately define the population nor the intervention for addressing the concerns. It is voiced more as a global type of question. Here is the PICOT analysis:

  Population: Full-time nursing staff employees
  Intervention: Use of 12-hour shifts with primary care model
  Comparison: Use of 8-hour shift with team nursing care model
  Outcome: Improved staff retention rate and improved patient satisfaction findings
  Time: Not used in this question

Revised Searchable Question: For full-time nursing staff employees, will the use of 12-hour shifts with a primary care nursing model improve the staff retention rate and patient satisfaction findings, when compared to 8-hour shifts using a team nursing approach?

between getting evidence about exactly your group of patients and getting all the evidence about all groups of patients" (p. 13). Care must be given to providing enough specificity to ensure that the search addresses the appropriate population while not excluding relevant information.

The depiction of the intervention for the question is another key aspect that necessitates careful thought and attention. This facet is the clear determination of the topic under consideration. It does not have to be an action step (and, therefore, an activity), but rather is the key topic for clarification. This aspect of the query should seek to potentially include "any exposure, treatment, patient perception, diagnostic test, or prognostic factor" (Melnyk & Fineout-Overholt, 2005, p. 29). Clarification of this aspect within the questioning process reduces the potential for having to backtrack later when the results are not as clearly delineated as anticipated.

The third aspect of the question formation—the comparison of interest—is an optional facet within the questioning process. Within this component, the comparison of different treatment options would be analyzed. In many situations, alternative treatment decisions may not be available. The lack of supplementary preferences does not restrict the development of EBP guidelines.

The fourth aspect for consideration in foreground questions is the outcome of interest. According to Dawes et al. (2005), it is very important to carefully consider this aspect to determine exactly the outcome that is expected.

The final aspect on which to reflect is time. Timing for the outcome of interest is a principal characteristic to prudently contemplate. While time is not included in all PICOT questions, it is valuable for inclusion on those questions that can be directly affected by the passage of time.

Having presented these considerations for preparing the question(s) for concentrating the evidence-based search, it must be acknowledged that too specific a question can also be a major problem. According to Gennaro, Hodnett, and Kearney (2001), "A one-size-fits-all technical procedural protocol will not help" (p. 236). There is no single way to ask a searchable question. The PICOT format fosters clarification of the heart of the area for investigation. The overarching motivation must be the narrowing of the investigation to allow for the effective determination of evidence to strengthen the delivery of holistic nursing care for the client population.

As our thoughts move to the **research process**, the use of different types of questions for various research types must be clarified. Questions focusing on how many or how much are frequently answered through the use of quantitative studies. According to DiCenso et al. (2005), a quantitative question involves three components—population, intervention/exposure, and outcomes. Questions that are directed toward discovering how people feel or experience a specific state of affairs or environments are answered through the use of qualitative research designs. Qualitative questions are worded to include only two parts—population and situation (DiCenso et al., 2005). These questions focus on characteristics that provide a foundation for composing EBP questions and analyzing research results to confirm EBP practices.

Research Utilization

In the past, much lip service has been given to the need for nurses to apply research to practice. More recently, with the emergence and acceptance of EBP, the literature regarding **research utilization** in the clinical arena has proliferated. The need for improved patient outcomes, decreased healthcare costs, greater patient safety, and higher patient satisfaction are driving forces for the use of scientific data in the decision-making process of nursing care provision (**Table 1-3**).

As a result of the promotion of using research as a basic component in nursing practice, one might ask, "Is nursing research being applied to nursing practice?" Surprisingly, the answer is both "yes" and "no." Logic seems to dictate that if EBP can improve patient care, EBP should be implemented. Some healthcare organizations are beginning to incorporate EBP in their institutions. Unfortunately, obstacles for the use of EBP often focus primarily on research utilization.

Obstacles to Using Research

Much of the literature discusses *barriers* to using research for the guidance of practice. *Webster's II New College Dictionary* (1999) defines a barrier as "something that hinders or restricts; a boundary; limit" (p. 91).

Table 1-3
Suggested Resources to Support the Retrieval and Appraisal of Evidence
Agency for Healthcare Research and Quality (www.ahrq.gov)   Cochrane Database of Systematic Reviews (www.update-software.com/publications/cochrane)   Institute of Medicine of the National Academies (holds the documents produced by the IOM related to patient safety; www.iom.edu)   Joanna Briggs Institute (www.joannabriggs.edu.au)   The Joint Commission (http://jointcommission.org)   Medscape (integrated information and educational tools; www.medscape.com/nurseshome)   Morrisey, L. J., & DeBourgh, G. A. (2001). Finding evidence: Refining literature searching skills for the advance practice nurse. *AACN Clinical Issues, 12*(4), 560–577.   National Comprehensive Cancer Network (www.nccn.org)   National Guidelines Clearinghouse (www.guideline.gov)   National Library of Medicine Web site, which allows free searches of MEDLINE through PubMed (www.ncbi.nlm.nih.gov/entrez/query.fcgi)   Oncology Nursing Society (ONS)—EBP Online Resource Center "Evidence Search" section (http://onsopcontent.ons.org/toolkits/evidence/ProcessModel/references.shtml)   Registered Nurses' Association of Ontario (RNAO), Best Practice Guidelines (www.rnao.org/Page.asp?PageID = 861&SiteNodeID = 133)   Sarah Cole Hirsh Institute (http://fpb.case.edu/Centers/Hirsh)   School of Health and Related Research (ScHARR), University of Sheffield—Netting the Evidence (www.shef.ac.uk/scharr/ir/netting)   Schulmeister, L., & Vrabel, M. (2000). Searching for information for presentations and publications. *Clinical Nurse Specialists, 16*(2), 79–84.   Sigma Theta Tau Virginia Henderson Library. (www.nursinglibrary.org/portal/main.aspx)   Studentbmj.com: International Medical Student's Journal (http://studentbmj.com/back_issues/0902/education/313.html)   University of Alberta—Evidence Based Medicine Tool Kit (www.ebm.med.ualberta.ca/ebm.html)   University of North Carolina at Chapel Hill Health Sciences Library (www.hsl.unc.edu/services/tutorials/ebn/index.htm)
Note: Access verified February 17, 2009.

A barrier seems to imply a structure that impedes success. Perhaps another word better defines the utilization of research to nursing practice—*obstacle*. An **obstacle** is "one that opposes, stands in the way of or diverts passage or progress" (*Webster's II New College Dictionary*, 1999, p. 755). An obstacle can be overcome. As a result, the term "obstacle" will be used instead of "barrier" when discussing reasons for not employing research utilization in evidence-based nursing care.

The nurse strives to identify ways to overcome each impediment in the path to success; thus it becomes a challenge to overcome the hindrance and be successful. The use of theories can be viewed as a barrier within the application of research, for example. The complexity of theories and functionality of using theories within the field of research can be perceived as a challenge by the nurse providing care at the bedside. An in-depth discussion of theories is beyond the scope of this textbook, although a general dialogue about the use of theories within the research process will be provided in several chapters. Nurses at the bedside do need to understand the connection between theory, research, and practice.

? Think Outside the Box

www.

Discuss the role of clinical expertise in evidence-based practice.

While it may seem simple to apply research to practice, it is actually a complex problem. Three major categories of obstacles deter nurses from readily incorporating research into their practice—education, beliefs/attitudes, and support/resources. Staffileno and McKinney (2011) and Whitmer, Auer, Beerman, and Weishaupt (2011) suggest many nurses don't have enough time, support, mentoring or sufficient education to use EBP in their practice.

Education

Educational preparation ranks high on the list of obstacles to using research for the guidance of practice. Omery and Williams (1999) suggest that the more education a nurse has, the greater the chance the nurse will use research in providing patient care. The majority of nurses (57%) practicing in the United States are prepared at the associate degree (ADN) or diploma level, and most ADN programs do not include research in their curricula (Estabrooks, 1998). If, as Estabrooks suggests, nurses practice as they were taught, then few nurses today have knowledge about research. It is common to hear, "That's the way I was taught." Considering that the average age of nurses is 47, the fallacy of that line of thinking becomes apparent; such a nurse may have been taught 20 to 25 years ago. Research may appear to be too "mystical" and have no relevance to nurses educated during that time period.

Another aspect of educational preparation that influences a nurse's use of research is the way in which research is taught. Even though baccalaureate and graduate programs include research courses in their curriculum, many graduates continue to resist engaging in or exploring research. Learning research can be likened to learning a foreign language. Carroll et al. (1997) state, "Researchers often present their findings in technical language that is difficult to understand" (p. 209). It is a common misperception that only an academician at a state-of-the-art university can conduct research. The idea that research is practical and beneficial, if linked to clinical practice, appears to be poorly explained to novice nurses. It is therefore no wonder nurses do not understand research, much less want to use it in their practice. Without adequate motivation to use all aspects of an educational program, nurses are unwilling to translate research to practice.

Beliefs/Attitudes

A major portion of the literature attributes the lack of research use by nursing professionals to beliefs and attitudes regarding research. Several authors (Carroll et al., 1997; Cronenwett, 2002; Jolley, 2002; Omery & Williams, 1999; Pravikoff et al., 2005) suggest that negative attitudes about research use represent obstacles for incorporating EBP into nursing care. This is true of both healthcare organizations and individual nurses. If organizations perceive that research has a lack of value for their operations (Jolley, 2002), then little support will exist for EBP within the organization. If nurses feel intimidated (Yoder, 2005) or lack confidence in their ability to use research (Cronenwett, 2002), then nurses will not actively incorporate research into their practice.

Support/Resources

The third major category of obstacles to the incorporation of EBP is support and resource availability. Too often, administrators list "cost" as a reason for limiting or hindering the use of EBP. When a nursing shortage exists, staffing becomes a major issue. Allowing staff adequate time to do the requisite reading to update their clinical or EBP knowledge or to attend continuing nursing education offerings is not always possible in such circumstances.

Another problem relates to the lack of access to or availability of research materials. Many organizations do not have a library, librarian, or personnel familiar with accessing current research findings. Nurses who lack computer skills may not know how to conduct online searches. For this reason, without the assistance of a library, librarian, or information technology personnel, nurses may not seek out EBP data. Both new and older generations of nurses have little, if any, expertise in using search engines. Even when a nurse has the requisite knowledge and skill to be able to conduct EBP database searches, state and federal policies may prevent the searches from being conducted within the healthcare organization. For example, privacy issues relating to HIPAA guidelines inhibit access to the World Wide Web from agency computer systems.

One can easily understand why EBP has a steep learning curve, as practitioners struggle to overcome these obstacles. Lack of nursing educational preparation, lack of value assigned to research by organizations and individual nurses, and lack of support/resources must be critically examined, and solutions to these problems must be found, if nursing is to promote widespread use of EBP. According to Vratny and Shriver (2007), "Leadership, enthusiasm, mentorship, clinical inquiry, and reflective practice are what really make evidence-based practice grow, thrive, and come to light" (p. 166).

In the future, as agencies support nurses in recognizing the extent of improvement possible in clinical care and patient outcomes through the use of EBP, nurses will seize the opportunity to move nursing care forward and seek empowerment as part of their professional growth. Of course, expecting all organizations and every nurse to conduct research is unrealistic. Nevertheless, use of research in EBP provides the opportunity for research utilization by all.

Responsibility for Using Research

Given the formidable obstacles to research, why do research at all? Few would argue with the premise that having evidence to improve patient outcomes is desirable. As Brockopp and Hastings-Tolsma (2003) say, "Professional nurses have the responsibility to participate in the promotion of evidence-based practice. Such expectations are both societal and professional" (p. 459). A better-informed consumer will inevitably demand higher-quality care. Thus, given their greater accessibility to healthcare information, today's healthcare consumers expect nurses to use the most current data available to provide quality care. To do so, nurses must continuously explore new evidence and incorporate that evidence into nursing practice. Carroll et al. (1997) have suggested, "The possession of a body of knowledge from research is the hallmark of a profession" (p. 208). Fain (2009) recommends that nurses take an active role in developing a body of knowledge. As a relatively new profession, nursing has the responsibility to generate scientific data and to use that data to achieve optimal outcomes. EBP uses the best clinical data available in making decisions about nursing care. Thus the profession demands that nurses not only be responsible for the use of research, but also participate in research to add to the body of nursing knowledge through EBP.

According to Kitson (2007), "Health administrations across the world are looking to understand how best to improve the quality, effectiveness, and safety of the health care they deliver" (p. S1). Two key movements in health care have led to this quest for excellence: quality/safety initiatives and the evidence-based practice innovation. By striving to acquire a foundation of knowledge while holding fast to honesty, integrity, and respect for the wide variety of perspectives and experiences within the healthcare delivery system, nursing can establish a firm base on which to build the practice of health care for each individual patient encountered.

Overcoming obstacles to the use of research in practice can improve patient outcomes, decrease costs, and increase the body of knowledge for the nursing profession as a whole. Nursing practice leads to research questions, and vice versa. Practice and research as evidence confirmation are inseparable pieces of the puzzle of EBP, as depicted in Figure 1-1. Posing questions about nursing care frequently generates scientific data, which in turn often generate further questions to be explored.

The Importance of Generating Evidence

Discovering Significant Evidence

As stated earlier, to practice nursing based on "how we are taught" assumes that there is no further need to produce evidence. That dangerous assumption was investigated as early as 1975, when Ketefian's study revealed that nurses did not use research for making decisions about nursing care (Polit & Beck, 2008).

Lack of innovation and failure to develop a rationale for nursing care will result in a decrease in respect for nursing as a profession. Currently, consumers of health care list nurses/nursing as one of the most respected roles in today's society (Jones, 2010). Consequently, generating and using scientific evidence can only improve the image of nursing and provide better outcomes from nursing care.

Another force underlying the need for generating evidence, and its incorporation into practice, is the increasing cost of health care. Healthcare costs are spiraling upward at an uncontrollable rate that demands nurses perform their work in the most cost-effective way.

As Bucknall (2007) notes, "Without an assessment of the extent to which the facts are relevant and contribute to a particular conclusion, they remain simply facts rather than evidence" (p. S61). Each and every fact must be carefully gauged to ensure that the cost of delivering the care remains within an acceptable level while still leading to high-quality, high-safety health care. In fact, the nursing profession cannot afford to ignore innovative approaches in nursing care that will reduce costs while simultaneously improving outcomes.

Impact on Practice

The potential impact of using research in evidence-based nursing practice is enormous. No longer can nurses rely on "how I was taught" or a "gut feeling." Research provides tangible scientific data to promote optimal patient outcomes. The nurse at the bedside must be an integral participant in the development of EBP. Nurses are the individuals who observe what works and what does not work in the real world of health care. The expertise that this hands-on practice brings to the research process is of paramount importance to the effective development of a body of nursing knowledge.

Patients interact with nurses and, as surveys indicate, trust them with their care. As a result, nursing practice that incorporates research also increases patient satisfaction. In turn, assisting a patient to recover health brings satisfaction to the nurse and helps keep the cost of health care at an acceptable level.

Within the current healthcare environment, nurses are expected to embrace continuous performance improvement (CPI) processes such as Six Sigma and the plan–do–check–act (PDCA) cycle. These continuous improvement processes are being driven by the IOM's *Health Profession Education: A Bridge to Quality* (2003) document, which identified five core areas of concern: providing patient-centered care, working in interdisciplinary teams, employing evidence-based practice, applying quality improvement, and utilizing informatics. According to Finkelman and Kenner (2007), "The report [IOM] recommends (1) adopting transformational leadership and evidence-based management, (2) maximizing the capability of the workforce, and (3) creating and sustaining cultures of safety" (p. 8). As a result, nurses are confronted with the challenges of transforming care at the bedside (TCAB); situation, background, assessment, recommendation (SBAR) communication strategies; electronic medical records (EMR); and other healthcare trends such as the ACA, IOM/RWJF and Carnegie Foundation reports. Change is imperative for each of us working within the healthcare field. It is our responsibility to become knowledgeable about the evidence that is available as we select mechanisms to address these core areas and national imperatives to change and transform care provided by nurses.

Nurses must ask targeted, concise questions about the nursing care that is being provided. According to Rolston-Blenman (2009), "Successfully embracing a culture of change and innovation requires enlisting nurses to champion the objectives and empowering them to design the tools they need for success on the frontline" (p. 25). Settling for the status quo is no longer acceptable. Instead, nurses must take the lead in querying the healthcare delivery venue as to the appropriateness and safety of the care being provided. According to Yoder (2008), "By deploying the broadest range of solutions possible, organizations can significantly improve communication among providers, decrease care delays, and enable clinicians to spend more time with patients, all of which can lead to improved outcomes" (p. 26). Evidence-based nursing practice requires that each nurse develop this "inquiring mind" posture to ensure that the resulting patient outcomes are of high quality, safe, and appropriate in the current healthcare arena.

Nursing is truly both an art and a science. EBP not only provides elements of each aspect, but also contributes to the profession's overall development. As a result, EBP improves everyday practice by providing empirical data to guide nursing interventions. In addition, prompted by national developments mentioned above, nurses need to collaborate with physicians and other healthcare providers to improve patient outcomes. Generating evidence for use by all professionals requires teamwork and collaboration, as silos of research are no longer the standard approach. As a result, partnerships of individuals and agencies allow for more efficient use of resources and decreased costs.

Summary Points

1. Recent national legislation and reports have had an impact on the importance of evidence-based practice (EBP) and research utilization.
2. A core body of nursing knowledge is derived from the process in which research is incorporated into practice; this process has been called best practice, quality of care, and evidence-based practice.
3. EBP is a process of utilizing confirmed evidence (research and quality improvement), decision making, and nursing expertise to guide the delivery of holistic patient care.
4. The PICOT acronym provides a mechanism for posing forceful, clinical questions to generate scientific questions.
5. Obstacles for research utilization can be categorized into three areas: education, beliefs/attitudes, and support/resources.
6. Generating evidence adds to the core of nursing knowledge, which promotes nursing as a profession.
7. The combination of nursing practice and research is essential to developing EBP.
8. Safe, effective patient care is not a luxury, but rather a necessity.

RED FLAGS

- Within the documentation of a research project, certain decisions concerning the planning and implementation of the process must be supported by rationales. In EBP, randomized controlled trials are viewed as the most powerful evidence. As a result, some research aspects are viewed as stronger designs (quantitative, experimental, and randomized sampling) than other facets of the process. In this text, the designation of a *red flag* will reflect features of the research project that are less stringent than others. These areas are not strictly forbidden within research, but rather are concerns that need to be taken into account. Within the documentation, these aspects should be supported by rationales reflecting the thought process for utilization of those pieces.
- When a nurse is appraising an article for inclusion in an EBP situation, the presence of red flags should be seen as an opportunity to assess the justification for the decisions made by the research team. If the research team has provided an adequate justification for its research decisions, a study characterized by multiple red flags can still be a strong study. The documentation of the research report by a researcher is a process of validation and justification of the various judgments made during the planning process. The researcher has the responsibility to document the reasoning for the decisions incorporated into the study such as ethics, sampling, design, and data collection.
- Red flags are areas within the documentation of the study that may raise concerns. These areas are not items that should never be done, but rather are items that should be supported by sound, clear rationales as to why the researcher used the research components.

Multiple Choice Questions

www

1. One of the primary foundations for evidence-based nursing practice is
   A. Medical knowledge.
   B. Research results.
   C. Everyday health care.
   D. Textbook information.

2. Within the process of providing evidence-based nursing care, which types of research results are incorporated to ascertain the plan of treatment?
   A. Personal experiences and medical knowledge
   B. Client values and medical knowledge
   C. Personal experiences and client values
   D. Medical knowledge and identified challenges

3. As a novice nurse on a medical–surgical hospital unit, you want to get involved in a research study that is being proposed for your unit. Because your hospital is involved with evidence-based nursing practice, which aspects of EBP are essential for you to have?
   A. Sound bedside nursing skills
   B. Basic knowledge of your unit
   C. Method for accessing published information
   D. Fundamental safety knowledge

4. Which of the EBP components carries the greatest weight in determining the management of the clinical situation?
   A. Thought process
   B. Client preferences
   C. Research
   D. The situation

5. Evidence comes in many forms. Examples of the data that could best be utilized for EBP are
   A. Quality improvement data and integrated reviews.
   B. Integrated reviews and non-peer-reviewed journal articles.
   C. Collegial relationships and lay journals.
   D. Verbal data and practice guidelines.

6. When developing a question to drive the compilation of evidence for a specific practice situation, the five components that can be used to focus the investigation are
   A. Patient, situation, intervention, comparison, and practice.
   B. Situation, intervention, comparison, outcome, and time.
   C. Patient, intervention, comparison, outcome, and time.
   D. Patient, situation, intervention, outcome, and data.

7. A nurse working in a cancer follow-up setting has been asked to consider the development of a transition program to help young people adjust to the adult program. The initial question suggested for use in focusing the identification of evidence is "What is it like to have care transferred from a pediatric center to an adult clinic?" Which aspects of this question need to be strengthened to make it more searchable?

   A. Population and outcome
   B. Population and intervention
   C. Intervention and outcome
   D. Comparison and outcome

8. Research utilization has often been

   A. Neglected in the literature.
   B. Denied by publishers.
   C. Reported in the literature.
   D. Spurned by EBP.

9. Obstacles to using nursing research in practice include lack of

   A. Education, beliefs/attitudes, and support/resources.
   B. Faculty, knowledge, and cost.
   C. Time, beliefs/attitudes, and consumers.
   D. Outcomes, values, and motivation.

10. As a nurse on a medical–surgical hospital unit, you begin to question the amount of time your hospital policy requires for taking a patient's oral temperature. Your hospital uses an EBP approach to nursing care. Which hospital resources would you expect to be able to connect with to assist with the accessing of a computer?

    A. Ward clerk or CNA
    B. Doctor or lawyer
    C. Charge nurse or supervisor
    D. Librarian or library

11. You are a BSN-prepared nurse who wants to initiate a research project on your unit. To get the other nurses to participate, you would

    A. Ask the doctors what they think.
    B. Check the educational level of other nurses on the unit.
    C. Ignore your desire to learn more at this time.
    D. Give a presentation to your peers on the benefits of research.

12. In the past, nurses were often taught that while research might be a good thing to do, only faculty could do research because

    A. Faculty members are the only ones prepared to do research.
    B. Most nurses have not been taught research.
    C. Most nurses don't need to use research.
    D. Faculty members know what's best for nursing.

13. Many nurses don't understand research because

    A. Research isn't necessary for their practice.
    B. Most nurses are too old.
    C. Research is like a foreign language.
    D. Patients don't expect them to use research.

14. Research is often not valued because

    A. It costs too much.
    B. Administration wants it.
    C. Search engines are easy to access.
    D. Staffing is not an obstacle.

15. Nurses have a responsibility to use research because

    A. Doctors order it done.
    B. Administrators don't have time for research.
    C. Research is nice to know.
    D. Research is the "hallmark of a profession."

16. The ACA, IOM/RWJF and Carnegie Foundation reports are national movements to

    A. Reaffirm current nursing practice.
    B. Ignore current nursing practice.
    C. Transform current nursing practice.
    D. Eliminate current nursing practice.

Discussion Questions

1. You are a public health nurse working in an outpatient hospice facility. You are responsible for clients and their families in a six-county area. During the course of a week, you have from six to ten clients or their families who experience stressful situations related to the disease process. These families and their loved ones experience anguish and guilt as they confront and deal with the terminal nature of the healthcare situation. You have been asked to explore the following question: *How do others in this type of situation deal with the numerous stressful challenges?* Which type of searchable question could you develop to drive the data search related to this request?

2. As a BSN staff nurse, you are excited that your hospital wants you to participate in an evidence-based project. You have been chosen to chair a taskforce. How would you approach this task?

3. You are an ADN-prepared staff nurse at an acute care facility who has enrolled in an RN-BSN program. One of the key messages presented by the RN-BSN program is the importance of evidence-based nursing practice. In your first course in the program, you are asked to identify an evidence-based topic for development. The faculty members instruct you to select a topic that will be functional in your workplace. Which types of activities would you carry out to aid in the selection of this topic?

Suggested Readings

www

Harvey, G., Loftus-Hills, A., Rycroft-Malone, J., Titchen, A., Kitson, A., McCormack, B., & Seer, K. (2002, March). Getting evidence into practice: The role and function of facilitators. *Journal of Advanced Nursing, 37*(6), 577–588.

Hewitt-Taylor, J. (2002, December). Evidence-based practice. *Nursing Standard, 17*(14–15), 47–52, 54–55.

McCormack, B., Allison, K., Gill, H., Rycroft-Malone, J., Titchen, A., & Seers, K. (2002, April). Getting evidence into practice: The meaning of "context." *Journal of Advanced Nursing, 38*(1), 94–104.

Newhouse, R. P. (2006, July/August). Examining the support for evidence-based nursing practice. *Journal of Nursing Administration, 36* (7–8), 337–340.

Rycroft-Malone, J. (2003, July). Consider the evidence. *Nursing Standard, 17*(45), 21.

Rycroft-Malone, J. (2004). The PARIHS framework: A framework for guiding the implementation of evidence-based practice. *Journal of Nursing Care Quality, 19*(4), 297–304.

Rycroft-Malone, J., Kitson, A., Harvey, G., McCormack, B., Seers, K., Titchen, A., & Estabrooks, C. (2002). Ingredients for change: Revisiting a conceptual framework. *Quality and Safety in Health Care, 11*(2), 174–180.

References

Agency for Healthcare Research and Quality (AHRQ). (2000). *Outcomes research fact sheet, AHRQ Publication No. 00-P011*. Retrieved from http://www.ahrq.gov/clinic/outfact.htm

Benner, P., Sutphen, M., Leonard, V., & Day, L. (2010). *Educating nurses: A call for radical transformation*. San Francisco, CA: Jossey-Bass.

Brockopp, D. Y., & Hastings-Tolsma, M. T. (2003). *Fundamentals of nursing research* (3rd ed.). Sudbury, MA: Jones and Bartlett.

Bucknall, T. (2007). A gaze through the lens of decision theory toward knowledge translation science. *Nursing Research, 56*(4S), S60–S66.

Burns, N., & Grove, S. K. (2009). *The practice of nursing research: Appraisal, synthesis, and generation of evidence* (6th ed.). St. Louis, MO: Saunders Elsevier.

Cannon, S., & Boswell, C. (2010). Challenges and opportunities for teaching research. In L. Caputi (Ed.), *Teaching nursing: The art and science* (2nd ed.). Glen Ellyn, IL: College of DuPage Press.

Carroll, D. L., Greenwood, R., Lynch, K. E., Sullivan, J. K., Ready, C. H., & Fitzmaurice, J. B. (1997). Barriers and facilitators to the utilization of nursing research. *Clinical Nurse Specialist, 11*(5), 207–212.

Ciliska, D., Cullum, N., & Marks, S. (2001). Evaluation of systematic reviews of treatment or prevention interventions. *Evidence-Based Nursing, 4*(4), 100–104.

Cronenwett, L. R. (2002, February 19). Research, practice and policy: Issues in evidence-based care. *Online Journal of Issues in Nursing* [Online serial], *7*(2). Retrieved from http://www.nursingworld.org/MainMenuCategories/ANAMarketplace/ANAPeriodicals/OJIN/Columns/KeynotesofNote/EvidenceBasedCare.aspx

Davies, B. L. (2002). Sources and models for moving research evidence into clinical practice. *Journal of Obstetric, Gynecologic, & Neonatal Nursing, 31*(5), 558–562.

Dawes, M., Davies, P., Gray, A., Mant, J., Seers, K., & Snowball, R. (2005). *Evidence-based practice: A primer for health care professionals* (2nd ed.). Edinburgh, Scotland: Elsevier Churchill Livingstone.

DiCenso, A., Cullum, N., & Ciliska, D. (1998). Implementing evidence-based nursing: Some misconceptions. *Evidence-Based Nursing, 1*(1), 38–40.

DiCenso, A., Guyatt, G., & Ciliska, D. (2005). *Evidence-based nursing: A guide to clinical practice*. St. Louis, MO: Elsevier Mosby.

Estabrooks, C. A. (1998). Will evidence-based nursing practice make practice perfect? *Canadian Journal of Nursing Research, 30*(11), 15–36.

Fain, J. A. (2009). *Reading, understanding, and applying nursing research: A text and workbook* (3rd ed.). Philadelphia, PA: F. A. Davis.

Ferguson, L., & Day, R. A. (2005). Evidence-based nursing education: Myth or reality? *Journal of Nursing Education, 44*(3), 107–115.

Fineout-Overholt, E., & Melnyk, B. (2005). Building a culture of best practice. *Nurse Leader, 3*(6), 26–30.

Finkelman, A., & Kenner, C. (2007). *Teaching IOM: Implications of the Institute of Medicine reports for nursing education*. Silver Springs, MD: American Nurses Association.

Fonteyn, M. (2005). The interrelationship among thinking skills, research knowledge, and evidence-based practice. *Journal of Nursing Education, 44*(10), 439.

Gennaro, S., Hodnett, E., & Kearney, M. (2001). Making evidence-based practice a reality in your institution: Evaluating the evidence and using the evidence to change clinical practice. *American Journal of Maternal/Child Nursing, 26*(5), 236–244.

Institute of Medicine (IOM). (2003). *Health professions education: A bridge to quality.* Washington, DC: National Academies Press.

Institute of Medicine (IOM). (2011). *The future of nursing: Leading change, advancing health.* Washington, DC: National Academies Press.

Jolley, S. (2002). Raising research awareness: A strategy for nurses. *Nursing Standard,* 16(33), 33–39.

Jones, J. M. (2010). *Nurses top honesty and ethics list for 11th year.* Retrieved from http://www.gallup.com/poll/145043/Nurses-Top-Honesty-Ethics-List-11-Year.aspx

Kitson, A. L. (2007). What influences the use of research in clinical practice? *Nursing Research,* 56(4S), S1–S3.

Magee, M. (2005). *Health politics: Power, population, and health.* Bronxville, NY: Spencer Books.

Malloch, K., & Porter-O'Grady, T. (2006). *Introduction to evidence-based practice in nursing and health care.* Sudbury, MA: Jones and Bartlett.

Mason, D. J., Leavitt, J. K., & Chaffee, M. W. (2012) *Policy & politics in nursing and health care* (6th ed.). St. Louis, MO: Elsevier Saunders.

Melnyk, B. M. (2003). Finding and appraising systematic reviews of clinical interventions: Critical skills for evidence-based practice. *Journal of Pediatric Nursing,* 29(2), 125, 147–149.

Melnyk, B. M. (2004). Integrating levels of evidence into clinical decision making. *Journal of Pediatric Nursing,* 30(4), 323–325.

Melnyk, B. M., & Fineout-Overholt, E. (2005). *Evidence-based practice in nursing and healthcare: A guide to best practice.* Philadelphia, PA: Lippincott Williams & Wilkins.

Newhouse, R. P., Dearholt, S. L., Poe, S. S., Pugh, L. C., & White, K. M. (2007). *Johns Hopkins Nursing evidence-based practice: Model and guidelines.* Indianapolis, IN: Sigma Theta Tau International.

Omery, A., & Williams, R. P. (1999). An appraisal of research utilization across the United States. *Journal of Nursing Administration,* 29(12), 50–56.

Oncology Nursing Society. (2005). *EBP process.* Retrieved October 29, 2005, from http://onsopcontent.ons.org/toolkits/evidence/Process/index.shtml

Polit, D. F., & Beck, C. T. (2008). *Nursing research: Generating and assessing evidence for nursing practice* (8th ed.). Philadelphia, PA: Lippincott Williams & Wilkins.

Porter-O'Grady, T. (2006). A new age for practice: Creating the framework for evidence. In K. Malloch & T. Porter-O'Grady (Eds.), *Introduction to evidence-based practice in nursing and health care* (pp. 1–29). Sudbury, MA: Jones and Bartlett.

Pravikoff, D. S., Tanner, A. B., & Pierce, S. T. (2005). Readiness of U.S. nurses for evidence-based practice. *American Journal of Nursing,* 105(9), 40–51.

Rolston-Blenman, B. (2009). Nurses roll up their sleeves at the bedside to improve patient care. *Nurse Leader,* 7(1), 20–25.

Rutledge, D. N., & Grant, M. (2002). Introduction. *Seminars in Oncology Nursing,* 18(1), 1–2.

Staffileno, B. A., & McKinney, C. (2011). Getting "research rich" at a community hospital. *Nursing Management,* 42(6), 10–14.

Titler, M. G., Everett, L. Q., & Adams, S. (2007). Implications for implementation science. *Nursing Research,* 56(4S), S53–S59.

Vratny, A., & Shriver, D. (2007). A conceptual model for growing evidence-based practice. *Nursing Administration Quarterly,* 31(2), 162–170.

Webster's II new college dictionary. (1999). Boston, MA: Houghton Mifflin.

Whitmer, K., Auer, C., Beerman, L., & Weishaupt, L. (2011). Launching evidence-based nursing practice. *Journal for Nurses in Staff Development,* 27(2), E5–E7.

Yoder, L. (2005). Evidence-based practice: The time is now! *Medsurg Nursing,* 14(2), 91–92.

Yoder, L. (2008). Evidence-based design. *Nursing Management,* 39(12), 26–29.

Chapter 2

Overview of Evidence

Carol Boswell

Chapter Objectives

At the conclusion of this chapter, the learner will be able to

1. Explain the importance of understanding the need and functionality of evidence for performing quality health care
2. Identify different qualities for classification of information as evidence
3. Discuss various methods for grading evidence

Key Terms

- Case-controlled
- Case report
- Case series
- Consensus
- Decision making
- Editorials
- Evidence
- Expert opinion

- Forensic science
- Ideas
- Observations
- Opinions
- Quality improvement
- Research
- Research utilization

Introduction

In today's media environment, the idea of evidence is regularly discussed on television shows such as CSI, NCIS, and 60 Minutes, to name just a few of the shows. Everywhere we look, the concept of "what does the evidence say" can be seen and considered. Individuals on these different programs spend excessive time and energy to obtain the best evidence possible. The idea is not to just get some information but to get as much of the total unbiased information as possible. Alligood (2011) noted "nurse scholars have forged ahead developing nursing science in various forms while embracing challenges regarding the nature of the science from without and within the discipline" (p. 195). Health care needs to base the provision of treatment on the evidence which provides the best outcomes for the unique situation. To start this discussion, a definition of evidence is required. Dictionary.com (n.d.) defines **evidence** as "that which tends to prove or disprove something; ground for belief; proof; something that makes plain or clear; an indication or sign" (p. 1). Adding clarity and providing the groundwork for understanding is key to the selection of healthcare activities that will advance the provision of quality nursing care. Evidence is that foundation on which sound nursing and health care can be based to allow for authentic management of the care provided. As patients and family members realize that the care provided by the healthcare professional is established on trustworthy, responsible, and reliable information, compliance with the plan of care can be supported and embraced. Vanhook (2009) acknowledged that "it's imperative that nurses feel empowered to question nursing practice and have available the resources to support the search for evidence to guide patient care" (p. 10). An environment for nurses which is supportive of autonomy and investigation allows the individual to enhance their nursing knowledge while exemplifying professional preparation and ensuring practical outcomes. Within the sphere of evidence-based practice (EBP), nurses must realize the importance of embracing the quest for the best information available to provide the optimum care for the patient. Stillwell, Fineout-Overholt, Melnyk, and Williamson (2010) maintain that nurses must embrace an attitude of investigation and analysis, along with a culture which truly accommodates and utilizes evidence-based practice. As nurses develop a spirit of inquiry, innovative and novel questions will be incorporated into the day-to-day process for providing quality, effective health care.

Vanhook (2009) discusses the confusion which exists between EBP and research. Evidence-based practice has four components which carry weight—nursing confirmation (evidence), **decision-making** process, nursing experience (clinical), and holistic patient care (patient preferences). **Research**, on the other hand, is a systematic process of inquiry for the development of generalizable knowledge. Evidence-based practice,

quality improvement, and research, while complementary, have unique outcomes which are crucial for the advancement of the profession of nursing. Mensik (2011) identified another aspect along these same lines: "it is important to recognize that EBP is an outcome, not a process" (p. 176). Too often the idea of EBP takes on the concept of processing information rather than the conclusion and effect resulting from the information collected. As a consequence, returning to the idea of understanding what evidence can involve becomes critical to the end product. Taking the time and energy to effectively consider the evidence is imperative. The proof and/or indications which can be pulled together to determine the best line of action becomes the driving force, rather than the amount of research which may have been done. By taking into account the research findings, quality improvement outcomes, and the evidence-based practice activities, nurses can integrate the critical components to allow for the provision of safe and quality health care. Mensik (2011) discovered only 10% of the care provided on a daily basis by nurses is currently founded in any research or evidence. The goal established by the Institute of Medicine is for a minimum of 90% of clinical practice to be founded on evidence by the year 2020 (Mensik, 2011). To get to this level within the next few years, the nursing profession must come to grips with the idea of evidence from multiple venues.

Evans (2003) acknowledged the fact that a common attitude is that research is not without errors and biases. This attitude leads many people to question the integrity of research findings. As a result, the need to grade the evidence—research and other forms—becomes a necessity. The grading process allows each team to carefully and cautiously consider the evidence presented in light of the unique clinical environment.

The Institute of Medicine's *Future of Nursing* report was summarized by Albert and Fulton (2011) to address four central recommendations. While not all of the four recommendations concern evidence, two recommendations can be supported by these processes: research, and evidence-based practice. First, nurses are encouraged to utilize their full extent of education and knowledge. Understanding the nature of evidence and using it appropriately to change and support quality health care is foundational to this recommendation. Second, the report demanded that nurses be key players and full partners in the redesigning of health care. Changes must be based upon evidence. We can no longer accept the idea that care is based on "how we have always done it." The manner in which health care is provided must be established on facts and proof, instead of habits and opinions. Selker et al. (2011) stated the healthcare system must learn "to use evidence-based approaches for prevention, diagnosis, and treatment, and also [learn] from the care it delivers to develop new evidence" (p. 2). An understanding that evidence is not stagnant is paramount in understanding how evidence can be used to advance the provision of appropriate and effective health care.

Foundations for Evidence-Based Practice

As nurses begin the work of understanding evidence-based practice, a firm appreciation for the interconnectedness of the different aspects within EBP, research, and quality improvement becomes essential. Each of these aspects has unique characteristics, but all serve to advance the quality of care provided within the healthcare setting. An appreciation for the consistencies and differences among these concepts is important to establish a foundation on which to best use the evidence. Evidence-based practice can be viewed as the "umbrella" under which evidence is to improve healthcare delivery. Proehl and Hoyt (2012) stated "evidence-based practice involves critical appraisal of the available research, the formulation of recommendations based on the findings of well-designed and executed studies, and an indication of how solid the evidence is to support the practice" (p. 2). While this statement is correct, the critical appraisal within EBP must involve more than just the available research. It needs to embrace all evidence obtainable pertaining to the matter of interest. Evidence-based practice sets the stage for the research, **research utilization**, and quality improvement activities. Since EBP includes multiple decision-making efforts, the evidence-based practice process is the underpinning for the utilization of evidence for the optimal provision of safe and effective health care in any venue.

To get a clear understanding of the interconnectedness of EBP and research, a flowchart is provided here to conceptualize the relationship (see **Figure 2-1**). Whether an individual is considering research activities or quality improvement efforts, the initial step is always the identification of the problem to be addressed. As a problem is identified, a PICOT (Population, Intervention, Comparison, Outcome, Time) statement is formed. The PICOT statement (which was introduced in Chapter 1) is an organized, effective framework for structuring the problem into a manageable format. This PICOT statement drives the review of the literature, with each part of the PICOT statement providing key words to narrow the search for relevant articles during the literature review. This allows for a truly in-depth evaluation of the accessible evidence relevant to the topic under investigation. While most of the evidence will be available through the literature, other forms of evidence can be accessed and included in this part of the process. All evidence pertinent to the topic should be included within the review. Once the literature has been collected and reviewed, gaps and consistencies within the literature can be determined.

Based on these gaps or consistencies, the next step toward establishing a thorough foundation constructed on the evidence can be embraced. These gaps and consistencies can either lead to a research study or a quality improvement project. If the evidence indicates that a policy, procedure, or protocol needs to be investigated, a quality

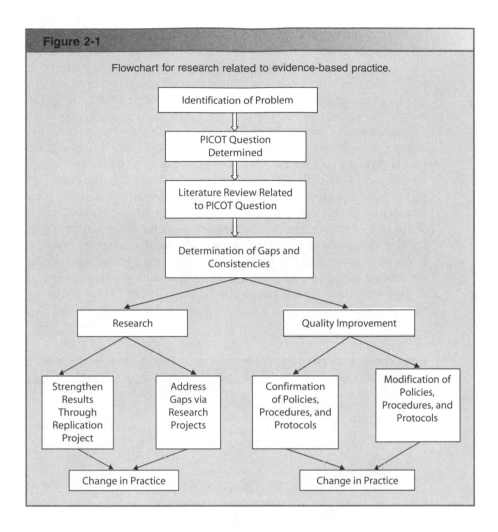

Figure 2-1

Flowchart for research related to evidence-based practice.

Identification of Problem

PICOT Question
Determined

Literature Review Related
to PICOT Question

Determination of Gaps and
Consistencies

Research | Quality Improvement

Strengthen Results Through Replication Project

Address Gaps via Research Projects

Confirmation of Policies, Procedures, and Protocols

Modification of Policies, Procedures, and Protocols

Change in Practice

Change in Practice

improvement process is instituted for that purpose. When the evidence found through the literature review and evidence analysis reflects that a standard of practice for that topic has been determined, the application of that standard to the bedside setting is the quality improvement action required. As is noted in Figure 2-1, the quality improvement can either confirm a policy, procedure, and/or protocol already in place or it can drive the modification of those documents. Either way, the change resulting from the EBP analysis is a local change and/or modification rather than a more global alteration.

On the other side of the flow sheet, the gaps and consistencies may identify the need for further evidence to provide a foundation for the topic under investigation. If the gaps and consistencies suggest that further research is required to arrive at an answer for the identified problem, a full research project should be planned and implemented. When the evidence is not strong enough to denote the best practice for a topic, additional research projects are required to provide that foundation for the management of the identified challenge. Both aspects of the process are focused on changing and/or improving the practice provided at the bedside.

If research is the direction in which the nurse should proceed, the best process for arriving at a sound conclusion should be determined (see **Figure 2-2**). As a research endeavor is planned, the methodology for best addressing the problem must be selected. The flowchart in Figure 2-2 identifies the steps commonly followed when conducting quantitative or qualitative research. The steps are similar for both types of research, but they do reflect the uniqueness of the research approaches. Both of these research methodologies will be discussed in detail in future chapters within this book. At this point, the general flow within the process is strategic for understanding how and why the levels and strengths of evidence are assigned to these types of decision-making processes. Due to the systematic decision-making activities incorporated

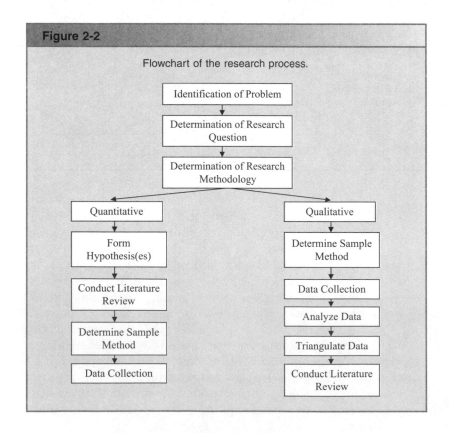

Figure 2-2

Flowchart of the research process.

into the different research methodologies, the assignment of degrees of strength for the resulting evidence/findings have been made.

Within the process of quality improvement, the focus for the course of action is primarily local or regional in nature. Selker et al. (2011) champion "continuous improvement as the foundation for a learning system that discovers and applies the best possible evidence to the care of individual patients, their communities, and the institutions in which they receive care" (p. 2). This aspect of health care is bringing the standards to the bedside setting. As a result, the process is confirming what is done within the general area and/or modifying the current level of practice to incorporate the standard of practice. Quality improvement works to validate the current practices while ensuring that continuity of health care is provided. The process of quality improvement can be visualized within **Figure 2-3**. Many quality improvement plans are available in the literature. The basic process is for the question to be asked, current structures examined, changes made accordingly, and evaluation of those changes within the local venue, followed by communication of the next steps related to the process. Quality improvement is the process of bringing standards

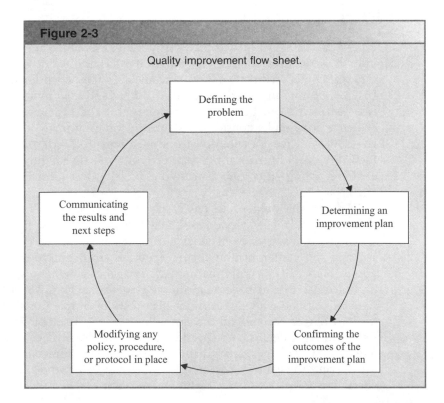

Figure 2-3

Quality improvement flow sheet.

Defining the problem

Communicating the results and next steps

Determining an improvement plan

Modifying any policy, procedure, or protocol in place

Confirming the outcomes of the improvement plan

of practice to the actual bedside or practice arena. Within this process, the functionality of the standard within a variety of settings is addressed. Some settings have more resources than others; thus, the implementation of the standards must be carefully considered to validate the best practices within the uniqueness of the practice venue.

Whether a project is research or quality improvement, the beginning component is assessing the current state of the evidence. Vanhook (2009) proposes that the evolution toward EBP requires a cultural change process to occur within the hearts and minds of the individuals involved. Individuals directly responsible for the safe and quality care of the patient must embrace the entire process of evidence-based practice for it to become a commonplace tradition within the provision of health care. "What evidence is available?" and "How good is the evidence?" are key questions in this context. Understanding what is evidence and determining how to evaluate the evidence is necessary for the process. The querying of evidence to support the different procedures used in the advancement of health care, along with the questioning of the validity and reliability of that evidence, must be foremost and fundamental for each and every provider of care.

Qualities of Evidence

Paget et al. (2011) noted "obtaining the highest-value care for each individual requires establishing common goals and expectations for care through shared deliberation that marshals the best information" (p. 2). Determining which evidence to accept and how much weight is to be placed on the evidence requires that the characteristics of evidence be carefully considered. Evidence comes in many forms and levels. All evidence does not have the same foundation and/or strength. Each piece of information must be carefully and thoroughly considered regarding the foundation on which the information is established.

Within the field of **forensic science**, the idea of evidence is dominant. Evidence is viewed as the data upon which judgments and decisions are made. To be beneficial, evidence has to be established by scrutiny and contemplation of the materials from multiple vantage points. Mick (2011) notes that regulatory agencies demand supporting information and benchmarking as evidence of compliance with standards. Sound evidence is more than just the simple decisions set forth by one or two individuals. Sound evidence is based on hard and fast particulars, details, and specifics that can be confirmed from different views of the same materials. Within the forensic science discussion of evidence, it is classified as having class and individual characteristics. Class characteristics are established on the physical qualities that are shared by a group of like items. Individual characteristics are those qualities that are unique to the specialized entity.

Within the discussion of evidence, several factors need to be carefully considered. Initially, the meticulousness of the material is important to consider. Alligood (2011) stresses the challenge for evidence-based practice is ensuring that theories are made explicit enough so that nursing research and evidence can support the meaning suggested. The data that is under consideration must represent the wholeness of what is known about a topic. Care must be given to strive to organize the most relevant materials for review. Once the materials are collected, the distinctiveness of the results should be focused on that identified topic. The distinguishing traits of the results along with the topic need to be evaluated and contemplated. Another aspect to consider is the frequency that the results are seen. When the same results are observed without regard to person, place, or situation, the results are viewed with increased confidence. When multiple sources in various venues are found to come to the same conclusions about a topic, the reliability of the findings are strengthened. This aspect can also be viewed as the persistence in the result. Persistence and consistency within the results add support and strength to the quality of the evidence. A final aspect to carefully consider when contemplating evidence is the likelihood of any alternative explanations for the results obtained. As alternative explanations are removed, the remaining justification for the findings gains power and influence.

While evidence is frequently perceived as primarily research-related, the field of EBP acknowledges that other forms of evidence such as case studies and expert opinion are valuable within this process (Armola et al., 2009). Using the factors and concepts from forensic science concerning evidence, greater latitude in regard to accepting and utilizing these other beneficial forms can be exercised. Research cannot and will not answer all of the questions concerning health care. Mensik (2011) notes that the primary objective for research projects is the development of generalizable original knowledge. Alternative styles of evidence must be carefully considered.

Case studies are one form of evidential material. The consideration of case studies can have several different dimensions. A case scrutinizes the lives of individuals, dealings, resolutions, episodes, phases, projects, and/or other systems to determine the uniqueness of the situation. Case studies do not follow rigid sets of rules. The case or situation drives the consideration of the aspects identified. Case series and case reports can be intermeshed with case studies. Each type of case scenario adds additional depth to the evidence. A **case series** incorporates several case studies that have resulted in similar outcomes. Thus, the findings can be combined to provide additional strength to the results documented. A **case report** is the documentation of the aspects identified within a situation. The strength of this evidence is based on the clarity of the report provided. In addition to the outcomes, the situation and environment where the case occurred lends depth and influence to the resulting materials.

Another form of evidence that can be considered is **expert opinion**. Expert opinion is the furnishing and/or contributing of applicable and significant information by an individual who is viewed as an authority based upon a set of criteria. Different rules can be utilized to identify the expert based upon the materials being sought. While biases are possible due to the nature of the evidence provided by the expert, the expectation is for the expert to qualify any opinion based upon what is known about the topic under investigation.

In conjunction with the topic of expert opinion, the definition of idea, editorial, and opinion must be clarified. An idea encompasses thoughts, convictions, and/or principles. An idea can be based upon potentially or actually existing foundations. **Ideas** are considered to be individual work, thus their influence can be minimal. **Editorials** are the statements of the opinions of an owner, manager, or similar individual. Again, the weight of this type of evidence is based upon the perceived biases associated with the thoughts and statements. Finally, **opinions** represent a person's beliefs, judgments, and/or values about a designated subject. Opinions can be viewed as evidence but these have the same caveats as noted with ideas and editorials. Opinions are attitudes and viewpoints that do not rest on adequate foundations to be viewed as completely unbiased.

A third type of evidence that can be considered is **observation**. Observations begin with the individual striving to attentively perceive and/or scrutinize a situation. Following the inspection and surveillance, the observer will document those aspects pertinent to the topic or activity being observed. This process can have biases associated with the observations. To minimize this concern, observations are often placed into the context of when, where, and how the observations were gathered. Documentation of the observation requires the clear determination of what constitutes an observed activity. For example, there are multiple non-verbal behaviors which could be recorded for non-compliance. By designating which behaviors will be counted and which will not, the quality of the evidence can be increased.

A final example of alternate forms of evidence is a **consensus**. A consensus occurs when individuals involved in the process come to a common understanding. A consensus usually is understood to mean that the majority has reached the agreed resolution. Since the evidence (consensus) is based on a majority and not the complete agreement, the strength of the results can be questionable. With the other forms of evidence, attention to factors and types of evidence must be integrated into the classification of the data. Each and every type and piece of evidence, whether provided by research or via some other avenue, must be thoroughly and unconditionally scrutinized to ensure the validity of the claims being made.

The steps within EBP must be followed as the evidence is collected. Stichler (2010) advocates that the initial step "in finding a quality answer is to review the literature for previous research and ask experts in the field for their opinions" (p. 348). To get to the correct evidence for a topic, the quality of the journey toward that evidence is important. Mick (2011) supports this idea since the current health care environment is transitioning toward forecasting and predictive measures instead of depending on historical and/or descriptive data. The quality of the evidence is becoming increasingly critical.

Nursing knowledge pulls from these concepts in regard to evidence to validate and modify the care provided. Mensik (2011) reminds the profession that knowing comes from four generally accepted patterns—empirics, aesthetics, the ethical, and the personal. These styles of appreciating the information around us provide various vantage points by which to consider the material put forth as evidence. Empiric knowledge transpires from the science of nursing and encompasses the formal research aspects. Gawlinski and Miller (2011) champion the expectation of research as the "most powerful tools for advancing the science of nursing and improving the quality of patient care and outcomes" (p. 190). Formal research does hold the position as the strongest form of evidence. Aesthetics knowing embraces those facts and information that reflects emotion and awareness of the beauty and art around us. This aspect takes in the idea that data must be interpreted within the environment that it was formed or discovered. To remove the information out of that setting can and does modify the application of the findings. The third form of knowing is ethical. The incorporation of ethical knowing within the venue of evidence brings in the ideas of right and wrong. Mensik (2011) connects ethical knowing with the delivery of "care on the basis of the values of the patient, not solely on the science or personal belief" (p. 175). The ethical aspect incorporates the patient's desires into the utilization of the evidence. The final type of knowing is personal knowledge. Personal knowledge and clinical expertise are critical components within EBP. Personal knowing allows for the participants in the process of healthy living to be actively engaged and involved. These individuals are not passive members but enthusiastic contributors in the consideration of the evidence and the plan of care. The question becomes the key within this process of accessing the evidence. A well-prepared question with clinical relevance focuses the search for evidence within these different forms of knowing (Blazeck, Klem, & Miller, 2011; Burns & Chung, 2010). The type of question facilitates the types of evidence to be sought. It also promotes the evaluation of that evidence using these different forms of understanding the knowledge. For some questions, empiric knowing would be important. For other queries, the ethical and/or aesthetic component could be the driving force toward the level of evidence needed.

As the concept of evidence becomes understandable and transparent, attention must be directed toward classifying the different levels of evidence to allow for consistency within the discussion. Without a uniform means of evaluating the evidence, communication of the nature of the evidence will be confusing and disoriented. Mensik (2011) demands that nurses become increasingly aware of their current practice—what is and is not known through evidence—supported by research conclusions appropriate to the distinctive interventions which can be utilized. Nurses need to embrace a standardized objective approach for use when evaluating evidence of all natures—research, quality improvement, expert opinion, case studies, and so on.

Evidence Grading Methods

One topic drawing an increasing amount of attention as part of the movement toward incorporation of research critiques into EBP is the grading of evidence. Armola et al. (2009) acknowledge that the use of grading tools "assist[s] practitioners to determine whether statements about clinical practice were based on research or other reliable evidence" (p. 71). A quick Internet search can provide multiple levels for consideration. According to Steelman, Pape, King, Graling, and Gaberson (2011), over 40 evidence-rating methods were discoverable in 2011. As a result of finding this many rating tools, the Association of periOperative Registered Nurses (AORN) board elected to evaluate the different methods using the Agency for Healthcare Research and Quality's (AHRQ) three domains of evidence—quality, quantity, and consistency. Within the study conducted by Steelman et al., only eight tools out of the 40 methods were found to address these three domains. Two additional tools were also identified for a total reviewed of ten. Within this scoring of the different methods, the AORN group identified only one method that addressed the five criteria that were evaluated: the Oncology Nursing Society (ONS) Putting Evidence into Practice (PEP) schema.

After the critique of the article is completed, the information assessed is awarded a specific grade based on the strength of the evidence presented in the publication. For the most part, the "levels of evidence" categories developed by the various organizations are compatible, with only minor differences. Each of the different formats currently being used to score and/or grade evidence categorize the evidence documents from strongest to least supported evidential materials (Burns & Chung, 2010). Since all of the individual hierarchies reflect this grading of the evidence, it becomes critical to carefully examine the assorted tools to determine which criteria fits within the practice area of the individual. Stichler (2010) maintains that while the rating hierarchies are provided to allow for the critical appraisal of studies, they are not established to allow for a value judgment about the quality of any study. Each grouping has unique characteristics based upon the agency or organization responsible for the determination of the categories.

Numerous organizations, AHRQ, Joanna Briggs Institute, and Cochrane Collaboration, among others, have developed "levels of evidence" hierarchies in an effort to help reviewers categorize the strengths and weaknesses of various studies. One such hierarchy developed by United States Prevention Service Task Force (USPSTF) can be seen in **Figure 2-4**. Within this ladder, quantitative and

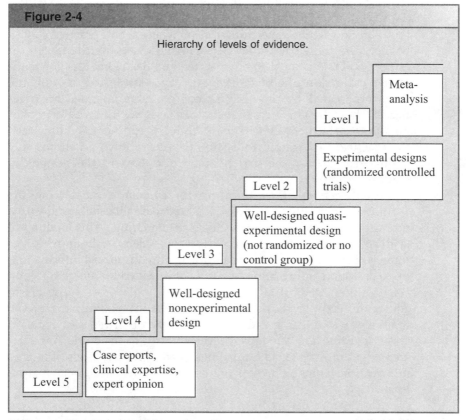

Figure 2-4

Hierarchy of levels of evidence.

Level 1 — Meta-analysis

Level 2 — Experimental designs (randomized controlled trials)

Level 3 — Well-designed quasi-experimental design (not randomized or no control group)

Level 4 — Well-designed nonexperimental design

Level 5 — Case reports, clinical expertise, expert opinion

Source: Adapted from United States Prevention Service Task Force (USPSTF). (2009). *Slide presentation from the AHRQ 2008 annual conference.* Retrieved from http://www.ahrq.gov/about/annualmtg08/090808slides/Lin2.htm

qualitative types of research design are designated as a specific level within the hierarchy of research study designs. Evans (2003) supports this process since "confidence in the findings of research has important implications for those developing practice guidelines and clinical recommendations, or implementing the result of research in their area of practice" (p. 78). One drawback with this ranking is the lack of classification of mixed method studies. Reviewers must make their own decisions about classifying such studies as quantitative or qualitative, because no level for mixed method studies has been established. Another concern raised with this hierarchy relates to the four levels given to research results and the classifying of all other types of evidence as level 5. The message from this rank order is that research is the only valid evidence mechanism.

Since the ONS PEP schema was identified as meeting specific criteria for evaluating the evidence, it can serve as an effective foundation for use within the clinical arena. This tool is used after the selection of articles and evidence is determined. The use of this tool is to aid in the determination of whether the practice should be included in the day-to-day performance of health care (Steelman et al., 2011). Within the schema, specific decision rules for summative evaluation of a body of evidence is established to guide the reviewers in making the designations of: recommended for practice, likely to be effective, benefits balanced with harms, effectiveness not established, effectiveness unlikely, and not recommended for practice. Each rating tool should be carefully and thoroughly evaluated to determine which one works best in the designated clinical setting.

Another type of classification for evidence comes from the Turning Research Into Practice (TRIP) database (accessible at http://www.ebmpyramid.org/samples/complicated.html). This levelling of evidence provides three basic divisions. Evidence falls into one of three global categories—filtered information, unfiltered information, or background information/expert opinion (Harvey Cushing/John Hay Whitney Medical Library, n.d.). While this process appears to address different levels, the hierarchy shows that six out of the seven levels speak to research endeavors. Again, all other types of evidence are placed into the one lowest level within the structure. This hierarchy does provide an additional designation for the levels of filtered information which addresses the critical analysis and meta-analysis levels.

The Joanna Briggs Institute (JBI) (2012a, 2012b) has moved toward the use of the FAME (Feasibility, Appropriateness, Meaningfulness, Effectiveness) level of evidence and the AGREE (Appraisal of Guidelines Research and Evaluation) collaboration. Within the JBI approach to levels of evidence, evidence documents are scored based on four criteria—feasibility, appropriateness, meaningfulness, and effectiveness. Effectiveness relates to whether an intervention performs as expected. Appropriateness considers the psychosocial aspects of the intervention. It is concerned with the impact the activity will have on the consumer and whether it will be accepted by the individual. According to Evans (2003), feasibility "encompasses the broader environmental issues related to implementation, cost, and practice changes" (p. 79). Meaningfulness considers the effect of the intervention on the individual. Within each of these areas, a document would be scored from 1–4. Level 1 is the strongest level of evidence. In addition to these four components, each document is also assessed for economic evidence. The majority of this ranking focuses on meta-synthesis of research. As the grid is examined, aspects such as **case-controlled**, observations, expert opinion, and consensus can be found only in the lowest levels of the document. In conjunction with the level of evidence ranking, JBI developed a practice focus ranking document which accompanies the Appraisal of Guidelines Research and Evaluation (AGREE) Collaboration. This document grades the evidence used within the guideline from level A to level C based on the appropriateness of application to a practice setting. By having this document alongside the levels of evidence (FAME) document, individuals can look toward the application within the practice setting.

AHRQ has also developed a "tool for evaluating the strength of the evidence" (United States Prevention Services Task Force, 2009); see **Figure 2-5**. With this tool, the evidence is assigned a level of strength based on the anticipated benefit and/or harm to the patient. Mensik (2011) states that this tool serves to address the routine clinical aspects of evidence-based practice. As this rating schedule is used, the process looks at the application of any evidence into the practice arena. None of the five levels speak to the idea of research. Each level clarifies a different amount of benefit or harm for the patient from the use of the service. Differences in classifications using this tool continue to be a problem since individual opinions have to be used to rank or assign the levels.

SUNY Downstate Medical Center (n.d.) provides an evidence pyramid as a means of classifying and/or ranking evidence. This pyramid has nine levels. Within these levels, the ranking progresses from systematic reviews and meta-analyses at the top to in vitro ("test tube") research at the base. Within the middle range on the pyramid, the levels of case series, case reports, and ideas, editorials, and opinions are listed. While the framework is interesting, the placement of research at both the top and bottom of the pyramid is confusing.

Figure 2-5

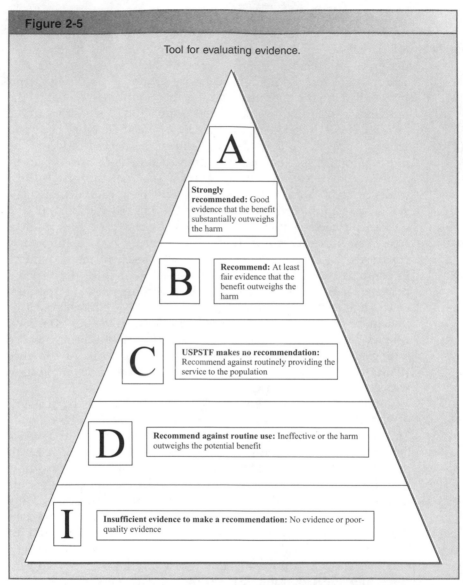

Tool for evaluating evidence.

Source: Adapted from United States Prevention Service Task Force (USPSTF). (2009). *Slide presentation from the AHRQ 2008 annual conference.* Retrieved from http://www.ahrq.gov/about/annualmtg08/090808slides/Lin2.htm

Animal research and in vitro research tends to be quantitative research which is held to be strong evidence by other ranking groups. No rationale was provided as to why the pyramid develops from quantitative research to expert sources, and finally ending back with quantitative research designs.

? **Think Outside the Box**

1. Look at the different types of evidence. List the strengths and weaknesses for each type of evidence. Can you identify any other types of evidence which should be considered when establishing healthcare practice?
2. Select four different forms of evidence. Use at least two of the different rating tools to evaluate the four pieces of evidence. Which tool was easiest to use? Which provided the best review of the evidence? Which tool was difficult to use and why?
3. Debate the use of a rating tool. Do healthcare professionals need to rate all of the evidence they use? Is the rating of evidence just added work which does not meet the needs of the clinical workplace?

With the integration of evidence-based practice into the research critique process, the classification of research projects in terms of the "level of evidence" and the strength of the evidence using instruments such as the AHRQ tool seeks to improve the clarity of the information available for making clinical decisions about the modification of policies, procedures, and clinical guidelines.

Conclusion

Vanhook (2009) stated "nurses and nurse leaders have the opportunity to advance nursing practice and improve patient outcomes unlike any time in the past. Our historical roots are embedded in patient observations, hypotheses development, data collection, data analysis, and conclusions leading to improved patient care" (p. 9). Each nurse must accept the challenge of investigating the evidence which is available to support and advance the practice of nursing care and health care at the local setting. No longer can health care be provided based on the "way we have always done it." Each nurse must recognize and acknowledge the responsibility for advancing the evidence of how and why the interventions are done. Only when this process is done will health care be able to provide quality health management. Within this process the use of the hierarchies to grade the different evidence is important but serves only as a guide rather than a set of rigid rules (Evans, 2003). The careful consideration of evidence quality is based upon logical steps and criteria. Agencies must consider the different formats available to determine which one works best in each setting. The primary responsibility is to question the evidence and not just accept it because it is there. Nurses must be willing to evaluate and confront the data to ensure that the care provided does rise to the appropriate level to advance the quality of the health care provided.

Summary Points

1. Evidence includes that which can be proven and/or disproven. It is an indication or sign related to a topic.
2. Taking the time and energy to effectively consider the evidence is imperative.
3. The proof and/or indications which can be pulled together to determine the best line of action becomes the driving force, instead of the amount of research which may have been done.
4. A grading process allows one to carefully and cautiously consider the evidence presented in light of a unique clinical environment.
5. A firm appreciation for the interconnectedness of the different aspects within EBP, research, and quality improvement is paramount.
6. A critical appraisal for evidence-based practice must consider more than just the available research.
7. Whether an individual is considering research activities or quality improvement efforts, the initial step is always the identification of the problem to be addressed.
8. Each piece of information must be carefully and thoroughly considered concerning what is the foundation on which the outcome is established.
9. Persistence and consistency of results add support and strength to the quality of the evidence.

Red Flags

- All evidence must be carefully and thoroughly questioned prior to the acceptance of the validity of the information.
- Sources of evidence should provide enough information concerning the development of the materials along with the outcomes for others to be able to evaluate the quality of the evidence.

Multiple Choice Questions

1. What type of evidence is paramount to use when providing health care?

  A. Outcomes based on the unique situation
  B. Opinions held by multiple individuals
  C. Research is the only form of evidence
  D. The weight of the evidence is not as important as the amount

2. Four aspects which are included in evidence-based practice are

  A. Research, decision-making processes, time, and patient preferences.
  B. Evidence, decision-making processes, clinical setting, and patient mix.
  C. Evidence, decision-making processes, nursing experiences, and holistic patient care.
  D. Research, nursing process, nursing experiences, and nursing care.

3. What aspect within the process of evidence-based practice controls the path of the literature review?

  A. Determination of the question
  B. Use of MeSH terms
  C. Location of adequate research articles
  D. Determination of a rating system to be used

4. Quality improvement activities result in what type of changes?

  A. Generalizable
  B. Global
  C. Broad, dynamic
  D. Local, regional

5. Whether the evidence is gained by research or other sources, the information must be scrutinized for

  A. Uniqueness.
  B. Individuality.
  C. Validity.
  D. Reliability.

6. The type of knowing which considers the emotions and awareness of beauty and art is called

  A. Empirics.
  B. Aesthetics.
  C. Ethical.
  D. Personal.

7. When the information is presented as a close examination of individuals, trans-actions, solutions, events, and projects, the type of evidence is listed as

   A. Case studies.
   B. Opinions.
   C. Editorials.
   D. Observations.

8. Information provided as feelings, convictions, and/or values are designated as which form of evidence?

   A. Editorials
   B. Observations
   C. Ideas
   D. Opinions

9. When the evidence is understood to represent the outcome resulting from the discussion by a majority of the participants, it is what type of evidence?

   A. Editorials
   B. Observations
   C. Expert opinions
   D. Consensus

10. What reason is key for using a level of evidence hierarchy to rate evidence considered for EBP reviews?

    A. Understanding what is in the evidence
    B. Clarifying that only research evidence is used
    C. Determining the risk and benefit of the research
    D. Categorizing the strengths and weaknesses of the evidence

11. The AHRQ tool for evaluating the strength of the evidence is used to determine

    A. The anticipated benefit and/or harm to the patient.
    B. Only the benefit for the nurse.
    C. Gaps and consistencies in the research.
    D. The harm for the nurse.

12. Which of the different rating scales serves to address the clinical routine aspect of EBP?

    A. Turning Research into Practice (TRIP)
    B. Joanna Briggs Institute's FAME
    C. AHRQ strength of the evidence tool
    D. SUNY Downstate Medical Center's pyramid

13. The four types of knowing are designated as

    A. Deontology, empiric, clinical, and aesthetics.
    B. Empirics, aesthetics, ethical, and personal.
    C. Facts, opinions, case studies, and consensus.
    D. Decision making, clinical, ethical, and client.

14. The AGREE (Appraisal of Guidelines Research and Evaluation) Collaboration tool is used to

    A. Grade the evidence used within the guideline.

    B. Score the research articles to be used for a guideline.

    C. Establish the anticipated benefit and/or harm of the guideline.

    D. Provide an additional tool to be used at the bedside.

15. The ONS method, the Putting Evidence into Practice (PEP) schema is used to

    A. Identify the research that was used in the process.

    B. Rate the collective evidence that supports a recommendation.

    C. Establish the risk and/or benefit of an activity.

    D. Rank the research articles for use with a guideline.

Discussion Questions

1. The Institute of Medicine's *Future of Nursing* report identified four central recommendations to advance the nursing profession and health care. The four recommendations were: (1) nurses function at their full extent of knowledge and education; (2) nurses become active at the decision-making table; (3) seamless academic progression for nurses to advance within the educational systems, and (4) adequate and reliable data on which to advance health care. Carefully and thoughtfully consider these four recommendations in light of the use of evidence-based practice. How can the nursing profession best address these four central recommendations related to evidence-based practice?

2. Steelman et al. (2011) listed the task force recommendations for implementing the use of a rating scale within a site. The recommendations included: determining the steps for completing an evidence review, establishing a consensus minimum for those involved in the review, developing educational materials to be used to update staff and committee members on the process, and allocation of resources for the process. Based on these recommendations, what guidelines would you develop to be used in your setting to select and incorporate a rating system for evidence review?

Suggested Readings

Newhouse, R. P. (2008). Evidence synthesis: The good, the bad, and the ugly. *Journal of Nursing Administration, 38*(3), 107–111.

Oermann, M. H. (2012). Building evidence for practice: Not without dissemination. *MCN: The American Journal of Maternal Child Nursing, 37*(2), 77.

Riley, J. K., Hill, A. N., Krause, L. B., Leach, L. B., & Lowe, T. J., (2011). Examining nurses' attitudes regarding the value, role, interest, and experience in research in an acute care hospital. *Journal for Nurses in Staff Development, 27*(6), 272–279.

Thiel, L., & Ghosh, Y. (2008). Determining registered nurses' readiness for evidence-based practice. *Worldviews on Evidence-Based Nursing, 5*(4), 182–192.

References

Albert, N. M., & Fulton, J. S. (2011). Four rights for focusing clinical nurse specialist research: Right focus, right projects, right level, and right resources. *Clinical Nurse Specialist,* 25(4), 165–168.

Alligood, M. R. (2011). Nursing theory-guided research. *Nursing Science Quarterly,* 24(3), 195–196.

Armola, R. R., Bourgault, A. M., Halm, M. A., Board, R. M., Bucher, L., Harrington, L., . . . Medina, J. (2009). AACN levels of evidence: What's new? *Critical Care Nurse,* 29(4), 70–73.

Blazeck, A., Klem, M. L., & Miller, T. H. (2011). Building evidence-based practice into the foundations of practice. *Nurse Educator,* 36(3), 124–127.

Burns, P. B., & Chung, K. C. (2010). Developing good clinical questions and finding the best evidence to answer those questions. *Plastic and Reconstructive Surgery,* 126(2), 613–618.

Evans, D. (2003). Hierarchy of evidence: A framework for ranking evidence evaluating healthcare interventions. *Journal of Clinical Nursing,* 12(1), 77–84.

Evidence. (n.d.). *Dictionary.com unabridged.* Retrieved from http://dictionary.reference.com/browse/evidence

Gawlinski, A., & Miller, P. S. (2011). Advancing nursing research through a mentorship program for staff nurses. *AACN Advanced Critical Care,* 22(3), 190–200.

Harvey Cushing/John Hay Whitney Medical Library. (n.d.). *Evidence-based practice (EBP) resources.* Retrieved from http://www.ebmpyramid.org/samples/complicated.html

Joanna Briggs Institute. (2012a). *Grades of recommendation.* Retrieved from http://www.joannabriggs.edu.au/Grades%20of%20Recommendation

Joanna Briggs Institute. (2012b). *Levels of evidence FAME.* Retrieved from http://www.joannabriggs.edu.au/About%20Us/JBI%20Approach/Levels%20of%20Evidence%20%20FAME

Mensik, J. S. (2011). Understanding research and evidence-based practice: From knowledge generation to translation. *Journal of Infusion Nursing,* 34(3), 174–178.

Mick, J. (2011). Data-driven decision making: A nursing research and evidence-based practice dashboard. *Journal of Nursing Administration,* 41(10), 391–393.

Paget, L., Han, P., Nedza, S., Kurtz, P., Racine, E., Russell, S., . . . Von Kohorn, I. (2011). *Patient-clinician communication: Basic principles and expectations* [Discussion paper]. Institute of Medicine of the National Academies.

Proehl, J. A., & Hoyt, K. S. (2012). Evidence versus standard versus best practice: Show me the data! *Advanced Emergency Nursing Journal,* 34(1), 1–2.

Selker, H., Grossmann, C., Adams, A., Goldmann, D., Dezii, C., Meyer, G., . . . Platt, R. (2011). *The common rule and continuous improvement in health care: A learning health system perspective* [Discussion paper]. Institute of Medicine of the National Academies.

Steelman, V. M., Pape, T., King, C. A., Graling, P., & Gaberson, K. B. (2011). Selection of a method to rate the strength of scientific evidence for AORN recommendations. *AORN Journal,* 93(4), 433–444.

Stichler, J. F. (2010). Evaluating the evidence in evidence-based design. *Journal of Nursing Administration,* 40(9), 348–351.

Stillwell, S. B., Fineout-Overholt, E., Melnyk, B. M., & Williamson, K. M. (2010). Evidence-based practice, step by step: Asking the clinical question: A key step in evidence-based practice. *American Journal of Nursing, 110*(3), 58–61.

SUNY Downstate Medical Center. (n.d.). *Guide to research methods.* Retrieved from http://library.downstate.edu/EBM2/2100.htm

United States Prevention Service Task Force (USPSTF). (2009). *Slide presentation from the AHRQ 2008 annual conference.* Retrieved from http://www.ahrq.gov/about/annualmtg08/090808slides/Lin2.htm

Vanhook, P. M. (2009). Overcoming the barriers to EBP. *Nursing Management, 40*(8), 9–11.

Chapter 3

Overview of Research

Sharon Cannon and Margaret Robinson

Chapter Objectives

At the conclusion of this chapter, the learner will be able to

1. Discuss the evolution of evidence-based practice, nursing research, and current healthcare trends
2. Identify the value of using models and frameworks in nursing research
3. Differentiate between basic and applied research
4. Delineate sources for nursing research

Key Terms

➤ Applied research
➤ Basic research
➤ Best practices
➤ Bundling
➤ National Center for Nursing
  Research (NCNR)

➤ National Institute of Nursing
  Research (NINR)
➤ National Institutes of Health (NIH)

Introduction

The roots of research utilization can be traced back to the time of Florence Nightingale in the mid-1800s. Over the past 150 years, nursing research has encompassed a variety of models, settings, and foci. The following historical perspective illustrates the trajectory of nursing research.

Historical Perspective

Evolution from Nightingale to Present Time

Florence Nightingale's work on sanitation in the 1800s was one of the early efforts at linking environmental variables to clinical outcomes. In the early 1900s, the focal point of nursing research was on nursing education. In the 1940s, the concentration shifted to the availability and demand for nurses in time of war. A major milestone occurred in 1952 when the first edition of the journal *Nursing Research* was published. In the 1970s, clinical outcomes again reemerged as a focus for nursing research, and the *Nursing Studies Index* by Virginia Henderson was produced. Today, through evidence-based practice (EBP), the focus is on the application of research findings to clinical decision making in an effort to improve individual patient outcomes.

❓ Think Outside the Box

Explore the various approaches used to generate knowledge in your practice area. For example, which information has been used to determine the method of catheterizing a laboring mother? Which information serves as the basis for the range of blood sugars used in elderly patients who are newly diagnosed with diabetes?

Florence Nightingale's *Notes on Matters Affecting the Health, Efficiency and Hospital Administration of the British Army* (1858) was one of the first published works that outlined the clinical application of nursing research (Florence Nightingale Museum Trust, 2003; Riddle, 2005). Florence Nightingale created a polar-area diagram (or coxcomb) to display data related to the causes of mortality in the British Army during the Crimean War (**Figure 3-1**). This early pie chart used color graphics to depict deaths secondary to preventable disease, war injuries, and all other causes. Using these data, Nightingale calculated the mortality rate for contagious diseases such as cholera and typhus. Her statistical analysis demonstrated the need for sanitary reform in military hospitals.

Figure 3-1

Polar-area diagram.

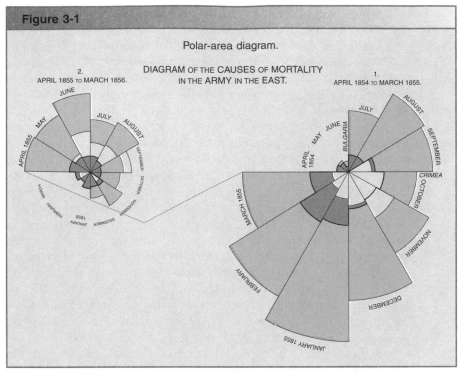

2.
APRIL 1855 TO MARCH 1856.

DIAGRAM OF THE CAUSES OF MORTALITY
IN THE ARMY IN THE EAST.

1.
APRIL 1854 TO MARCH 1855.

Source: Nightingale, F. (1858). *Notes on matters affecting the health, efficiency and hospital administration of the British army.* London, UK: Harrison and Sons. As cited in Riddle, L. (2005). *Polar-area diagram: Biographies of women mathematicians.* Retrieved from http://www.agnesscott.edu/lriddle/women/ nightpiechart.htm

? **Think Outside the Box**   www

What would Florence Nightingale say about nursing research and evidence-based practice today?

The American Nursing Foundation, established in 1955, was devoted exclusively to the promotion of nursing research:

> The primary objectives of the foundation were to increase public knowledge and understanding of professional nursing, practical nursing and the arts and sciences on which the health of the American people depended. The foundation was to conduct studies, surveys and research; provide research grants to graduate nurses; make grants to public and private nonprofit educational institutions; and publish scientific, educational and literary works. (Kalisch & Kalisch, 1986, p. 651)

Federal support for nursing research began in 1946, with the creation of the Division of Nursing within the Office of the Surgeon General. In 1955, the **National Institutes of Health** (NIH) established the Nursing Research Study Section. A 1983 study entitled *Nursing and Nursing Education: Public Policy and Private Actions*, published by the Institute of Medicine (IOM), recommended that nursing research be included in the mainstream of health-related research. With growing public support, the Health Research Extension Act of 1985 authorized the development of the **National Center for Nursing Research** (NCNR) at the NIH. The NIH Revitalization Act of 1993 elevated NCNR to an NIH Institute and established the **National Institute of Nursing Research** (NINR, 2006a).

"The National Institute of Nursing Research supports basic and clinical research to establish a scientific basis for the care of individuals across the lifespan—from the management of the patient during illness and recovery to the reduction of risks for disease and disability, and the promotion of healthy lifestyles" (NINR, 2006b, p. 1). The strategic planning process at NINR identified areas of focus for prospective nursing research (**Table 3-1**). In April 1993, the Board of Directors of the American Nurses Association (ANA) adopted a position statement that acknowledged that "research based practice is essential if the nursing profession is to meet its mandate to society for effective and efficient patient care" (ANA, 1993, p. 1). It went on to identify the role of nursing research for the ADN-, BSN-, MSN-, and doctoral-prepared practitioner. The position statement outlined a process whereby clinicians identify relevant clinical problems for investigation and researchers design studies to address these problems (**Table 3-2**).

Table 3-1
Areas of Focus for Nursing Research
Chronic illnesses
Quality and cost-effectiveness of care
Health promotion and disease prevention
Management of symptoms
Adaptation to new technologies
Health disparities
Palliative care at the end of life
Source: National Institute of Nursing Research. (2006b). *Mission statement.* Retrieved from http://www.ninr.nih.gov/AboutNINR/NINRMissionandStrategicPlan

Table 3-2

Research Roles at Various Levels of Nursing Education
Associate Degree
Helping to identify clinical problems in nursing practice Assisting with the collection of data within a structured format Using nursing research findings appropriately in clinical practice in conjunction with nurses holding more advanced credentials
Baccalaureate Degree
Identifying clinical problems requiring investigation Assisting experienced investigators to gain access to clinical sites Influencing the selection of appropriate methods of data collection Collecting data and implementing nursing research findings
Master's Degree
Collaborating with experienced investigators in proposal development, data collection, data analysis, and interpretation Appraising the clinical relevance of research findings Creating a climate in the practice setting that promotes scholarly inquiry, scientific integrity, and scientific investigation of clinical nursing problems Providing leadership for integrating findings into clinical practice
Source: American Nurses Association. (1993, Adopted April 1994). *Position statement: Education for participation in nursing research.* Retrieved from http://nursingworld.org/MainMenuCategories/Policy-Advocacy/Positions-and-Resolutions/ANAPositionStatements/Archives/rseducat14484.html

? Think Outside the Box

www.

Discuss the barriers you might encounter when trying to implement evidence-based practice and research utilization in your area.

Early nursing research focused on the development of the profession of nursing, not the clinical practice of nursing. In 1970, a study conducted by Lysaught "revealed that little nursing research has been conducted on the actual effect of nursing interventions and that nursing had few definitive guidelines for its practice. The study recommended that investigation of the impact of nursing care on the quality, effectiveness and economy of health care be conducted" (Polit & Hungler, 1978, p. 11). Thus began a new era in which clinical practice emerged as a priority for nursing research.

In the 1980s, clinical pathways were introduced into nursing practice. Clinical pathways are a plan of care developed by a multidisciplinary team that outlines the sequential care that should be provided to a predictable group of patients. Early clinical pathways focused on high-volume admissions in the acute care setting, such as elective surgeries and routine obstetrical care. Clinical pathways should incorporate the applicable research. However, the intent of a clinical pathway is to manage the progression of an individual patient through a clinical event. These pathways emerged in response to shifting payment methods for health care and focused on the critical path whose steps must be accomplished for the patient to have a cost-effective and timely discharge. Measures of success were, generally, a reduction in the total cost to provide care and a reduction in the average length of stay for each patient. In the late 1990s, a growing concern arose that many hospitals had adopted clinical pathways without strong evidence that they were clinically or economically effective.

The emergence of EBP takes the application of research one step further to focus on outcomes-based practices. The emphasis is now on the assessment and evaluation of clinical practices that have demonstrated their ability to improve morbidity and mortality for patients. Frequently, multiple interventions have been identified that together enhance the clinical outcome; this practice has come to be known as **bundling**. A bundle is a group of interventions related to a disease or care process that, when executed together, result in better outcomes than when the interventions are implemented individually. Evidence suggests that consistently implementing these practices with all patients who have a specific disease or procedure can improve patient outcomes (Institute for Healthcare Improvement, 2006). In 2005, the Institute for Healthcare Improvement introduced care bundles for the prevention of central-line infection and ventilator-acquired pneumonia as part of the 100,000 Lives Campaign. In this case, the outcomes-based practices focus on a single aspect of care that is known to have serious complications.

Blending evidence-based research and applying it to clinical practice and patient outcomes was a goal of the work of the IOM in its landmark publication *To Err Is Human: Building a Safer Health System* (1999). In the preparation of this report, research in human factors was applied to health care in an attempt to understand where and why systems or processes break down. Specifically, the report's authors looked at how practices in healthcare settings could be made safer so as to prevent adverse outcomes for patients.

In 2004, the IOM expanded on its original work to look at the work environment of nurses in its publication *Keeping Patients Safe: Transforming the Work Environment of Nurses*. This report further described the need for bundles of mutually reinforcing patient safety defenses as part of the effort to reduce errors and increase patient safety. It described "bundles of changes" that are needed within four aspects of care— (1) leadership and management, (2) the work force, (3) the work process, and (4) organizational culture—to strengthen patient safety.

As EBP emerged, a major shift occurred beginning in 2010. National trends discussed in Chapter 1 began to emphasize patient outcomes, cost containment and reimbursement related to hospital readmissions. In addition, demand for patient involvement in healthcare decision making is emphasized ever more; no longer would health care be "doing for" the patient, but rather it would be "doing with" the patient. The importance of EBP and research is currently focused on patient-centered care. As a result of the Affordable Care Act (ACA), the recent establishment of the Patient Centered Outcomes Research Institute (PCORI) is a prime example of efforts to make the patient the center of care and the provision of outcomes specific to the patient (National Pharmaceutical Council, 2012).

Recent changes in Medicare/Medicaid reimbursement have also forced healthcare organizations to reexamine how services are provided. Gold (2011) indicates the ACA is also the impetus for the provision of Accountable Care Organizations (ACOs) and is regulated by the Centers for Medicare and Medicaid Services (CMS). A major area of concern for CMS is quality reporting and performance of ACOs which include: "(1) patient experience of care; (2) care coordination; (3) patient safety; (4) preventive health and (5) at-risk population/frail elderly health" (Gordon, 2011, p. 1).

Obviously, research and EBP will play a significant role in patient-centered care and ACOs in the future. Quality Assurance/Quality Improvement (QA/QI) initiatives will provide the necessary evidence for generating knowledge about what does and does not work. Nursing EBP and research will be heavily involved in the years to come.

? Think Outside the Box

Which model and/or theoretical frameworks do you think can be most appropriate for a medical/surgical unit?

Purpose of Nursing Research

The major rationale for conducting research is to build a body of nursing knowledge, thereby promoting improvement in patient outcomes. This is accomplished by using results of research in the provision of nursing care that is based on scientific data rather than on a hunch, gut feeling, or "the way I was taught." As a profession, nursing must hold its members accountable for providing safe, cost-effective, and efficient care. EBP that incorporates research findings is a model for nurses to use in their practice.

Theory, Research, and Practice

Parker and Smith (2010) define theories as "organizing struct
our reflections, observations, projections and inferences" (p. 7
(2009) defines research as "a systematic inquiry into a subject tl
various approaches (quantitative and qualitative methods) to answer
questions and solves problems" (p. 5). Research can be more readily
considered a specific explanation. Fawcett and Garity (2009) have an
interesting approach to theories and EBP. They suggest that "theories
can be thought of as evidence" (p. 6). The theory becomes evidence to
guide practice. Research is therefore equal to theory development.

When considering the relationship between theory and research,
one could conclude that theory gives direction to research, which in
turn guides practice. As a result, many nursing research projects
include a nursing theory/theoretical framework and concepts to
guide the research and provide implications for nursing practice.

The evolution of the relationship of theory to research to practice
has been ongoing since the days of Florence Nightingale. The current
emphasis in research is on translational research and implementation
science. These changes move theory into a new dimension for application to practice. If translational research is seen as a method to move
a theory into another dimension, and if implementation science is
perceived as supporting evidence-based practice and research utilization, then the relationship to practice is further enhanced and becomes
stronger. Thus, implementing research (evidence) and theory into
practice (translation) optimizes EBP.

It is beyond the scope of this text to examine theory in depth.
Sometimes a theory is not identified for a research or evidence-based
project; however, a theory is still important. The researcher or nurse
using evidence to guide nursing care must, at the very least, incorporate a model, framework, plan, or system that gives direction to the
project. Van Achterberg, Schoonhoven, and Grol (2008) connect
models to research and theories for implementation of EBP.

Models and Frameworks

Nursing research provides a way to explain and predict the care that
nurses provide, including the underlying rationale. As a result, models
of nursing care and their frameworks provide ample opportunities for
the generation of new nursing knowledge. As Malloch and Porter-
O'Grady (2006) indicate, "Professional Care Models give nurses
responsibility and authority to provide patient care. In addition, nurses
are accountable for coordinating care and ensuring that continuity of
care is provided across the continuum. Patients' unique needs are
addressed to achieve outcomes" (p. 236).

Webster's II *New College Dictionary* (1999) defines a model as "a preliminary pattern serving as the plan from which an item not yet constructed will be produced; a tentative description of a theory or system that accounts for all its known properties" (p. 704). Many nursing care models and research models are problem-solving processes that begin with a question. Nurses ask clinical questions on a daily basis and often conduct research on an informal basis. When a nurse observes the same phenomena occur with multiple patients having the same diagnosis over time, a pattern emerges. The nurse has, through experience, validated his or her observations, just not in a formal, structured research model. As Burns and Grove (2009) state, "A framework is an abstract, logical structure of meaning. It guides the development of the study and enables you to link the findings to the body of knowledge used in nursing" (p. 126). When a theory is not used, a care model, plan, or system is needed in evidence-based practice and research. A model, plan, or system then functions as a framework.

Validation of Best Practices

Best practice is a term used by many different types of professionals in many different settings. The definition of best practices varies depending on the meanings assigned to the words *best* and *practices*. In this text, *best practices* is defined as those nursing actions that produce the most desirable patient outcomes through scientific data.

? Think Outside the Box

Most of the research projects associated with evidence-based practice tend to be examples of applied research. Brainstorm about some possible projects that would be classified as basic research.

For best practices, research utilization supports decision making for nursing practice through a problem-solving process. Reaffirmation through scientific data validates the desired outcomes and reinforces best practices. This is an excellent example for reality testing. While a wealth of information is available, nurses have little time to look for it, and therefore often practice as they were taught. There may be times when a nurse thinks or feels that the result of an action is accurate, when it actually is not. Burns and Grove (2001) cite an example related to patient consumption of oxygen. The nurse's sense might be that getting a patient up to the bedside commode results in more oxygen consumption than when the patient uses a bedpan. However, research has shown this to not be accurate. Thus, reality can be tested through scientific inquiry, which leads to validated best practice.

Fineout-Overholt and Melnyk (2005) suggest that "best practice" is a term used by more than healthcare providers. According to these authors, "without well-designed research, best practices cannot claim universal application" (p. 27); consensus builds best practices that are achieved through evidence.

Simpson (2005) suggests that through EBP, nurses could overlook the truth about nursing practice. Nurses need to look at what practice is and what is really done. Perhaps, research and practice need to merge to have a major impact on practice. Through this merger, practice and research would combine to actually become a validated best practice. Hopp and Rittenmeyer (2012) promote the term "best available research evidence" for making decisions on the best evidence (p. 13).

Basic Versus Applied Research

Basic research can be defined as research to gain knowledge for knowledge's sake (Brockopp & Hastings-Tolsma, 2003; Burns & Grove, 2009; Fain, 2009). Another way to look at basic research is that it tests theories (Fawcett & Garity, 2009). Sometimes basic research is also called bench research, such as laboratory experiments intended to elucidate cell structure. Simply stated, basic research is often useful later when, for example, a researcher addresses how a new drug being tested affects a cell's structure. Fain (2009) indicates that basic research is conducted with little concern for how it might ultimately be applied to practice.

? Think Outside the Box

www

Using Florence Nightingale's ideas, apply these ideas to research and evidence-based practice.

In contrast, **applied research** directly impacts practice and modifies current practice. Most nursing research is applied research that assists in decision making related to nursing care. Applied research occurs in multiple settings and with diverse populations. This can also include the development of new approaches for care. Modification, development, and evaluation of nursing care of best practice form the heart of EBP. Applied research builds a body of knowledge for nursing practice and guides the nurse in providing patient care. An example of applied research in nursing would be a study that generates new information about the use of soap and water versus hand cleansing gels in preparation for a sterile dressing change. An applied research project might indicate that soap and water is more effective in preventing potential wound infections. The nurse would then use the applied research results in preparation for doing a sterile dressing change.

As can be seen, basic research differs from applied research primarily in terms of its focus and intent. Basic science (also known as bench science) is conducted in a laboratory and seeks to add to the knowledge base. Applied research is grounded in the practice area and its application to practice. Fain (2009) suggests that while basic research and applied research are quite different, they can be considered to form a continuum where basic research is required for interpretation of findings of applied studies. One might say that basic research in nursing is building a body of knowledge (theory) and that applied research is the application of the theory to the clinical arena (practice).

Sources for Nursing Research

Most nursing research comes from two primary sources: academia and healthcare settings. One might expect that nurses doing research in academic settings would focus only on educational research and that those conducting research in health care would focus only on practice settings. Although that distinction may hold true in some cases, most often both arenas produce research for both education and practice, because they are closely aligned with each other. This intertwining is most evident in the nursing position papers published by two major nursing organizations.

Academia

A major thrust of research in education is the evaluation of programs, technologies, and instructional design. Research in education flourished from the mid-1980s until about 2001, when funding for nursing education withered. An Act of Congress specified that no funding from the NCNR could be distributed for research in nursing education (Diekelmann, 2001). As a result, nurse educators had to seek funding outside the discipline, where the competition was intense. Consequently, little nursing education research was conducted. Nurse-educator researchers turned to research in clinical practice. Although that effort translated into some positive gains for clinical practice, it drastically affected the research needed to support innovative programs, teaching/learning activities, and other aspects of nursing education.

Since 2000, when the National League for Nursing (NLN) was reorganized, increased emphasis and financial support have been directed toward research in nursing education. In its reorganization, the NLN recognized the need for a "quality nursing education that prepares the nursing workforce to meet the needs of diverse populations in an ever changing healthcare environment . . . and change the landscape related to funding for nursing education research . . . to lead in promoting evidence-based teaching in nursing . . ." (NLN, n.d., p. 1). This commitment to nursing education research is also expressed in the NLN's mission and goal statements. Nurse educators have recognized the need to continue seeking external funds from outside the discipline. Grant funding has also come from several government agencies and foundations. The current impetus for obtaining funding from outside sources is a direct result of the nursing shortage and reports on health care generated by agencies such as the IOM. Because the nursing shortage appears destined to last for years to come, research in nursing education has a promising future. The relationship with EBP will likely remain in the forefront when such research in nursing education is carried out.

? **Think Outside the Box**   `www`

There are many nursing theories available within the literature. Search the literature to find evidence of nursing research utilization of a selected theory.

Healthcare Settings

For healthcare settings to serve as a source for nursing practice, a process for research is necessary. Figure 2-2 details the steps to commonly follow when conducting quantitative or qualitative research in healthcare settings. The flow chart assists the nurse in identifying the best process for obtaining a sound conclusion for the best method to address the problem. Using the flow chart, the nurse would identify the problem, determine the research question and the research methodology (either quantitative or qualitative). All of these specific steps will be addressed in future chapters. It is important to note that outcomes of research and EBP determine what works and what doesn't work. In many ways the research process is similar to the nursing process of assess, plan, implement and evaluate. According to Cronenwett (2002), in 1999 Marita Titler observed that outcomes achieved in a research study might not be replicated with multiple caregivers in the natural clinical setting. The variable demands on the bedside nurse and multiple comorbidities that exist in the hospitalized patient can make it difficult to replicate findings. Cronenwett (2002) has noted that "evidence for practice mounts slowly over time, as scientists discover first what works in controlled environments and second what works in daily clinical practice" (p. 3). Today, it is our challenge to move from a focus solely on research development to the use of valid and reliable evidence in clinical practice. Nurses have been identified as champions in the adoption of EBP. It is equally important that healthcare institutions implement mechanisms that diffuse available evidence into the practice environment.

Summary Points

1. Florence Nightingale's work emphasized clinical applications of nursing research through the creation of a polar area diagram.
2. From 1900 to 1940, nursing research focused on nursing education.
3. In the 1950s, the first issue of *Nursing Research* was published with the notion to share research information with colleagues. Also, the American Nursing Foundation was established to promote nursing research.
4. The 1960s focused on models and frameworks of nursing practice.
5. In the 1970s, Virginia Henderson introduced the Nursing Studies Index.
6. In the 1980s, the Institute of Medicine recommended that nursing research be included in health-related research. In addition, the National Center for Nursing was established.
7. In the 1990s and 2000, both the National League for Nursing and American Nurses Association developed position papers on research-based practice.
8. In 2004, the Institute of Medicine published *Keeping Patients Safe: Transforming the Work Environment for Nurses*, which focused on the need for bundles of mutually reinforcing patient safety defenses as part of the effort to reduce errors and increase patient safety.
9. Recent national trends such as the ACA have had a major impact on the way care is delivered and emphasizes the importance of QA/QI.
10. Models and frameworks of professional practice are validated through research.
11. EBP incorporates research as a professional care model.
12. Basic research is gaining knowledge for knowledge's sake.
13. Applied research directly impacts practice.
14. Sources for research in nursing can be found in academic and healthcare settings.
15. The research process can be defined by a series of detailed steps.

RED FLAGS

- Research projects should be grounded by a model or theoretical framework to anchor the concepts identified within the project.
- Assumptions about best practices must be based on scientific evidence, rather than just on everyday consensus of opinion or intuition.

Case Scenario

Incorporation of EBP into bedside nursing generally requires a change in nursing practice. Change theory models point out that each change process inevitably has potential barriers to effective implementation of the desired change. To more effectively implement EBP, one must identify these barriers to implementation of change. Fink, Thompson, and Bonnes (2005) conducted a nursing research project in an attempt to better understand barriers to implementation of nursing research among inpatient nursing units at a large university-affiliated Magnet hospital:

> The purpose of this study was to examine the effect of multifaceted organizational strategies on registered nurses' (RNs) use of research findings to change practice in an academic hospital. The specific aims were to (1) identify nurses' attitudes and perceptions about organizational culture and research utilization, (2) identify perceived barriers and facilitators to nurses' use of research in practice, and (3) determine which factors are correlated with research utilization. (Fink et al., 2005, p. 121)

Survey tools, including the BARRIERS to Research Utilization Scale and the Research Factor Questionnaire, were used to gather data. The majority of respondents (83%) were registered nurses who held a baccalaureate or advanced degree in nursing. The results demonstrated an improvement in nurses' perception after implementation of multifaceted interventions. The authors also identified journal club participation as a major strategy to facilitate the use of research in clinical nursing practice.

www

Case Scenario Questions

1. How might the findings vary in an academic teaching facility that was not a Magnet hospital?

2. How might the findings vary in a community-based hospital setting?

3. How might the findings vary in an outpatient or procedural-based nursing practice?

4. How might the findings vary in a hospital setting that has primarily associate-degree nursing graduates?

5. What would you anticipate would be the findings in your own clinical practice environment?

6. If you implemented a journal club, do you believe that would increase the use of research findings in your clinical practice area? Why or why not?

Multiple Choice Questions

1. The research role of the baccalaureate degree nurse includes
   A. Identifying clinical problems that require investigation, assisting experienced investigators to gain access to clinical sites, and collecting data.
   B. Creating a climate in the practice setting that promotes scholarly inquiry, scientific integrity, and scientific investigation of clinical nursing problems.
   C. Collaborating with experienced investigators in proposal development, data collection, data analysis, and interpretation of results.
   D. Providing leadership in integrating research into practice.

2. Potential areas of nursing research identified by the National Institute of Nursing Research include
   A. Stem cell research.
   B. Application of pharmaceuticals in clinical practice.
   C. Chronic illness, health promotion, disease prevention, and end-of-life care.
   D. Healthcare literacy.

3. The first issue of *Nursing Research* was published in
   A. 1858.
   B. 1952.
   C. 1985.
   D. 1992.

4. The Nursing Studies Index, the first annotated index of nursing research, was the work of
   A. Florence Nightingale.
   B. Virginia Henderson.
   C. Marita Titler.
   D. Dorothea Orem.

5. The American Nurses Association position statement acknowledges that
   A. Researchers identify clinical problems and study them.
   B. Faculty members identify clinical problems and study them.
   C. Clinicians identify clinical problems and researchers design them.
   D. Faculty members and researchers identify clinical problems and study them.

6. Clinical pathways are developed by
   A. Nursing teams.
   B. Physician teams.
   C. Educator teams.
   D. Multidisciplinary teams.

7. A bundle is a group of interventions related to a disease or care process that

   A. Results in better outcomes than when the interventions are implemented together.
   B. Results in diverse outcomes when the interventions are implemented individually.
   C. Results in confusing information about a single disease or care process.
   D. Provides insufficient evidence to alter clinical practice related to individualized interventions.

8. Professional care models give nurses

   A. Accountability.
   B. Authority.
   C. Responsibility.
   D. All of the above.

9. Best practice is an excellent example of which kind of testing?

   A. Cognitive
   B. Reality
   C. Didactic
   D. Evaluation

10. Basic research is also known as bench research and is defined as research to gain knowledge for

    A. Use in academia.
    B. Use in clinical practice.
    C. Knowledge's sake.
    D. Use in biochemistry.

11. Applied research builds a body of knowledge for nursing practice because it is the basis of

    A. Evidence-based practice.
    B. Clinical pathways.
    C. Nursing process.
    D. Nursing diagnosis.

12. Sources for nursing research come primarily from two sources:

    A. Business and occupational settings.
    B. Academic and healthcare settings.
    C. Both urban and rural settings.
    D. Pharmaceutical and business settings.

13. Best practices in nursing can be defined as

    A. A well-written plan of nursing care.
    B. A systems approach to nursing care.
    C. Nursing actions that produce desirable patient outcomes.
    D. A way for nurses to justify their care.

14. The Institute of Medicine's publication *Keeping Patients Safe* focuses on

    A. Building a safer health system.

    B. Processes to report medication errors.

    C. Transforming the work environment for nurses.

    D. Healthcare reform.

15. Theories are

    A. A guide for research and practice.

    B. Considered to be a specific explanation of an idea.

    C. Not essential to research or EBP.

    D. Static and do not change over time.

16. QA/QI data are now considered

    A. Valid research to guide practice.

    B. Valid evidence to guide practice.

    C. Generalizable to all practice.

    D. Unlimited to any practice.

17. The research process allows for

    A. The best method to address the problems.

    B. Little comparison of outcomes.

    C. Limited measures of evaluation.

    D. Extra time for the nurse at the bedside.

Discussion Questions

www

1. Identify potential opportunities for you to use EBP in your current clinical setting.
2. Identify barriers to implementing EBP in your clinical setting.
3. Identify three clinical problems requiring investigation in your nursing practice. What steps might you take to begin to explore these identified problem areas?
4. Compare your QA/QI data to national standards.

Suggested Readings

Booth, W. C., Colomb, G. G., & Williams, J. M. (2003). *The craft of research* (2nd ed.). Chicago, IL: University of Chicago.

Dimsdale, K., & Kitner, M. (2004). *Becoming an educated consumer of research: A quick look at the basic methodologies of research design.* Retrieved from http://www.air.org/files/Becoming_an_Educated_Consumer_of_Research.pdf

Gerrish, K., & Lacey, A. (2006). *The research process in nursing* (5th ed.). Oxford, UK: Blackwell.

Gold, J. (2011). *FAQs on ACOs: Accountable Care Organizations explained.* Retrieved from http://www.kaiserhealthnews.org/stories/2011

Johnson, B., & Webber, P. (2005). *An introduction to theory and reasoning in nursing* (2nd ed.). Philadelphia, PA: Lippincott Williams & Wilkins.

Kilbom, J., & Cogdill, S. (2004). Writing abstracts. *St. Cloud State University and LEO: Literacy Education Online.* Retrieved from http://leo.stcloudstate.edu/bizwrite/abstracts.html

Shirey, M. R. (2006, July/September). Evidence-based practice: How nurse leaders can facilitate innovation. *Nursing Administration Quarterly, 30*(3), 252–265.

van Meijel, B., Gamel, C., van Swieten-Duijfjes, B., & Grypdonck, M. H. F. (2004, October). The development of evidence-based nursing interventions: Methodological considerations. *Journal of Advanced Nursing, 48*(1), 84–92.

References

American Nurses Association (ANA). (1993). *Position statement: Education for participation in nursing research*. Retrieved from http://nursingworld.org/MainMenuCategories/Policy-Advocacy/Positions-and-Resolutions/ANAPositionStatements/Archives/rseducat14484.html

Brockopp, D. Y., & Hastings-Tolsma, M. T. (2003). *Fundamentals of nursing research* (3rd ed.). Sudbury, MA: Jones and Bartlett.

Burns, N., & Grove, S. K. (2001). *The practice of nursing research: Conduct, critique, and utilization* (4th ed.). Philadelphia, PA: W. B. Saunders.

Burns, N., & Grove, S. K. (2009). *The practice of nursing research: Appraisal, synthesis, and generation of evidence* (6th ed.). St. Louis, MO: Saunders Elsevier.

Cronenwett, L. R. (2002, February 19). Research, practice, and policy: Issues in evidence-based care. *Online Journal of Issues in Nursing, 7*. Retrieved from http://www.nursingworld.org/MainMenuCategories/ANAMarketplace/ANAPeriodicals/OJIN/Columns/KeynotesofNote/EvidenceBasedCare.aspx

Diekelmann, N. (2001). Funding for research in nursing education. *Journal of Nursing Education, 40*(8), 339–341.

Fain, J. A. (2009). *Reading, understanding, and applying nursing research* (3rd ed.). Philadelphia, PA: F. A. Davis.

Fawcett, J., & Garity, J. (2009). *Evaluating research for evidence-based nursing practice*. Philadelphia, PA: F. A. Davis Company.

Fineout-Overholt, E., & Melnyk, B. (2005). Building a culture of best practice. *Nurse Leader, 3*(6), 26–30.

Fink, R., Thompson, C., & Bonnes, D. (2005). Overcoming barriers and promoting the use of nursing research in practice. *Journal of Nursing Administration, 35*(3), 121–129.

Florence Nightingale Museum Trust. (2003). *The passionate statistician*. Retrieved August 19, 2009, from http://www.florence-nightingale.co.uk/cms/index.php/florence-royal-commission

Gold, J. (2011). *FAQs on ACOs: Accountable care organizations explained*. Retrieved from http://www.kaiserhealthnews.org/stories/2011

Gordon, J. H. (2011). *Overview, issues raised and probable controversies*. Retrieved from http://www.accountablecarenews.com/issues/acnewsspecial0411.pdf

Hopp, L., & Rittenmeyer, L. (2012). *Introduction to evidence-based practice: A practical guide for nursing*. Philadelphia, PA: F. A. Davis Company.

Institute for Healthcare Improvement (IHI). (2006). *100K lives campaign*. Retrieved June 29, 2009, from http://www.ihi.org/IHI/programs/campaign/campaign.htm

Institute of Medicine (IOM). (1983). *Nursing and nursing education: Public policies and private actions*. Washington, DC: National Academies Press. Retrieved from http://www.nap.edu/openbook.php?isbn=0309033462

Institute of Medicine (IOM). (1999). *To err is human: Building a safer health system*. Washington, DC: National Academies Press.

Institute of Medicine (IOM). (2004). *Keeping patients safe: Transforming the work environment of nurses*. Washington, DC: National Academies Press.

Kalisch, P. A., & Kalisch, B. J. (1986). *The advance of American nursing* (2nd ed.). Boston, MA: Little, Brown.

Malloch, K., & Porter-O'Grady, T. (2006). *Introduction to evidence-based practice in nursing and health care.* Sudbury, MA: Jones and Bartlett.

National Institute of Nursing Research (NINR). (2006a). *A brief history of the NINR.* Retrieved from http://www.ninr.nih.gov/AboutNINR/NINRHistory/

National Institute of Nursing Research (NINR). (2006b). *Mission statement.* Retrieved from http://www.ninr.nih.gov/AboutNINR/NINRMissionandStrategicPlan

National League for Nursing (NLN). (n.d.). *NLN mission statement.* Retrieved from http://www.nln.org/aboutnln/ourmission.htm

National Pharmaceutical Council. (2012). *The patient-centered outcomes research institute resource guide.* Retrieved from http://www.npcnow.org/Public/Research___ Publications/Publications/pub_cer/The_Patient_Centered_Outcomes_ Research_Institute_Resource_Guide.aspx

Nightingale, F. (1858). *Notes on matters affecting the health, efficiency and hospital administration of the British army.* London, UK: Harrison and Sons.

Parker, M. E., & Smith, M. C. (2010). *Nursing theories and nursing practice* (3rd ed.). Philadelphia, PA: F. A. Davis Company.

Polit, D. F., & Hungler, B. P. (1978). *Nursing research: Principles and methods.* Philadelphia, PA: J. B. Lippincott.

Riddle, L. (2005). *Polar-area diagram: Biographies of women mathematicians.* Retrieved from http://www.agnesscott.edu/lriddle/women/nightpiechart.htm

Simpson, R. L. (2005, December). Leader to watch. *Nurse Leader, 3*(6), 10–14.

van Achterberg, T., Schoonhoven, L., & Grol, R. (2008). Nursing implementation science: How evidence-based nursing requires evidence-based implementation. *Journal of Nursing Scholarship, 40*(4), 302–310.

Webster's II new college dictionary. (1999). Boston, MA: Houghton Mifflin.

Chapter 4

Ethics for Nursing Research and Evidence-Based Practice

Jane Sumner and Sharon Cannon

Chapter Objectives

At the conclusion of this chapter, the learner will be able to

1. Explain why ethical theories used in nursing practice are important for nursing research
2. Acknowledge how international and national ethical principles have influenced ethical nursing research
3. Discuss the impact of the history of human experimentation on nursing research today
4. Delineate the ethical implications in each step of the research process
5. Identify specific ethical issues when various research methodologies are utilized

Key Terms

- ➤ Code of ethics
- ➤ Deontology
- ➤ Ethical theories
- ➤ Ethics
- ➤ Honesty
- ➤ Human experimentation

➤ Informed consent

➤ Institutional review board (IRB)

➤ Justice

➤ Respect

➤ Teleology

➤ Trustworthiness

➤ Vulnerable subjects

Introduction

This chapter will focus on ethics in two areas: research and evidence-based practice. The literature for ethics and research are plentiful. However, literature regarding ethics in evidence-based practice is just emerging. There are similarities and differences in ethics for research and evidence-based practice. Since ethics in research is abundantly found in the literature, ethics in research will be examined first.

Nurses practice within a unique social world with norm, controls, rules, and regulations. Nurses, under the mandate of caring, are required to do no harm to patients. Nurse researchers are further constrained by this principle. The following statement encapsulates all the principles important for ethical nursing research; the most important and critical principle is the protection of the rights of all and any individuals participating in biomedical research.

> No one shall be subjected to torture or to cruel, inhuman or degrading treatment or punishment. In particular, no one shall be subjected without his free consent to medical or scientific experimentation. (United Nations Organization, 2002)

Nurse researchers, acting as social scientists, examine the human condition in relation to health and illness. They, too, are governed by all the ethical principles encompassed within biomedical research. Both the International Council of Nurses (ICN) and the American Nurses Association (ANA) have developed ethical codes that control the practice of the nursing profession. As the ANA (2001) made clear in its opening preamble to the **Code of Ethics** for Nurses, nurses have a "professional mandate to society for effective and efficient care" (p. 1). This is doubly true for the nurse researcher, whom the Code identifies as having to be qualified to conduct research, regardless of the particular role (e.g., principal investigator, clinical research coordinator, or member of an institutional review board). This means the researcher must understand all the elements required to maintain the highest ethical standards. The nurse researcher must understand what is morally and ethically appropriate to study and disseminate so as to protect the vulnerable—a group that includes everyone who participates as a subject and who trusts the nurse researcher will be ethical. "All research has ethical dimensions, and all research must be ethical" (Cipriano Silva, 2006, p. 178).

Nursing research, which lies within the domain of social science, is critical for the development of nursing knowledge. As a social science, nursing research is concerned with the human condition and, as such, is directed and controlled by all international ethical codes. The pursuit of nursing research requires participants to respect the specific ethical constraints and standards that are discussed below. The following text discusses the ethical issues in each step of the research process. Universal **ethical theories** and their relevance to nursing research are presented, as well as theories that underpin all the health disciplines. A brief review of the history of **human experimentation** and the need for ethical practice is provided as well.

Ethical Theories

Ethics is described as "a philosophical study of morality" (Deigh, 1995, p. 244), but the line between morality and ethics is often blurred. Not infrequently, little distinction is made between the two. However, the original meanings of the words "moral" and "ethics" may assist in separating the two. Moral is a "custom" (from the Latin *mos, moris*), which suggests that it is not a constant, but rather will change over time. With this premise, then, one can argue that the norms of a society, which are based on a moral perspective that everyone agrees to and is expected to live by, have the potential to change over time. Ethics comes from the Greek *ethos*, meaning "character," which can be applied to both the individual and the individual's behavior. When combined, "custom" and "character" lead to a "right way" to lead one's life.

"In relation to social research [ethics] refers to the moral deliberation, choice and accountability on the part of researchers throughout the research process" (Edwards & Mauthner, 2002, p. 14). Ethics are the standards by which a society lives and acts, and they have embedded within them various principles. The principles most relevant to nursing are (1) the value of life, (2) goodness or rightness, (3) justice or fairness, (4) truth telling or honesty, and (5) individual freedom (Thiroux, 1980).

The value of life refers to recognition of the importance of life, preserving life when appropriate but also accepting the reality of death. Issues that arise within this principle and that nurses confront include abortion, assisted suicide, and euthanasia.

Goodness or rightness is more difficult to pin down. Immanuel Kant (1724–1804) indicated that goodness means that we promote goodness over badness, that we cause no harm, and that we prevent badness or harm. Florence Nightingale supported this perspective when she said, "Hospitals should do the sick no harm" (Tschudin, 1992, p. 54).

Justice or fairness does not occur if we are not good. After all, doing good includes treating all equally and with equal distribution.

Truth telling or **honesty**, Tschudin (1992) suggested, may be the most difficult principle to live by, partly because truth is interpreted differently by different people. Truth is conveyed in communication that involves at least two participants, both of whom are speaker and listener, and who may hear things differently from the intention of the speaker. However, Tschudin cites Benjamin and Curtis (1986), who stated that "a person of integrity . . . is one whose responses to various matters are not capricious or arbitrary, but principled. One of the qualities most of us admire in others and try to cultivate in ourselves is personal integrity" (p. 59).

Finally, regarding the principle of individual freedom, "We need to use freedom to preserve life, do right and be good, act justly and tell the truth" (Tschudin, 1992, p. 59). Both societal and individual freedoms exist, ensuring just action and the doing of right and good. Societal pressures or limitations on freedoms may constrain the individual from acting justly and doing good.

Tschudin (1992) points out that ethics are identified as either normative or descriptive. Normative ethics are prescriptive ethics; they relate to the standards that have been laid down and are generally accepted in any society as the guidelines for what one should do. From normative ethics emerges the code by which a profession lives, which is particularly true in nursing. In contrast, descriptive (or scientific) ethics arise from what people do. Tschudin (1992) suggests that a code of ethics subscribed to by physicians tends to derive from scientific ethics as these clinicians investigate illness with the aim of curing of it. Regardless of which type of ethical theory is accepted by a group or profession (i.e., physicians or nurses), the principles of goodness, justice, and truth are entwined. These values, along with individuals' behavior, underpin their specific code of ethics.

? Think Outside the Box

Consider the various ethical theories. Which one seems to align with your nursing practice and why?

Utilitarianism (Teleology)

Aristotle is regarded as a teleologist, although he does not necessarily take a wholly utilitarian perspective (utilitarianism is identified somewhat more narrowly than teleology). The **teleology** theory is closely associated with Jeremy Bentham and John Mill (Mill, 1967), two English philosophers. Simply put, it relates to the means justifying the ends and consequences of the actions, which may be either good or bad. Bentham and Mill (Mill, 1967) emphasized the duty of "good action" on the basis of happiness, or the greatest happiness that required the right action. Three propositions form the basis of utilitarianism:

1. Actions are judged right or wrong based on the "virtue" of their consequences.
2. In assessing the consequences, all that is of concern is the amount of happiness that results.
3. When calculating happiness or unhappiness, no one person's reaction is more important than the reaction of anyone else (Rachels, 1995).

According to the views espoused by advocates of utilitarianism, the only thing that matters in the final analysis is the consequences. Rachels (1995) states that utilitarianism, with its adherence to the principle of utility, is the standard for judging right and wrong and firmly "rejects corruption" (p. 115). This perspective reduces—if not eliminates—feelings, desires, and "intuition" (p. 115) from rational and moral decision making.

While this ethical theory is applied in healthcare delivery, it is perhaps somewhat difficult to apply and of limited use, except in weighing all the consequences of an action before it occurs, and in making the decision whether the end truly justifies the means. In many instances, this would not be the case if one is to do no harm to the patient. However, if adherence to the principle of utility is applied, then it can be assumed that reason will trump feelings and emotions.

The implication for nursing is that all nursing actions should be focused on doing the right thing or good (beneficence), rather than on doing harm (maleficence). In relation to nursing research, Edwards and Mauthner (2002) describe ethical theory as the situation in which the right thing is that research produces new knowledge, providing the human subject is not put at increased risk during the process of conducting the research.

Deontology

In **deontology**, the theory focuses on the intrinsic nature or "rightness" of the action itself, and some actions are seen as right and others as wrong. With "right" action, the individual is obligated to act regardless of the consequences. Kant is believed to be the first to put duty at the forefront of moral behavior (Norman, 1998). In particular, Kant believed that because humans are "rational" entities, they are entitled to be treated with dignity, they always have value, and they must never be used as means—they are always ends. With this thinking comes responsibility, and Kant made clear his position that individuals must take responsibility for their actions.

Kant also defined "oughts" of reasoned behavior as "act only according to that maxim by which you can at the same time will that it should become a universal law" (Kant, 1785, cited by Rachels, 1995, p. 110). The limitation of this perspective is that a universal law should be upheld without exception, which makes it difficult or impossible to take into account the context for the behavior. The obligated duties of deontology are as follows:

- Duties of fidelity
- Duties of reparation
- Duties of gratitude
- Duties of justice
- Duties of beneficence
- Duties of self-improvement
- Duties of nonmaleficence (Ross, 1954, as cited by Norman, 1998)

If one understands the meanings of these duties, then it is not difficult to accept why deontology is more easily accepted within the healthcare delivery system, and particularly in the nursing profession, with its strong sense of duty and obligation to the patient.

Embedded in this ethical theory is the freedom of the individual but also consideration for the common good. "A right action is only right if it is done out of a sense of duty, and the only good thing without any qualification is a person's goodwill: the will to do what one knows to be right" (Tschudin, 1992, p. 51). Nursing has the obligation to protect the vulnerable patient—and therein lies the cause for justice. Edwards and Mauthner (2002) describe this theory as "actions governed by principles" (p. 20), to include honesty, respect, and justice. For the nurse researcher, the obligation is to protect the human subject through demonstration of respect and honesty.

Values Theories

Principles of ethics not uncommonly used in health care include (1) respect, (2) autonomy, (3) beneficence (or nonmaleficence), and (4) justice. All ethics codes related to human experimentation stress

respect for persons, both from the perspective of individual autonomy and by emphasizing the rights of those with diminished autonomy to the same protections. Autonomy refers to the ability to make careful choices. In relation to research, a potential subject should receive all the information required to make an informed decision.

Beneficence refers to the practice of maximizing benefits while minimizing risks. In relation to research, as stated by the Council for International Organizations of Medical Sciences (CIOMS, 2002), "this principle gives rise to norms requiring that the risks of research be reasonable in light of the expected benefits ... the research design be sound . . . investigators competent to perform the research and to safeguard the welfare of the research subjects." Another term for beneficence is nonmaleficence, or the doing of no harm to the individual. Beneficence is identified as an obligation, and every effort must be made to ensure the well-being of the research subject. *The Belmont Report* (National Institutes of Health [NIH], 1979) indicated that the principle of beneficence applies to society at large as well as to specific investigators. Thus there are obligations inherent in all human research projects that have implications measured in terms of long-term effects for the society at large.

Finally, the principle of **justice** is particularly applicable to the "vulnerable," but is more widely viewed as the "ethical obligation to treat each person in accordance with what is morally right and proper, to give each person what is due to him or her" (CIOMS, 2002, p. 11). *The Belmont Report* (NIH, 1979) describes what is due as "(a) to each person an equal share, (b) to each person according to individual need, (c) to each person according to individual efforts, (d) to each person according to societal contribution, and (e) to each person according to merit." "Equal" in this instance implies equity, although clearly at times not everyone will be equal. Nevertheless, there should be equity or justice in distribution of whatever is distributed. The implication of "distributive justice," to which both CIOMS and *The Belmont Report* refer, is that the issues of vulnerability of human subjects must be addressed as the same for everyone.

In human studies, nursing and medical practitioners are tending to vulnerable populations simply by virtue of the illnesses that brought patients to the attention of healthcare providers. CIOMS (2002) describes vulnerability as a "substantial incapacity to protect one's own interests owing to such impediments as lack of capability to give informed consent, lack of alternative means of obtaining medical care or other expensive necessities, or being a junior or subordinate member in a hierarchical group" (p. 11). Human subjects are therefore vulnerable before they are invited to participate in research projects, and this imposes further ethical obligations on the researcher to protect them.

Virtues Theory

Virtues are regarded as character traits. Norman (1998) cites Hume's (1751) list of virtues, which gives insight into these traits:

- Qualities useful to others: benevolence, justice, and fidelity
- Qualities useful to their possessor: discretion, industry, frugality, strength of mind, and good sense
- Qualities agreeable to their possessor: cheerfulness, magnanimity, courage, and tranquility
- Qualities agreeable to others: modesty and decency (p. 55)

Rachels (1995) adds "courage, self-control, generosity, and truthfulness" (p. 159) to this list, and suggests that moral philosophers can frame these virtues within the larger question of "what is the right thing to do" (p. 160) for the moral agent in "habitual action" (p. 163). Nevertheless, these characteristics, while important, do not offer a complete ethical theory. They assist in explaining how they can influence moral reasoning and behaviors. Rachels indicates that they may provide moral motivation, but it is important to realize that emotion may be an influence and that care is required to maintain impartiality. The virtue characteristics clearly play a role in determining how ethical theories are interpreted and utilized, but the theory itself does not depend on virtues themselves.

Historical Overview

The twentieth century has seen an explosive increase in human research, with a need for ethical oversight and controls. Significant medical breakthroughs, however, have occurred throughout history as a result of experimenting upon other human beings. For example, in 1789 in England, Edward Jenner first inoculated his son, aged 1 year, with swinepox against smallpox, a lethal disease. This vaccination method proved to be ineffective, and later Jenner used cowpox on other human subjects. This approach was successful and led the way for effective inoculation against smallpox (Reich, 1995). Despite his undoubted achievement, Jenner's work raises a number of key ethical issues:

- No consent was obtained from the subject.
- No understanding was established as to whether the agents used (i.e., swinepox and cowpox) were safe for human use.
- Research was performed on a minor who would have had no understanding of what was happening, although the argument could be made that because the researcher was the father of the child, it was a nonissue. However, this practice would be deemed unacceptable today.

Nevertheless, throughout Western European history, there is evidence of the relevance of ethical behaviors in human research. Moses Maimonides (1135–1204), a physician and philosopher, "instructed colleagues always to treat patients as ends in themselves, not as means for learning new truths" (Reich, 1995, p. 2248). Claude Bernard, writing in France in 1865, stated

> Morals do not forbid making experiments on one's neighbor or one's self . . . the principle of medical and surgical morality consists in never performing on man an experiment which might be harmful to him to any extent, even though the result might be highly advantageous to science, i.e., to the health of others. (Reich, 1995, p. 2249)

However, recognition of the need for regulated ethical constraints emerged as a result of horrific episodes during the twentieth century. The worst documented atrocities were probably the Nazi experiments that were conducted mainly on prisoners during World War II. These experiments included "putting subjects to death by long immersion in subfreezing water, deprivation of oxygen to learn the limits of bodily endurance, or deliberate infection by lethal organisms in order to study the effect of drugs and vaccines" (Reich, 1995, p. 2253). In addition, "Nazi experimental atrocities included investigation of quicker and more effective means of inducing sexual sterilization (including clandestine radiation dosing and unanesthetized male and female castration and death)" (Reich, 1995, p. 2258).

In addition to these appalling events, highly unethical human research studies were performed in the United States. The most infamous was the Tuskegee Syphilis Study (Centers for Disease Control and Prevention [CDC], 2011), which involved African American males suffering from secondary syphilis; the treatment of penicillin (the recommended and available medication) was deliberately withheld from these patients so that the progression of the disease could be studied. The Tuskegee study, which was initiated in the mid-1930s, was not halted until 1972, when a newspaper published an account of it. At no time were the human subjects fully informed about the study, and in some instances they appear to have been deliberately misinformed. Among the many sad aspects of the study was the fact that subjects more than likely, in all innocence, infected others, because their syphilis was not being treated. Therefore, maleficence was directed not only toward the study subjects, but also toward their families, which compounded the researchers' ethical lapses.

Instances of human drug testing or usage with inadequate ethical oversight have also occurred. Thalidomide, a widely used sedative in the 1950s (though not in the United States), was given to some pregnant women to control morning sickness. When the tragic mal-formations of their fetuses were made public, thalidomide was removed from the market for this particular use. Thalidomide was one of a group of drugs for which it is evident that there was already knowledge about the potential for teratogenicity (malformation of fetuses). Yet because this drug had been "widely praised, advertised, and prescribed on the grounds that it was unusually safe" (Dally, 1998, p. 1197), it was never properly tested for safety before human use. Instead, because of the highly effective advertising campaign conducted by the drug's manufacturer, the medical community ignored the evidence and went on using thalidomide. This case high-lights another aspect of the relevance of stringent ethical controls in human research studies.

More recently, the inadequate design of a medical research study at Johns Hopkins School of Medicine led to the death of one of the subjects. In this instance, prior to the initiation of the study on the inhalation of the drug hexamethonium, a limited and sketchy review of the literature was performed using only a medical index website. Such reviews are limited in terms of how far back they can search. The failure to explore the full history of the drug resulted in a healthy 24-year-old female losing her life: A review of the literature from an earlier period would have revealed potential hazards in association with this drug and its proposed route of administration. This case points to the importance of the careful design and organization of a study before it is initiated. Fault lay at many levels, not the least of which was the researcher, but also perhaps with Johns Hopkins' research review board (Perkins, 2001).

Interestingly, the World Medical Association in 1964 first made ethical principles for medical research involving human subjects public in the Declaration of Helsinki. Specifically, in section B, Basic Principles for All Medical Research, item #11 states, "Medical research involving human subjects must conform to generally accepted scien-tific principles, be based on a thorough knowledge of the scientific literature, [and] other relevant information . . ." (World Medical Asso-ciation, 1964–2004). Clearly, in the Johns Hopkins study, the study design did not adhere to international standards.

? **Think Outside the Box** www

Consider several examples of human experimentation that have occurred during the history of medical research. Have these projects resulted in beneficial outcomes for society? Can human experimentation be justified when the greater good of society is at stake? Defend your thoughts.

Research Ethics

The core ethical issue in medical research is the need for voluntary consent of the potential research subject so that a fully informed individual participates. Many efforts have been made to address this issue, but perhaps the most significant progress came from the Nuremberg Trials, in which the Nazi war crimes were investigated. The result was the Nuremberg Code of 1946, in which it is stated, "the voluntary consent of the human subject is absolutely essential ... This means that the person involved should have legal capacity to give consent ... the research subject should be so situated as to be able to exercise free power of choice" and human subjects "should have sufficient knowledge and comprehension of the elements of the subject matter involved as to make an understanding and enlightened decision" (Reich, 1995, p. 2253).

In the United States during the 1960s, different agencies within the federal government began more stringently regulating funded research on human subjects. On July 1, 1966, the National Institutes of Health, through the Public Health Service, assigned "responsibility to the institution receiving the grant for obtaining and keeping documentary evidence of informed patient consent" (Reich, 1995, p. 2254). It also mandated "review of the judgment of the investigator by a committee of institutional associates not directly associated with the project" (Reich, 1995, p. 2254). Finally, the "review must address itself to the rights and welfare of the individual, the methods used to obtain informed consent, and risks and potential benefits of the investigation" (Reich, 1995, p. 2254).

In 1973, Congress formally recognized the importance of ethical standards in human research when it created the National Commission for the Protection of Human Subjects of Biomedical and Behavioral Research, whose mission was to protect the rights and welfare of research human subjects. Research oversight by the federal government continues with a constant updating of regulations, which can be found in the Code of Federal Regulations, Title 45 and 21—specifically in the Protection of Human Subjects Rule (U.S. Department of Health and Human Services [DHHS], 2005). Federal efforts to improve the safeguards to human subjects in research continue apace, culminating most recently with the Health Insurance Portability and Accountability Act (HIPAA).

ICN has followed suit, making the need for protection of human rights very clear in its own Code of Ethics, which focuses on four principal elements: (1) the nurse and people; (2) nurses and practice; (3) nurses and the profession; and (4) nurses and coworkers. Ethical behaviors within these relationships are expected at all times, not just in areas of research. The second statement in the "nurses and people" element of the ICN Code of Ethics (2006) reads as follows: "In providing care, the nurse promotes an environment in which the human rights, values, customs and spiritual beliefs of the individual, family and community are respected" (p. 2). As a social science, nursing research must demonstrate ethical values that reflect the values of the profession at any one time (Jeffers, 2005). Human rights, equity, and justice are stressed specifically in relation to educators and researchers. The "nurses and the profession" element of the ICN's Code of Ethics states that the researcher must "conduct, disseminate and utilize research to advance the profession" (p. 7). Although ethics is not named directly here, its importance is inherent in the entire document.

ANA (2001) has its own *Code of Ethics for Nurses*, in which specific vulnerable populations are identified. These populations include children, the elderly, prisoners, students, and the poor. The Code was published in 1994, copyrighted in 1997, and updated and republished in 2001. It also indicates that the nurse clinician identifies clinical problems that need examining and the researcher designs the study in association with the clinician. What is clear in this statement is that research topics in nursing should be focused on practice, which in itself should provide an ethical underpinning for nursing research.

Environment for Ethical Research

Most nurse researchers are associated with institutions having ethical regulations already in place that the researcher is required to follow. This offers protection to the institution, the researcher, and the human subjects. The research institution housing the project typically has an office for reviewing all research proposals, usually called the **institutional review board** (IRB). The main purpose of an IRB is to protect human subjects, especially vulnerable populations such as children, prisoners, pregnant women, handicapped or mentally disabled persons, or economically/educationally disadvantaged persons. The issues that receive the most intense IRB scrutiny relate to thorough evaluation by the research team of the risks and benefits of the project, the provision of sufficient protection for human subjects, and the implementation of sufficient monitoring of the project once approval is given to proceed (Rothstein & Phuong, 2007). In addition, this office is most helpful in ensuring that the researcher submits all the required paperwork, including the proposal for the study, the consent form that study participants will sign, the budget, and whatever tools the researcher will be using in data gathering (e.g., surveys or instruments, or interview guides in the case of qualitative studies).

The DHHS Code of Federal Regulations controls the IRB offices in various types of healthcare organizations. The membership of the

IRB must have at least five members of different backgrounds who also have the competence to review research proposals. It is expected that the membership will have cultural and gender diversity, as well as an awareness of local community mores. Thus, not only will there be healthcare professionals on the board, but there will also be members who are "unaffiliated" with the institution; at least one member must have scientific interests, and one may not (Rothstein & Phuong, 2007). The members are expected to be knowledgeable about all federal guidelines and regulations. When reviewing a proposal, an IRB member may not have involvement with the project (DHHS, 2005). Unfortunately, there have been instances when IRB members have had some sort of conflict of interest or lack of objectivity that renders the board less capable of being just, fair, and protective of human subjects (Rothstein & Phuong, 2007).

The IRB members meet once a month to review all proposals, which they have already carefully scrutinized, and they may request further information to make informed decisions. When the IRB is satisfied that the researcher will provide full protection of the human subjects, the researcher is given permission to proceed and the project is given an identifying number. The researcher must report progress back to the IRB every 12 months. The IRB members expect the researcher to follow the protocol exactly as laid out in the proposal. If the project has more than one researcher, all must be listed on the protocol and, if requested by the institution, the curriculum vitae (CV) of each must also be attached. The issues of specific concern for ensuring ethical research are that the risks to the subjects are minimized (or are at least reasonable, providing the expected outcomes or benefits can be attained); subject selection is equitable; informed consent is sought from participants; and issues relating to data collection and storage, privacy, and confidentiality are managed according to regulations (DHHS, 2005).

The researcher is expected to be competent to perform the research. Lenz and Ketefian (1995) indicate that in 1989, the Institute of Medicine's Committee on the Responsible Conduct of Research was concerned that there was "a lack of formal training in scientific ethics and the responsible conduct of science as a deficit in the training of scientists and clinicians" (p. 217). Although baccalaureate degree programs and higher levels of nursing education include courses on research, it is not until a student is writing either a master's thesis or a doctoral dissertation that he or she begins to understand the process that ensures that the research is ethical and legal.

According to Ketefian and Lenz (1995), "Scientists have traditionally valued their independence in the conduct of their research. In the main, society and academic institutions have to be willing to give certain freedoms and latitude . . . in return, increased accountability is . . . demanded" (p. 268). However, an institution does not want its reputation sullied by sloppy, illegal, or unethical research. Research **trustworthiness**, reliability, and usefulness are utterly dependent on the credibility of the researcher, the work, and the institution. The rules and regulations are generally the most rigorous when an institution receives federal funding. In such cases, the IRB office is insistent on all requirements being met. Ultimately, the research has to be honest.

Although multiple brakes are now applied in an attempt to prevent unethical research from occurring, some continue to have concerns that there is still the potential for inadequate protection of human subjects. Wood, Grady, and Emanuel (2002) believe that the review process is "bureaucratic and inefficient" (p. 2) and suggest that IRB members are overworked, frightened by the possibility of federal audits, and do not always understand "ambiguous regulations" (p. 2). They continue: "Federal regulators are aggravated by the limited scope of their authority and variable adherence to regulations" (p. 2), and their concerns are not limited to these particulars. For the nurse researcher, however, adherence to the ethical standards for human subject protection applied by the organization for which the researcher works and the codes of ethics developed by ICN and ANA is crucial, regardless of external concerns.

Developing a Researchable Topic

Although nurse researchers may have curiosity about and interest in many topics they believe have the potential for expanding the body of nursing knowledge, some topics may not be realistically researchable for a number of reasons. The critical factor relates to protection of the **vulnerable subject**. As nurses, we are deeply and intimately involved with human beings at their most vulnerable, and the research topic may well pose a further increase in those individuals' vulnerability. When developing a researchable topic, the nurse researcher is called upon to utilize "ethical sensitivity" so as to decide what is appropriate, to have the "ability to perceive rightness and wrongness" (Weaver, 2007, p. 142), and to know what one is doing that affects the welfare of another person either directly or indirectly.

Issues related to the researcher also determine whether a topic is researchable. Volker (2004) indicates that attempting to research certain topics could put the researcher at risk "for loss of professional license, legal actions, imprisonment and peer ostracism" (p. 119). The types of topics that pose a threat to the researcher, according to Volker (2004), include those examining "social deviance, [those impinging] on powerful social interests, or [those examining] a deeply personal sacred value held by study participants" (p. 117). Nurses should not be studying illegal activities as a general rule, of course. Volker uses the example of a patient requesting assistance with suicide—an issue that nurses confront in their practice. A topic such as this presents problems when considering a research project; as the ANA's 1994 statement on assisted suicide states, "Nursing has a social contract with society that is based on trust, and therefore patients must be able to trust that nurses will not actively take human life" (p. 4). Volker does not state that the topic of assisted suicide cannot be examined in a research project, but rather that careful vigilance must be exercised to ensure the study design is meticulously developed to protect both the researcher and the research subject. The ANA Code of Ethics also makes it very clear that the nurse researcher "has a duty to question and if necessary to report or refuse to participate in research they deem morally objectionable" (ANA, 1994).

In legally sensitive research projects, further measures can be sought that protect the researcher against "compelled disclosure" (Anderson & Hatton, 2000, p. 249) or breaking confidentiality covenants (Volker, 2004) and that offer additional protection for the study subjects. In particular, a Certificate of Confidentiality may be issued by DHHS in such cases. Federal law states that a Certificate of Confidentiality

> may authorize persons engaged in biomedical, behavioral, clinical, or other research (including research on the use and effect of alcohol and other psychotic drugs) to protect the privacy of individuals who are the subject of such research by withholding from all persons not connected with the conduct of such research the names or other identifying characteristics of such individuals. Persons so authorized to protect the privacy of such individuals may not be compelled in any Federal, State, or local civil, criminal, administrative, legislative, or other proceedings that identify such individuals. (Public Health Service Act, 42 USC 163, 1988)

Volker (2004) makes it clear that "researchers who engage in socially sensitive research must be prepared for scrutiny by diverse professional and lay parties who have varying agendas and interests" (p. 123). Research projects are usually undertaken in institutions that have a well-developed ethical structure and that are highly conscientious in following federal guidelines and regulations, to protect the vulnerable patients under their care. As a consequence, the researcher, as he or she develops the project, has resources immediately available for advice and consultation, including the IRB, professional colleagues, attorneys, and an ethics committee.

? **Think Outside the Box**

www

Vulnerable populations are always with us. Can you think of some additional ones that are emerging in the current healthcare environment? Explain why you see these groups as vulnerable. Which issues need to be considered when determining the vulnerability of a group of people?

The topic that the nurse researcher chooses should be one of real interest to him or her. The researcher should be willing to allocate the preparatory time and effort to ensure that the project meets all of the institution's ethical guidelines. Ethical behavior requires intellectual honesty of the researcher—giving credit due to others, not using ideas from others without acknowledgment, and not initiating data collection before institutional approval has been given. Plans for seeking funding for the study, the study design, methodology, data collection, and the dissemination of results (even if insignificant) at the conclusion of the study are also critical parts of developing the topic for research.

In discussing the Canadian system of protecting human subjects, Pilkington (2002) makes it clear that if a research project is not scientifically valid, then it is unethical to involve human subjects. It is the responsibility of the IRB (known as a "research ethics board" in Canada) to ensure that a study is scientifically valid. In defining whether a research project is scientifically valid, Pilkington (2002) states bluntly, "If a study does not hold substantial promise of answering a significant question(s), thereby generating valuable knowledge, then there is no justification for exposing persons to the actual or potential risks and inconvenience of participation" (p. 197). Scientific validity, therefore, influences how a researchable topic is developed to be an ethical research study.

Developing Researchable Questions

Although the nurse researcher may have a burning interest in a particular topic, developing the question(s) appropriately is most important when gearing up for a formal study. This development is necessary to narrow down the topic to a specific focus, clarify the methodology, determine whether the topic has embedded in it useful questions that will give shape to the study, and ensure that significant research results will emerge and add to the body of nursing knowledge. The questions should be broad enough to obtain results, yet not so broad so as to yield diffuse and possibly meaningless results.

Thorough reading on the subject can assist in developing questions that meet these criteria. This preliminary investigation can help identify the gaps in the literature and hone the researcher's thinking about what it is specifically that he or she wants to investigate.

Communication with both clinician colleagues and fellow nurse researchers can also assist in refining the questions.

The ethical component of this endeavor derives from ANA's demand for effective and efficient care of the patient. If the research design is faulty at any level—and specifically the question development level—then one must ask if the results will improve the efficiency and effectiveness of patient care.

Participant Recruitment and Informed Consent

Vulnerable populations are always a concern for all research regulatory bodies, but there are some populations who are particularly vulnerable—the very young, the frail elderly, prisoners, the mentally incompetent, and women. In addition, issues related to socioeconomic status, education, and language may contribute to a specific population's vulnerability (Anderson & Hatton, 2000; Rogers, 2005). The researcher must be sensitive to these issues as well as to the points specifically outlined in federal regulations. This can make recruitment more difficult and the need for true **informed consent** crucial. Very specific regulations can be found in the *Belmont Report* (NIH, 1979), the *International Ethics Guidelines for Biomedical Research Involving Human Subjects* (CIOMS, 2002), and the DHHS's *Protection of Human Subjects* document (2005), including sections relating to the protections needed for specific vulnerable populations.

The key ethical issue embedded in informed consent is that the individual always has the freedom of choice to participate or not participate, and may withdraw from the study at any time. It is important to note that the term "valid consent" is more recently being used instead of "informed consent." Valid consent is thought to be more informative of the process. This freedom of choice is built on a series of components:

- The language is simple enough to be clearly understood.
- The potential subject adequately comprehends the project.
- The subject has had to time to think about the study and its potential risks and benefits, and to discuss it with family members.
- The consent is not coerced.
- The written consent is documented.

CIOMS (2002) discusses "inducements" to participation, which can be identified as coercion and, therefore, are not appropriate.

Several authors have expressed concern over how to achieve the consent and indicate that, in fact, obtaining consent should be a continuous process throughout a research project. In other words, the researcher should regularly check in with the subject to ensure that he or she is still a willing and informed participant (Edwards & Mauthner, 2002; Miller & Bell, 2002). The only payment or compensation allowed includes the costs of transportation or loss of earnings due to participation in the research project. It is unethical to offer more financial incentives, as they may encourage a potential subject to consent against his or her better judgment. It is also unethical for the researcher to receive compensation from a pharmaceutical company to conduct a study.

Research using child participants encompasses all the usual ethical issues relating to informed consent, privacy, and confidentiality, but includes several other factors that may compound the issues: Children exist in a natural power hierarchy with adults, but are able to communicate and understand according to their interpretation of the world around them (Kirk, 2007). Children must believe they are part of the project, but researchers must be alert to the specific child's "agenda" and continually check back with the child to ensure that he or she wants to continue to participate. Parents are also involved with providing informed consent, but researchers must ensure that children do understand what they are getting into and that their consent is given freely. In some instances, only one parent's consent is required, although two parents' consent is preferable. On occasion, a child and parents may not agree on continued participation; in general, it is the child's decision that is accepted in such cases.

The success of the study may depend on the warmth, interest in the child, and rapport established by the researcher, so that the child trusts the researcher. These characteristics have been demonstrated to be critical in longitudinal studies with children (Ely & Coleman, 2007), particularly when ill children are subjected to discomforting treatments. A slightly different issue arises with teenagers who, while still legally minors, have the right to give informed consent without parental consent (Roberson, 2007). Parents still have legal responsibility "to ensure the child [receives] appropriate medical care, [but] there is also the ethical need to 'respect the rights and autonomy of every individual, regardless of age'" (Kunin, 1997, cited by Roberson, 2007, p. 191).

Recruiting the desired composition and number of participants may require establishing multiple research sites, which can create some problems for the researcher, even as it confers some distinct advantages to the study: Such studies are "likely to produce generalizable, high quality results . . . [increase the] likelihood of attracting funding . . . [provide access to] a broader range of practice settings and patient with a wider range of diagnoses . . . [and] expedite data collection" (Twycross & Corlett, 2007, p. 35). Multisite research enables experts to work together and perhaps close the theory–practice gap. Of course, there are some notable difficulties in conducting multisite studies, including those related to establishing and maintaining collaborative, trusting relationships with one's colleagues; meeting face-to-face; overcoming organizational cultural differences; and having to gain IRB approval at each site.

Data Collection and Data Analysis

Protection of vulnerable human subjects remains the critical ethical issue with data collection and analysis. First and foremost, the privacy and confidentiality of the subjects must be protected, which means that the data must be locked securely in a safe place at all times. Data may include audiotapes, surveys, or videotapes, among other media.

Videorecording is becoming more popular for data collection because of "its inherent accuracy and reliability as a record of events and detailed, nuanced levels of observation and analysis permitted" (Broyles, Tate, & Happ, 2008, p. 59). Additional ethical issues must be addressed when such data collection methods are used, however— namely, privacy; participant burden and safety; storage, location, and condition of storage of recordings; maintenance of the recordings in storage; access to recordings; use of the recordings as part of a presentation; and whether the actual taping will interfere with clinical care. The IRB will make decisions on all these issues and may require that faces be blurred and/or eyes are covered with a black box in the final recording.

Each institution has specific guidelines about how long data files must be kept. Lutz (1999) has raised the issue of premature destruction of original data, predominantly in studies on particularly vulnerable populations (e.g., battered women). According to this author, such destruction could occur if the researcher were concerned about court subpoenas that could compromise the participants' safety. However, premature destruction could lead to institutional accusations of scientific misconduct, which suggests that the researcher has a fine line to walk between ethical and unethical actions.

Ethical analysis and interpretation depend on the honesty and trustworthiness of the researchers. Although healthcare organizations make every effort to ensure ethical behaviors within their research environments, ultimately it rests with the researchers to ensure that the project is indeed conducted ethically in all areas, including analysis, interpretation, and dissemination of results. The opposite of ethical behavior is scientific misconduct, which brings dishonor to both the individual and the institution, and renders the research project meaningless. In addition, concern for the welfare of the vulnerable human subjects is negated when misconduct occurs. Scientific misconduct, an extremely serious issue, is defined by DHHS as follows:

> Fabrication, falsification, plagiarism or other practices that seriously deviate from those that are commonly accepted within the scientific community for proposing, conducting or reporting research. It does not include an honest error or honest differences in interpretations or judgments of data. (Commission on Research Integrity, 1995, p. 1)

Lutz (1999) has cited Macrina (1995), who states that falsification involves results being manipulated or tampered with, fabrication refers to "totally unfounded results" (p. 90) being produced, and plagiarism is "theft of another person's ideas" (p. 90). History makes evident that falsification, fabrication, and plagiarism are unconscionable and utterly unethical.

? Think Outside the Box

Determine if your school or hospital has an institutional review board (IRB). Which criteria do the board members use when approving a research project?

Issues in Quantitative and Qualitative Research

There is concern in qualitative research about the increased risk for ethical lapses inherent with this research methodology. As Birch and Miller (2002) state, this "type of research relationship may involve acts of self-disclosure, where personal, private experiences are revealed" (p. 92) and is never value free or "value neutral" (Christians, 2003, p. 213). The researcher must be aware of this potential and approach this type of research by making every attempt to acknowledge any personal biases.

In qualitative research, interviews are commonly used to gather data, resulting in face-to-face exposure for both the researcher and the researched. The dialogue serves as the research data that are then analyzed and interpreted. The vulnerable patient immediately becomes more vulnerable as the researcher delves into his or her lived experience. Anonymity and confidentiality are inevitably compromised in the interaction between researcher and human subject, which means there is an even greater need for data security and constant awareness on the part of the researcher of these issues. Honesty and trustworthiness of the research are even more important in such cases. Firby (1995) has stated, in relation to an IRB giving permission for a qualitative research project, "We should not simply assume that because research has been accepted by a committee it is morally justifiable in its methods" (p. 41). The moral obligation of nursing is to do good, and to do no harm. Therefore, qualitative nursing research must meet that obligation.

In contrast to qualitative research, quantitative research, which initially arose from the objective methodology of the Enlightenment's scientific paradigm, is more apt to be value neutral. The quantitative researcher is less likely to engage in face-to-face self-disclosure, which protects both him or her and the subject. The facts should speak for themselves. However, the researcher must be alert to the potential for his or her biases to influence the interpretation of data. Nevertheless, there remains the ethical principle of justice and the need for informed consent for human participants in such studies.

External Pressures

Conducting research studies is never easy, but various pressures making it more difficult may push the researcher toward unethical behaviors. According to Lutz (1999), these pressures include limited funding, the competition for achieving tenure for faculty, and "increasing emphasis on producing research reports" (p. 92).

The Health Insurance Portability and Accountability Act (HIPAA) is designed to protect patients against unauthorized disclosure of their health and medical records. At the same time, it adds another source of pressure for nurse researchers, as passage of HIPAA has led to some new concerns related to health research. According to Erlen (2005), these regulations were written for healthcare delivery organizations, and not for universities per se; nevertheless, the latter organizations have had to develop their own policies and procedures that meet the requirements of HIPAA. At times it has proven difficult to draw "clear boundaries," and universities have tended to err on the side of caution by providing for additional protection of human subjects, privacy, confidentiality, and informed consent. This has meant additional training for anyone who wishes to engage in research. The institution's IRB office sets the policy for how the researchers of that institution can proceed while adhering to HIPAA regulations.

HIPAA and its ramifications are key ethical considerations for the nurse researcher. With the drive for evidence-based research to underpin practice, the nurse researcher needs to be aware that study data and their interpretation must be shared, but within the constraints of HIPAA. To meet these criteria, data must contain no identifiers of an individual in a sample. Thus, subjects may be given a code number or letter. Only the researcher maintains a list linking the sample identifiers with their associated codes, and this document must be kept secure at all times.

Evidence-Based Practice and Ethical Implications

Now that we have explored ethics in the research process, let's examine ethics and evidence-based practice (EBP). In the clinical environment, considerable effort is being made to implement evidence-based nursing practice. Such practice is derived from several elements, including experiential knowledge on the part of the nurse (i.e., knowing what works in practice and why); having clinical judgment and skills of critical inquiry; knowing the individual patient both as a human being and in terms of his or her pattern of responses to what is occurring; and knowledge of current scientific research findings (Borsay, 2009; Redman, 2007; Tanner, 2006). Evidence-based practice is designed to reduce unthinking, ritualistic practices in nursing care (Siedlecki, 2008).

Quality improvement (QI) is constantly performed in healthcare organizations: Data are gathered in order to improve patient outcomes through "local innovations in and assessment of the processes and systems of care delivery" (Redman, 2007, p. 217). This process is designed for rapid implementation of change. It is different from the slower rigorous, empirical research approach, which is more deliberative and follows a "fixed protocol with a clearly defined method and . . . a period of analysis after completed data collection" (Lynn et al., 2007, p. 668). Quality improvement is not empirical research. There is some concern, however, related to the ethics of human subject protection in QI practices (Grady, 2007; Lynn et al., 2007). To date, there has been no standard established regarding whether there should be a separate IRB process for QI.

Changes that are derived from QI are not regarded as the strongest evidence in EBP. Rather, EBP is dependent on generalizable scientific evidence (Batalden & Davidoff, 2007). The research utilized in evidence-based nursing practice utilizes well-tested scientific study data from studies that have undergone the required ethical scrutiny.

Developing an Evidence-Based Project

Similar to some nurses interested in researchable topics, other nurses may want to pursue EBP projects. Much interest has been generated in QI, patient autonomy, quality of life, and end of life issues. Future chapters will discuss the specific process of developing an EBP project. However, there are ethical issues to be addressed prior to, during, and after the completion of EBP projects that parallel ethical issues in research projects.

Evidence-based practice is a broad area that encompasses more than scientific research. In fact, research is considered to be one aspect of EBP. Not all nurses have the knowledge and skill to conduct research but that does not mean they don't encounter clinical situations that arouse their curiosity. As a result, they may wish to pursue information to improve nursing care. Developing an EBP topic also requires sensitivity to vulnerable populations, confidentiality, and existing federal and state guidelines, as well as professional regulations to practice nursing. Keeping all this in mind, the nurse should choose an EBP topic which is of specific interest to him or her to improve nursing practice. EBP projects also require the nurse to meet the institution's ethical guidelines.

Developing EBP Questions

In Chapter 1, the PICOT format was discussed and an in-depth examination of developing an EBP question is included in Chapter 5. Nurses must consider the ethics of asking an EBP question. The topic selected must be narrow enough to produce results that will improve patient care. At the same time, the design must be carefully planned to eliminate the potential of harm to participants.

Participant Recruitment

Protection of human subjects is as important to EBP projects as it is to research. Thus, vulnerable populations are a concern for EBP projects. For example, if you want to collect data about fall rates in your institution, the population might include the elderly and/or children. Ethically, you must ensure that patient privacy and confidentiality are protected. Even if you are only conducting a retrospective chart review of patients who have fallen, you must still keep all patient information in confidence and not reveal any patient identification information.

It is also necessary to ensure that participants in an EBP project will be honest in their responses. If a nurse is investigating nurses' medication errors in his or her institution, nurses in the institution must report that a medication error is made. If the nurses making the errors do not report them for fear of reprisal, the information about the number, type, or reasons for the error(s) will not be accurate, and recommendations to decrease medication errors will not be effective. The EBP project must also be ethical in all areas, including design, implementation, and evaluation. EBP projects require the same ethical rigor required in research.

Data Collection and Data Analysis

Data collection for EBP generally focuses more on institutional benchmarks to improve patient outcomes, patient satisfaction, communication techniques, hospital readmissions, and staff/physicians satisfaction, to name just a few. An example might be a hospital that wants to decrease the occurrences of pressure ulcers. To accomplish that, the hospital wound care nurse obtains permission to adapt the Braden Scale as part of the nursing assessment of skill. The wound care nurse then educates the staff regarding the use of the Braden Scale and how it is mandatory to chart this assessment so that pressure ulcers can be prevented by early detection. After 1 month, the wound care nurse performs a chart review to determine if nurses used the Braden Scale, charted the skin assessment results, and if the number of new pressure ulcers decreased. The wound care nurse may also compare the results with other hospitals in the same geographic area or with other hospitals of the same size and same general population. Thus, data analysis does not necessarily involve statistical tests/methods as seen in research projects.

Data collection and data analysis for EBP projects such as the one described, requires the same ethical considerations for protection of human subjects. Many hospitals request patients to allow their information to be used to promote better outcomes and/or for teaching purposes. To be ethical in the example given, the wound care nurse must protect patient confidentiality, remove patient identifying information, and report results in the aggregate (group) and not as individuals.

? Think Outside the Box

Should EBP projects need to be approved by an IRB? List the reasons why or why not IRB approval is necessary.

Issues in Evidence-Based Projects

As in research projects, anonymity and confidentiality in EBP projects is paramount. The person(s) responsible for EBP projects must protect the human subjects and must do no harm. In addition, they must be alert to any bias that may influence how the data is interpreted.

Internal Pressures

Because EBP projects are often specific to an institution, care must be taken to avoid pressure from individuals within the organization who want to show positive results. The EBP project must ensure that policies and procedures are followed and that data is accurately represented. Training regarding such things as HIPAA are necessary to ensure no violations occur.

Publication of Research or EBP

A further ethical dimension is encountered when, at the end of the research or EBP project, it is time to publish the results: Journals accept only peer-reviewed manuscripts (Ketefian & Lenz, 1995). Peer referees are required to evaluate the scientific merit of the research study as well as the manuscript's acceptability for a particular journal. To warrant publication, the findings are expected to contribute new knowledge to the practice of nursing (Driever & Pranulis, 2003). Without that expectation, the research is inappropriate, if not unethical. Those who review manuscripts for publication must have the knowledge and expertise to evaluate the work appropriately (Pilkington, 2002).

An emerging literature is focusing on issues related to publication. Conn (2008) discusses how pressure may be put on the author to change results because the manuscript reviewers resist "unexpected outcomes" (p. 161) and want revisions that are not consistent with the results. The authors may need to make changes, but those changes should not come at the expense of reliable data results. Freda and Kearney (2005) discuss how editors can face ethical issues when articles have been published in more than one journal; when data are published in more than one journal with no changes; or when there is evidence of author misconduct, demand for credit for someone "undeserving" of credit, lack of IRB approval, or misconduct related to lack of informed consent or an undeclared conflict of interest.

A recent study by Henley and Dougherty (2009) revealed another potential problem related to publication of research results: discrepancies in the quality of the reviews submitted by many persons who serve as peer reviewers. According to these authors, "Peer review is the mainstay of the editorial process" (p. 18). The key issues of concern within a paper were poor reviews related to the study's theoretical framework (47.2%), literature review (35.15%), discussion and interpretation of results (22%), and data analysis/presentation (21.9%). In terms of usefulness of the written comments to the author, 14.4% of peer reviews were deemed poor. Finally, in terms of usefulness to the editor, 12.2% of peer reviews were poor or inadequate. These authors recommended formal training and a probationary period for all potential reviewers.

A further ethical issue relates to who should be listed as first author when multiple researchers participated in the study. Generally, the principal investigator is listed as first author. However, in the case of multiple authors, negotiation determines the first author named on various publications. Ketefian and Lenz (1995) point out that listing authors in order of their extent of effort made is the most ethical way of recognizing authorship. These authors also suggest that it is unethical to publish the same manuscript or article in multiple journals. It is appropriate to publish several articles on the same study, provided that each manuscript is written with a different focus. In addition, all contributions and funding sources for an article must be acknowledged.

Emerging Issues in Research and EBP

The prevalence of EBP projects has caused much controversy about whether EBP and research are separate. One school of thought is that research is not a component of EBP; the other side of course is that research is one aspect of EBP. Much depends on the definition of each. Proponents of research argue that EBP is specific to an institution, has no theoretical framework and data is not able to be statistically tested and analyzed. Proponents of EBP state that EBP is broader, includes research where appropriate and that data collected from specific institutions can be compiled and added to national data banks providing information that has broad implications. Ethical considerations for both will continue to be required regarding protection of human subjects, regardless of the prevailing school of thought.

Although nurses generally have not been involved in animal, genetic, or biological material research in the past, this situation is changing and is likely to continue to do so as more transdisciplinary, translational research occurs. The issues of concern with animals include ensuring that the least harm and suffering is inflicted, using animals only when absolutely necessary, using the fewest animals possible, and, when seeking IRB permission, ensuring that someone on the board understands the implications of animal research. In relation to genetic and biological materials research, the same moral and ethical obligations apply as when dealing with any human subjects (Cipriano Silva, 2006).

An environment that has been neglected as a site for study in the past, but is likely to draw increasing attention from researchers in the future because of the aging of the U.S. population, is the community-based care facility (i.e., nursing home). All of the usual ethical research issues apply in this setting, but some additional concerns may arise relating to ensuring the quality of life, safety, and satisfaction of those residing in nursing homes, and ensuring that the study will not impose an undue burden on the participants. Proxies may be required to give consent for resident participation if the resident is mentally incompetent or extremely frail; however, use of proxies requires that the proxy holder have the authority to give this type of consent, and he or she must be adequately informed of the study's focus. In a study by Cartwright and Hickman (2007), it was discovered that community-based facility administrators had limited understanding of the protections established by an IRB that gives consent to a study, although most seemed aware of federal and state statutory requirements in terms of informed consent. In an attempt to overcome these deficits, Cartwright and Hickman developed a Bill of Rights for Community-Based Research Partners that could prove valuable for similar institutions.

Conclusion

The lessons learned from the history of human experimentation have led to the development of ethical codes, both nationally and internationally. These controls are crucial for the protection of vulnerable human subjects. Indeed, ensuring adequate protection of human subjects requires that particular care be taken in each step of the research or EBP process. The obligations inherent within nursing demand the "moral deliberation, choice and accountability" (Edwards & Mauthner, 2002, p. 14) of the nurse researcher. Nurses in their practice are tending to humans at their most vulnerable, and this level of understanding adds to the responsibility of the nurse as researcher or EBP project director. Achieving valid research and EBP that enhances nursing knowledge is dependent on adherence to the highest ethical standards. The key components necessary to ensure that these ethical standards are met, as described in this chapter, should provide a useful guide for all nurses embarking on a research or EBP project.

Summary Points

1. History provides many lessons on the importance of protection of vulnerable human subjects. These history lessons have led to the development of national and international ethical codes of conduct.
2. Both the International Council of Nurses (ICN) and the American Nurses Association (ANA) acknowledge the obligations of the nursing profession to the vulnerable human and, as such, stress ethical standards in nursing research.
3. Ethical theories guide the standards of nursing research.
4. Some populations are more vulnerable than others (e.g., children); as such, they must be provided with the utmost protection during the research or EBP project.
5. Each step of the research process involves meeting ethical standards.
6. The privacy and confidentiality of the human subject must always be guaranteed.
7. Informed consent must be given by a human subject participant who truly understands to what he or she is consenting.
8. The honesty and trustworthiness of the nurse researcher or EBP project directors are crucial in ensuring valid—and valuable—results are derived from any study.

RED FLAGS

- Every study must address the ethical aspects of that study. Documentation of this focus may be demonstrated through a statement reflecting IRB approval of the study.
- Every study must speak to how the subjects will be protected from harm—physical and/or psychological—during the research process.

Critical Discussion: Ethical Issues in Nursing Research and EBP Projects

www.

1. You are not the principal investigator in a research study of incarcerated women who are HIV positive or have AIDS, but you are one of the researchers who has received permission to interview some of the women who volunteered to participate. One woman gives you inappropriate information about another prisoner, whom she states propositioned her for sex; the interviewee claims this prisoner has AIDS. As you leave the prison, the warden asks you to relate what happened during this interview. Discuss your responsibilities as a researcher in this sensitive study. A number of critical elements must be taken into account: the interviewee divulging information about another prisoner's possible HIV/AIDS status and behaviors, confidentiality and protection of human subjects, the warden's request, and your ethical responsibility to the study and to your institution.

2. You are the principal investigator studying young teenagers (10–14 years old) who are receiving aggressive treatment for life-threatening cancers. One 11-year-old boy has had many bouts of chemotherapy, which have made him acutely ill. His parents would like the child to participate in the study, but he refuses. What he shares could potentially be of use in treating other young teenagers. Clearly, there are some issues of consent here. Discuss what you should do.

3. You are one of a group of nurse researchers who are participating in a multinational study. The sample will include people of many different ethnic groups, all of whom speak different languages, and will include women and children. You understand the process of IRB review in your own institution, but many other issues arise when one is participating in international studies. Among the issues of concern here are the need for an interpreter, confidentiality, local permission requirements, management of the study in the foreign country, recruitment of persons into the study, and protection of human subjects in a different country. How can these issues be resolved so that the study may be conducted?

4. Your hospital wants to decrease the rate of falls in patients older than 65 years of age. You have been asked to conduct an EBP project regarding these patient outcomes. What are some ethical considerations you must incorporate into this project?

Multiple Choice Questions

1. When developing a nursing research project, why is it important to remember the ethical constraints?

    A. The study will not be approved by the institutional review board without these constraints.
    B. The protection of human subjects underlies all human research projects.
    C. The results will not be trustworthy and replicable.
    D. The nurse researcher will not be able to get funding for the project and, therefore, will not be able to complete the project.

2. The atrocities performed on prisoners in Nazi Germany violated which ethical principles?

    A. Value of life, justice, and respect
    B. Beneficence, nonmaleficence, and value of life
    C. Autonomy, nonmaleficence, and respect
    D. Justice, autonomy, and nonmaleficence

3. Protection of vulnerable individuals is a critical ethical component in human research studies. How did Edward Jenner fail to meet this standard when he tested swinepox on his 1-year-old son?

    A. He thought the new knowledge overrode any concern he should have for the rights of his son.
    B. He did not know any better.
    C. He ignored the point that he could not get informed consent from his son, who was particularly vulnerable.
    D. Give that smallpox was such a lethal disease at that time, it was better for Jenner to ignore his son's vulnerability so to gain new knowledge.

4. The Tuskegee Syphilis Study lasted many years, and none of the human subjects were properly informed about the study's conduct. Which ethical principle was egregiously ignored in this study?

    A. Autonomy
    B. Respect
    C. Nonmaleficence
    D. Justice

5. Why does an ethical research environment assist with ensuring scientific integrity?

    A. Within this environment, expectations for scientific integrity are laid out.
    B. Federal regulations related to ethical standards are adhered to, increasing the likelihood of integrity.
    C. The researcher always works within an ethical environment, which encourages the practice of ethical research behaviors.
    D. Scientific integrity ensures funding, which means that the study will be completed.

6. Why do federal regulations specify that the makeup of the institutional review board should reflect cultural and gender diversity and an awareness of local mores?

   A. This practice ensures that all research projects presented to the IRB will receive fair examination and not be denied without discussion.
   B. Gender studies have not been common until recently, and females react differently to different treatments.
   C. Awareness of local customs and culture means that both IRB members and researchers understand issues of concern in a non-American population.
   D. There is now great interest in researching healthcare issues in persons of different cultures.

7. Why is it important that the researcher be competent to conduct research?

   A. It is not ethically appropriate for an incompetent person to conduct research.
   B. An incompetent researcher will not be able to get informed consent from the vulnerable subject, which is unethical.
   C. An incompetent researcher should always work with someone who is competent, so that he or she can learn the process.
   D. Research is a complicated process that has to be learned.

8. What is the issue of greatest concern when developing a research project?

   A. The competence of the researcher to do the research
   B. The availability of funding
   C. The protection of the vulnerable subject
   D. Informed consent

9. A Certificate of Confidentiality may be required to protect both the researched and the researcher. Why?

   A. The nurse researcher will not lose his or her license to practice and do research because of the sensitive topic being researched.
   B. If the research topic is particularly sensitive, this certificate protects patients from divulging issues uncomfortable to them.
   C. The certificate protects the researcher and the researched from being coerced by governmental authorities to reveal sensitive information.
   D. The certificate means that no information is shared with those who should not be informed.

10. Why do research questions have to be developed carefully?

   A. The wrong question for the study means the wrong answer.
   B. Carefully developed and refined questions focus the research project.
   C. Without careful development of the questions, the research results will be meaningless.
   D. It is unethical not to develop questions carefully.

11. Informed consent is a crucial issue in research projects because

A. Research results will be more meaningful.

B. The researcher will be adhering to international codes of ethics from which federal regulations are drawn.

C. The project will be rejected by the IRB, because the subject is not informed about the study.

D. The consenting subject will understand what the research is about and will have the choice to participate (or not).

12. Scientific misconduct on the part of the researcher is very serious. What constitutes scientific misconduct?

A. Lying about the project to subjects when seeking informed consent

B. Fabrication, falsification of data, and plagiarism

C. Attributing only partial authorship to other contributors when they have done most of the work

D. Making false claims about a project being funded when the researcher is talking about his or her work

13. HIPAA, which was designed to protect all humans and their medical records in this era of electronic paperless records, has imposed another restraint on conducting research. Why?

A. It is more difficult to obtain IRB permission to conduct a research project.

B. With paperless medical records, there are no data to analyze, even when interview data and surveys are involved.

C. The regulations protect against unauthorized disclosure; although IRB permission includes this protection, additional care is taken under HIPAA.

D. HIPAA ensures that highly sensitive data (e.g., HIV/AIDS status) is not disclosed.

14. Privacy and confidentiality are always issues in human subject research. What are the important steps to ensure that they are protected?

A. The researcher does not talk about what the subject shares until the project's results are published in a peer-reviewed journal.

B. All data are kept securely locked in a safe place and destroyed when the study is completed.

C. Care with replication studies must be taken so that original data are not shared in the second study.

D. All data are kept securely locked in a safe place and may be destroyed only according to IRB instructions.

15. Both the International Council of Nurses and the American Nurses Association make it clear that the ethical standards of the profession require the same obligations from the nurse researcher. Why?

A. For the protection of vulnerable clients and patients
B. For the protection of the nurse researcher
C. Because of an obligation inherent within the nursing profession
D. Because practice on which these ethical standards are built focuses nursing research

16. In developing a question for an EBP project involving the fall rate of patients 65 years of age and older, the initial ethical consideration should be

A. The age of the researcher.
B. The number of falls.
C. The age of the population.
D. The sample size of the population.

17. EBP projects in your institution are not required to obtain IRB approval. However, as the nurse in charge of an EBP project, you must still

A. Maintain anonymity and confidentiality of patient information.
B. Maintain professionalism in gathering patient information.
C. Provide all staff access to the patient information.
D. Provide patient information obtained to the hospital board of directors.

Discussion Questions

www

1. Several nurses are working together to develop a research project. Only one is doctorally prepared; the others have either a master's degree or a baccalaureate degree. The preparatory work is to be shared equally among all the nurses. As the project evolves, it turns out that those who do not have a doctorate do all the work. At a meeting, the doctorally prepared nurse insists that she be listed as the principal investigator for the grant to be submitted and as the first author on all publications. She bases her request on a belief that the reviewers of the grant would "pay more attention to the application" if the principal investigator has a doctoral degree. Discuss the ethical issues embedded in this situation.

2. The protection of human subjects lies at the heart of any research project. Part of this protection entails the need to obtain informed consent. A female nurse wants to do a qualitative study investigating what it means for males to live with diabetes mellitus and the resultant impotence. Qualitative research usually involves interviewing the human subject— and sexual impotence is a particularly sensitive subject. How should the nurse explain the study to her potential sample to ensure that the consent is truly informed and that the subjects will not drop out of the study because of extreme discomfort during the interview? What are the ethical issues involved?

3. Codes of ethics in human research, developed partly as a result of the atrocities of the mid-twentieth century, continue to be refined. The dictionary definitions of "moral" and "ethics" suggest that the meanings of these terms can and will change and the evolving codes support this idea. Yet codes of ethics are based on some universal theories and values theories. Discuss why, despite the universality of these theories, the codes continue to evolve.

4. You have an idea for an EBP project that your hospital has approved regarding the fall rates of pediatric patients on your unit. Discuss the ethics involved with this particular population. How would you incorporate ethics in the data collection, analysis, and report of the project?

Suggested Readings

American Association of Critical Care Nurses (AACN). (2005). *Ethics in critical care nursing research*. Retrieved from http://classic.aacn.org/AACN/research.nsf/0/daddec18fb7e925788256826007dec91?OpenDocument

Goldman, E. (2001, May). *Vulnerable subjects*. Retrieved June 29, 2009, from http://poynter.indiana.edu/sas/res/vs.pdf

Im, E.-O., & Chee, W. (2002, July/August). Issues in protection of human subjects in Internet research. *Nursing Research*, *51*(4), 266–269.

International Council of Nurses (ICN). (2006). *The ICN code of ethics for nurses*. Retrieved from http://www.icn.ch/about-icn/code-of-ethics-for-nurses/

Lanter, J. (2006). Clinical research with cognitively impaired subjects. *Dimensions of Critical Care Nursing*, *25*(2), 89–92.

Levine, C., Faden, R., Grady, C., Hammerschmidt, D., Eckenwiler, L., & Sugarman, J. (2004). The limitations of "vulnerability" as a protection for human research participants. *American Journal of Bioethics*, *4*(3), 44–49.

National Institutes of Health (NIH). (1979). *The Belmont report: Ethical principles and guidelines for the protection of human subjects of research*. Retrieved from http://www.hhs.gov/ohrp/humansubjects/guidance/belmont.html

Rogers, B. (2005). Research with protected populations: Vulnerable participants. *AAOHN Journal*, *53*(4), 156–157.

Smith, L. (2001, May/June). Ethics and the research realist. *Nurse Educator*, *26*(3), 108–110.

United Nations Organization. (2002). International covenant on civil and political rights, article 7. Universal declaration of human rights. In Council for International Organizations of Medical Sciences (CIOMS). *International ethics guidelines for biomedical research involving human subjects*. Retrieved from http://www.cioms.ch/publications/layout_guide2002.pdf

U.S. Department of Health and Human Services (DHHS). (1998). *Sponsor–investigator–IRB interrelationship*. Retrieved from http://www.fda.gov/RegulatoryInformation/Guidances/ucm126425.htm

U.S. Department of Health and Human Services (DHHS). (2005). *Protection of human subjects rule, 45 C.F.R. 46*. Retrieved from http://www.hhs.gov/ohrp/humansubjects/guidance/45cfr46.html

World Medical Association (WMA). (1964–2004). *World Medical Association: Declaration of Helsinki: Ethical principles for medical research involving human subjects*. Retrieved from http://www.wma.net/en/30publications/10policies/b3/17c.pdf

References

American Nurses Association (ANA). (1994). *Position statement: Assisted suicide.* Washington, DC: Author.

American Nurses Association (ANA). (2001). *Code of ethics for nurses.* Retrieved from http://www.nursingworld.org/MainMenuCategories/EthicsStandards/CodeofEthicsforNurses/Code-of-Ethics.aspx

Anderson, D. G., & Hatton, D. C. (2000). Accessing vulnerable populations for research. *Western Journal of Nursing Research, 22*(2), 244–251.

Batalden, P. B., & Davidoff, F. (2007). What is "quality improvement" and how can it transform healthcare? *Quality and Safety in Health Care, 16*(1), 2–3.

Benjamin, M., & Curtis, J. (1986). *Ethics in nursing* (2nd ed.). New York, NY: Oxford University Press.

Birch, M., & Miller, T. (2002). Encouraging participation: Ethics and responsibilities. In M. Mauthner, M. Burch, J. Jessop, & T. Miller (Eds.), *Ethics in qualitative research* (pp. 91–106). London, UK: Sage.

Borsay, A. (2009). Nursing history: An irrelevance for nursing practice? *Nursing History Review, 17*(1), 14–27.

Broyles, L. M., Tate, J. A., & Happ, M. B. (2008). Videorecording in clinical research: Mapping the ethical terrain. *Nursing Research, 57*(1), 59–63.

Cartwright, J. C., & Hickman, S. E. (2007, October). Conducting research in community-based care facilities: Ethical and regulatory implications. *Journal of Gerontological Nursing, 33*(10), 5–11.

Centers for Disease Control and Prevention (CDC). (2011). *The Tuskegee timeline.* Retrieved from http://www.cdc.gov/tuskegee/timeline.htm

Christians, C. G. (2003). Ethics and politics in qualitative research. In N. K. Denzin & Y. S. Lincoln (Eds.), *The landscape of qualitative research: Theories and issues* (2nd ed., pp. 208–244). Thousand Oaks, CA: Sage.

Cipriano Silva, M. (2006). Ethics of research. In J. Fitzpatrick & M. Wallace (Eds.), *Encyclopedia of nursing research* (2nd ed., pp. 177–180). New York, NY: Springer.

Commission on Research Integrity. (1995). *Integrity and misconduct in research* (Department of Health and Human Services, Publication No. 1996–746–425). Washington, DC: U.S. Government Printing Office.

Conn, V. S. (2008). Staying true to the results. *Western Journal of Nursing Research, 30*(2), 161–162.

Council for International Organizations of Medical Sciences (CIOMS). (2002). *International ethics guidelines for biomedical research involving human subjects.* Retrieved from http://www.fhi360.org/training/fr/retc/pdf_files/cioms.pdf

Dally, A. (1998). Thalidomide: Was the tragedy preventable? *Lancet, 351*(9110), 1197–1199.

Deigh, J. (1995). Ethics. In R. Audi (Ed.), *The Cambridge dictionary of philosophy* (pp. 244–249). Cambridge, UK: Cambridge University Press.

Driever, M. J., & Pranulis, M. F. (2003). New challenges for issues in clinical nursing research. *Western Journal of Nursing Research, 25*(8), 937–947.

Edwards, R., & Mauthner, M. (2002). Ethics and feminist research: Theory and practice. In M. Mauthner, M. Burch, J. Jessop, & T. Miller (Eds.), *Ethics in qualitative research* (pp. 14–31). London, UK: Sage.

Ely, B., & Coleman, C. (2007). Recruitment and retention of children in longitudinal research. *Journal for Specialists in Pediatric Nursing, 12*(3), 199–202.

Erlen, J. A. (2005). HIPAA: Implications for research. *Orthopedic Nursing*, 23(2), 139–142.

Firby, P. (1995). Critiquing the ethical aspects of a study. *Nurse Researcher*, 3(1), 35–41.

Freda, M. C., & Kearney, M. H. (2005). Ethical issues faced by nursing editors. *Western Journal of Nursing Research*, 27(4), 487–499.

Grady, C. (2007). Quality improvement and ethical oversight. *Annals of Internal Medicine*, 146(9), 680–681.

Henley, S. J., & Dougherty, M. C. (2009). Quality of manuscript reviews in nursing research. *Nursing Outlook*, 57(1), 18–26.

Hume, D. (1751). *An enquiry concerning the principles of morals*. Oxford, UK: Oxford University Press.

Institute of Medicine (IOM). (1989). *The responsible conduct of research in the health sciences*. Washington, DC: National Academies Press.

International Council of Nurses (ICN). (2006). *The ICN code of ethics for nurses*. Retrieved from http://www.icn.ch/images/stories/documents/about/icncode_english.pdf

Jeffers, B. R. (2005). Research environments that promote integrity. *Nursing Research*, 54(91), 63–70.

Kant, I. (1785). Fundamental principles of the metaphysics of morals. In J. Rachels (1995), *The elements of moral philosophy* (2nd ed., pp. 107–131). New York, NY: McGraw-Hill.

Ketefian, S., & Lenz, E. R. (1995). Promoting scientific integrity in nursing research. Part II: Strategies. *Journal of Professional Nursing*, 11(5), 263–269.

Kirk, S. (2007). Methodological and ethical issues in conducting qualitative research with children and young people: A literature review. *International Journal of Nursing Studies*, 44(7), 1250–1260.

Kunin, T. F. (1997). Ethical issues in longitudinal research with at-risk children and adolescents. Cited in A. J. Roberson. (2007). Adolescent informed consent: Ethics, law, and theory to guide policy and nursing research. *Journal of Nursing Law*, 11(4), 191–196.

Lenz, E. R., & Ketefian, S. (1995). Promoting scientific integrity in nursing research. Part I: Current approaches in doctoral programs. *Journal of Professional Nursing*, 11(5), 213–219.

Lutz, K. F. (1999). Maintaining client safety and scientific integrity in research with battered women. *Image: Journal of Nursing Scholarship*, 31(1), 89–93.

Lynn, J., Baily, M. A., Bottrell, M., Jennings, B., Levine, R., Davidoff, F., . . . James, B. (2007). The ethics of using quality improvement methods in health care. *Annals of Internal Medicine*, 146(9), 666–673.

Macrina, F. L. (1995). *Scientific integrity: An introductory text with cases*. Washington, DC: ASM Press.

Mill, J. A. (1967). *Utilitarianism*. London, UK: Longmans.

Miller, T., & Bell, L. (2002). Consenting to what? Issues of access, gate-keeping and informed consent. In M. Mauthner, M. Burch, J. Jessop, & T. Miller (Eds.), *Ethics in qualitative research* (pp. 53–69). London, UK: Sage.

National Institutes of Health (NIH). (1979). *The Belmont report: Ethical principles and guidelines for the protection of human subjects of research*. Retrieved from http://www.hhs.gov/ohrp/humansubjects/guidance/belmont.html

Norman, R. (1998). *The moral philosophers: An introduction to ethics* (2nd ed.). Oxford, UK: Oxford University Press.

Perkins, E. (2001). Johns Hopkins tragedy: Could librarians have prevented a death? *Information Today*, 18(8), 51, 54. Retrieved http://newsbreaks.infotoday.com/nbreader.asp?ArticleID=17534

Pilkington, F. B. (2002). Scientific merit and research ethics. Nursing Science Quarterly, 15(3), 196–200.

Public Health Service Act, 42 USC~163. (1988). Cited in D. L. Volker (2004), Methodological issues associated with studying an illegal act: Assisted dying. Advances in Nursing Science, 27(2), 117–128.

Rachels, J. (1995). The elements of moral philosophy (2nd ed.). New York, NY: McGraw-Hill.

Redman, R. W. (2007). Knowledge development, quality improvement, and research ethics. Research and Theory for Nursing Practice: An International Journal, 21(4), 217–219.

Reich, W. T. (Ed.). (1995). Encyclopedia of bioethics. New York, NY: Simon & Schuster Macmillan, pp. 2248–2259.

Roberson, A. J. (2007). Adolescent informed consent: Ethics, law, and theory to guide policy and nursing research. Journal of Nursing Law, 11(4), 191–196.

Rogers, B. (2005). Research with protected populations: Vulnerable participants. AAOHN Journal, 53(4), 156–157.

Ross, W. D. (1954). Kant's ethical theory. Oxford, UK: Oxford University Press.

Rothstein, W. G., & Phuong, L. H. (2007). Ethical attitudes of nurse, physician and unaffiliated members of institutional review boards. Journal of Nursing Scholarship, 39(1), 75–811.

Siedlecki, S. L. (2008). Making a difference through research. AORN Journal, 88(5), 716–729.

Tanner, C. A. (2006). Thinking like a nurse: A research-based model of clinical judgment in nursing. Journal of Nursing Education, 45(6), 204–211.

Thiroux, J. P. (1980). Ethics, theory and practice. Encino, CA: Glencoe.

Tschudin, V. (1992). Ethics in nursing: The caring relationship. Oxford, UK: Butterworth Heinemann.

Twycross, A., & Corlett, J. (2007). Challenges of setting up a multi-centered research study. Nursing Standard, 21(49), 35–38.

United Nations Organization. (2002). International covenant on civil and political rights, article 7. Universal declaration of human rights. In Council for International Organizations of Medical Sciences (CIOMS), International ethics guidelines for biomedical research involving human subjects. Retrieved from http://www.fhi360.org/training/fr/Retc/pdf_files/cioms.pdf

U.S. Department of Health and Human Services (DHHS). (2005). Protection of human subjects rule, 45 C.F.R. 46. Retrieved from http://www.hhs.gov/ohrp/humansubjects/guidance/45cfr46.html

Volker, D. L. (2004). Methodological issues associated with studying an illegal act: Assisted dying. Advances in Nursing Science, 27(2), 117–128.

Weaver, K. (2007). Ethical sensitivity: State of knowledge and needs for further research. Nursing Ethics, 2(4), 141–155.

Wood, A., Grady, C., & Emanuel, E. J. (2002). The crisis in human participants research: Identifying the problems and proposing solutions. Retrieved from http://bioethics.georgetown.edu/pcbe/background/emanuelpaper.html

World Medical Association (WMA). (1964–2004). World Medical Association Declaration of Helsinki: Ethical principles for medical research involving human subjects. Retrieved from http://www.wma.net/en/30publications/10policies/b3/17c.pdf

PICOT, Problem Statement, Research Question, Hypothesis

Lucy B. Trice and Kathaleen C. Bloom

Chapter Objectives

At the conclusion of this chapter, the learner will be able to

1. Discuss processes involved in identifying a researchable problem in nursing practice
2. Write an effective problem statement
3. Discuss essential characteristics needed to pose a research question
4. Identify the criteria for establishing research variables
5. Contrast the various types of hypotheses
6. Explain the differences between conceptual and operational definitions
7. Critically evaluate research questions and hypotheses found in research reports for their contribution to the strength of evidence for nursing practice

Key Terms

➤ Associative hypothesis

➤ Categorical variable

➤ Causal hypothesis

➤ Complex hypothesis

➤ Confounding variable

➤ Continuous variable

➤ Demographic variable

➤ Dependent variable

➤ Dichotomous variable

➤ Directional hypothesis

➤ Discrete variable

➤ Extraneous variable

➤ Hypothesis

➤ Independent variable

➤ Nondirectional hypothesis

➤ Null hypothesis

➤ Problem statement

➤ Research hypothesis

➤ Research question

➤ Simple hypothesis

➤ Variable

Introduction

Every research study begins with a problem the researcher would like to solve. For such a problem to be researchable, it must be one that can be studied through collecting and analyzing data. Some problems, although interesting, are by their nature not appropriate research problems because they are not researchable. Problems involving moral or ethical issues are not researchable, as the solutions to these problems are based on an individual's values. For example, one could not research a question such as "Should marijuana use be legalized?" because the answer to the question depends on one's values rather than on a clearly right or wrong answer. This is not to say that marijuana use cannot be studied. One could study people's opinions regarding marijuana use. For example, one might ask the question, "Do cancer patients hold more favorable opinions regarding legalization of marijuana use than the general public?" The need to avoid moral/ethical questions as a research topic applies to both quantitative and qualitative studies.

Other factors influence whether a problem is researchable using quantitative methods. For a problem to be considered researchable by quantitative methods, the **variables** to be studied must be clearly defined and measurable. This clarity is necessary to apply statistical measures that will identify relationships among the variables. Qualitative studies are not subject to the same restriction, as the purpose of these studies is to describe in detail the phenomenon of interest as it is perceived by the study subjects. In other words, qualitative studies are descriptive in nature and are not concerned with relationships among variables.

Identifying Researchable Problems

There are a number of sources from which researchable problems can arise. Personal experience, whether as a healthcare professional or as a consumer of health care, is a rich source. For example, reviewing procedure manuals might raise the question, "Does one procedure for giving mouth care apply to all patients?" In considering such diverse groups of patients as those with endotracheal or nasogastric tubes in place; those with full-blown AIDS, often accompanied by buccal mucosal lesions; and cancer patients on chemotherapy, one might ask, "Does one size fit all, or should separate procedures be established for each case?" Thus, as many authors point out (Macnee & McCabe, 2008; Norwood, 2010; Polit & Beck, 2010; Schmidt & Brown, 2012), practice experience is a major source for identifying gaps in knowledge that would benefit from research.

The nursing literature can also be a valuable source for researchable problems, particularly for the novice researcher (Burns & Grove, 2007; Norwood, 2010; Polit & Beck, 2010). For example, the researcher might identify a topic of interest and then review the nursing research literature to determine which kinds of studies have been done in that area. Seeing how other researchers have approached a problem can often spark new ideas or perhaps point to studies that would benefit from replication. In addition to offering such indirect assistance in the development of a **problem statement**, the research literature, including unpublished dissertations and theses as well as published research articles, provides direct assistance through specific suggestions for future research in the area. These suggestions may be offered under a special heading for future research, or they may be part of the discussion of the findings.

Social issues often give rise to topics relevant to healthcare research (Norwood, 2010; Polit & Beck, 2008, 2010). For example, the feminist movement raised questions about gender equity in health care and in healthcare research. The civil rights movement led to research on minority health problems in general and to explorations of the differences in effectiveness of medical treatment in different ethnic groups.

Shifts in the U.S. population including increasing numbers of elderly, and increasing numbers of individuals with one or more chronic diseases, also provide impetus for healthcare research. For example the emergence of conditions such as Alzheimer's Disease has led to research dealing with the nursing care of these patients, as well as research in how best to give "care for the caregiver" (Elliott, Burgio, & DeCoster, 2010). The rising epidemic of obesity at all ages of the population, and especially in childhood, highlights the need for research into methods to promote skill building with regard to healthy lifestyles (Melnyk, 2008). The Institute of Medicine's report on professional education suggests that these shifts in population and changing face of our society also demand a revamping of professional education to better deal with these issues (Institute of Medicine Board on Health Care Services, 2003).

? Think Outside the Box

Using the following examples, develop problem statements, research questions, and/or hypotheses for each one. (1) Which information has been used to determine the method of catheterizing a laboring mother? (2) Which information serves as the basis for the range of blood sugars used within newly diagnosed elderly diabetics? (3) Which items need to be included into the formation of a problem statement, research question, and hypothesis?

The research priorities of the profession, and particularly of the funding bodies interested in healthcare research, are also a primary source for generating researchable problems (Burns & Grove, 2011; Norwood, 2010). For example, the National Institute of Nursing Research (NINR, n.d.) is the largest federal funding body dedicated specifically to nursing research. The NINR has as its mission "to promote and improve the health of individuals, families, communities, and populations" (p. 4). The Institute supports both clinical and basic research, and also provides funding for researcher training. The ongoing funding priorities of the NINR are listed in **Table 5-1**. Further elaboration within each priority is provided in the NINR strategic plan located on the Institute's website: http://www.ninr.nih .gov/AboutNINR/NINRMissionandStrategicPlan

Table 5-1
Funding Priorities of NINR
1. Health Promotion and Disease Prevention 2. Advancing Quality of Life: Symptom Management 3. Palliative and End-of-Life Care 4. Innovation
Source: National Institute of Nursing Research (NINR). (n.d.). *NINR mission.* Retrieved from http://www.ninr.nih.gov/AboutNINR/NINRMissionandStrategicPlan

Determining Significance of the Problem

Once the problem of interest has been identified, and before going any further, the researcher must determine the significance of the problem to nursing as well as the feasibility of studying the problem. Significance refers to whether a problem is worth studying. A number of authors agree on the criteria that can be used to determine the significance of a problem to nursing (Burns & Grove, 2011; LoBiondo-Wood & Haber, 2010; Polit & Beck, 2008):

- Will nursing's stakeholders (patients, nurses, healthcare community) benefit from the findings of the study?
- Will the findings be applicable to practice, education, or administration?
- Will the findings extend or support current theory, or generate new theory?
- Will the findings support current nursing practice or provide evidence for changing current practice and/or policies?

Some authorities recommend that two additional criteria be considered when determining the significance of a problem:

- Will the findings address nursing research priorities? (Burns & Grove, 2007; Polit & Beck, 2010)
- Will the results of the proposed study build on previous findings? (Burns & Grove, 2011; Polit & Beck, 2008, 2010)

If the research problem does not meet the majority of these criteria, it should be reworked or, if that is not possible, simply abandoned. The single most important of these criteria is perhaps the first one: Will nursing's stakeholders (patients, nurses, healthcare community) benefit from the findings of the study? If this question cannot be answered with a resounding "yes," then the problem is probably not worth studying. Nursing is a discipline that takes pride in research aimed at benefitting patients and changing practice for the better. In the move to evidence-based practice (EBP), benefit to patients and applicability to practice—and especially support for current practice or evidence for changing current practice—are paramount in assessing the significance of a research problem. According to Farrell (2006), "Practices are sorely needed that are based on sound evidence" (p. 119).

Examining Feasibility of the Problem

Feasibility refers to whether the study can be done. It includes considerations such as cost of the study, availability of study subjects, time constraints, availability of facilities and equipment, cooperation of others, interest of the researcher, and expertise of the researcher (Burns & Grove, 2009, 2011; LoBiondo-Wood & Haber, 2010; Norwood, 2010; Polit & Beck, 2008).

Cost

EBP has emerged from the desire of the majority of healthcare providers (both institutions and individuals) to do what is right for the patient and what will result in more good than harm (Craig & Smyth, 2002). The evidence for EBP is gathered through research (DiCenso, Guyatt, & Ciliska, 2005; Schmidt & Brown, 2012)—and all research studies cost money to some degree. It is the researcher's task to obtain support for the research from the institution in which it will be conducted as well as from potential funding bodies, both within the institution itself and in outside agencies. When seeking this support, the researcher must present a clear picture of the value of the research in terms of patient outcomes versus the costs involved. The current economic climate, which emphasizes the link between outcomes value and resources expenditure, demands nothing less (Malloch & Porter-O'Grady, 2006). In the final analysis, the deciding factor with regard to feasibility of a particular study may be how much the study will cost versus the funds and other necessary support that are available to the researcher.

Availability of Subjects

The type and number of study subjects will vary depending on the purpose and design of the study. Larger numbers of participants are generally needed for quantitative studies if the findings are to be considered significant, whereas smaller numbers of subjects are appropriate for studies using a qualitative design. Clearly, a sufficient number of subjects must be available for the study to be feasible.

Time Constraints

Studies done in connection with the pursuit of academic degrees (e.g., research projects, theses, dissertations), of necessity, have a time frame for their completion. The same is true for studies supported by grant monies, as well as studies for which grant monies are being sought. For a study to be considered feasible, it must have the possibility of being completed within the applicable time constraints.

Availability of Facilities and Equipment

The need for special facilities and equipment can add greatly to the cost of a study. Although not all studies require specialized equipment or facilities, for those that do, both the cost and the availability of these items must be taken into consideration when determining the feasibility of the study.

Cooperation of Others

All studies require a certain amount of cooperation from others. The researcher may need referrals from others to obtain research subjects, for example, or to arrange for use of laboratories or other kinds of facilities. Student researchers in particular often need assistance with data entry in quantitative studies, data transcription in qualitative studies, and statistical analysis. These types of assistance are frequently offered to student researchers without a fee; however, obtaining the assistance requires cooperation from those providing these services. The study subjects themselves must also cooperate in a sense, if the data are to be collected in a timely manner. Thus cooperation of these important others is an essential ingredient of a feasible study. Securing that cooperation falls squarely on the shoulders of the researcher. In their discussion of obtaining cooperation from various others, Burns and Grove (2001) contend that researchers need to maintain objectivity throughout the course of the study, avoiding a tendency to take themselves too seriously; "a sense of humor is invaluable" (p. 426).

Interest of the Researcher

Conducting research, although often rewarding when the final results are in, is nevertheless hard work. To embark on a study that is not of fairly profound interest to the researcher is foolhardy at best, and at worst it can lead to failure to complete the study. If the researcher is not interested in doing the research, then carrying out the study is not generally feasible.

Expertise of the Researcher

Ideally, the researcher should have prior knowledge and experience in the field of study in question. This is not to say that a study would be considered not possible solely because it is a new area of study for the researcher. Certainly, seasoned researchers frequently "branch out" into new areas of study. When less experienced researchers are involved, however, Polit and Beck (2008) caution that difficulties may arise in developing and carrying out a study on a topic that is totally new and/or unfamiliar.

Addressing Nursing Research Priorities

If the body of knowledge that deals with the practice of nursing is to be expanded, the major focus of nursing research should be on issues that influence patient outcomes. Further, it is through this type of research that we will gather the evidence to document the quality and effectiveness of nursing care (Moorhead, Johnson, Maas, & Swanson 2008). The specific areas of focus, in terms of patient outcomes, vary widely. As noted elsewhere, doing research can be costly, so it behooves the researcher to attempt to match his or her research interests not only with those of the institution where the individual works, but also with the priorities established by funding agencies. The major federal funding agency dedicated to nursing is NINR. Other funding bodies with research priorities relevant to nursing include the Agency for Healthcare Research and Quality; private organizations such as the Kellogg Foundation and the Helene Fuld Health Trust; professional organizations such as the American Nurses Foundation and Sigma Theta Tau International; and nursing specialty organizations such as the Association of Perioperative Registered Nurses and the American Association of Critical Care Nurses, to name a few. Taking care to address the funding priorities of a particular organization enhances the possibility of obtaining from that organization the funding needed to complete the research project.

Problem Statement

The problem statement presents the idea, issue, or situation that the researcher intends to examine in the study. The statement should be broad enough to cover the concern prompting the study, yet narrow enough to provide direction for designing the study. It can be conceptualized in the form of a declarative sentence or a question. In some cases, the term "research question" is used interchangeably with "problem statement."

? **Think Outside the Box**

Formulate a conceptual and operational definition for catheterization, laboring mother, blood sugar, and newly diagnosed elderly diabetic.

The problem statement is the foundation of the study, and as such is usually preceded by several paragraphs of background information that set the stage for the proposed study. These paragraphs identify the significance of the problem, present justification that the problem is researchable, and provide supporting documentation from the literature.

This general discussion of the problem culminates in the problem statement. The problem statement is often further clarified by including the purpose and goal(s) of the study, all of which are derived from the problem statement.

Research Question

Although the terms "**research question**" and "problem statement" are sometimes used interchangeably, the research question is often more specific than the problem statement. Additionally, research questions (rather than hypotheses) are frequently used to guide studies that are exploratory in nature and aimed at describing variables or perhaps identifying differences between groups in relation to these variables. Research questions also guide studies that examine relationships among the variables being studied but do not test the nature of these relationships. Studies designed to test the nature of the relationships among variables are generally guided by hypotheses rather than research questions (Burns & Grove, 2009; Fain, 2009).

Research questions can be used to guide both quantitative and qualitative studies. Quantitative studies are often initiated to answer several questions derived from the problem of interest, each focused on a specific variable to be measured in the population. For example, West et al. (2011) were interested in obesity prevention, and specifically how to prevent regaining weight initially lost during a weight loss regimen. Most weight loss methods focus on behavioral skill refinement, i.e., changing food choice and/or eating patterns. These same methods are used in maintenance programs, but with disappointing results (Wing et al., 2008). West and her colleagues devised a study to compare the efficacy of a motivation-focused treatment versus a skill-based treatment in maintaining weight loss (2011). The following research questions might be used to guide this study:

1. Does a motivation-focused intervention affect weight maintenance in individuals who have recently lost weight?
2. Does a skill-based intervention affect weight maintenance in individuals who have recently lost weight?
3. Do individuals who follow a motivation-focused intervention maintain their weight loss for a longer time period than those who follow a skill-based intervention?

Questions 1 and 2 are narrowly focused, dealing with one **independent variable** (participation in a motivation-focused intervention and participation in a skill-based intervention, respectively) and the **dependent variable** (weight maintenance). The third question,

while more complex, gets at the heart of the matter: Does one intervention work better than the other?

Qualitative studies, by their nature, explore phenomena about
which little is known. Burns and Grove (2007) point out that the
research questions guiding these types of studies are limited in number
and generally broad in scope, and they include variables or concepts
that are more complex than those guiding quantitative studies. For
example, Karlsson, Bergbom, and Forsberg (2012) investigated the
lived experiences of adult intensive care patients who were conscious
while undergoing mechanical ventilation. Using a qualitative approach
(namely phenomenology), they conducted in-depth interviews with
12 patients who were determined to be conscious while they were
being mechanically ventilated. The interviews took place approximately 1 week following their discharge from the intensive care unit.
The research question guiding this study might be stated as follows:
What are the essential themes common to the experience of being
conscious while undergoing mechanical ventilation? The concepts in
this question are much broader than those cited for the earlier quantitative example. Qualitative studies, because they are designed to get
at understanding behavior and the values/perceptions that underlie it
are particularly important as a starting point for designing and implementing nursing interventions (Ketefian & Redman, 2013).

Components of the Problem Statement

A well-written problem statement for a quantitative study, whether
written as a declarative statement or a question, has at a minimum,
two components: the population of concern and the variable(s) to be
studied. The PICOT format described elsewhere, has the advantage of
clarifying more fully the population of the study as well as the inter-
vention/comparison of interest, the outcome desired, and the time
frame involved. For example, a researcher might be interested in
investigating the use of pet therapy to increase morale in hospitalized
patients. As stated, the population (hospitalized patients) is fairly
broad and does not provide a lot of direction for the literature search
or for the study design. Depending on the specific concern and age
group under investigation, the researcher could narrow the population by age (e.g., hospitalized patients between the ages of 6 and
10 years) or other characteristics, such as disease and/or treatment
(e.g., hospitalized patients between the ages of 6 and 10 years undergoing treatment for cancer). The variables of interest would be pet
therapy and morale. Following the PICOT format, the population of
interest (P) would be hospitalized patients between the ages of 6 and
10 years undergoing treatment for cancer; the intervention of interest
(I) would be pet therapy; the comparison of interest (C) would be

no pet therapy; the outcome of interest (O) would be increased morale; and the time (T) would refer to time of hospitalization.

Strictly speaking, the term "variable" refers to measurable qualities or characteristics of people, things, or situations that can change, vary, or fluctuate. For example, blood pressure, pulse rate, anxiety level, and degree of pain are all characteristics of people that can vary from one person to another. A child's reaction to the presence (or absence) of a parent in the hospitalized child's room during painful procedures can vary from one hospitalized child to another. Variables are the foundation of quantitative studies; they constitute what is being studied in the designated population.

Researchers often want to know what causes or influences a particular phenomenon or, in some cases, what alleviates or diminishes that phenomenon. For example, one might want to know if a hospitalized child's anxiety level during a painful procedure would be lessened if a parent were present during the procedure. In this case, there are two variables of interest: the child's anxiety level and the presence of a parent during the painful procedure. The researcher is investigating the effect that the presence of a parent has on the child's anxiety level during a painful procedure. Because the variable "presence of a parent" is having an effect on the variable "child's anxiety level," it is termed the independent variable. By the same token, the variable being affected (i.e., child's anxiety level) is termed the dependent variable. In a study investigating more than one variable, the variable(s) that is (are) acting on, influencing, or causing an effect on the other variable(s) is (are) called the independent variable(s), and the variable(s) being acted on is (are) called the dependent variable(s) (Burns & Grove, 2011; LoBiondo-Wood & Haber, 2010; Norwood, 2010; Polit & Beck, 2010).

Other types of variables that can affect the outcome of the study but are not the variables the researcher is investigating are referred to as **extraneous variables**. In the example cited earlier, the age of the child could affect his or her anxiety level, regardless of whether a parent is present in the room, and therefore would be considered an extraneous variable. The researcher could control for the variable of age by limiting the study population to a particular age group. Another variable that might affect the child's anxiety level, regardless of whether a parent is present in the room, is the nature of the painful procedure. The procedure could be specified to control for this variable. With any study, it is important to identify and control for extraneous variables; otherwise, the study results may be confusing and inaccurate. Most studies have extraneous variables of one sort or another. It is important for the researcher to recognize and control for these variables, either in the study design or through statistical procedures, to preserve the validity of the study results. If a study cannot control for an extraneous variable, the variable is then termed a **confounding variable**.

The term "**demographic variable**" refers to characteristics of the subjects in the study. Data on these characteristics are usually collected during the study and are then used to describe the study group. Many different kinds of demographic information can be collected, including details about age, gender, ethnicity, educational level, marital status, and number of children. The types of demographic data collected depend on the purpose of the study; however, at a minimum, data on age, gender, and ethnicity should be gathered.

? Think Outside the Box   www

Why is it necessary to have a problem statement, research question, or hypothesis? What benefit does it provide? Is one better than others? Which restrictions arise related to the use of the problem statement, research question, or hypothesis?

If a variable can take on a wide range of values (from 0 to 100 or larger), it is often referred to as a **continuous variable**. A continuous variable is not limited to whole-number values. Examples of continuous variables include age, weight, salary, and blood pressure. In contrast, variables that can take on only a finite number of values, usually restricted to whole numbers, are referred to as **discrete variables**. For example, respiratory rate would be considered a discrete variable, as it can take on only whole-number equivalents; although variation in respiratory rate can occur from person to person, a finite number of these variations are compatible with life.

Categorical and dichotomous variables are similar because they represent characteristics that can be measured only in the sense that they are either present or not present. These kinds of variables are often assigned a number for identification, but the number does not represent a quantity. For example, ethnicity might be divided into white, African American, Hispanic, Native American, Pacific Islander, and Asian American, with each classification assigned an identifying number. The assigned number, however, would have no meaning other than identifying the occurrence of each race, perhaps to facilitate counting the number of occurrences of that particular race in the study. In this case, race would be considered a **categorical variable**, with each race included in the study representing a category. If only two categories are possible for a categorical variable, it may be referred to as a **dichotomous variable**. For example, gender is considered a dichotomous variable, as two categories are possible—male and female.

Table 5-2	
Problem Statements	
Declarative Statement Format	**Question Format**
Music therapy decreases the level of maternal anxiety during cesarean section.	Does music therapy decrease the level of maternal anxiety during cesarean section?
Nursing home residents who participate in regular exercise have fewer falls than those who do not.	Do nursing home residents who participate in regular exercise have fewer falls than those who do not?
Participation in a support group improves morale in family caregivers of Alzheimer's patients.	Does participation in a support group improve morale in family caregivers of Alzheimer's patients?
Diabetic patients who perceive of themselves as obese will participate in a weight management program.	Will diabetic patients who perceive of themselves as obese participate in a weight management program?
The number of medication errors made by nurses increases when the number of medications per patient is greater than three (3).	Does the number of medication errors made by nurses increase when the number of medications per patient is greater than three (3)?

Writing the Problem Statement

As noted previously, problem statements for quantitative studies may be written in the form of a declarative statement or a question (**Table 5-2**). The two components that must be included in every problem statement are the population of interest and the variable(s) to be measured. For example, if we were interested in studying the effect of presence of a parent on anxiety level in children undergoing painful procedures, we might construct a problem statement in the form of a question: "Does the presence of a parent affect the anxiety level in children ages 3–5 years undergoing initiation of intravenous therapy?" Alternatively, the same problem could be stated as a declarative statement: "The presence of a parent affects the anxiety level in children ages 3–5 years undergoing initiation of intravenous therapy." Both statements contain a population of interest (children ages 3–5 years undergoing initiation of intravenous therapy) and two variables (presence of a parent—independent variable; anxiety level of the child—dependent variable). The only difference between the two is the form of the statement—one is presented as a question and the other as a declarative statement. Note also that the elements of the PICOT format are readily apparent in each of these examples as well as those in Table 5-2.

? Think Outside the Box

Identify the elements of the PICOT format for each of the problem statements in Table 5-2.

Hypotheses

A research question asks whether a relationship exists between variables in a particular population. In contrast, a **hypothesis** stipulates or predicts the relationship that exists. For example, if the research question is "Does the presence of a parent in the room affect the anxiety level in children ages 3–5 years undergoing initiation of intravenous therapy?", then we might develop several hypotheses:

1. The presence of a parent in the room affects the anxiety level in children ages 3–5 years who undergo initiation of intravenous therapy.
2. The presence of a parent in the room reduces the anxiety level in children ages 3–5 years who undergo initiation of intravenous therapy.
3. The presence of a parent in the room has no effect on the anxiety level in children ages 3–5 years who undergo initiation of intravenous therapy.
4. The presence of a parent in the room increases the anxiety level in children ages 3–5 years who undergo initiation of intravenous therapy.

The advantage of a hypothesis over a research question is that the hypothesis puts the question into a form that can be tested. It is the nature of hypotheses to predict relationships among or between variables. For a hypothesis to be testable, it must stipulate a relationship between at least two variables in a given population.

Within EBP, the research question format incorporates the population of interest, the intervention, a comparison of interest, outcomes, and timing to ensure clarity of the subject (note that these are the components of the PICOT format). This process can also be applied to developing one or more hypotheses for a research study. Each hypothesis should contain the population of interest, the independent variable(s), the dependent variable(s), and the comparison of interest, all of which should lead to the outcome of the study.

Hypotheses and Qualitative Studies

Hypotheses are used in quantitative studies but are not appropriate for qualitative studies. By their nature, they present the researcher's opinion in the form of a prediction about the outcome of the study. In qualitative studies, however, researchers focus on the viewpoints of the subjects participating in the study rather than on their own. Thus the participants' viewpoints, rather than the researcher's hypothesis, guide the qualitative study. Generally, the purpose of qualitative studies is to explore new concepts and ideas about which little is known, or to discover new meanings for concepts. In keeping with this purpose, researchers using qualitative methods take great care to set aside their preconceived notions about the phenomena under investigation. A hypothesis would be a disadvantage in a qualitative study, because it would predict the outcome of the study and potentially bias the results. Thus, while qualitative studies may generate hypotheses that can then be tested using quantitative methods, they are not themselves guided by research hypotheses.

Types of Hypotheses

A testable hypothesis, also called the **research hypothesis**, predicts the relationship between two or more variables in a population of interest. All four of the hypotheses in the previous example could be considered testable.

Hypotheses may be directional, nondirectional, or null:

- A **directional hypothesis** predicts the path or direction the relationship will take. In the preceding example, both hypothesis 2 and hypothesis 4 are directional hypotheses. Hypothesis 2 predicts a decrease in anxiety with the presence of a parent, and hypothesis 4 predicts an increase in anxiety with the presence of a parent.
- A **nondirectional hypothesis** predicts a relationship but not the path or direction of the relationship. Hypothesis 1 in the previous example is a nondirectional hypothesis; it states that the presence of a parent affects the anxiety level in children ages 3–5 years but does not stipulate the direction of the effect.
- A **null hypothesis**, also called a statistical hypothesis, predicts that no relationship exists among or between the variables in the study. When inferential statistics are used to analyze data, the assumption is that the null hypothesis is actually being tested. Because this is understood, many researchers do not state the null hypothesis when reporting their findings in the literature. In the previous example, hypothesis 3 is stated in the null form.

Hypotheses may also be classified as simple or complex: A **simple hypothesis** specifies the relationship between two variables, whereas a **complex hypothesis** specifies the relationships between and among more than two variables. In the previous example, all four of the hypotheses could be classified as simple hypotheses. In each case, there are only two variables—the presence of a parent and the anxiety level in children ages 3–5 years. An example of a complex hypothesis might be "Religious beliefs, presence of social support, and ethnic background affect the perception of pain in patients who are terminally ill with cancer." Here there are four variables—religious beliefs, the presence of social support, ethnic background, and perception of pain. Complex hypotheses may also be termed multivariate hypotheses for the simple reason that they contain more than two variables.

? Think Outside the Box

Describe a problem in which a null hypothesis would be used and state the null hypothesis.

In addition, hypotheses may be categorized as associative or causal. These terms reflect the relationship between or among the variables in the hypothesis. For example, in an **associative hypothesis**, the hypothesis is stated in a way indicating that the variables exist side by side, and that a change in one variable is accompanied by a change in another. However, there is no suggestion that a change in one variable causes a change in another—merely that the variables change in association with each other (Reynolds, 1971).

In contrast, a **causal hypothesis** is stated in a way indicating that one variable causes or brings about a change in one or more other variables (Burns & Grove, 2011). As one might expect, the variable inducing the change is referred to as the independent variable, and the variable being changed is the dependent variable. Causal hypotheses may also be called directional hypotheses. Continuing with the example of the presence of a parent in the room with a child during a painful procedure and its effect on the child's anxiety level, two of the hypotheses can be termed causal—hypothesis 2 and hypothesis 4. Hypothesis 2 predicts a decrease in anxiety (dependent variable) with the presence of a parent in the room (independent variable), and hypothesis 4 predicts an increase in anxiety (dependent variable) with the presence of a parent in the room (independent variable).

Defining Variables for the Study

The variables to be studied in quantitative research projects are generally defined in two ways—conceptually and operationally. The conceptual definition is a broad, more abstract definition that is generally drawn from relevant literature, particularly the theoretical literature; the researcher's clinical experience; or, in some cases, a combination of these sources. The conceptual definition is similar to a dictionary definition in that it provides the general meaning associated with the variable, but it is more in-depth and broader in scope. Although considered the starting point, conceptual definitions rarely give direction regarding how the variable will actually be measured for the study. The operational definition, by contrast, stipulates precisely how the variable will be measured, including which tools will be used, if applicable. If a conceptual definition is abstract, an operational definition is concrete. This concreteness is necessary to allow for precise measurement of the variable(s) of interest in the study.

Evidence-Based Practice Considerations

Stommel and Wills (2004) point out that the ability to apply research findings to practice is an expected competency of advanced practice nurses. However, if we accept that it is the desire of all practitioners of nursing to provide "only that care that makes a positive difference in the lives of those whom they serve" (Porter-O'Grady, 2006, p. 1), then it is clear that all professional nurses—from the new graduate to the seasoned veteran—should have the ability to apply research findings to practice. Inherent in this ability is an understanding of how the research process unfolds and what constitutes good research.

Further, Melnyk and Fineout-Overholt (2011) maintain that "the goal of EBP is to use the highest quality of [research] knowledge in providing care to produce the greatest impact on patients' health status" (p. 75). To accomplish this, practitioners—and particularly staff nurses who are at the bedside caring for patients on a daily basis—must have the tools to critically analyze research so as to make appropriate EBP decisions. To critically analyze research, these staff nurses must possess a working knowledge of the language of research; recognize a researchable problem statement; distinguish between and among variables, identifying independent versus dependent variables; determine the population of interest; and above all, recognize a well-conducted study, one whose findings are worth consideration for applying to practice. In its purest and best form, EBP happens at the bedside. The burden of implementation rests squarely on the shoulders of the staff nurse.

For more information on EBP, visit the following site: http://journals.lww.com/ajnonline/pages/collectiondetails.aspx?Topical CollectionId=10

Summary Points

1. Every study begins with a problem the researcher would like to solve.
2. There are many sources for researchable problems, including personal experience, the nursing literature, social issues, and the research priorities of funding bodies.

3. The significance of the problem to nursing and the feasibility of studying the problem are important aspects to consider before embarking on any research project.
4. The problem statement presents the issue or situation to be examined and should identify the population of interest as well as the variables that will be studied.
5. Variables may be classified in a variety of ways: (a) independent versus dependent, (b) continuous versus discrete, (c) extraneous, (d) confounding, (e) categorical, and (f) dichotomous.
6. The problem statement may be written as a question or as a declarative sentence.
7. Placing the problem statement in the PICOT format helps to clarify the population, variables, outcome and time frame involved.
8. Hypotheses predict the relationship between or among variables.
9. Hypotheses may take many forms: (a) directional versus nondirectional, (b) simple versus complex, (c) associative versus causal, and (d) null.
10. Variables to be studied are generally defined both conceptually and operationally.
11. For nurses to pursue evidence-based practice, they must understand the research process and all of its components.

RED FLAGS

- Quantitative studies address research problems, research questions, and/or hypotheses.
- Qualitative studies do not use hypotheses, but rather explore research problems and research questions. If a qualitative study discusses a hypothesis, thought should be given to its focus and validity.
- A hypothesis must have at least one independent variable and one dependent variable; it is usually stated in a declarative statement format rather than as a question.
- Key variables within a study should have at least the operational definition provided for consideration.

Multiple Choice Questions

1. Developing a research study to investigate the availability of health care for minority children whose families are on welfare is an example of a research problem generated primarily from

   A. Practice.
   B. Social issues.
   C. Healthcare trends in society.
   D. Theory.

2. Problems involving moral or ethical issues are not researchable because

   A. They are too costly to perform.
   B. Most researchers are not interested in these studies.
   C. They are based on individual values.
   D. Data collection is problematic.

3. Determining if studying the problem will lead to results that are applicable to nursing practice is essential when analyzing the _____ of the problem.

   A. Feasibility
   B. Profitability
   C. Cost
   D. Significance

4. Which of the following topics would be inappropriate for a researchable problem?

   A. The morality of abortion as a form of birth control
   B. The relationship between cigarette smoking and weight loss
   C. The effect of severe dietary restrictions on well-being
   D. The relationship between religious beliefs and pain perception

5. Which of the following is the best example of a problem statement containing all parts of the PICOT format?

   A. Children whose parents stay with them experience less pain.
   B. Hospitalized patients who have a relative with them experience less pain than those who do not.
   C. Hospitalized children ages 3–5 years whose parents stay with them during painful procedures experience less pain than those who do not.
   D. Patients who have a relative with them during a transfusion will experience less anxiety than those who do not.

6. Which of the following best represents a well-constructed problem statement?

   A. What affects pain perception?
   B. Obesity negatively impacts self-image in first graders.
   C. This study will compare the effectiveness of antacids.
   D. Does time of day affect appetite?

7. The two essential parts of the research problem statement are the population and the
   A. Setting.
   B. Theory.
   C. Concepts.
   D. Variables.

8. The research question is "Obesity increases the risk of type 2 diabetes in teenage boys." Which of the following is/are the independent variable(s)?
   A. Teenage boys with type 2 diabetes
   B. Gender and obesity
   C. Obesity
   D. Type 2 diabetes, obesity, and gender

9. The research question is "Does massage therapy increase satisfaction during cesarean delivery?" Which of the following is/are the dependent variable(s)?
   A. Massage therapy
   B. Satisfaction
   C. Music therapy and satisfaction
   D. Satisfaction and type of delivery

10. Which statement by a fellow student best describes a confounding variable?
   A. "It can take on a wide range of values."
   B. "A variable that is restricted to whole numbers."
   C. "It describes the characteristics of the study subjects."
   D. "A variable that can't be controlled."

11. Which of the following best represents a dichotomous variable?
   A. Blood pressure
   B. Age at death
   C. Gender
   D. Weight

12. Which of the following represents a simple hypothesis?
   A. Exposure to pet therapy increases appetite in elderly patients.
   B. Family support and positive attitude decrease symptoms of dysreflexia in spinal cord injured patients.
   C. Social support, balanced diet, and regular exercise decrease the incidence of postpartum depression.
   D. Daily exercise and eliminating carbohydrates from the diet will result in a significant weight reduction in obese diabetic patients.

13. What is the difference between a null hypothesis and a directional hypothesis?

   A.   One is a declarative sentence; the other is a question.
   B.   One assumes a relationship; the other denies that one exists.
   C.   One is researchable; the other is statistical.
   D.   One includes at least two variables; the other does not.

14. Which statement best represents the relationship between a causal and an associative hypothesis?

   A.   They are the opposite of each other.
   B.   One is written in as a question, the other as a declarative sentence.
   C.   One assumes a relationship, the other denies that one exists.
   D.   They are similar to each other.

15. An operational definition of a variable is one that is:

   A.   Broad and abstract.
   B.   Narrow and abstract.
   C.   Concrete and continuous.
   D.   Narrow and concrete.

Discussion Questions

1. You work in a cardiology clinic that treats patients who have coronary artery disease and are recovering from a myocardial infarction. Many of these patients have hypertension and are overweight, and you have noticed that some of them have more difficulty following their medical regimens than others. You want to develop a research study to investigate this problem. How would you go about doing so? What would be a possible problem statement?

2. You are a BSN student enrolled in a research course. The instructor has given you the following problem statement: "Does completion of a mandatory health promotion course affect the incidence of smoking cessation among college students who smoke?" Develop four hypotheses that might be drawn from this problem statement: a null hypothesis, a directional hypothesis, a nondirectional hypothesis, and an associative hypothesis. Can all of these hypotheses be developed? If any of them cannot be developed, why not?

3. Read the following abstract and then provide the following information:
   A. Identify the population of interest.
   B. Identify the variables.
   C. Construct a research question that could have guided this study.
   D. Construct a null hypothesis.
   E. Construct a directional hypothesis.

   Abstract: Hypertension Treatment and Control Within an Independent Nurse Practitioner Setting
   Objective: To assess blood pressure (BP) control among patients with hypertension managed by nurse practitioners (NPs) versus physicians.
   Study Design: Cross-sectional study.
   Methods: Retrospective medical record reviews were conducted at 3 independent NP-based practices and at 21 physician-based practices. Investigators at each practice identified a sample of patients 18 years or older with a hypertension diagnosis. The primary outcome was controlled BP.
   Results: The propensity score-matched cohort (623 in each group) had similar baseline characteristics. Among the NP cohort, 70.5% had controlled BP compared with 63.2% among the physician cohort; the mean number of antihypertensive medications was lower among NP-treated patients. The adjusted odds of controlled BP were slightly lower for physician-treated patients.
   Conclusions: Comparable controlled BP rates were observed among patients with hypertension receiving care from an NP versus a comparison group receiving care from a physician; the groups had similar baseline characteristics. Our findings support the increasingly important role of NPs in primary care (Wright, Romboli, DiTulio, Wogen, & Belletti, 2011).

Suggested Readings

Beitz, J. (2006). Writing the researchable question. *Journal of Wound, Ostomy, & Continence Nursing, 33*(2), 122–124.

Fineout-Overholt, E., Melnyk, B., & Schultz, A. (2005). Transforming health care from the inside out: Advancing evidence-based practice in the 21st century. *Journal of Professional Nursing, 21*(6), 335–344.

Hudson-Barr, D. (2005). From research idea to research question: The who, what, where, when and why. *Journal for Specialists in Pediatric Nursing, 10*(2), 90–92.

Law, R. (2004). From research topic to research question: A challenging process. *Nurse Researcher, 11*(4), 54–66.

Library of Washington. (n.d.). *The basics in research 101* [Archived]. Retrieved from http://guides.lib.washington.edu/content.php?pid=55083&sid=2465031

References

Burns, N., & Grove, S. K. (2001). *The practice of nursing research: Conduct, critique, and utilization* (4th ed.). Philadelphia, PA: W. B. Saunders.

Burns, N., & Grove, S. K. (2007). *Understanding nursing research: Building an evidence-based practice* (4th ed.). St. Louis, MO: Saunders/Elsevier.

Burns, N., & Grove, S. K. (2009). *The practice of nursing research: Appraisal, synthesis, and generation of evidence* (6th ed.). St. Louis, MO: Saunders/Elsevier.

Burns, N., & Grove, S. K. (2011). *Understanding nursing research: Building an evidence-based practice* (5th ed.). St. Louis, MO: Saunders/Elsevier.

Craig, J. V., & Smyth, R. L. (2002). *The evidence-based practice manual for nurses.* London, UK: Churchill Livingstone.

DiCenso, A., Guyatt, G., & Ciliska, D. (2005). *Evidence-based nursing: A guide to clinical practice.* St. Louis, MO: Mosby.

Elliott, A. F., Burgio, L. D., & DeCoster, J. (2010). Enhancing caregiver health: Findings from the resources for enhancing Alzheimer's caregiver health II intervention. *Journal of the American Geriatrics Society, 58*(1), 30–37.

Fain, J. A. (2009). *Reading, understanding, and applying nursing research* (3rd ed.). Philadelphia, PA: F. A. Davis.

Farrell, M. P. (2006). Living evidence: Translating research into practice. In K. Malloch & T. Porter-O'Grady (Eds.), *Introduction to evidence-based practice in nursing and health care* (pp. 107–124). Sudbury, MA: Jones and Bartlett.

Institute of Medicine Board on Health Care Services. (2003). *Health professions education: A bridge to quality.* Washington, DC: National Academies Press. Retrieved from http://books.nap.edu/openbook.php?record_id=10681

Karlsson, V., Bergbom, I., & Forsberg, A. (2012). The lived experiences of adult intensive care patients who were conscious during mechanical ventilation: A phenomenological-hermeneutic study. *Intensive and Critical Care Nursing, 28*(1), 6–15.

Ketefian, S., & Redman, R. (2013). Nursing science in the global community. In W. K. Cody (Ed.), *Philosophical and theoretical perspectives for advanced nursing practice* (5th ed., pp. 279–289). Burlington, MA: Jones & Bartlett.

LoBiondo-Wood, G., & Haber, J. (2010). *Nursing research: Methods and critical appraisal for evidence-based practice* (7th ed.). St. Louis, MO: Mosby/Elsevier.

Macnee, C. L., & McCabe, S. (2008). *Understanding nursing research: Reading and using research in evidence-based practice* (2nd ed.). Philadelphia, PA: Lippincott Williams & Wilkins.

Malloch, K., & Porter-O'Grady, T. (2006). *Introduction to evidence-based practice in nursing and health care.* Sudbury, MA: Jones and Bartlett.

Melnyk, B. M. (2008). The worldwide epidemic of child and adolescent overweight and obesity: Calling all clinicians and researchers to intensify efforts in prevention and treatment. *Worldviews on Evidence-Based Nursing, 5*(3), 109–112.

Melnyk, B. M., & Fineout-Overholt, E. (2011). *Evidence-based practice in nursing & healthcare: A guide to best practice* (2nd ed.). Philadelphia, PA: Lippincott Williams & Wilkins.

Moorhead, S., Johnson, M., Maas, M., & Swanson, E. (2008). *Nursing outcomes classification (NOC)* (4th ed.). St. Louis, MO: Mosby.

National Institute of Nursing Research (NINR). (n.d.). *NINR mission.* Retrieved from http://www.ninr.nih.gov/AboutNINR/NINRMissionandStrategicPlan

Norwood, S. L. (2010). *Research essentials: Foundations for evidenced-based practice*. Boston, MA: Pearson.

Polit, D., & Beck, C. (2008). *Nursing research: Generating and assessing evidence for nursing practice* (8th ed.). Philadelphia, PA: Lippincott Williams & Wilkins.

Polit, D., & Beck. C. (2010). *Essentials of nursing research: Appraising evidence for nursing practice*. Philadelphia, PA: Wolters Kluwer Health/Lippincott Williams & Wilkins.

Porter-O'Grady, T. (2006). A new age for practice: Creating the framework for evidence. In K. Malloch, & T. Porter-O'Grady (Eds.), *Introduction to evidence-based practice in nursing and health care* (pp. 1–29). Sudbury, MA: Jones and Bartlett.

Reynolds, P. (1971). *A primer in theory construction*. Indianapolis, IN: Bobbs-Merrill.

Schmidt, N. A., & Brown, J. M. (2012). *Evidence-based practice for nurses: Appraisal and application of research* (2nd ed.). Sudbury, MA: Jones & Bartlett.

Stommel, M., & Wills, C. (2004). *Clinical research: Concepts and principles for advanced practice nurses*. Philadelphia, PA: Lippincott Williams & Wilkins.

West, D. S., Gorin, A. A., Subak, L. L., Foster, G., Bragg, C., Hecht, J., . . . Wing, R. R. (2011). A motivation-focused weight loss maintenance program is an effective alternative to a skill-based approach. *International Journal of Obesity 35*, 259–269.

Wing, R. R., Papandonatos, G., Fava, J. L., Gorin, A. A., Phelan, S., McCaffery, J., & Tate, D. F. (2008). Maintaining large weight losses: The role of behavioral and psychological factors. *Journal of Consulting and Clinical Psychology, 76*(6), 1015–1021.

Wright, W. L., Romboli, J. E., DiTulio, M. A., Wogen, J., & Belletti, D. A. (2011). Hypertension treatment and control within an independent nurse practitioner setting. *American Journal of Managed Care, 17*(1), 58–65.

Chapter 6

Literature Review: Searching and Writing the Evidence

Carol Boswell and Dorothy Greene Jackson

Chapter Objectives

At the conclusion of this chapter, the learner will be able to

1. Define the concept of literature review
2. Discuss the purpose of a research/evidence-based practice literature review
3. Differentiate research articles from nonresearch articles
4. Recognize the importance of collaboration with a library specialist
5. Identify steps for conducting a literature review using electronic retrieval methods
6. Identify guidelines for evaluating research articles
7. Identify steps for writing a literature review
8. Relate the literature review to evidence-based nursing practice

Key Terms

➤ Annotated bibliography

➤ CINAHL

➤ Database

➤ Discursive prose

➤ Literature review

➤ Medical Subject Headings (MeSH)

➤ MEDLINE

➤ Reference librarian

➤ Research article

➤ Search engine

Introduction

This chapter provides practical guidelines for conducting and writing a literature review for an evidence-based proposal in nursing. Guidelines and tips are given for selecting appropriate databases for electronic retrieval of research review articles. Steps are given for the process of writing and organizing data based on evidence and issues in nursing practice. Why is this idea of literature review so very important in the current climate of health care? According to Duncan and Holtslander (2012), skills associated with information acquisition are of paramount importance. Yet students and practicing nurses declare insecurity and uncertainty in the process of conducting library searches for appropriate materials. When the latest computer literate generations, the so-called "Generation X" and "Millennials," voice these concerns, more attention must be directed to facilitating the process, if evidence-based practice is to be the standard.

Definition and Purpose of the Literature Review

The **literature review** is a written, analytic summary of research findings on a topic of interest. It is a comprehensive compilation of what is known about the phenomenon. The review is guided by the researcher's curiosity about a particular subject and gaps in the knowledge about the subject area. The purpose for developing and presenting a review of the literature emerges from a desire to document the knowledge and ideas currently established concerning the identified topic. The ensuing document conveys the strengths and weaknesses ascertained from the review of the pertinent literature (Taylor, 2012). Each literature review must be characterized by designated concepts and ideas such as the PICOT and/or research objective/purpose.

The literature review is intended to assess the evidence regarding the research topic by identifying and synthesizing studies that examine the subject of interest. Taylor (2012) states that a literature review must not be merely a descriptive inventory of the available information, nor is it to be a collection of synopses. The main purpose of the literature review is to identify what is known and unknown about an area that has not been totally resolved in practice. A second purpose is to determine how an issue can be resolved and managed based on research evidence. The literature review provides the background and the context within which the research is conducted. It lays out the foundation of the study. Specifically, a good review of the literature does the following:

- Identifies a research problem and indicates how it can be studied
- Helps clarify and determine the importance of a research problem
- Identifies what is known about a problem and identifies gaps (what is unknown) in a particular area of knowledge
- Provides examples based on documented studies for resolving a nursing issue
- Provides evidence that a problem is of importance
- Identifies theoretical frameworks and conceptual models for organizing and conducting research studies
- Identifies experts in the field of interest
- Identifies research designs and methodologies for conducting like studies
- Provides a context for interpretation, comparison, and critique of study findings (Norwood, 2000; Polit & Beck, 2008)

Taylor (2012) sets out four aspects which need to be identifiable within a literature review. The first is the expectation that the literature review is directed toward an identified topic of interest. The author of a literature review must not ramble in the hope of eventually addressing the needed information concerning a topic of interest. Thought and attention to the flow and appropriateness of each entry into the review is based upon a directed process. Second, the review needs to provide both what is known and what continues to be unknown about the topic. The final document should balance these two aspects to provide a complete picture of the current state of the topic under consideration. As a third aspect, controversial perceptions within the literature need to be delineated for consideration. A literature review which does not provide all sides to the question does not effectively consider the entire topic. All subjects have at least two sides to the arguments involved in the process. Finally, the summarization of the complete literature foundation on the topic should facilitate the development of any further needed research or EBP projects. Literature reviews can be provided in either a **discursive prose** format or as an **annotated bibliography**. When provided as discursive prose, the material is provided in sections organized by themes or identified trends, not as a summary of the different research projects identified. The annotative bibliography begins with a succinct discussion of each research report, and also includes the themes and concepts embedded within a crucial assessment of the information provided.

The Literature Review Within the Evidence-Based Practice and/or Research Process

Within an evidence-based practice process, the literature review serves to identify the evidence that is currently available related to the challenge identified. For this process, the PICOT question is determined which drives the literature search. From the evidence which can be located on the topic, a decision concerning the next steps within the process—either research or quality improvement—can be determined. From the literature review which provides the gaps, limitations, or foundation of knowledge on a topic, a person can identify what more is needed within the scientific investigation of the phenomena. Enough evidence may be available to restrict the need for further research. On the other hand, the evidence may be directed into a narrow scope which then demonstrates the need for a broader look at the topic through a directed research process.

The literature review usually happens early during the research process. In qualitative research, however, this step may come at the end of the study. Initially, the researcher has a hunch or curiosity about something observed in practice. Soon this idea is translated into a research problem or research question. Shortly thereafter, the review of the literature is conducted to see what has happened in other situations where the problem has occurred.

In terms of its placement in a research article, the review of the literature usually follows the statement of the research problem or the research question. The reason the review comes early in the research process is because it sets the stage (lays the foundation) for the rest of the study. As mentioned earlier, the review of the literature provides the theoretical framework for how the current study will be structured, helps to frame the research question into a research hypothesis, and identifies what will be studied and measured in the study.

For example, suppose there is a unit in a local 340-bed hospital in which no nurse has resigned or left the staff in 15 years. This unit exists in a setting where the nursing shortage is rampant and the attrition rate is at an all-time high. A newly hired nursing administrator becomes curious about this unit. She calls the director of the unit to visit and discuss the reason turnover is so low on this unit. From conversations with several other staff members of this unit, the administrator formulates in her mind the theory that a good manager is the most important link to the low attrition rate on the unit. Although a low attrition rate does not seem to be a problem requiring research, this idea can be translated so that some insight is gained to answer the administrator's question, "Is the staff's perception of the nurse manager associated with the attrition or retention rate on a unit?" Searching the literature for studies about managers and retention or attrition can further illuminate this research question. The literature review may then describe what has been found to be true from other similar settings by conducting a survey of nurses who have worked in the same facility or unit for at least 15 years. The new administrator could use this survey or questionnaire to conduct a small research study on her hospital's unit.

This hypothetical example illustrates the importance of the literature review and demonstrates how it fits within the rest of the research process. The process used in the study came from the review of the literature.

According to the University Library (2012), the formula for commencing a literature review requires that a problem be formulated to drive the selection of materials. Without clearly denoting the problem or challenge, the identifying of materials for inclusion into the review becomes problematic. The second aspect which is needed is the tangible acquisition of the materials relevant for the subject being investigated. Ensuring that each document included in the review addresses a component of the subject is imperative. After the materials are assembled for consideration, each document must be evaluated to ascertain the connection between it and the subject matter under investigation. As the review is being done, four facets are important to consider. Initially within the review, the author's credentials and arguments need to be carefully considered for relevance and provenance. Second, the author's viewpoints should be evaluated for bias. Another area to consider is the inclusion of contradictory data along with the supportive data. Persuasiveness is another facet that should be carefully weighed during a literature review: Are the themes identified and set forth by the author convincing? Finally, the review should ultimately contribute significantly to the understanding of the identified topic. The final piece of the formula for completing the review entails the documentation of the findings and conclusions as they pertain to the investigated topic. The dissemination of the findings and conclusions is vital for the next steps within either the evidence-based practice process or a research endeavor.

Differentiating a Research Article from a Nonresearch Article

Many good sources of very valuable information that may contribute to nursing practice exist. However, for the purposes of illuminating the value of evidence-based knowledge, this text focuses primarily on data from original research. It is often difficult to locate original research, especially when little research has been published in a particular area. If that is the case, the lack of previous studies serves as an opportunity, as it can stimulate the development of research data for that particular issue.

The importance of research derives from the fact that it has been conducted using a consistently acceptable scientific method known and respected by the research world. It is not just someone's opinion, but rather has been examined critically. **Research articles** consistently contain components that are required by a scientific decision-making process. **Table 6-1** describes components of a research article.

It is sometimes tempting to choose nonresearch information or evidence when conducting the review of literature. For example, reports from state agencies, various nursing organizations, or websites

---

Table 6-1

Components of a Research Article

- **Title:** The title describes what the study was about.
- **Abstract:** The abstract is a brief summary of the problem of interest to the researcher. It describes, in approximately 120 words, what took place in the research study and makes a brief statement about the outcome. It helps to determine relevance to the reader who is conducting a search of the literature.
- **Introduction/literature review:** This component gives the background of the research topic and explains why it is important, based on a selective review of relevant literature. It compares and contrasts other research articles and summarizes what is already known and not known about the topic.
- **Purpose of the study/hypothesis/problem statement:** The purpose explains the aim of the study. It is the hypothesis or the research question that the author wants to answer or support.
- **Methodology/procedures/research design:** This component tells what happened. It describes in detail what actions the author took to carry out the study. The method describes the procedure for how the research was conducted and how the information was analyzed or statistical testing was done. It also describes the population, including how it was selected; the setting where the research took place; the number of participants in the study; the type of study, either qualitative or quantitative; and the tools used to collect the data or the method used to attain the information in the study.
- **Major findings/results/analysis/discussion:** This component describes the outcome of the study.
- **Summary/conclusion/ideas for future studies/implications:** This component highlights major findings of the study and identifies the gaps in the study or any areas that need further research. Recommendations for policy or practice are discussed in this section.
- **Works cited/references/acknowledgments:** The reference list should be organized in a recognized literary format (such as APA) or other recognized reference formats.

may present information that is very important to a body of knowledge, yet has not been critically examined in a research study. Some nationally conducted surveys may provide very important information, but may not be considered true research because not all the people in a particular population were included or not enough people returned the surveys. Unless all of the critical components are incorporated in the research process, the information obtained in the investigation should not be considered research. All evidence does have value but each has a different level of value based upon several aspects which are addressed elsewhere. As these other forms of evidence are considered within a literature review, the level and/or strength of the evidence becomes increasingly important.

Very often individuals will state that they are "going to research" a topic; searching the literature is not considered research, but rather a mechanism for providing background information for the research project. The use of the word "research" to describe following a line of investigation does not hold the same meaning as the process of conducting a research study. Whether an individual is conducting an evidence-based practice review or a research literature review, the person will need to ultimately become very well versed on the evidence available on the topic of interest.

Conducting a Literature Review Search

The guidelines presented in this section of the chapter are targeted toward the novice researcher. It is advised that the student researcher seek the help of a professional librarian at the beginning of a research project and throughout the research process when it is necessary to access comprehensive information from appropriate sources. Most literature searches can be done by electronic retrieval. Researchers can find most of the material they need from doing their own personal searches; however, the most comprehensive searches are done with the help of professional library personnel. Many librarians are credentialed or specially trained in working with particular databases or particular aspects of data management and retrieval.

? Think Outside the Box `www`

In your current clinical setting, which types of evidence materials are used as the foundation of policies? Discuss the appropriateness and effectiveness of these types of evidence. What levels of evidence are used in the process? How much evidence is needed for a policy to be deemed as "based on evidence" at your facility?

Some of the special types of librarians include research, law, medical, government documents, and consumer health librarians. Many librarians play an integral role in research. Nurses should consider their own expertise when starting a research project or conducting research literature reviews.

The Importance of Library Specialists in Conducting a Literature Review

Finding pertinent articles that deal with the topic at hand may be a complex task and may require the expertise of a research librarian. Librarians are able to assist users at finding information in a timely manner. As a result of their education, training, and experience, they are well versed on the databases, including the way in which the information is catalogued and organized. They understand the terminology needed to retrieve the information that is most relevant to the user. Their specialized knowledge may help the user conduct a more comprehensive search from multiple sources. Librarians' search expertise makes them highly skilled at weeding out irrelevant documents that otherwise might inundate the user and cause the researcher to spend unnecessary time chasing down blind alleys. Leedy and Ormrod (2012) strongly encourage all levels of researchers and seekers of evidence to effectively use the **reference librarian**. The world of library resources is exploding with new and innovative means for accessing the evidence available for consideration. The reference librarian must become a key person who is regularly engaged in accessing the evidence to ensure that the materials compiled present the best confirmation and proof available.

Nevertheless, with the advancement of the electronic library, conducting a search is much easier for the beginning researcher than ever before. The beginning researcher must set aside time to learn the process and become comfortable with the search process. With a little help from expert information specialists (librarians) and guidance from a good mentor, the beginning researcher can conduct literature searches and write a literature review that provides evidence supporting a meaningful research proposal or project.

All levels of researchers must understand when and where to ask for help. Anyone can complete an effective literature search, the key is determining what are effective articles to include, which articles are not needed, and when should an expert such as the resource librarian be used. Developing that collaboration with strategic mentors is paramount within the process.

The Research Idea

The first step in conducting a literature review is brainstorming about an idea or an area of interest with colleagues and mentors. The nurse's practice area is probably one of the most common sources for a research idea in the nursing field. Important issues in nursing provide abundant ideas for research. For example, the nursing shortage, the cost of health care, the quality of care for uninsured persons, and new delivery methods identified in federal legislative bills are all broad areas that may generate a researchable topic. Ideas may also come from reading professional journals or from the news media. As we realize that the majority of research at this time tends to be done within teams of peers who have a common interest, ideas to help provide the foundation for the brainstorming sessions can be determined. During a brainstorming session, every idea should be put on the table for consideration. Once a thorough list of ideas is developed, further development of the selected thinking can be done by the group to clarify and cultivate the research and/or evidence-based practice idea.

In addition, articles in professional journals may end with the phrase, "additional research is needed to explore the nature of …" Here is a snapshot of one such article: "More research is needed on how organizational structures influence empowerment of leaders" (Force, 2005, p. 341). In this example from an article on the relationship of managers and nurse retention, the author sets forth an idea for further research. Often, the conclusion of an article marks the starting point for other research ideas.

The Research Question

Most nurses have a hunch or curiosity about some aspect of nursing science or patient care. It is helpful to formulate that idea into a question that, if answered, would contribute to the field of nursing. Each research or evidence-based practice project should initially answer the question of "So what?" In answering this question, the importance of the project is confirmed before time is wasted on ideas that do not have valid foundations. Formulation of a research question is covered elsewhere. For the purposes of this text, asking a simple question based on the area of interest helps the novice researcher focus on topics and key concepts for conducting the literature search. Utilizing the PICOT format which is discussed elsewhere provides crucial components beneficial for conducting a successful literature search. For example, the student researcher may be curious about how long it takes the new baccalaureate-prepared nurse graduate to feel comfortable in a management position. A possible question could be, "What is the role transition time for baccalaureate-prepared nurse graduates in management positions in a small hospital?"

Reading is another very important source of research ideas. In the article cited earlier, the author suggested that more research should be conducted to explore how organizational structure can influence nurse retention. The author implied that there is a gap in the literature about this idea or that more should be known about this idea. Because the focus of the article was nurse retention, examples of questions stemming from that need could be "What is the impact of the organizational structure on nurse retention?" and "What is the relationship between nurses' perceptions of empowerment and retention?" Of course, after undertaking further reading, the researcher may have different ideas. Thus, the research question must not be etched in stone. As additional information is acquired from the literature, the evolution of the research project occurs.

Forming an initial question is a good place to start the process of conducting the literature review search. Without the identification of the problem and the development of an initial question, the literature review could become overwhelming and convoluted. This process of stating the initial idea and problem allows for commitment to a specific focus for the preliminary work. To start the literature review, it is important to distinguish between databases and search engines.

Definition of Database

It is appropriate at this juncture to define a **database** and to indicate how it is different from a search engine. Let's start by saying that Google and Yahoo are examples of search engines and MEDLINE is a database. "A **search engine** is a collection of software programs that collect information from the Web, index it, and put it in a database so it can be searched" (Ackerman & Hartman, 2003, p. 47). The job of a search engine is to retrieve the information in a format that is accessible visually on screen at an on-site library or in downloadable, readable (full-text) written format.

Leedy and Ormrod (2012) provide selected broad tactics for conducting useful searches via search engines. To limit the search, utilize at least two key words. One method used to denote crucial words in the search utilizes the addition of the plus sign (+) before the selected word. By using this designation, the search engine concentrates the search on the designated word. A final idea for narrowing the search provided by a search engine is to place quotation marks around any phrase which is principal to the quest. Sources identified by search engines need to be carefully considered concerning the quality and accuracy of the material found within the site. Some websites are closely monitored while others are open to general access and publication of information.

In contrast, a database is an organized body of related information arranged for speed of access and retrieval (Database, n.d.). A database is a storage location, like a library, where information is stored, catalogued, maintained, and updated systematically. Many of the databases used within literature searches are available online at this time. These sources include indexes, abstracts, encyclopedias, dictionaries, and other universal reference tools. Databases allow an individual to narrow the focus for the search using strategic words, titles, author names, years, languages, and combinations of these elements.

Two main types of databases are available—bibliographic and full text. Bibliographic databases give directions on where to find the information, whereas full-text databases contain the information itself. In other words, the full-text type of database contains the article itself in a downloadable format. In recent years, more major databases have added an increased number of full-text capabilities.

Databases Useful to Nursing

The two most useful databases for nursing literature are Medical Literature Analysis and Retrieval System Online (**MEDLINE**) and the Cumulative Index to Nursing & Allied Health Literature (**CINAHL**) (**Table 6-2**). MEDLINE provides literature related to medicine, nursing, and dentistry. The focus of information in MEDLINE is biomedicine, but this database also contains the citations that are provided in CINAHL. The CINAHL database provides authoritative coverage of the literature related to nursing and allied health.

The MEDLINE database is generally considered the premier bibliographic database for providing access to the North American biomedical literature. It stores and indexes more than 11 million articles from an

Table 6-2
Databases Useful in Nursing
Medical Literature Analysis and Retrieval System Online (MEDLINE)
Cumulative Index to Nursing & Allied Health Literature (CINAHL)
Cochrane Library
Nursing & Health Sciences: A Sage Full-Text Collection
Nursing Journals (Proquest Nursing Journals)
Test and measurement databases, theses, and dissertations
PsycINFO
AID Search

excess of 4,800 catalogued titles (ProQuest, 2012). The database is probably updated more frequently than any other database of its type—daily, Monday through Friday (National Library of Medicine [NLM], n.d.). The NLM website (www.nlm.nih.gov), which contains nursing and medical citations, can be accessed free of charge from the Internet. In other words, library privileges are not required, only access to the Internet. Thus this website is an excellent place to start a literature search.

The MEDLINE database uses a controlled vocabulary. This means that information is catalogued according to specific words or subject headings as in a dictionary. Although most people start searches using fundamental words, this type of search does not yield the most comprehensive results. The dictionary for finding the words that most appropriately define or match the search term or concept in MEDLINE is the **Medical Subject Heading (MeSH)** database guide. This feature can be accessed from the NLM/PubMed website, adjacent to the left search boxes in most cases. PubMed is a service of the NLM that includes more than 16 million citations from MEDLINE and other life science journals dating back to the 1950s. PubMed includes links to full-text articles and other related resources (NLM, n.d.).

This example illustrates the difference between a key word search and a subject heading search. The key words "patient visitation" might be used to locate journal articles focusing on how nurses perceive open visitation in intensive care units. When the term "patient visitation" was used to search in MEDLINE, 15 citations were retrieved (at the time of this book's writing). When the subject or controlled vocabulary term found in the MeSH database guide (dictionary) was used ("visitors to patients"), 1,830 citations were located. Knowing how a database stores information is very important in conducting effective and relevant searches. Using dates, types of nursing units, or other strategies can narrow this search.

CINAHL is probably the most popular database used by nurses. It indexes more than 5,000 journals; 777 full-text journals and magazines; 277 full-text books and monographs; 134 full-text evidence-based care sheets; 169 full-text quick lessons; 167 full-text continuing education unit reports, and more than 360 full-text research instruments recorded from 1937 to the present (CINAHL Information Systems, n.d.). CINAHL houses nursing publications, including the *American Journal of Nursing* and the publications of the National League for Nursing. It also indexes journals in the allied health fields related to physical therapy, occupational therapy, cardiopulmonary technology, emergency service, physician assistant health education, radiology technology, medical laboratory technology, medical records, surgical technology, and medical assistants. Other selected journals related to biomedicine, consumer health, and librarianship health sciences are included as well (CINAHL Information Systems, n.d.).

CINAHL publications can be searched using EBSCOhost and Ovid and are available for use only through a library. EBSCOhost provides approximately 200 full-text and secondary databases (EBSCO Publishing, n.d.). It accesses databases in business, medical, public, and nursing publications.

Just as in MEDLINE, records in CINAHL are indexed by a controlled vocabulary or subject headings. Subject headings provide descriptors of the terms listed in the database. Searching by the terms or subjects used in the database yields results that are more relevant to the topic being searched. Subject headings can be viewed by clicking the CINAHL Headings button on the EBSCOhost toolbar. To begin the search, the subject heading term should be entered in the Find field. Searches using this tool can also be done by using key words. The EBSCOhost system matches articles with appropriate subject terms by a process called mapping.

CINAHL can also be accessed using the Journals@Ovid Full Text database. This database contains research articles, book and media reviews, and full-text nursing articles. Information in this database is searched by using key words.

A number of other databases are useful in nursing. These include the Cochrane Library, Nursing & Health Sciences: A Sage Full-Text Collection, Nursing Journals (Proquest Nursing Journals), PsycINFO, AID Search, tests and measurements databases, theses and dissertations, and free Internet databases (**Table 6-3**):

- Cochrane Library: A regularly updated collection of evidence-based medicine databases. These databases include systematic reviews of subjects, including economics, health interventions, controlled trials, and methodologies.
- Nursing & Health Sciences: A Sage Full-Text Collection: Includes full text of 24 journals published by Sage.
- Nursing Journals (Proquest Nursing Journals): Full-text journals.
- PsycINFO: Includes journals from the social sciences.
- AID Search: Includes journals and reports dealing with AIDS treatment and research.
- Tests and measurements databases.
- Mental Measurements Yearbook.
- Health and Psychosocial Instruments.

? **Think Outside the Box**

Which databases have you used in your literature searches? Discuss the pros and cons of those databases you are familiar with using.

Table 6-3
Full-Text Databases Useful in Nursing
• Academic Search Premier (http://www.epnet.com): Designed for academic institutions; contains full-text scholarly publications; source—EBSCOhost research database.
• AIDSinfo (http://www.aidsinfo.nih.gov): Federally approved HIV/AIDS research information for patients and healthcare providers.
• CINAHL Plus with Full Text.
• www.epnet.com/thisTopic.php?topicID=172&marketID=1.
• Cumulative Index to Nursing and Allied Health (CINAHL).
• The Cochrane Collaboration (http://www.cochrane.org): Evidence-based medicine systematic reviews.
• Health and Psychosocial Instruments (HAPI): Evaluation and measurement instruments in health; available through Ovid Technologies.
• Health and Wellness Resource Center (http://www.gale.com/HealthRC): Informational sources, magazines, videos, journals, and newspapers on health and disease.
• Health Reference Center Academic (http://www.gale.com/customer_service/sample_searches/hrca.htm): Articles on fitness, pregnancy, medicine, nutrition, diseases, public health, occupational health and safety, alcohol and drug abuse, HMOs, prescription drugs, and more. The material contained in this database is intended for informational purposes only.
• Journals@OVIDFullText (http://www.ovid.com/site/about/terms.jsp?top=42): The second generation of *Ovid Full Text*, which combines all the capabilities of *Ovid Full Text Collections* with several important features and functions.
• MEDLINE with MeSH (http://www.ncbi.nlm.nih.gov/entrez/query.fcgi?DB=pubmed): Medical Literature Analysis and Retrieval System Online (MEDLINE) is the U.S. National Library of Medicine's (NLM) premier bibliographic database that contains more than 16 million references to journal articles in life sciences, with a concentration on biomedicine.
• Health Sciences: A Sage Full-Text Collection (http://csa.tsinghua.edu.cn/factsheets/sagenurs-set-c.php): A searchable database of bibliographic records and full-text journal articles.
• Proquest Nursing Journals (http://www.proquest.com/products_pq/descriptions/pq_nursing_journals.shtml): Designed to meet the needs of students and researchers at academic institutions; includes information on obstetrics, nursing, geriatrics care, oncology, and more.

Basics of Searching

Any review of published articles about a topic is only as good as what has been searched. In other words, "the first requirement for writing a good literature review . . . is to do a good literature search" (Kellsey, 2005, p. 526). An effective place to start is to identify concepts from the research question that can be the focus of the search. For the research question mentioned earlier ("What is the relationship between nurses' perception of empowerment and retention?"), concepts include empowerment and nurse retention. These words can be used as the search terms.

Successful searching takes some planning and thought. According to Duncan and Holtslander (2012), individuals encounter the highest amount of frustration as a result of unsuccessful queries which then result in the need for requerying. Using the incorrect and incomplete terms within the query can result in large, unmanageable search results to work through to get to the key articles. Because search engines locate an enormous number of documents, the results can sometimes be overwhelming. A clear search strategy is necessary to narrow the results to relevant, usable information. In developing an effective search strategy, it is important to identify the main concepts from the research question or topic and determine any synonyms for these terms. For the sample research question, "What is the relationship of nurses' perceptions of empowerment and retention?" the concepts are "nurses," "empowerment," and "retention." Other alternate words include "power" and "authority" (for "empowerment") and "retaining" (for "retention"). Duncan and Holtslander (2012) provide several strategies for narrowing the search words. Those strategies include "verifying concepts in the course textbook, using thesauri, noting the key words or subject headings identified from located papers, consulting specialized nursing or other pertinent dictionaries, and checking Wikipedia or Google Scholar" (p. 26). These tactics along with the use of selected terms from cited references, retrieved papers, and sources such as Web of Science databases can aid an individual in locating the articles and evidence that is needed to support a change in practice or validate a current practice.

The following steps outline the basics of conducting a search from electronic sources. The researcher should consider the use of MEDLINE while following these steps.

1. Select a topic of interest and identify the concepts or search terms. Think in terms of controlled vocabularies or subject headings for databases when selecting the topic. Subject headings yield more precise results than key words.
2. Access the NLM/PubMed website using the Internet browser.
3. Locate the MeSH database guide to the left of the main PubMed page.
4. Type the search term in the MeSH search box.
5. Select the subject heading from MeSH that matches the search term and place it in the PubMed search box. It will be necessary to switch back from the MeSH database guide to the main PubMed page. This can be done by selecting PubMed from the toolbar drop-down menu.
6. Choose limit options as appropriate by date, author, and title.
7. To combine search strategies, use "and" or "or" in the search box. "And" is more restrictive (reduces the number of citations), and "or" is less restrictive.

Other Key Information

When searching for basic information, textbooks can sometimes be helpful and acceptable. A textbook often provides a foundation, a framework, or a gold standard by which other sources are measured.

For example, when studying about health disparities, the book that contains the premier report is *Unequal Treatment: Confronting Racial and Ethnic Disparities in Health Care* (Smedley, Stith, & Nelson, 2003). It provides data sources, initial research findings, and suggested models that attempt to explain some of the issues surrounding this problem. From reading this book, it is possible to identify the gaps in the literature and the authors of major articles describing the research in this area. Leedy and Ormrod (2012) recommend a very pertinent idea: try to access primary sources of material. Anytime material is extracted from one source to insert into another source, bias can be introduced. Even when care is given to ensuring accuracy, the interpretation of material reflects a unique view of the material which may be contradictory to the original interpretation. Seeking the primary discussion of the material is imperative for getting the accurate picture which was originally gleaned from the analysis of the information presented. This type of information can also be used as background for the research proposal. If the requirements for the proposal include the use of recent information (not more than five years old), for example, then research journal articles should be used.

Another point to keep in mind is that the more precise the search, the fewer the number of resources that will be retrieved. The more general the search, the larger the number of articles that will be retrieved. After conducting the initial search, the researcher should review the abstracts of the articles and determine if more or less information is needed. The search should then be modified based on how the materials match the research question.

Evaluating the Literature

Evaluation of what has been published is an important and sometimes complex process. Many sources refer to this process as "critiquing the literature." The term "evaluation" is used here because it is more representative of what takes place and does not seem as overwhelming. Beginning researchers may find this an intimidating process, because they have far less experience than the authors of the original works. This concern may not always be the case, of course. Many times, the reader has more clinical knowledge than some of the people writing the articles. It is necessary to build on the analytical skills that most nurses have and to draw from the practice experience. The good thing about nursing is that there is enough variety and specialization in practice and academia for every nurse to have something of value to offer. Thus, it is important that beginning researchers believe they have the skills necessary to raise questions about what is published. Accessing and studying the material available on a topic is very important.

The other side of that coin is also knowing when to stop accessing and studying to begin the next phases. Repetition is the significant term to remember in regard to when to stop. When the material read and analyzed begins to demonstrate a repetitive pattern of material, accessing additional resources can be stopped. At a later time, a further search may need to be done to confirm that no new information has been published since the initial cyclic pattern was found.

A good place to locate information for evaluation of the literature is in the discussion section of an article, where the authors talk about the limitations of the study. Other tools to evaluate articles may be provided in the classroom setting from nursing faculty.

The evaluation process consists of a review of the components of the study and a comparison of the study with other studies related to the same research topic. The driving force behind the evaluation is the need to determine whether the study supports the research question identified and whether it identifies gaps in the literature that support the gap the beginning researcher or student has in mind.

It is generally accepted that the components of the study that should be reviewed include (1) the purpose of the study, (2) the sample size and selection, (3) the design of the study (methods used), (4) the data collection procedures, (5) the analysis of the data, and (6) the author's conclusion. The theoretical framework is also an important section to review, although it is sometimes not included due to space restrictions imposed by the publisher. However, it remains an important part of the study, as it provides structure for conducting the study and explaining the results. Conceptual framework is not addressed in this text.

A discussion of the areas selected for evaluation follows. These areas correspond to the headings in the "Gaps in the Literature" table (**Table 6-4**).

Article

When choosing articles from the literature, the researcher should be aware of the authors' credentials. It is important to identify where they work and how to contact them if you have questions about what they have written. Oftentimes, their email addresses are available. Many authors are helpful and willing to give ideas to beginning researchers on request. The article usually provides some brief background about the authors that informs the reader about their credibility in writing about the research topic. It is important to document the citation of the article and contact information of the author. It may seem painstaking at the time, but it is time well spent to document all the information about how to locate the article, such as the author, date of publication, title of article, title of the work containing the article, volume, and page numbers of the article.

Table 6-4

Gaps in the Literature

Article (Title, author, journal, publication date, contact information for author)	Purpose (Why study was conducted)	Sample (Number of participants, demographics, other characteristics, geographic location)	Methods (Design, instruments or questionnaires, data collection, data analysis)	Major Findings (Results, statistical significance, conclusions)	Limitations (Factors that may complicate the interpretation of the findings)	Gaps (Suggestions for further study that support the research question)

Purpose

The purpose of the study explains why the study is being done. It is distinct from the problem, in that the problem addresses what the study is about (Nieswiadomy, 2012). This is an appropriate section for the researcher to determine what he or she wants to do with the findings of the study. For example, if the problem of the study is obesity in third-grade students in public schools, the purpose could be to determine if the environment of the school and the age of the children may contribute to food consumption choices. The findings could then be used to make changes in the school or to enhance healthy behaviors in the children while they are at school.

The purpose of the study is usually located in the first few paragraphs of the study. Identifying the purpose may help later in grouping similar types of studies and also in organizing the writing of the literature review.

Sample/Population

The sample is a representation of the entire population of interest. All persons in the world cannot be studied, so a representative sample is selected that may have characteristics similar to the general population being studied. For example, caregivers may be the population of interest. Because it is impossible to study all the caregivers in the world, a sample with similar experiences could be chosen. To choose a manageable sample size, the sample may be narrowed to those caregivers who care for their spouses and live in a particular county of Texas.

? Think Outside the Box

> Select a topic. Discuss the specific steps you would use to conduct a literature review on that topic. Which words would you use to do the search, and why? Which databases would you use, and why?

The sample/population section of the study describes the study participants. The author describes demographic characteristics (e.g., age, gender, race, ethnicity, educational level, geographic location, income level) of the persons who will be in the study. The description of the sample and how it was selected helps the researcher make statements about the generalizability of the study—that is, whether similar findings would be obtained in other locations under the same or similar conditions. How the sample was selected may affect the study findings. If the participants were randomly selected using random tables or computer software, the findings are more likely to be generalizable to other similar subjects. In contrast, if the sample was selected based on who showed up at the announcement of the study (known as a convenience sample), it is less likely that the findings could be generalized to other groups.

This section can be documented by providing just a few statements, such as "persons 65 years of age and older caring for their 65-and-older spouses with Alzheimer's disease in their home in rural west Texas."

Methods

The methods section of the study describes the strategy for how the study is conducted. In quantitative research, the methods section includes (1) the inclusion criteria, explaining how the participants were selected; (2) the exclusion criteria, explaining why subjects were not selected; (3) the sample size and whether it was adequate; (4) the design; (5) the instruments or surveys used; (6) data collection procedures; and (7) data analysis (Portney & Watkins, 2008).

The design describes whether the investigation was a descriptive, correlational, exploratory, or experimental study. (Research study designs are covered elsewhere in this text.) The main points of interest for the reader in the methods section should be whether the methods used to collect the data were controlled for any outside conditions that could confuse the findings of the study and whether the methods affected the accuracy of the findings. For example, if the study focuses on the relationship of weight to blood pressure, the researcher must have ensured that the weight scales and blood pressure machines were calibrated and functioning properly. The procedure for how this was done should also be described in the study. If the condition of the measuring instruments is not standardized, it will be impossible to know whether the findings were accurate. Thus the methods section of the article should include a description of the conditions under which the weights and blood pressures were measured and the person taking the measurements. If surveys or questionnaires were used, the researcher should discuss how the reliability and validity of these instruments were determined when used with other subjects.

Put simply, the design identifies the number of subjects, the number of groups, the type of intervention, and the conditions under which the intervention was performed (Portney & Watkins, 2008). This section of the study helps the reader interpret the degree of accuracy or validity of the findings.

The analysis of the data describes the statistical tests that were used to test the research hypothesis. For example, if the study sought to determine the relationship between two variables, a correlational test would be done. If the study sought to determine the difference between two variables, the test would be a t-test. The reader should make note of the type of testing and compare it with the testing done in other studies; he or she should also determine if the appropriate test was done to match the research hypothesis.

Major Findings

The findings (or results) may overlap with the discussion section of the study, but it is most appropriate for the results to stand alone. The results section should be reported without the researcher's interpretation (Portney & Watkins, 2008). This is a factual section that may be explained with tables and charts. It is important for the reader to determine whether the results match the purpose of the study and the research question. In addition, the reader should make note of any statistically significant results and the tests that were used.

Limitations

The limitations of the study describe the elements that may have complicated the results. For example, suppose a study was done to measure improvement in test scores after an instructive video on electrical safety on small appliances in the workplace was presented to the study participants. A pre-test was given before the video was shown, and a post-test was given one week after the video presentation. If the scores were low on the post-test, a limitation could be that there was too much of a time lapse between the test, the instruction, and the post-test. Discussing this limitation of the study may suggest ways to improve the study if it is later replicated. Limitations may also help to identify gaps in the literature that could be considered in other studies.

Gaps in the Literature

This section is of greatest importance for the review of the literature; however, it cannot be given due diligence unless all the other parts of the research study are examined first. The discussion and conclusion section of the article is generally where most of the suggestions for future research are presented. Suggestions for future research usually represent gaps in knowledge about the research topic. Perhaps a particular group suffers a worse outcome than other populations, relative to a particular disease condition. The gap in the literature might then be that no studies have examined the nature of this problem.

The discussion and conclusion section is where authors most often compare their findings with other studies, offer alternative explanations, or offer support for existing practice (Portney & Watkins, 2008). This section is a reflection of the authors' interpretation and experience, biases, and interests relevant to the findings of the study at hand. The authors discuss unanswered questions and point out gaps in the knowledge on the research topic.

The reader should examine this section very carefully for missing pieces of knowledge and for what is unknown about the research area, looking for information that justifies the research being proposed. This information could be gaps related to unanswered questions regarding gender, age, ethnicity, characteristics of healthcare facilities, geographic locations, differences in disease outcomes, or any combination of variables that have not been examined. These would represent gaps in the literature.

Writing the Literature Review

The literature review is not a list of article summaries, but rather a well-written synthesis of information about a topic that includes a discussion on the research that has been done and the evidence gathered, the methodologies, the strengths and weaknesses of findings, and gaps that require more knowledge. The approach to writing the review should be to convince the reader that the information supports the need for the proposed study. The format for writing the review may vary depending on the purpose of the review. If the review is conducted for a class assignment, the student should follow the grading criteria. If the review is part of a grant proposal, it is usually succinct and points out various themes, conceptual models, theories that explain the research question, and gaps in the literature that support the need for the grant.

Unfortunately, it is all too easy to get bogged down while actually writing the review. The researcher usually reads numerous articles before settling on those used in the literature review. One manageable tool of organization is an outline. Others have recommended the use of grids or matrices for organizing the review of the articles, or index cards for categorizing the materials read (McCabe, 2005; Polit & Beck, 2008). One way of developing headings for an outline is to mark notes on the articles or to use the variables identified for the study. After reading the articles chosen for the review, it is helpful to go back and write in the margins adjacent to pertinent information in the text or to list on the first page of the article the reasons why the article was chosen (e.g., good questionnaire, clearly written design, independent and dependent variables listed and defined, similarities to another study).

? **Think Outside the Box**   www

Select a research article. Examine which aspects from the article must be documented within the summary provided for a literature review.

Answering Key Questions

A good written review should answer some basic questions. Listed here are questions developed from the information found in most published research studies. These questions are based on experiences of the author from a confluence of reading, conducting, and critiquing research reviews and information learned from graduate courses in nursing and library science.

- What was the main focus of the articles (research question, purpose, objectives)?
- Did the articles represent recent (less than five years old) as well as classic studies?
- What were the designs of most of the studies (research questions, methodology, sample size, population characteristics, and pertinent conclusion)?
- Which studies did not positively support the research question?
- What were the target populations of most of the studies (e.g., nurses in emergency departments, medical–surgical units, operating rooms)?
- Which models or conceptual frameworks were used to explain the structure of the studies?
- What were the general findings and limitations in most of the studies?
- Which articles were the most similar in findings, design, or other features?
- Which gaps were identified in the articles?
- What was the overall conclusion for the literature review that supports the research question and need for your proposal?

An Outline for Writing the Review

Discussion of the preceding questions should be helpful in providing organization to the review. The following outline provides further guidance for developing headings and completing the written review. The components of the outline include (1) the purpose, (2) a description of the search strategy, (3) the themes or categories of similar types of articles, (4) limitations, (5) gaps in what is known about a research area, and (6) a discussion and conclusion. A more detailed description of an outline for organizing the writing of the review appears in **Table 6-5**.

Other Writing Tips

When writing a literature review for a class, it is important to follow the grading criteria and the objectives of the course. The length of the

Table 6-5

Outline for a Literature Review

I. Purpose of the review
II. Description of how search was conducted
  A. Databases used
  B. Key words and subject headings
  C. Rationale or criteria for articles chosen in the review
    1. Articles five years old or less
    2. Classic articles or books
III. Themes of articles
  A. Similarities in articles that support the research question
    1. Purposes, designs, target populations, tools of measurement (e.g., questionnaires, methodologies)
    2. General findings
  B. Conceptual framework, models, or theories that explain the research described in the articles
  C. Inconsistencies in articles
    1. Articles that do not provide positive support for the research question identified
IV. Limitations
  A. Components identified by the authors of the articles that were limitations in the studies
V. Gaps in the articles
  A. Gaps identified by the authors of the articles
VI. Discussion and conclusion
  A. Summary statement of how articles support the proposal
  B. Identification of gaps perceived and how the proposal will meet the needs of some aspect of nursing practice

review, in terms of the number of pages, depends on the criteria and purpose of the review. The student should follow the headings and subheadings of the writing style required by the course (e.g., American Psychological Association [APA] or other sources). Paraphrase the crucial points of the articles and avoid using too many direct quotes. Also, be aware that lengthy writing does not necessarily mean comprehensive writing. Being able to synthesize what is called for in the writing and to give the reader what was promised in the purpose of the writing is what is most important.

Linking the Literature Review to Evidence-Based Nursing Practice

Evidence-based practice is an important issue in nursing today. Nurses need to know why they do what they do. Although many support the idea of intuition, the profession must provide logical explanations for the actions of nursing based on scientific findings. The literature review provides the foundation for good research. To make sound decisions, today's nurses must be well-read. The research presented in the literature review may provide nurses with the background they need to make informed choices in practice. The ability to critically analyze scientific literature is a skill every nurse should develop, and a skill that is central to deciding whether to incorporate new information into practice based on the strength of the evidence.

? **Think Outside the Box**

Discuss how you would determine the credibility of information found on the Internet.

Summary Points

1. The literature review is the foundation of the research proposal.
2. A good literature review begins with a good literature search that is assisted by a professional librarian.
3. The assistance of an expert librarian may both enhance the relevance of material found and reduce the amount of time spent conducting the search.
4. A database search using subject headings yields more precise information than a key word search.
5. The literature review identifies what is known and unknown about the research topic.
6. The review should focus on original research studies dealing with the selected topic.
7. The literature review identifies gaps in the literature.
8. The gaps in the literature should support the research question.

RED FLAGS

- Literature summaries should provide enough information about the different sources related to sample size, methodology, and results to allow for a clear understanding of the application of that information to the current project.
- Within the literature review, the sources used should be predominantly primary sources, not secondary sources.
- The current expectation is for references to be within the five-year limit unless the article is a classical/benchmark study.
- When Internet sources are used, the credibility of the information must be reflected in the literature review.
- Gaps in the literature review should be identified.

Multiple Choice Questions

1. A literature review is
   A. Everything that is known about a subject.
   B. An analytical summary of research findings.
   C. All approved data on a research topic.
   D. A compilation of all positive results of research.

2. The purpose of the literature review is to
   A. Identify a problem that has not been resolved.
   B. Clarify the importance of a research problem.
   C. Identify gaps in the literature.
   D. All of the above.

3. The literature review should occur
   A. Near the end of the research process.
   B. Shortly before the analysis of the problem.
   C. Early in the research process.
   D. None of the above.

4. When conducting a literature review, it is advisable to
   A. Seek most information from the Internet.
   B. Gather all data from books.
   C. Gather all data from journals.
   D. Seek assistance from a librarian.

5. Evidence-based nursing literature provides the nurse with the ability to
   A. Choose only those practice activities based on evidence.
   B. Describe and analyze published research results.
   C. Use textbook information.
   D. Problem-solve all nursing issues.

6. A database differs from a search engine in the following manner:
   A. A database stores the information.
   B. A search engine takes you to the information.
   C. Databases are specialized by area of knowledge.
   D. All of the above.

7. The database that is considered the premier bibliographic database for providing access in the North Americas for biomedical literature is
   A. Google.
   B. MEDLINE.
   C. CINAHL.
   D. Yahoo!

8. It is appropriate to use key word searches in which of the following contexts?

   A. Evidence-based medicine
   B. Ovid
   C. MEDLINE
   D. Evidence-based nursing

9. The purpose section of a research study usually

   A. Tells the geographic location of the study.
   B. Tells why the study was done.
   C. Is the methodology of the study.
   D. Tells what the study is about.

10. The gaps in the literature are

    A. Missing pieces in the knowledge of the research area.
    B. Questions about the research that have not been explained.
    C. Suggestions for future research made by the author.
    D. All of the above.

11. The main difference between a research article and a nonresearch article is

    A. A research article reports statistics on surveys and a nonresearch article does not.
    B. A research article describes research by the original author.
    C. A nonresearch article describes the methods of how the study was conducted.
    D. A nonresearch article conducts analysis and statistical testing on the data presented in the article.

Discussion Questions

1. You are interested in seeing what has been written about using dietary supplements to treat bone loss in postmenopausal women. You have been told that appropriate MeSH headings include "dietary supplements" and "osteoporosis, postmenopausal," but you want to use the MeSH database to verify these terms. You also know that you want only English-language articles, so you limit your search by using the Limits function and setting Language to English. Execute your search and examine the results. (This exercise was provided by Dr. Jeffrey Huber, personal communication, Texas Woman's University, 2003.)

2. To gain a greater understanding of evidence-based nursing, conduct a search to retrieve references to the published literature about aspirin use for prevention of myocardial infarction. Choose the full-text Nursing Collection produced by Ovid. Develop a search strategy for this topic. Review your results.

Suggested Readings

Ahern, N. R. (2005). Using the Internet to conduct research. *Nurse Researcher 13*(2), 55–70.

American University Library. (n.d.). *Questions to ask yourself about materials you are including.* Retrieved from http://www.library.american.edu/Help/tutorials/lit_review/materials.html

University of California, Berkeley Library. (n.d.). *Finding historical primary sources.* Retrieved from http://www.lib.berkeley.edu/instruct/guides/primarysources.html

University Libraries, University of Maryland. (n.d.). *Primary, secondary and tertiary sources.* Retrieved from http://www.lib.umd.edu/guides/primary-sources.html

The Writing Center. (n.d.). *Literature reviews.* University of North Carolina at Chapel Hill. Retrieved from http://writingcenter.unc.edu/resources/handouts-demos/specific-writing-assignments/literature-reviews

Yale University Library. (2006). *Primary sources at Yale.* Retrieved from http://www.library.yale.edu/instruction/primsource.html

References

Ackerman, E., & Hartman, K. (2003). *Searching and researching on the Internet and the World Wide Web* (3rd ed.). Wilsonville, OR: Franklin, Beedle & Associates.

CINAHL Information Systems. (n.d.). *The CINAHL database.* Birmingham, AL: EBSCO Industries. Retrieved from http://www.ebscohost.com/academic/cinahl-plus-with-full-text

Database. (n.d.). *American heritage dictionary of the English language* (4th ed.). Boston, MA: Houghton Mifflin. Retrieved from http://education.yahoo.com/reference/dictionary/entry/database

Duncan, V., & Holtslander, L. (2012). Utilizing grounded theory to explore the information-seeking behavior of senior nursing students. *Journal of the Medical Library Association, 100*(1), 20–27.

EBSCO Publishing. (n.d.). *EBSCOhost.* Birmingham, AL: EBSCO Industries. Retrieved from http://www.ebscohost.com/biomedical-libraries

Force, M. (2005). The relationship between effective nurse managers and nursing retention. *Journal of Nursing Administration, 35*(7–8), 336–341.

Kellsey, C. (2005). Writing the literature review: Tips for academic librarians. *College Research Library News, 66*(7), 526–527.

Leedy, P. D., & Ormrod, J. E. (2012). *Practical research: Planning and design* (10th ed.). Boston, MA: Pearson.

McCabe, T. F. (2005). How to conduct an effective literature search. *Nursing Standard, 20*(11), 41–47.

National Library of Medicine (NLM). (n.d.). *PubMed.* Bethesda, MD: Author. Retrieved from http://www.ncbi.nlm.nih.gov/sites/entrez

Nieswiadomy, R. M. (2012). *Foundations of nursing research* (6th ed.). Boston, MA: Pearson.

Norwood, S. L. (2000). *Research strategies for advanced practice nurses.* Upper Saddle River, NJ: Prentice Hall Health.

Polit, D. F., & Beck, C. T. (2008). *Creating and assessing evidence for nursing practice* (8th ed.). Philadelphia, PA: Lippincott Williams & Wilkins.

Portney, L. G., & Watkins, M. P. (2008). *Foundations of clinical research: Applications to practice* (3rd ed.). Upper Saddle River, NJ: Prentice Hall Health.

ProQuest. (2012). *Medline/Medline full text: Key facts.* Retrieved from http://www.proquest.com/en-US/catalogs/databases/detail/medline ft.shtml

Smedley, B. D., Stith, A. Y., & Nelson, A. R. (2003). *Unequal treatment: Confronting racial and ethnic disparities in health care.* Washington, DC: National Academies Press.

Taylor, D. (2012). *The literature review: A few tips on conducting it.* Retrieved from http://www.writing.utoronto.ca/advice/specific-types-of-writing/literature-review

University Library. (2012). *Write a literature review.* Retrieved from http://library.ucsc.edu/help/howto/write-a-literature-review

Chapter **7**

Sampling

Kathaleen C. Bloom and Lucy B. Trice

Chapter Objectives

At the conclusion of this chapter, the learner will be able to

1. Discuss basic concepts related to sampling
2. Contrast inclusion and exclusion criteria in the sampling process
3. Distinguish between probability and nonprobability samples
4. Identify types of sampling strategies used for qualitative and quantitative research
5. Discuss approaches to determining sample size
6. Critically evaluate sampling plans found in research reports for their contribution to the strength of evidence for nursing practice

Key Terms

➤ Accessible population

➤ Cluster sampling

➤ Convenience sampling

➤ Exclusion criteria

➤ External validity

➤ Inclusion criteria

➤ Internal validity

➤ Nonprobability sampling

➤ Population

➤ Probability sampling

➤ Purposive sampling

➤ Quota sampling

➤ Random sampling

➤ Representative sample

➤ Sample

➤ Sampling error

➤ Simple random sampling

➤ Snowball sampling

➤ Stratified random sampling

➤ Systematic random sampling

➤ Target population

➤ Theoretical sampling

Introduction

Keeping in mind that evidence-based practice (EBP) is about integrating the strongest research evidence with clinical expertise and patient needs (Malloch & Porter-O'Grady, 2010; Melnyk & Fineout-Overholt, 2011), it is time to examine the research design decisions made in terms of sampling. Regardless of the topic of the research, every investigator must make decisions about which subjects will provide data to answer the research question. This is done through the development of a sampling plan—a process that involves making choices about who or what to include in the sample, how to select the sample, and how many subjects to include in the sample for a particular study. The choices made in developing the sampling plan are critical in designing high-quality clinical studies to build evidence-based nursing practice. Careful appraisal of the sampling plan in a published research study is critical to determining both the quality of the evidence and the applicability of the findings to nursing practice.

A **population** is the entire set of elements that meet specified criteria. An element may be a person, a family, a community, a medical record, an event, a laboratory specimen, or even a laboratory animal. Often called the **target population**, this set encompasses every element in the world that met the sampling criteria, such as all pregnant adolescents, preterm infants, persons with diabetes, or children who are chronically ill. The **accessible population**, by comparison, is that portion of the target population that the investigator can reasonably reach. It might include pregnant adolescents enrolled in an alternative high school in the southeastern United States, persons with diabetes who are enrolled in diabetic education at a local hospital, or children with a chronic illness who are enrolled in a summer camp. The sample, drawn through a specified sampling strategy from the accessible population,

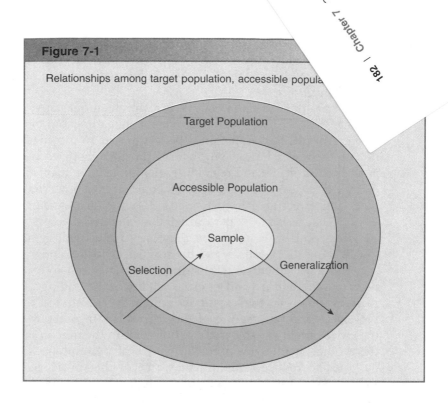

Figure 7-1

Relationships among target population, accessible popula...

Target Population

Accessible Population

Sample

Selection

Generalization

consists of those elements from whom or about whom data are actually collected (**Figure 7-1**).

Why Sample?

Researchers use **samples** rather than populations for reasons of efficiency and cost-effectiveness. It would be almost impossible, and generally impractical, to conduct a study on the entire population, even though this is the population to which the investigator would like to be able to generalize the conclusions. Sampling strategies, therefore, have been designed to select a subset of the population to represent the entire population.

The overarching concern in evaluating a sample in quantitative research is how well the sample represents the target population. A **representative sample** is one that looks like the target population in terms of important characteristics. Decisions with respect to sampling strategies are made in an effort to reduce sampling error. **Sampling error** is the difference between data obtained from the sample and data that would be obtained if the entire population were included in the study. Thus, to the extent that the sample from which data was collected possesses important characteristics of the accessible and target populations, the findings can be used to develop EBP with these populations.

The major concern in evaluating a sample in qualitative research is how well the sample represents the phenomenon of interest. In other words, the sample must be appropriate to provide information on the research problem. The data provided by the sample needs to be both sufficient and relevant. For example, in a qualitative study of the experience of becoming a father, researchers interviewed first-time fathers recruited from prenatal classes (Chin, Daiches, & Hall, 2011). The researchers performed the interviews between 4 and 11 weeks post-birth and found these new fathers willing and eager to talk about their feelings and the realities of fatherhood.

Two key elements in evaluating quantitative research are issues related to the internal and external validity of the findings. **Internal validity** refers to the extent to which the results of the study present an accurate picture of the real world. In other words, did the independent variable make a difference in the outcome, or were there other factors at work? The choice of a sampling strategy is designed to reduce sampling bias, one of the threats to internal validity. Sampling bias is evident when groups of people are either underrepresented or overrepresented in a sample. When assessing the sample in a study, the researcher should ask, "Did any characteristics of the sample influence the outcomes of the study?" Another threat to internal validity is a change in the world or within research participants themselves during the course of the study. Imagine, for example, the effects of the events on and after September 11, 2001, or in the aftermath of Hurricane Katrina, on emotional, mental, and physical health and how they might affect study outcomes.

External validity, in contrast, refers to issues with generalizability of the findings from the research beyond the sample and situation that were studied. In other words, to whom and under which circumstances could the findings from this study be applied? When assessing the sample in a study, the researcher should ask, "How well does this group reflect the population as a whole?"

Internal and external validity do not apply in the same way to qualitative research. In qualitative studies, the sample is evaluated as to whether it is representative of the phenomenon of interest, rather than representative of the population as a whole. When assessing the sample in a qualitative study, the researcher should ask, "Did the sample chosen have the ability to talk about a phenomenon or an experience from the perspective of someone who was affected by it?"

Whom to Sample?

The responsibility of the investigator is to specify the sampling criteria or the characteristics necessary to be part of the research sample. It is these criteria that determine the target population. Sampling criteria may be very broad or very specific. These criteria are established to minimize bias or to control for irrelevant variability in the sample. Choosing a sample based on carefully selected criteria increases the strength of the evidence, thereby enhancing the ability to generalize the findings.

The researcher must make two different types of decisions—whom should be considered for inclusion in the sample and whom should be excluded from the sample. **Inclusion criteria** (sometimes called eligibility criteria) are those characteristics that must be met to be considered for participation in the study. Here, the investigator specifies what the sample will look like and which characteristics all study participants will have in common.

Exclusion criteria are not the polar opposite of the inclusion criteria, but rather those characteristics that, if present, would make persons ineligible to be in the sample, even though they might meet all of the inclusion criteria. These exclusions limit the representativeness of the sample and, therefore, the generalizability of the findings. As such, exclusion criteria should be specified after careful consideration. They should represent only those conditions or characteristics that might potentially make a difference in the outcome.

The specification of inclusion and exclusion criteria should not be taken lightly because of potential bias resulting in threats to internal validity and limitation of generalizability. Each criterion should be based on sound reasoning and be grounded in the goal of eliminating a potentially confounding effect on the outcome of the study. For example, in a study of the impact of home visits by mental health nurses on postpartum depression in Japanese women, the researcher used the following criteria when selecting the sample:

> Japanese women aged 18 years or older. Women were excluded if they lived outside the district, had delivered prematurely (before 36 weeks' gestation), if their infant had any congenital or serious disease, if they did not have a singleton birth, or if they had received any antidepressant or other specific treatments during the study period. (Tamaki, 2008, p. 420)

? Think Outside the Box

What are the potential threats to generalizability in the Tamaki (2008) example above?

How to Sample?

There are two categories of sampling strategies—probability and non-probability sampling. **Probability sampling** employs specific strategies designed to yield an unbiased (i.e., representative) sample by giving each element the possibility of being selected. The elements, which are each potential members of a sample, are chosen at random (by chance). **Nonprobability sampling** does not include random selection of elements and, therefore, has a higher possibility of yielding a biased (i.e., nonrepresentative) sample. In this case, researchers use elements that are accessible and available, and there is no way of estimating the probability that an element will be included in the sample.

? **Think Outside the Box**   www

Differentiate among the following terms: target population, accessible population, representative sample, population, and sample.

The researcher makes the choice of whether to use a probability or nonprobability strategy based on the problem under investigation and the purpose of the study. Quantitative studies can use either probability or nonprobability sampling strategies. All decisions made about sampling in quantitative studies are based on maximizing the representativeness of the sample. Qualitative studies, because of their very nature, employ nonprobability sampling strategies. All decisions made about sampling in qualitative studies are based on maximizing the representativeness of the phenomenon of interest.

Probability Sampling Strategies

Probability sampling is the most well-respected type of sampling for quantitative studies, because it is more likely to produce a representative sample. It is not the same thing as random assignment, however. Random assignment is the process of randomly placing subjects in an experimental study in different treatment groups. **Random sampling** involves processes in which each element of the population has an equal chance of being in the sample. Four probability sampling strategies are commonly used: (1) simple random, (2) stratified random, (3) cluster, and (4) systematic random.

Simple random sampling is a process in which the researcher defines the population, lists and consecutively numbers all elements of the population, and then randomly selects a sample from this list.

Table 7-1				
Excerpt from a Table of Random Numbers				
39634	62349	74088	65564	16379
14595	35050	40469	27478	44526
30734	71571	83722	79712	25775
64628	89126	91254	24090	25752
42831	95113	43511	42082	15140
80583	70361	41047	26792	78466

Source: Excerpted from http://www.mrs.umn.edu/~sungurea/introstat/public/instruction/ranbox/randomnumbersII.html

The most simplistic method of simple random sampling is to put all of the numbers in a "hat" and draw out the desired number of elements. Obviously, this technique would work only for a study with a very small number of elements.

The random selection of the sample may also be accomplished by using a table of random numbers (**Table 7-1**). With this strategy, the researcher begins at any point on the list of numbers and reads consecutive numbers in any direction, choosing those numbers that correspond to the numbered elements in the population until the desired sample size is reached. For example, if you have a list of 50 elements from which to choose a random sample of 15, each element would be numbered from 01 to 50. If you closed your eyes and pointed at the data in Table 7-1 and your finger ended up on the numeral 91254, deciding to go across the rows to the right, the first two-digit number would be 91 (**91**254), which is not in your range of possibilities. The next two-digit number would be 25 (91**25**4); that element would be selected, as would 42 (91254 **42**090), and 40 (24**0**90). The next two-digit number would be 90 (240**90**), which is not in your range, followed by 25 (**25**752), which you have already selected, and 75 (25**75**2), which is not in your range. Thus the next elements selected would be 24 (25752 **24**831), 28 (42**831**), and 31 (428**31**). This process would continue until 15 elements were selected. Simple random selection is not widely used, because it is rather cumbersome and inefficient. Furthermore, it is rare to have the ability to list every element in the population.

Stratified random sampling is a variation on the simple random sampling technique. When the composition of a population with respect to some characteristic important to the study is known, the population is divided into two or more strata (groups) based on that characteristic. Simple random selection is then used to pick elements from each group. This selection strategy makes each group homogenous as far as the characteristic of interest is concerned. Examples of characteristics upon which stratification may be made include gender, age, ethnicity, occupation, education, and so forth. For example, if a researcher wanted a sample of 100 people to be stratified in terms of gender, the elements would be divided based on gender, and a random selection of 50 people from each list would be chosen for the sample.

If desired, the researcher may use proportional sampling to ensure that the sample accurately reflects the composition of the population on the characteristic by which the population was stratified. If, for example, 60% of the known population is male, the researcher might want to randomly select 60 males and 40 females for a total sample of 100. Proportional sampling is not generally a wise choice if the strata are of extremely disproportionate sizes. To demonstrate how this technique works, consider a study of substance use and body mass index in southern Taiwan (Liu et al., 2010). In this study, proportional stratified random sampling was used to select 10,247 adolescents from junior high schools and high schools. Stratification was based on where the participant lived (urban versus rural) and the type of institution (middle school versus high school). In this way, the researchers ensured representation of adolescents from all strata without underrepresenting or overrepresenting either urban or rural dwelling adolescents, or those from junior high or high schools. **Cluster sampling,** also called multistage sampling, is a probability sampling strategy in which not all of the elements of the population need to be known. This strategy employs random selection of first larger sampling units (clusters), then successively smaller clusters, either by simple or stratified random selection techniques. It is a particularly efficient strategy when the population is large and spread out over a large geographic area. For example, in a rapid assessment of the health impact and the needs of the citizens of three Texas communities after Hurricane Ike struck in 2008, 30 clusters (neighborhoods) were identified and 7 households in each cluster were interviewed (Zane et al., 2010). Interviewing the entire target population (all households in the two counties) would have been an impossible task. By identifying and selecting neighborhoods and then households within neighborhoods, however, researchers could conduct an overall assessment in a short period of time.

? **Think Outside the Box**

Why is the use of a randomly selected population a stronger sampling method than the use of a nonrandomized sample? Discuss the value of having the strongest sampling method possible for the research to be conducted.

Systematic random sampling is a probability sampling technique in which elements are randomly selected from the population at predetermined, fixed intervals. The researcher first determines the desired sample size and then decides on the sampling interval. If the researcher has a list of the elements in the population, the sampling interval is determined by dividing the total population by the desired sample size. Suppose the population includes 750 individuals and the sample size is 50; in this case, the sampling interval would be 15. The researcher selects the first element randomly and then selects every fifteenth element thereafter to obtain the 50 elements for the sample. If the list is exhausted before the sample size is reached, counting resumes at the top of the list. This technique produces a random sample in a more efficient manner than is possible with simple randomization. For example, in a study of factors in adolescence predicting homelessness in young adulthood, systematic random sampling was used to select adolescents from a list of high schools in the United States (van den Bree et al., 2009). Interviews were then held with these individuals in 1994–1995 and again in 2001.

Nonprobability Sampling Strategies

The second broad category of sampling strategies is nonprobability sampling. These techniques are less likely to produce samples that are representative of the population. Nonetheless, they are more widely used in many disciplines, including nursing, because such samples are generally easier to obtain. Commonly used nonprobability sampling strategies include (1) convenience sampling, (2) quota sampling, (3) purposive sampling, (4) snowball sampling, and (5) theoretic sampling.

Convenience sampling is the process of selecting elements to be in the sample simply because they are readily available. Also called accidental sampling, it is the simplest and potentially least representative of all the sampling strategies. It is also currently the most frequently used sampling strategy in nursing research studies.

Quota sampling begins with the researcher identifying strata of the population and then determining the number of elements in each stratum necessary to proportionately represent the population. Actual selection of elements from each stratum is then accomplished in the same way as in convenience sampling. In a study of menopausal symptoms in black women, quota sampling was used to ensure equal numbers of women from specific age categories assumed to represent three menopausal states—premenopausal, perimenopausal, and postmenopausal (Im, Lee, & Chee, 2010). **Purposive sampling**, also called judgmental sampling, is a sampling strategy in which participants are handpicked by the researcher, either because they are typical of the phenomenon of interest or because they are knowledgeable about the issues under investigation. This strategy is often used when the researcher desires a sample consisting of experts. McCabe (2011) used this strategy to recruit 100 school nurses and 200 school teachers in her evaluation of their perceptions of fatigue among school children.

Snowball sampling, also known as network sampling, is a sampling strategy in which participants already in the study are asked to provide referrals to potential study subjects. Doherty and Scanell-Desch (2008), for example, in describing the recruitment of the 10 women in their study of the lived experience of widowhood during pregnancy, stated:

> One investigator obtained the name of a September 11th widow from a nursing colleague. This woman was pregnant at the time of her husband's death, agreed to participate in the study, and referred the researchers to other potential participants. The investigator also obtained the names of several pregnant military widows from a retired military nurse. (p. 104)

Snowball sampling is a particularly good strategy to use when potential participants in the study are challenging to find, as might be the case with vegetarians, drug abusers, persons engaged in prostitution, people with a specific disability or rare condition, and homeless individuals.

Theoretical sampling is generally restricted to qualitative research methods, especially in conjunction with grounded theory. It is most analogous to the purposive sampling strategy. As the study unfolds and the interviews conducted with the first few participants are analyzed, conceptual categories and themes are identified. Subsequent decisions as to who will provide data and which data will be gathered are then based on who has already been sampled and which data have already been provided. Sampling and data collection continue until all of the categories and themes are "saturated"—that is, no additional categories or themes are emerging and no new facets of existing categories and themes are uncovered. Busby and Witucki-Brown (2011), for example, used theoretical sampling to select the 15 participants for a grounded theory explanation of how emergency response personnel utilize situational awareness in their management of multiple casualty incidents.

How Many to Sample?

Once the researcher has decided whom to sample and how the sampling will be done, it is time to make the decision about how many elements need to be in the sample. The question of sample size is a crucial one when the objective is the ability to generalize the findings to a larger population. The generally accepted recommendation is to sample as many elements as possible. It is wise to remember, however, that the validity of a study begins with the design. Even the largest of samples cannot make up for faulty design.

? Think Outside the Box

Convenience sampling is the most commonly used sampling method. Which steps would you expect to see used within a study to strengthen the study in this type of sampling method?

Quantitative Studies

Several factors are taken into consideration when decisions are made about desired sample size in quantitative studies, including factors related to (1) the population, (2) the study design, (3) measurement, and (4) practicability.

Population Factors

Population-related factors that influence required sample size include the homogeneity of the population as well as the expected rate of the phenomenon, event, or outcome being measured and the anticipated attrition rate. In a population that is fairly homogenous (i.e., in which sampling elements are very similar to one another), the required sample size is generally smaller than if the population were more heterogeneous. Similarly, if the phenomenon, event, or outcome occurs frequently, a smaller sample size is needed than if occurrences are infrequent.

In longitudinal studies, attrition may be a problem. When this phenomenon is anticipated to occur, researchers often "over-enroll" participants in the research. If, for example, a study were expected to have an attrition rate of 20% (i.e., if 100 subjects were to begin the study, only 80 would complete it), then the researcher would enroll 120 participants so as to have the desired 100 at completion.

Design Factors

Design factors influencing sample size include the type of study, the number of variables, and the sampling strategy. Quantitative studies, in general, require larger sample sizes than do qualitative studies. Some differences also occur in relation to the quantitative designs themselves. First, a study that is more complex requires a larger sample size. For example, a study employing a longitudinal data collection plan needs to enroll increased numbers of participants at the beginning because of the increased possibility of losing subjects over the course of the study (sample attrition). Second, as the number of variables being measured increases, so does the needed sample size. Third, the sampling strategy itself can affect the required sample size. Stratified random sampling and quota sampling techniques, for example, allow the researcher to use smaller sample sizes than would be needed in studies employing simple random or convenience sampling, because some of the representativeness is already built into the stratification procedure.

Measurement Factors

Measurement factors that influence sample size include the sensitivity of the research instruments and the effect that the process has on the outcome. Data collection instruments in which measurement error is minimal are said to be precise. The less precise the instrument, the larger the sample size might need to be. Because interval-level data are generally more precise, from a sample size perspective it is best to measure at that level if at all possible, because a smaller sample size may be used.

Practical Factors

Practical factors such as cost and convenience also influence sample size. Although population factors, design factors, and measurement factors certainly affect the ideal sample size, it is these practical factors that often prove most influential. When this is the case, adjustments in design and/or sampling strategies need to be made to strengthen the internal validity of the study.

Given these factors discussed, how do researchers determine the sample size needed for a particular study? Some use the "rule of 30": There should be 30 subjects for each group or 30 subjects for each variable. This notion is based on the central limit theorem, which asserts that, in a randomly generated sample of 30 or more subjects, the mean of a characteristic will approximate the population mean (Hinkle, Wiersma, & Jurs, 1988). It is essential to remember, however, that representativeness is more important than sample size. The "rule of 30" should, therefore, be considered the minimum acceptable sample size rather than the ideal.

The gold standard in determining sample size is power analysis, a statistical calculation of the number of subjects needed to accurately reject the null hypothesis (Fitzner & Heckinger, 2010). The actual calculation of sample size is beyond the scope of this text. The most commonly used significance level is 0.05 and the standard power is 0.80. The effect size is estimated based on pilot studies undertaken by the researcher or on reports in the literature drawn from previous studies on the same or similar problems. Performing the power analysis prior to conducting a study strengthens the study's credibility concerning the size of the sample utilized. For example, here is the description of the power analysis for a study of the impact of a relative's clinic on next-of-kin satisfaction with care received by patients in critical care:

> The study was powered to detect a difference in mean satisfaction score of 0.5, assuming a 50% response rate, 150 participants in each group and a standard deviation of 1.0 using an unpaired two-tailed t-test. The alpha and beta levels selected were 0.05 and 0.2, respectively. (Steel, Underwood, Notley, & Blunt, 2008, p. 122)

Power analysis formulas are sometimes applied after the fact to determine the power of a test given the sample size and results obtained. Sometimes the formula is used on a post hoc basis to determine the optimal sample size. For example, in a study comparing outcomes of care for an ulcer on a leg in a sample of 104 patients who chose either a nurse-led clinic or home care, the post hoc analysis revealed only a 48% power to find a difference in treatment (Harrison et al., 2011).

Qualitative Studies

Qualitative studies generally employ relatively small, nonrandom samples. Because the aim of qualitative research is to describe and analyze the meanings and experiences of particular individuals or groups, large sample sizes are not generally appropriate or feasible in these scenarios. Instead, the sample size should be sufficient to provide enough information to answer the research question based on the notion of data saturation. Participants continue to be enrolled in a study until no new information is being uncovered; that is, redundancy occurs in all subsequent data collection encounters.

Redundancy may be achieved with a limited number of participants when the sample is homogenous. For this reason, it is not unusual to have very small sample sizes in phenomenologic studies. For example, Goldbort, Knepp, Mueller, and Pyron (2011) had nine participants in their study of the nurses' experiences working with women who had traumatic birthing processes, and Underhill and Dickerson (2011) interviewed nine participants for their study of the experience of women with a hereditary risk of breast cancer who were participating in a breast surveillance program.

? **Think Outside the Box**

What would be the implications of the "rule of 30" applied to qualitative research?

In contrast, for ethnographic or grounded theory studies, in which the sample is usually more heterogeneous, larger sample sizes are generally the norm. For example, an ethnography approach was used with 32 women who shared their perspectives on the 1-month postnatal practices in China (Holroyd, Lopez, & Chan, 2011), and 30 registered nurses supplied the data upon which a grounded theory of end-of-life care was developed (McCallin, 2011).

Specific Evidence-Based Practice Considerations

Evidence-based clinical decisions are essential for the practice of nursing. Melnyk and Fineout-Overholt (2011) have rightly asserted, "The goal of EBP is to use the highest quality of knowledge in providing care to produce the greatest impact on patients' health status and healthcare" (p. 75). It is imperative, therefore, to have the ability to critically examine the available research and to determine the strength of the evidence. Several guiding questions can help direct reading about and critiquing sampling plans. While these questions are similar in some respects in both quantitative and qualitative research, they differ in many other respects (**Table 7-2**).

Quantitative Evidence Critique

A well-written quantitative research report contains a detailed explanation of the sampling strategy (including sample size determination)

Table 7-2
Guidelines for Critiquing the Sample for Evidence-Based Practice
Quantitative Research Studies
1. How and when was the desired sample size determined?
2. Was the sample size adequate to answer the research question?
3. What were the inclusion and exclusion criteria?
4. Was the sampling strategy one of probability or nonprobability? Was this strategy appropriate to the research question?
5. Is the sample for the study clearly described?
6. Are there potential biases in the sample selection or the sample itself that could have an effect on the outcome of the study?
7. Is the sample representative of the target population? Is it representative of your own patients?
Qualitative Research Studies
1. Which sampling strategy was used to choose the participants?
2. Was the sample size adequate to answer the research question?
3. Is the sample for the study clearly described?
4. Is the sample representative of the phenomenon of interest?

and the inclusion and exclusion criteria together with the rationale for their use. Kahre, Fortune, Hurley, and Winsett (2011), for example, provided the following description of the sampling plan in their comparison of measures for pain relief for IV insertion:

> Sample size was calculated using software for power and sample size calculations with estimated standard deviation of change scores at 0.80 power. Nine subjects per group were needed to detect a medium difference. A sample size of 40 healthy adult subjects was estimated to provide an adequate sample size for subgroup analyses. Inclusion criteria for eligibility to participate were licensed registered nurses (RN) aged 21 years or older, palpable veins in hand, forearm or antecubital bilaterally, no allergy to benzyl alcohol or lidocaine, and normal healthy adult as defined in the American Society of Anesthesiologists' (ASA) Physical Status Classification System. (p. 311)

The well-written quantitative research report also thoroughly describes the demographic characteristics of the sample that actually participated in the study:

> The sample included 56 subjects with a mean of 18.6 ± 10.6 years as an RN. Forty-eight (86%) were Caucasian females. Mean years in direct care were 7.5 ± 4.7 years, and the subjects reported a mean of 5.2 ± 4.4 years of IV starts as part of their job description. (Kahre et al., 2011, p. 312)

Descriptions such as these allow the reader to determine the representativeness of the sample for their own population and establish the strength of the evidence for implementing the findings.

Qualitative Evidence Critique

A well-written qualitative research report also contains a detailed explanation of the sampling strategy as well as a description of the sample obtained. Stewart, Masuda, Letourneau, Anderson, and McGhan (2011), for example, described the plan they used to recruit participants in their study of the support needs of children with asthma and allergies as follows:

> Participants were recruited using existing clinical and community networks in each province (e.g., pediatric asthma and allergy clinics, pharmacies, community organizations, registries). Members of the Community Advisory Committee facilitated recruitment by identifying potential participants. Criteria for inclusion in the study

were: physician-diagnosed asthma and/or severe anaphylactic allergies, 6 to 12 years of age, and able to speak English. (p. 69)

Evaluating the Evidence for Implementation

Once the sample characteristics and size have been critically analyzed, the next step in determining appropriateness for consideration for EBP is to establish whether this evidence, however good, is applicable in the local situation. For example, in the study of smoking cessation intervention for pregnant women, Stotts et al. (2009) designed an intervention employing the use of ultrasound and motivational interviewing that was effective in decreasing smoking among light smokers. The sample was primarily Caucasian, married or living with a partner, and had at least a high school education.

A nurse who wanted to implement a smoking cessation program with a population that was primarily from ethnic minority groups would need to carefully consider whether the strategy designed by these researchers could be applied in the local setting. An alternative in this situation would be to examine the smoking cessation strategies employed in the study conducted by Hennrikus et al. (2010), whose sample was predominately from ethnic minorities, unmarried, and unemployed, with 65% having a high school education or less. The mobilization of support within pregnant women's social networks as described in the Hennrikus et al. study might be more appropriate for pregnant women in ethnic minorities.

? **Think Outside the Box**   www

> Specific evidence-based practice considerations: Identify the demographic characteristics of a sample that would be representative of the population with whom you are currently working in a clinical course.

Sampling Decisions for an Evidence-Based Project

After identifying the clinical question or problem on which to build an evidence-based project and deciding, based on the strength of the evidence, on an appropriate intervention or change in practice, a sampling decision must be made. Based on the information contained in this chapter, it should be clear that the best (i.e., the strongest) sampling technique would be a random assignment of patients to either the nursing intervention or the standard of care. If it were not possible to randomize the participants, then a nonrandom sampling plan would be appropriate if efforts to build in representativeness through matching or purposive sampling procedures were used.

Final Comments on Sampling

Although they are only one component in the overall research process, sampling decisions affect both the internal validity and the external validity of a study. As such, critical analysis of the sampling strategy, the sample size, and the quality of the sample are essential in determining the relevance of the results of one study, or a group of studies, to EBP for nurses.

Summary Points

1. Sampling allows a researcher to draw conclusions about the research problem under investigation based on information from a portion of the population, rather than the whole population.
2. The researcher selects a sample from an accessible population that is representative of the target population to whom the findings may be generalized.
3. Probability sampling strategies employ random selection of elements of the population. Probability strategies include simple random, systematic random, stratified random, and cluster sampling.
4. Nonprobability sampling strategies employ nonrandom selection of elements of the population. Nonprobability strategies include convenience, quota, purposive, snowball, and theoretical sampling.
5. Sampling decisions in quantitative research are made based on the desire to have a representative sample. Sampling strategies include both probability and nonprobability strategies.
6. Sampling decisions in qualitative research are made based on the desire to obtain data that are representative of the phenomenon of interest. Sampling strategies are almost always nonprobability strategies.
7. Critiquing studies to determine their relevance for evidence-based practice (EBP) involves evaluation of the sampling plan, sampling strategies, and sample size for their appropriateness to the research question and the research design.

RED FLAGS

- Randomization of a sample group strengthens a study. Bias within the sampling process is decreased by randomization.
- The appropriate sample size for a quantitative study is best established by performing a power analysis before the study gets under way.
- Convenience and snowball sampling methodologies are weak sampling methods owing to their higher potential for lack of generalizability and potential for bias.
- At the least, inclusion criteria should be documented for review within the research report. Both inclusion and exclusion criteria should be provided.
- Failure to utilize the "rule of 30" can weaken a study.
- Inadequate or unclear description of the sampling strategy results in confusion when others attempt to understand the study's conclusions.
- Failure to use a sampling strategy that would produce a sample size appropriate for the particular research method leads to a limitation for the study.
- Attempts to generalize findings past the representativeness of the sample are inappropriate.
- Failure to acknowledge limitations resulting from sample size or sample selection decisions is problematic.

Multiple Choice Questions

1. A researcher who wishes to study the impact of having a child with cystic fibrosis on family functioning contacts the local chapter of the Cystic Fibrosis Foundation for assistance in finding parents to interview. Parents of children with cystic fibrosis in the local chapter are the:
    A. Target population.
    B. Accessible population.
    C. Sample.
    D. Participants.

2. In a study of the use of simulation in nursing education, the researcher specifies that participants must be nursing students 18 years of age or older who are in their first clinical nursing course. These specifications are an example of
    A. Demographic variables.
    B. Exclusion criteria.
    C. Extraneous variables.
    D. Inclusion criteria.

3. A sample that accurately reflects the characteristics of the population is known as a
    A. Random sample.
    B. Purposive sample.
    C. Representative sample.
    D. Probability sample.

4. Which of the following types of studies would require the largest sample size?
    A. Experimental study
    B. Descriptive survey
    C. Grounded theory
    D. Ethnographic study

5. A researcher has decided to conduct a satisfaction survey among all of the patients who presented to the emergency department over a 2-month period of time. This is an example of
    A. Stratified random sampling.
    B. Cluster sampling.
    C. Convenience sampling.
    D. Purposive sampling.

6. In a study of nursing students' attitudes toward caring for patients with hypertension who are noncompliant with their medications, the researcher randomly selected a sample of nursing students from a list of all students enrolled in each of five nursing programs that had been randomly selected from one state. Because the sample was randomly selected, to which population can the findings be generalized?
   A. Nursing students in the programs that were randomly selected
   B. Nursing students in the state from which the programs were randomly selected
   C. Nursing students in the United States
   D. All nursing students

7. Power analysis is conducted to
   A. Determine a large effect size.
   B. Estimate sample size.
   C. Test for internal validity.
   D. Set the level of significance.

8. Determination of the appropriate sample size in qualitative research is based on the principle(s) of
   A. Power analysis.
   B. The "rule of 30."
   C. Saturation and redundancy.
   D. Convenience.

9. Which of the following would be the strongest method for assigning 50 subjects to treatment and control groups in an experimental study?
   A. Group subjects according to attending physician.
   B. List subjects alphabetically, divide the list in half, place the first 25 names in the treatment group and the last 25 in the control group.
   C. Assign each participant a number, place even numbered participants in the treatment group and the odd numbered in the control group.
   D. Assign each participant a number, place the numbers in a box, draw numbers from the box, alternating placement in either the treatment group or the control group.

10. In interpreting quantitative research results, the representativeness of the sample is most closely tied to
    A. Internal validity.
    B. External validity.
    C. Sample validity.
    D. Research validity.

Discussion Questions

1. You are a nurse working in the labor and delivery suite in an academic medical center. You are interested in nonpharmacologic pain management for your patients and would like to implement an evidence-based change project on your unit. Which particular sampling concerns will you examine in the research studies about nonpharmacologic pain management for laboring patients?

2. You are a BSN student enrolled in a research course. The instructor has given you the following problem statement: "Does music affect the perception of pain in patients who have undergone hip replacement?" Describe one probability sampling plan and one nonprobability sampling plan for answering this question.

3. Read the excerpt below from an article describing a study to test a social support intervention for mothers of children newly diagnosed with type 1 diabetes mellitus and answer the following questions:
   1. What is the sampling strategy used?
   2. What were the inclusion and exclusion criteria?
   3. What are the sample characteristics?
   4. Is this sample representative?
   5. How could the sampling strategy be improved?

   > Mothers [of children newly diagnosed with type 1 diabetes mellitus] were recruited from 2 regional pediatric diabetes clinics in the northeastern United States. Those who agreed to participate were randomly assigned . . . to an experimental or control group . . . Parents were recruited for participation in the study by the diabetes team members in the hospital or clinic . . . The mothers were predominantly married (83%) and white (88%). The mothers' mean ± SD age was 36 ± 6 years (range, 22–57) . . . with the majority having at least a high school education (mean ± SD, 14 ± 2 years; range, 12–22). Almost half (49.4%) were employed full-time, 19.3% were employed part-time, and the rest (31.3%) were not employed outside the home. (Sullivan-Bolyai et al., 2010, pp. 91–92).

Suggested Readings

Abrams, L. S. (2010). Sampling "hard to reach" population in qualitative research: The case of incarcerated youth. *Qualitative Social Work, 9*(4), 536–550. doi:10.1177/1473325010367821

Claudio, L., & Stingone, J. A. (2008). Improving sampling and response rates in children's health research through participatory methods. *Journal of School Health, 78*(8), 445–451. doi:10.1111/j.1746-1561.2008.00328.x

Hedges, C., & Bliss-Holtz, J. (2006). Not too big, not too small, but just right: The dilemma of sample size estimation. *AACN Advanced Critical Care, 17*(3), 341–344. doi:10.1097/01256961-200607000-00013

Shields, L., & Twycross, A. (2008). Sampling in quantitative research. *Paediatric Nursing, 20*(5), 37.

Trochim, W. (2006). *Research Methods Knowledge Base: Sampling.* Retrieved from http://www.socialresearchmethods.net/kb/sampling.php

References

Busby, S., & Wituki-Brown, J. (2011). Theory development for situational awareness in multi-casualty incidents. *Journal of Emergency Nursing, 37*(5), 444–452. doi:10.1016/j.jen.2010.07.023

Chin, R., Daiches, A., & Hall, P. (2011). A qualitative exploration of first time fathers' experiences of becoming a father. *Community Practitioner, 84*(7), 19–23.

Doherty, M. E., & Scannell-Desch, E. (2008). The lived experience of widowhood during pregnancy. *Journal of Midwifery & Women's Health, 53*(2), 103–109.

Fitzner, K., & Heckinger, E. (2010). Sample size calculation and power analysis: A quick review. *Diabetes Educator, 36*(5), 701–707. doi:10.1177/0145721710380791

Goldbort, J., Knepp, A., Mueller, C., & Pyron, M. (2011). Intrapartum nurses' lived experience in a traumatic birthing process. *MCN, American Journal of Maternal Child Nursing, 36*(6), 373–380. doi:10.1097/NMC.0b013e31822de535

Harrison, M. B., VanDenKerkhof, E., Hopman, W. M., Graham, I. D., Lorimer, K., & Carley, M. (2011). Evidence-informed leg ulcer care: A cohort study comparing outcomes of individuals choosing nurse-led clinic or home care. *Ostomy Wound Management, 57*(8), 38–45.

Hennrikus, D., Pirie, P., Hellerstedt, W., Lando, H. A., Steele, J., & Dunn, C. (2010). Increasing support for smoking cessation during pregnancy and postpartum: Results of a randomized controlled pilot study. *Preventive Medicine, 50*(3), 134–137. doi:10.1016/j.ypmed.2010.01.003

Hinkle, D., Wiersma, W., & Jurs, S. (1988). *Applied statistics for the behavioral sciences* (2nd ed.). Boston, MA: Houghton-Mifflin.

Holroyd, E., Lopez, V., & Chan, S. W. (2011). Negotiating "doing the month": An ethnographic study examining the postnatal practices of two generations of Chinese women. *Nursing & Health Sciences, 13*(1), 47–52. doi:10.1111/j.1442-2018.2011.00575.x

Im, E. O., Lee, S. H., & Chee, W. (2010). Black women in menopausal transition. *Journal of Obstetric, Gynecologic, and Neonatal Nursing, 39*(4), 435–443. doi:10.1111/j.1552-6909.2010.01148.x

Kahre, C., Fortune, V., Hurley, J., & Winsett, R. P. (2011). Randomized controlled trial to compare effects of pain relief during IV insertion using bacteriostatic normal saline and 1% buffered lidocaine. *Journal of Perianesthesia Nursing, 26*(5), 310–314. doi:10.1016/j.jopan.2011.05.009

Liu, T. L., Yen, J. Y., Ko, C. H., Huang, M. F., Wang, P. W., Yeh, Y. C., & Yen, C. F. (2010). Associations between substance use and body mass index: Moderating effects of sociodemographic characteristics among Taiwanese adolescents. *Koahsiung Journal of Medical Sciences, 26*(6), 281–289.

Malloch, K., & Porter-O'Grady, T. (2010). *Introduction to evidence-based practice in nursing and health care* (2nd ed.). Sudbury, MA: Jones and Bartlett.

McCabe, M. A. (2011). Perceptions of school nurses and teachers of fatigue in children. *Pediatric Nursing, 37*(5), 244–250, 255.

McCallin, A. M. (2011). Moderated guiding: A grounded theory of nursing practice in end-of-life care. *Journal of Clinical Nursing, 20*(15–16), 2325–2333. doi:10.1111/j.1365-2702.2010.03543.x

Melnyk, B. M., & Fineout-Overholt, E. (2011). *Evidence-based practice in nursing and healthcare: A guide to best practice* (2nd ed.). Philadelphia, PA: Lippincott Williams & Wilkins.

Steel, A., Underwood, C., Notley, C., & Blunt M. (2008). The impact of offering a relatives' clinic on the satisfaction of the next-of-kin of critical care patients: A prospective time-interrupted trial. *Intensive Critical Care Nursing, 24*(2), 122–129. doi:10.1016/j.iccn.2007.08.002

Stewart, M., Masuda, J. R., Letourneau, N., Anderson, S., & McGhan, S. (2011). "I want to meet other kids just like me": Support needs of children with asthma and allergies. *Issues in Comprehensive Pediatric Nursing, 34*(2), 62–78. doi:10.3109/0146 0862.2011.572638

Stotts, A. L., Groff, J. Y., Velasquez, M. M., Benjamin-Gamer, R., Green, C., Carbonari, J. P., & DiClemente, C. C. (2009). Ultrasound feedback and motivational interviewing targeting smoking cessation in the second and third trimesters of pregnancy. *Nicotine and Tobacco Research, 11*(8), 961–968. doi:10.1093/ntr/ntp095

Sullivan-Bolyai, S., Bova, C., Leung, K., Trudeau, A., Lee, M., & Gruppuso, P. (2010). Social support to empower parents (STEP): An intervention for parents of young children newly diagnosed with type 1 diabetes. *Diabetes Educator, 36*(1), 88–97. doi:10.1177/0145721709352384

Tamaki, A. (2008). Effectiveness of home visits by mental health nurses for Japanese women with post-partum depression. *International Journal of Mental Health Nursing, 17*(6), 419–427. doi:10.1111/j.1447-0349.2008.00568.x

Underhill, M. L., & Dickerson, S. S. (2011). Engaging in medical vigilance: Understanding the personal meaning of breast surveillance. *Oncology Nursing Forum, 38*(6), 686–694. doi:10.1188/11.ONF.686-694

van den Bree, M. B., Shelton, K., Bonner, A., Moss, S., Thomas, H., & Taylor, P. J. (2009). A longitudinal population-based study of factors in adolescence predicting homelessness in young adulthood. *Journal of Adolescent Health, 45*(6), 571–578. doi:10.1016/j.jadohealth.2009.03.027

Zane, D. F., Bayleyegn, T. M., Haywood, T. L., Witz-Beckham, D., Guidry, H., Sanchez, C., & Wolkin, A. F. (2010). Community assessment for public health emergency response following Hurricane Ike—Texas, 25–30 September 2008. *Prehospital & Disaster Medicine, 25*(6), 503–510.

Chapter **8**

Quantitative
Research Design

Sharon Cannon

Chapter Objectives

At the conclusion of this chapter, the learner will be able to

1. List characteristics of quantitative designs
2. Discuss descriptive designs
3. Identify control for quantitative designs
4. Compare experimental, nonexperimental, time-dimensional, and quasi-experimental designs
5. Compare and contrast research design, quality improvement programs, and root cause analysis
6. Select a quantitative design for research utilization in an evidence-based practice clinical situation

Key Terms

➤ Comparative design

➤ Control

➤ Correlational design

➤ Dependent variable

➤ Descriptive design

➤ Experimental design

➤ Independent variable

➤ Manipulation

➤ Meta-analysis or meta-synthesis

➤ Nonequivalent control group

➤ Nonexperimental design

➤ Quality improvement project

➤ Quantitative design

➤ Quasi-experimental design

➤ Randomization

➤ Research design

➤ Root cause analysis

➤ Secondary analysis

➤ Sentinel events

➤ Time-dimensional design

Introduction

The most commonly used **research design** is a quantitative design. But precisely what is a quantitative design? This question, as well as the characteristics and types of designs for use in evidence-based practice (EBP) clinical situations, are discussed in this chapter.

Before exploring the characteristics of a study design, it is necessary to define quantitative research. Quantitative research is often identified with the traditional scientific method that gathers data objectively in an organized, systematic, controlled manner so that the findings can be generalized to other situations/populations (Brockopp & Hastings-Tolsma, 2003; Burns & Grove, 2009; Fain, 2009; Polit & Beck, 2008). A design is a plan on how to proceed; thus a quantitative research design can be defined as an objective, systematic plan or blueprint to gather data that has application to other situations/populations. **Quantitative design** may be (1) experimental, (2) nonexperimental, or (3) quasi-experimental. Studies utilizing an **experimental design** use treatment and control groups; those with a **nonexperimental design** generate questions for experimental design; and studies having a **quasi-experimental design** lack randomization or may not include a control group.

Characteristics of Quantitative Research Design

The characteristics of quantitative design center on the why, where, who, what, when, and how questions. The quantitative researcher must state why (purpose) the study is being done, where (setting) the study is being conducted (i.e., laboratory, hospital, or clinic), who (subjects) is being studied (i.e., animals or humans), what type of data is being collected, when the data are to be collected, and how (design) the data are to be collected.

Within the framework of these questions, quantitative research looks for cause and effect in an experiment. When considering potential causes and effects, different groups participating in the study are viewed in terms of being either treatment or control groups. **Control** is one of the most common and important characteristic of quantitative design. To understand the concept of control, it is necessary to understand variables. A variable can be a quality, characteristic, attribute, or property of a person, thing, or situation (Burns & Grove, 2009; Polit & Beck, 2008). The two types of variables found in quantitative research are dependent and independent variables. The **dependent variable** is the outcome caused or influenced by the independent variable; the **independent variable** is a treatment, intervention, or experiment. Consider the situation in which a nurse researcher studies the effect of patient teaching (independent variable) about wound care in an attempt to reduce the likelihood of wound infection (dependent variable) when the surgical patient is discharged from the hospital. In this example, the teaching is what affects the rate of wound infection.

? **Think Outside the Box**   www

Considering these examples, which type of research design could be used to provide the strongest methodology possible:
- What information has been used to determine the method of catheterizing for a laboring mother?
- What information serves as the basis for the range of blood sugars used within elderly persons who are newly diagnosed with diabetes?
- What nursing model would be useful in a critical access type of agency?

Closely connected to the issue of control is **manipulation** of the independent variable. The researcher wants to make sure that the treatment is the only explanation for the outcome. In the example given above, the nurse researcher wants to ensure that the patient education on wound care delivered prior to discharge is the reason why the rate of wound infections in discharged surgical patients decreases. Control or manipulation in this situation would involve providing patient education to surgical patients who are not taking antibiotics when discharged from the hospital. Because patients who are taking antibiotics would be least likely to develop a wound infection, the use of antibiotics would be a variable that might skew the results.

Another important characteristic of quantitative research is randomization. **Randomization** is the assignment of subjects to a group in such a manner that each subject has an equal opportunity of being selected to participate in the study. In the example previously given about wound care, the researcher might have two groups: The control group would include those subjects who did not receive any wound care education, whereas the experimental group would include those subjects who did receive patient education. Randomization would occur when the patients were assigned to either group in a way that each patient had an equal opportunity for inclusion in either group. This could be done by selecting every third patient discharged to be a member of a group. Another way to randomize the sample might be to give each patient a number, draw the numbers out of a hat, and alternate assignment to the groups. Randomization helps to eliminate bias. For example, the nurse who thinks that only her patients should be in the treatment group would be biased; randomization of subjects would eliminate that possibility. Although randomization strengthens a study, be aware that not all studies can be randomized. Randomization can be costly and time-consuming, and there may not be enough participants to randomize them effectively.

In any quantitative research study, it is important to control the influence of extraneous variables, such as gender, age, and ethnicity. Randomization provides for internal validity of a study because the groups are equal at the beginning of the study. External validity is achieved when the outcome can be applied (generalized) to the target population; generalization helps strengthen the study results. Using the wound care example, control of the extraneous variable could involve not providing patient education to pediatric patients, but rather providing it only to adult patients.

Manipulation, control, and randomization are three essential characteristics of quantitative research design. These characteristics enable the researcher to be confident that the outcome is caused by the intervention and not by other variables, and that it can be generalized to a target population.

Descriptive Design

Descriptive design examines the characteristics of just one sample population. According to Burns and Grove (2009), this type of research design may be used for theory development, practice problems, rationale for current practice, generating hypotheses, or clinical decision making based on what others are doing. Examples of descriptive design include comparative (looking at differences in two or more groups), time-dimensional (occurring over an extended period of time), cross-sectional (stages of development simultaneously), trends and events, and correlational (relationships) designs. A descriptive design delineates or explains the variables being studied and provides flexibility in examining a problem from many different angles. However, be aware that data obtained in quantitative, descriptive designs are limited to participant responses to things such as blood pressure equipment or scores on a survey. The two most commonly used types of descriptive designs are comparative and correlational.

The **comparative design** involves no manipulation or control of the independent variable, with the dependent variable being the only variable measured in two or more groups (Brink & Wood, 2001). This type of design can also be retrospective in nature. Using the wound care example, a comparative design would assign patients with wounds to a group of surgical patients or to a group of patients with wounds resulting from trauma to compare the rates of post-discharge infections. The research question might be, "Is the rate of infection higher in trauma patients than in surgical patients?" The patients' past histories would then be examined for prior surgeries or trauma wounds. Cause and effect remain the focus of this design, in that the two groups being compared for infection rates are identified according to the type of wound.

? Think Outside the Box   www

Explore the idea of control within a quantitative design methodology. Which aspects of the study design are important to consider and why?

Perhaps the most widely used type of descriptive design is the correlational study. Simply stated, a **correlational design** examines the relationships between two or more variables within a situation without knowing the reason for the relationship. The researcher may use this design when there is uncertainty about whether the variables are related and, if so, how they are related. However, the researcher assumes that the variables *are* related and seeks to discover and explain that relationship. Correlational designs do not conclude that only one variable causes another, because the independent variable cannot always be controlled (Polit & Beck, 2008).

Another aspect of a correlational design is that it is "ex post facto," meaning "from after the fact" (Polit & Beck, 2006). For example, a study that compares a variable occurring in the past with a variable occurring currently would be characterized as using a retrospective correlational design. In other words, a study that looks at a variable after the fact is a retrospective study. For instance, the nurse researcher might conduct a chart review on all discharged surgical patients to determine if any patient education on wound care occurred prior to discharge from the hospital and then to check whether any of those patients were readmitted for a wound infection.

Prospective correlational designs are usually considered stronger than retrospective designs, because the researcher may be able to control or rule out explanations for some outcomes (Polit & Beck, 2008). These designs require the researcher to assume cause and effect and to implement the study under those assumptions.

Correlational designs may also be predictive in nature. In this type of study, one variable occurs prior to another variable—that is, the independent variable occurs prior to the dependent variable. Again using the wound care example, a predictive correlational study research statement might be, "The rate of wound infection will decrease 1 week post discharge after receiving the wound care educational program in the outpatient clinic."

Experimental Design

Experimental design looks for cause and effect (outcome). Obviously, there must be a preceding cause and a relationship between the cause and the outcome without any influencing variables to warrant the conclusion that a cause-and-effect relationship exists.

Several issues related to experimental design should be addressed before discussing the designs themselves. The first issue is that not all variables can be manipulated. In the prior wound care example, not every patient has a wound. As such, the researcher cannot inflict a wound on all individuals so as to obtain a large random sample.

Another issue is that of ethics. Consider the famous Tuskegee Syphilis Study (Centers for Disease Control and Prevention, n.d.), an experiment that was conducted over 40 years to examine the progress of syphilis in adult black males. Many of the subjects in this study were not even aware that they were participants. Also, even though an effective treatment for syphilis (penicillin) was available, not all subjects with syphilis in this study were given penicillin. To satisfy ethical concerns, some variables should not be manipulated.

Feasibility is another issue in experimental design. Some experiments may be too expensive, require cooperation from individuals from multiple key areas, require too much time, or not have enough subjects for participation. When considering the feasibility of a proposed study, careful attention should be given to what types of resources might be needed to conduct the research project.

In experimental design, another significant issue is the Hawthorne effect. Simply stated, the Hawthorne effect arises when the subjects know that they are part of the study and change their behavior accordingly; that is, the act of observing changes the observed's behavior. While it is not possible to prevent the Hawthorne effect from occurring, thought needs to be given to how to minimize the influence that attention has on the outcome to the study.

Keeping in mind these issues, we now move on to an examination of experimental design. The most classic experimental design is a pre-test/post-test design. With this approach, subjects are assigned to one of two groups: a control (comparative) group that does not receive the treatment (intervention) or an experimental group that does receive the treatment. In the wound care example, patients would be assigned to a group that receives no specific wound care instructions (control group) or to the group that receives patient education regarding wound care (experimental group).

Another experimental design of considerable importance in the healthcare arena is the randomized controlled trial (RCT). The RCT is considered the true experiment. This design may involve two, three, or four groups. The tests used may involve both a pre-test and post-test, a post-test only, or repeated measures (**Figure 8-1**).

Figure 8-1

Experimental design examples.

Pre-test/Post-test

$\quad$ R $\quad$ O_1 $\quad$ X_1 $\quad$ O_2

$\quad$ R $\quad$ O_1 $\quad$ X_2 $\quad$ O_2

Two-Group Post-test Only

$\quad$ R $\quad$ X_1 $\quad$ O_1

$\quad$ R $\quad$ X_2 $\quad$ O_1

Three Groups

$\quad$ R $\quad$ X_1 $\quad$ O_1

$\quad$ R $\quad$ X_2 $\quad$ O_1

$\quad$ R $\quad$ O_1

Four Groups

$\quad$ R $\quad$ O_1 $\quad$ X_1 $\quad$ O_2

$\quad$ R $\quad$ X_1 $\quad$ O_2

$\quad$ R $\quad$ O_1 $\quad$ X_2 $\quad$ O_2

$\quad$ R $\quad$ X_2 $\quad$ O_2

Note: O = Outcome/measurement; R = Random assignment; X = Treatment/intervention.

Nonexperimental Design

Some studies do not lend themselves to an experimental design; that is, manipulation of variables is not possible, nor is randomization controlled. Studies with this kind of nonexperimental design occur in the here and now and are observational rather than interventional in nature. Two types of nonexperimental designs used in EBP are secondary analysis and meta-analysis.

Secondary analysis follows the course implied by its name: It examines data obtained in another study and allows researchers to examine large and small data sets collected via different approaches. A secondary analysis asks new questions about data previously collected for another purpose. For example, a nurse researcher interested in the effects of patient education on decreased wound infection rates might examine one or several previously conducted studies. By analyzing a variable that had not been studied previously, such as the age of the patient, a secondary analysis might show a relationship to wound healing, especially for geriatric patients.

Meta-analysis also looks at previous studies. Brockopp and Hastings-Tolsma (2003) indicate that meta-analysis, through calculation of statistics, can help researchers establish the existence of bias and confounding variables in the cause-and-effect relationship identified in multiple studies. Polit and Beck (2006) suggest that a data set is "the total collection of data for all sample members for analysis" (p. 642). The data set analysis carried out as part of a meta-analysis is similar to that performed for individual studies through statistical tests. The key facet of meta-analysis is the application of statistics to multiple studies looking at the same phenomenon (Burns & Grove, 2009). Stated another way, meta-analysis for quantitative designs is intended to "to utilize statistical methods to merge the outcomes of independent projects" (Hopp and Rittenmeyer, 2012). Meta-analysis for quantitative designs focuses on statistical methods and is not to be confused with **meta-synthesis** of qualitative designs which focuses on individual studies which are pooled.

? **Think Outside the Box**

> If you have elected to use a nonexperimental design, how can you strengthen the confidence in the research project's findings?

Although secondary and meta-analyses are of particular importance for research utilization in EBP, caution should be taken when considering their findings. Not all studies focus on the same subject, and information may even be missing from some studies. Care should be taken before drawing conclusions or making generalizations in applying findings to specific populations because bias can result, especially in studies with small sample sizes. The researcher should keep in mind the adage that "one size does not fit all."

Time-Dimensional Design

When establishing a research project, attention must always be given to the dimension of time. The determination of when and how long data are to be collected is an essential component to any research design, and this process is termed **time-dimensional design**. If data have already been collected, then the study is considered to utilize a retrospective design. An example of a retrospective design would be that of a chart review. Perhaps a new procedure has been implemented to decrease length of stay (LOS). The nurse might go to the Medical Records department and conduct a chart review for the average LOS for patients who did not receive the new procedure versus those who did receive it.

A second type of time-dimensional design comprises a cross-sectional design. The cross-sectional design measures only what is currently in existence; it does not examine anything that happened in the past or future. An example of this design could be a retrospective chart review of lung cancer patients for the past five years to discover how long they had smoked cigarettes. Many cross-sectional studies are retrospective in nature, but they all collect data at a specific point in time.

The third type of time-dimensional design is the longitudinal study. As is implied by the name, a study with a longitudinal design relies on data that are collected at various intervals over time. The times for data collection may be short or long depending on the rate of change. This design is useful to examine changes that occur over time and assist in determining causality (Polit & Beck, 2008). Longitudinal designs are considered stronger than cross-sectional study designs because longitudinal designs allow for the possibility that changes and trends might emerge. However, longitudinal studies also face the extra danger of having subjects drop out over time, and they are generally more expensive to manage.

Each of the time-dimensional designs has its own set of advantages and disadvantages that must be considered by the researcher. In addition, the strengths and weaknesses of each study design must be considered before the results of the studies are applied to practice.

Quasi-Experimental Design

Given that randomization is often not possible in research studies, quasi-experimental design is the most frequently used quantitative research design. With this approach, the independent variable is still manipulated, but there is no randomization or control group. The purpose of quasi-experimental design is to examine causality, though it is acknowledged that this design is not as strong as the experimental design, which has a control group and randomization. Nevertheless, quasi-experimental design is considered stronger than descriptive design, and it is more practical when true experimental design is not possible.

Types of quasi-experimental design include (1) post-test only with nonequivalent groups, (2) one-group pre-test/post-test, (3) untreated control group with pre-test/post-test, (4) removal treatment and reversal treatment, (5) nonequivalent control group, and (6) time series. The two most commonly used designs—nonequivalent control group and time series—are discussed here.

The **nonequivalent control group** design (sometimes called a comparison group) compares two groups that are not randomized. The initial baseline measurement (O_1) is used to determine if the subjects assigned to groups are similar. A treatment/intervention (X) is applied, and then a second measurement (O_2) is performed to see if the outcome is a result of the treatment/intervention (**Figure 8-2**).

Using the prior example of wound care, all patients would be assigned to group 1 or group 2. A pre-test assessment would be conducted. The intervention (patient education program) would then be implemented. Each group would then be tested to see if its members experienced a decreased infection rate (outcome). When using this type of study design, the nurse researcher should keep in mind potential confounding factors such as the Hawthorne effect as well as the threat of history. History, in this instance, refers to some other variable that might have occurred. In the wound care experiment, an example of the history variable might be the patients who received additional instruction by the doctor's office staff prior to undergoing surgery or again after the educational program was administered.

The second quasi-experimental design to be discussed is the time-series design. This type of study may be conducted over a long period, in which case it is also called a longitudinal study. With a time-series design, participants are not randomized, nor is a control group used. Data are collected at various intervals prior to the treatment as well as after the treatment (see Figure 8-2). Returning to the wound care example, in a time-series design, the first observation might be

---

Figure 8-2

Quasi-experimental design examples.

Nonequivalent Control Group

$O_1 \quad X \quad O_2$ ①

$O_1 \quad O_2$ ②

Note: O_1 = Baseline measurement; X = Treatment/intervention; O_2 = Outcome

measurement.

Time Series (Simple)

$O_1 \quad O_2 \quad O_3 \quad X \quad O_4 \quad O_5 \quad O_6$

Note: O_1, O_2, O_3 = Baseline measurements at various levels; X = Treatment/intervention;

O_4, O_5, O_6 = Outcome measures at various intervals.

---

on days 2 and 3 postoperatively, with a subsequent observation being recorded on the day of discharge. The educational program would then be conducted. The next three measurements might be on days 5, 7, and 9 postoperatively.

A variable that should be considered as an alternative explanation for the outcome measurement within time-series studies is maturation. Maturation refers to change that occurs throughout the entire span of time that the experiment is conducted. It might be a result of the repetition of testing, which might influence the scores that follow. For instance, if the patients were tested about wound care knowledge prior to receiving the educational program, they might become aware of what was needed for wound care to prevent infection just because of the questions used to test their baseline knowledge.

? Think Outside the Box

Discuss how you would use the ranking of research designs' strength in evidence-based practice.

Another area of concern with the time-series design is the potential for attrition of subjects. Because the study occurs over time, subjects may drop out of the study for various reasons. As a result, the sample size may be too small when the study ends, causing the study's findings to not be generalizable to other situations or populations.

The two quasi-experimental designs discussed here offer a practical approach when an experimental design is not possible. Nurse researchers should be alert to the possible threats of the quasi-experimental design that can lead to other reasons for the study's outcomes.

Control

As indicated earlier in this text, control of variables is critical when the researcher is seeking to determine the extent of a cause-and-effect relationship for the treatment/intervention applied as part of a study. Randomization helps control extraneous variables, both internal and external, to a research project, especially when the study employs an experimental design.

In studies using nonexperimental and quasi-experimental designs, which do not have randomization or control groups, using subjects who are similar helps control extraneous variables that can influence the outcome. As a result, history, maturation, and attrition threats must be considered when designing the research project so as to maintain control. Variables can be controlled through the establishment of specific inclusion/exclusion criteria for selection of subjects, timing of test intervals, use of scripts for data collectors, and the setting in which the study is conducted.

Research Design, Quality Improvement Projects, and Root Cause Analysis

Care must be taken when designing quantitative research. Even though research and **quality improvement (QI) projects** or activities are focused on patient outcomes, they are different processes (Kring, 2008). QI results can provide direction for improving practice but are not necessarily considered true "scientific inquiry." For example, chart reviews may reveal a trend but do not inspire the same level of confidence as results produced from a quantitative retrospective research design. QI projects can and often do contribute additional evidence, and it may even give significance to previous findings. Nevertheless, research designs take a more rigorous approach toward producing results and have more significant implications for practice. Both research design and QI projects may have implications for evidence-based practice, however, and their relationship should be considered within the totality of quantitative research design.

Root cause analysis (RCA) began in 1949 when the U.S. military wanted to examine system and equipment failures. Other industries, such as the space, manufacturing, and automotive industries, then began to realize the importance of RCA (Dunn & Renner, 2012). Simply stated, RCA identifies whether a failure is due to system-related or human error. For instance, when a plane crashes, the RCA determines whether there was a system/equipment error or pilot error. In health care, RCAs are used to investigate adverse events or **sentinel events,** since the Joint Commission mandated the use of RCAs in 1997 (Agency for Healthcare Research and Quality [AHRQ], 2012). RCAs have a significant impact for designing research and QI projects to eliminate errors and provide safer health care to patients. Examples of errors can range from nurse staffing issues to incorrect dosage calculations, and from amputations of the wrong limb to lack of appropriate policies/procedures. Research design and QI projects can provide evidence for RCA and thus improve patient safety.

? **Think Outside the Box**   www

What could an RCA reveal about a patient who had the wrong leg amputated? What could be considered a system failure? What could be considered a personnel failure? What research design would be most appropriate to investigate this type of error?

Evidence-Based Considerations

Utilization of quantitative research design in EBP requires the nurse to be able to comprehend the various designs and understand both their benefits and their shortcomings. Whether the nurse is participating in research or is applying research findings in practice, the type of design is essential to guide clinical decision making. The concepts of randomization and control in quantitative research provide information about generalization of outcomes in experimental, nonexperimental, and quasi-experimental studies to current practice.

If a nurse wants to look at the relationship between an educational program and the rate of wound infections, a correlational design would be appropriate. In contrast, if a nurse wants to examine the effect of a wound care educational program in producing a decreased rate of wound infections, the appropriate quantitative design would be experimental or quasi-experimental. Use of a secondary analysis or meta-analysis is another way a nurse might use quantitative research to validate existing practice or the need to change practice.

Manipulation, control of variables, and randomization are essential components of quantitative research. Extraneous variables in the practice setting must be examined carefully so that the evidence obtained will be applicable to nursing practice. Thus, knowing whether the research design is experimental, quasi-experimental, or nonexperimental influences the strength and generalizability of a study's findings to the current practice being considered. This point is of particular significance when conducting a secondary analysis or meta-analysis of research for the purpose of making clinical decisions.

Quantitative research design and QI projects are important when examining evidence to improve practice. Nurses need to make sure they fully understand the distinctions between QI and quantitative research designs, as well as how both are relevant in EBP.

Summary Points

1. Quantitative research is often identified as corresponding with the traditional scientific method, which gathers data objectively in an organized method to allow findings to be generalized to other situations/populations.
2. A quantitative research design is an objective, systematic plan to gather data.
3. Characteristics of quantitative designs center on *why, where, who, what, when,* and *how* questions.
4. Quantitative research examines relationships for cause and effect in an experiment.
5. Manipulation of the independent variable, control of extraneous variables, and randomization are essential to quantitative research.
6. In comparative designs, there is no manipulation or control of the independent variable.
7. The most commonly used descriptive design is the correlational design, which examines relationships between two or more variables within a situation without knowing the reason why the relationship exists.
8. Correlational designs may be ex post facto, prospective, or predictive.
9. Experimental designs look for cause and effect (outcome).
10. Issues such as ethics, inability to manipulate all variables, feasibility, and the Hawthorne effect must be addressed when considering studies with experimental designs.
11. The most classic experimental design is the pre-test/post-test design.

12. The randomized controlled trial (RCT) is considered to be a true experimental design.
13. Two types of nonexperimental designs are used in evidence-based practice (EBP): secondary analysis and meta-analysis. Both look at previously completed studies and create data sets from those earlier studies to be analyzed in a different approach.
14. Quasi-experimental designs are used most frequently because the independent variable can still be manipulated even when no randomization or control group is possible.
15. The two most commonly used quasi-experimental designs are the nonequivalent control group and time-series designs.
16. The nonequivalent control group design compares two groups whose members are not randomized.
17. The time-series design is not randomized, and there is no control group. Data are gathered at various intervals.
18. Control of threats such as history, maturation, and attrition is of prime importance in quantitative designs and is of significance when making clinical decisions based on outcomes from quantitative research.
19. Understanding the implications for utilization of quantitative research in EBP requires a working knowledge of quantitative design.
20. Quality improvement projects and quantitative research are important in confirming evidence for EBP.
21. Root cause analysis (RCA) and quality improvement (QI) have a relationship with research design and EBP.

RED FLAGS

- For a study to be classified as an experimental (quantitative) design, the design must incorporate control, randomization, and an intervention.
- Experimental (quantitative) design is considered to be the strongest research design. Quasi-experimental (quantitative) design has less strength, and non-experimental (quantitative) design has the least strength.
- When a small sample size is used for a quantitative study, the results of the study need to be examined closely for their generalizability to other populations.
- Prospective designs are stronger than retrospective design formats.
- Control of variables is critical when results are related to cause and effect.
- A comparative design does not involve any manipulation or control of the independent variable.
- Sentinel/adverse events require a root cause analysis (RCA) to improve.

Multiple Choice Questions

1. Which of the following characteristics is not part of a quantitative research design?

   A. Randomization
   B. Manipulation
   C. Saturation
   D. Control

2. Which of the following is not an independent variable?

   A. Outcome
   B. Treatment
   C. Intervention
   D. Experiment

3. Quantitative research is often identified with which method of gathering data?

   A. Triangulation
   B. Saturation
   C. Ethnography
   D. Scientific

4. Nonexperimental designs generate _____ for _____ designs.

   A. Answers; quasi-experimental
   B. Questions; experimental
   C. Solutions; quantitative
   D. Problems; experimental

5. One of the most common and important characteristics of a quantitative design is

   A. The dependent variable.
   B. The independent variable.
   C. Control.
   D. The relationship.

6. Manipulation of which variable is connected to control?

   A. Independent
   B. Dependent
   C. Extraneous
   D. Attribute

7. Randomization helps to eliminate

   A. Confounding data.
   B. Ethics.
   C. Subjects.
   D. Bias.

8. Generalization can _____ a study.

    A. Weaken
    B. Strengthen
    C. Shorten
    D. Lengthen

9. A comparative design has

    A. No manipulation and control of the dependent variable.
    B. Only measurement of the dependent variable.
    C. No manipulation and control of the independent variable.
    D. Both B and C.

10. A correlational study looks at the

    A. Cause of two or more variables.
    B. Relationship of two or more variables.
    C. Effect of two or more variables.
    D. Both A and C.

11. Issues related to experimental design include

    A. Manipulation of all variables, ethics, and feasibility.
    B. The Hawthorne effect, ethics, and sample size.
    C. Treatments, interventions, and no manipulation of variables.
    D. Feasibility, the Hawthorne effect, and research questions.

12. An example of a randomized controlled trial (RCT) design is as follows (where R = randomization, O = measurement, and X = treatment):

    A. R   O   X   O
    B. O   X   O
    C. O   O   X   O   O
    D. O   O   O   X   O   O   O

13. Meta-analysis is the examination of multiple studies through statistical analysis to establish

    A. The nonexistence of bias.
    B. New data sets for analysis.
    C. The nonexistence of confounding variables.
    D. Correlation of the variables.

14. A quasi-experimental design is one in which

    A. The dependent variable is manipulated with randomization and a control group.
    B. The independent variable is manipulated with randomization and a control group.
    C. The independent variable is manipulated with no randomization and no control group.
    D. The dependent variable is manipulated with no randomization and no control group.

15. The initial baseline measurement in a nonequivalent control group is used to determine if the subjects assigned to the group are

    A. Different.

    B. Equal.

    C. Bonded.

    D. Similar.

16. The research design that collects data at various intervals is called a(n)

    A. Long study.

    B. Time-series study.

    C. Experimental study.

    D. Nonexperimental study.

17. An area of concern in a time-series design is

    A. Randomization.

    B. Control.

    C. Manipulation.

    D. Maturation.

18. Some ways of controlling variables for nonexperimental or quasi-experimental designs are

    A. Timing of test intervals and the setting.

    B. Randomization of subjects and control groups.

    C. Flexible inclusion and exclusion criteria.

    D. Control of history and maturation.

19. In evidence-based practice, a nurse using quantitative research for clinical decision making must be most knowledgeable about how

    A. To calculate statistics.

    B. To write research reports.

    C. The study design applies to practice.

    D. To design a research study.

20. Using research in practice requires the nurse to be most aware of

    A. Limited funding.

    B. Generalizability of the results to current practice.

    C. Exclusion of subjects.

    D. The credentials of the researcher.

21. Quality improvement (QI) projects are considered

    A. The same as scientific inquiry.

    B. Different from scientific inquiry.

    C. To focus on only patient satisfaction.

    D. A rigorous approach for research.

22. Root cause analysis (RCA) had its origin in

    A.   Dental industry.

    B.   Mechanical engineering.

    C.   Military industry.

    D.   Business industry.

23. The Joint Commission mandated RCAs in

    A.   1967

    B.   1977

    C.   1987

    D.   1997

Discussion Questions

1. You are a nurse in a pre-op holding area in which all patients are classi-fied as "nothing by mouth" (NPO) after midnight to prevent possible aspiration. You wonder why that policy is necessary, and you and a surgi-cal team want to design a research project to investigate the potential for providing at least some liquid nourishment to pre-op patients. The team decides to do a two-group post-test only design.
   a. Using the example above (all surgical patients being NPO after midnight), how would you and the surgical team conduct a meta-analysis?
   b. Using a nonequivalent control group design in the NPO scenario, explain how this design would be constructed.
2. A medication error resulted in a sentinel event on your unit. How would you go about implementing a root cause analysis (RCA)?

Suggested Readings

www

Bott, M., & Endacott, R. (2005). Clinical research: Quantitative data collection and analysis. *Intensive & Critical Care Nursing, 21*(3), 187–193.

Chulay, M. (2006). Good research ideas for clinicians. *AACN Advanced Critical Care, 17*(3), 253–265.

Freshwater, D. (2005). Integrating qualitative and quantitative research methods: Trend or foe? *Journal of Research in Nursing, 10*(3), 337–338.

Kinn, S., & Curzio, J. (2005). Integrating qualitative and quantitative research methods. *Journal of Research in Nursing, 10*(3), 317–336.

Onwuegbuzie, A., & Leech, N. (2005). Taking the "Q" out of research: Teaching research methodology courses without the divide between quantitative and qualitative paradigms. *Quality & Quantity, 39*(3), 267–295.

Walker, W. (2005). The strengths and weaknesses of research designs involving quantitative measures. *Journal of Research in Nursing, 10*(5), 571–573.

Yoder, L. (2005). Evidence-based practice: The time is now! *MedSurg Nursing, 14*(2), 91–92.

References

Agency for Healthcare Research and Quality (AHRQ). (2012). *Patient safety primers: Root cause analysis.* Retrieved from http://psnet.ahrq.gov/primer.aspx?primerID=10

Brink, P. J., & Wood, M. J. (2001). *Basic steps in planning nursing research from question to proposal* (5th ed.). Sudbury, MA: Jones and Bartlett.

Brockopp, D. Y., & Hastings-Tolsma, M. T. (2003). *Fundamentals of nursing research* (3rd ed.). Sudbury, MA: Jones and Bartlett.

Burns, N., & Grove, S. K. (2009). *The practice of nursing research: Appraisal, synthesis, and generation of evidence* (6th ed.). St. Louis, MO: Saunders Elsevier.

Centers for Disease Control and Prevention (CDC). (n.d.). *The Tuskegee timeline.* Retrieved from http://www.cdc.gov/tuskegee/timeline.htm

Dunn, E. J., & Renner, C. (2012). *Root cause analysis: Faculty development* [Presentation slides]. Retrieved from www.med.cornell.edu/risk-management/best_practices/Root CauseAnalysis.ppt

Fain, J. A. (2009). *Reading, understanding, and applying nursing research* (3rd ed.). Philadelphia, PA: F. A. Davis.

Hopp, L., & Rittenmeyer, L. (2012). *Introduction to evidence-based practice: A practical guide for nursing.* Philadelphia, PA: F. A. Davis.

Kring, D. L. (2008). Research and quality improvement: Different processes, different evidence. *MedSurg Nursing, 17*(3), 162–169.

Polit, D. F., & Beck, C. T. (2006). *Essentials of nursing research methods, appraisal and utilization* (6th ed.). Philadelphia, PA: Lippincott Williams & Wilkins.

Polit, D. F., & Beck, C. T. (2008). *Nursing research: Generating and assessing evidence for nursing practice* (8th ed.). Philadelphia, PA: Wolters Kluwer/Lippincott Williams & Wilkins.

Chapter 9

Qualitative and Mixed Research Methods

Donna Scott Tilley and JoAnn Long

Chapter Objectives

At the conclusion of this chapter, the learner will be able to

1. Define qualitative and mixed methods research
2. Describe the various qualitative research methodologies
3. Describe the various mixed method research methodologies
4. Discuss analysis of qualitative and mixed method study data
5. Contrast the goals and distinctive features of qualitative and mixed methods research
6. Discuss the advantages of qualitative and mixed methods research
7. Discuss issues of methodological rigor in qualitative and mixed methods research

Key Terms

➤ Action research

➤ Bracketing

➤ Case study

➤ Content analysis

➤ Convergent validity

➤ Ethnography

➤ Grounded theory

➤ Mixed method research

➤ Nesting

➤ Phenomenology

➤ Purposeful sampling

➤ Qualitative research

➤ Rigor

➤ Saturation

Introduction

Humans are by nature complex. Much of what drives human decision making and behavior is difficult to understand, much less measure. Thus, understanding the complex nature of humans is a challenging task. **Qualitative research** methods are based on the assumption that truth is dynamic and offers an avenue for exploration of elements of humanity that are not feasible using quantitative research methods. Mixed method research offers a diverse approach to research which values and draws upon both objective and subjective knowledge. This chapter will present an overview of qualitative research methods and mixed method research. This text will discuss the history of qualitative research in nursing; compare quantitative and qualitative research paradigms; present an overview of the most commonly used qualitative designs in nursing research; discuss sampling, data collection, and data analysis for both qualitative and mixed method research; and guide the reader in the application to one's nursing practice.

Qualitative Research

The word "qualitative" means that one is examining the quality of something rather than the quantity, amount, intensity, or frequency. Examining the quality of something implies a level of subjectivity. Denzin and Lincoln (1998) stated that the qualitative researcher stresses the socially constructed nature of reality, the intimate relationship between the research and the subject of the research, and the situational factors that shape inquiry. Thus, the social experience shapes the meaning of reality.

Nursing has traditionally focused on the person as a whole. This holistic approach to the person lends itself well to qualitative methods. As a result, qualitative methods have become increasingly common in nursing research. Qualitative methods continue to gain recognition as being valuable to the science of nursing, as qualitative studies contribute to areas in which little research has been done or variables for quantitative research have yet to be defined. With the increased use of qualitative methods, efforts to design qualitative methodologies that offer holistic understanding of persons while still offering reliability and validity are also improving.

A Brief History of Qualitative Methods

Research, as we know it, was founded in the natural sciences with a positivist approach. Simply stated, the positivist approach requires objectivity and neutrality to test theories and hypotheses. The underlying assumption is that truth is something that can be known.

Alternatively, qualitative research methods are rooted in the disciplines of sociology, anthropology, and philosophy with the underlying assumption that truth can only be approximated. In the 1920s and 1930s, social scientists such as Mead (1935) and Malinowski (1922) put structure to what had previously been an unstructured process of qualitative research. Researchers at the Chicago School, in adopting and formalizing processes of qualitative social study, gave credibility to this new qualitative paradigm of research (Holloway & Wheeler, 2010).

In the 1960s, qualitative research saw increased use when new qualitative approaches, such as grounded theory (Glaser & Strauss, 1967) were introduced. In the 1970s, it was increasingly common to see journals publishing exclusively qualitative research reports. Nurse researchers began adopting the qualitative paradigm to inform their practice. Today, there are well over 100 journals that publish only qualitative research, many of which are specific to nursing. Reputable research journals worldwide routinely publish research drawn from both the quantitative and qualitative paradigms.

Comparing Qualitative and Quantitative Methods

It is not uncommon for both researchers and consumers of research to have strong opinions about the value of quantitative or qualitative methods. Those who favor quantitative methods may dismiss qualitative studies as lacking reliability, validity, and structure. Those who favor qualitative methods may claim that quantitative studies are shallow or don't paint a complete and accurate picture of a phenomenon. In truth, both types of research have great scientific merit.

Morse (1991) identified three features that distinguish the qualitative research approach from the quantitative approach. First, qualitative research approaches phenomena from the "emic" perspective.

That is, the perspective of the participant provides the source of meaning rather than the perspective of the researcher. Second, qualitative research utilizes a holistic approach to the participant. The participant brings values and life experiences that affect his or her perspective on the phenomena of interest. Although quantitative methods often seek to minimize the impact of these values and experiences, qualitative methods embrace these individual differences. Finally, qualitative methods are inductive and interactive rather than deductive. Quantitative methods require that the researcher not deviate in the data collection process from one subject to another; qualitative methods allow the researcher to adapt his or her inquiry as understanding of the phenomena grows.

The consumer of research may also note that research participants are described differently in these two types of studies. Quantitative researchers typically refer to the individual of interest in a study as a subject. Qualitative researchers may refer to the individual of interest in a study as an informant or a participant.

Qualitative and quantitative methods differ significantly in acceptable sample size. Sample sizes in qualitative studies are generally smaller than in quantitative studies. Because the focus of the qualitative data is on the quality of the data collected, each participant is a source of a large volume of data. Thus, a smaller sample size is reasonable and common.

The differences between qualitative and quantitative methods are significant, but, in many cases, combining both methods is a viable option for researchers. A researcher might choose to combine methods in order to supplement the data, validate the data, or determine in pilot studies the best approach to data collection with a larger group.

Approaches to Qualitative Research

There are many rich and varied designs from which to choose when planning a qualitative study. The more commonly used designs will be discussed here. Many qualitative designs share common features, particularly with regard to sampling strategies, data collection techniques, and data analysis.

Case Study

A **case study** is an in-depth examination of individuals or groups of people. Case study may be used when insight into a unique situation is needed (Rosenberg & Yates, 2007). For example, a researcher interested in end-of-life issues could conduct a case study of a person recently diagnosed with terminal cancer. The investigator might choose to conduct a case study of nurses at a hospice agency. An examiner might also choose to examine a series of similar cases in order to inquire about the phenomenon, population, or general condition. This would be called a "collective case study" (Stake, 1998).

The researcher engaging in a case study is typically seeking to understand what is common about a case as well as what is unique about a case (Stake, 1998). Stake stated that in order to fully understand commonalities and unique features of a case, the researcher is likely to explore case features such as the following:

- The nature of the case
- The historic background of the case
- The physical setting
- Other contexts, including economic, political, legal, and aesthetic
- Other cases through which this case is recognized
- Those informants through whom the case is known

A case study might include data such as temperatures or pain ratings (quantitative), along with data about the person's experience of pain and discomfort (qualitative). Together, such data paint a more complete picture of the disease experience.

Data analysis in case studies, as with other qualitative methods, involves **content analysis**, in which the researcher looks for patterns and themes. For example, the researcher might identify the themes of "social isolation" and "mistrust and jealousy" in a case study of an adult male who has abused his spouse (Scott Tilley, Rugari, & Walker, 2008).

The readers or consumers of a case study should expect to be able to apply the findings from a case to their practice when the researcher has clearly delineated the case by defining the object of the study, identified patterns of data, and developed generalizations or assertions about the case. They should avoid applying findings from a case to their practice when the case is single or is a poor representation of a population, or when a single case as a negative example is applied to general populations. For example, a single case about intractable pain that is poorly managed should not be used to guide policy. Conversely, several cases illustrating effective management of pain through the use of guided imagery might well be used to guide policy about the use of guided imagery in a hospice agency.

Ethnography

Ethnography involves collection and analysis of data about groups. The ethnographer seeks to understand the culture of the group or to gain an understanding of the values, norms, and rules that characterize the group. For ethnography, groups of interest may be organizational, experiential, ethnic, and geographic. Ethnography is an excellent way to understand the norms of groups of interest to nursing. For example, there are outstanding ethnographies of organizations such as groups of patients or caregivers with specific illnesses (e.g., HIV and AIDS), specific healthcare delivery settings (e.g., nursing homes, critical care units).

Data collection for ethnography is usually accomplished through reading of documents within the culture, conducting interviews, observation, or a combination of all these methods. Key informants or people who are most knowledgeable about the culture are usually a primary source of interview data.

The reader or consumer of studies based on this method might find practice applications if the ethnography informs one how to:

- Behave when with a certain group
- Approach a person within the group
- Recognize and respond to needs of a person within the group

For example, a nurse might find ethnographic data of the experiential group of parents of children with Cystic Fibrosis (CF) helpful in the provision of care to a child with the disease. This ethnography might provide the nurse with insight about the needs of the parents, how the parents can access assistance within the community of parents of children with CF, and what experiences and feelings are common among the parents of children with CF.

Grounded Theory

Grounded theory is a general methodology for developing new theory that is inherent in data systematically gathered and analyzed (Denzin & Lincoln, 1998). There is an explicit expectation of theory development and theory verification in this method.

? Think Outside the Box   www

Carefully consider the idea of saturation. Discuss how you can determine that saturation has occurred within a research project.

Data analysis in grounded theory is systematic and deliberate. The process begins with open coding, which involves categorizing the information and examining properties and dimensions of the data (Strauss & Corbin, 1998). The next step is axial coding, in which the researcher identifies relationships between categories and subcategories. Selective coding, the final step in data analysis, is the integration of concepts around a core category and the filling in of categories in need of further development and refinement (Strauss & Corbin, 1998). **Saturation** is a concept of relevance in data analysis as well as data collection, as the researcher continues data analysis until no new codes or categories emerge.

The final product of the grounded theory method is a theory that is established in data about the phenomenon of interest. The consumer of grounded theory research could expect to apply the model while developing interventions for a population. For example, reading a grounded theory about the attachment patterns of elderly adults might guide the nurse who is assisting a family in relocating their aging parent from a home environment to an assisted-living environment.

Narrative Inquiry

Narrative inquiry, sometimes known as storytelling, is a qualitative research method that seeks to understand the meaning that participants ascribe to their experiences. Telling the story of their experience, say with illness or provision of health care, allows the participant to reflect on the experience from their own point of view to inform others about the experience. Meanings are derived by both the participant and the researcher. Narrations can come from patients, lay or professional care providers, parents, or other parties with stories that can serve to inform practice.

Phenomenology

As the name implies, **phenomenology** is the study of events and trends from a human perspective. Phenomenology seeks to develop an understanding of lived experience. The first-hand report or description of one's experience of the phenomenon is central to understanding the phenomenon. The meaning one creates in the world is socially constructed and is rooted in the experiences of the person.

Data collection in phenomenology is done through unstructured interviews and inductive analysis. The guiding question in a phenomenological study typically centers on the essence, structure, or lived experience of a phenomenon. Data analysis occurs simultaneously with data collection. The researcher is identifying patterns and themes and developing new questions as data emerges.

The reader or consumer of a phenomenological study can use the findings to understand the experiences of clients who are experiencing a similar event. For example, reading a phenomenological study about the lived experience of a victim of sexual assault might assist the emergency department nurse in communicating more effectively and providing meaningful education to a client who has been sexually assaulted.

Sampling Strategies in Qualitative Research

In contrast with quantitative research, which requires a careful sample plan that is designed before the study commences and seeks homogeneity of subjects, the sampling strategy in qualitative research is often an intra-project process which seeks to maximize variation of participants, saturation of data, and verification of data (Strauss & Corbin, 1998). Each of these components will be discussed in detail.

Researchers in qualitative studies often sample for variation. Even when a homogeneous sample is sought, for instance patients with breast cancer, researchers often seek informants with slightly different experiences who can provide diverse perspectives. Sometimes also called criterion sampling, **purposeful sampling** is designed to select participants who are able to inform the researcher on elements of the phenomenon that remain poorly understood (Strauss & Corbin, 1998).

Sample sizes are rarely decided upon before commencing a qualitative study. Rather, a reasonable sample size may be estimated based on similar studies. Sampling is continued until data saturation is reached. The qualitative researcher knows that data saturation has been attained when no new themes or concepts arise, or there is redundancy of data. Consumers of qualitative research may perceive that a small sample size in a qualitative study is a serious limitation of the study. In truth, sample sizes in qualitative studies are often expected to be small. There are vast amounts of data generated in a qualitative study and analyzing data from hundreds of participants may not be feasible or necessary. Given the longer time researchers often spend with participants, data saturation may be reached with a small number of subjects. Depending on the study design, goal of the study, phenomena of interest, and other factors, a reasonable sample size for a qualitative study might be as small as five or six participants.

To verify data, qualitative researchers will often seek out negative cases as they near completion of data collection. This is similar to the notion of purposeful sampling but the researcher seeks participants or cases in which the emerging theory or emerging interpretations of data can be challenged. Seeking negative cases is both a sampling strategy and a method of assuring rigor in qualitative research.

Approaches to Qualitative Data Collection

The most common approaches to data collection in qualitative studies are interviews and observations. Interviews may occur once or be done in a series.

In general, interviews are not neutral in nature. The interviewer naturally introduces a variable into interviews by virtue of his or her race, class, ethnicity, gender, education, and experience. Structured interviews may follow a script of questions established prior to beginning data collection. Structured interviews allow little room for variation in response. The interviewer must remain neutral in the structured interview. The semi-structured interview is commonly used in qualitative research. Using a semi-structured interview, the researcher uses a list of fairly broad questions with prompts. Rather than being an interested listener, the interviewer may engage in the conversation more than in a structured interview.

Interview of groups, or focus groups, require a researcher who is experienced in the conduct of focus groups. Like individual interviews, group interviews can be structured or semi-structured. Group interviews are not meant to replace individual interviews. They are an alternative way to collect data and should be conducted only when the question is appropriate or as a way to determine a direction for semi-structured interview questions for individuals.

Observation is an acceptable but less common method of data collection in qualitative research. Elements that may be observed can include:

- Appearance
- Clothing
- Interactions
- Roles
- Exits
- Routines
- Rituals
- Temporal elements
- Organization
- Interpretations

Bracketing is a concept common to all qualitative methods, though all researchers may not describe using this process in their study. Bracketing is also known as phenomenological reduction. In bracketing, the researcher identifies his or her own personal biases and beliefs about the phenomenon and sets them aside in order to fully understand the experience of the informants. Bracketing typically commences during data collection and continues through the data analysis process. For example, researchers interested in the phenomenon of preconception health practices of women in abusive relationships would likely bracket by making a conscious decision to temporarily suspend their beliefs and attitudes about how women should plan for pregnancy as well as what they believe about the experience of being in an abusive relationship. They would make a decision to be open to what the participants had to say about this phenomenon without making pre-judgments or assumptions about the phenomenon.

Approaches to Qualitative Data Analysis

Qualitative data analysis is often a tedious and time-consuming process. With most qualitative methods, the data collection and data analysis processes are occurring simultaneously. As new data evolve, new questions emerge. This is part of the reason for the lack of structure in interview guides.

Although many qualitative researchers prefer to analyze data by hand, there are many software programs available to assist in the organization and coding of data. Data collection to saturation implies a level of data analysis as data collection occurs.

From the brief descriptions of data analysis in the methods previously described, one can see that qualitative data analysis can be quite complex. While quantitative data analysis usually involves numbers and statistics, qualitative data analysis involves deep examination of large volumes of written data.

The qualitative research methods of grounded theory, phenomenology, and ethnography require specific steps in data analysis. Other qualitative methods have no specific "rules" for the analysis of data. In such cases, a researcher might simply state that content analysis was conducted. Content analysis is a generic term for the process of data being analyzed and categories of data being created by experts.

Methodological Rigor in Qualitative Research

Both qualitative and quantitative research methods require the researcher to strive for **rigor**, or the criteria for trustworthiness of data and interpretation of data. The major methods for ensuring rigor are intricately linked with reliability and validity checks. The four criteria for rigor as presented by Lincoln and Guba (1985) include (a) credibility, (b) transferability, (c) dependability, and (d) conformability. Lincoln and Guba (1985) provided pioneer work in the area of qualitative research, particularly in the area of methodological rigor. A discussion follows on how each criterion can be achieved to establish the trustworthiness of a study.

Credibility, or the truth value of data and data analysis, can be achieved in a proposed study through several methods. First, when possible, the data should be taken back to subjects to ensure accuracy. Upon coding of data, the coded data can be checked with available participants. Additionally, coded data can be reviewed by experts in both the area of research and in the method used for the study. These checks usually consist of validation of data, validation of findings, and checking of interpretations.

Transferability refers to the applicability of findings to other populations in different contexts. Often, this is accomplished by providing a thorough description of the sample, setting, and data in the report to allow the reader to determine the transferability of the study's findings.

Dependability in qualitative research can also be described as auditability. If other researchers can follow the investigator's decisions throughout the study and come to similar conclusions, the study is auditable (Lincoln & Guba, 1985). Thus, an audit trail also provides an element of rigor to any study. The audit trail documents the development of the project and provides an adequate amount of evidence for interested parties to reconstruct the process by which the investigators reached their conclusions (Morse, 1998).

Confirmability represents freedom from bias, or neutrality (Lincoln & Guba, 1985). It is important to analyze data in a way that keeps researcher biases, assumptions, and perspectives separate. These elements should be clearly identified early in the proposal process. Reviewing the analyzed data with informants or study participants and review by experts also serves to mitigate the effects of researcher bias.

Although there are many ways to establish the quality of qualitative data, researchers can select the appropriate criteria for the topic under investigation. It is not necessary for all of these criteria to be incorporated into each study project. Application of any research results to practice, whether qualitative or quantitative, must be considered in light of the study's reliability, validity, and generalizability.

Understanding and Using Qualitative Study Results

There is virtually no area within nursing that does not lend itself to qualitative study. Nursing practice should be guided by nursing theory that is solidly grounded in research data. Qualitative studies are often the first step in the development of a theoretical framework for a phenomenon that has not been fully explored. Andrews and Waterman (2005) collected interview and observation data using the grounded theory approach in their study about how hospital-based staff used vital signs and the Early Warning Score to predict physiologic deterioration in clients. The authors reported that quantifiable evidence is the most effective means of referring patients to doctors and improving communication between professionals. The authors concluded that the Early Warning Score leads to successful referral of patients by providing an agreed-upon framework for assessment, increasing confidence in the use of medical language, and empowering nurses.

Qualitative research affords an opportunity to explore human issues that have previously been understood by way of assumption or simply not understood. For example, the high turnover and burnout rate of nursing staff has historically been assumed to be a function of long hours, physically strenuous work, and lack of power. The combined qualitative and quantitative studies of Cohen-Katz, Wiley, Capuano, Baker, and Shapiro (2004) have illuminated the causes of nursing burnout and led to system-wide changes to help nurses manage stress and burnout.

Qualitative studies often offer immediate clinical applicability. These studies are a source of rich descriptions of a wide range of physical and psychosocial experiences of healthcare consumers. By gaining a deeper understanding of those experiences, nurses can counsel, plan interventions, and develop programs to meet the needs of clients in similar conditions.

A study to describe the experience of managing lymphedema in breast cancer survivors provides an example (Fu, 2005). A descriptive phenomenological method was used to explore how 12 breast cancer survivors managed lymphedema in their daily lives. Findings of the study provided an insightful alternative to the compliance approach to lymphedema management. Instead of merely evaluating breast cancer survivors' degree of compliance with treatment, the author suggested that researchers and practitioners should also assess the impact of the presence or absence of the women's intentions on lymphedema management.

Qualitative research brings increased knowledge to the evidence-based practice of nursing. Qualitative research methods are often used to develop theories needed to guide future quantitative studies. Qualitative studies can illuminate issues that are poorly or inaccurately understood. Finally, qualitative studies often offer immediate clinical applicability and can guide teaching and practice.

Mixed Method Research

Broadly defined, **mixed method research** is a combination of quantitative and qualitative research methods and techniques for collecting and analyzing data which together make possible an increase in the understanding to be gained from the research data (Creswell, Klassen, Plano Clark, & Klegg Smith, 2010). This form of research is also referred to in the literature by several other names—multimethod, triangulated, and integrated designs.

Mixed method research is often possible within the clinical arena. For example, nurses may believe that the dryness of quantitative research needs to be tempered with the "touchy-feely" aspects of qualitative research. Within the realm of evidence-based nursing practice, a nurse might realize that the time spent in the surgical holding area causes increased stress to the patients. A study could collect physiologic data related to stress, such as blood pressures and time in the surgical holding area, as well as observed signs of stress and emotional data (e.g., verbal comments about the experience while in the surgical holding area awaiting the surgical procedure). The conclusions resulting from the collection of both types of data would reveal each aspect of the individual's experiences while in the surgical holding area. This mixed method study would provide needed data to facilitate the provision of evidence-based nursing practice within the institution.

Quantitative research, which is considered the foundational method, permits the researcher to make inferences only about the data that are being examined. These studies, however, are not designed to detect contextual nuances, which may produce a biased understanding of the variables being studied. By comparison, qualitative research spreads a much broader net, allowing for in-depth examination of elements of a phenomenon not considered when research is conducted using quantitative methods. Because both quantitative and qualitative methods have strengths and weaknesses, neither can perfectly establish the full truth about phenomena of interest to nursing (Polit & Beck, 2011). Joining methods is done to reduce the biases associated with one design alone, provide insight into the complexity of the problem under study, and introduce rigor into the study design (Creswell et al., 2010). This form of research entails more than just the combination of two or more methods in a single study. Multimethod (mixed method) research implies the integration of both numbers and narrative, pragmatically offering enhanced results in terms of quality and span (Shaw, Connelley, & Zecevic, 2010). An example of what is meant by multimethod research can be seen when a questionnaire includes both closed-ended questions (numbers) to provide quantitative data and open-ended questions (narrative) that require qualitative analysis.

Simply stated, mixed method design views both quantitative and qualitative research as useful and important, while avoiding the constraints that might hamper a study carried out using a single research methodology (Chow, Quine, & Li, 2010). Researchers must carefully consider each of the different pieces to determine the optimal method for addressing the research problem identified.

? Think Outside the Box

Carefully consider the idea of mixed method studies. Which elements would need to be present to reflect effective use of quantitative methods in a qualitative research project? Explain your answer.

As the field of research has advanced, the use of mixed method has sometimes been referred to as "**action research**" and/or "participatory research." It is seen as a research technique that may be useful in the implementation of evidence-based practice (Munten, van den Bogaard, Cox, Garretsen, & Bongers, 2010). This form of research may be employed to facilitate a change in strategy based on feedback about what is being observed in real time (Goodnough, 2008; Ponic, Reid, & Frisby, 2010). With the advancement of mixed method research attention must be given to the optimal avenue to get at the information being sought to address the identified problem and/or challenge.

Components of Mixed Method Procedures

In using mixed method procedures, the researcher attempts to blend a combination of methods (qualitative and quantitative) that have complementary strong points, while defusing the non-overlapping weaknesses. Bliss (2001) has stated, "A common misconception about mixed method research is that it requires a blending of contradictory or competing research paradigms" (p. 331). This view is also supported by Johnson and Onwuegbuzie (2004): "Mixed methods research is an attempt to legitimate the use of multiple approaches in answering research questions, rather than restricting or constraining researchers' choices (i.e., it rejects dogmatism)" (p. 17).

Although quantitative and qualitative methods each have an established focus, the two are neither contradictory nor competing. Within the delivery of the methodology, the two research designs are frequently meshed within the sampling, data collection, and analysis aspects of the research project. Although these aspects are the current levels, the process does not restrict the versatility or variety of the potential combinations within the two methodologies. Bliss (2001) has noted that "mixed method research seems to offer an opportunity to deepen our insights, sharpen our thinking, develop sensitive methods, and accelerate our advances" (p. 331). By allowing the researcher to identify a combination of methods, this process merges the best of both worlds of research to address the identified healthcare problem in the optimal manner available to the profession. The primary restriction on the joining of the methodologies is the obstruction occurring through lack of vision and risk taking on the part of the researcher.

According to Creswell, Fetters, and Ivankova (2004), mixed method (multimethod) research possesses the potential for rigor, methodologic effectiveness, and investigation within the primary care setting. Even though rigidity is not a problem within this kind of research, the aspects of each methodology employed must still be carefully considered and weighted by the researcher. Within any of the research designs, each method has identified strengths and limitations. As a researcher tries to maximize the complementary points while modifying the limitations, certain concerns emerge to be considered.

According to Patton (1990), one of the main advantages of using the mixed method approach to research is the idea of triangulation. This principle states that the validity of the results from the use of various research approaches determines the appropriateness of the resulting outcomes of the analysis. A mixed method design allows for the utilization of words, pictures, and narrative within the data collection process. Each of these qualitative aspects of the study augments the data provided via the statistical process. Numbers provide the precision, while the words, pictures, and narrative supply the textural aspects of the experience.

As a result of having this intensity of data available for data analysis of the event, an extensive and more comprehensive array of research questions and/or hypotheses can be answered. Put simply, the researcher is not limited regarding the breadth of the questions to be searched within the study. Because both quantitative and qualitative aspects of the issue are being addressed through the mixed methods, the research team draws from the different designs to develop the optimal research project to address the identified problem.

An example of how the use of mixed methodologies uncovers perceptions that might otherwise be missed is illustrated in the work published by Chen and Goodson (2009), who studied barriers to adopting genomics into public health education. On the one hand, qualitative data were collected from a small number (n = 24) of public health educators through personal interviews. Quantitative data, on the other hand, were collected using a large (n = 1,607), web-based survey method. The combined data gathered via the two methods highlighted barriers that extended beyond a lack of knowledge to more nuanced and complex issues of incompatibility of the individual's personal ethics and beliefs about genomics as factors in the adoption of genomics into public health education.

An additional strength visualized by the use of a mixed methodology for a research project relates to the enthusiasm of the evidence. This resulting power from the in-depth evidence comes about from the triangulation (convergence and corroboration) of the results identified (Johnson, n.d.). Because the evidence is managed through several different processes, the truth of the results may be strengthened.

A further strength associated with use of mixed method strategies can be seen when complementary insights and perceptions arise that might have been missed if only one research methodology were employed. The use of both quantitative and qualitative methodology allows the researcher to pull together a wider and deeper understanding about the identified research problem, as it is considered from multiple viewpoints.

Mixed method strategies are not without limitations, however. When both quantitative and qualitative methods are employed, the researcher must be well versed in both methodologies, especially if the two methods are managed concurrently. If the researcher does not feel competent to implement both methods, a research team may be required to complete the process effectively. The combination of the two methods should not be engaged in haphazardly. When this strategy is selected for implementation, care must be given to learning about the various methods and tactics to allow for the successful incorporation of the necessary approaches. Mixed methodology research can also be especially expensive to complete due to the use of teams, and it can result in additional time-consuming steps.

When an investigator elects to use this methodology, rationales for the decisions made must be documented and supported. These rationales need to be based on a thorough understanding of the relevant characteristics of both the quantitative and qualitative methodologies. Clear justification for the selection of a mixed method approach to the research problem must be provided to ensure that the research community comprehends the reasons for the decisions. These rationales are most often cited in the introduction section of the study report, the study aims discussion, or the overview of the section on methods to be used. As a researcher initiates this discussion concerning the rationales, the priority of the data collection process must be one key aspect that is presented clearly and concisely. This dialogue addresses the question of whether the quantitative and qualitative data are both emphasized equally. Regardless of the direction a researcher elects to go with the prioritization of the data, understandable and succinct logic for the choice should be carefully and thoroughly documented within the project.

Creswell et al. (2004) have elaborated on the labor-intensive process needed for the involvement of multiple points of data collection and analysis. This process should not be seen as an easier way of arriving at results but rather as a process for obtaining richer and more thorough information about the phenomenon under investigation. Johnson and Onwuegbuzie (2004) contend that the fundamental piece driving this process should be the research question or identified problem. From the identified research problem, a researcher ought to be free to select those research methods that best address the research questions, thereby taking the best opportunity to obtain meaningful answers. If a single research design is considered the best option, then a researcher should utilize that design methodology. When the research problem is viewed as progressively complex, however, all avenues of research methodology should be contemplated to identify the best manner to successfully gain a thorough understanding of the phenomenon.

Types of Mixed Method Strategies

As researchers conceptualize using both quantitative and qualitative methodologies, at least three aspects of this process need to be considered: implementation, prioritization, and integration Each of these three aspects results in one of two subtypes of mixed method models— within-stage or across-stage methods. Within-stage methods reflect the use of quantitative and qualitative approaches within one or more stages of the research process. An example of this method would be the inclusion of both open-ended questions and closed-ended questions on the same tool for administration at the same time. Across-stage mixed method approaches involve mixing the two research designs transversely between at least two of the stages within the research endeavor. Returning to the example given earlier concerning the surgical holding room, the use of physiologic data collected while the individual is in the holding area, followed by development of a narrative regarding how the experience was perceived after the surgical process, is an example of the use of across-stage mixed methods. With this approach, the data are not collected at the same time but rather data collection at each stage builds on data collection from the other stages.

In addressing the implementation question, the principal decision relates to whether the two methods—quantitative and qualitative— will be executed at the same time or sequentially. The research question aids in this choice. At times, the information discovered within one of the methods is perceived as a valuable foundation for the gathering of the data within the following method. For example, to determine the extent of research used within an acute care facility, researchers could conduct focus groups with a select group of nurses to determine perceived barriers to the use of research. Based on the data collected via the focus groups, a questionnaire could be developed and given to all staff nurses to determine their level of agreement with the information identified by the focus group members. In this scenario, the qualitative data results and analysis are seen as critical forces determining the data to be collected within the quantitative piece of the project. When neither type of data is needed to drive the data collection, quantitative and qualitative data can be collected concurrently. The surgical holding area example could be considered from this viewpoint. If the nurse collected physiologic data of blood pressures, observation of stressed behaviors, and time in the surgical holding area, while also questioning the individual about his or her perceptions of being in the holding area, the data would be collected concurrently. The determination of the appropriateness of this implementation comes directly from the identified research problem and resulting research questions and hypothesis.

If the decision is to conduct both the quantitative and qualitative data collection aspects at the same time, the process tends to be used to confirm, cross-validate, or corroborate findings within a single study (Creswell, 2003). Even when the two methods are conducted simultaneously, the question concerning how the information will be delivered must still be answered. If one method is embedded into the other method, then the process is termed "**nesting**," where the less predominant method is implanted into the other method.

An example of nesting would be the inclusion of open-ended questions at the conclusion of a previously validated quantitative tool. An advantage of using concurrent design for the mixed method process is the shortened data collection time period. Because all of the data are collected at one phase, the expense and time allocation can be reduced.

Within the concurrent implementation of the methodology, each piece of data is weighted equally within the data analysis phase. That is, for concurrent implementation, neither quantitative nor qualitative data are awarded a higher priority relative to the other; each aspect is judged on its own merits. Within this approach to mixed methods research, data integration begins during the data collection phase and continues through the data analysis phase and into the data interpretation phase. The data are interconnected for the initiation of the research process. When concurrent processing is selected for the research project, the investigator must be competent in both methodologies. This proficiency in both methods is imperative, because the researcher must ensure that the protocols for the quantitative and qualitative processes are appropriately carried out at each juncture of the research process.

Data Collection Procedures

In research methods of all types, the collection of data refers to information collected and organized by the researcher. Research data are collected in an effort to measure specific variables that are relevant to the study (Macnee, 2004).

One often thinks first of data taking the form of numbers or statistics. Many preliminary steps must occur prior to the collection of such data in quantitative research. Polit and Beck (2008) describe the data collection plan in quantitative research as including the following steps:

1. Determining the data that need to be gathered
2. Considering the type of measurement to be used for each variable
3. Identifying the instruments available to capture each variable
4. Developing data collection forms/protocols
5. Collecting and managing the data

In mixed method research, data collection may also take non-quantitative forms. Narratives, verbal feedback from focus groups, transcripts, and videotapes are examples of sources of non-quantitative data (Vogt, 2005). The purpose of qualitative data collection in mixed record research may vary. For example, qualitative data may be collected for the purpose of developing questions in a quantitative survey or instrument. This step assists in developing a more comprehensive understanding of the dimensions of a construct under study or in generating hypotheses.

The rationale for the data collection process used in mixed method research studies should be stated clearly: Why and how did using one or more methods of collecting and integrating data contribute to the purpose of the study? The specific data that are collected by quantitative and qualitative methods, and the priority and emphasis given to each type of data, are determined by the researchers and driven by the research problem and goals of the study (Creswell et al., 2004). Johnson and Onwuegbuzie (2004, p. 21) describe their mixed method process as having eight distinct steps:

1. Determine the research question.
2. Determine whether a mixed design is appropriate.
3. Select the mixed method or mixed model research design.
4. Collect the data.
5. Analyze the data.
6. Interpret the data.
7. Legitimate the data.
8. Draw conclusions (if warranted) and write the final report.

Johnson and Onwuegbuzie's (2004) mixed method process focuses on data collection. Data collection in multimethod studies is frequently carried out such that quantitative and qualitative components of the study are kept separate during the actual conduct of the study and are combined only later in the interpretation and reporting of results (Creswell et al., 2004; Polit & Beck, 2011).

To illustrate this idea, consider the research reported by Long et al. (2006), in which quantitative methods were used to measure the differences among fruit, vegetable, and fat consumption before and after a web-based intervention to prevent diabetes in adolescents. Qualitative methods were employed to understand adolescent perceptions and satisfaction with learning about healthy eating through a technology-based medium. In this pilot study, the researchers identified statistical analysis and significance testing of the effectiveness of the intervention as being research priorities. Structured interviews and checklists were used in combination with a computer-based self-report questionnaire to quantitatively measure fruit, vegetable, and fat intake in adolescents. The authors also used qualitative methods to collect data and analyze research questions of importance to the study. In particular, were adolescents satisfied—that is, how did they feel about learning how to prevent type 2 diabetes through the use of the World Wide Web? For the qualitative data collection, the researchers observed adolescent behavior during the study and held focus groups (unstructured group interviews) after the completion of the intervention (Long et al., 2006). They recorded data during the intervention by collecting field and interview notes to record the observations and the feedback obtained from the participants (Long et al., 2006).

Data Analysis and Validation Procedures

How data are analyzed is inextricably tied to the type of information that has been collected. Quantitative data will, at minimum, be counted and described. Inferential statistical analysis will be applied depending on the type and level of data available to the researcher. Qualitative data analysis also takes multiple forms, but it generally involves the coding of narrative themes for depth of understanding. It is not surprising, therefore, that analysis of mixed method research mirrors the variety seen in analyses of both quantitative and qualitative methodologies.

To illuminate this point, consider the subset of data analysis in the study conducted by Long et al. (2006), which compared the results from two quantitative measurements of fruit, vegetable, and fat intake for **convergent validity**. Quantitative data from a computer-based self-report and from a structured interview were compared statistically (triangulated) and determined to have a small to medium correlation (Long et al., 2006). This form of mixed methodology is generative, and it assisted the researcher in determining the need for further development of the measurement methods used to determine fruit, vegetable, and fat consumption in an adolescent population. In the same study, the qualitative feedback obtained from observations of student enjoyment with using the web-based educational intervention and verbal feedback from focus groups was analyzed and coded thematically to capture observed variances among learners, raising new questions about the population and about how to best provide meaningful health education to this group.

? Think Outside the Box

1. Debate the benefits and restrictions involved in using a mixed methodology for a research project.
2. How would you handle a PICOT question format when using a mixed methodology?
3. Consider a clinical situation that you have confronted. How could you address the clinical problem using both a quantitative method and a qualitative method?
4. Debate which types of rationales are necessary when a mixed methods approach is used.

In summary, both quantitative and qualitative research designs can be combined through the use of a mixed method approach to data collection and analysis. The specific data collected by both methods and the emphasis given to each should be determined based on the research problem and the goals of the study. A research team whose members are experienced with use of both types of methods is important to the success of mixed method research. While each of the methods has its own strengths and weaknesses, mixed method research offers the opportunity for a more complete investigation into the problem being studied (Creswell et al., 2004; Elliott, 2004; Ramprogus, 2005). Given the complexities and the nature of the problems of interest to nursing, mixed method research holds promise for advancing evidence-based understanding that might lead to enhanced quality patient care.

Evidence-Based Practice Considerations

Problems of interest to nursing are characteristically complex in nature. Nurses in clinical practice need to know how to find, evaluate, and use research so that they can implement best practices at the bedside (Lander, 2005). Understanding mixed method research is important, as it holds the potential for promoting methodologically sound studies that capture complexities which might otherwise be overlooked. According to Rolston-Blenman (2009), "Clinical stakeholders must participate in planning and championing the changes taking place. Staff must feel they have a voice in making decisions" (p. 21). Through the use of mixed methods (action research), the staff at the bedside can actively participate in different aspects of research, resulting in better management of the problems so identified. According to Myers and Meccariello (2006), "It's critical to help nurses understand how crucial their role is in the research process and how they can improve patient care by validating their own trial and error experiences" (p. 24). Each day, individuals must realize the importance of connecting the research process to key activities that occur within the workplace—one patient at a time. This permeation of the workplace with a critical thinking mindset allows for the deep consideration of multiple problems at the ground-zero level. Taking advantage of the strengths of qualitative and quantitative research design methods, while planning for ways to overcome the limitations of the research designs, allows the discipline of nursing to advance the body of knowledge toward practice confirmed by evidence and practice.

Conclusion

Qualitative research lends itself well to the study of complex human issues. Qualitative research is the study of the quality of something rather than the quantity, amount, or frequency of something. Subjectivity is an expected trait of a qualitative study. Qualitative and quantitative research methods differ in many ways. As described previously, qualitative studies approach phenomena from the emic perspective— the perspective of the participant provides the meaning rather than the perspective of the researcher. Qualitative methods are inductive, as opposed to the deductive approach of quantitative methods. Although quantitative methods seek to minimize differences among subjects, qualitative methods embrace differences among participants. Sample size in qualitative research is often small compared with the requisite larger sample sizes in quantitative research.

? Think Outside the Box

1. Look at the table below, which compares quantitative and qualitative research designs. Which other aspects can you identify that might be added to this table to further delineate the differences and similarities between these two research design methods?

Differences Between Quantitative and Qualitative Research Methods

	Point of View	Attachment to Participant	Process of Inquiry	Sample
Quantitative	Etic—analyzed without considering their role as a unit within a system	Seeks to minimize the differences among subjects	Deductive	Large sample size required
Qualitative	Emic—analyzed with consideration of their role as a unit within the system	Embraces different perspectives of each participant	Inductive	Individuals; a small sample size is typical

2. Discuss how sample sizes for qualitative versus quantitative research projects differ. How do researchers determine optimal sample size for qualitative studies as opposed to quantitative studies?
3. Think for a moment about your current workplace. Identify one problem, process, or policy in your work area whose improvement by the healthcare team would favorably affect patient outcomes. Once you have identified a problem, list ideas about which quantitative data would assist you and your colleagues in solving the problem. Further consider those aspects of the issue in which your understanding would be enhanced through collection of qualitative data. How could you apply best practices to solve the problem you identified using aspects of both research methods? Now consider an unmet educational need of new staff members on your unit. How might an "action research" mixed method approach assist you in understanding and meeting the changing educational needs of new staff members?

Case studies, ethnography, grounded theory, and phenomenology are methods used within qualitative research to seek the essences of the situation being investigated. In data collection and analysis, saturation occurs when no new themes or codes emerge or the data analysis becomes redundant. The reliability and validity of qualitative research can be ensured by verifying credibility, transferability, dependability, conformability, adequacy of data, and appropriateness of data.

Mixed method design (called multimethod, triangulated, and integrated design) is an amalgamation of quantitative and qualitative research methods and techniques used to collect and analyze data. In mixed method studies, two research patterns are regularly interlocked within the sampling, data collection, or analysis aspects of the project. The use of both methods permits the researcher to develop a wider and deeper understanding of the identified research problem as a result of the consideration of the problem from multiple viewpoints.

The fundamental force driving the use of mixed method research continues to be the clear and concise identification of the research problem. The investigator must rigorously examine the issue of whether the two research designs should be conducted concurrently or sequentially.

Triangulation allows the researcher to fully understand a phenomenon of interest through validation or supplementation of data. The term "triangulation" is used to describe the situation in which data are analyzed for the purpose of corroborating data from multiple methods. Justification for the ordering and prioritization of the different methods must be documented, with rationales being presented for each of the decisions made concerning the research process. During collection and analysis of data in mixed method research, quantitative and qualitative data are often treated as independent components in the research design.

Summary Points

1. Qualitative research is the study of the quality of something rather than the quantity, amount, or frequency of something. Subjectivity is an expected trait of a qualitative study.
2. Qualitative research is conducted from the emic perspective; quantitative research is conducted from the etic perspective.
3. Sample size in qualitative research is often small compared with the requisite larger sample sizes in quantitative research.
4. The criteria for reliability and validity of a qualitative study include credibility, transferability, dependability, conformability, adequacy of data, and appropriateness of data.
5. Mixed research methods—combinations of qualitative and quantitative methods—are used to supplement or validate data.
6. Saturation occurs in data collection or analysis when there is repetition or redundancy in the themes or patterns in the data.
7. Mixed method design (called multimethod, triangulated, and integrated design) is an amalgamation of quantitative and qualitative research methods and techniques used to collect and analyze data.

8. In mixed method studies, two research patterns are regularly inter-locked within the sampling, data collection, or analysis aspects of the project.

9. The use of both methods permits the researcher to develop a wider and deeper understanding of the identified research problem as a result of the consideration of the problem from multiple viewpoints.

10. The fundamental force driving the use of mixed method research con-tinues to be the clear and concise identification of the research problem.

11. The criteria used when choosing the combination of methods for inclusion in a mixed method study are related to implementation, pri-oritization, and integration needs.

12. The investigator must rigorously examine the issue of whether the two research designs should be conducted concurrently or sequentially.

13. Justification for the ordering and prioritization of the different methods must be documented, with rationales being presented for each of the decisions made concerning the research process.

14. During collection and analysis of data in mixed method research, quan-titative and qualitative data are often treated as independent components in the research design.

15. The term "triangulation" is used to describe the situation in which data are analyzed for the purpose of corroborating data from multiple methods.

RED FLAGS

- Care must be given to explaining how different research methodologies are entwined as a single project.
- A lack of a rationale for using mixed methods is problematic.
- Any indication that quantitative and qualitative methods are competing with each other reflects lack of planning.
- When the rationale for weighting of the methods is not provided, then concerns must be raised about the results of the data analysis.
- The data collection process for each of the two research methodologies should be kept distinctive.
- If data collection methods are improperly conducted for the identified research methodology, then the validity of the results must be questioned.
- Attention must be given to the auditability of the data collected via a qualitative methodology.
- Within a qualitative research report, the reader should be able to pick out aspects that demonstrate credibility, transferability, dependability, and confirmability of the research.
- Qualitative research designs use an inductive reasoning process.
- Patterns and/or themes coming from the data should be documented and supported by the discussion.
- Given that qualitative research deals with volumes of written data, the documentation of statistic results would cause concern when evaluating a project.

Multiple Choice Questions

1. Qualitative research examines which of the following characteristics of a phenomenon?

    A. Frequency
    B. Quantity
    C. Quality
    D. Intensity

2. Which of the following best illustrates the emic perspective in research?

    A. Finding a quality of a phenomenon and looking for examples of the quality
    B. Taking an outsider's view of a phenomenon
    C. Exploring the way members of a group view themselves
    D. Validating perspectives about a group through interviews

3. Which of the following types of studies is considered qualitative research?

    A. Delphi technique
    B. Cross-sectional design
    C. Ethnography
    D. Survey

4. Combining qualitative and quantitative methods in a single study is known as

    A. Systematic analysis.
    B. Transferability.
    C. Prospective design.
    D. Triangulation.

5. A researcher explores the phenomenon of how nurses make decisions about when to discuss end-of-life issues with clients. From this research, a model is developed to explain the decision-making process. Which type of research does this represent?

    A. Grounded theory
    B. Ethnography
    C. Phenomenology
    D. Case study

6. A researcher examines the norms, rules, and values of the staff of a large long-term care facility. Which type of research does this represent?

    A. Grounded theory
    B. Ethnography
    C. Phenomenology
    D. Case study

7. A researcher conducts a study in which participants are asked to describe the lived experience of being a caregiver of a parent with Alzheimer's disease. Which type of qualitative study does this represent?

    A. Grounded theory
    B. Ethnography
    C. Phenomenology
    D. Case study

8. Which of the following statements is true with regard to comparing qualitative and quantitative research methods?

    A. Qualitative studies often require a larger sample size than quantitative studies.
    B. Qualitative studies don't require evidence of reliability and validity.
    C. Qualitative studies don't allow for the use of computerized data analysis.
    D. Qualitative research is often inductive in nature, whereas quantitative research is deductive in nature.

9. When writing up a research project, the researcher describes in detail the audit trail used as conclusions about data were drawn. Which criterion for reliability and validity was met?

    A. Credibility
    B. Transferability
    C. Dependability
    D. Confirmability

10. When writing up a research project, the researcher describes in detail the sample, setting, and data. Which criterion for reliability and validity was met?

    A. Credibility
    B. Transferability
    C. Dependability
    D. Confirmability

11. When writing up a research project, the researcher describes in detail how biases, assumptions, and personal perspectives were identified and set aside, or bracketed. Which criterion for reliability and validity was met?

    A. Credibility
    B. Transferability
    C. Dependability
    D. Confirmability

12. The researcher collecting data notices that she is beginning to hear the same things repeatedly and that no new themes are emerging. The researcher recognizes that what has occurred?

    A. Triangulation
    B. Saturation
    C. Quantizing
    D. Redundancy

13. Another term used within the literature for mixed method design is

    A. Quantitative design.

    B. Qualitative design.

    C. Multimethod design.

    D. Experimental design.

14. When a researcher endeavors to use mixed method design to answer an identified research problem, the blending of the methods is based on

    A. Combining the methods to capitalize on their strong points while negating their flaws.

    B. Combining the methods to blend both their strengths and their weaknesses.

    C. Separating the strengths from the weaknesses within the different designs.

    D. Separating the weaker method from the stronger method.

15. The research designs are merged within which sections of the report on the research project?

    A. Introduction, sampling, and problem identification

    B. Problem identification, data collection, and analysis

    C. Sampling, data collection, and analysis

    D. Introduction, data collection, and analysis

16. The primary restrictions related to the researcher that prevent the use of mixed method research are

    A. Lack of understanding about the methods and the research community.

    B. Lack of willingness to engage in the use of, and lack of confidence in, one research method.

    C. Lack of vision and risk taking.

    D. Lack of willingness and overconfidence.

17. A nurse identifies individuals who seem to comply better with a treatment plan when several different teaching methods are used within the discharge planning process. In developing a mixed method design for researching which educational methods work best, a question concerning the type of data to be collected is confronted. Which of the following groups of data collection methods represents a mixed method format?

    A. Likert scale tool with a demographic component

    B. Observation of teaching sessions with videotaping

    C. Focus group discussion with audiotaping

    D. Likert scale tool with focus group discussion

18. The determination of the mixed method design approach must address the meshing of the qualitative and quantitative methodologies through the use of which of the following criteria?

    A. Implementation, prioritization, and integration

    B. Implementation, analysis, and investigation

    C. Analysis, prioritization, and integration

    D. Collection, prioritization, and analysis

19. A researcher has elected to conduct a mixed method research project. Within this project, the decision has been made to conduct the two types of data collection concurrently, with each type of data having equal weight within the analysis process. Based on these decisions, what must the researcher make sure is done for the reporting of the process?

    A. Establish a team to aid in the management of the study.
    B. Reevaluate the decision, because quantitative research is the stronger method.
    C. Ensure that confidentiality is maintained within the process.
    D. Document the rationale for the decisions made within the process.

20. Triangulation in mixed method research is utilized for the purposes of supporting _____ validity.

    A. Criterion
    B. Convergent
    C. Construct
    D. Variable

21. The data collected in mixed method research and the emphasis given to each type of data should be determined by the _____ and goals of the study.

    A. Source of funding
    B. Preference of the research team
    C. Research problem
    D. Literature

22. Qualitative data analysis seeks _____ in understanding a phenomenon.

    A. Rigor
    B. Depth
    C. Numbers
    D. Statistics

23. A primary reason for using mixed research methodologies is the opportunity to _____ that might otherwise be overlooked.

    A. Catch complexities
    B. Define concepts
    C. Describe problems
    D. Uncover opportunities

24. In mixed method research, the collection of quantitative and qualitative data is often treated

    A. Synchronously.
    B. Stringently.
    C. Independently.
    D. Statistically.

25. An advantage of using a mixed method design for a research study is to
    A. Increase the biases associated with the use of two designs.
    B. Provide insight into the complexity of the problem under study.
    C. Impart rigor to the examination of the intricacies of the problem under study.
    D. Decrease the impartiality associated with the use of one design.

26. Limitations related to the use of mixed method strategies include the
    A. Cost and additional time required.
    B. Extensive and comprehensive research questions involved.
    C. Vivacity of the evidence provided.
    D. Complementary insights and perceptions provided.

Discussion Questions

www

1. You are the nurse manager of a perinatal care unit. You have read a phenomenology research report on the positive effects of music on the labor and delivery process for mothers. Consider the following: The study is one of many of this type with similar findings, there were five informants in the study, and the researcher did not provide a discussion of reliability and validity in the write-up. Will you use this study to support the practice of ensuring that all labor and delivery rooms are equipped to play music throughout the labor and delivery process? Support your answer.

2. You are the charge nurse on a medical–surgical floor. After reading several qualitative research reports on pet therapy, you approach your nurse manager about the possibility of implementing a pet therapy program on your floor. Your nurse manager states that no changes should be made based on qualitative research, because the sample sizes are always too small. What is your best response?

3. You are reading a research report about a long-term care facility. The researcher describes in detail the demographics of administration, staff, and clients. There is a lengthy discussion about how problems are solved in the facility, how various departments communicate, and how the facility values family involvement in client care. Which type of qualitative study does this represent? Support your answer.

4. A nurse on the labor and delivery unit wants to study the effects of having small children participate with the family in the delivery process on the bonding process between mother and child. For this study, the nurse has determined that a questionnaire will be mailed out to families who elect to have their toddlers in the delivery room during the delivery of a sibling. The questionnaire will include both open-ended questions and closed-ended (Likert-type) questions. Which aspects of the study should be considered to provide a rationale for selecting this mixed method strategy?

5. A researcher working within a hospital striving to gain Magnet status wants to study the barriers to use of research at the bedside. For the design of this study, the individual is considering using a mixed method format. Which pieces of the design should be considered as the researcher prepares the study?

6. A group of researchers has developed a new instrument to assess the degree of destruction noted within decubitus ulcers (pressure ulcers). As part of their study, they are planning to compare the new instrument with instruments currently used within their acute care setting. Which components of the mixed method strategies need to be carefully considered as the researchers develop the study design?

Suggested Readings

Bader, M. K., Palmer, S., Stalcup, C., & Shaver, T. (2002). Using a FOCUS-PDCA quality improvement model for applying the severe traumatic brain injury guidelines to practice: Process and outcomes. *Online Journal of Knowledge Synthesis for Nursing, Clinical Column*, Document No. 4C.

Balas, E. A., & Boren, S. A. (2000). Managing clinical knowledge for health care improvements. In V. Schattauer, J. Bemmel, & A. T. McCray (Eds.), *Yearbook of medical informatics* (pp. 65–70). Stuttgart, Germany: Schattauer.

Borkan, J. M. (2004). Mixed methods studies: A foundation for primary care research [Editorial]. *Annals of Family Medicine, 2*(1), 4–6.

Classen, S., & Lopez, E. (2006). Mixed methods approach explaining process of an older driver safety systematic literature review. *Topics in Geriatric Rehabilitation, 22*(2), 99–112.

Foss, C., & Ellefsen, B. (2002, October). The value of combining qualitative and quantitative approaches in nursing research by means of method triangulation. *Journal of Advanced Nursing, 40*(2), 242–248.

Freshwater, D. (2005). Book review: Integrating qualitative and quantitative research methods: Trend or foe? *Journal of Research in Nursing, 10*(3), 337–338.

Freshwater, D., Walsh, L., & Storey, L. (2002, February). Prison health care part 2: Developing leadership through clinical supervision. *Nursing Management, 8*(9), 16–20.

Grassley, J. S., & Nelms, T. P. (2008). The breast feeding conversation: A philosophic exploration of support. *Advances in Nursing Science, 31*(4), E55–E66.

Halcomb, E., & Andrew, S. (2005). Triangulation as a method for contemporary nursing research. *Nurse Researcher, 13*(2), 71–82.

Hanson, W. E., Creswell, J. W., Clark, V. L., Petska, K. S., & Creswell, J. D. (2005). Mixed methods research designs in counseling psychology. *Journal of Counseling Psychology, 52*(2), 224–235.

Happ, M. B. (2009). Mixed methods in gerontological research. *Research in Gerontological Nursing, 2*(2), 122–127.

Happ, M. B., Dabbs, A. D., Tate, J., Hricik, A., & Erlen, J. (2006, March/April). Exemplars of mixed methods data combination and analysis. *Nursing Research, 55*(2 Suppl.), S43–S49.

Harland, N., & Holey, E. (2011). Including open-ended questions in quantitative questionnaires—theory and practice. *International Journal of Therapy and Rehabilitation, 18*(9), 482–486.

Kinn, S., & Curzio, J. (2005). Integrating qualitative and quantitative research methods. *Journal of Research in Nursing, 10*(3), 317–336.

Kreutzer, J. S., Stejskal, T. M., Godwin, E. E., Powell, V. D., & Arango-Lasprilla, J. C. (2010). A mixed methods evaluation of the Brain Injury Family Intervention. *NeuroRehabilitation, 27*, 19–29.

Law, M., Stewart, D., Letts, L., Pollock, N., Bosch, J., & Westmoreland, M. (1998). *Guidelines for critical review of qualitative studies.* Retrieved from http://www.usc.edu/hsc/ebnet/res/Guidelines.pdf

Melnyk, B. M., & Fineout-Overholt, E. (2006, Second Quarter). Advancing knowledge through collaboration. *Reflections on Nursing Leadership, 32*(2), 1–5.

Melnyk, B. M., Fineout-Overholt, E., Stetler, C., & Allen, J. (2005). Outcomes and implementation strategies from the first U.S. evidence-based leadership summit. *Worldviews on Evidence-Based Nursing, 2*(3), 113–121.

Miller, S. I., & Fredericks, M. (2006). Mixed-methods and evaluation research: Trends and issues. *Qualitative Health Research, 16*(4), 567–579.

O'Neill, R. (2006). *The advantages and disadvantages of qualitative and quantitative research methods.* Retrieved from http://www.learnhigher.ac.uk/analysethis/main/quantitative1.html

Onwuegbuzie, A. J., & Leech, N. L. (2005). Taking the "Q" out of research: Teaching research methodology courses without the divide between quantitative and qualitative paradigms. *Quality & Quantity, 39*(3), 267–295.

Paton, B., Martin, S., McClunie-Trust, P., & Weir, N. (2004). Doing phenomenological research collaboratively. *Journal of Continuing Education in Nursing, 35*(4), 176–181.

Priest, H., Roberts, P., & Woods, L. (2002). An overview of three different approaches to the interpretation of qualitative data. Part 1: Theoretical issues. *Nurse Researcher, 10*(1), 30–42.

Rapport, F., & Wainwright, P. (2006). Phenomenology as a paradigm of movement. *Nursing Inquiry, 13*(3), 228–236.

Sale, J. E. M., Lohfeld, L. H., & Brazil, K. (2002). Revisiting the quantitative–qualitative debate: Implications for mixed-methods research. *Quality & Quantity, 36*(1), 43–53.

Schifferdecker, K. E., & Reed, V. A. (2009). Using mixed methods research in medical education: Basic guidelines for researchers. *Medical Education, 43*(7), 637–644.

Shih, F. J. (1998). Triangulation in nursing research: Issues of conceptual clarity and purpose. *Journal of Advanced Nursing, 28*(3), 631–641.

Silverstein, L. B., Auerbach, C. F., & Levant, R. R. (2006). Using qualitative research to strengthen clinical practice. *Professional Psychology: Research & Practice, 37*(4), 351–358.

Vishnevsky, T., & Beanlands, H. (2004). Qualitative research. *Nephrology Nursing Journal, 31*(2), 234–238.

Williamson, G. R. (2005). Illustrating triangulation in mixed-methods nursing research. *Nurse Researcher, 12*(4), 7–18.

References

Andrews, T., & Waterman, H. (2005). Packaging: A grounded theory of how to report physiological deterioration effectively. *Journal of Advanced Nursing, 52*(5), 473–481. doi:10.1111/j.1365-2648.2005.03615.x

Bliss, D. Z. (2001). Mixed or mixed up methods? *Nursing Research, 50*(6), 331.

Chen, L. S., & Goodson, P. (2009). Barriers to adopting genomics into public health education: A mixed methods study. *Genetics in Medicine, 11*(2), 104–110.

Chow, M. Y., Quine, S., & Li, M. (2010). The benefits of using a mixed methods approach—quantitative and qualitative—to identify client satisfaction and unmet needs in an HIV healthcare centre. *AIDS Care, 22*(4), 491–498.

Cohen-Katz, J., Wiley, S. D., Capuano, T., Baker, D. M., & Shapiro, S. (2004). The effects of mindfulness-based stress reduction on nurse stress and burnout: A quantitative and qualitative study. *Holistic Nursing Practice, 18*(6), 302–308.

Creswell, J. W. (2003). *Research design: Qualitative, quantitative, and mixed method approaches* (2nd ed.). Thousand Oaks, CA: Sage.

Creswell, J. W., Fetters, M. D., & Ivankova, N. V. (2004). Designing a mixed methods study in primary care. *Annals of Family Medicine, 2*(1), 7–12.

Creswell, J. W., Klassen, A. C., Plano Clark, V. L., & Klegg Smith, C. (2010). *Best practices for mixed methods in the health sciences.* Retrieved from http://obssr.od.nih.gov/scientific_areas/methodology/mixed_methods_research/pdf/Best_Practices_for_Mixed_Methods_Research.pdf

Denzin, N. K., & Lincoln, Y. S. (Eds.). (1998). *Collecting and interpreting qualitative materials.* Thousand Oaks, CA: Sage.

Elliott, J. (2004). Multimethod approaches in educational research. *International Journal of Disability, Development and Education, 51*(2), 135–149.

Fu, M. R. (2005). Breast cancer survivors' intentions of managing lymphedema. *Cancer Nursing, 28*(6), 446–459.

Glaser, B. G., & Strauss, A. L. (1967). *The discovery of grounded theory: Strategies for qualitative research.* Chicago, IL: Aldine De Gruyter

Goodnough, K. (2008). Moving science off the "back burner": Meaning making within an action research community of practice. *Journal of Science and Teacher Education, 19*(1), 15–39.

Holloway, I., & Wheeler, S. (2010). *Qualitative research in nursing and healthcare* (3rd ed.). Ames, IA: Wiley-Blackwell.

Johnson, R. B. (n.d.). *Chapter 14: Mixed research: Mixed method and mixed model research* [Online lecture]. Retrieved from http://www.southalabama.edu/coe/bset/johnson/dr_johnson/lectures/lec14.htm

Johnson, R. B., & Onwuegbuzie, A. J. (2004). Mixed methods research: A research paradigm whose time has come. *Educational Researcher, 33*(7), 14–26.

Lander, J. A. (2005). Finding, evaluating, and using research for best practice. *Clinical Nursing Research, 14*(4), 299–302.

Lincoln, Y. S., & Guba, E. G. (1985). *Naturalistic inquiry.* Beverly Hills, CA: Sage Publications, Inc.

Long, J. D., Armstrong, M. L., Amos, E., Shriver, B., Roman-Shriver, C., Feng, D., . . . Blevins, M. W. (2006). Pilot using World Wide Web to prevent diabetes in adolescents. *Clinical Nursing Research, 15*(1), 67–79.

Macnee, C. L. (2004). *Understanding nursing research: Reading and using research in practice.* Philadelphia, PA: Lippincott Williams & Wilkins.

Malinowski, B. (1922). *Argonauts of the western Pacific: An account of native enterprise and adventure in the archipelagos of Melanesian New Guinea.* New York, NY: E. P. Dutton & Co.

Mead, M. (1935). *Sex and temperament in three primitive societies.* New York, NY: Morrow.

Morse, J. M. (1991). *Qualitative nursing research: A contemporary dialogue.* Newbury Park, CA: Sage Publications.

Morse, J. (1998). Designing funded qualitative research. In N. K. Denzin & Y. S. Lincoln (Eds.), *Strategies of qualitative inquiry* (pp. 56–85). Thousand Oaks, CA: Sage Publications.

Munten, G., van den Bogaard, J., Cox, K., Garretsen, H., & Bongers, I. (2010). Implementation of evidence-based practice in nursing using action research: A review. *Worldviews on Evidence-Based Nursing, 7*(3), 135–157.

Myers, G., & Meccariello, M. (2006). From pet rock to rock-solid: Implementing unit-based research. *Nursing Management, 37*(1), 24–29.

Patton, M. Q. (1990). *Qualitative evaluation and research method* (2nd ed.) [Online]. Newbury Park, CA: Sage. Retrieved from http://onlinelibrary.wiley.com/doi/10.1002/nur.4770140111/abstract

Polit, D. F., & Beck, C. T. (2008). *Nursing research: Generating and assessing evidence for nursing practice* (8th ed.). Philadelphia, PA: Lippincott Williams & Wilkins.

Polit, D. F., & Beck, C. T. (2011). *Nursing research: Generating and assessing evidence for nursing practice* (9th ed.). Philadelphia, PA: Lippincott Williams & Wilkins.

Ponic, P., Reid, C., & Frisby, W. (2010). Cultivating the power of partnerships in feminist participatory action research in women's health. *Nursing Inquiry, 17*(4), 324–335.

Ramprogus, V. (2005). Triangulation. *Nurse Researcher, 12*(4), 4–6.

Rolston-Blenman, B. (2009). Nurses roll up their sleeves at the bedside to improve patient care. *Nurse Leader, 7*(1), 20–25.

Rosenberg, J. P., & Yates, P. M. (2007). Schematic representation of case study research designs. *Journal of Advanced Nursing, 60*(4), 447–452.

Scott Tilley, D., Rugari, S. M., & Walker, C. A. (2008). Development of violence in men who batter intimate partners: A case study. *The Journal of Theory Construction & Testing, 12*(1), 28–32.

Shaw, J. A., Connelly, D. M., & Zecevic, A. A. (2010). Pragmatism in practice: Mixed methods research in physiotherapy. *Physiotherapy Theory and Practice, 26*(8), 510–518.

Stake, R. (1998). Case studies. In N. K. Denzin & Y. S. Lincoln (Eds.), *Strategies of qualitative inquiry* (pp. 86–109). Thousand Oaks, CA: Sage Publications.

Strauss, A., & Corbin, J. (1998). *Basics of qualitative research: Techniques and procedures for developing grounded theory* (2nd ed.). Thousand Oaks, CA: Sage Publications.

Vogt, W. P. (2005). *Dictionary of statistics and methodology: A nontechnical guide for the social sciences* (3rd ed.). Thousand Oaks, CA: Sage Publications.

Chapter 10

Data Collection

Carol Boswell

Chapter Objectives

At the conclusion of this chapter, the learner will be able to

1. Contrast a researcher's decision to use accessible data versus new data
2. Distinguish various forms of data collection processes

Key Terms

➤ Accessible data

➤ Biophysiological data

➤ Closed-ended questions

➤ Data collection

➤ Focus group

➤ Interview

➤ In vitro

➤ In vivo

➤ Meta-analysis

➤ Novel data

➤ Observation

➤ Open-ended questions

➤ Primary data

➤ Questionnaire

➤ Secondary data

➤ Systematic review

➤ Test

Overview of Data Collection Methods and Sources

Data come in many forms and are obtained through multiple methodologies. **Data collection** becomes a foundational piece within all aspects of the research process. The data collection process should drive the tool selection, aid in the determination of the research methodology, speak to the questions about sampling, and drive the selection of the statistical/evaluation process for the study. As a result, the process of collecting data essentially establishes boundaries for a project. As a researcher begins to conceptualize the implementation of a research project, the question of the appropriate facts required for addressing the PICOT question(s), research question(s), research purpose(s), and/or hypothesis(es) becomes critical. According to LoBiondo-Wood and Haber (1998), "The major difference between the data collected when performing patient care and the data collected for the purpose of research is that the data collection method employed by researchers needs to be objective and systematic" (p. 308). Although many methods of data gathering are available, all of them are implemented in the same manner, regardless of the anticipated project. The objectivity and organization of the data collection process provide for generalizability of a research project's resulting outcomes to a broader population. By carefully building the research project around the data that will best address the question raised within the study, each aspect of the research process becomes increasingly appropriate to gather the information needed to answer the burning question.

The specification of the outcome for each phase of the data collection plan is mandatory. When all aspects and/or variables of the data required for the study are established prior to the initiation of the study, the selection of the appropriate data collection method can be effectively addressed as part of this specification. This process decreases the potential for unintentionally omitting a key component of the data. Because data collection is fundamental to the entire process, careful consideration for the use of a mixture of types can prove to be a valuable option as the decisions about data collection methods are made.

Before delving into a discussion of the functions of data collection source and data collection tools/instruments, it is helpful to have an understanding of the definitions of selected concepts. The term "source" within the data collection process of research focuses on the processes used to collect the data. These sources can be any tool or instrument, any process such as interviewing, observation or focus groups, where information can be accessed. The sources for data collection can be varied but require a connection with the participants. Data collection "tools/instruments" comprise the actual physical devices employed to collect the information that is under investigation.

The use of a tool/instrument does not mandate a direct connection with the participants, as these tools could be delivered by mail or through the Internet. Tools and instruments can be hard copy collection forms such as tests and questionnaires, but can also be tools which provide physiological data such as laboratory equipment, weight scales, and x-ray reports.

There are several major methods of data collection:

- Tests
- Questionnaires
- Interviews
- Focus groups
- Observations
- Biophysiological data
- Systematic reviews
- Existing or secondary data

The data set identified by the researcher for any selected study can usually be accessed by several of these methods.

According to Polit and Beck (2008), the researcher must try to determine which data will effectively address the question under investigation, describe the sample characteristics, establish methods for controlling extraneous variables, analyze impending biases, recognize subgroup effects, and check for manipulation of the data. Creswell (2003) reinforces this notion by identifying the data collection steps to include (1) establishing the boundaries for the study, (2) accumulating the data through the appropriate methodologies, and (3) clarifying the process for recording and managing the data collected. As a result, the researcher has the responsibility to understand the different formats of data collections, the strengths and weaknesses of the different methods, and the specific needs recognized for the topic under evaluation.

Accessible Data Versus Novel Data

As the researcher begins the process of clarifying the data collection process, a key question arises concerning the type of information that will be used to satisfy the question being investigated. Two types of data can be identified—accessible (existing) or new (novel). The aspects of each of these data types need to be conscientiously considered as the researcher determines the data collection process.

Accessible data may also be called existing data; it provides an essential source for use in research endeavors. This information may be located in pre-existing reports (e.g., hospital records, databases, narrative journaling documents, historic documents), and it can be used as the basis for a secondary analysis of the data gathered in a previous study or of records developed for some other reason, such as hospital patient records and national databases. The use of pre-existing records, often called a retrospective chart/record review, is common in nursing research because these documents are an economical and convenient source of information. Questions do arise with this form of data, however, as the records' biases and incompleteness cannot be thoroughly established. Secondary analysis of data allows for the use of data collected for a prior project to test one or more different hypotheses and illuminate fresh relationships evident within the data. When pre-existing data can be used, this practice does eliminate the time-consuming and costly process subsumed within the practice of research of collecting the data before beginning the analysis process. The use of accessible (existing) data serves as the foundation for evidence-based practice. Meta-analyses, synthesis analyses, and meta-syntheses, which use obtainable research reports as their underlying database, integrate the material to provide the foundation for evidence-based protocol guidelines.

New or **novel data** comprise original information collected for a specific study. This type of data is unique to the question or questions under investigation. The researcher needs to judiciously determine each component of data needed for the particular question(s). Within the time sequence allocated for the research project, all of the various pieces of data must be collected. The data collection plan should address each aspect of the needed information so that at some point during the process, it is all collected for use during the analysis process.

Another way to classify data is either as primary data or secondary data. Primary (novel) data are data generated through the actual conducting of an original study. **Primary data** provides direct access into the actual process being reported. The information comes from the source without any additional interpretations or modifications. In contrast, secondary (accessible) data are pulled from existing data and documents (Social Dimensions of Watershed Planning, 2006). **Secondary data** is information interpreted by the second reviewer. Each reviewer tends to include their individualized analysis of the information as it applies to a given situation. Thus, additional biases from the further interpretation of the materials may be introduced. This process of using accessible or secondary data is termed "data mining."

Key Categories of Data for Nursing Studies

Within any research design, the data collection process must be matched to the stated study aims and/or purpose and reflect the particular strategies implemented during the study. Many data sources are available for use. They include secondary data from national surveys and other secondary data sources such as Medicaid, demographic indicators, nonclinical program data, clinical program data, public comments, informant groups, questionnaire/interview surveys, screenings, and epidemiology surveys. Researchers must carefully and thoroughly contemplate the various methods of data collection and the various sources of data, thereby ensuring they select the most appropriate options.

Orcher (2005) identified two feasible incentives for using established instruments. Established tools are identified as validated tools based on the number of times that the tool has been successfully used while fostering a reliable body of research. By using a validated tool for a study, the results can be compared and contrasted to the prior studies which used the tool. As tools are used in subsequent studies, the validity and reliability of the tool is further established for different populations. Each of the two incentives can have a profound impact on the quality of the research study outcomes:

■ Initially, time and energy should be expended to ensure that the data collected are appropriate for the study question(s) and the methodology is effective in capturing the total picture needed to address the research problem.
■ Care should be given to identifying any confounding variables that could adversely affect the research outcomes.

? Think Outside the Box

Using the provided examples, select a data collection method and justify your selection:
- Which information has been used to determine the use of 6-hour NPO status prior to an outpatient surgical procedure versus a 12-hour NPO status level?
- Which information serves as the basis for the range of blood sugars used within newly diagnosed adolescent diabetics?
- Which information could be used to determine the cause of patient falls?

Significant Facets of Data Collection Schemes

As the investigator establishes the data collection methodology for a study, questions concerning the consistency of the data collected from each participant become of paramount importance. The basic idea is that the data should be collected in the same manner for each of the participants so that unique environmental, societal, and physical effects are diminished. Concerns related to the Hawthorne effect, for example, must be carefully thought about to minimize the potential of participants modifying their behaviors because they are affected—either positively or negatively—by being included in a study. As studies of the Hawthorne effect have shown, the simple act of being selected to participate in a project can result in the modification of the behavior being evaluated. Because this effect is real, researchers must carefully consider all aspects of the data collection process to diminish the likelihood that the resulting modifications will be so pronounced that the data collected are of little value.

Another important aspect within the data collection process is interrater reliability. In those studies that employ more than one data collector, the goal is to ensure accuracy, such that each of the data collectors accumulates the information in the exact same way. According to Melnyk and Fineout-Overholt (2005), "It is important to train observers on the instrument that will be used in a study so that there is an interrater reliability or agreement on the construct that is being observed at least 90% of the time" (p. 277). If the 90% rate cannot be accomplished, the researcher and data collectors must establish a level of agreement for the specific project that considers the element of chance. Items which have to be carefully considered within this process are the need to use the same questions by each data collector, the ordering of the question delivery, and the acceptability of providing interpretations to the participants. If one data collector does these items but another does not, the results could be affected.

Now let's turn the attention to the different data collection methods. In the remainder of this text, for each method, an overview of the method expectations, strengths of the method, and limitations resulting from its use are discussed.

Test Methods

Overview

The use of **tests** within the research process is a fairly common methodology used to ascertain the explicit intelligence, talents, behaviors, or cognitive endeavor that is under investigation. Frequently, the terms "tool," "instrument," and "standardized test" are used interchangeably to describe this research method. These devices are used within research to appraise characteristics, aptitude, accomplishments, and performance. The use of self-reporting strategies when the goal is collection of vast amounts of research information appears to be an effective process. Directness and versatility are two key benefits associated with the use of tests (especially standardized tests) to discover the information that is sought within a research project.

The Educational Testing Service (ETS) *Testlink Test Collection Database* (2012) contains descriptions of more than 25,000 instruments, including research and unpublished instruments. Another resource for locating possible tools is a review of literature on a topic. Other research reports may also provide insight concerning tools that have been used in other research projects about an identified topic.

When a tool cannot be located to address a particular topic, the eight steps identified by Orcher (2005, p. 121) for building an appropriate instrument can be used:

1. Develop a plan.
2. Have the plan reviewed.
3. Revise the plan in light of the review.
4. Write items based on the plan.
5. Have the items reviewed.
6. Revise the items in light of the review.
7. Pilot test the instrument.
8. Revise the instrument in light of the pilot test.

Because an instrument is essential in addressing a topic, the development of a unique instrument can be a suitable alternative when the researcher cannot locate an appropriate one for data collection.

Strengths

Because tests are structured, a comparable motivation encouraging completion of the tool is presented for each participant, thus allowing for consistency during the data collection process. Each potential participant is offered the same benefits for agreeing to participate in the study. The equivalency of the measurement across research populations is another benefit from using this form of data collection. According to the Harvard Family Research Project (2004), tests and assessments provide additional valid and reliable data, as they tend to reduce the identification of perceptions and opinions. Because the functionality of a test is established through its validity and reliability, the usability of the tool within multiple population samples certifies the effectiveness of that tool. As tools are used repeatedly, the availability of reference group data grows, providing additional support for the tool and the data collected via use of that tool.

Another advantage to using tests relates to the administration process for the tool. Frequently, tests can be dispensed within a group setting, which saves time, expense, and energy. When the data can be collected in a group setting, the response rate is higher, due to the greater control exerted with this type of administration. Interrater reliability is improved since the instructions for the tool completion are given to the group rather than repeated for each individual.

An additional reward for using tests within the data collection process is the accessibility of an extensive assortment of tests. The wide variety of tests available for use in research projects reflects the many content areas that might be investigated. For this reason, the identification of a functional tool that is appropriate for use within a research project requires a persistent quest for the most applicable instrument. Because the same instrument/tool can be used both prior to and after an intervention has been delivered, changes in the results from both phases of the study can be compared.

The final advantage of tests within the research process derives from the practicality of undertaking data analysis because of the quantitative features of the data accumulated through use of this methodology. Because quantitative data are numerical in nature, those data can be easily used within the calculations used for statistical analysis.

? Think Outside the Box

Discuss the ethical aspects of using covert data collection methods.

Limitations

Although tests have multiple strengths related to their use in research, several limitations must also be considered with this methodology. If a test requires that a fee be paid for each individual taking the test, the expense can be excessive should a large sample be required. In addition, standardized tests must be evaluated for the presence of biases within the construction of the tool. These biases may be directed toward a certain group of individuals or a unique population. Because these tests are structured, this data collection method does not lend itself to open-ended and probing-type questions as easily as other methods do.

Another area the researcher must consider is the management of incomplete test documents. Will these incomplete forms be omitted from the data analyzed, or will the answered questions still be included? Does the inclusion of incomplete forms skew the results? When no responses are provided for selected aspects within any research instrument/tool, the appropriate management of the potential distortion of the results should be considered.

A final area of potential weakness or limitation with the use of tests relates to the problems encountered when an instrument/tool lacks psychometric data. Psychometric data are the validity and reliability measurements for the tool/instrument. It is the process of validating the tool for the anticipated use. If the tool does not measure what is being evaluated, then the use of the tool would be a limitation since the results could not be authenticated. In such cases, the project does not guarantee the validity or reliability for the device. When a tool lacks the foundational psychometric data, the use of the tool in other projects can provide validity and reliability of the tool, but it cannot certify the appropriateness of the tool for all uses.

Questionnaire Methods

Overview

When a questionnaire is the tool used for data collection, the data collection method is a survey process. A survey necessitates the querying of individuals through the use of some device that contains questions to be answered. A **questionnaire** is a data collection tool completed by a participant, where the researcher has the intent to discover what the individual thinks about a specific item. Questionnaires can be employed to gather information concerning knowledge, attitudes, beliefs, and feelings. Because it is a self-reporting device, a questionnaire can be provided as a paper-and-pencil device, a telephone survey, or a structured document uploaded onto the Internet, such as those generated through companies such as SurveyMonkey. As a result, the device can be administered in person, by mail, by telephone, or through an Internet delivery method.

According to Brink and Wood (2001), questionnaires limit the replies possible, because they involve directed answers to prearranged questions. Several types of questions can be incorporated into the questionnaire format, including dichotomous (yes/no), multiple choice, cafeteria, rank order, forced-choice ratings, checklists, calendar, and visual analogue (Polit & Beck, 2008). The researcher should consider the question format while assessing the applicability of different tools.

Should a researcher elect to develop a tool specific for the topic under investigation, several facets of the instrument should be vigilantly contemplated in designing the questionnaire (**Table 10-1**). Of course, the entire tool must address the research focus as well as be appropriate for the target population. These two items are fundamental to the process of developing the different questions and the format for the tool. The language employed within the instrument must be free of jargon, use familiar words, and be easily understood

Table 10-1

Design Tenets for Questionnaires

- Ensure that the tool addresses the research purpose, objectives, goals, and questions.
- Carefully consider the target population who will use the questionnaire so that the tool is easy to use.
- Use simple, familiar language without jargon and with correct grammar.
- Compose each question to be understandable, concise, and reasonably brief.
- Consider sequencing the questions from impersonal to personal, less sensitive to more sensitive, and broad to specific.
- Avoid using questions that hint at or direct responses, use double negatives, or embarrass the participant.
- Verify that each question addresses only a single topic.
- Structure the tool by beginning with questions that stimulate interest and group questions by topics.
- Cautiously word questions dealing with painful situations.
- Incorporate into the question all information necessary to address the issue under investigation.
- Construct the tool with the questions in the same order for each testing session to provide consistency in delivery and data collection.
- Ascertain the necessary format to accumulate the appropriate information: open-ended questions, closed-ended questions, mutually exclusive and exhaustive response categories, response categories for closed-ended questions (rating scales, ranking, semantic differential, checklists).
- Use various items and approaches to appraise conceptual ideas.
- Carefully consider the use of reverse wording on some of the questions to eliminate the possibility of a "response set."
- Determine the coding and/or weighting of the responses prior to the administration of the tool.
- Conduct a pilot test of the tool with a select group of the target population to confirm the applicability of the tool.

by the potential participants. Each statement should be short and specific, while addressing only one concept. Care must be given to the wording to prevent any leading of the participants toward a specific response.

According to Boswell (2010), "Good questions endeavor to scrutinize, evaluate, translate, illuminate, and reflect relationships about the multiple fragments of data assembled on any given topic" (paragraph 1). While neutral wording for each statement should be the goal, the use of active verbs in the statement is conducive to analysis, synthesis, and evaluation of the situation, thus resulting in an optimal response (Boswell, 2010).

The type of questions (open-ended versus closed-ended) is one of the initial concerns to be addressed in terms of the format of the instrument. **Open-ended questions** leave the direction of the answer up to the individual participant. This type of questioning is more frequently used to assess qualitative types of issues and exploratory research. In contrast, **closed-ended questions** force a response, because the researcher provides the answers. Closed-ended questions lend themselves to the collection of quantitative data and quantitative (confirmatory) research.

When developing closed-ended questions, the tool developer must ensure that the categories used for the answers are mutually exclusive and exhaustive. An example of a mutually exclusive category is the classification of years of service to an organization. The potential choices must not overlap, because overlapping of categories would cause confusion. Therefore, the ranges would need to be stated as follows:

Years of service: Less than 3, 4–6, 7–9, 10–12

For categories to be exhaustive, every possible option must be presented as a potential selection piece. In the ranges provided in the preceding example, individuals who had worked 13 or more years would not be provided with an option that they could select. However, keep in mind that the researcher may not want a certain range. In such a case, the researcher will need to provide a rationale for the exclusion. An example of when a lack of a specific range might be appropriate is when the researcher opens the year range to include every year possible.

The tool developer needs to carefully consider the information that is being sought through the use of the questionnaire. As that decision is confirmed, the tool should then address each and every potential aspect of the information being collected. For example, the types of response categories are an important consideration with closed-ended questionnaires. The instrument developer should consider several types of responses, including rating scales, ranking, semantic differential, and checklists (**Table 10-2**). Ultimately, the type of information that is being collected should drive the choice of response categories used for the tool.

Strengths

The use of questionnaires for data collection has several advantages. A primary reason for using this methodology is the ability to access a larger sample in a group setting at a minimum expense. Participants also seem to favor the use of questionnaires because this method of data collection provides a greater sense of anonymity. The use of questionnaires can also be time-sensitive to the participant. As the process is begun, the researcher can state that the completion of the questionnaire should take a designated amount of time. Thus, the participant can then determine if they have that amount of time to use for the process. Another advantage identified by Brink and Wood (2001) is the potential to collect an enhanced quantity of data with an extensive variety of topics using a standard format. A final advantage to the use of this data collection method is the opportunity to determine the validity and reliability of the tool, thereby strengthening the overall design of the research project.

Table 10-2

Different Types of Questionnaire Responses	
Type of response	**Example of response**

Rating scales	On a scale of from 0 to 10, with 10 being the most severe pain you can imagine and 0 being no pain at all, where does your current pain level fall?
	
	    0 1 2 3 4 5 6 7 8 9 10
	    No pain Most severe pain

Ranking	Nurses rank different things at different levels. Below is a list of items that many nurses value in the workplace. Please designate their order of significance to you by placing "1" beside the most significant, "2" beside the next most significant, and so on. _____ Salary _____ Competent peers _____ Effective workplace _____ Management workload _____ Opportunities to advance
Semantic differential	On each of the combinations provided, place an "X" to reflect how you see yourself function related to the two associated terms. Competent !__!__!__!__!__!__!__! Incompetent Pleasant !__!__!__!__!__!__!__! Unpleasant Responsible !__!__!__!__!__!__!__! Irresponsible Successful !__!__!__!__!__!__!__! Unsuccessful
Checklists	Please check all of the applicable characteristics you think a nurse should have in order to participate in evidence-based practice (EBP). Critical thinking abilities _____ Energy _____ Knowledge about searching _____ Years of nursing experience _____ Desire for EBP _____

Limitations

The use of questionnaires as a data collection method does present some notable problems, however. To ensure adequate sampling, the tool must be short and to the point. Long, cumbersome questionnaires result in individuals electing to not complete the tool, which in turn requires enrollment of additional sample participants to complete the research project and can delay the project.

Another limitation resulting from the use of questionnaires in data collection is the potential for participants to be nonresponsive to selected items within the tool. This nonresponsiveness to items results in a dilemma for the researcher, as the inclusion of an incomplete questionnaire becomes an important question to address prior to the actual use of the tool within a study.

A final limitation resulting from the use of this method is the time-consuming nature of the data collection process. For open-ended questions, the differences within the verbal responses must be carefully considered and correlated. This process is time-consuming because the verbal responses are not preselected responses. Determinations concerning the comparability between terms must be made carefully, and supported by documentation to reflect the thought processes used. For closed-ended questions, the establishment of the data set, the process of data input, and the actual inputting of the quantitative data must be considered and planned, because it requires focused time to manually enter each piece of data.

Interview Methods

Overview

Brink and Wood (2001) identified the key variation between questionnaires and **interviews** as the presence of an individual to conduct the interview; this "personal touch" is the basic difference between the two data collection methods. Otherwise, the expectations and concerns about interview questions are the same as arise in the development of a questionnaire or survey.

Within this compilation design, the use of an interviewer to direct the questioning process requires that trust and rapport be developed between interviewer and interviewee. The interviewer has to present a positive, supportive manner to engage the individual being queried. If the individual does not perceive the environment to be appropriate, the data collected may be skewed. Thus the environment selected for the session is of paramount importance. Because the questions are presented by the interviewer, the ordering of the questions and the environment wherein the questions are presented should allow for openness from the interviewee and the increased depth of the resulting responses. If a room is too hot, too cold, too noisy, or too open, the participant may elect not to continue the interview or may be less open to engaging in dialogue. According to the Harvard Family Research Project (2004), "Questions [in an interview] are generally open-ended and responses are documented in thorough, detailed notes or transcription" (p. 3).

Interview data collection can pull together information from both the quantitative and qualitative realms. When quantitative information is sought from the interview process, the questions are completed through the use of a structured format. Frequently, closed-ended questions are administered by means of a standardized test. Each question is asked in the same pattern or flow. The environment of the interview is controlled in an attempt to reduce the effect of confounding environmental variables.

If the purpose of the planned data collection is to seek qualitative information, the entire process can be managed in a less structured manner. Often, the questions used for this type of interview are geared more toward the open-ended type. When an informal conversational interview format is used, the process is impulsive and freely structured. An interviewer serves as a mediator who guides participants as they move between topics. To better facilitate the process, the interviewer should initiate the discussion with a subject matter that is significant but not problematic.

The flexibility of the interview process is perceived as both an advantage and a disadvantage for this data collection method. Because of the openness of the data collection process, the interviewer collects not only verbal data, but also nonverbal data. By juxtaposing the nonverbal communication with the verbal statements, clarification related to the meanings of the comments and data is improved and facilitated. The disadvantage is related to the wealth of data that can be collected and then must be utilized or analyzed to determine the appropriateness of the material. The volume of data collected can make the data analysis process overwhelming and cumbersome.

Strengths

One of the initial strengths noted with the interview data collection design is the resulting powerful and abundant information accumulated, which paints an extensive portrait of the issue at hand and may have far-reaching implications. Another benefit gained from using this design is the ability, through the use of communication, to highlight issues that may present themselves only during the course of discussion as the interview progresses. The ability to measure attitudes, probe feelings, pose follow-up questions, gather internal meanings and ways of thinking, and control the depth of information amassed are other advantages associated with the use of the interview data collection method. An extra advantage is that interviews allow for the collection of data without the requirement that the participant be able to read or write.

Limitations

The interview data collection process does present some limitations that must be considered as a researcher decides which method to use. This methodology for gathering information can be both expensive and time-consuming. Conducting individual interviews requires time-intensive interactions and close observation of the nonverbal communication that helps to clarify the verbal responses. The interviewer must be able to elicit the information expected for the research project. Related to this limitation of the interviewer is interrater reliability. When more than one interviewer is used to collect the data, the interviewer could alter and/or transform the data collected by the use of various processes. When the data is not collected in the same manner by each interviewer or data collector, bias may be introduced. Another weakness to consider is the potential for the participants to say what they perceive is appropriate or socially desirable, instead of what they actually believe. In addition, the sample size is often small when the interview methodology is used, making generalizations to a larger population more difficult. Finally, analysis of the open-ended, subjective data collected via interviews requires time and thought to ensure that the results are valid and supported by the information.

Focus Group Methods

 Overview

Although **focus groups** share many of the characteristics discussed in relation to interviews, a focus group entails a type of "coordinated interview," in which approximately 6 to 12 homogeneous individuals are led in the discussion of a selected topic at the same time. According to Shaha, Wenzel, and Hill (2011), "focus groups—moderated group discussions designed to allow research participants to exchange, discuss, agree, or disagree about opinions, attitudes, and experiences— are an increasingly popular way of eliciting the attitudes or opinions of populations regarding sensitive, under-investigated topics" (p. 78). Each focus session tends to last approximately one to three hours. To facilitate the data collection process, the sessions typically are audiotaped or videotaped for analysis at a later time.

The focus group leader should understand where the session should come together in regard to the data to be collected. This leader must ensure that the research topic is adequately covered during the discussion. The focus group leader challenges are to persuade everyone to share in the dialogue, motivate conversation, channel the progression between the different topics, stay impartial and endeavor to not interject any biases into the discussion while maintaining control of the discussion.

Many different features within the process need to be controlled and manipulated. The participants must understand that their opinions and experiences are important, such that no answers are inappropriate within the context of the subject under investigation. Care concerning the setting for the focus group should address comfort, privacy, and convenience. Although the session is recorded in some manner, the focus group leader and researcher must ensure that the participants feel secure in the knowledge that the recording will be used only to pull out the information provided.

The researcher should also give thought and consideration to the membership of the group. Shaha, Wenzel, and Hill (2011) suggest that the researcher should consider group members' educational background, job positions, and/or work environments. When these items are not taken into consideration, problems with feasibility, power, confidentiality, and integrity can develop. A homogeneous grouping with regard to gender, age, and socioeconomic status enhances the generalizability of the resulting data. Putting thought into the size and composition of each focus group is essential to maximize the effectiveness of the data collection process.

As the focus group is pulled together, the focus group leader should begin the session with a personal introduction concerning the research team members, purpose for the session, discussion about why the session is important, and what type of administrative support is in place. It is also important that the members of the focus group understand that any participation is completely voluntary on their part. For the session to be successful, members must feel comfortable in discussing their attitudes and opinions on the topic without fearing any type of repercussions. During the session, the focus group leader and/or research team member must make sure that distractions such as background noises are removed. Time must be allowed for the initial development of trust between the members of the focus group and the group leader. Without this trust, the information obtained can be biased and compromised.

Strengths

Many of the same advantages listed previously for interviews also hold true for the focus group data collection method. Because the collection of data is done in an open and revealing manner, exploration of ideas and concepts can grow and develop as the session progresses. As members of the focus group discuss the different aspects presented through the process, the moderator can probe the in-depth information for additional understanding of the phenomenon. Each individual is allowed to react to other participants without having to carry the entire data collection process by himself or herself.

Limitations

Limitations of this design process relate to the sizing and management of the focus groups. The moderator must be adept at conducting the process. Getting the right moderator, organizing the appropriate focus group members, conducting the session, and completing the management of the data can also be quite expensive. Within each group, extrovert personalities must be controlled, while involvement of introvert personalities is encouraged.

Observation Methods

Overview

According to Wood and Ross-Kerr (2006), "**Observation** is a method of collecting descriptive, behavioral data and is extremely useful in nursing studies because one can observe behavior as it occurs" (p. 171). The entire process of observing individuals results in an interactive engagement. Frequently, what a person says and what a person does can be two different pieces of information. Observation allows for the confirmation of what is said by the viewing of specific behaviors and activities. It is an articulation of individualism, character preconceptions, and beliefs. Each individual assesses a situation based on his or her unique background and philosophy of life. As a result, the selectivity of this type of data collection must be highly patterned by the expectations of the study. Clarity related to the behavioral information under investigation is imperative.

LoBiondo-Wood and Haber (1998) specified four conditions needed for the use of observation as a data collection method:

- "Observations undertaken are consistent with the study's specific objectives,
- Standardized and systematic plan for the observation and the recording of data,
- All of the observations are checked and controlled, and
- Observations are related to scientific concepts and theories" (p. 312).

The complexity of the process requires attention to be given to the operationalization of the variables. The variables are frequently the behaviors being observed. Consequently, the individual characteristics and conditions (traits, symptoms, verbal communications, nonverbal conditions, activities, skills, or environmental aspects) should be clearly and distinctly documented for the integrity of the data collection process. Another issue that arises with this type of data collection process is whether the observer will be directed to try to provoke some behavior/action by the individuals being observed.

? Think Outside the Box

www

After selecting an evidence-based topic, develop open-ended and closed-ended questions that could be used to address the topic. Debate the benefits of using open-ended versus closed-ended question formats.

Both quantitative and qualitative observations can be used within this research effort. Because generalizability of the results is desired, a checklist of the behaviors/observations is frequently used to provide a structure for the analysis phase of the process. Put simply, quantitative observations require the standardization of those items to be counted or not counted. Likewise, clear directions related to the operational definitions of the selected behaviors must be given. When these behaviors are unmistakably defined, the observational sessions produce the quantitative data expected from the research process. The definition should include the "who, what, when, where, why, and how" for the behavior on which data are to be collected within the study. As an example, if one piece of data that a researcher wants to collect is the number of times a person made eye contact during a lecture presentation, clarification is needed as to what duration of eye contact would be counted. In this case, the researcher might establish that each time the lecturer made eye contact with a student for at least 45 seconds, the contact would be counted.

In contrast to quantitative observation, qualitative observation is investigative and open-ended. The resulting information provides massive amounts of field notes to analyze.

Four diverse observer roles create a continuum of data collection with the observation methodology:

- *Complete participant.* The observer takes the role of member within the sample; the data is collected via a covert (hidden) process; the members of the group are not informed about the data collection process.
- *Participant-as-observer.* The observer continues to work from within the group but collects the data through an overt (informed) process; the members of the group are aware that the observer is taking on the dual roles of member of the group and spectator.
- *Observer-as-participant.* The observer does work from within the group but spends more time in the role of spectator, instead of member of the group; data are collected in an overt manner.
- *Complete observer.* The observer is totally in the role of watcher; covert observations are used to collect the data.

? Think Outside the Box

Using a PICOT question format, describe how you would collect data for the topic you addressed in the PICOT question.

For each data collection session, the researcher takes time to conscientiously consider which of these depths of observation is appropriate for the study population. Because some of the methods require covert (undercover) data collection, the researcher must also justify why this clandestine method is needed. In these situations, the question is raised as to the necessity of collecting information without the individual's knowledge and the ethics of that undisclosed process. The researcher must diligently document the manner in which the individuals would be protected from harm.

On the other side of the picture, when the participants know they are being watched, the researcher has to work to ensure that behaviors are not modified due to this knowledge (the Hawthorne effect). Frequently, the course of action used to ensure that individuals are behaving naturally is related to the length of time the observations are occurring. The researcher/observer may have to be immersed in this situation of being observed for a long period of time so that the participants become comfortable with him or her being there. As their comfort with the researcher's presence increases, the individuals return to their normal behaviors, allowing the observer to then see the normalcy of the situation.

Strengths

According to the Harvard Family Research Project (2004), the observation method provides "highly detailed information from an external perspective on what actually occurs in programs" (p. 3). The depth of the information obtained is the primary benefit from collecting data in this manner. Having someone watch the activity under investigation allows events that might otherwise be undetected in everyday life to be identified and discussed. Observation as a data collection process is seen as an effective method for understanding important related items of a designated setting. Another advantage of this method is that it can be used with any individual regardless of educational preparation. Thus the behaviors, attitudes, and involvement of individuals who may have weaker verbal skills can be evaluated and researched.

Limitations

The limitations of this data collection practice flow from the time-consuming, labor-intensive, and expensive nature of completing the observation process. Interrater reliability of the observers and the training of these individuals have equally important implications for the quality of the resulting data. Without the assurance that the observers are knowledgeable about the entire process, the excellence of the data may be questioned.

Bias is a major problem that must be addressed throughout the observation period. Researchers and observers should be upfront about the presence of any biases that might potentially compromise the integrity of the study results. It becomes imperative that all biases are identified and reported. Because biases cannot be completely removed, the acknowledgment of the existence of the predispositions provides validation of the results. Consumers of the research results can then be aware that these preconceptions were recognized.

Secondary (Existing) Data Methods

Overview

The data collection process using secondary (existing) data builds on the information collected from another study. Because it takes the data compiled for another reason and applies it in a different manner, this method of reevaluating should be carefully considered and contemplated. The researcher must explain which pieces of the primary data will be used in reassessment of the information. Within this process, the researcher reconsiders a part of the information accumulated through some other manner in an attempt to address a follow-up type of question.

The data used for these secondary assessment projects might include documents, physical data, and/or archived research data, for example. When documents are used, they could include personal documents, such as letters, diaries, or family pictures, as well as official documents, such as attendance records, budgets, annual reports, newspapers, yearbooks, minutes, or client records.

Strengths

The advantages of using this method to assess existing records result from the availability of the records. A data collection process that relies on secondary data can be completed without any intrusion into the lives of people. The extra time gained by using the sources already assembled can be devoted to collecting key pieces of information that previously were overlooked or not valued.

In addition, the reevaluation of documents allows for exploration of alternative conclusions. The environmental aspects and historic perceptions can augment the interpretation of the data. A fuller evaluation of the information can be completed, thereby providing a more comprehensive understanding of the phenomena under investigation.

By using previously collected records, researchers can identify trends, because the entirety of the incident can be manipulated. For the most part, the use of secondary (existing) data is also less expensive than collection of primary data.

Limitations

Some of the weaknesses of this data collection method revolve around the restrictiveness of the data sources. The only data that can be collected and analyzed are the data that were initially amassed. The researcher cannot add questions and can access only the information that has been compiled. Among the other barriers presented by the use of secondary data is the potential for the data to be out-of-date.

Another obstacle a researcher may encounter related to this type of data collection results from the restriction on accessing certain documents. If the documents are controlled to protect individual privacy, access to the information could be problematic.

An additional hindrance ensuing from this method is the limitation resulting from the sample used for the initial data collection. Specifically, the original sampling inclusion and exclusion criteria could negatively affect the secondary assessment of archived research data.

A final problem with the use of secondary (existing) data is the lack of open-ended or qualitative data related to the question. The researcher would need to acknowledge the unavailability of this type of data, which might or might not affect the quality of the project. If the project did not require the inclusion of qualitative data, then a secondary assessment of data would be appropriate. If qualitative data were desired to paint the total picture of the occurrence under investigation, the likelihood of accessing the original sample to gain further data would be highly problematic, if not impossible. Thus the reevaluation of secondary sources for additional results can pose difficulties because of the lack of initially collected information relating to the topic under current discussion.

Biophysiological Methods

Overview

The final type of data collection method is the use of biological indicators to organize the data being sought for the research activity. The research community views biophysiological measures as objective data. Researchers may use the **biophysiological data** collection process either alone or in combination with other methods.

This method of data collection necessitates the use of specialized equipment to establish the physical and/or biological condition of the subjects. Two types of biophysiological methods are possible:

- **In vivo:** Requires the use of some apparatus to evaluate one or more elements of a participant. Examples of the types of items evaluated include blood pressure measurements, electrocardiograms, temperatures, muscular activity, and respiratory rates and rhythms.
- **In vitro:** Requires the extraction of physiological materials from the participants, frequently via a laboratory analysis. Examples of the types of items within this realm include bacterial counts and identifications, tissue biopsies, glucose levels, and cholesterol levels.

This type of data collection process is frequently used with experimental and quasi-experimental research designs. Typically, the data are used to advance the implementation of specific nursing actions. Because of the type of information collected through this method, the research projects gathering biophysiological data tend to be more structured and controlled.

? Think Outside the Box

www

Discuss the challenges involved in using in vitro and in vivo data collection methods.

Strengths

The advantages of using this kind of data collection are the objectivity, precision, and sensitivity of the information compiled. The facts acquired from the use of specialized equipment have the tendency to be viewed as having increased independence from bias and subjectivity. As a result, the research community views this level of data with enhanced respect.

Limitations

The disadvantages related to the use of the specialized apparatus include the cost of obtaining the measurements and calibrating the instruments, which can be enormous with some data collection processes. Also, the acquisition of data by instrumentation requires specialized knowledge and training to be able to accurately gather the data. Additional research assistants may be required to perform the testing processes, leading to escalating costs, greater time commitments, and concerns related to interrater reliability.

A final problem resulting from this type of data collection is the potential reluctance of the accessible population to participate in such a study. Some members of the accessible population may decline to allow the physiological and biological measurements. The researcher must obtain informed consent from each individual prior to the collection of data and/or samples for analysis.

Systematic Analysis

With the increasing focus on evidence-based practice, systematic reviews and meta-analysis reviews are becoming commonplace in the literature. These different forms of pulling the evidence together provide a clean synthesis of current knowledge about a topic. The Institute of Medicine of the National Academies (2011) define a **systematic review** as a process identifying, selecting, assessing, and synthesizing the findings from similar but individualized studies. This process of data collection allows for the clarification of what is known and not known about an identified topic. Within the data collection process, another method utilized within evidence-based practice is **meta-analysis**. According to materials developed by Northern Arizona University (2001), a meta-analysis is a process of merging the outcomes from multiple studies related to one primary topic. The strength of each set of conclusions is determined to provide an overall view of the evidence available on the identified topic. The methods used within the various studies, along with the quantification of the findings from the studies, are condensed into a summary document related to the topic under investigation. The effect size within a meta-analysis seeks to establish the relevance of the tests, treatments, and methods used in the research studies under consideration. These documents are then used to provide the context for the next steps in the research process and the determination of the reliability of the evidence related to that topic.

The Institute of Medicine of the National Academies (2011) developed the Standards for Systematic Reviews. The standards are developed to provide direction to individuals for completing a systematic review in an effective and manageable approach. Hemingway and Brereton (2009) identified five aspects that demonstrate a high-quality systematic review. To generate an effective review, all relevant published and unpublished evidence should be included within the document. After all the evidence is compiled, inclusion criteria as to which pieces of evidence are to be included in the review must be determined. It is not possible to include everything, so care must be given to the determination of the inclusion criteria to allow for effective evidence to be included. After the selection of the evidence to be included in the review, each piece and report must be assessed for the quality of that evidence toward the goal of the review. As the appraisals are completed on each of the studies, incorporation of the results into an unbiased report of those findings is imperative. Following the synthesizing of the results, an interpretation of the findings in a balanced and impartial summary is the culmination of the review. Effective consideration of any flaws in the evidence must be noted within a high-quality systematic review.

Systematic reviews must be completed with a peer-reviewed protocol to allow for replication of the review as needed. Hemingway and Brereton (2009) stated that, looked "at individually, each article may offer little insight into the problem at hand; the hope is that, when taken together within a systematic review, a clearer (and more consistent) picture will emerge" (p. 2). The process for completing a review requires that each member of the review team carefully and appropriately assess each of the selected articles/documents utilizing the agreed upon criterion. To effectively conduct a systematic review, five steps should be followed. The first step within the process is the formation of a suitable and fitting review question. Within the healthcare question, attention to the principle objective, along with the phenomena of interest, is critical. Once the question is clearly worded, a search of the literature and other sources of evidence is initiated. Since systematic reviews need to be unbiased, the search for evidence must be accomplished in any venue where the evidence for that topic could be located. Furthermore, it is essential that each and every view of the topic is included in the search. The third component within the review process is an assessment of the studies. Using the inclusion criteria, specific documents are selected to be included in the review. From this point, the researcher performs a critical appraisal of each document to determine the strength of the evidence based on the methodological quality of that study. Some questions which can be used to drive the appraisal of each document are:

- Is the subject defined adequately to allow the development of the review?
- How thorough was the search for studies and evidence?
- Did the inclusion criteria provide a clear and concise description to be used that allowed for the fair application of the criteria?
- Is the review conducted as a blinded or independent review to decrease biases?
- How was missing information managed within the review?
- Do the included studies and documents reflect similar effects? If not, why?

■ Did the review speak to the idea of robustness of the process?
■ Were the recommendations supported by the strength of the quality of the evidence? (Hemingway & Brereton, 2009).

Once the overview of the documents is determined, the combining of the findings is carefully and thoughtfully integrated into the review. Care and attention to the depth and quality of the review must be established. Two types of systematic reviews used in the research field are meta-synthesis and meta-analysis. A meta-synthesis is a review which primarily focuses on qualitative data. A meta-analysis utilizes quantitative data to address a clinical effectiveness problem. The process for either type of analysis includes the same steps listed above. The difference between these two is the types of studies and evidence considered within the review. The analysis would be directed by the research method used in the different documents utilized in the review.

Achievement of the Data Collection Strategy

Each of the data collection strategies profiled in this chapter has both benefits and limitations. The researcher must carefully consider the PICOT question, research purpose, research question/hypothesis, research design, sampling method, cost considerations, and time restrictions as he or she identifies the appropriate data collection plan. According to the Harvard Family Research Project (2004), "Using multiple methods to assess the same outcomes [e.g., using surveys and document review to assess program management] provides a richer, more detailed picture" (p. 5). Although it certainly adds to the richness of the results, the use of multiple methods of data collection also increases the resources (cost, personnel, and tools) required to carry out the project.

Each researcher must carefully consider the many different strategies available for accessing the information needed to address the identified research problem. In singling out the appropriate data collection process, justification for those choices needs to be documented. Because each method has its own set of strengths and limitations, the primary objective for the researcher is to substantiate the rationale for the choices made to dispatch the research challenge.

In determining the strategy, the objectives of the project, along with the type of data required, should be taken into account during the decision-making process. If the strategy for a research or evidence-based project has been determined to be the use of a tool, several aspects must be considered. The selection of a tool, the questions that need to be developed, and the method for implementing the tool/questions must all be contemplated. In addition, the environment of the data collection process is just as important as the individual questions to be addressed. Within the environment, the participants must be made to feel secure with the process, or the resulting data could be compromised.

Evidence-Based Practice Considerations

Within the realm of evidence-based practice (EBP), the focus is more on the idea of outcome measures. According to Melnyk and Fineout-Overholt (2005), "The effectiveness and usefulness of outcomes measurement is affected by: the quality of the data, the consistency and accuracy of the data collection process, the commitment and ability of those collecting the data and making decisions based on findings, and the timing of data collection" (p. 306). The principal issues for data collection, as viewed from the EBP perspective, are the quality of the process and the content of the data collected. Each choice made by a researcher concerning the data to be collected, the method or methods to be used, and the environment used to collect the data must be founded on reliable, sensible judgments. The rationales for these decisions can make or break the study by determining the validity and reliability of the results produced by the study. If the decisions are not supported by appropriate thought processes and planning, then the entire inquiry is in jeopardy.

A researcher need not select the strongest data collection methods possible, but researchers must select the optimal strategies for getting the data needed to answer the questions asked and provide an appropriate justification for each of those decisions. The key is to make a decision and justify the selection with sound reasoning and a sound decision-making process. The entire research or evidence-based process rests on the quality of the data. The data form the foundation on which the results, recommendations, and outcomes of a study are based; the merit of the data becomes the underpinning for the research or evidence-based conclusions. The researcher must provide a sound rationale and strong support for the decisions made concerning the data collection process.

Summary Points

1. Data come in many varieties, and data collection is achieved through numerous methodologies.
2. Data collection sources are items or strategies for accumulating the information desired.

3. Data collection tools are the tangible devices used to complete the collection of the data.
4. The major methods of data collection are tests, questionnaires, interviews, focus groups, observations, secondary (existing) data, and biophysiological data.
5. Attention must be given to the information that actually exists and the information that is accessible. These two types of data may not be the same.
6. The basic objective in research is to collect the data in the same manner for each of the participants so that unique environmental, societal, and physical dimensions are diminished.
7. Another key aspect of the data collection process is the establishment of interrater reliability when more than one data collector is used to gather evidence.
8. Tests are used to ascertain the specific knowledge, talents, behaviors, and/or cognitive capabilities under investigation.
9. A questionnaire/survey is a data collection tool that is completed by a participant and allows the researcher to discover what the individual thinks about a specific item.
10. When interviews are used as the data collection process, establishing trust and rapport between interviewer and interviewee is essential.
11. Environmental aspects of the study setting must be taken into account when planning to conduct interviews and/or focus groups.
12. Observation allows for the confirmation of what is said by viewing the participant's specific behaviors and activities.
13. Several ethical issues need to be carefully considered as the method of observation is determined.
14. A data collection process that uses secondary (existing) data builds on the information collected from another study or document.
15. Systematic reviews are key components within the documentation of evidence.
16. A systematic review is a process identifying, selecting, assessing, and synthesizing the findings from similar but individualized studies.

RED FLAGS

- Tools used for quantitative data collection should have documentation of their validity and reliability indices.
- If desired, effective discussion of the entire data collection process should be provided in the report of the study results to allow for replication of the study.
- The use of appropriate tools to collect the information being sought must be addressed.
- The type of information needed to satisfy the research question must be reflected in the study design.
- The potential for a Hawthorne effect must be evaluated.
- If two or more data collectors are used within a study, interrater reliability must be established.
- Systematic reviews should document the different steps taken to ensure the quality of the review process.

Multiple Choice Questions

1. Which of the following examples is *not* a data collection source used as a mechanism for amassing the information?

   A. Focus group discussions
   B. Observations
   C. Work excitement instrument
   D. Project progress reports

2. Which of the following processes is *not* a major method of data collection?

   A. Observations
   B. Open-ended questions
   C. Secondary (existing) data
   D. Tests

3. When considering the different data collection schemes, researchers must be careful to contemplate the presence of the Hawthorne effect. The Hawthorne effect is defined as a process in which the:

   A. Participant does not modify his or her behavior to meet the expectations of the study.
   B. Researcher modifies his or her behavior because of conducting the study.
   C. Researcher modifies the participants' behavior based on the data collected.
   D. Participant modifies his or her behavior as a result of engagement in the study.

4. As a researcher, you are attempting to gather data about the effects of a drug on individuals between the ages of 20 and 40 years. On the developed tool, the age ranges are provided as follows: 20–25; 25–30; 30–35; 35–40. Which problem is evident in this set of responses related to the question seeking to know a person's current age?

   A. The categories are not mutually exclusive.
   B. The categories are not exhaustive.
   C. The categories are written in a closed-ended format.
   D. There is no problem with this set of response categories.

5. Which of the following are tenets for use when designing a questionnaire?

   A. Use a variety of items and approaches to appraise conceptual ideas.
   B. Ensure that each question addresses the entire scope of the topic.
   C. Use simple but appropriate jargon for the designated topics.
   D. Both A and B.

6. Which of the following is a method of data collection?

    A.   Experimental
    B.   Grounded theory
    C.   Observation
    D.   Cross-sectional

7. When developing questions for an instrument, a researcher should be careful in the wording to

    A.   Provide hints toward the response.
    B.   Use jargon as needed.
    C.   Use single-topic questions.
    D.   Use cultural aspects to provide context.

8. Both open-ended and closed-ended questions are used to collect data for research endeavors. Which of the following statements is true?

    A.   Open-ended questions are used to collect primarily quantitative data.
    B.   Closed-ended questions are used to collect quantitative data information, because the researcher provides the answers for selection.
    C.   Open-ended questions provide confirmatory information, because the data are focused by the question.
    D.   Closed-ended questions are used to collect exploratory data, because the information is left up to the individual.

9. Open-ended questions provide primarily _____ data.

    A.   Confirmatory
    B.   Exhaustive
    C.   Qualitative
    D.   Quantitative

10. Which of the following statements is true concerning observation?

    A.   Clear directions related to the operational definitions of the selected behavior must be determined.
    B.   Ethical considerations are a minor concern within this method of data collection.
    C.   Observation data collection strategies result in manageable amounts of field notes to analyze.
    D.   Within observational sessions, the observer is always known to the participant.

11. When creating a questionnaire, it is essential to do each of the following *except*

    A.   Be concise and reasonably brief.
    B.   Code and weight the responses prior to the administration of the tool.
    C.   Conduct a pilot testing of the tool with a select group of the target population.
    D.   Use double-negative questions regularly within the tool.

12. A researcher decides to use observation as the data collection method for a study. To effectively collect the needed data from college-age students, the researcher enrolls in a selected college course to be able to observe and collect data about the behaviors of the students. The researcher is using which observation role?

A. Complete participant
B. Participant-as-observer
C. Observer-as-participant
D. Complete observer

13. A class of preschool children is observed via a one-way mirror for a research project designed to determine the aggressive behaviors of boys and girls. The parents of the students are not informed about the research project, as no intervention is planned. Which type of data is being collected?

A. Quantitative
B. Covert
C. Overt
D. Time sequence

14. Which of the following terms best describes data compiled for another reason and applied in a different manner?

A. Primary data
B. Secondary data
C. Novice data
D. Experimental data

15. Which of the following biophysiological tests is an example of in vivo data?

A. Complete blood count
B. Urinalysis
C. Respiratory rate
D. Bacterial count

16. A systematic review considers

A. Reports about clinical standards.
B. Research and other documents which address the topic being reviewed.
C. Only opinion documents that address a topic of interest.
D. Only quantitative research reports.

Discussion Questions

1. A researcher begins to develop the demographic section for use within a project. The three questions developed are the following:

   A. How many years have you been practicing professional nursing?
      * 0–5 years
      * 5–10 years
      * 10–15 years
      * More than 15 years

   B. What is your highest nursing degree?
      * ADN
      * BSN
      * MSN
      * Doctorate

   C. I have never been identified in a legal case.
      * Yes
      * No

   Which problems are present within these three questions that need to be corrected?

2. A researcher initially planned to use covert data collection techniques (observing a class of teenagers via a one-way mirror) for a research project designed to determine the aggressive behaviors of boys and girls. Neither the parents nor the students were to be informed about the research project, as no intervention was planned. Which other observational role might the researcher use to make the data collection process an overt one?

3. A researcher has decided to conduct a structured interview with nursing students concerning their perceptions of what tasks constitute the provision of spiritual care within an acute care setting. Write three open-ended questions and three closed-ended questions related to this idea.

Suggested Readings

Ahern, N. R. (2005). Using the Internet to conduct research. *Nurse Researcher*, *13*(2), 55–70.

Colling, J. (2004, June). Coding, analysis, and dissemination of study results. *Urology Nursing*, *24*(3), 215–216.

Duffy, M. E. (2005). Systematic reviews: Their role and contribution to evidence-based practice. *Clinical Nurse Specialist*, *19*(1), 15–17.

Halcomb, E., & Andrew, S. (2005). Triangulation as a method for contemporary nursing research. *Nurse Researcher*, *13*(2), 71–82.

Happ, M. B., Dabbs, A. D., Tate, J., Hricik, A., & Erlen, J. (2006). Exemplars of mixed methods data combination and analysis. *Nursing Research*, *55*(2), S43–S49.

Holopainen, A., Hakulinen-Viitanen, T., & Tossavainen, K. (2008). Systematic review—A method for nursing research. *Nurse Researcher*, *16*(1), 72–83.

Institute of Medicine of the National Academies. (2011). *Standards for systematic reviews: Report at a glance.* Retrieved from http://iom.edu/Reports/2011/Finding-What-Works-in-Health-Care-Standards-for-Systematic-Reviews/Standards.aspx

Kitchenham, B. (2004). *Procedures for performing systematic reviews* (Joint Technical Report TR/SE-0401). Keele, UK: Keele University. Retrieved from http://csnotes.upm.edu.my/kelasmaya/pgkm20910.nsf/0/715071a8011d4c2f482577a700386d3a/$FILE/10.1.1.122.3308%5B1%5D.pdf

Kuipers, P., & Hartley, S. (2006). A process for the systematic review of community-based rehabilitation evaluation reports: Formulating evidence for policy and practice. *International Journal of Rehabilitation Research*, *29*(1), 27–30.

Priest, H., Roberts, P., & Woods, L. (2002). An overview of three different approaches to the interpretation of qualitative data. Part 1: Theoretical issues. *Nurse Researcher*, *10*(1), 30–42.

Vishnevsky, T., & Beanlands, H. (2004). Qualitative research. *Nephrology Nursing Journal*, *31*(2), 234–238.

Examples of Data Collection

Questionnaires:

Palese, A., Tomietto, M., Suhonen, R., Efstathiou, G., Tsangari, H., Merkouris, A., . . . Papastavrou, E. (2011). Surgical patient satisfaction as an outcome of nurses' caring behaviors: A descriptive and correlational study in six European countries. *Journal of Nursing Scholarship, 43*(4), 341–350.

Interviews:

Adhiambo Onyango, M., & Mott, S. (2011). The nexus between bridewealth, family curse, and spontaneous abortion among southern Sudanese women. *Journal of Nursing Scholarship, 43*(4), 376–384.

Focus groups/interviews:

Wood, E. B., Hutchinson, M. K., Kahwa, E., Hewitt, H., & Waldron, D. (2011). Jamaican adolescent girls with other male sexual partners. *Journal of Nursing Scholarship, 43*(4), 396–404.

Secondary data analysis:

Nantsupawat, A., Srisuphan, W., Kunaviktikul, W., Wichaikhum, O. A., Aungsuroch, Y., & Aiken, L. H. (2011). Impact of nurse work environment and staffing on hospital nurse and quality of care in Thailand. *Journal of Nursing Scholarship, 43*(4), 426–432.

References

Boswell, C. (2010). Questioning students to develop critical thinking. In L. Caputi (Ed.), *Teaching nursing: The art and science, Volume 2* (2nd ed., pp. 423–453). Glen Ellyn, IL: College of DuPage Press.

Brink, P. J., & Wood, M. J. (2001). *Basic steps in planning nursing research: From question to proposal* (5th ed.). Sudbury, MA: Jones and Bartlett.

Creswell, J. W. (2003). *Research design: Qualitative, quantitative, and mixed method approaches* (2nd ed.). Thousand Oaks, CA: Sage Publications.

Educational Testing Services. (2012). *Testlink test collection database.* Retrieved from http://1340.sydneyplus.com/ETS_Test_Collection/Portal.asp

Harvard Family Research Project. (2004). Detangling data collection: Methods for gathering data. *Out-of-School Time Evaluation Snapshot, 5,* 1–6. Retrieved from http://www.hfrp.org/publications-resources/browse-our-publications/detangling-data-collection-methods-for-gathering-data

Hemingway, P., & Brereton, N. (2009). *What is a systematic review?* Hayward Medical Communications. Retrieved from http://www.whatisseries.co.uk

Institute of Medicine of the National Academies. (2011). *Finding what works in health care: Standards for systematic reviews.* Retrieved from http://iom.edu/Reports/2011/Finding-What-Works-in-Health-Care-Standards-for-Systematic-Reviews.aspx

LoBiondo-Wood, G., & Haber, J. (1998). *Nursing research: Methods, critical appraisal, and utilization* (4th ed.). St. Louis, MO: Mosby.

Melnyk, B. M., & Fineout-Overholt, E. (2005). *Evidence-based practice in nursing and healthcare: A guide to best practice.* Philadelphia, PA: Lippincott Williams & Wilkins.

Northern Arizona University. (2001). *Module 2: Methods of data collection: Chapter 2* [Online lesson]. Retrieved from http://www.prm.nau.edu/prm447/methods_of_data_collection_lesson.htm

Orcher, L. T. (2005). *Conducting research: Social and behavioral science methods.* Glendale, CA: Pyrczak Publishing.

Polit, D. F., & Beck, C. T. (2008). *Nursing research: Generating and assessing evidence for nursing practice* (8th ed.). Philadelphia, PA: Lippincott Williams & Wilkins.

Shaha, M., Wenzel, J., & Hill, E. E. (2011). Planning and conducting focus group research with nurses. *Nurse Researcher, 18*(2), 77–87.

Social Dimensions of Watershed Planning. (2006). *Conducting a social profile: Step 3: Selecting data collection methods.* Retrieved from http://www.watershedplanning.illinois.edu/profile_steps/step3.cfm

Wood, M. J., & Ross-Kerr, J. C. (2006). *Basic steps in planning nursing research: From question to proposal* (6th ed.). Sudbury, MA: Jones and Bartlett.

Chapter 11

Reliability, Validity, and Trustworthiness

James Eldridge

Chapter Objectives

At the conclusion of this chapter, the learner will be able to

1. Identify the need for reliability and validity of instruments used in evidence-based practice
2. Define reliability and validity
3. Discuss how reliability and validity affect outcome measures and conclusions of evidence-based research
4. Develop reliability and validity coefficients for appropriate data
5. Interpret reliability and validity coefficients of instruments used in evidence-based practice
6. Describe sensitivity and specificity as related to data analysis
7. Interpret receiver operand characteristics (ROC) to describe validity

Key Terms

➤ Accuracy

➤ Concurrent validity

➤ Consistency

➤ Construct validity

➤ Content-related validity

➤ Correlation coefficient

➤ Criterion-related validity

➤ Cross-validation

➤ Equivalency reliability

➤ Interclass reliability

➤ Intraclass reliability

➤ Objectivity

➤ Observed score

➤ Predictive validity

➤ Receiver operand characteristics

➤ Reliability

➤ Sensitivity

➤ Specificity

➤ Stability

➤ Standard error of measurement

➤ Trustworthiness

➤ Validity

Introduction

The foundation of good research and of good decision making in evidence-based practice (EBP) is the **trustworthiness** of the data used to make decisions. When data cannot be trusted, an informed decision cannot be made. Trustworthiness of the data can only be as good as the instruments or tests used to collect the data. Regardless of the specialization of the healthcare provider, nurses make daily decisions on the diagnosis and treatment of a patient based on the results from different tests to which the patient is subjected. To ensure that the individual makes the proper diagnosis and gives the proper treatment, the nurse must first be sure that the test results used to make the decisions are trustworthy and correct.

Working in an EBP setting requires the nurse to have the best data available to aid in the decision-making process. How can an individual make a decision if the results being used as the foundation of that process cannot be trusted? Put simply, a person cannot make a decision unless the results are trustworthy and correct.

This text presents five concepts to help the nurse determine whether the data upon which decisions are based are trustworthy: reliability, validity, accuracy, sensitivity, and specificity. Each defines a portion of the trustworthiness of the data collection instruments, which in turn defines the trustworthiness of the data, ensuring a proper diagnosis or treatment.

Reliability and validity are the most important qualities in the decision-making process. If either of these qualities is lacking in the data, the nurse cannot make an informed decision and, therefore, is more likely to make an incorrect decision. Since an incorrect decision in the medical field can have catastrophic consequences for the patient, one can see why reliability and validity are so important. But what do these concepts mean? What would happen if the same test was run on a person several times but the results were different each time? In the case of varying results, a decision becomes ambiguous because the results are unclear.

- Reliability = the instrument consistently measures the same thing.
- Validity = the instrument measures what it is intended to measure.

Reliability is defined as the consistency or repeatability of test results. Other descriptors used to indicate reliability include "consistency," "repeatability," "objectivity," "dependability," and "precision." Accuracy is a function of reliability: The better the reliability, the more accurate the results. Conversely, the poorer the reliability, the more inaccurate are the results which increases the chance of making an incorrect decision. Furthermore, accuracy is affected by the sensitivity and specificity of the test. **Sensitivity** can be defined as how often a test measures a "true" positive result, while **specificity** determines the capability of the test for determining "true" negative results. The greater the sensitivity and specificity is for a test, the more accurate the test results. The concepts of sensitivity and specificity will be discussed in more detail later in the text.

Validity is defined as the degree to which the results are truthful. It depends on the reliability and relevance of the test in question (**Figure 11-1**). Relevance is simply the degree of the relationship between the test and its objective, meaning that the test reflects what was reported to be tested.

An example of relevance is the measurement of the height of a patient. A nurse uses a stadiometer (a ruler used to measure vertical

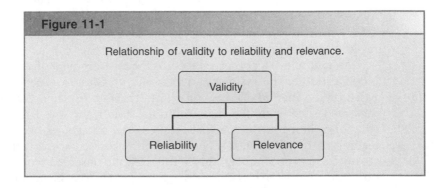

Figure 11-1

Relationship of validity to reliability and relevance.

Validity

Reliability

Relevance

distance) to establish a patient's height. Is the stadiometer a relevant height measurement device? Height is the vertical distance from the floor to the top of the head, and a stadiometer measures vertical distance from the floor to any point above the floor; thus the stadiometer is a relevant measure of height.

Validity cannot exist without reliability and relevance, but reliability and relevance can exist independently of validity. **Figure 11-2a** depicts the case in which there is a high degree of reliability and a low degree of relevance. In this representation, even when reliability is high, validity is low, due to the lack of relevance. This figure shows that under the most reliable test, a low degree of relevance decreases the validity of the test.

Figure 11-2b depicts the situation in which there is a high degree of relevance and a low degree of reliability. In this representation, even when relevance is high, validity is low due to the lack of reliability. Even when a nurse uses what might be considered the most relevant test for the situation, if the instrument has a low degree of reliability, it will also have a low degree of validity.

Figure 11-2c shows the desired capacity for an instrument—to have both a high degree of reliability and a high degree of relevance, thereby creating a high degree of validity. Whereas the other examples show that a test can be reliable but not relevant, or relevant but not reliable, a valid test will always have some degree of reliability and relevance. When validity is absent, the results of the testing are not truthful and making an informed or evidence-based decision is impossible. However, when validity is present, a nurse can be assured that the decision is based on truthful evidence.

Reliability as a Concept

As previously described, reliability focuses on the repeatability or consistency of data. To understand the theoretical constructs of reliability, one must understand the concept of the **observed score**. By definition, the observed score is the score that is seen; stated in other terms, the observed score is the actual score printed on the readout of an instrument.

An example of an observed score is the measurement of a patient's blood pressure. The systolic and diastolic pressures are determined based on the aneroid dial or digital liquid crystal display (LCD) readings associated with the first sound (systolic) and the last sound (diastolic) heard in the brachial artery. If the first sound occurs at a reading of 130 mmHg, this is the systolic observed score. If the last sound occurs at 85 mmHg, this is the diastolic observed score. These observed scores for blood pressure are not the true blood pressure

Figure 11-2

Relationship among reliability, relevance, and validity.

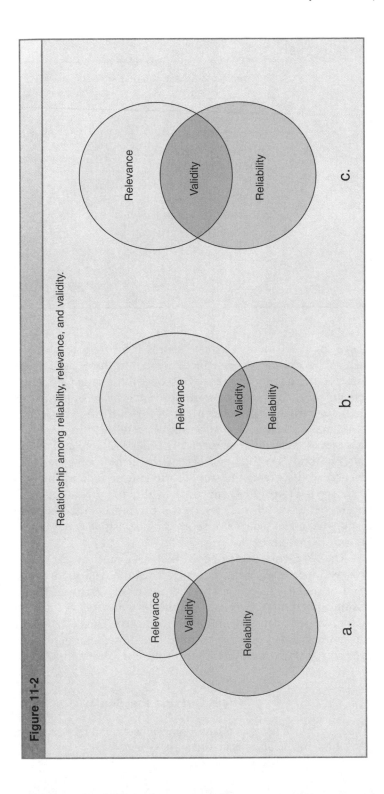

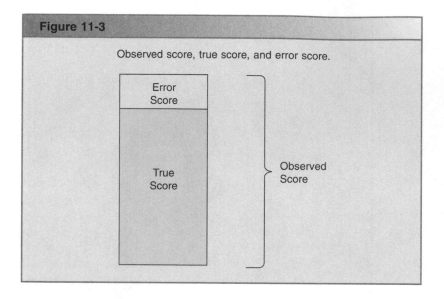

Figure 11-3

Observed score, true score, and error score.

scores for the patient, as those scores ultimately depend on factors such as the amount of error incorporated in the type of sphygmomanometer, the quality of the stethoscope, the quality of hearing of the person taking the blood pressure, the experience of the person taking the measurements, and placement of the cuff over the artery. Each of these nuances can add or subtract error within the readings, which increases the variability between the observed score and the true score. This variability can be described as the error score, thereby defining the observed score as the sum of the true score and the error score. As shown in **Figure 11-3**, any error within the measurement decreases the degree to which the observed score reflects the true score. Note that the net effect of an error score can be positive or negative, depending on the nature of the error.

The true score exists only in theory, because all data collected are observed score data. A nurse can think of the true score as the perfect score of a test—that is, a score without any error and void of any misinterpretation. Of course, the world is not perfect and therefore, neither are any data that might be collected. Thus a true score exists and never changes for a given period of time; changes occur only in the error score, which then determines the observed score.

? Think Outside the Box

www

Discuss the elements of trustworthiness as related to making decisions about the data found within a research study.

Figure 11-4

Theoretical calculation of reliability.

$$\text{Reliability} = \frac{S^2 \text{ true}}{S^2 \text{ observed}} = \frac{S^2 \text{ observed} - S^2 \text{ error}}{S^2 \text{ observed}}$$

Reliability is the degree to which the observed score of a measure reflects the true score of that measure. Therefore, reliability could theoretically be calculated as the proportion of observed score variance that consists of true score variance (**Figure 11-4**).

In this equation, if no error exists, then the observed score variance and the true score variance are equal, and the reliability coefficient is 1.0. Conversely, when the observed score variance and the error score variance are equal, the reliability coefficient is 0. Therefore, reliability always falls within the range of 0–1.0, with a perfect reliability equaling 1.0 and no reliability equaling 0. For research purposes, high reliability measures are desired if at all possible. The general rule is that reliability coefficients greater than 0.80 are considered to be high. Note that if the reliability coefficient is calculated to be greater than 1 (e.g., 1.15), a calculation error has been made, because the range of reliability is always between 0 and 1.0.

Forms of Reliability

Although the purpose of the theoretic concept of reliability is to determine the relationship between the true and observed scores of a measurement, practical use of this concept allows a nurse to determine the relationship only between two or more observed scores. The relationship between these observed scores allows an individual to estimate reliability and to determine a range for the true score. The outcome of the calculation of the relationship between two or more observed scores is known as the **correlation coefficient**. The correlation coefficient is the practical calculation of the theoretic expression of the proportion of observed score variance that consists of true score variance, as described previously.

Given this basic understanding of reliability as a concept, it is now time to learn about the forms of reliability. Globally, reliability can be described as either interclass reliability or intraclass reliability. The most basic description of **interclass reliability** is the reliability between two and only two variables or trials, whereas **intraclass reliability** is the reliability between more than two variables or trials. The limiting factor that separates the two forms of reliability is the number of variables or trials that can be used in the calculation of the correlation coefficient. The number of variables also determines which statistical equation is used to develop the correlation coefficient. Each of these considerations has its place in EBP depending on the number of variables a nurse uses to calculate the reliability coefficient.

Interclass Reliability

Interclass reliability is the reliability between two measures that are presented in the data as either variables or trials. Four types of interclass reliability are distinguished:

- Consistency
- Stability
- Equivalency
- Internal consistency

Each of these reliability coefficients is developed using a Pearson Product Moment (PPM) correlation. Most statistical packages or spreadsheet software can calculate PPM correlations; therefore, the actual equation is not included in this text. Although each interclass reliability coefficient uses the same formula, the calculated reliability coefficient is defined by the type of variables to be compared and the methods used for interpretation of the results. This concept becomes more evident as the types of interclass reliability are further defined.

Consistency

One type of interclass reliability to report is the consistency of a measure. **Consistency** simply describes the degree to which you can expect to get the same results when measuring a variable more than once on a single day. Consistency reliability is sometimes described as test–retest reliability, because it compares two trials of a single measure. An example of testing for consistency would be running two tests on a single blood sample from each subject to measure hemoglobin using a single hemoglobin analyzer. The question is whether the results from the hemoglobin analyzer are consistent within a single day. In **Table 11-1**, the subjects' hemoglobin from a single sample of blood was measured twice, and the reliability coefficient was calculated to be 0.996.

This coefficient simply means that 99.6% of the observed score variance is true score variance. Because the reliability coefficient is close to 1.0, the reliability of the instrument is high. The initial question with this data was whether or not the machine was consistent.

Table 11-1

Consistency and Stability of the ACTdif Analyzer		
Subject Number	Test 1 (g/dL)	Test 2 (g/dL)
1	14.10	14.00
2	12.20	12.10
3	11.90	11.90
4	14.50	14.40
5	13.80	13.90
6	13.20	13.10
7	13.50	13.60
8	14.00	14.10
9	11.10	11.00
10	9.60	9.90
		$r = 0.996$

The results demonstrate that it was consistent, with a consistency reliability coefficient of $r_{xx'} = 0.996$.

Stability

When results of trials or tests are collected over two or more days, consistency becomes **stability**. Suppose we take the same data from Table 11-1, this time imagining that the samples were tested over a 2-day period. The question now becomes whether a blood sample is stable over a 2-day period. Notice that the results remain constant, because nothing has changed except the theoretical timing of the tests. The reliability coefficient is still 0.996, but this time a nurse would interpret the results as the samples being stable over a 2-day period, with a stability reliability coefficient of $r_{xx'} = 0.996$.

Both consistency and stability have their place in EBP. In the current example of hemoglobin testing, the consistency of the measures is described by determining that, for any time during a single day, the data would be repeatable. A nurse can expect the same results as long as no other factors have occurred in the interim, such as acute onset of anemia. In other words, the nurse is sure that the hemoglobin analyzer will give the same measure of hemoglobin for the same sample within the same day. Notice that nowhere in this example of consistency do we assume that the measurement gives the *correct* amount of hemoglobin, only that it indicates the presence of the *same* amount of hemoglobin. To determine if this is the correct amount of hemoglobin, the relevance and the validity of the instrument would have to be known.

When discussing this example in terms of stability, the key determination relates to the length of time that the blood samples remain stable. Hemoglobin analyzers usually have instructions that indicate the time frame for running samples before differing results would be seen. In most instances, the time frame is usually 24 hours. A question might arise concerning how the manufacturer determined this time frame. The answer simply is that the manufacturer developed a stability coefficient using the same techniques described previously.

Again, notice that nowhere in the example of stability is there any mention of the correctness of the amount of hemoglobin over a 24-hour period; the only consideration is that it is the same amount of hemoglobin measured for a 24-hour period. To determine whether this is the correct amount of hemoglobin over the 24-hour period, the relevance and the validity of the instrument and the measures would need to be determined.

Equivalency

Another type of interclass reliability to report is equivalency. This kind of reliability allows a person to report whether one type of test is equivalent to another. **Equivalency reliability** is calculated in the same manner as the consistency and stability coefficients described previously, except that a PPM correlation between two forms of a single test is calculated, rather than a single variable over two trials.

An example of testing for equivalency reliability would be comparing two methods of blood pressure measurement to determine if they are equivalent. In this case, the question is whether the systolic blood pressure results determined by an automatic blood pressure cuff are equivalent to those recorded from manual blood pressure measures using a stethoscope and sphygmomanometer. As shown in **Table 11-2**, subjects' systolic pressure was measured once with an automatic cuff and once using manual methods. The reliability coefficient was calculated to be 0.959.

Table 11-2		
Equivalency of Automatic Versus Manual Systolic Pressure Readings		
Subject	Automatic Cuff Systolic (mmHg)	Manual Method Number Systolic (mmHg)
1	150.00	155.00
2	130.00	128.00
3	125.00	129.00
4	124.00	120.00
5	122.00	125.00
6	148.00	144.00
7	133.00	135.00
8	146.00	143.00
9	117.00	120.00
10	121.00	120.00
		$r = 0.959$

This coefficient simply means that 95.9% of the observed score variance consists of true score variance. Because the reliability coefficient is close to 1.0, the reliability between the instruments is high. The initial question with these data was whether automatic cuff readings are equivalent to manual readings of systolic blood pressure. A person can now report that the two methods are equivalent, with an equivalency reliability coefficient of $r_{xx'} = 0.959$. These results indicate that either an automatic cuff or manual methods are acceptable for measuring systolic blood pressure, because they are equivalent. No matter which method is used, a nurse can expect to get similar measures from a single individual. Notice again that there is no mention of the correctness of the data, only the similarity of the data. To determine if the blood pressure measures are correct, the relevance and the validity of the measures would need to be determined.

Internal Consistency

The final type of interclass reliability discussed here is the internal consistency of written tests. Internal consistency reliability is sometimes described as split-halves reliability, because it entails comparing two halves of a written test. To calculate the internal consistency of a written instrument, the instrument responses are divided into two equal halves. The sum of each half is calculated to make the comparison.

The simplest means for dividing a test in half is to compare the sum of the odd-numbered question responses with the sum of the even-numbered question responses. If possible, the questions should be matched between each half, based on their content and difficulty. Another possible method is to make the a priori assumption that both halves are equal because the questions were randomly placed in order during the development of the written test. As with the other types of interclass reliability, the PPM correlation is used to develop the reliability coefficient.

Data for a 10-item pain questionnaire are presented in **Table 11-3** to demonstrate the principle of internal consistency. Each item of the pain questionnaire is scored from 0 (strongly disagree) to 5 (strongly agree). The questionnaire is then divided into odd and even scores, with the sum of the scores for the odd-numbered items and the sum of the scores for the even-numbered items presented in the table. The question under consideration is whether this questionnaire has internal consistency. As with the previous types of reliability, the reliability coefficient is reported; here, it is 0.761. This coefficient simply means that 76.1% of the observed score variance consists of true score variance. Notice that the internal consistency is lower than in previous examples. The fact that the reliability coefficient is lower does not

	Table 11-3	
	Internal Consistency of a Ten-Item Pain Questionnaire	
Subject	**Odd-Numbered Item Scores**	**Even-Numbered Item Scores**
1	25.00	21.00
2	18.00	14.00
3	16.00	18.00
4	12.00	14.00
5	10.00	10.00
6	18.00	19.00
7	15.00	18.00
8	12.00	9.00
9	14.00	15.00
10	17.00	13.00
		$r = 0.761$

mean that the questionnaire is not reliable—just that it is less reliable than it could be.

? Think Outside the Box

www

Look around your clinical setting. Which tools or instruments are present, and how are they typically used for data collection? Do they include surveys of employees, patients, or consumers? Are the tools or instruments used appropriately?

The initial question for these data was whether the pain questionnaire was internally consistent. We can now report that it has some internal consistency, with a reliability coefficient of $r_{xx'} = 0.761$, but there is at least some error present in the questionnaire. In other words, the questionnaire is not perfectly consistent internally, so the results from using the questionnaire will not be an accurate reflection of the true score. This does not mean that this questionnaire should not be used, but rather that a person needs to be careful in the interpretation and use of the results of the questionnaire. When using written item tests, individuals can actually estimate how reliability will change as a result of adding items to the questionnaire. To estimate a new reliability for a written questionnaire with added items, the Spearman–Brown prophecy formula (**Figure 11-5**) could be used. Where $r_{kk'}$ is the new reliability coefficient, $r_{xx'}$ is the original reliability coefficient, and k is the total items on the new questionnaire divided by the number of items on the original questionnaire, the

---

Figure 11-5

Spearman–Brown prophecy.

$$r_{xx'} = \frac{k \times r_{xx'}}{1 + r_{xx'}(k-1)}$$

Spearman–Brown prophecy can be determined. In the example given in Table 11-3, the reliability coefficient was 0.761. To calculate the reliability of the questionnaire if 10 questions were added, a person would solve for $r_{kk'}$ using the following information shown in **Figure 11-6**.

The original reliability coefficient is 0.760 and the number of total items on the new questionnaire divided by the total items on the original test is 2. Notice that by increasing the number of items on the questionnaire to 20, the new reliability coefficient for the questionnaire becomes 0.864. This coefficient is higher than the original value. Thus, adding items to the questionnaire improves this tool's internal consistency and strengthens the interpretation of its results. As discussed earlier, as reliability and relevance increase, so does validity. If the questionnaire being used has a high degree of relevance, the addition of more questions to the questionnaire (assuming they are relevant) would increase the reliability of the questionnaire, thereby improving the validity of its results.

Intraclass Reliability

Now that we have an understanding of interclass reliability, it is time to move on to intraclass reliability. As discussed earlier, the basic difference between interclass reliability and intraclass reliability is the number of variables that can be analyzed. Interclass reliability testing allows for the reliability analysis of only two variables, whereas intraclass reliability testing allows a researcher to develop a reliability coefficient for more than two variables.

Suppose we wanted to measure the reliability among three different pain scales. One of the scales requires only 2 minutes for

---

Figure 11-6

Spearman–Brown prophecy example.

$$r_{xx'} = \frac{2 \times 0.761}{1 + 0.0761(2-1)}$$

completion, the second scale requires 10 minutes for completion, and the third scale requires 30 minutes for completion. The nurse would prefer to use either the 2-minute or 10-minute scale for efficiency, but the 30-minute scale is currently being used. Although the data could be analyzed using three PPM correlations to determine the equivalency reliability coefficients for these tools, this kind of analysis would miss a very important portion of the error: In the PPM inter-class analysis, the statistic estimates only the error between the items, but it ignores the error within the item that reflects the differences in individuals taking the test.

In contrast, the intraclass reliability coefficient uses analysis of variance (ANOVA) to determine not only the error *between* the tests, but also the error *within* the tests. Using ANOVA allows for construction of a better estimate of the overall reliability of the scales and the errors that reduce the observed score variance, which is the true score variance. Thus, whereas PPM analysis allows for only a two-dimensional view of reliability, ANOVA supports a three-dimensional view of reliability. Notice that the basic terms of reliability remain the same. In the current example, a nurse is still estimating the equivalency of the scales, but now an error that might exist within each individual scale is included.

Figure 11-7 shows the equation used in determining a reliability coefficient using ANOVA. In this equation, a reliability coefficient is developed using the mean square between scales and the mean square within scale data from the ANOVA table.

Table 11-4 presents data for the example of the three pain scales. These ANOVA data include the between-cells mean square of 2908.233 and the within-cells mean square of 35.100. As shown in **Figure 11-8**, the reliability coefficient is determined by substituting the numbers represented in the table into the ANOVA equation for reliability (Figure 11-7).

In this example, the equivalency reliability is 0.988 for the three scales. We can now state that the 2-minute pain scale is equivalent to the 10-minute pain scale and the 30-minute pain scale. The evidence for replacing the longer 30-minute test with the more efficient 2-minute test is now documented, because the tests are equivalent. The same

---

Figure 11-7

Intraclass reliability coefficient using ANOVA.

$$r_{xx'} = \frac{MS_{between} - MS_{within}}{MS_{between}}$$

Table 11-4				
Intraclass Reliability Using ANOVA				
		Scale		
Subject Number	2-Minute Scale	10-Minute Scale	30-Minute Scale	
1	15.00	35.00	60.00	
2	12.00	30.00	51.00	
3	9.00	22.00	40.00	
4	10.00	25.00	42.00	
5	11.00	19.00	43.00	
6	14.00	31.00	45.00	
7	6.00	20.00	38.00	
8	3.00	15.00	33.00	
9	12.00	22.00	45.00	
10	11.00	21.00	45.00	
Source of Variation	SSq	DF	MSq	F
Between cells	5816.467	2	2908.233	82.86
Within cells	947.700	27	35.100	
Total	6764.167	29		

ANOVA reliability equation can be used to determine consistency, stability, and equivalency, depending on the intended use of the data.

Objectivity

An area of intraclass reliability that many times is overlooked is the measure of **objectivity**. Objectivity is the reliability of scores assigned by judges, multiple observers or reviewers. In theory, if three individuals see the same performance, they should score the performance based on the merits of the performance, such that their scores are not affected by internal biases that each may possess. When no bias is evident, the scores should be similar among the judges.

A good example of objectivity (or lack of objectivity) comes from the 2002 Winter Olympics figure skating competition, in which three judges rated the performance of the Canadian skating pair. Two of the judges assigned scores of 9.9 and 9.8 for the pair's performance, but a third judge scored the pair at 7.8. If no biases were associated

Figure 11-8
Intraclass reliability coefficient using ANOVA.
$$r_{xx'} = \frac{2908.233 - 35.10}{2908.233} = 0.988$$

with the scoring method, then the third judge should have been expected to score the performance in the 9.7–9.9 range.

Objectivity also has relevance for EBP. The Apgar score—a tool for assessing the health of newborn infants—offers an example of objectivity in healthcare practice. If three medical professionals are in the delivery room, the Apgar scores each assigns to the newborn should be equivalent. This factor can be tested using the same ANOVA techniques described in the previously given pain scale example, albeit with scores for each observer, rather than each scale, being used. A researcher could determine if the Apgar scores are objective. If they are not, the researcher could meet with the observers to determine where differences occurred.

By now, it should be clear that the same formula (either PPM or ANOVA, depending on the number of trials) is used to determine the reliability of any measure. The only difference in the results relates to the interpretation based on the intended use of the data.

Accuracy

Another item that is important when determining the intraclass reliability of a test is the test's **accuracy**. The measure of the accuracy of a test is known as the **standard error of measurement** (SEM). The SEM reflects the fluctuation of the observed score attributable to the error score. Computing the SEM allows a researcher to determine confidence intervals for the observed score based on the standard deviation of the test and its reliability. The relationship between the true score and the observed score was discussed earlier in this text. The SEM allows a researcher to provide a range for which the true score is present.

The equation shown in **Figure 11-9** is used to calculate the SEM. Notice that in this equation, the reliability coefficient of the test and the standard deviation of the sample are used.

? Think Outside the Box

On most clinical units, many different tools are regularly used, such as thermometers, glucometers, sphygmomanometers, and weight scales. Are these tools accurate? How can you be sure that they are reliable and valid for what they are being used to evaluate? *Are* they valid and reliable tools?

Figure 11-9
Standard error of measurement. $$SEM = s\sqrt{1 - r_{xx'}}$$

> **Figure 11-10**
>
> SEM for consistency of a hemoglobin analyzer.
>
> $$SEM = 1.496 \sqrt{1 - 0.996}$$
> $$= \pm 0.0946 \text{ mg/dL}$$

The SEM can be determined for any of the prior examples. For Table 11-1, the standard deviation of the sample is 1.496, and the reliability coefficient is 0.996. Using the equation in Figure 11-9, we can compute the SEM as ± 0.0946 mg/dL (**Figure 11-10**).

In a normal distribution, 68% of the sample scores fall between ± 1 standard deviation of the mean. Thus, for this example, we have 68% confidence that the hemoglobin scores will fall between ± 0.0946 mg/dL of the measured score. If a ± 2 standard deviation from the mean is used, a 95% confidence interval for the scores is expected. To find the SEM for ± 2 standard deviations from the mean, we multiply the SEM by 2 (the number of standard deviation units). In our example, we have 95% confidence that the true hemoglobin score will fall between ± 0.1892 mg/dL of the measured score. If a blood sample is run in the analyzer and the hemoglobin level is found to be 14.0 mg/dL, we would therefore have 95% confidence that the true score is between 13.1080 mg/dL and 14.1892 mg/dL. Notice that as the standard deviation increases for a set of scores, the SEM increases. Also, as the reliability of a set of scores decreases, the SEM increases. To proclaim a tool as giving an accurate measure, test scores need a relatively low standard deviation and a high reliability coefficient.

Up to this point, we have examined accuracy as it relates to continuous data. But what happens when a test uses nominal data—how do we determine its accuracy? In the case of nominal data, we use the χ^2 (chi-square) statistic and its corresponding phi coefficient as a measure of accuracy. Think of the phi coefficient as a correlation or reliability coefficient for nominal data. A χ^2 statistic and its corresponding phi coefficient would most likely be used when you are trying to determine whether a new test is equivalent to a "gold standard" test. All of the same rules apply just as they have in the previous discussion of reliability for continuous data; however, now you are simply determining the accuracy of the new test based on its "pass or fail" performance compared to the "gold standard" test.

Be aware that reliability and accuracy can be sensitive to situational changes; although a test is reliable in one situation or within one group, it may not always be reliable when the situation or group changes. This consideration is especially important concerning written items. Factors that can affect reliability and accuracy include the following issues:

- Fatigue. Fatigue of the person taking the test or collecting the data can decrease reliability.
- Practice. The more practiced a person becomes at taking a test or in collecting data, the more reliability is improved.
- Timing. The more time that passes between test administrations, the more the reliability of the test is decreased.
- Homogeneity of the testing conditions. The more homogeneous the testing conditions (e.g., same room, same time taken to collect data, same time of day), the better the reliability.
- Level of difficulty. The more difficult a test or data collection procedure, the lower the reliability.
- Precision. The more precise the measurement (1/100 or 1/1000 decimal), the better the accuracy.
- Environment. Environmental changes such as ambient pressure or temperature variations can decrease reliability.

The more control maintained over these factors, the better the reliability and accuracy of the resulting data. Accuracy and reliability improve the decision-making process in EBP.

Receiver Operand Characteristics (ROC) and Accuracy

When discussing nominal data, historically the use of the chi-square (χ^2) statistic determines accuracy; however, newer statistical methods such as **receiver operand characteristics** (ROC) curves are being implemented in the field of nursing to determine accuracy of test results (Zou, O'Malley, & Mauri, 2007). ROC analyses were first developed for the armed services during World War II as a method for determining the accuracy of radar signals. More recently, this statistical method is being adapted to the medical field for defining the accuracy of diagnostic tests. ROC analysis determines the sensitivity and specificity (accuracy) of a diagnostic test to predict a specific outcome of disease the test is reported to measure. Most of the time, ROC analysis uses dichotomous variables much like a 2×2 χ^2 statistic, however the analysis can also be used when an ordinal grading system is available for determining disease severity. The most basic form of ROC analysis uses a 2×2 method for determining accuracy of positive and negative results from a specific diagnostic test compared to whether or not the patient actually possesses the disease. **Table 11-5** represents the conceptual nature of a dichotomous diagnostic test comparing the positive and negative test results to actual disease state of a patient (nondiseased or diseased).

Table 11-5

Conceptual Nature of a Dichotomous Test		
	Disease State	
Test Result	**No Disease**	**Disease**
Negative test result	True negative	False negative
Positive test result	False positive	True positive

In Table 11-5, a perfectly accurate test would indicate only true negative results and true positive results; however as discussed previously, there is always some inherent measurement error in diagnostic tests. The ROC analysis allows the medical provider a means to quantify this error and determine in which area of the figure the error is greatest. Unlike the standard error of measurement (SEM) which gives the researcher a global characterization of the measurement error, ROC analysis allows the researcher to determine the sensitivity (rate of true positive results) and the specificity (rate of true negative results) for any diagnostic test.

Calculations for sensitivity and specificity are fairly simple to develop. The researcher needs to know the rates or number of individuals within each of the four groups (true negative, false negative, true positive and false positive). **Table 11-6** simplifies the variables necessary to calculate sensitivity and specificity.

In Table 11-6, TN represents the number of individuals who do not have the disease and have negative test results on the diagnostic test (true negatives). FP represents the number of individuals who do not have the disease but have positive results on the diagnostic test (false positives). FN represents the number of individuals who have the disease but have negative test results on the diagnostic test (false negative). TP represents the number of individuals who have the disease and have positive results on the diagnostic test (true positives). To calculate sensitivity (the probability of the test to correctly predict

Table 11-6

Variables for Calculating Sensitivity and Specificity			
	Disease State		
Test	**No Disease**	**Disease**	**Total**
Negative	TN	FN	TN + FN
Positive	FP	TP	FP + TP
Total	TN + FP	FN + TP	n

true positive scores), the formula used is TP / (TP + FN). To calculate specificity (the probability of the test to correctly predict true negative scores), the formulas used is TN / (TN + FP). Many reasons might be discussed for why ROC analyses might be used, but one of the most common reasons is to determine if a less invasive and less expensive diagnostic test will provide as good or better results when compared to the "gold standard" diagnostic test for a given disease.

For an example of calculating sensitivity and specificity of a diagnostic test, let's assume a new diagnostic test was developed for assessing the presence of carpal tunnel syndrome. The test uses a tactile response of the index fingers by touching the fingers with a thin monofilament line while conducting Phalen's test for carpal tunnel syndrome. The response from the patient is simply YES, they feel the thread (positive MPT) or NO, they do not feel the thread (negative MPT). Previously each patient was diagnosed for the presence (positive EDS) or absence (negative EDS) of carpal tunnel syndrome via an electrodiagnostic neural conduction study. The data for the test is found in **Table 11-7**.

To determine the sensitivity of the modified Phalen's test, the equation would be 39/46 where the 39 represents the number of individuals that reported a positive MPT and a positive EDS score, while the 46 represents the total positive EDS scores. The sensitivity of the modified Phalen's test is 0.848, or 84.8% probability of predicting true positive tests. To determine the specificity of the modified Phalen's test, the equation would be 20 / 21 where the 20 represents the number of individuals that reported a positive MPT and a negative EDS score, while the 21 represents the total negative EDS scores. The specificity of the modified Phalen's test is 0.952, or 95.2% probability of predicting true negative tests. The conclusion from this data is that the modified Phalen's test can accurately predict both true positive and true negative tests.

The philosophical discussion that occurs when using ROC analysis in the healthcare field is what should be considered acceptable values for sensitivity, specificity, and overall accuracy. Acceptable values are often dependent on the severity of the disease state. If the disease

Table 11-7			
Sensitivity and Specificity of the Modified Phalen's Test			
	Negative EDS	**Positive EDS**	**Total**
Negative MPT	20	7	27
Positive MPT	1	39	39
Total	21	46	66

is a life threatening disease, then sensitivity values should be above 85%, while specificity values may be somewhat lower. If the disease or diagnosis is mundane, then sensitivity values may be lower, but specificity values should be higher. The overall accuracy of a test should still follow the general rules of reliability and exceed 80%.

Validity

To this point in the text, the knowledge necessary to understand the reliability and accuracy of the data collected has been provided. The fact that a test has accuracy and reliability does not mean that the test is valid, however. A valid test is defined as a test that truthfully measures what it purports to measure. Validity can be classified as either logical or statistical in nature. Logical validity requires inference and understanding of the subject being measured. Statistical validity uses statistical formulas to compare the test in question with a specific criterion or known valid measure. In EBP, validity is further delineated into three types: content-related validity, criterion-related validity, and construct-related validity. Depending on the measure, either one type or several types of validity can be used to determine if a measure is valid.

Content-Related Validity

Content-related validity is based on the logical thought process and interpretation of the measure. Many people refer to this quality as face or logical validity. The American Psychological Association (APA, 1985) defines content-related validity as "demonstrating the degree to which the sample of items, tasks, or questions on a test is representative of some defined content" (p. 10). A humorous restating of this concept is the cliché, "If it looks like a duck and quacks like a duck, then it must be a duck." A valid test using content-related validity should logically measure the content being reported.

Consider the pain scale example introduced earlier in this chapter. Content-related validity would assume that if it logically asks questions concerning the specific nature and degree of pain for a patient, then it must be measuring the pain of the individual. Another example arises with the stadiometer: If the stadiometer is a ruler, and a ruler measures distance, then it must logically be able to measure height. Both of these examples show the use of a logical thought process to validate the measure as a truthful representation of what the instrument reports to measure.

The fact that a test has content validity does not always mean that the test is valid. Other nuances may add error to the test and negate the test's content validity. Consider the practice of measuring of blood pressure at the arm, which is an accepted, valid method for measuring blood pressure. But what happens when the person obtaining the measurement is inexperienced or does not place the cuff in the proper position? The result will be an invalid measurement owing to the use of an improper measurement procedure. Any deviations in measurement procedures decrease the reliability of the test, thereby invalidating the data collected with the instrument.

The criteria for content-related validity can be traced back to the process used in developing the test, the interpretation of the results, and a well-defined protocol for collection of the data. In developing content-related validity, the researcher needs to be aware of extraneous factors that can affect the outcome of the test and render the test invalid. Whenever content-related validity for an instrument is relied upon, a set of strict guidelines concerning the use and collection methods of the instrument need to be in place to ensure that the validity of the instrument is not rendered useless by these factors.

Criterion-Related Validity

Criterion-related validity is based on a comparison between the test being used and some known criterion. According to the APA (1985), criterion-related validity involves "demonstrating test scores are systematically related to one or more known criteria" (p. 11). Criterion-related validity is the statistical validity identified earlier in this section (Terms such as "statistical validity" and "correlational validity" are sometimes used as synonyms for "criterion-related validity.") The same statistical technique used to determine reliability (i.e., PPM) is used to develop a validity coefficient.

Consider the following example: measurement of oxygen saturation of arterial blood in patients. The criterion for arterial saturation would be blood gas analysis from an arterial line; however, this type of measurement brings the risk of complications and should not be used during a routine office visit. An alternative method for measuring oxygen saturation is via an infrared monitoring device that attaches to the fingertip. The infrared monitor is minimally invasive, can be used with the general population without risk, and is supposedly valid for estimating arterial oxygen saturation. To verify that the alternative method of infrared monitoring is valid, a researcher would identify a small sample of patients, subject those patients to both tests, and compare their actual blood gas results with the infrared monitoring scores. The PPM would be calculated to quantify the comparison, which would be between the alternative test to be used and the known criterion. The results would have a validity coefficient associated with the infrared monitoring model instead of a reliability coefficient. Interpretation would be done in the same manner used to interpret the reliability coefficient.

Criterion-related validity can be subdivided into **concurrent validity** and **predictive validity**, based on the time between the collection of data using the alternative method test to be validated and the criterion measurement. Concurrent validity can use the PPM statistic for validity coefficient development. With predictive validity, however, the researcher is not limited to using the PPM correlation; a linear or logistic regression can be used to develop a validity coefficient. Concurrent validity coefficients are developed simultaneously for the criterion and the alternative method test, whereas predictive validity is not limited by time.

The arterial blood oxygen saturation testing described previously is an example of concurrent validity. In this example, both criterion and alternative method measures are collected at the same time to develop the validity coefficient.

The criterion in predictive validity can be measured years after the collection of alternative method test data. Testing for the occurrence of heart disease is an example of predictive validity. A patient's total cholesterol, high-density lipoprotein (HDL) cholesterol, and low-density lipoprotein (LDL) cholesterol levels, along with other measures, are used to predict the future occurrence of atherosclerosis. Atherosclerosis—the criterion in this example—does not occur until later in life, whereas the lipid profiles, which are the alternative method test, are collected years earlier. In the predictive validity example, if a PPM correlation is used, the validity coefficient might be low because the criterion measure is a nominal value. In this case, a researcher might use logistic regression techniques to predict the probability of occurrence and develop the validity coefficient from the probability of occurrence, rather than simply from the dichotomous variable (i.e., either a person does or does not have heart disease). A good point to remember is that whenever the criterion is a continuous variable, there is a better chance of having a high validity coefficient due to the possibility of improved true score variance and lower error score variance.

❓ Think Outside the Box

Discuss how you could make sure that each person who collects data as part of a research project does the collection in the same manner to ensure reliability of the study results.

When a dichotomous or nominal variable is used as the criterion, a researcher should expect to have a lower validity coefficient, due to a decline in true score variance and an increase in error score variance. An example of this mystery is presented in **Table 11-8**.

Table 11-8			
Effects of Variable Scale on Validity Coefficient			
Subject Number	Heart Disease (Yes or No)	Probability of Heart Disease	Total Cholesterol Level
1	0	40%	145
2	1	75%	200
3	1	89%	225
4	0	45%	170
5	0	30%	160
6	1	65%	195
7	0	40%	165
8	1	85%	250
9	1	88%	300
10	0	50%	180

Heart disease and total cholesterol $r = 0.777$

Probability of heart disease and total cholesterol $r = 0.879$

In this example, the criterion measure of atherosclerosis is presented both as a dichotomous variable and as a probability of occurrence based on a logistic regression formula. The alternative test for the validity coefficient is the total cholesterol levels of the subjects collected when they were 40 years of age. Notice that when a continuous variable is used as the criterion in this example, the validity coefficient is 10% higher compared with use of a dichotomous criterion. When using dichotomous variables as measures of validity, a researcher can expect to have lower validity coefficients than when using continuous variables. This decline in the validity coefficient reflects the lack of variability within the dichotomous measure—the lack of variability decreases the effectiveness of determining the true score of the measure. If the true score measure is decreased, then the error score measure is increased, which also affects reliability.

Many times, **cross-validation** techniques are used to develop a validity coefficient from a predictive validity criterion. Cross-validation simply implies that the researcher uses one group of subjects to develop the regression equation to predict the criterion and then gathers data from a second separate, but similar, group to develop the actual validity coefficient. Cross-validation techniques are generally used in developing new prediction models for a criterion.

ROC Analysis for Determining the Criterion-Related Validity of Diagnostic Exams

Since predictive analysis as a subsidiary of criterion-related validity compares an alternative method test to a criterion measurement for developing a validity coefficient, one can logically infer that ROC analysis may be used not only to describe the accuracy of a diagnostic test, but also as a measure of the validity of a diagnostic test. When using ROC analysis for validation of testing, the evidence-based practitioner can develop an inherent validity coefficient which quantifies the predictive quality of the alternative test to predict the presence or absence of the disease. An inherent validity coefficient quantifies the ability of the alternative diagnostic test to identify true positive and true negative results. The inherent validity coefficient is calculated using the equation

$$(\text{True positive tests} + \text{True negative tests}) \ / \ n$$

In the case of the modified Phalen's test from Table 11-7, the inherent validity is $(20 + 39)/66 = 0.893$ or 89.3% probability of correctly identifying true positive and true negative disease states (Bilkis, Loveman, Eldridge, Ali, Kadir, & McConathy (2012).

Construct Validity

The most abstract of validity procedures is **construct validity**. Construct validity refers to the concept of "focusing on test scores that are associated with a psychological characteristic" (APA, 1985, p. 9). In practice, construct validity attempts to develop validity for measures that exist in theory but are unobservable.

The best example of this type of validity in EBP is the measure of pain perceived by a patient. Although we know pain exists, direct measurement of pain is somewhat convoluted and is affected by the psychological traits, tolerance levels, and perceptions of the patient. The tool most commonly used to measure pain today is the analog pain scale, which measures pain on a one-dimensional scale of 1 to 10. To develop a more precise pain scale that measures several dimensions of pain and has a high validity coefficient, constructs must be developed that can measure these traits associated with pain. Thus we can think of construct validity as the combination of content validity and statistical validity to develop a validity coefficient for an abstract variable such as pain.

To develop construct validity of a variable, the variable must first be defined as specifically as possible. The researcher would then need to identify all of the constructs associated with the variable and to define them as specifically as possible. These definitions would prove helpful in developing the measurement scales and tools to quantify the variable. In the case of the pain example, pain might be defined as the degree to which a physical symptom causes discomfort at greater than normal levels for a patient. In using this definition, the constructs associated with this variable need to be identified and defined. Notice in the definition of pain that the term "degree" is used, which assumes that some type of quantifiable scale with specific unit differences is available to quantify the intensity and severity of the variable. Also, the term "discomfort" is used in the definition, which assumes that some type of non-well-being exists. In this case, intensity is one construct, severity is another construct, and discomfort is the final construct that needs to be defined and measured.

To start the process of developing a pain scale, think about the physical pain that you have experienced previously in relation to the constructs of intensity, severity, and discomfort. If your experience with pain is limited, you might seek the help of others who have more experience with pain or investigate current publications in pain research to help you with the definition and development of these constructs. For the current example, assume the definitions for your constructs are as follows:

- Intensity is the degree of pain.
- Severity is the degree of debilitation associated with pain.
- Discomfort is the degree of the measure associated with the patient's pain tolerance.

In this example, it is assumed that these three constructs are measurable and part of the content that defines the overall construct of pain.

Once you have defined the constructs, you need to determine the type of scale that can be used to measure each one. For intensity, you might decide to use a scale of 0 to 10, where 0 is defined as the absence of pain and 10 is defined as the most excruciating pain imaginable. For severity, you might have to develop a scale using terms that reflect a decline in functional capacity associated with debilitation. For discomfort, you might use a scale that reflects the type of pain, such as sharp, dull, or throbbing.

After developing the scales for the constructs that are included in the measurement of pain, you must determine how each scale should be weighted to reflect the absolute construct of pain. Again, you might want to rely on personal experience when developing your construct weights; alternatively, you might wish to seek expert opinions or explore previous research to help in developing your weighting system.

When you have accomplished this last step, you have a measure that logically measures pain (content validity). You are ready to test the merits of the measure by applying it to comparable groups to determine the statistical validity of the measure. In using statistical validation measures, you are attempting to prove the following hypothesis: Those individuals with diseases that are not associated with pain should score low on the new pain scale, and those individuals with diseases or disorders associated with a high level of pain should score high on the new pain scale. By combining the logical validation of the pain scale with the statistical interpretation of the pain scale, you have developed construct validity for a measure of pain. As you become more comfortable with the process of developing construct validity for abstract or unobservable measures, you will find that the greater the number of definable constructs, the greater the validity gained by the measure.

Conclusion

This chapter focused on two key principles that determine trustworthiness of research data: reliability and validity. Whereas reliability and relevance can exist independently of each other, validity cannot exist without the presence of both reliability and relevance.

The two basic statistical techniques used to determine reliability and validity are the PPM correlation and the ANOVA test. As with most techniques, the selection of which to use is based on the number of variables being compared. When there are only two variables, a researcher would use PPM; when more than two variables are being compared, the ANOVA technique would be used. Both techniques generate a coefficient between an absolute value of 0 and 1.0, and the presence of a coefficient greater than 1.0 signifies an error in the calculations.

The interpretation of the coefficient is the only change that should occur regardless of the technique used. In the case of reliability, the coefficient can be used to interpret the consistency, stability, equivalency, or objectivity of the measure depending on which aspects were used to determine the estimate. A researcher can also use the reliability coefficient in conjunction with the standard deviation of the sample to determine the accuracy of the measure using the SEM equation. With reliability and accuracy determined, a nurse can be sure that comparable measures are similar and can be interpreted as consistent, stable, equivalent, or objective within a defined range of error. In the case of validity, these techniques can be used to develop a validity coefficient for concurrent validity or predictive validity based on the time between the collection using the alternative method test, or a validity coefficient for construct validity to improve the interpretation of the measure beyond simple content validation.

Summary Points

1. Trustworthiness of study data is only as good as the instruments or tests used to collect the data.
2. Reliability and validity are the most important concepts in the decision-making process when designing research studies.

. Reliability is the determination that an instrument consistently measures the same thing.

4. Validity is the determination that an instrument measures what it is supposed to measure.

5. Validity cannot exist without reliability and relevance.

6. Reliability and relevance can exist independently of validity.

7. The correlation coefficient is the degree (positive or negative) of the relationship between the variables.

8. Interclass reliability is the consistency between two measures that are presented in the data as either variables or trials.

9. The three types of interclass reliability are consistency, equivalency, and internal consistency.

10. Intraclass reliability allows for the development of a reliability coefficient for more than two variables.

11. Within intraclass reliability, objectivity and accuracy need to be considered.

12. The three types of validity are content-related validity, criterion-related validity, and construct-related validity.

13. Content-related validity is the level at which a sample of items, tasks, or questions represent the defined content.

14. Criterion-related validity reflects the demonstration that test scores are systematically related to one or more identified measures.

15. Criterion-related validity is subdivided into concurrent validity and predictive validity.

16. Construct-related validity concentrates on the test scores that are associated with a psychological characteristic.

17. A receiver operand characteristics (ROC) analysis can be used for determining the criterion-related validity of diagnostic exams.

RED FLAGS

- If reliability and validity are missing from the data, an informed decision concerning the trustworthiness of the results of a research study cannot be made.
- If validity is documented in a study without any indication of reliability and relevance, concerns about the trustworthiness of the results should be raised.
- If a tool is documented as being used within a study, the report should provide information concerning the validity and reliability indices for the tool.

Multiple Choice Questions

www

1. When making good decisions in evidence-based practice, _____ of the data is necessary.

   A. Confirmability
   B. Trustworthiness
   C. Independence
   D. Timing

2. Reliability is defined as the case in which an instrument

   A. Consistently measures the same thing.
   B. Measures what it is supposed to measure.
   C. Measures demographic data.
   D. Consistently measures the same sample.

3. Reliability and relevance may exist

   A. With dependence on validity.
   B. With only independence of validity.
   C. Independently of validity.
   D. None of the above.

4. A valid test will _____ have some degree of reliability and relevance.

   A. Never
   B. Sometimes
   C. Frequently
   D. Always

5. When measuring blood pressure, the actual score is the

   A. Observed score on the instrument.
   B. Estimated score determined by the nurse.
   C. Perfect score without error.
   D. First sound heard by the nurse.

6. Reliability coefficients greater than _____ are considered to be high.

   A. 0.50
   B. 0.60
   C. 0.70
   D. 0.80

7. As an example of consistency and stability in EBP, when a urinalysis is done four times in a 24-hour period, the urine sample needs to be the _____ amount.

   A. Correct
   B. Same
   C. Smallest
   D. Largest

8. Dividing scores on a pain questionnaire (with 0–5 items) into odd-numbered and even-numbered scores is a mechanism that can be used to determine

   A. External consistency.
   B. Relevance.
   C. Internal consistency.
   D. Validity.

9. A research study was developed to consider the assessment of skin color. Nurses on a medical–surgical unit were asked to record their judgments of the skin color from four pictures of individuals with differing skin tones. This process is an example of which area of reliability measurement?

   A. Accuracy
   B. Objectivity
   C. Feasibility
   D. Equivalency

10. Which test is used to establish the measurement of the accuracy related to reliability?

    A. ANOVA
    B. Standard error of measure (SEM)
    C. Pearson Product Moment (PPM) correlation
    D. Reliability coefficient

11. To establish a test as an accurate measurement of reliability, the test scores need a relatively _____ standard deviation and a _____ reliability coefficient.

    A. High; high
    B. Low; low
    C. Low; high
    D. High; low

12. Factors that can affect the reliability, objectivity, and accuracy of a tool or test include

    A. Practice, timing, and environment.
    B. Fatigue, subjects, and environment.
    C. Precision, homogeneity of the test conditions, and the researcher.
    D. Sequencing, practice, and level of ease.

13. Validity can be classified as

    A. Universal.
    B. Concise.
    C. General.
    D. Logical.

14. A criterion for content-related validity determination is

    A. The inclusion of extraneous variables.
    B. Establishment of brief guidelines for using the tool.
    C. A well-defined protocol for data collection.
    D. The clarification of nuances that might add errors.

15. A researcher was comparing alternative methods for establishing a child's core body temperature for a study. The testing included the measurement of anal, oral, and aural temperatures. This example reflects which type of validity determination?

    A. Construct-related validity
    B. Criterion-related validity
    C. Content-related validity
    D. Predictive validity

16. A study presented the results from the development of a new tool. This tool was established to measure the level of anxiety perceived by children. Which type of validity would this study need to document for the tool?

    A. Content-related validity
    B. Criterion-related validity
    C. Construct-related validity
    D. Concurrent validity

Discussion Questions

Use the following data to answer questions 1–4.

Patient #	Oral Temperature (°F)	Temperature (°F)
1	98.6	98.7
2	99.4	99.3
3	101.2	101.3
4	98.6	98.6
5	100.5	100.7
6	99.7	99.4
7	101.0	101.1
8	98.4	98.6
9	102.9	102.5
10	103.1	102.9

Patient #	Oral Temperature (°F)	Tympanic Temperature (°F)
1	98.6	98.7
2	99.4	99.3
3	101.2	101.3
4	98.6	98.6
5	100.5	100.7
6	99.7	99.4
7	101.0	101.1
8	98.4	98.6
9	102.9	102.5
10	103.1	102.9

1. Is tympanic temperature a similar measure of temperature?
2. Which type of reliability coefficient have you developed with these data?
3. What is the accuracy of tympanic temperature?
4. Is tympanic temperature a valid measure of patient temperature based on the information provided in the second table?
5. Using the example of the pain scale provided in the text, define and develop five additional constructs that might be used to measure pain.

Suggested Readings

Baumgartner, T., & Jackson, A. J. (1999). *Measurement for evaluation in physical education and exercise science* (6th ed.). Dubuque, IA: McGraw-Hill.

Cunningham, G. K. (1986). *Educational and psychological measurement.* New York, NY: Macmillan.

Glass, G. V., & Hopkins, K. D. (1996). *Statistical methods in education and psychology* (3rd ed.). Englewood Cliffs, NJ: Prentice Hall.

Golafshani, N. (2003). Understanding reliability and validity in qualitative research. *Qualitative Report, 8*(4), 597–607.

MedicalBiostatistics.com. (n.d.). *Sensitivity-specificity, Bayes' rule and predictivities.* Retrieved from http://www.medicalbiostatistics.com/Sensitivity-specificity.pdf

Morrow, J. R., Jackson, A. W., Disch, J. G., & Mood, D. P. (2000). *Measurement and evaluation in human performance* (2nd ed.). Champaign, IL: Human Kinetics.

Thomas, J., & Nelson, J. (2005). *Research methods in physical activity* (5th ed.). Champaign, IL: Human Kinetics.

References

American Psychological Association (APA). (1985). *Standards for educational and psychological testing.* Washington, DC: Author.

Bilkis, S., Loveman, D. M., Eldridge, J. A., Ali, S. A., Kadir, A., & McConathy, W. (2012). Modified Phalen's test as an aid in diagnosing carpal tunnel syndrome. *Arthritis Care & Research, 64*(2), 287–289. doi:10.1002/acr.20664

Zou, K. H., O'Malley, A. J., & Mauri, L. (2007). Receiver-operating characteristic analysis for evaluating diagnostic tests and predictive models. *Circulation, 115*(5), 654–657.

Chapter **12**

Data Analysis

James Eldridge

Chapter Objectives

At the conclusion of this chapter, the learner will be able to

1. Identify the types of statistics available for analyses in evidence-based practice
2. Define quantitative analysis, qualitative analysis, and quality assurance
3. Discuss how research questions define the type of statistics to be used in evidence-based practice research
4. Choose a data analysis plan and the proper statistics for different research questions raised in evidence-based practice
5. Interpret data analyses and conclusions from the data analyses
6. Discuss how quality assurance affects evidence-based practice

Key Terms

➤ Analysis of variance (ANOVA)

➤ Central tendency

➤ Chi-square

➤ Interval scale

➤ Mean

➤ Median

➤ Mode

➤ Nominal scale

➤ Ordinal scale

➤ Qualitative analysis

➤ Quality assurance

➤ Quantitative analysis

➤ Ratio scale

➤ Statistical Package for the Social Sciences (SPSS)

➤ t-test

Introduction

So far in this text, the authors have methodically explained how to move from the formulation of the hypothesis to the data collection stage of a research project. Data collection in evidence-based practice (EBP) might be considered the easiest part of the whole research experience. The researcher has already formed the hypothesis, developed the data collection methods and instruments, and determined the subject pool characteristics.

Once the EBP researcher has completed data collection, it is time for the researcher to compile and interpret the data so as to explain them in a meaningful context. This compilation and interpretation phase is completed using either quantitative data analysis or qualitative data analysis techniques. **Quantitative analysis** is defined as the numeric representation and manipulation of observations using statistical techniques for the express purpose of describing and explaining the outcomes of research as they pertain to the hypothesis. In other words, quantitative analysis uses numerical values to explain the outcomes of a research project. In contrast, **qualitative analysis** techniques use logical deductions to decipher gathered data dealing with the human element and do not rely on numerical values or mathematical models to explain the results. In other words, qualitative analysis uses words and phrases to explain the outcomes of a research project.

An example of the contrast between these two types of analyses would be a research project involving the study of a specific treatment for the reduction of pressure induced bed sores during convalescent care. To determine if the treatment was effective, data would be collected to compare two groups of individuals who were bed ridden. One group would receive the treatment, while the other group would not receive the treatment. Using a scale that quantified the number and size of bed sores, the researcher would collect numerical data to determine if differences were apparent between the treatment group and the no treatment group. This would be a form of quantitative analysis.

Using the same group of subjects, the researcher could also observe the patients' movement characteristics, attitude, and facial expressions during both pre-treatment and post-treatment phases and the nursing staff could chronicle their improvement through the use of a written journal. This process would be a form of qualitative analysis.

In the example using quantitative analysis techniques, the researcher could report significant differences between the end treatment values of the treatment and no treatment groups—for example, there was a significant difference between the mean post-treatment occurrences of pressure ulcers of the treatment group compared to those of the no treatment group. In the qualitative analysis example, the researcher would state the results in a different way—for example, the treatment group exhibited more positional changes during bed rest, with an observed decline in localized long-term pressure points in a single area of the body, skin blood flow changes, rashes, and blisters; furthermore, the patients had a better attitude and were less likely to gripe at the nurse while undergoing the post-test procedures.

Notice that in the qualitative analysis example, no mention of statistical differences is made; only a description of the observed differences and changes is included. The only time a researcher can report a significant difference is when he or she has used quantitative analysis techniques to interpret the data. In this text, the learner will discover when and how to use these two techniques in the reporting and explanation of a project's results.

Quantitative Analysis

Measurement Scales

As described previously, quantitative analysis requires the use of numeric data to describe and interpret the results. It is often referred to as statistical analysis; in reality, however, statistical analysis is a subunit of quantitative analyses. Before a researcher can understand the nuances of quantitative analysis, he or she must first understand the types of numeric data that are available for analysis. Numeric data are classified into four measurement scales: (1) nominal, (2) ordinal, (3) interval, and (4) ratio. These four scales are listed here in hierarchical order, with the nominal scale being the least precise measurement scale and the ratio scale being the most precise measurement scale in describing results.

The **nominal scale** is the simplest of the measurement scales, because it is used for identification or categorization purposes only. This level of measurement lacks numeric order, magnitude, or size. Examples of nominal scales include race, gender, and patient identification number.

A scale for race might collect data in the following way: Anglo equals 1, African American equals 2, Hispanic equals 3, and other race equals 4. In this scale, the number assigned to each race is indicative of group identification only, with no other assumption of magnitude, order, or size. The reason that we use the numerical scale rather than the word terms for race is because most statistical analysis packages have a difficult time interpreting word terms, especially when capitalization and misspellings occur.

The second measurement scale in the hierarchy is the **ordinal scale**. This scale is more precise in measuring items as compared to the nominal scale. It incorporates order or ranking, yet lacks magnitude and size. A researcher using an ordinal scale is unable to make direct comparisons between ranks, because he or she does not know whether the difference between a ranking of 1 and 2 is very small or very large. The only known aspect is that a ranking of 1 is greater or better than a ranking of 2. A medical example of an ordinal scale is the transplant recipient list for a donor heart. A transplant recipient is given a number that identifies his or her order on the list based on symptoms, severity, cross-matching/typing, and time of request. When a donor heart becomes available, the person ranked highest on the list who meets the criteria of proper cross-matching/typing, being symptomatic, with the highest level of illness severity, and the longest time on the donor list receives the heart. Potentially, two patients with the same symptoms, severity, and cross-matching/typing might be separated in the order only by the time (sometimes a few seconds) at which they were placed on the list. Thus the different aspects have no magnitude or set units of measure between each numeric value. This example illustrates how an ordinal scale represents order but lacks magnitude and size. For both nominal and ordinal scales, mathematical calculations have no meaning, because the scales are unable to represent the magnitude and size of the variable.

The final two scales of measurement in the hierarchy are considered continuous scales, because each incorporates both order and magnitude within its description. Continuous scales allow for mathematical calculations so as to give the results meaning. Researchers can truly describe significant differences because each number in the scale represents a unique place of order within the scale, and there is equal distance between it and the number directly above and below it in the order.

? Think Outside the Box

Compare and contrast quantitative versus qualitative research techniques for analyses.

The third scale of measurement is the **interval scale**. This scale is more precise than the nominal and ordinal scales because it incorporates both order and magnitude within the description; at the same time, it lacks a defined size or, for want of a better term, an "absolute" zero point. An example of the interval scale is the Fahrenheit temperature scale. The degrees in the Fahrenheit scale are ordered from high to low. Each degree within the scale has an equal distance from the next degree; however, the point taken as zero in the scale is arbitrary. Using the term "arbitrary zero" in a scale means that the zero point is not defining a complete lack of quantity, but rather just serves as a starting point for the measurement. In the Fahrenheit scale, the point chosen as zero is arbitrary, because you can actually have a score that is below zero. This same consideration also applies when using the Celsius scale for temperature.

The final and most precise scale in the hierarchy is the **ratio scale**. This scale combines the attributes of the interval scale with the addition of an absolute zero point. The best example of a ratio scale is weight, whether measured in pounds or kilograms. The weight scale has order: 1 pound weighs less than 2 pounds. It has magnitude, and the difference between 1 pound and 2 pounds is the same as the difference between 2 pounds and 3 pounds. Finally, it has an absolute zero point, in that 0 pounds means there is a complete absence of weight.

This section of the text has opened with the description of the measurement scales because the measurement scale used determines the type of statistical analysis performed. It is important to understand that the more precise a scale, the more stable the statistic used to calculate the outcome implies. Consider the measure of pain. When determining pain, a physician might use a nominal pain scale that implies only the absence or presence of pain (1 = pain, 0 = no pain), or a physician could use the ratio analog pain scale that implies degrees of pain. If the physician used a nominal scale, no differences between the groups (treatment versus no treatment) could be identified, because all of the patients in both groups still exhibited pain at the end of the study. In the analog pain example, however, the physician used a ratio scale so that the degree of pain could be measured. Although none of the patients completely lacked pain, it is clear that the group receiving the treatment had a lower degree of pain at the end of the study when compared with the no treatment group. Remember, precision not only adds reliability and validity to the study, but it also enhances the statistical power and enthusiasm of the results.

Descriptive Statistics: Nominal and Ordinal Data

The first step and lowest order of any quantitative analysis is the description of the data in numeric terms. As described earlier, the measurement scale used for each item on an instrument determines

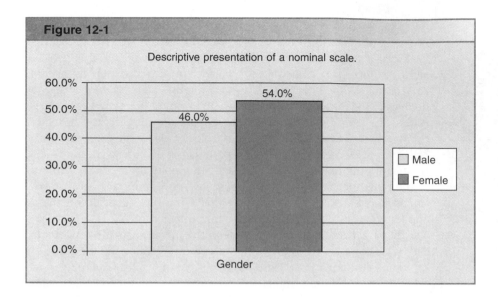

Figure 12-1

Descriptive presentation of a nominal scale.

how the data are presented in a descriptive form. Reporting of data for instrument items that use a nominal or ordinal scale usually takes the form of frequencies or percentages of the response for the item. For example, demographic data for a sample might be reported using variables such as gender, race, marital status, or educational status. Data of this type are presented in the form of percentages, such as the percentage of males and females in the sample (**Figure 12-1**).

Novice researchers often make the mistake of reporting nominal or ordinal data in the form of means; this is absolutely incorrect. Because nominal and ordinal data have no magnitude or size, measures of central tendency such as a mean and standard deviation are meaningless with these data.

Interval and Ratio Data

Central Tendency
What is **central tendency**? Central tendency is a way to allow the researcher to show the audience how the scores are distributed around a central point. Central tendencies are described in three ways: the mean, the median, and the mode.

The **mean**, or average, of a set of scores is determined by the sum of the scores divided by the total number of scores. Consider the example of taking a patient's systolic blood pressure five times. The systolic scores are 125, 130, 122, 128, and 130 mmHg. Notice that these scores are ratio scale data, because there is an absolute zero point (meaning no pressure or the absence of any pressure might be

---

Figure 12-2

Mathematical representation of the mean.

$$\text{Mean} = \frac{\sum x}{n}: \text{where } X \text{ is the observed score and } n \text{ is the number of scores}$$

$$= \frac{\sum 125, 130, 122, 128, \text{ and } 130}{5}$$

$$= \frac{635}{5}$$

$$= 127$$

---

measured). The calculation of the mean of these scores is shown in **Figure 12-2**.

The average (mean) for the systolic pressure scores is 127 mmHg. Notice that 127 mmHg does not appear in the set of original scores. Rarely does the mean actually equal one of the scores in the observed list; rather, it represents a best estimate of the central point of all the measured scores. Measurement error is inherent in all instruments. The mean allows a researcher to develop a central point within the data, incorporating the error within the measure. The process and rationale for doing so are explained in more detail in the discussion of the standard deviation that appears later in this text.

The **median** is the second measure of central tendency. The median is the middle score of a set of data. It represents the 50th percentile; thus it allows the researcher to show the exact point at which half of the scores fall above the median and half of the scores fall below the median. In the previous systolic pressure example, the median of the scores 125, 130, 122, 128, and 130 is 128 mmHg. Notice that in these readings, the score of 128 is the second to the last score. If the median is the middle number, then how can 128 be the median score? A specific point needs to be made when determining the median. The data should always be ordered from lowest to highest when determining the median. In this case, the data for systolic pressure should be ordered as follows: 122, 125, 128, 130, and 130.

The final measure of central tendency is the **mode**. The mode is the most frequently observed score within a variable's data. In the previous example, the systolic pressure of 130 mmHg is the mode of the data because it occurs twice, while all other scores appear only once. Whereas the mean is the most stable measure of central tendency (meaning it represents the absolute possible middle score), the mode is the least stable measure of central tendency (meaning it represents only the most frequently occurring score). As a researcher increases the number of observations within a variable, the chances are that the mean, median, and mode will be more representative or equal to each other.

Variability

A second issue when describing interval and ratio data is the variability of the data. Variability describes how the data vary between each score and also from the mean. There are two types of variability that the EBP research might report: the range of the data and the variance or standard deviation of the data.

The range of the data is calculated by subtracting the lowest score for the variable from the highest score for the variable. In the previous example involving systolic blood pressures, the range of the data is 130–122 mmHg, or 8 mmHg. This calculation simply means that the highest score and lowest score vary by only 8 mmHg. When reporting this range, the reader can infer that because the mean of the data was 127 mmHg and the range was 8 mmHg, then the scores ranged from 123 to 131. In such a case, the reader of the report must assume that the variability was uniform. This rating reflects that the scores varied from the mean evenly: In other words, the upper scores varied 4 mmHg from the mean, and the lower scores varied 4 mmHg from the mean. With the aforementioned assumption, the reader infers some error, because the actual scores ranged from 122 to 130 mmHg. When reporting the range of 8 mmHg and the mean of 127 mmHg, however, the range was 123 to 131 mmHg.

One other point to remember is that the range is unstable if the data being used include numerous outliers, either above the mean or below the mean. For example, in the systolic pressure example, assume that the data were 125, 130, 122, 128, and 160 mmHg. The mean for these data is 133 mmHg (approximately 6 mmHg higher than the mean found in the first example), and the range is 38 mmHg. Notice that the inclusion of a single high value increased the range by 30 mmHg. Also notice that when interpreting the data, the reader would assume falsely that with a mean of 133 mmHg, the data would range from 114 to 152 mmHg. In this case, the description of the data is lacking, because the outlier of 160 mmHg negatively affects the description.

The second measure of variability in describing data is the standard deviation, which is the square root of variance. Variance is the measure of the spread of scores around the mean based on the squared deviations of the observed scores from the mean of the data. The concept of a standard deviation allows a researcher to develop a description of the scores' variability from the mean based on a normal distribution. The standard deviation, which can be determined using the formula in **Figure 12-3**, provides the ability to describe the data based on a normal distribution and the percentage of the normal distribution expected to occur between each standard deviation unit.

Figure 12-3

Mathematical representation of standard deviation.

$$\sqrt{\frac{\Sigma x^2 - \frac{(\Sigma x)^2}{n}}{n-1}}$$ where X is the observed score and n is the number of scores

---

As shown in **Figure 12-4**, the researcher can more fully describe the pattern of the data by using both the mean and the standard deviation. The standard deviation can be interpreted as meaning that the reader of the data can expect 68.26% of the observed scores to fall plus or minus one standard deviation from the mean. Conversely, the reader can expect less than two-tenths of 1% of the scores to fall plus or minus one standard deviation from the mean. In presenting both the mean and the standard deviation, a researcher describes the data in terms of a normal distribution, allowing the reader of the results to get a mental picture of how the scores compare to the normal distribution.

Consider the systolic pressure example once again. With scores of 122, 125, 128, 130, and 130 mmHg, the mean is 127 mmHg, with a standard deviation of 3.46 mmHg. When data are presented in this form, the reader can visualize that 68.26% of the scores fell between 123.54 and 130.46 mmHg. The reader can also determine from the mean and the standard deviation that less than 0.26% of the scores were less than 116.62 mmHg or greater than 137.38 mmHg. In looking at the data described in this manner, the reader begins to understand that most of the scores from this sample were within the normal range for systolic blood pressure.

? Think Outside the Box

Discuss how statistics can be used in your evidence-based practice.

This type of analytical presentation emphasizes the verbal descriptions that are made when describing the sample demographics. ("The sample when beginning the study had normal systolic blood pressures.") Some people might shy away from reporting the mean and the standard deviation in their research reports because of math phobia. This fear is unwarranted, because most statistical software packages make the process of computing these values very simple. In the current world of research, most researchers utilize a statistics software package, such as the **Statistical Package for the Social Sciences (SPSS)**, to complete all of the calculations for the data collected.

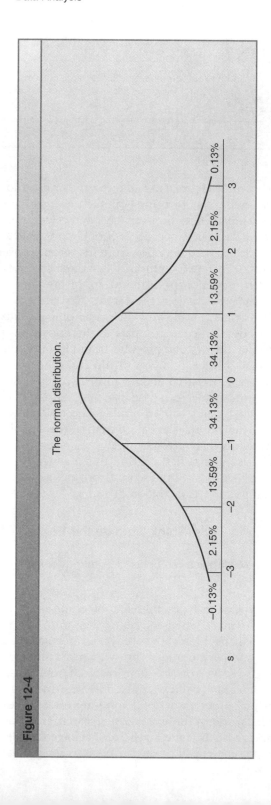

Figure 12-4

The normal distribution.

Table 12-1	
Hemoglobin Scores	
Patient ID	**Hemoglobin**
1	14.10
2	12.20
3	11.90
4	14.50
5	13.80
6	13.20
7	13.50
8	14.00
9	11.10
10	9.60

From this point forward in this text, all data analysis is described to the student. To finish the lesson on the mean and standard deviation, the student is asked to determine the mean and standard deviation of a set of scores for hemoglobin content (**Table 12-1**). In this example, all of the scores would need to be totaled and divided by 10.

Inferential Statistics

Once a researcher has described the study subjects through descriptive analysis, it is time to quantitatively analyze and present the data for the results. To accomplish this task, a researcher must understand not only the scales of measurement, but also the type of variable. Research design typically includes two types of variables—the dependent variable and the independent variable. The dependent variable is the criterion that determines the entire purpose of the research. The independent variable is the variable that affects the change in, or is related to, the dependent variable. A dependent variable can be categorized as the outcome variable or the effect variable, while the independent variable is categorized as the manipulated variable or the cause variable. **Table 12-2** lists other differences between the dependent and independent variable.

An example of a statement using an independent variable and a dependent variable would involve a researcher attempting to determine if there is a difference between use of a statin drug and use of niacin alone in reducing cholesterol level. The dependent variable in this case is cholesterol level (the outcome measured in mg/dL); the independent variable is the type of treatment (statin or niacin). Determining which variable is the dependent variable and which is the independent variable is only the first step in identifying the statistic to use for data analysis, however. The second step is to determine the

Table 12-2	
Differences Between Dependent and Independent Variables	
Independent Variable	**Dependent Variable**
Cause	Effect
Manipulated	The consequence
Measured	Outcome
Predicted to	Predicted from
Predictor	Criterion
x	*y*

scale of measurement for both the dependent variable and the independent variable. The scale of measurement for each of these variables then determines the proper statistic for analysis of the data. General guidelines for choosing the proper statistic based on the measurement scale of the dependent and independent variables are presented in **Table 12-3**.

Chi-Square

Whenever the dependent variable is scaled nominally, the **chi-square** statistic is typically used for its analysis. The chi-square (χ^2) value suggests whether an association exists between nominally scaled variables.

An example of a research design that warrants a chi-square analysis would be the case in which a researcher wants to know if there are differences between men and women in undergoing annual checkups (yes or no). The dependent variable for these data is whether the person underwent an annual checkup, while the independent variable is gender. With the use of a statistical software package, the chi-square value could be calculated quite easily. Once the calculation is completed, the determination of any difference between men and

Table 12-3		
Statistical Choice for Measurement Scales of Dependent and Independent Variables		
Independent Variable	**Dependent Variable**	**Statistical Test**
1 nominal	1 nominal	Chi-square
1 nominal (2 groups)	1 continuous	*t*-test
1 nominal (2 groups)	1 continuous	One-way ANOVA
2 nominal	1 continuous	Two-way ANOVA
ANOVA = analysis of variance.		

women in terms of whether they underwent an annual checkup could be made by reviewing the **chi-square** statistic and the significance of the test. Generally, most research studies seek to find statistical differences at the $p < 0.05$ level. Anything greater than 0.05 is considered not significant.

This is an appropriate time to point out that in data analysis, the results are either significant or not significant. The p value does not impose magnitude. Therefore, even if the results have a significance of 0.0001, this finding does not mean that the results are "extremely" significant—just that they *are* significant.

t-Test

Now that we have described the analysis of a nominally scaled dependent variable, it is time to learn how to determine which test to use for a continuous scaled dependent variable. Review Table 12-3 to refresh your memory. The number of nominal variables and levels within the nominal variables for the independent variable determines which statistic (t-test or analysis of variance [ANOVA]) should be used.

If the independent variable has one nominal variable with two groups (e.g., gender), the researcher would use a **t-test** to determine statistical differences between the groups. Two types of t-tests can be calculated—the independent t-test and the dependent t-test. An independent t-test is used when a single continuous dependent variable is being compared, while a dependent t-test allows a researcher to compare two continuous variables as long as the variables are related.

An example of a dependent t-test would be a comparison of the pre-treatment and post-treatment cholesterol levels of a group of individuals receiving a statin drug as single-agent therapy. Interpretation of the t-test statistic is the same for both variables; the nuance relates to the number of dependent variables and whether they are related.

The independent t-test statistic determines if a difference is present in a single dependent variable between the two groups. An example of a research design that warrants a t-test analysis would be a researcher who wants to know if there are differences between men and women in terms of their hemoglobin content. The dependent variable for these data is hemoglobin content, which is a ratio-scaled continuous variable; the independent variable is gender. Data are provided in **Table 12-4** to assist in determining the answer to this question.

Once the results are input and statistics are calculated using a statistical software package, the determination of the difference between men and women in hemoglobin levels could be identified by assessing the significance of the test. Again, remember that most research studies seek to find statistical differences at the $p < 0.05$ level.

Table 12-4

Quantitative Analysis: Data for *t*-Test Analysis

Patient ID	Gender	Hemoglobin
1	Male	14.10
2	Female	12.20
3	Male	11.90
4	Female	14.50
5	Female	13.80
6	Female	13.20
7	Male	13.50
8	Male	14.00
9	Male	11.10
10	Female	9.60

? Think Outside the Box

Describe the different numerical values used in the clinical setting. Discuss which level of measurements each of those types of values represent (i.e., blood pressure readings, fasting blood sugars, weights). Differentiate among the different measurement scales that you use on a daily basis. Does this understanding change the way you think about the values that you use when delivering care?

ANOVA

The final statistical analysis to be discussed for interpreting data is the **analysis of variance** (**ANOVA**). As described previously in the t-test section, the number of nominal variables and levels within the nominal variables for the independent variable determine which statistic (t-test or ANOVA) should be used. If the independent variable has one nominal variable with more than two groups (e.g., race), an ANOVA test would be used to determine statistical differences.

Two types of ANOVA can be calculated—the one-way ANOVA and the two-way ANOVA. The one-way ANOVA is used when a research study is comparing a single nominal independent variable. The two-way ANOVA allows the researcher to compare two nominal independent variables. An example of a two-way ANOVA would involve comparing men and women (one independent variable) by trial (pre-treatment versus post-treatment; the second independent variable) in terms of their cholesterol levels. This example would be considered a 2 × 2 design, which is used in many clinical trials.

Interpretation of the ANOVA statistic is the same for both variables; the nuance relates to the number of independent variables. The one-way ANOVA statistic determines whether a difference is present in a single dependent variable among the several groups within a single independent variable.

An example of a research design that warrants an ANOVA analysis would be a researcher who wants to know if there are differences among people of various ethnicities in terms of their hemoglobin content. The dependent variable for these data is hemoglobin content, which is a ratio-scaled continuous variable, while the independent variable is race (White, African American, or Hispanic). Data are provided in **Table 12-5** to assist in answering this question. Notice that in the data entry for race, the variables are dummy coded (1 = white, 2 = Hispanic, and 3 = African American). These are treated as nominal scale variables.

To determine if there is a difference among people of these races in terms of their hemoglobin levels, the significance of the test would

Table 12-5		
	ANOVA Model	
Patient ID	**Race**	**Hemoglobin**
212	1	8.119
172	2	16.029
183	2	14.569
152	2	17.624
153	2	15.242
154	2	19.942
182	2	16.111
186	2	14.230
213	3	16.951
237	1	12.400
105	1	12.350
106	1	12.106
107	1	11.811
149	1	12.972
150	1	13.930
151	1	12.038
181	2	13.703
227	2	16.433
228	2	13.446
128	2	14.953
129	2	12.624
130	2	13.169
142	2	14.987
159	2	12.596
170	3	15.996
171	3	11.476
179	1	11.233
187	1	12.253
222	1	14.090
173	1	14.060

need to be calculated using a statistical software package. Again, remember that most research studies seek to find statistical differences at the $p < 0.05$ level.

A final note about ANOVA techniques: When completing either a one-way ANOVA or a two-way ANOVA, the statistical program will require the ANOVA to be defined as a one-tailed or two-tailed test. This simply means that the researcher must determine whether the differences among the data are expected to occur in a single direction on the normal curve or in both directions on the normal curve. A single-tailed test suggests that the expected differences for all groups will occur in a single direction, either above the mean (an increase) or below the mean (decrease). A two-tailed test assumes that group differences are expected to change in a bidirectional manner, where one group may have a decrease from the mean while another group may have an increase from the mean. An example of a single-tailed test would be the measurement of body temperature with the onset of a disease. The researcher might expect that body temperature will increase from the normal temperature of 98.6°F only with the onset of a disease, so the ANOVA in this study will be a single-tailed test.

An example of a two-tailed test would be the measurement of body weight among a dieting group and a control group. The researcher might expect that body weight will decrease in the dieting group, whereas it will increase with the control group, so the ANOVA will be a two-tailed test.

Reporting the Results of Quantitative Analysis

The final step in the quantitative analysis of data is disseminating the results in an intelligible form. Put simply, a researcher must thoroughly describe the sample using the descriptive analysis techniques. Once the sample is described, each inferential statistic needs to be described within the results. The a priori probability value (usually $p < 0.05$) must be stated. Finally, the statistical tests need to be reported, including what their probability is and whether these results are significant. These analyses allow a researcher to develop the discussion by comparing the results of the study with the findings from other research and inferring whether these results have substantial implications for practice.

Qualitative Analysis

The second major form of analysis that an EBP researcher may perform is a qualitative analysis. As described previously, qualitative analysis incorporates observation and language to develop an in-depth description of the results. Where quantitative analysis describes results and outcomes based on numeric data, inferential statistics, and sample size, qualitative analysis relies on the observational method of the researchers and their ability to describe the in-depth intricacies of the observations to explain outcomes and develop theories for the research. The final outcome of most qualitative analyses is not based on significant differences from the numeric data, but rather consists of a refined conceptual framework of the research that is improved through logical reasoning.

Another way to think about the difference between quantitative and qualitative analysis is to frame it in the terms of the reasoning process. Quantitative analysis uses the deductive reasoning process—that is, a top-down method of analysis. With this approach, the researcher begins with a theory on a topic, then narrows the scope to one or more hypotheses, and finally hones in on conformational results collected from a specific sample. In contrast, qualitative analysis most times uses the inductive reasoning process—a bottom-up analysis that goes in the opposite direction of the deductive process. With this approach, the researcher starts with observations of a specific pattern and, from those observations, develops hypotheses and theories. Once these theories are developed, then the quantitative method can be used to test those theories and generalize the results to a population. Many times, the final outcome of a qualitative analysis is not a set of specific results, but rather a set of specific questions or hypotheses in need of quantitative analysis.

Two types of qualitative analysis apply to the EBP provider—the case study and the program evaluation. Each of these types of analysis occurs at some time during a nurse's professional practice. Each has commonalities and distinct characteristics that are based in the foundation of observation. The major skills that all EBP researchers must possess to ensure well-derived products from qualitative analyses are good language skills and keen observational techniques.

Notice that observation is the key element in all qualitative analyses. As a result, most qualitative research plans focus on small groups of individuals to develop the conceptual framework that encompasses the final deductions, unlike quantitative analyses that use large samples to derive the results. Also, comparison data are minimal, because qualitative analysis, although not restrained by the assessment of significant differences, lacks the distinct comparable traits that are inherent in the use of quantitative analysis.

The Case Study

The case study is the most commonly practiced type of qualitative analysis occurring in EBP research. Case studies are individualized and personal. Many of the case studies gleaned from EBP eventually lead to larger quantitative analysis trials. In developing a case study, the researcher's initial response is to assume that all aspects of the case are important and to take a broad overview of the topic in an attempt to explain the outcomes.

In any qualitative analysis, focus on the conceptual framework determines the success or failure of the end product. The conceptual framework explains the dimensions of the study, the key factors, the variables, and the relationship among different variables. The EBP researcher must focus on and define the conceptual framework prior to implementing a case study. Effective preparation and focus can help eliminate unnecessary observations and shorten the time for completion of the study.

To develop a conceptual framework for a case study, or any other qualitative analysis, the EBP nurse must be well-versed in the area of study and thoroughly familiar with research previously conducted on the topic (i.e., the literature). The conceptual framework many times starts as a new observation that piques the curiosity of a researcher. In the process of becoming interested, the researcher begins to focus his or her observations, collecting data through a written journal or diary of the observations, and then attempts to develop a coherent framework that explains the novel observations. In nursing practice, patient files may be reviewed and described to develop the conceptual framework for the analysis.

Once a conceptual framework sets the boundaries of the analysis, the research questions must be developed. This is done in the same manner as in any research—through review of the literature and comparison of the case with the previous findings of other research. Case studies, like program evaluations, must be described in depth to improve the impact of their findings. A lack of depth in such descriptions may lead subsequent reviewers of the research to discard it as being poorly substantiated.

Once the conceptual framework is completed and the research questions are defined, it is time to develop the means to explain the observations in the context of the questions. A researcher should focus and include only those material observations that are relevant. Inclusion of minutiae and irrelevant observations in the report of a study tend to detract from the impact of the overall analysis. The relevant findings should be described in detail and previous research should be used, when available, to help derive the conclusions. The end product of the effective completion of this process is often the identification of questions needing further study.

The Program Evaluation

The program evaluation is another method of qualitative analysis that the EBP researcher may use to evaluate a specific program rather than an individual case. Program evaluation allows the EBP researcher to observe the workings of a specific program, rather than a single case, and develop explanations for the success or failure of the program.

Like the case study, the program evaluation needs a well-defined conceptual framework through which to judge success or failure. Many times the program evaluator will ask the program participants to complete a self-study exercise listing the items that each participant perceives as important to the successful implementation of the program. The evaluator will then review the self-study and compare it with previously successful programs that incorporated the same conceptual framework. The researcher may also review characteristics of the site where the program implementation occurs to determine if site-specific barriers are present that might potentially hamper the successful implementation of the program.

The end product of a program evaluation should include well-defined areas of success within the program and identification of all observed barriers in the program that might increase the likelihood of failure. The final product of a program evaluation should include well-founded conclusions that will improve the likelihood of successful implementation of the program. Many times the end product will either help strengthen the implementation of the program or determine that, in the present state and site reference, the program needs to be reconceptualized.

Quality Assurance

Quality assurance analysis is becoming one of the most important analyses required of the EBP researcher in the healthcare setting. Patients, insurance companies and regulatory agencies demand that programs, hospitals, and clinics provide ever increasing evidence of the quality of the health care available to the public. Quality assurance analysis is not a recognizable single technique for analyzing data, but is the process that allows the EBP researcher to guide them in developing the necessary outcome measures that will provide the evidence of quality health care.

Quality assurance analyses may include using both quantitative and qualitative statistical techniques. These statistical techniques will define the degree to which quality exists in the healthcare services provided to the patient or the community. The ultimate outcome of a quality assurance analysis is to help the EBP researcher determine strengths and weaknesses associated with the healthcare service and allow for the development of quality improvement practices that may improve the likelihood of desired health outcomes or improve the process of efficiently delivering the healthcare service. The Institute of Medicine (IOM, 2010) defines healthcare quality as being effective, safe, patient-centered, timely, efficient, and equitable. Two specific elements expected from measuring healthcare quality are the assessment of the effects of the healthcare service on improved health status and the assessment of the degree to which the healthcare services adhere to evidence-based practices and processes as defined by current scientific research, professional body consensus statements, and/or patient preferences.

The ultimate goal of quality assurance is to provide feedback to the EBP researcher for the development of quality improvement initiatives. To this end, the EBP researcher must carefully define the desired measures of quality. To aid in the development of a quality assurance measure, the EBP researcher must first determine if the measure will assess outcomes or processes associated with health care. There are advantages and disadvantages to both types of quality measures. Process measures are easily benchmarked, tend to use readily accessible data, require smaller sample sizes, take less time to accumulate the data, and can provide clear feedback to the provider; however, process measures must have well-defined criteria for patient inclusion and may be difficult to summarize due to lack of available comprehensive data. Outcome measures use easily defined populations, tend to be more specific, produce clearer results concerning patient survival, health changes and well-being, and can be compared across conditions; however, outcome measures require much larger sample sizes, tend to be more labor intensive, require collection of data beyond that which is collected for clinical or billing purposes, and feedback generally cannot be interpreted for changes in processes. Once the type of measurement is defined as an outcome measure or a process measure, the EBP researcher can then decide which of the six measurable characteristics of quality (efficacy, efficiency, safety, timeliness, equity, and/or patient-centered) will be incorporated in the measure. Finally, the EBP researcher must ensure that the defined measure has adequate validity and reliability. Well-defined and developed quality assurance measures will result in effective treatments and policies, thereby improving healthcare services and healthcare delivery.

Conclusion

Data analysis is one of the most stressful aspects of the research process because of the complexity of the endeavor. Table 12-3 is designed to help address some of the confusion related to which tests to use. Care must be taken to select the appropriate data analysis test, thereby ensuring the broad applicability of the study's findings. For quantitative data, focus on the level of measurements for the different variables is of paramount importance. Consideration of the appropriate central tendency measurement has application when determining which statistical test to use. For most researchers, the statistical tests are calculated using statistical software. The researcher must then make sense of the results that are provided.

Summary Points

1. Quantitative analysis uses numeric values to explain the outcome of a research project.
2. Qualitative analysis uses words or phrases to explain the outcomes of a research project.
3. Nominal scales use only group identification or categories to organize data.
4. Ordinal scales use ranking to organize data.
5. Interval scales have an arbitrary zero point.
6. Ratio scales have an absolute zero point.
7. Measures of central tendency include the mean, median, and mode.
8. Variability of the data describes how data vary between each score and from the mean.
9. The standard deviation statistic provides the ability to describe data based on a normal distribution and the percentage of the normal distribution expected to occur between each standard deviation unit.
10. A chi-square test is used to analyze data when the dependent variable is scaled nominally, to determine if an association exists between the variables.
11. A t-test is used to analyze data that include one nominal variable with two groups.
12. ANOVA is used to analyze data that include one nominal variable with more than two groups.
13. Case studies often lead to larger quantitative analysis trials.
14. Quality assurance is a means of assessing the outcomes and processes of health care in terms of efficacy, efficiency, safety, timeliness, equity, and patient-centeredness.

RED FLAGS

- Means are not calculated for nominal data.
- Large standard deviations imply a wide range within the individual scores. This result suggests there is greater variability and less consistency within the resulting data.
- Outliers within the data set can skew the results of analysis of those data.
- If the data consist of a nominal level of measurement for the variable, the chi-square (χ^2) statistic would be the statistical test of choice.
- Chi-square (χ^2) tests reflect association between variables.

Multiple Choice Questions

1. Which statistic is often used for nominally scaled variables?

   A. t-test
   B. ANOVA
   C. Chi-square
   D. Pearson product moment

2. What level of measurement is most often associated with categorical data such as gender?

   A. Nominal
   B. Ordinal
   C. Interval
   D. Ratio

3. Which inferential procedure is appropriate when there is one nominal-scale dependent variable and one nominal-scale independent variable?

   A. Chi-square
   B. t-test
   C. One-way ANOVA
   D. Factor analysis

4. Inferential statistics are used to decide if differences among treatment groups are due to the

   A. Significance.
   B. Dependent variable.
   C. Confounding variable.
   D. Independent variable.

5. Selection of the appropriate statistical technique is based on

   A. The research question.
   B. The level of measurement of the independent variable or variables.
   C. The level of measurement of the dependent variable or variables.
   D. All of the above.

6. What do statistically significant findings imply?

   A. The results are very important.
   B. The results are not very important.
   C. The results are likely due to chance differences among groups.
   D. The results are likely due to real differences among groups.

7. A researcher investigated the relationship between vitamin C (none, 500 mg, 1,000 mg) and workers (office, outdoors) in terms of the frequency of colds. Which of the following is (are) the dependent variable(s)?

   A.   Colds
   B.   Vitamin C
   C.   Colds and workers
   D.   Vitamin C and workers

8. Which of the following is an inferential statistic?

   A.   Mode
   B.   t-test
   C.   Standard deviation
   D.   Range

9. Which statistical test has a dependent variable that is nominal in nature?

   A.   Chi-square
   B.   t-test
   C.   ANOVA
   D.   Two-way ANOVA

10. The standard deviation is

   A.   The square of the mean deviation.
   B.   The square of the variance.
   C.   The square root of the variance.
   D.   The square root of the sum of squares.

11. The t-test is used to

   A.   Adjust for initial differences within the groups.
   B.   Estimate the error of prediction.
   C.   Test whether two groups differ significantly.
   D.   Test whether more than two groups differ significantly.

12. Use of a one-tailed versus a two-tailed test of significance of the difference between two samples is determined by

   A.   Whether there is expected overlap between the error curves of the two sample distributions.
   B.   Whether the difference is expected to be in one direction only.
   C.   The size of the samples relative to population size.
   D.   Whether the subjects were matched or chosen randomly.

Discussion Questions

1. A nurse has decided to research the following PICOT question: "Adult clients who are admitted to the cardiac unit with congestive heart failure are more likely to develop nosocomial infections than other cardiac clients admitted to the cardiac unit." A quantitative research design is planned for this project. From the PICOT question, determine the variables, the levels of measurement of each variable, and the statistical test to be used.

2. A research study assessing vital signs for 15 clients resulted in the following results.

Client Number	Oral Temperature (°F)	Pulse (Beats per Minute)	Respirations (Breaths per Minute)	Blood Pressure
1	97.6	80	12	160/80
2	98.6	60	20	154/90
3	98.6	54	32	132/60
4	99.0	92	16	90/62
5	98.0	86	18	200/140
6	98.4	84	22	116/76
7	99.2	74	28	132/80
8	100.0	72	18	124/78
9	98.6	90	20	140/90
10	98.6	88	32	160/90
11	98.6	64	30	100/50
12	98.8	68	20	118/84
13	98.4	74	18	120/88
14	98.2	50	14	132/74
15	97.6	100	32	190/110

Calculate the mean, median, mode, range limits, range, and presence of outliers for each of the vital sign indices.

3. A research project is envisioned to analyze preintervention and postintervention cholesterol levels for a group of high school students participating in an after-school athletic program. Which type of statistical test could be used for this study and why?

Suggested Readings

American Psychological Association (APA). (2001). *Standards for educational and psychological testing* (5th ed., pp. 8–9). Washington, DC: Author.

Baumgartner, T., & Jackson, A. J. (1999). *Measurement for evaluation in physical education and exercise science* (6th ed., pp. 57–109). Dubuque, IA: McGraw-Hill.

Colling, J. (2004). Coding, analysis, and dissemination of study results. *Urology Nursing, 24*(3), 215–216.

Cunningham, G. K. (1986). *Educational and psychological measurement.* New York, NY: Macmillan.

Glass, G. V., & Hopkins, K. D. (1996). *Statistical methods in education and psychology* (3rd ed., pp. 31–77). Englewood Cliffs, NJ: Prentice Hall.

Happ, M. B., Dabbs, A. D., Tate, J., Hricik, A., & Erlen, J. (2006). Exemplars of mixed methods data combination and analysis. *Nursing Research, 55*(2), S43–S49.

Institute of Medicine (IOM). (2010). *The future of nursing: Leading change, advancing health.* Washington, DC: National Academies Press.

Magee, T., Lee, S., Giuliano, K., & Munro, B. (2006). Generating new knowledge from existing data: The use of large data sets for nursing research. *Nursing Research, 55*(2S), S50–S56.

Morrow, J. R., Jackson, A. W., Disch, J. G., & Mood, D. P. (2000). *Measurement and evaluation in human performance* (2nd ed., pp. 65–70). Champaign, IL: Human Kinetics.

Owen, S., & Froman, R. (2005). Focus on research methods. Why carve up your continuous data? *Research in Nursing & Health, 28*(6), 496–503.

Priest, H., Roberts, P., & Woods, L. (2002). An overview of three different approaches to the interpretation of qualitative data. Part 1: Theoretical issues. *Nurse Researcher, 10*(1), 30–42.

Rubin, H. R., Pronovost, P., & Diette, G. B. (2001). The advantages and disadvantages of process-based measures of health care quality. *International Journal for Quality in Health Care, 13*(6), 469–474.

Seibers, R. (2002). Data in abstracts of research articles: Are they consistent with those reported in the article? *British Journal of Biomedical Science, 59*(2), 67–68.

Thomas, J., & Nelson J. (2005). *Research methods in physical activity* (5th ed., pp. 110–212). Champaign, IL: Human Kinetics.

Reference

Institute of Medicine (IOM). (2010). *The future of nursing: Leading change, advancing health.* Washington, DC: National Academies Press.

Chapter 13

The Research Critique Process and the Evidence-Based Appraisal Process

Carol Boswell and Sharon Cannon

Chapter Objectives

www

At the conclusion of this chapter, the learner will be able to

1. Provide a rationale for completing a research critique
2. List the necessary elements in a research critique
3. Examine the evidence-based appraisal
4. Evaluate evidence needed for clinical decision making
5. Use evidence-based practice guidelines to manage holistic nursing practice

Key Terms

www

➤ Critique

➤ Hypothesis

➤ Qualitative research

➤ Quantitative research

Rationale for Doing a Research Critique

When a critical question in nursing practice has been posed, the immediate reaction is often itself a question: What's in the literature? A common assumption made by most people is that the printed words are absolute or true. This assumption is even more commonplace when the literature is a researched study. Unfortunately, not all published research is scientifically sound. As a result, it is imperative that a nurse be able to critically assess a report.

According to Burns and Grove (2009), in the 1940s and 1950s nursing research generated critiques that were less than pleasant. Consequently, little nursing research was undertaken until the 1980s and 1990s. No studies are without some imperfections, but that is not a valid excuse for failure to conduct research. The basic concept of research management is that the researcher makes decisions about the research plan and justifies those decisions. If the researcher has done a good job with the justifications, then the strength of the results is supported. When poor justifications for the research decisions are evident, the strength of the results must be questioned. As a result of this realization, scrutiny focusing on the limitations and strengths of studies are now commonplace. This shift from criticism to analysis provides a more positive approach to examining the usefulness of the scientific data generated. Nurses must critically contemplate and evaluate studies, particularly research studies to determine the appropriate application to practice. Melnyk and Fineout-Overholt (2010) support this sentiment in relation to research and evidence-based practice (EBP). In EBP, research provides the evidence that guides clinical practice in making decisions about the care nurses provide.

? Think Outside the Box

www

Looking critically at the evidence required of nurses today, how could you start the process of gaining confidence in doing research critiques? What are some of the reasons for doing research critiques?

According to Polit and Beck (2008), a research **critique** is a mechanism to provide feedback for improvement. They suggest that nurses who can critically review a study make valuable contributions to the body of nursing knowledge. Individuals conducting critiques need to be aware of biases that they could insert into their review. Care needs to be given when looking at sources to determine the effectiveness of the material for practice, so that changes in practice are based on material that has minimum biases within the review of the material.

Finally, considering a rationale for a research critique can be found in the definition of the word "critique" as offered by *Merriam-Webster Learner's Dictionary* ("Critique," 2012): "a careful judgment in which you give your opinion about the good and bad parts of something (such as a piece of writing or a work of art)" (p. 1). If one thinks of nursing as both an art and a science, then a critical review of nursing research can be seen as a work of art. Studies withstanding the test of time through careful exploration of findings and implementation allow nurses to practice the art and science of the profession. Each nurse is asked to regularly and consistently examine how and what they are doing in light of the evidence to ensure that the care provided is current. By examining the different articles for positive and negative items within the discussion, gaps and consistencies can be determined. Since research is a significant aspect of EBP, the research critique will be discussed first.

Elements of a Research Critique

Perhaps, before considering the elements of a research critique, we should discuss the types of critiques. Burns and Grove (2009) have identified nine types of critiques, ranging from a student critique to the critique of research proposals:

- Students learn to critique in their nursing education programs.
- Practicing nurses analyze studies for evidence on which to base the care provided.
- Educators approach critiques from the aspect of improving instruction.
- Nurse researchers focus on building a program of research emphasizing the review of studies in one specific area.
- Abstracts are frequently reviewed for use in presenting research findings.
- Presenting research at meetings, conferences, and workshops allows participants to verbally critique studies.
- Several nursing journals publish critiques of published articles, with the authors of the original article subsequently responding to concerns raised with the critique. These types of critiques often take the form of letters to the editor.
- An article submitted for publication in a peer-reviewed journal undergoes a review by peers who assess the quality of the study.
- Requests for funding for research studies from agencies such as the National Institute of Nursing Research (NINR) are subjected to scrutiny.

Critiques are essential to EBP and are expressed in the various forms just discussed.

Regardless of the type of critique, each critique includes certain elements. Brink and Wood (2001) have suggested that "the purpose of a research critique is to determine whether the findings are usable for you" (p. 57). Some general questions can be associated with the elements of a critique.

Study Purpose

The first element of a research critique generally involves determining the purpose of a study. Questions to be asked about this element include the following:

- Is the purpose understandable?
- Is it appropriate to your practice?
- Is a need for the study clearly stated?
- Will the study improve nursing practice and add to the body of nursing knowledge?

Answers to these questions guide the critique. If the responses are negative, then the notion of applying the study to practice is questionable. The purpose section should clearly and effectively present the importance of the need to complete this study on this topic. When the goal of the study is not evident with the initial information, the article may be overlooked as not connected to the material being sought. This determination is based on that key, preliminary clarification of the "why" statement. The reasons for the study must be unmistakably declared within the first few paragraphs of the article.

Research Design

A second element involves the design of the research. Questions to ask about this element include the following:

- Is there a framework/theory to guide the study?
- If there is no framework/theory, are you able to identify how data will be evaluated?
- Do the authors provide a clear discussion of how data will be collected and maintained?
- Who will be studied?
- What is the plan for conducting the study?
- Are the research plan decisions adequately justified?

Constructing the different components for a research study with the rationales for the decisions made along with the generating of the research project is a multifaceted and intricate enterprise. Adequate planning is important to allow the use of the best evidence for incorporation in nursing practice. A well-thought-out design allows for assurance that the evidence has practicality. The research design can be likened to a set of instructions allowing the builder to put together the pieces of a puzzle resulting in a usable product. The determination of the rationales as to how and why decisions within the research process were made is imperative to the successful development of a sound and reasonable research application. The justification for the decisions made provide the foundation for users of the research to determine the reasonableness of the results and outcomes recommended.

? Think Outside the Box

www

Which aspects of a research article do you perceive as important, and why? Which aspects of the article seems to be the hardest to locate, and why?

Literature Review

Another element to consider is the literature review focusing on the problem presented. The literature review should speak to the gaps and consistencies found within the evidence. A resourceful and constructive literature review provides clarity as to what has been done and what continues to be needed.

Questions to ask about this element include the following:

- Is the literature review thorough and detailed?
- Is the literature review current—that is, has the literature been published within the last 5 years?
- Are there benchmark publications?
- Are the majority of sources primary or secondary?
- Is the literature review well organized, including an introduction and a summary?
- Does the literature review include a section for a model/theory?

A thorough literature review allows for assessment of the credibility of the present study. Of major importance in beginning a research study is the need to ask, "What has been written about the problem?" The literature review provides the foundation for the study's significance and relationship to practice. Benchmark publications are valuable since they serve as the foundation for the ongoing investigation on the topic of interest. Those publications which have been deemed as underpinning and supporting of the ongoing work are paramount to successful progression to the next level of knowledge concerning a topic of interest.

Research Question/Hypothesis

The next element of a research critique is the research question(s) or **hypothesis**(es). This element of the critique is of extreme importance, as it should reflect the purpose of the study. Research questions in EBP are the "who, what, when, where, why, and how" guiding the nursing care provided to patients. Thus it is essential to assess the following issues:

- Is the research question clearly stated?
- Does it match the purpose of the study?
- Are the decisions made about the research question adequately justified?
- Is there a theory/framework/model discussed that establishes a relationship with the question?

A study can contain a hypothesis rather than a research question. In some studies, the research purpose may be the only statement provided. Whether it is a research purpose, research question, and/or hypothesis, it is important that the connection to the study purpose is evident. The expectation that the study purpose is evident in all aspects of the development of the study is crucial. Polit and Beck (2008) define a hypothesis as "a prediction about the relationship between two or more variables" (p. 755). Simply put, a hypothesis may predict, propose, suppose, explain, or test a quality, property, or characteristic of people, things, or settings. We have talked about or discussed "hypothetical situations." A hypothesis proposes a solution. Questions to ask about a hypothesis and/or research questions include the following:

- Are the independent and dependent variables described?
- Is the hypothesis clearly stated?
- Does the hypothesis reflect the purpose of the study?
- Are the decisions made regarding the hypothesis adequately justified?
- Is there a theory/framework/model discussed that establishes a relationship with the hypothesis?

The establishment of the research question or hypothesis is paramount to the focus of the study. Each aspect of the wording within the questions or hypotheses needs to be clear and concise to allow for the effective concentration of the research endeavor. The PICOT statement should play a part toward the development of the research question or hypothesis. The PICOT process drives the literature review and can evolve into the research question or hypothesis, based on the outcomes of the literature review. From the gaps and consistencies identified during the literature review within the EBP process, the research question/hypothesis can be structured to advance toward the next level the body of knowledge concerning the topic under investigation.

Study Sample

Another element of the research critique focuses on the sample. Sampling questions address the different aspects of the population. Each aspect within the clarification of the sampling design should be supported by rationales within the dissemination of the study. Questions regarding the sample should include the following:

- Who is identified as the target population?
- How were the subjects chosen (e.g., randomly, conveniently)?
- Who is included (e.g., males, females, children, adults)?
- Who is excluded (e.g., elderly, pregnant women, minorities)?
- How large is the sample?
- Are the decisions made regarding the sampling plan adequately justified?
- Were ethical considerations clearly addressed within the sampling process?

Answers to these questions can help the nurse decide if decisions about patients and clinical problems are practical for their unique setting. By looking at these aspects of the sampling plan generalization to a population can be supported. Clarification of the sample population must be denoted. Each aspect of the sampling process should be carefully and thoroughly described within the discussion of the project.

Data Collection

Data collection embraces many aspects that are critical to the success of the research study. Essential to the critique is a description of how the data were collected. Questions about this element include the following:

- What steps were taken to collect the data?
- How often were data collected and for how long?
- Which instruments or tools were used?
- Who designed the tools?
- Are the tools valid and reliable?

▓ Are the tools adequately described so that readers can understand what the scores means?

▓ Were data analysis procedures appropriate?

▓ Are the plans for data collection and analysis decisions adequately justified?

▓ Were ethical considerations adequately addressed within the data collection process?

Data collection gives information about the research question or hypothesis. Quantitative data, for example, are often collected by a survey mechanism that provides a score for analysis. In such a case, a clear understanding of how and where the data were collected, the description of the instrument (tool) that was used, and how the results were statistically analyzed is essential. In contrast, the data collected for a qualitative study are presented in narrative format. Qualitative data utilizes collection methods which must include a discussion of how potential biases were addressed.

? **Think Outside the Box**   `www`

Frequently, the theoretical foundation for a study seems to be omitted in research articles due to page restrictions imposed by the journal. Debate the importance of including the theoretical foundation for a study in the report of its findings.

Study Results

Clear discussion of the results from a study is essential. Results must be placed within the context of where and when they were collected. A critique should provide the results of the study. Questions about results include the following:

▓ Is the research question answered or the hypothesis supported?

▓ Were there limitations listed and explained?

▓ Can generalizations to a wider population be made?

▓ Did the results support what was reported in the literature?

▓ Were there any unexpected findings?

▓ Did the outcomes affirm the theory used as the basis of the study?

The elements of the critique summarize the study, including what was found and how the findings might be applied to similar situations. The summary of the findings needs to be carefully presented to allow for generalization to other settings and populations. Care must be given to this aspect within the report of the study outcomes to provide an understanding for where and how the results can be used within the practical world of health care.

Study Recommendations

The final element of the research critique is the section presenting the author's recommendations. Since the author understands what this study means, it is the author's responsibility to provide guidance as to where the next steps should be directed. With the in-depth work pivotal from the study completion, avenues which were identified but not addressed and/or unexpected outcomes are key areas that should be recommended for further study. Questions for this element include the following:

- Are suggestions for further use in practice included?
- Is there an identified need for further research?
- Could you make a change in your practice based on the results of this study?
- What are the benefits to using the information learned?

The necessary elements in a research critique can be organized as answers to a series of questions. Utilizing a logical format for reporting the decisions made as the study was planned, along with the results that were obtained, provides a foundation for moving healthcare research forward. This process of carefully and thoroughly considering all aspects within a reported study demonstrates accountability for advancing health care and patient safety. Those questions then form the basis for the process of conducting a research critique. As the individual investigates the quality of a study, these questions can provide a beginning place for the critique. A validated study should successfully address the majority of these questions in a positive and constructive manner. The idea of reporting the results of any study is to allow colleagues to carefully assess the outcomes to identify ways to improve patient care.

Process for Conducting a Research Critique

The word "critique" can also be defined as "a critical review or commentary, especially one dealing with works of art or literature; a critical discussion of a specific topic; the art of criticism" ("Critique," n.d.). Although "research critique" is the term frequently used, several other terms—such as "critical analysis," "review," "evaluation," and "appraisal"—can also be associated with the process. Any of these terms could be, and are, used as the method for assessing a published research article.

To gain a true understanding and appreciation of the process of a research critique, one must recognize the expectations for conducting the process. As the definition implies, it is undertaken to allow individuals to carefully and thoroughly examine a research endeavor. The outcome is not anticipated to be a negative grilling of the project to identify all of its shortcomings. Wood and Ross-Kerr (2006) affirm this point: "In your best judgment, you decide if what you have read will serve your purpose" (p. 65). The materials should be practical and applicable to your individual practice setting and the patient situation.

Studies should be scrutinized for their merits, limitations, implications, and consequences. Each and every report should be assessed with a critical eye toward each unique setting. The resulting critique should be impartial, presenting both strengths and challenges. Any review should have a goal of providing constructive recommendations related to how the study might be improved, along with where the results/outcomes could be used within health care. It is envisioned as a review or analysis of the research undertaking. Both the strengths and challenges within the process of conducting the research study are judiciously examined to verify that the ending results can truly be generalized to the target population.

❓ Think Outside the Box

www

If nurses do not value research, their engagement with the critique process and their participation in research studies are decreased. Identify steps and incentives that might be used to get you and your peers involved in doing research critiques or research projects.

By completing an effective research critique, a reviewer becomes aware of both the strengths and the shortcomings of the research project. As a consequence of identifying these concerns, the assessor can efficiently incorporate the results into practice based on this in-depth knowledge of the study findings. Thus the incorporation of the results into nursing practice is based on an understanding of the comprehensiveness of the study.

Every study has limitations, because researchers must inevitably make multiple methodological judgments that influence the significance, integrity, and value of the resulting research outcomes (San Jose State University, 2005). No study in humans is ever perfectly conducted, and even nonhuman studies frequently have limitations and weaknesses. It is true that research conducted on laboratory animals can be controlled with greater success than projects in which humans are the subjects. Put simply, when working with laboratory animals, the variables can be manipulated. If the same project were envisioned using human subjects, however, the ethical ramifications could be increased, because manipulation of the variables for human subjects might result in damages. Thus, the ethical nuances of human research must be considered when the results are proposed to be incorporated into practice.

? Think Outside the Box   www

> Look at some research articles. Can you identify within them any discussion related to patient preferences that is part of evidence-based practice? Discuss your thoughts about your findings.

Another factor—the austere style of journal articles—also triggers some concerns. The amount of space allocated to articles within journals is prescribed by the companies that publish those journals. As a result of these restrictions regarding page length and word count limits, key elements within the research process must be succinctly presented. Depth of discussion about the basic research principles must, therefore, be limited or even omitted. Unfortunately, discussions of the operational definitions for key variables; models, plans, and systems; and conceptual or theoretical frameworks are often omitted due to space restrictions. Classic research studies include a description of the theory/framework and concepts underlying the study, but many other studies use a model, plan, or system for the research.

Another aspect of the process that deters nurses from participating in research critiques is the unfamiliar jargon. Statistical aspects are quite intimidating to many practicing nurses. The definitions used within research to discuss sampling, variables, hypotheses, and quantitative and qualitative methods are typically foreign to the practicing nurse. Although many of these are common terms, such as "independent," "dependent," "convenience," and "variable," they often take on new meanings within a research project. This specificity of the terms within research leads to conflict and misunderstanding for novice evaluators of research. In the future, nurses will be increasingly confronted with the expectation that they will center their practice on evidence. Because nurses must become proficient at reading and understanding research reports to incorporate their findings into EBP, they need to take a deep breath now and plunge into the critiquing process.

The most valuable advice for developing expertise in this process is to continue doing research critiques, because practice does diminish the confusion and overwhelming nature of the process. By reading research articles, nurses become increasingly accustomed to the format and terminology. Evidence-based nursing practice mandates that nurses begin to build a knowledge base by the "steady diet" approach—specifically, by digesting at least one research report each week. By accepting the challenge to become comfortable with research reports, nurses will find that the different aspects of the report become more familiar, even commonplace—and, therefore, less threatening. Not all nurses will strive to carry out research activities, but it is imperative that all nurses become comfortable with the use of research results to advance the discipline of nursing and ultimately improve nursing care.

Initially, some general areas of the research study must be considered. The author(s) of the study needs to be evaluated. Precisely who is completing the research, including those persons' job titles and qualifications to conduct the project, needs to be carefully contemplated. After the author information is pondered, an assessment of the study title provides valuable information. The title of the project should provide a clear, concise description of the project. It should stimulate a prompt perception of the fundamental nature of the paper.

At this point, the abstract is examined to further clarify the focus for the research endeavor. The abstract should condense the main points from the research project. A quick read of the abstract and discussion sections should provide valuable insight into the complexity of the study and its applicability to a unique practice setting.

Four key aspects to carefully address when initiating a research critique are:

- Recognizing the purpose and problem, while resolving if the design and methodology are consistent with the study intent
- Verifying that the methodology is utilized appropriately
- Contemplating if the outcomes and conclusions are credible and confirmed by the findings
- Reflecting on the report's overall quality, strengths, and challenges, and whether they contribute to the knowledge base and offer suggestions for improvement

Research critiques can take many different pathways. The principle idea is to make sure that, regardless of the tool or process used, each aspect of the research process is carefully examined for appropriateness. An example of the research critique process should involve the following steps:

1. Reading the entire study carefully and with purpose
2. Examining the organization and presentation of the different components for logical flow
3. Identifying any term you don't understand by seeking clarification as to the meaning of the term
4. Highlighting and examining each step of the research process
5. Identifying the strengths and challenges without bias
6. Considering modifications for future studies
7. Determining how well the study followed the expectations for an ideal study

Table 13-1	
Critique Worksheet	
Areas for Consideration	**Comments Concerning Completeness of the Information Provided**
Title of the study	
Author credentials	
Purpose of the study	
Timeliness of literature used	
Literature review addressed each of the variables	
Theory/framework, concepts, and the relationship to nursing	
Research question or hypothesis	
Dependent and independent variables listed	
Definitions given	
Tools and their reliability and validity information (quantitative)	
Data collection methods and triangulation of process (qualitative)	
Sample description	
Study ethics description (i.e., institutional review board [IRB] information)	
Data collection procedures	
Data analysis	
Results, recommendations, and implications for practice	

In **Table 13-1**, an example of a critique worksheet is provided. Some worksheets provide areas for comments while others may have checkmark boxes to complete. Any format that addresses the different areas which need to be included in a critique can be used to help the individual develop confidence in completing a review of a scholarly article.

These guidelines are fairly general, but they do provide a place to start. A careful, general reading of the entire study must be the beginning point for any critique. The examiner initially should read the complete research report to gain an awareness of the study and its input to knowledge improvement. A second reading of the document allows the focus to be directed toward the questions appropriate to each stage of the critiquing process. The use of a photocopy of the article may facilitate the research critique process, because areas can be highlighted, questions can be added to the margin, and key points can be circled. For individuals just beginning the process of critiquing articles, the use of note-taking and comment-making in the margin allows for the questions to be directed to the correct place within the article.

As the reader begins this initial review of the research project, he or she will develop a feel for the organization of the article, along with the manner of presentation for the entire research process. At this point, the examiner will become aware of the complexity of the identified material. To become somewhat relaxed with the content, he or she should expect to read the article several times. Each time the article is read, the examiner comes to terms with a different aspect of the article. Frequently, an initial question relates to the researcher's ability to verbalize the process in a manner that nurses can understand and be able to utilize in practice. The reader may also find that some of the initial questions raised in the introductory section are answered in other sections within the article. After this general overview of the article, a more critical examination of the document can then be completed.

Each aspect within a research article is examined to identify areas of concerns and assets (**Table 13-2**). The evaluator will benefit from

Table 13-2

Rules for an Ideal Study

Research problem	• Significance of problem noted • Clarification of aim of study • Practicality of study • Clarity, significance, and documentation
Review of literature	• Organization of literature • Progression toward study question through previous research reports • Rationale and direction for the study presented
Study conceptual framework/theory	• Clear link between conceptual framework/theory and research question/purpose • Any maps/models logically presented
Research questions or hypotheses	• Expressed appropriately and clearly • Logically related to the research purpose/aim and framework/theory
Variables	• Concepts identified within the framework/theory used • Variables operationally defined • Conceptual definition consistent with operational definition of each variable
Research design	• Design appears appropriate • Clearly defined protocol for conducting research project • Any treatment closely scrutinized to guarantee consistency • Threats to internal validity minimized • Logically connected to the sampling method and statistics used
Sampling method	• Method appropriate to result in representative sample • Biases identified • Human rights protected • Setting described and appropriate for target population
Measurements	• Instruments sufficient for measuring the study variables • Instrument validity and reliability levels • Instrument scoring techniques clearly described
Data collection	• Techniques for using observation clearly described • Methods for recording measures clearly described • Interrater reliability described when appropriate • Process clearly, consistently, and ethically described
Data analysis	• Procedures suitable for the type of data collected • Analysis procedures clearly portrayed • Outcomes offered in a comprehensible way

Source: Modified from San Jose State University. (2005). *Reading and critiquing research.* Retrieved December 26, 2006, from http://www.sjsu.edu/upload/course/course_969/Reading_and_CritiquingResearch.ppt

taking the time to highlight each of the steps of the research process, spotlighting the hypothesis(es), literature review, sample, ethical considerations, and research design. During this focused examination, any limitations identified by the researchers should be noted. Another area to recognize explicitly is the operational definitions, which reflect the standards used within the research project to clarify the specific variables. After noting the operational definition for each variable, a reviewer should not have many additional terms that require explanation. The evaluator should define any term that continues to be unfamiliar to enable him or her to better understand the entire process.

Every reader should develop a habit of looking up unfamiliar terms instead of skipping over them, which simply causes those terms to remain unfamiliar. The objective of critiquing any research report is to become familiar with the language and procedures used regularly within the scheme.

At this point in the research critique, the reviewer attempts to identify the strengths and limitations of the research process described in the report. The reviewer should be aware that the limitations so identified might actually be a consequence of the lack of space allowed within the documentation of the research endeavor rather than representing the intended omission of the aspect. All journal articles have space limitations, which can result in some items being cut because of space considerations rather than because they were lacking in the study.

One major challenge for novice research readers is the evaluation of statistics. In considering this aspect of any research process, the key point is to ask for help. To better understand the material presented in articles, it could be suggested that reviewers either find someone to provide help in this area or obtain a book similar to *Statistics for Dummies* to aid in the assessment of the statistical data. Nurses who practice evidence-based nursing are not expected to become statisticians. Nurses are, however, expected to acknowledge their limitations and seek help from statisticians and others as needed to improve their evaluation of research results for incorporation into everyday nursing practice.

One means of utilizing the expertise of peers and colleagues is through establishment of a journal club. The journal club members can select a different article on a regular basis. The group then completes the review/critique. By using the group to complete the work, each participant grows in their own knowledge and confidence to be able to complete a review individually.

As nurses are asked to become involved with the critiquing of research articles for EBP, several formidable factors emerge and must be dealt with. Several Internet sites are available to use as resources for exploring the development of research critiques geared toward

EBP (see this text's Companion Website, using the access code found in the front of the book).

Critically Assessing Knowledge for Clinical Decision Making

The various aspects of EBP are of fundamental importance in considering the assessment of knowledge related to clinical decision making. As nurses, the evidence required to steer a competent and effective practice does not occur after reviewing a single independent study. Changes within best practices is based upon a sound base of evidence, not just the results from a single study. The practicing nurse comes to the research critique process with a foundation of clinical experience. Thus the critique of the research endeavor is tempered by this clinical expertise. Yoder (2005) suggests that "clinical decisions require that one use a problem-solving approach to clinical practice that integrates a systematic search for and critical appraisal of the relevant evidence to answer the clinical questions" (p. 91). Every nurse has been taught a problem-solving methodology. During the review of research, it becomes essential for nurses to utilize this critical thinking framework, which has already been incorporated into practice, to validate and conceptualize the research critique process. The idea behind a research critique is to provide a systematic process for critically appraising research projects. Within this process, nurses must become comfortable with looking at all aspects of the various studies to assess any strengths and limitations that might be apparent. Carefully considering these different aspects of the report facilitates critical thinking concerning the results reported and the applicability of those results to the workplace.

One aspect of paramount importance to be considered within any research critique is the determination of the sampling process. According to Pajares (2007), "The key word in sampling is representative" (Section VI.E.4). Determining the appropriateness of the sampling method is critical in any study appraisal. When a convenient sampling method is used, the rationale and limitations related to this methodology must be meticulously discussed.

Evaluating Quantitative Research Evidence

Quantitative research reports tend to be slightly easier to critique because of the concreteness of the quantitative research design. The various aspects of quantitative research reports document the expectations for all of the various elements of the article—that is, the introduction, literature review, hypothesis(es), sampling, research design, statistical testing, and discussion. Although each of these areas includes considerable levels and components, the clarity of the descriptions of these aspects is more distinct than in qualitative methodologies.

According to Carter (2006), the critiquing of quantitative research reports should address four basic areas: comprehension, comparison, analysis, and evaluation. Each of these four levels of review adds a different dimension to the resulting scrutiny. Comprehension and comparison provide the overall appraisal of the report. Analysis then takes the investigation of the report to the level of reflecting on the continuity among the different parts (Carter, 2006). At this point of assessing the report, the principal concern is whether the hypothesis flows into decisions made about the sample, and whether that sample is appropriately managed by the research design. The final aspect of the review carefully considers the meaning and significance of the study process for implementation into nursing practice. The focus here is to determine whether the findings, implications, and recommendations presented in the study report are truly supported and presented.

A key aspect of this review process that is unique to the quantitative research appraisal is the use of a conceptual or theoretical framework (Pajares, 2007). Although it can be provided in any of the research methodologies, this framework is essential in all quantitative research endeavors. Having said this, within printed articles documenting quantitative research, the discussion of the conceptual/theoretical framework is frequently omitted to satisfy the journal's page length requirements. Of course, the omission could also reflect the researcher's failure to include a conceptual/theoretical framework as part of the study design. The total omission of this framework would be a marked limitation within a quantitative research methodology. When a lack of theoretical foundation for a study is determined (yet the study outcomes appear to be applicable to your setting), sending a query to the authors about the issue may be helpful to determine the status of the theoretical foundation.

Evaluating Qualitative Research Evidence

When evaluating **qualitative research** efforts, the examination of the entire process assumes a slightly different perspective from that employed with a quantitative research undertaking. Assessment of the clarity of the purpose and statement of the phenomenon remains consistent with that of any other methodology critique. These components must be presented upfront. From that point onward, the specificity of the qualitative design must be considered. Broad research questions, instead of hypotheses, are frequently employed within this type of research design. The literature review may follow the data collection process rather than driving the research attempt from its inception. A framework may or may not be clearly presented as part of the study report. Qualitative research reviews must carefully discuss the researcher–participant relationship, because this aspect is a critical component of the data collection process. Ethical considerations also play significant roles in determining the appropriateness of this methodology.

Carter (2006) has detailed five standards to keep in mind when conducting a qualitative research critique. First, the research report must present a comprehensible depiction of the research environment, data collection process, sampling process, and the researcher's thought process. A second standard relates to the importance of congruence among the methodological aspects. According to Carter (2006), this section should indicate "rigor in documentation, procedural rigor, ethical rigor, and auditability" (Critique of qualitative research, 2). The third standard is the analytical preciseness: The researcher's thoughts and decisions related to the data should be evident in the report. The fourth standard stresses the importance of addressing the theoretical connectedness presented within the report. The fifth standard identified suggests that the relevance (value of the study) needs to be apparent within the documentation of the research project. Appropriate examination of each of these facets within a research report should yield a strong, valid depiction of the research project.

The data collection aspect of the study is a crucial component of the presentation of qualitative research projects. The reader must be walked through the entire process, from identification of the participants to the management of the data collected from them. The congruence of these data with the research purpose, question, and tradition needs to be assessed. The researcher is obliged to discuss how the field engagements and observations ought to build trust and ensure validity of the data collected. Another aspect that should be identifiable within the report is the ongoing and concurrent nature of data collection and analysis. Because data collection and analysis occur in tandem in qualitative research, the codes used as categories and the process utilized to determine data saturation must be explicitly discussed in the report. The research report should also address triangulation, peer review of the research process, articulation of researcher biases, member checking, and external audit by expert consultants.

A final aspect that must be noted within qualitative research reports is the sampling data. Because the sample population in such studies is usually small and focused, a description of this population is critical to allowing the reader to determine if the study findings are generalizable to other populations.

Qualitative research often employs additional terminology that must be defined and clarified, which can cause further confusion and frustration. As a result, the critique of qualitative research tends to be an area that is best entered into after learning how to conduct critiques of quantitative research. Put simply, qualitative research tends to be less structured than quantitative research.

Evaluating Mixed Method Evidence

Mixed method research embraces both quantitative and qualitative design aspects. According to Creswell (2003), the mixed method approach takes advantage of the strengths of both quantitative and qualitative research by employing sequential, concurrent, and transformative strategies of inquiry. As a critique of a mixed method research study is undertaken, the reader must, therefore, consider the presentation of both methodologies within the discussion. A unique aspect of a mixed method research critique is the expectation of a stated rationale for the use of this method.

The quantitative and qualitative data in a mixed method research report are frequently presented separately, which allows the reader to concentrate on one type of data prior to considering the other type. Quantitative data are customarily presented first, followed by the qualitative data. The discussion section should integrate the two types of data, thereby strengthening the study's findings. When a transformative study design is employed, this section should address the advancement of the agenda for change or reform that has developed as a result of the research.

? Think Outside the Box

www

Can you think of any data other than research that can be used as evidence for nursing practice? Identify data that nurses provide in their practice.

Employing EBP Guidelines: Instruments for Holistic Practice

EBP requires that multiple related articles be correlated to provide a sum of evidence rather than a single data set. Contradictory evidence must be reconciled through the evaluation and association of data from multiple quality research projects. Of course, this process of reconciling contradictory evidence and multiple research discussions generates additional questions that need to be investigated at some point in time.

According to the Oncology Nursing Society (2005), the EBP process comprises six steps:

1. Identify the problem.
2. Find the evidence.
3. Critique the merit, feasibility, and utility of the evidence.
4. Summarize the evidence.
5. Apply the ideas to practice.
6. Evaluate the results.

Each of these steps, with the exception of the application to practice (Step 5), can be visualized within the research critique process. Research critiques require the identification of the problem; an examination of the literature review; a critique of the merits, feasibility, and use of the research process; summarization of the research process; consideration of the applicability of the research results to practice; and evaluation of the results.

The Evidence-Based Appraisal

Evidence comes from many different sources. The first part of this text examined the research critique process which is part of evidence-based practice. Now let's examine other important elements for nurses to use in their nursing practice.

Expert Opinion

When there is no definitive data available, nurses often turn to experts with knowledge needed about a specific aspect of nursing care. There does exist a body of thought that expert opinion is not valuable. However, when there is no valid answer, expert opinion is considered a viable alternative. Expert opinion may be expressed in books, conferences, forums, reports or even from expert clinicians in practice. Most often, textbooks and expert clinicians are the only valid resources when scientific data is not readily obtained.

Hopp and Rittenmeyer (2012) suggest the use of the term "local data." This type of data may be internal to an organization such as patient/employee satisfaction surveys, audits, or employee performance evaluations. Of particular interest to local data is quality improvement (QI)/quality assurance (QA). Hospitals and clinics, accredited by the Joint Commission and other accreditation agencies, compile QI/QA data. This data is often reported to national agencies and allows for comparisons of how the local hospital clinic is doing compared to other agencies of like size and function. For example, the Agency for Healthcare Research and Quality (AHRQ) looks at access to care, costs, and patient outcomes. The Area Resource File (ARF) examines data specific to a county. The Hospital Consumer Assessment of Healthcare Providers and Systems (HCAHPS) is a national survey of patients about the quality of hospital care they receive (Mason, Leavitt, & Chaffee, 2012). The Joint Commission is particularly interested in sentinel events. Sentinel events may be medication errors, wrong-site surgery, suicide, operative and postoperative complications or even nurse staffing issues (Sorbello, 2008). Sentinel events require healthcare organizations to conduct a root cause analysis which is a structured process to examine why an adverse event occurred. A plan is then developed to ensure that the event does not occur again.

Each of the items discussed above demonstrates a variety of ways to obtain data that may not be the result of scientific research. The evidence-based appraisal is necessary to provide nurses with knowledge to improve their nursing practice through expert opinion and internal data. The evidence-based appraisal is an important aspect in the daily practice of nurses, whether it applies to patient/nurse satisfaction, cost, or patient safety.

Summary Points

1. Critiques of research are essential to EBP and allow nurses to practice the art and science of the profession.
2. There are nine types of critiques.
3. The necessary elements in a research critique can be compiled in a series of questions for the process of critiquing research.
4. Critiques should be balanced, identifying both strengths and limitations in the study report examined.
5. Journal articles have restrictions on page limits and word limits, which sometimes results in information being omitted.
6. Jargon in research reports often deters nurses from doing research critiques.
7. The critical appraisal of research is a skill to be developed through repeated practice.
8. General areas of the research study include author qualifications, study purpose, study design, the sample, the research methodology, the outcomes, limitations, and strengths of the research, and recommendations.
9. Nurses in EBP do not need to be statisticians, but they do need to be comfortable asking for help when evaluating the statistical analysis portion of a research report.
10. Quantitative research studies are concrete in nature and should include a theoretical framework.
11. Qualitative research studies contain broad research questions and are unstructured.
12. Mixed method research embraces both quantitative and qualitative aspects of study design.
13. Research critiques should consider the applicability of the research results to practice.
14. Evidence-based appraisals may include evidence from sources other than research.

RED FLAGS

- A critique is not a negative process, but rather should entail a careful examination of all aspects of the research process.
- A research critique should identify gaps within the study's research process.
- Future research possibilities should be identified as part of the original study and the critique of that study.
- Recommendations for advancement of the nursing profession should be documented in transformative research.
- For EBP, multiple related articles need to provide a sum of evidence rather than a single data set.
- Evidence-based appraisals are critical to patient safety and quality of patient care.

Multiple Choice Questions

1. Nurses must critically assess research studies to
   A. Understand that all research is scientifically sound.
   B. Determine the applicability of their findings to practice.
   C. Know that all studies are perfect.
   D. Identify a negative approach to research utilization.

2. Of the nine types of critiques, which of the following are considered essential to EBP?
   A. Student, practicing nurse, and peer review critiques
   B. Abstracts, presentations, and email critiques
   C. Program of research, letters to the editors, and lay-journal critiques
   D. National Institute of Nursing Research, educator groups, and newspaper critiques

3. The purpose of a study applies to EBP when it
   A. Adds to the body of nursing knowledge.
   B. Is complete and requires multiple readings.
   C. Is relevant to the authors.
   D. Is hard to find in the literature.

4. A hypothesis may be described by which of the following terms?
   A. Results, introduces, criticizes, reviews
   B. Findings, improvements, collections, sets
   C. Studies, plans, appreciates, concerns
   D. Proposes, predicts, supposes, tests

5. An essential component of a critique is a description of how the data were collected. Which of the following statements provides the best data collection description?
   A. Data collection was timely and used a tool developed by the researcher.
   B. Multiple tools were used to collect the data.
   C. The data was collected at 2-week intervals using a pre-test/post-test procedure.
   D. The score for the tool is easily understood and needs little description.

6. Results of the study should include
   A. Unexpected findings.
   B. Unanswered questions.
   C. Pictures of subjects.
   D. Endorsements of peers.

7. A research study recommendation should include

    A. No further need for research.

    B. No benefits for use in practice.

    C. Ways to change practice based on results.

    D. Ways to avoid using the results in other studies.

8. The definition of a research critique is understood to imply

    A. Analytical examination or commentary of a research report.

    B. A negative assessment related to the weaknesses of a research report.

    C. An analytical evaluation of the literature review.

    D. A positive assessment of the research design.

9. Although many aspects are discussed within a research critique, the basic aspects that the critique is attempting to identify are

    A. Hypothesis(es) and literature review.

    B. Strengths and limitations.

    C. Research design and sampling methodology.

    D. Shortcomings and critical problems.

10. Evidence-based nursing practice requires that nurses initiate a pattern to facilitate effective utilization of research results. The best method for improving a nurse's ability to incorporate research results into practice is

    A. Planning a monthly session to complete a literature review.

    B. Completing a critique of a single research project.

    C. Assessing at least one research report on a weekly basis.

    D. Reviewing abstracts from selected research projects.

11. Several basic guidelines can be used to make the research critiquing procedure less threatening. Which of the following reflects the utilization of these guidelines?

    A. The nurse reads the entire discussion section carefully to gain an overview of the research report.

    B. The nurse identifies shortcomings that are unfamiliar, to clarify the limitations within the study.

    C. The nurse reads the entire study meticulously to acquire a general understanding of the research report.

    D. The nurse identifies modifications for the selected research report.

12. Quantitative research design tends to be easier to critique due to the

    A. Length of the research reports.

    B. Incorporation of triangulation into the process.

    C. Use of convenient sampling methodology.

    D. Concreteness of the research design.

13. When attempting to critique a qualitative research endeavor, individuals must be able to

    A.   Easily identify the hypothesis(es).

    B.   Carefully assess the data collection and management processes.

    C.   Quickly determine the conceptual framework utilized.

    D.   Effectively understand the statistical results.

14. One unique aspect present in reports of mixed method research projects is a(an)

    A.   Rationale for the utilization of the method.

    B.   Clear delineation of the sampling method.

    C.   In-depth discussion of the methodology.

    D.   Listing of the strengths and limitations.

15. Sentinel events require

    A.   The nurse to be fired.

    B.   The hospital to ignore it.

    C.   A root cause analysis.

    D.   The doctor to be present.

Discussion Questions

1. You and your peers, as staff nurses, have found a research article that has the potential to change the way you practice. List questions about the report elements that could guide your critique of the study.

2. Select an article on a research project for your practice area and complete the critique worksheet in Table 13-1. After completing the critique of the article, give the article a "level of evidence" rating and a "strength of evidence" score. Would you change your practice based on the information in this article?

3. You are a manager on a medical–surgical acute care unit. Your facility is moving toward an EBP format. Each unit has been charged with establishing a process for involving the staff nurses in this transformation. You have decided to implement a journal club for staff nurses to review and critique research articles for potential inclusion in evidence-based policies. What would you set as the ground rules for the implementation of this journal club activity?

4. You are a circulating nurse when a patient is to have his left leg amputated, but the scrub nurse is preparing the right leg. You realize this could be a wrong-side surgical procedure. During your operating room orientation, you were given the hospital policy/procedure for making sure this does not occur. How would you proceed?

Suggested Readings

Daggett, L., Harbaugh, B. L., & Collum, L. A. (2005). A worksheet for critiquing quantitative nursing research. *Nurse Educator, 30*(6), 255–258.

Pellechia, G. L. (1999). Dissemination of research findings: Conference presentations and journal publications. *Topics in Geriatric Rehabilitation, 14*(3), 67–79.

Riley, J. (2002). Understanding research articles. *Tar Heel Nurse, 64*(3), 15.

Valente, S. (2003). Critical analysis of research papers. *Journal for Nurses in Staff Development, 196*(3), 130–142.

References

Brink, P. J., & Wood, M. J. (2001). *Basic steps in planning nursing research: From question to proposal* (5th ed.). Sudbury, MA: Jones and Bartlett.

Burns, N., & Grove, S. K. (2009). *The practice of nursing research: Appraisal, synthesis, and generation of evidence* (8th ed.). St. Louis, MO: Saunders Elsevier.

Carter, K. (2006). *How to critique research*. Retrieved March 14, 2012, from http://www.runet.edu/~kcarter/Course_Info/nurs442/chapter12.htm

Creswell, J. W. (2003). *Research design: Qualitative, quantitative, and mixed methods approaches* (2nd ed.). Thousand Oaks, CA: Sage.

Critique. (n.d.). In *The American heritage dictionary of the English language*. Retrieved from http://education.yahoo.com/reference/dictionary/entry/critique

Critique. (2012). In *Merriam-Webster Learner's Dictionary*. Retrieved from http://www.learnersdictionary.com/search/critique

Hopp, L., & Rittenmeyer, L. (2012). *Introduction to evidence-based practice: A practical guide for nursing*. Philadelphia, PA: F. A. Davis.

Mason, D. J., Leavitt, J. K., & Chaffee, M. W. (2012). *Policy & politics in nursing and health care* (6th ed.). St. Louis, MO: Elsevier Saunders.

Melnyk, B. M., & Fineout-Overholt, E. (2010). *Evidence-based practice in nursing and healthcare: A guide to best practice* (2nd ed.). Philadelphia, PA: Lippincott Williams & Wilkins.

Oncology Nursing Society. (2005). *Evidence-based process*. Retrieved from http://onsopcontent.ons.org/toolkits/evidence/Process/index.shtml

Pajares, F. (2007). *The elements of a proposal*. Retrieved from http://www.des.emory.edu/mfp/proposal.html

Polit, D. F., & Beck, C. T. (2008). *Nursing research: Generating and assessing evidence for nursing practice* (8th ed.). Philadelphia, PA: Lippincott Williams & Wilkins.

San Jose State University. (2005, March 1). *Reading and critiquing research*. Retrieved December 26, 2005, from http://www.sjsu.edu/upload/course/course_969/Reading_ and_Critiquing Research.ppt

Sorbello, B. C. (2008). Responding to a sentinel event. *American Nurse Today, 3*(10), 30–32. Retrieved March 11, 2012, from http://www.americannursetoday.com/assets/0/434/436/440/5426/5428/5442/5446/5b587e3d-6b56-4558-b2f7-05ab3738549b.pdf

Wood, M. J., & Ross-Kerr, J. C. (2006). *Basic steps in planning nursing research: From question to proposal* (6th ed.). Sudbury, MA: Jones and Bartlett.

Yoder, L. H. (2005). Evidence-based practice: The time is now! *Medsurg Nursing, 14*(2), 91–92.

Chapter **14**

Translational Research and Practical Applications

Carol Boswell

Chapter Objectives

At the conclusion of this chapter, the learner will be able to

1. Discuss the use of translational research principles within the process of systematic decision making
2. Construct a basic logic model for an identified project of individual choice

Key Terms

- Basic research
- Impact
- Logic model
- Outcomes
- Outputs
- Patient-oriented research
- Population-based research
- Translational research

Introduction

Many different concepts and ideas come together as investigators struggle with the idea of appreciating systematic decision making. Evidence-based practice, research, and quality improvement are all aspects that play a part in the development of critical decision making and the validation of successful and competent healthcare practices. These processes take diverse paths based upon the outcomes desired. At times, full experimental, basic research is the process required to get to the results sought. At other times, a quality improvement exercise is the way to gain the information essential for the advancement of quality practice. With each encounter of questions, the type and depth of evidence needed must be carefully and consciously considered. According to O'Brien (1998), individuals within the focus of structured inquiry are embracing the phrase, "If you want it done right, you may as well do it yourself." This idea, while interesting, does not hold with the current health environment of interprofessional engagement. The inclusion of strategic individuals to respond to the questions and challenges identified requires the different individuals to appreciate the multifaceted nature of systematic decision making.

Translational Research

Woolf (2008) describes **translational research** as a "'bench-to-bedside' enterprise of harnessing knowledge from basic sciences to produce new drugs, devices, and treatment options for patients" (para. 2). The idea of moving basic research from laboratory facilities to the actual bedside to aid in the day-to-day care of patients is critical for the healthcare community. The National Institutes of Health (NIH) embraced the idea of translational research in 2006 with the formation of centers to manage the process, and with the unveiling of the Clinical and Translational Science Award (CTSA) program (Rubio et al., 2010; Woolf, 2008). While translational research has been discussed since 2006, it continues to be complicated and obscure. Rubio et al. (2010) define translational research as fostering "the multidirectional and multidisciplinary integration of basic research, patient-oriented research, and population-based research, with the long-term aim of improving the health of the public" (p. 471). Within the process of implementing translational research, diverse components are integrated to focus the attention of the decision-making process toward the patient and populations. Several different types of research methodology can be incorporated into this delivery idea. **Patient-oriented**

research strives to provide knowledge advancement through the use of inclusion of groups of patients or healthy individuals to determine the patients' perceptions related to health care. For this methodology, the patient is the center for the entire process. Each aspect within the study focuses on the manner in which the patient will be impacted. From a different focus, **population-based research** seeks to mesh epidemiology, social and behavioral sciences, public health, quality evaluation, and cost-effectiveness into the research process to allow for a holistic outcome when answering critical questions. While the population of individuals is important within the study, the holistic nature of the research is a driving force. The problem tends to be examined from multiple fronts, instead of a single vantage point. **Basic research** embraces the research conducted within a laboratory setting to advance the knowledge on a topic for the sake of knowledge, without any focus on clinical practice at that point. Basic research is a foundation for the examination of questions. The process does not have to be linked to a group of people or a situation. It is research to discover information.

Translational research has two areas of focus. The initial area relates to basic research. During this phase of investigation, the pre-clinical studies along with human trials are used to establish the foundation for further development of the information. The second focus within translational research strives to move the outcomes determined through basic research to actual adoption at the bedside as examples of best practices for the community. The process of moving the basic research to the bedside encompasses nurses at all levels. As basic research is completed, the nurse at the bedside takes on the challenge of implementing the process with patients in unique settings. As new medications, procedures, and equipment are developed and studied using basic research strategies, the bedside nurse becomes the tool for implementing those innovations into clinical practice in an effective and organized manner. With the incorporation of each new skill and/or instrument, the translational aspect of research becomes critical. The process for making it functional in the clinical setting requires the expertise of the nurse working in collaboration with the patient for the optimum outcome. Each aspect of the process is crucial and imperative. The first phase provides the foundation of evidence on which to structure the best practices for the day-to-day delivery of health care. The central and noteworthy consequences from the totality of the translational research process address the "cost-effectiveness of prevention and treatment strategies" (Rubio et al., 2010, p. 472). By embracing a focus toward prevention and treatment that is cost-effective, the ultimate outcome is improved health for the public.

When reading about translational research, the initial stage that incorporates the basic research and patient-oriented research is identified as T1. This process undertakes the challenge to move new knowledge and understanding about disease processes identified within the laboratory setting into new areas. Those novel areas include the diagnosis, treatment, and prevention of the disease progression within patients. The timely movement of identified strategies for the management of diseases is needed within the healthcare arena to support the prevention and aid in the supervision of the disease within individuals.

The second phase (T2) assimilates the identified results from laboratory research into the practical management at the bedside. This transformation of results from the clinical, laboratory setting into the judicious guidance of healthcare delivery allows for the up-to-date harnessing of knowledge to advance health care. Woolf (2008) notes that this process supports the involvement of disciplines that utilize clinical epidemiology, evidence synthesis, communication theory, behavioral science, public policy, finances, organizational theory, system redesign, and informatics. Each of these different applications necessitates that the investigator carefully considers the implications within the human world of change and conflict. The uniqueness of the individual patient comes into the picture as the laboratory results are moved into the practical world.

Action research is a term identified along with patient-oriented research that integrates the ideas of best practices, patient inclusion, inclusion into practice, and evidence-based practice. O'Brien (1998) speaks about action research as assimilating interested individuals into the process of identifying a problem, ascertaining a method for confirming it, and testing the outcomes. Since action research is a practical application of systematic inquiry, the process reflects the evolution of solutions toward the bedside for quality management of disease processes.

Within the process of translational research—basic research, population-based research, and patient-oriented research—each plays a part toward the goal of moving research outcomes to bedside implementation for the advancement of disease prevention and management. Basic research and population-based research are not totally translational in nature (see **Figure 14-1**). As a result, these two types of research do not reside completely within the realm of translational research. On the other hand, patient-oriented research "fundamentally addresses issues that have the potential to translate to clinical practice and therefore, affect health" (Rubio et al., 2010, p. 474). All aspects of patient-oriented research support and advance the concept of translational research.

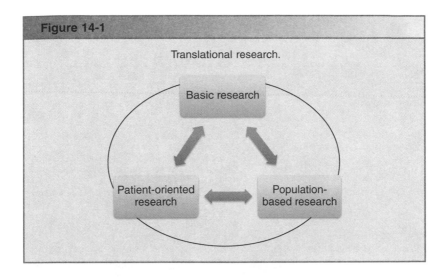

Figure 14-1

Translational research.

Logic Modeling

With the advancement of translational research, the innovative application of planning, implementation, and evaluation have been advocated and sponsored. One decisive concept incorporated within the movement toward best practice and evidence-based practice has been the logic modeling process. Different terms may be used for this process such as program theory, logical framework, theory of change, or program matrix. A **logic model** is a step-by-step roadmap for getting to the desired result. **Table 14-1** lists the multiple definitions provided for this process. Each of the definitions speaks to the idea that the logic model is utilized to advance a project in a focused, organized manner. Whether the modeling is used for a research endeavor, quality improvement project, or evidence-based practice venture, the aspects included within the model help to pull the needed components together to provide a clear and concise visual of the steps within the planned activity. **Figure 14-2** provides a simple version of a logic model framework. Each aspect builds upon the previous components to provide a template for planning, implementation, and evaluation. The model encourages the connection of strategies to the results. It also advocates timely and knowledgeable communication regarding the project and/or task. The sequencing of events related to the resources needed for a project, activities involved in a project, and the changes/benefits resulting from a project should be depicted within the tool. According to the W. K. Kellogg Foundation (2004) the declaration of the resources and activities reflects the planned work while the **outputs, outcomes,**

Table 14-1

Definitions for Logic Modeling

Source	Definition
University of Wisconsin-Extension. (2003, section 1, p. 2).	• Simplified picture of the projected program • Logical relationships found within the process • Program theory of action which reflects the different activities within the project • Denotes the underlying rationales for the activities selected to advance the project • Provides core for the planning, implementation, management, communication, and evaluation of the project
California Living 2.0. (2009, p. 1).	• Process used to create a graphic picture for how you think your work will lead to a collective vision for your community • Shows relationships among resources, strategies, and changes
Innovation Network, Inc. (n.d., p. 2).	• Commonly-used tool to clarify and depict a program within an organization • Logical framework • Theory of change • Program matrix
W. K. Kellogg Foundation. (2004, p. III).	• Defines a picture of how your organization does its work— the theory and assumptions underlying the program • Links outcomes with program activities • Facilitates thinking, planning, and communications about program objectives and actual accomplishments

Figure 14-2

Logic model template.

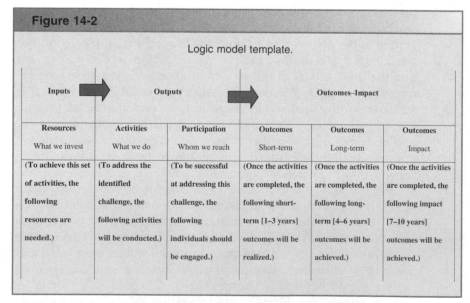

Resources	Activities	Participation	Outcomes	Outcomes	Outcomes
What we invest	What we do	Whom we reach	Short-term	Long-term	Impact
(To achieve this set of activities, the following resources are needed.)	(To address the identified challenge, the following activities will be conducted.)	(To be successful at addressing this challenge, the following individuals should be engaged.)	(Once the activities are completed, the following short-term [1–3 years] outcomes will be realized.)	(Once the activities are completed, the following long-term [4–6 years] outcomes will be achieved.)	(Once the activities are completed, the following impact [7–10 years] outcomes will be achieved.)

Source: Concepts in this table were adapted from the W. K. Kellogg Foundation's *Logic Model Development Guide* (2004) and University of Wisconsin-Extension website (2003).

and **impact** demonstrate the intended results. Each aspect endorses and promotes the next step.

Three different categories of logic modeling are available for agencies to use (W. K. Kellogg Foundation, 2004). Each of the unique types emphasizes discrete strengths. The theory approach model spotlights change theory that influences the designing and planning of a program. This model strives to provide a vivid justification for the development of a new program. Its intent is to "make a case" for the program through the use of the different components found within the model. This model type is frequently utilized by grant funders and individuals involved with grants. A second category is the outcome approach model. This type is also utilized early in the planning phase but grapples with the connections between the resources and the activities. Within this model, short-term (1–3 years), long-term (4–6 years), and impact (7–10 years) outcomes are provided for the set of activities. This category is most effective when designing effective evaluations. The third type of logic modeling is called activities approach models. The attention in this modeling process concentrates on the implementation strategies needed to accomplish the project. This model is used for program supervision and administration.

The initial step in this process of establishing a logic model is the analysis of the challenge identified or the problem. The University of Wisconsin-Extension (2003) identifies six questions to use during this process of problem/challenge analysis:

- What is the problem?
- Why is this a problem? (What causes the problem?)
- For whom (individual, households, group, community, society in general) does this problem exist?
- Who is involved in the problem?
- Who has a stake in the problem? (Who cares whether it is resolved or not?)
- What do existing research and experience say? What do we know about the problem? (p. 10)

Each of these questions provides essential information as the problem/challenge is conceptualized. As bedside nurses are asked to implement innovative strategies to advance healthcare delivery, these questions are key to ensuring that the process is organized and timely. By using a tool such as the logic model, implementation of change within a clinical setting can be accomplished successfully. Significant progress, such as introducing a new instrument (e.g., an intravenous pump), can be organized and managed to ensure that the optimum result can be reached through the use of the new information. While this tool can be time consuming, it is crucial for the management of large projects addressing multiple sites and components. By addressing these questions, the focus for the project can be distinctly established and presented. Once the problem is determined clearly, a goal for the project can be formulated. The problem statements can also be classified as issue statements or situations. The problem statement usually addresses the ideas of *who, what, why, where, when,* and *how.* These components are also used in the PICOT and/or hypothesis statements. The problem statement and goal should be narrow in focus, while objectives used within the process can reflect the scope of the project. Each component should drive the subsequent aspects within the model. The goal statements should address the intended results and target populations in general terms.

The following steps within the framework are driven by "if–then" statements. Regarding resources, certain means and/or assets are needed to activate the project. Resources identify currently available assets and opportunities. Resources can also be viewed as inputs or program investments. Some of the common areas of resources are people, budgetary items, space, technology, equipment, and materials. From this idea, the framework moves to the idea of: **IF** these means and/or assets are used, **THEN** specific activities can be utilized to advance the project. Thus, activities that support and utilize the resources are listed within the plan. The determination of activities is not the "to-do" list, but should be the processes, strategies, methods, and/or action steps. The "to-do" list is provided within an action plan tool.

In relation to the activities, the statement is depicted: **IF** the activities are successful, **THEN** certain outputs such as products or services will be completed. These outputs should be measurable, perceptible, and ensuing from the activities. The outputs reflect the deliverables, units of services, or products resulting from the project. Usually within the outputs, quantity is addressed but quality is not.

Once the outputs are determined, the outcome declaration demonstrates: **IF** the deliverables are obtained, **THEN** the participants will be rewarded with certain benefits. The outcomes are the results, impacts and/or objectives for the project. Outcomes should be measurable and reflect the change that occurs from the project process. Outcomes can reflect who or what will undergo the expected change. The focus can embrace the individual (client-focused), family/community, systemic, or organizational. Olney and Barnes (2006) include within the individual level a focus toward cognitive, affective, skills, and quality-of-care outcomes. At the community level of the outcomes, environmental and social aspects need to be carefully considered and included as appropriate (Olney & Barnes, 2006).

The final aspect within the model is the impact. The statement that depicts the process is: **IF** the benefits are achieved, **THEN** the resulting change to the organization, community, or system can be expected. The output, outcome, and impact aspects manifest the intended results of the project. The outcomes and impact fall into three categories. Outcomes can be viewed as short-term (1–3 years) and intermediate (4–6 years) results while the impact (7–10 years) is understood to represent the long-term results. W. K. Kellogg Foundation (2004) utilized the acronyms SMART for the outcomes and impact statements. SMART represents: **S**pecific, **M**easureable, **A**ction-oriented, **R**ealistic, and **T**imed. When short-term outcomes, long-term outcomes, and impact statements are developed, these five aspects should be integrated into the record. Short-term outcomes address the individual while the long-term outcomes and impact statements tackle the idea of the community and/or populations. Both the short-term and long-term outcomes endeavor to change "attitudes, behaviors, knowledge, skills, status, or level of functioning expected to result from program activities" (W. K. Kellogg Foundation, 2004, p. 18). Impacts work to affect organizational, community, or system level modifications.

With some formats of the logic model, assumptions and external factors will be provided. Assumptions consider how and why the change activities will work with the identified community/population. Frequently, the assumptions will be viewed in a box directly below the input and output sections of the model to reflect the link between the sections. External factors are viewed as rationales, existing policy environments, risk factors, successful strategies, and other factors that can affect the outcomes and impacts recognized for the project.

Logic models are becoming an integral part within grants, research, quality improvement, and evidence-based practice projects. Since the models allow for concise and organized planning, implementation, communication, and evaluation, the different aspects provide an effective decision-making path for projects. For each and every project that necessitates multiple applications, the utilization of a logic model framework endeavors to organize and structure the process for success. By using this type of framework on large projects, each component needed within the implementation can be planned and controlled. One example of using this type of framework on a large project would be when an acute care setting is planning a move into a new construction area. The many different aspects that must be planned and organized to allow for a successful, smooth transition can be laid out within a logic model framework. This model provides a framework on which to clearly and distinctly address the different components required for effective and efficient planning, implementation, and evaluation. With all of the elements in one tool, the entire process moves with one voice toward success. Each member of the team can easily and productively identify the components needed within each phase of a project. Evaluation becomes increasingly operational, since the objectives and activities are organized within the framework. Strategic planning for the next steps can be openly developed on the foundation provided within the logic model management.

? **Think Outside the Box**

www,

Consider the idea that a new catheter kit is being introduced within the acute care setting, try to complete an action plan for this change from one type of catheter kit to the new one.

Action Plans

Once the logic model is carefully constructed, it can be used to formulate the action plan, for the day-to-day management of the project. The action plan (**Figure 14-3**) takes the objectives/outcomes, specifying the means to obtain concrete measurements of them. The action plan takes the form of the "to-do" list for the logic model. At this level of development, the clearly worded objectives are supported by measurable indicators, target levels, and timeframes. Also within the process, the key individuals who are responsible for each level are denoted. By thoroughly and painstakingly completing this level of clarity, the progression toward the goal is visibly noted. According to Community Toolbox (n.d.), an effective action plan should be complete, clear, and current. Pulling the activities from the logic model will help to determine the step-by-step process needed to advance the project. Taking the time and energy to effectively plan in an organized manner allows for successful management of the project. Carefully and thoroughly considering the different aspects of program and putting the results into an action plan allows:

- The development of credibility for the organization, group, or project.
- The group to be sure that all aspects are addressed.
- Improved understanding of the magnitude of the organization's potential.
- For efficiency related to time, energy, and resources.
- Accountability for the project being considered and implemented.

The action plan should be viewed as a working document. Leedy and Ormrod (2013) suggest that breaking full projects down into manageable pieces allows for several beneficial outcomes. By dissecting the

Figure 14-3

Action plan worksheet.

Target Completion Date	Action Step	Accountable Person(s)	Assigned Person(s)	Actual Completion Date

project into small activities, the ordering of the activities can be determined. For projects of small to moderate size, the use of an action plan provides the structure needed to move the project forward. As nurses at the bedside look to institute a quality improvement plan, the use of a planning tool to ensure that each of the different steps are in place to as all aspects are carefully and thoroughly considered. One medical–surgical unit elected to use the action plan format when the decision was made to convert from routine checking to hourly rounding on patients. For each of the different aspects used in the conversion to hourly rounding, specific target completion time periods, action steps, the accountable individual and assigned personnel were laid out on an action plan worksheet. By having this plan established, the process over the following months was organized and calculated. When the manager for the unit changed during the implementation of the quality improvement project, the plan provided structure and organization for the new manager to use. In addition, small successes as each activity is completed can be acknowledged. The division of the project into a series of actions provides the opportunity to establish multiple target dates to strive toward instead just one huge hurdle to confront. Self-confidence can be developed as the project is viewed by the group as moving forward. The communication of the completion of the smaller tasks toward the large project reflects the evolution toward the goal. While attempting to be as clear and complete as possible with the initial design, changes and situations may develop requiring a change within the action plan. The columns used within an action plan (Figure 14-3) need to address the key areas identified by the unique project. Since it provides the structure for the advancement of the project, each element within the plan should support and enhance the group's mission and goal. Another use for the action plan is the ability to present opportunities for communication across the group. Communication of the successes and challenges is paramount for the progression of the project. A final benefit from the use of an action plan relates to its ability to keep the project on track. Since columns are provided for timeline and accountability, the supervision of the project becomes apparent and to the point.

? Think Outside the Box

`www`

What type of projects are occurring within the facility you are connected with that could benefit from completing an action plan?

Conclusion

Evidence-based practice, research, and quality improvement must be organized and directed in an appropriate manner to facilitate the success of the process. Care must be given to tools and processes that can be used to advance the achievements of the selected challenges. Translational research, with two components of basic and applied research process, is established to move knowledge from the laboratory to the bedside. By moving the results of the different projects to actual implementation for the patients, quality and best practice become standards in the practice arena. Tools such as logic modeling and action plans are crucial and strategic instruments to advance the science of nursing and health care. These tools can be used to support and coordinate the different venues within the decision-making process. By using each and every tool and resource available, the evidence will become nature in the practice sites.

Summary Points

1. Evidence-based practice, research, and quality improvement are all aspects that play a part in the development of critical decision making and the validation of successful and competent healthcare practices.
2. The inclusion of strategic individuals to respond to the questions and challenges identified requires the different people to appreciate the multifaceted nature of systematic decision making.

3. Translational research has two areas of focus. The initial area relates to basic research. The second focus strives to move the outcomes determined through basic research to actual adoption at the bedside as examples of best practices for the community.

4. Within the process of translational research, basic research, population-based research, and patient-oriented research each play a part toward the goal of moving research outcomes to bedside implementation for the advancement of disease prevention and management.

5. Each aspect with a logic model template builds upon the previous components to provide a template for planning, implementation, and evaluation.

6. Three different categories of logic modeling are available for agencies to use—theory approach model, outcome approach model, and activities approach model.

7. The outputs reflect the deliverables, units of services, or products resulting from the project. Usually within the outputs, quantity is addressed but quality is not.

8. The outcomes are the results, impacts and/or objectives for the project. Outcomes should be measurable and reflect the change that occurs from the project process.

9. Logic models are becoming an integral part as a means for grants, research, quality improvement, and evidence-based practice projects.

10. Once the logic model is carefully constructed, it can be used to formulate the action plan for the day-to-day management of the project. The action plan takes the objectives/outcomes, and specifies the means to obtain concrete measurements of them.

RED FLAGS

- Each aspect within a logic model should build upon the prior pieces. No part stands alone.
- Within any decision-making process, attention to the entire process should be evident within the materials provided.

Multiple Choice Questions

1. Translational research strives to use a decision-making process to

   A. Move the results from the bench to the bedside.
   B. Identify selected topics for research.
   C. Restrict who can complete research to individuals understanding the entire process.
   D. Focus only on the use of basic research.

2. The focus of attention for the implementation of translational research is

   A. Patients only.
   B. Populations only.
   C. Patients and populations.
   D. Patients, animals, and populations.

3. The type of research conducted in a laboratory setting to advance the understanding of knowledge is

   A. Translational research.
   B. Patient-oriented research.
   C. Population-based research.
   D. Basic research.

4. Translational research has two areas of focus, which are

   A. Basic research and moving the outcomes to the best practices.
   B. Basic and patient-oriented research.
   C. Cost-effectiveness and communication.
   D. Understanding prevention and treatment options.

5. Terms used for logic modeling are

   A. Basic research, patient-oriented research, or program theory.
   B. Program theory, logical framework, or action plan.
   C. Logical framework, theory of change, or program matrix.
   D. Theory of change, action plan, or program matrix.

6. The logic modeling approach, which underscores the use of change theory to transform the design and plan for a program, reflects which approach?

   A. Theory approach
   B. Outcome approach
   C. Activities approach
   D. Action plan approach

7. The logic modeling approach, which concentrates on the implementation strategies to transform the program, reflects which approach?

   A. Theory approach
   B. Outcome approach
   C. Activities approach
   D. Action plan approach

8. The preliminary action taken for a logic model development is

   A. Determining the challenge/problem.
   B. Setting up the resources and activities to be done.
   C. Clarifying the impact of the process.
   D. Developing the action plan.

9. The outputs as used within a logic model depict the

   A. Action plan.
   B. Translational research.
   C. Deliverables and/or units of services.
   D. Activities.

10. The impact statements within a logic model tend to address

    A. Individuals.
    B. Clients.
    C. Action plans statements.
    D. Communities.

Discussion Questions www,

1. A medical–surgical unit at your hospital wants to change from using a team nursing model to a primary care nursing model. The unit director asks the group to develop a logic model tool to show the problem, goal, resources, activities, and short-term goals involved in making this type of change. You are one of the staff members charged with preparing these aspects for the logic model. Discuss the details of the logic model you prepared.

   Items to consider when completing this request:

   The initial step in this process of establishing a logic model is the analysis of the challenge identified or the problem. Once the problem is determined clearly, a goal for the project can be worded. The problem statements can also be classified as issue statements or situations. Usually the problem statement addresses the ideas of: *who, what, why, where, when,* and *how.* The problem statement and goal should be narrow in focus, while objectives used within the process can reflect the scope of the project. From the activities, the statement is depicted: **IF** the activities are successful, **THEN** certain outputs such as products or services will be completed. These outputs should be measurable, perceptible, and ensuing from the activities. Once the outputs are determined, the outcome declaration demonstrates: **IF** the deliverables are obtained, **THEN** the participants will be rewarded with certain benefits. The outcomes are the results, impacts and/or objectives for the project. Outcomes should be measurable and reflect the change that occurs from the project process. Outcomes can be viewed as short-term (1–3 years).

2. Using the SMART acronym, change the outcome and impact statements to include the needed information.

   Outcome statement: Registered nurses will enjoy 12-hour shifts.

   Impact statement: Having 12-hour shifts will improve the retention rate of registered nurses.

   Items to consider when completing this request:

   W. K. Kellogg Foundation (2004) utilized the acronym SMART for the outcomes and impact statements. SMART represents: **S**pecific, **M**easureable, **A**ction-oriented, **R**ealistic, and **T**imed.

Suggested Readings

Dillon, K. A., Barga, K. N., & Goodin, H. J. (2012). Use of the logic model framework to develop and implement a preceptor recognition program. *Journal for Nurses in Staff Development, 28*(1), 36–40.

Olney, C. A., & Barnes, S. (2006). *Collecting and analyzing evaluation data.* Seattle, WA: National Network of Libraries of Medicine Outreach Evaluation Resource Center.

Olney, C. A., & Barnes, S. (2006). *Getting started with community-based outreach.* Seattle, WA: National Network of Libraries of Medicine Outreach Evaluation Resource Center.

University of Wisconsin-Extension. (2003). *Enhancing program performance with logic models.* Retrieved from http://www.uwex.edu/ces/lmcourse

W. K. Kellogg Foundation. (2004). *Logic model development guide.* Battle Creek, MI: W. K. Kellogg Foundation. Retrieved from http://www.wkkf.org/knowledge-center/resources/2006/02/WK-Kellogg-Foundation-Logic-Model-Development-Guide.aspx

References

California Living 2.0. (2009). *Logic modeling & frequently asked questions.* Building Healthy Communities: The California Endowment. Retrieved from http://www.calendow.org/healthycommunities/pdfs/EvaluationLogicModeling_FAQs_9_11_09.pdf

Community Toolbox. (n.d.). *Developing an action plan.* Retrieved from http://ctb.ku.edu/en/tablecontents/sub_section_main_1089.aspx

Innovation Network, Inc. (n.d.). *Logic model workbook.* Washington, DC: Author. Retrieved from http://www.innonet.org/client_docs/File/logic_model_workbook.pdf

Leedy, P. D., & Ormrod, J. E. (2013). *Practical research: Planning and design* (10th ed.). Boston, MA: Pearson.

O'Brien, R. (1998). *An overview of the methodological approach of action research.* Retrieved from http://www.web.ca/robrien/papers/arfinal.html

Olney, C. A., & Barnes, S. (2006). *Including evaluation in outreach project planning.* Seattle, WA: National Network of Libraries of Medicine Outreach Evaluation Resource Center.

Rubio, D. M., Schoenbaum, E. E., Lee, L. S., Schteingart, D. E., Marantz, P. R., Anderson, K.E., . . . Esposito, K. (2010). Defining translational research: Implications for training. *Academic Medicine, 85*(3), 470–475.

University of Wisconsin-Extension. (2003). *Enhancing program performance with logic models.* Retrieved from http://www.uwex.edu/ces/lmcourse

W. K. Kellogg Foundation, (2004). *Logic model development guide.* Battle Creek, MI: W.K. Kellogg Foundation. Retrieved from http://www.wkkf.org/knowledge-center/resources/2006/02/WK-Kellogg-Foundation-Logic-Model-Development-Guide.aspx

Woolf, S. H. (2008). Commentary: The meaning of translational research and why it matters. *JAMA, 299*(2), 211–213.

Chapter **15**

Application of Evidence-Based Nursing Practice with Research

Sharon Cannon and Carol Boswell

Chapter Objectives

At the conclusion of this chapter, the learner will be able to

1. Synthesize key components from evidence-based nursing practice and research utilization to drive the provision of quality nursing care
2. Demonstrate proficiency in one component of evidence-based practice using the principles of the research process and evidence-based appraisal

Key Terms

➤ Evidence-based practice (EBP)

➤ Integrative reviews

➤ Meta-analysis

➤ Research utilization

➤ Systematic reviews

Introduction

Evidence-based practice (EBP) is defined as a process of utilizing confirmed evidence (research and quality improvement), decision making, and nursing expertise to guide the delivery of holistic patient care. The recent need for and acceptance of EBP is apparent in the literature. In a 2006 survey conducted by Sigma Theta Tau International (STTI, 2006), results suggested that a majority of the nurses needed evidence on a weekly basis to guide practice. Approximately 90% of the participants indicated a moderate to high level of confidence in EBP. The results of this survey again support the premise that EBP is a driving force for the use of scientific data in the decision-making process in the provision of nursing care. In addition, Finkelman and Kenner (2009) recommend nurses be actively engaged with patient safety issues and concerned about quality research, and that nurses must participate in the evaluation of nursing care as it is connected to safety and quality. Their pronouncement is a direct result of the Institute of Medicine's imperative to ensure patient safety. Nurses' involvement in gathering evidence to support safe, quality nursing care is essential for the future growth of the profession and, most importantly, to the patients receiving the care they deserve.

As the country moves forward with the implementation of the recommendations from the Institute of Medicine (*To Err Is Human: Building a Safer Health System* and *The Future of Nursing*) and the requirements included in the Patient Protection and Affordable Care Act (PPACA), attention to how best to address these recommendations and requirements is vital. Evidence-based practice is a problem-solving process that mandates the use of current evidence to ensure safe and appropriate health care for patients. Melnyk (2012) states that the "ultimate purpose of EBP is to improve healthcare quality and patient outcomes and reduce hospital costs" (p. 130). Combining the ideas of research and quality improvement to address areas of concern within healthcare delivery allows for optimal use of the information currently available. Care must be given to the incorporation of scientific inquiry concepts as a mainstay for nurses. Nurses should and must be willing to challenge the status quo as health care moves forward to address the problems and opportunities facing us. Nurses are the underpinning for addressing clinically relevant questions and solving the problems that are identified in a systematic and efficient manner.

Understanding the research process is the first step in using evidence in everyday nursing practice. Following the initial historical background provided about research in nursing in Chapter 1, the chapters of this book have focused on the research process. According to Gawlinski and Miller (2011), "research is one of the most powerful tools for advancing the science of nursing and improving the quality of patient care and outcomes" (p. 190). Examples of evidence-based practice have been given elsewhere to demonstrate how EBP is applied in specific components of the research process.

Difficulty in analyzing the evidence has been identified as a major obstacle to **research utilization**. The preceding chapters of this book have provided information that is intended to assist the modern-day nurse in the analysis of research findings, with their subsequent application to nursing care. This text is designed to "pull the pieces together" by suggesting a practical approach for research utilization in evidence-based nursing practice. Evidence-based practice and research utilization must become common place for the staff nurse at the bedside. Only when it develops into a practical and everyday part of health care will evidence truly become a mainstay of healthcare practice.

To get a clear understanding of the interconnectedness of EBP and research, a flowchart is provided in Chapter 2 to conceptualize the relationship (Figure 2-1). As a dilemma is acknowledged, a PICOT statement should be created. This PICOT statement propels the literature review. Each element in the PICOT statement provides strategic words to limit the search for applicable articles. Gaps and consistencies within the literature need to be determined to provide the pathway to the next phase of the process. These gaps and consistencies direct the process toward either a research study or a quality improvement project. If the evidence reveals that a policy, procedure, or protocol needs to be scrutinized, a quality improvement process would be commenced for that intent. If the gaps and consistencies indicate that supplementary research should be needed to achieve an answer for the recognized problem, a full research project would need to be designed and executed.

If a research project is the trajectory, the principal process for conducting a thorough project would need to be ascertained (Figure 2-2). As a research venture is considered, the methodology for best addressing the challenge would need to be selected. The flowchart in Figure 2-2 differentiates the steps generally followed when performing quantitative or qualitative research.

Process for Evidence-Based Practice

According to Myers and Meccariello (2006), "Outdated practices are barriers to decreased length of stay, favorable patient outcomes, and lowered costs" (p. 24). To move evidence-based nursing practice forward, a realistic approach for allowing bedside nurses to actively engage in the process must be determined and used. At each stage of providing holistic care, nurses have to be confident in asking the questions and seeking the best practices to advance the provision of

? **Think Outside the Box**   www.

Prior to a surgical procedure, patients are instructed to not take anything by mouth after midnight on the preceding day. Due to surgical schedules, some patients can go as long as 10–12 hours without any liquids.
- Based on the evidence, what time limit is the best choice to manage this health challenge for the patient scheduled to have a surgical procedure?
- List PICOT questions that could be generated from this scenario.
- Which ethical considerations would need to be addressed prior to conducting a research study on this topic?
- How would you incorporate patient preferences into the evidence-based practice?

effective nursing care. Nurses must seek the best evidence to make sure that the care provided represents the optimal health care available for the specified treatment plan. By determining a functional method for documenting an EBP search, nurses can then gain confidence in the overall process of conducting and implementing EBP.

The process for EBP determination is different from the process for research utilization. Research utilization is covered in Chapter 13, which describes how to complete an assessment of a single research report (i.e., a research critique). The research utilization process carefully examines a distinct study to determine the strengths and limitations assumed within that one study and decide whether to apply its findings to nursing practice. Research utilization becomes a key aspect within the overall process of EBP, but it is only one piece of the EBP puzzle. For a nurse to be able to effectively utilize EBP, it is clear that he or she must be able to perform research critiques. The idea that nurses need to be able to *use* research, while acknowledging that not everyone has to be able to *conduct* research, is imperative. To facilitate implementation of EBP, bedside nurses need to understand how to recognize those elements of a particular research process that either strengthen or limit the use of its results.

Armed with this understanding of the applicability of the research results to practice, a nurse can then determine which study results might be used to sustain best practices in EBP. Clearly, to make this determination, nurses do need to appreciate the intricacies of the research process. Bedside nurses should be able to identify the justifications that a researcher provides for selecting a specific method of sampling, data collection, research design, and data analysis. If a researcher has a valid explanation for the choices employed within a study, the results can be assigned a higher value and incorporated into practice. Having begun the work with research critiques discussed in Chapter 13, the nurse can then move to the next step of development to use those skills within the EBP process.

Melnyk and Fineout-Overholt (2011) suggest that the process of EBP involves five critical steps:

1. Raise the urgent clinical question using a format that includes the key aspects of the issue.
2. Assemble the most appropriate evidence that addresses the issue identified.
3. Evaluate the evidence critically to determine its validity, relevance, and applicability.
4. Assimilate the evidence into clinical practice.
5. Assess the changes resulting from the use of the best evidence.

Each of these steps must be conscientiously finished to come to a conclusion about the best practices for a nursing setting. If an EBP process does not include all of the five steps, the result does not take into consideration all of the available evidence related to the clinical question.

? Think Outside the Box

In recent years, more parents have begun seeking alternative birthing options. Some individuals elect to deliver at home due to the burden placed on them by rising healthcare costs. Others make this decision based on a desire to have a more natural birthing process. When complications occur during the birthing process, however, the baby may have to be admitted to an acute care setting. For newborn infants, the standard initial treatment process includes erythromycin eye ointment, injection of triple dye onto the umbilical cord, and a vitamin K injection. If the parents voice concerns about these procedures, which steps would a nurse need to take to provide evidence-based information to alleviate their fears?

- List PICOT questions that could be generated from this scenario.
- Which ethical considerations would need to be addressed prior to conducting a research study on this topic?
- Which key words would be used in a literature search to locate evidence related to this EBP question?
- Which type of research project could be developed to further study this concern?
- How would you incorporate patient preferences into the evidence-based practice?

Although many models for EBP are currently being evaluated and modified, **Table 15-1** summarizes the key points in a quick and easy organizational design for evidence consideration. This format allows the individual to pull the needed aspects from any group of articles to reflect the current knowledge available regarding the topic under consideration. Within this format, the initial step is to refine the question confronting the nurse. Careful time and attention should be given to clarifying the five aspects driving the EBP question. As discussed previously, the question should consider the following aspects of the research issue (PICOT):

P: Population of interest (required aspect)
I: Intervention of interest (required aspect)
C: Comparison of interest (recommended aspect)
O: Outcome of interest (required aspect)
T: Time (recommended aspect)

Each of these characteristics for the clinical question was discussed in earlier chapters. The development of a clear and concise clinical question is of vital significance since the question guides the comprehensive EBP and/or research process. Once the question is clarified, the nurse needs to work with the librarian to establish strategic words and terms to employ in accomplishing the literature review. Using appropriate terms for the diverse search engines facilitates the search results to ensure the appropriate materials are located for the subsequent analysis of the best practices. As Melnyk (2003) has stated, "Evidence-based practice is a problem-solving approach to clinical decision making that incorporates a search for the best and latest evidence, clinical expertise, and assessment, and patient preference and values within a context of caring" (p. 149). Concerns are being raised at this time as to what are "best practices." Proehl and Hoyt (2012) contend that the term "best practices" is an indistinct phrase that indicates that the practice is founded on data but not necessarily research. The data on which best practices is constructed tends to be based on data utilized by respected and highly valued organizations and/or practitioners.

Malloch and Porter-O'Grady (2010) have classified investigations of practices as **meta-analyses**, **systematic reviews**, or **integrative reviews**. The combining of these different study types identified through the literature review and search engine inquiry process provides the foundation for determining whether there is a need to change practice patterns. Meta-analysis incorporates a statistical technique to determine the rigorousness of the findings from multiple studies dealing with a focused question. A systematic review summarizes all quantitative evidence found through the literature search that is correlated to an identifiable research or clinical issue, employing a rigorous format to ensure completeness of the assessment. An integrative review also summarizes

Table 15-1

Format for Documenting Aspects of Evidence-Based Practice

Questions to Consider Within the Evidence-Based Practice Process

P (population of interest): _____

I (intervention of interest): _____

C (comparison of interest): _____

O (outcome of interest): _____

T (time): _____

Articles (Level of Evidence/ Evaluation of Strength of the Evidence)	Who Is Involved (Sample Size, Sampling Method, Population)	What Occurred (Qualitative, Quantitative)	Where Completed (Type of Agency, State, Country)	When (Year Research Done)	Why (Research Question)	How (Data Collection, Tool Used with Validity and Reliability, Statistical Tests, Qualitative Control)	Consistencies (How It Addresses the PICOT Question, How Alike with Other Studies Reviewed)	Gaps (How It Does Not Address the PICOT Question, What Did the Researchers State Still Needed to Be Studied)

Summary of Findings

Application of Findings to Evidence-Based Practice That Validates or Changes Policies and Procedures

prior research studies on a selected topic but, in addition, draws conclusions from the summary concerning the studies examined.

Evidence can be evaluated using two different formats. One method is the levels of evidence discussed in Chapter 2. The levels of evidence are based upon the research method design. If an article or information is not research, the classification of that data into the levels of evidence becomes complex. To determine the level of evidence, the available literature is ranked (Figure 2-4). For example, Level 1 evidence (meta-analysis) is considered to be the highest-level, most important evidence that can be gathered. While Level 1 evidence is the most desirable, the researcher should not toss out evidence classified as being at the other levels. Sometimes the only evidence that is available is a case study (Level 5). A case study can still provide evidence for clinical decision-making purposes, though it is not the strongest form of support. The depth of the justification for using this level of evidence provided by the researcher aids in the determination of the value of the results documented.

? Think Outside the Box

Evidence-based practice should cause members of the nursing profession to query their normal activities. A simple skill such as catheterizing an individual can result in an EBP question such as "How much urine should a nurse drain off the bladder at one time following a catheterization of a client?"

- List PICOT questions that could be generated from this scenario.
- Which ethical considerations would need to be addressed prior to conducting a research study on this topic?
- Which key words would be used in a literature search to locate evidence related to this EBP question?
- Which type of research project could be developed to further study this concern?
- How would you incorporate patient preferences into the evidence-based practice?

The second method for classifying evidence is based upon the perceived strength of the evidence. The strength of evidence classification looks into the risks and benefits of using the information for the client population. Healthcare agencies tend to focus more on this aspect of a procedure than what type of research design was used. Risks and benefits can allow increased bias to be used in the determination of the level. Once the level of evidence is established, the researcher needs to evaluate the strength of the evidence. A simple rating system for this aspect of evidence can be used (Figure 2-5). Depending on the study, the evidence may be very strong or insufficient. The rating tool provides the researcher with a means for further discriminating which studies have significance for the project being considered.

The form provided in Table 15-1 allows for either a systematic review or an integrative review. Once the PICOT question has been determined and the literature review completed, each of the identified articles/studies is carefully assessed. For each article (citation, level of evidence, and evaluation of strength of the evidence), who is involved (sample size, sampling method, population), what occurred (qualitative, quantitative, level of evidence), where completed (type of agency, state, country), when (year research was done), why (research question), and how (data collection, validity and reliability of any tool used, statistical tests, qualitative control [trustworthiness, confirmability, transferability]) are determined and documented. As these aspects of a research critique are completed on the different studies, consistencies (how the study addresses the PICOT question, how similar it is to other studies reviewed) and gaps (how the study does not address the PICOT question, what the researchers stated still needs to be studied) within the different studies begin to surface. The identification of consistencies within the various studies may either support the proposed changes in practice or confirm that best practices are currently being used. The detection of gaps within the studies suggests the need for further or more in-depth research into the topic under consideration. The idea of identifying consistencies and gaps within the different articles and research reports also incorporates the concept of similarities and omissions that may be present.

Figure 2-1 provides a schema for understanding the process underlying EBP. As a clinical problem is identified, individuals are directed to develop that problem concern into a PICOT format. The PICOT drives the evidence-based practice literature search and the subsequent review of the literature discovered. Following the completion of the literature review, the PICOT question can evolve into a research question/hypothesis or a quality improvement focus. The gaps and consistencies found within the review process help to clarify the question to be used for the research or quality improvement process. From the literature review, the focus for the management of the problem is confirmed. When consistencies are identified in the literature, the nurse can elect to repeat the research concentration to strengthen the evidence related to the clinical challenge. Conversely, when gaps in the literature are recognized, additional research projects will be needed to address the gaps found. The third potential outcome is that the literature review might result in either a confirmation or a change in the agency's policies and procedures. In such a case, a quality initiative project may be needed to validate the practices, though further research might not be necessary.

Thus, within an EBP-focused endeavor, the outcomes could be either research projects (to replicate prior work or to address gaps) or quality initiatives (to validate clinical practice). Should the outcome lead to a research study, the research must be conducted in compliance with sound research design. By comparison, for quality initiative projects, any of the many quality initiative models—for example, Six Sigma, plan–do–check–act (PDCA), define–measure–analyze–improve–control (DMAIC), Lean, and root cause analysis—can be utilized. The development of these models has been largely driven by manufacturing businesses, with the models subsequently being adapted to many quality improvement efforts and used in the healthcare arena to improve performance. Some methodologies, such as Six Sigma, rely heavily on statistics and research as their underpinnings. The Lean philosophy relies on standardization to improve both the process and the organization from a consumer approach.

Associations established from the results of the various studies need to be collected to add strength to the rationale for making any changes in policies and procedures related to the selected clinical question. If several studies produce equivalent results, then nursing practice should embrace the behavior as supported by evidence. Conversely, if multiple studies reflect a gap in knowledge related to the selected clinical question, then further research should be directed toward the identified segment of nursing practice. According to Pravikoff, Tanner, and Pierce (2005), "The finding that a lack of value for research in practice was the most frequently selected barrier to the use of research in practice is of greatest concern" (p. 48). When practicing nurses cannot or do not use research results to strengthen and sustain holistic nursing practice, the implementation of EBP at the bedside falls short of its potential.

After completing the grid portion of Table 15-1, time must be allocated to summarizing the findings. The nurse should pay careful attention to, and critically consider the meaning ensuing from the consistencies and gaps identified. This painstaking contemplation of the discovered omissions and similarities serves to narrow the focus of the next steps within the process. By taking the time and energy to summarize and synthesize the information collected, the nurse becomes well-versed in the current state of the clinical problem. Obtaining this clearer viewpoint related to the clinical problem allows the nurse to make an informed decision about what is needed next in dealing with this challenge.

The final section of Table 15-1 relates to the application aspect of EBP-related research. After completing each of these prior steps, the nurse has a basis for making recommendations for maintaining or changing a policy or procedure. The time taken to complete this exercise allows for any recommendations to be based on sound, factual data. The suggestions can then be effectively supported by a wealth of tested research endeavors. At this point, the nurse would take this review of the evidence and combine it with the decision-making method employed, personal expertise, and holistic client focus to drive quality, sound nursing care.

? Think Outside the Box

www,

Frequently, an insulin drip protocol will seek to maintain a serum blood sugar level between 70 and 110 mg/dL. At one healthcare agency, a pilot research project revealed that the mean blood sugar for patients dismissed from a cardiac intensive care unit after three months was 148 mg/dL. The nurses questioned the protocol ranges as a result of this pilot study result.

- List PICOT questions that could be generated from this scenario.
- Which ethical considerations would need to be addressed prior to conducting a research study on this topic?
- Which key words would be used in a literature search to locate evidence related to this EBP question?
- Which type of research project could be developed to further study this concern?
- How would you incorporate patient preferences into the evidence-based practice?

Conclusion

According to Yoder (2005), "Both EBP and QI initiatives require ongoing evaluation of the practice environment, the appropriate use of data collection and evaluation, and the dissemination of the information learned through excellent communication process both from the top down and the bottom up" (p. 92). A variety of resources are available to help the nurse in strengthening the healthcare organization's EBP foundations and activities (see this text's Companion Website using the access code found in the front of the book). The current healthcare community requires nurses and other healthcare providers to be diligent in the determination and provision of holistic health care. Whitmer, Auer, Beerman, and Weishaupt (2011) clearly identified that the utilization of a core group of individuals knowledgeable on EBP generates a foundation for the advancement of EBP within an organization. These champions for EBP must be given the time, educational opportunities, and resources to be able to effectively conduct EBP inquiries. The different treatments and plans of care put forth for clients must be based on factual, tested data. Each nurse must take responsibility for ensuring that the care provided is based on firm, accurate research data. These research data are then used to provide individualized health care to clients based on factual data, patient preferences, and nursing expertise.

? **Think Outside the Box**

www

Gather at least three of your peers and form a journal club. Select a topic of your choice and identify a PICOT question. Conduct an integrative review for the selected topic. What conclusions can you draw from the review? How will this new understanding change your practice?

Summary Points

1. Evidence-based practice (EBP) is the process of utilizing confirmed evidence (research and quality improvement), decision making, and nursing expertise to guide the delivery of holistic patient care.
2. Understanding the research process is the first step in using evidence in everyday nursing practice.
3. To move evidence-based nursing practice forward, a realistic approach for allowing bedside nurses to actively engage in the research process must be determined and used.
4. The process for research utilization carefully examines a distinct study to determine the strengths and limitations assumed within that one study.
5. Armed with an understanding of the applicability of the results to practice, a nurse can determine which studies can be used to sustain best practices in EBP.
6. The development of a clear and concise clinical question is of paramount importance, because this question directs the entire research process.
7. Meta-analysis uses a statistical technique to determine the rigorousness of the findings from multiple studies conducted to answer a focused question.

8. A systematic review summarizes all quantitative evidence found in a literature search that is correlated to an identifiable research or clinical issue, employing a rigorous format to ensure completeness of the assessment.

9. An integrative review summarizes prior research studies on a selected topic but, in addition, draws conclusions from the summary concerning the studies examined.

10. For each article (citation, level of evidence and evaluation of strength of the evidence), the who involved (sample size, sampling method, population), what occurred (qualitative, quantitative), where completed (type of agency, state, country), when (year research was done), why (research question), and how (data collection, validity and reliability of tools used, statistical analysis, qualitative control) are determined and documented as part of the evaluation process.

11. The identification of consistencies (how the research addresses the PICOT question; how similar the research is to other studies reviewed) within the various studies evaluated may either support potential changes in practice or confirm that best practices are currently being used.

12. The detection of gaps (how the research does not address the PICOT question; what the researchers stated still needed to be studied) within the studies evaluated suggests the need for further or more in-depth research endeavors on the topic under consideration.

13. Obtaining a clearer viewpoint related to the clinical problem allows the nurse to make an informed decision about what is needed next in this challenge.

14. Quality improvement activities are designed to incorporate research into the healthcare environment from a consumer approach.

RED FLAGS

- Research utilization and evidence-based practice are not the same thing.
- The recommendation for changing nursing practice must be based on sound evidence, not on the results from a single study.

Case Scenario 1

A Hispanic woman presents to the emergency room complaining of epigastric pain in atypical form, nausea, diaphoresis, and neck pain. The initial assessment reveals a 60-year-old, Hispanic female with a history of diabetes and hypertension. The client reports being a smoker with a family history of cardiac problems. She is 5 feet, 3 inches tall and weighs 185 pounds. She is a homemaker with no outside employment. For the most part, she reports a sedentary lifestyle and denies alcohol consumption.

The ER physician orders an EKG and cardiac panel to rule out an acute myocardial infarction. Other tests ordered include a chest X-ray, urinalysis, and standard chemistry (CBC, troponins, creatinine protein). The tests reveal elevated troponin and EKG changes with an elevation in the ST segment. The client is diagnosed with a full-blown myocardial infarction. The ER physician mobilizes the cath lab team and orders a cardiology consultation. The client is transported to the cath lab for an angiogram, which reveals two blocked cardiac vessels.

After a double angioplasty is performed, the client is transferred to the cardiac care unit (CCU). After she arrives in the unit, the nursing staff member assesses the client and determines that the angioplasty versus manual compression was completed with Perclose. The use of this closure for angioplasty has been a topic of debate in the CCU.

As a result of this case and others, the nursing staff elects to engage in an evidence-based practice activity to determine if the policies and procedures currently used on the unit reflect the best practices for this type of client and medical treatment plan. The PICOT question shown in **Table 15-2** was identified, and the EBP process was initiated.

As can be seen from the case study analysis in Table 15-2, there are gaps in the literature—specifically, a lack of actual research projects on the use of Perclose versus manual pressure. All of the literature reviewed consisted of case studies with reference to recommendations from the manufacturer of Perclose. However, the case study illustrates how EBP and research can lead to specific actions to improve nursing care, thereby improving patient outcomes.

Table 15-2

Documenting Aspects of Evidence-Based Practice

Questions to Consider Within the Evidence-Based Practice Process

P (population of interest): Hispanic adult 50 years or older
I (intervention of interest): Perclose usage for percutaneous arterial closure
C (comparison of interest): Manual pressure
O (outcome of interest): Decrease length of stay, decreased hematoma, decreased discomfort, decreased infection rate
T (time): Within 2 weeks from discharge from hospital

Articles (Level of Evidence/Evaluation of Strength of the Evidence)	Who Is Involved (Sample Size, Sampling Method, Population)	What Occurred (Qualitative, Quantitative)	Where Completed (Type of Agency, State, Country)	When (Year Research Done)	Why (Research Question)	How (Data Collection, Tool Used with Validity and Reliability, Statistical Tests, Qualitative Control)	Consistencies (How It Addresses the PICOT Question, How Alike with Other Studies Reviewed)	Gaps (How It Does Not Address the PICOT Question, What Did the Researchers State Still Needed to Be Studied)
Geary, Landers, Fiore, & Riggs. (2002). Management of infected femoral closure devices. *Cardiovascular Surgery*, 10(2), 161–163. Level of evidence: 5. Strength of evidence: B.	4 males, 1 female, age range 63–73, purposive sampling	Qualitative, case study	New York, acute care unit, outpatient general hospital	2002	Examined Perclose	Case study; no indication of prophylactic antibiotic use, *Staphylococcus* infection	Population correct for age; all had infections, suture placement, antibiotics	Little research; recommendations came from manufacturer; no indication of ethnicity or manual pressure
Heck, Muldowney, & McPherson. (2002). Infectious complications of Perclose for closure of femoral artery puncture. *Journal of Vascular and Interventional Radiology*, 13(4), 427–431. Level of evidence: 5. Strength of evidence: B.	2 females, 1 male, age range 40–76, purposive sampling	Qualitative, case study	Three different institutions	2002	No specific question documented; report of cases, 3 days post-op	Case studies	Age range exceeds PICOT range; 2 cases had staphylococcal infection, one from bacterial source; concerns about suture placement	Neither manual pressure nor ethnicity noted in this study; refers to published trials

Citation	Sample	Design	Setting	Year	Question	Findings	Relevance to PICOT	Comments
Tiesenhausen, Tomka, Allmayer, Baumann, Hessinger, Portugaller, & Mahler. (2004). Femoral artery infection associated with a percutaneous arterial suture device. *VASA: European Journal for Vascular Medicine, 33*(2), 83–85. Level of evidence: 5. Strength of evidence: B.	77-year-old male, purposive sampling	Qualitative, case study	Austria	2004	No specific question documented; single case	Add to data; infection identified 4 weeks post hospitalization; seen in ER prior to final admission to hospital with sepsis; Perclose carries risk of femoral artery infections	Age complies with PICOT; sterile field must be maintained	Neither manual pressure nor ethnicity noted in this study; refers to research
Dumont. (2007). Blood pressure and risks of vascular complications after percutaneous coronary intervention. *Dimensions of Critical Care Nursing, 26*(3), 121–127. Level of evidence: 4. Strength of evidence: B.	Convenience sampling, 150 subjects, mean age 62.4, 45% women, 92% white	Case-matched control design	South Atlantic state, tertiary care teaching facility	2006	Determine which variables are significant individual predictors of vascular complications post-PCI—1), comorbidities: 2), physician-sensitive procedural factors (hemostasis method [Perclose compared with manual compression for hemostasis]), and 3), nurse-sensitive procedural factors	Specific details not provided; data collected—body mass index, comorbidity, physician-sensitive procedurals, and nurse-sensitive procedural factors	Mean age within PICOT level; use of Perclose compared to manual pressure included; outcomes of interest addressed	Ethnicity not addressed
Lasic, Nikolsky, Kesanakurthy, & Dangas. (2005). Vascular closure devices: A review of their use after invasive procedures. *American Journal of Cardiovascular Drugs, 5*(3), 185–200. Level of evidence: 5. Strength of evidence: B.	Not a research article, so no sampling done	In-depth review of vascular closure devices	Not a research article	2005	Meta-analysis data related to complications and success rates; research reports discussed within the summary of the different closure devices	Not a research article	Outcomes related to Perclose usage provided	Not a research article, so no sampling done

(continues)

Table 15-2

Documenting Aspects of Evidence-Based Practice (continued)

Summary of Findings (Consistencies and Gaps from All Articles)

Perclose can reduce length of stay and improve outcomes. Proper use of Perclose and consideration of prophylactic antibiotic therapy should be implemented. All of the reviewed articles were case studies; no quantitative research was found, and no nurse-directed research was located. The length of time before infections were identified ranged from 3 days to 4 weeks. Use of sterile technique during the procedure is paramount.

Application of Findings to Evidence-Based Practice That Validates or Changes Policies and Procedures (Which policies and procedures does this information directly address and why?)

• All articles suggest prophylactic antibiotic use and strict adherence to the manufacturer's recommendations for ensuring a sterile surgical site.

• ER departments should review their policies concerning the assessment of post-angioplasty clients who present with vague symptoms, because the infection may be masked until it develops into a sepsis-type infection even as late as 4 weeks post procedure.

• Patient education should be addressed within policies to ensure that clients are taught to maintain a clean site at the incision area, to complete all antibiotic treatment ordered, and to report vague symptoms reflective of infections even up to 4 weeks post procedure.

Case Scenario 2

A school nurse wanted to determine if the placement of alcohol hand sanitizers within the elementary school buildings would decrease the incidences of illnesses. Illnesses for this project were based upon children's absentee patterns. The school nurse has to carefully consider the cost and instructional process that would be required as a result of the placement of these hand sanitizer units.

The case study analysis for **Table 15-3** reflects research has not been adequately carried out within the elementary school population. Research is available for acute care settings and other healthcare settings but not successfully within this setting. A foundation is established that the use of hand sanitizers are effective for the management of illnesses. Gaps are evident within this case study. A foundation for the use of hand sanitizers can be established with the understanding that application to this setting would need to be verified.

Table 15-3

Documenting Aspects of Evidence-Based Practice

Questions to Consider Within the Evidence-Based Practice Process

P (population of interest): Elementary school age children
I (intervention of interest): Use of hand sanitizer
C (comparison of interest): Requirement to wash hands
O (outcome of interest): Decreased incidence of illnesses
T (time): Not applicable

Articles (Level of Evidence/ Evaluation of Strength of the Evidence)	Who Is Involved (Sample Size, Sampling Method, Population)	What Occurred (Qualitative, Quantitative)	Where Completed (Type of Agency, State, Country)	When (Year Research Done)	Why (Research Question)	How (Data Collection, Tool Used with Validity and Reliability, Statistical Tests, Qualitative Control)	Consistencies (How It Addresses the PICOT Question, How Alike with Other Studies Reviewed)	Gaps (How It Does Not Address the PICOT Question, What Did the Researchers State Still Needed to Be Studied)
Vessey, J. A., Sherwood, J. J., Warner, D., & Clark, D. (2007). Comparing hand washing to hand sanitizers in reducing elementary school students' absenteeism. *Pediatric Nursing, 33*(4), 368–372. Level of evidence: 3. Strength of evidence: B.	Sample size—Part I = 383, Part II = 13; Sampling method—Part I: randomized cross over, Part II: convenient; Population—Part I: 2nd and 3rd graders, Part II: teachers, school nurses, and office personnel	Randomized cross-over design; mixed method	Elementary schools in Butte, Montana	Not stated; published in 2007	Compare the efficacy of a hand sanitizer to standard hand washing in reducing illness and subsequent absenteeism in school age children	Part 1: Data collected—absentee rates, two groups: cohort 1/phase 2—hand washing, cohort 2/ phase 1—hand sanitizer; cohort switched in second phase; Part 2: focus group	Population correct for age; intervention and comparison included in this article	The outcome was not directly associated with this one; article looked at absenteeism

Citation	Sample	Design	Setting	Date	Purpose	Tools/Statistical test	Intervention/Comparison	Population/Outcome
Foster, K. M., & Clark, A. P. (2008), Increasing hand hygiene compliance: A mystery? *Clinical Nurse Specialist, 22*(6), 263–267. Level of evidence: 1. Strength of evidence: B.	6 articles Topic—hand hygiene compliance strategies	Meta-analysis	Literature review	Published 2008	The purpose of this article is to investigate some of the evidence-based strategies for increasing hand hygiene compliance, focusing on system wide solutions to see if they might offer insight to the CNS and other organizational leaders	No tools were used, so no validity and reliability Statistical test for part 1—*t*-test; Control for part 2—audit trail, audio-taped	Articles were reviewed for study design/ procedures, sample size/ population, findings, and conclusions	Intervention and comparison aspects were present in the articles Population and outcome not addressed.
Fuller, C., Savage, J., Besser, S., Hayward, A., Cookson, B., Cooper, B., & Stone, S. (2011). "The dirty hand in the latex glove": A study of hand hygiene compliance when gloves are worn. *Infection Control and Hospital Epidemiology, 32*(12), 1194–1199. Level of evidence: 5. Strength of evidence: B.	N = 56 Healthcare workers in medical or care of the elderly ward and ICUs	Observational study	15 hospitals across England and Wales	October 2006–November 2009	Carried out a study of glove use and associated hand hygiene behaviors	Observed hand hygiene and glove usage during 249 one-hour sessions Tool—hand hygiene observation tool, rigorously standardized and validated; Statistical test—proportions of moments and adjusted odds ratios used	Intervention, comparison, and outcome aspects addressed	Age group not addressed by this article

(continues)

Table 15-3

Documenting Aspects of Evidence-Based Practice (continued)

Articles (Level of Evidence/ Evaluation of Strength of the Evidence)	Who Is Involved (Sample Size, Sampling Method, Population)	What Occurred (Qualitative, Quantitative)	Where Completed (Type of Agency, State, Country)	When (Year Research Done)	Why (Research Question)	How (Data Collection, Tool Used with Validity and Reliability, Statistical Tests, Qualitative Control)	Consistencies (How It Addresses the PICOT Question, How Alike with Other Studies Reviewed)	Gaps (How It Does Not Address the PICOT Question, What Did the Researchers State Still Needed to Be Studied)
Haessler, S., Connelly, N. R., Kanter, G., Fitzgerald, J., Scales, M. E., Golubchik, A., Albert, M., & Gibson, C. (2010). A surgical site infection cluster: The process and outcome of an investigation—The impact of an alcohol-based surgical antisepsis product and human behavior. *Anesthesia Analgesia, 110*(4), 1044–1048. Level of evidence: 4. Strength of evidence: B.	Sampling—convenience sampling; Sample size—77; Population—patients having a SSI according to National Healthcare Safety Network SSI criteria	Quality improvement methodology	Academic tertiary care medical and level 1 trauma center in New England	2007	The process by which quality improvement methodology was used to investigate and manage the surgical site infection cluster	Specific details not provided; data collected—body mass index, comorbidity, physician-sensitive procedurals, and nurse-sensitive procedural factors	Outcome addressed	Age, intervention and comparison not addressed

Summary of Findings (Consistencies and Gaps from All Articles)
The use of hand sanitizer can affect the number of illnesses reported by individuals. Research reports directed toward the use of these care items within an elementary school age population are not effectively documented at this time.

Application of Findings to Evidence-Based Practice That Validates or Changes Policies and Procedures (Which policies and procedures does this information directly address and why?)
Policies within an elementary school setting that might need to be reviewed include:
- Instructions to provide to children as to the proper way to use hand sanitizer systems
- Infection control measures that can be started
- Effective hand washing procedures

Critical Thinking Exercise

Multiple ideas related to potential clinical questions are provided for your consideration here. Select one of these situations to use in working through the process outlined in Table 15-1. The situations are presented in a brief manner in the following list. Take the chosen idea and develop a PICOT question to best meet the needs at a selected healthcare agency of your choice.

1. One possible clinical question relates to whether a relationship between adequate pain control and length of stay in a community hospital setting could be determined.

2. Another clinical situation for investigation involves the determination of any relationship between glucose control during the operative period and length of stay in an acute care setting.

3. An alternative clinical circumstance relates to the effect of a one-on-one diabetic education course on the patient's HbA_{1C} level.

4. When a medication error occurs, the value of full disclosure to patients and/or family members in building trust and restoring confidence, as opposed to nondisclosure, with a look at the impact on perceived quality of care, could be investigated.

5. An additional idea involves determining whether the length of time and frequency of visits to patients' rooms by nursing staff affect the number of calls and the perception of quality of care by the patient and/or family members.

6. Maternal/child nurses understand that certain treatments (prophylactic eye treatments, vitamin K injections, PKU tests) are provided for all newborn children. What happens to children born outside of an acute care setting (e.g., home births)? What rationales do we have to support these treatments?

7. Childhood immunization is a state-directed process that applies to all school-age children. Certain immunizations (MMR, polio, DPT) are designated at key times prior to and during the school-age years. What is happening with the growing number of home-schooled children? Are they receiving these immunizations? What happens when these children come into acute care settings without having received the expected childhood immunization series?

Suggested Readings

Brody, A. A., Barnes, K., Ruble, C., & Sakowski, J. (2012). Evidence-based practice councils: Potential path to staff nurse empowerment and leadership growth. *Journal of Nursing Administration, 42*(1), 28–33.

Coopey, M., & Clancy, C. M. (2006). Translating research into evidence-based nursing practice and evaluating effectiveness. *Journal of Nursing Care Quality, 21*(3), 195–202.

Marchiondo, K. (2006). Planning and implementing an evidence-based project. *Nurse Educator, 31*(1), 4–6.

Newhouse, R. P. (2006). Examining the support for evidence-based nursing practice. *Journal of Nursing Administration, 36*(7–8), 337–340.

References

Finkelman, A., & Kenner, C. (2009). *Teaching IOM: Implications of the IOM reports for nursing education* (2nd ed.). Silver Spring, MD: American Nurses Association.

Gawlinski, A., & Miller, P. S. (2011). Advancing nursing research through a mentorship program for staff nurses. *AACN Advanced Critical Care, 22*(3), 190–200.

Malloch, K., & Porter-O'Grady, T. (2010). *Introduction to evidence-based practice in nursing and health care* (2nd ed.). Sudbury, MA: Jones and Bartlett.

Melnyk, B. M. (2003). Finding and appraising systematic reviews of clinical interventions: Critical skills for evidence-based practice. *Journal of Pediatric Nursing, 29*(2), 125, 147–149.

Melnyk, B. M. (2012). Achieving a high-reliability organization through implementation of the ARCC model for systemwide sustainability of evidence-based practice. *Nursing Administration Quarterly, 36*(2), 127–135.

Melnyk, B. M., & Fineout-Overholt, E. (2011). *Evidence-based practice in nursing and healthcare: A guide to best practice* (2nd ed.). Philadelphia: Lippincott Williams & Wilkins.

Myers, G., & Meccariello, M. (2006). From pet rock to rock-solid: Implementing unit-based research. *Nursing Management, 37*(1), 24–29.

Pravikoff, D. S., Tanner, A. B., & Pierce, S. T. (2005). Readiness of U.S. nurses for evidence-based practice. *American Journal of Nursing, 105*(9), 40–51.

Proehl, J. A., & Hoyt, K. S. (2012). Evidence versus standard versus best practice: Show me the data! *Advanced Emergency Nursing Journal, 34*(1), 1–2.

Sigma Theta Tau International (STTI). (2006). *Results of EBN survey.* Retrieved from an email dated June 12, 2006, from Sigma Theta Tau International Honor Society of Nursing. NurseAdvance: Knowledge Solutions.

Whitmer, K., Auer, C., Beerman, L., & Weishaupt, L. (2011). Launching evidence-based nursing practice. *Journal for Nurses in Staff Development, 27*(2), E5–E7.

Yoder, L. (2005). Evidence-based practice: The time is now! *Medsurg Nursing, 14*(2), 91–92.

Glossary

Accessible data Data that can be linked into for use within a research study.

Accessible population Individuals and/or groups accessible for a specific participation study; frequently a nonrandom division of the target population.

Accuracy The correctness of the information used within the process.

Action plan A map describing the steps to be taken to accomplish a stated goal or outcome.

Action research Applied research that is attentive to the resolution of nursing personnel's identified challenges.

Analysis A process of organizing and synthesizing data in such a way that research questions can be answered and hypotheses can be tested.

Analysis of variance (ANOVA) Parametric statistical test used to determine the statistical differences between the means among two or more groups; another name for it can be F test; computed as either a one-way or two-way ANOVA.

Annotated bibliography A listing that summarizes the research and published information related to a given topic; presents a concise and succinct synopsis of the knowledge known on a topic.

Anonymity A situation in which the identity and data provided by the research participant are shielded from everyone, including the researcher.

Applied research   Research that concentrates on resolving functional questions to supply reasonably direct solutions.

Associative hypothesis   A hypothesis stated in a way that indicates that the variables exist side by side and that a change in one variable is accomplished by a change in another variable.

Assumption   A fundamental tenet that is recognized as truthful on the foundation of logic or reason but is devoid of evidence or confirmation.

Barrier   An object, goal, or thing that obstructs or inhibits; a maximum value; a cut-off point.

Baseline   The state or conduct of a participant preceding the initiation of a treatment regimen.

Basic research   Research designed to generate elemental knowledge and theoretic agreement about crucial human and foundational innate processes.

Best practice   Those nursing actions that produce the most desirable patient outcomes, as determined through scientific data.

Bias   Any pressure that generates an alteration in the outcomes of an inquiry.

Biased sample   A sample group that is analytically diverse from the target population.

Biophysiological data   Objective data that use a specialized piece of equipment to establish the physical and/or biologic condition of the subjects.

"Blind" review   The appraisal of a document in which the identities of the author and the reviewer are concealed from the other party.

Bracketing   To categorize or classify collectively; to incorporate or eliminate through the use of established specialized limitations.

Bundling   Multiple identified interventions that, taken together, enhance the clinical outcomes.

Case-controlled   Type of project pattern used in epidemiology; a type of observational analysis where two groups with varying outcomes are recognized and contrasted related to differing contributory characteristics.

Case report   The documentation of the aspects identified with a situation such as a case study.

Case series   Incorporates several case studies that have resulted in similar outcomes.

Case study   A qualitative research method that concentrates on supplying a comprehensive description and scrutiny of an identified case situation.

Categorical variable   A variable that diverges in type or kind but that has distinct values instead of values spaced along a continuum.

Causal-comparative research   A type of nonexperimental research design in which the principal independent variable under investigation is a categorical variable.

Causal hypothesis   A hypothesis stated in a way that indicates that one variable causes or brings about a change in another variable or variables.

Central tendency   Statistical qualities associated with quantitative data classified as the mean, median, or mode.

Chi-square test for contingency tables Statistical test employed to establish if an association recognized in a contingency table is statistically significant.

Clinical pathway A document that has been prepared and validated to provide the acceptable management of a disease process; components of the pathway uphold the standards of practice.

Clinical relevance Degree to which a research inquiry addresses a problem of significance to the practice of nursing.

Clinical research Research calculated to produce knowledge to direct nursing practice.

Clinical trial A research process that assesses the efficacy of an aspect of clinical management, usually in a large and heterogeneous sample of participants.

Closed-ended question A question that is set up to force specific responses through the options provided within the question.

Cluster sampling A method of sampling in which a sizeable group is divided into consecutive subsampling of smaller units; a style of sampling in which groups are randomly selected.

Code of ethics Underlying ethical assumptions that are recognized by a discipline or organization to direct researchers; management of the research related to the safe handling of human subjects.

Coding Classifying portions of qualitative data with either symbols, explanatory words, or categorical narrative designations.

Coercion Related to research endeavors, the specific and/or embedded use of threats and/or disproportionate rewards to get individuals to consent to take part in a proposed study.

Cohort Several individuals presenting with a recognizable categorization or common attribute.

Community-based participatory research Investigation accomplished through a uniform collaboration connecting conventionally educated researchers and members of a community.

Comparative design A design that does not entail any manipulation or control of the independent variable, such that the dependent variable is the only variable measured in two or more groups.

Comparison group A company of participants whose results related to a dependent variable classification are used as a foundation for appraising the results of the grouping of designated significance; phrase employed in place of "control group" for studies not applying an exact experimental plan.

Complex hypothesis A statement that specifies the relationship between and among more than two variables.

Concept Theoretical foundation for inspection of specific activities or characteristics.

Conceptual definition Characterization of the identified word, variable, or activity from the dictionary-specific explanation of the term.

Conceptual model   Systematic concepts or beliefs that are compiled in a logical representation based on their significance to a familiar premise; a conceptual framework.

Concurrent research   Scientific projects that incorporate both qualitative and quantitative aspects within the project. Both types of inquiry are occurring at the same time.

Concurrent validity   Validity verification that is based on the correlation between the calculated scores and criterion scores acquired at the same time.

Concurrently   Occurring at the same time (data or processes).

Confidence interval   A range of numbers assessed from the sample that has a specific likelihood or probability of containing the population limitation.

Confidence limits   The final limits of a confidence interval.

Confidentiality   Protection of study participants that results in the individuals' identities not being linked to the information they provided, meaning that the information can be provided only in the aggregate; not revealing the data collected from study participants to any person except the researcher and designated staff.

Confounding variable   A type of extraneous variable that is not controlled for. A confounding variable regularly fluctuates with the independent variable and affects the dependent variable.

Consensus   Individuals involved in a process come to a common understanding about the topic; the majority of individuals reach an agreed upon resolution or understanding.

Consistency   The extent to which the equivalent outcome can be anticipated when measuring a variable more than a single time.

Constant   A single quantity or status of a variable.

Construct validity   The degree to which a higher-order concept is characterized in a specific inquiry.

Consumer   A person who reads, evaluates, and appraises research conclusions while endeavoring to use and employ the results in practice.

Content analysis   The practice of categorizing and combining qualitative results to establish the materializing premises and perceptions.

Content-related validity   The extent to which the details in a tool effectively characterize the totality of the content that needs to be included.

Contingency table   A table that places data in cells produced by the juncture of two or more categorical variables.

Continuous variable   A term that can take on a wide range of values, such as from 0 to 100, or larger.

Control   The procedure for managing the extraneous influences that could affect the dependent variable.

Control group   Participants in an experiment who provide the baseline for the study, in contrast to the treatment group. Members of the control group do not receive the experimental treatment.

Convenience sampling The process of selecting individuals to be in the sample who are accessible and/or who volunteer; also called accidental sampling.

Convergent validity A type of construct validity.

Correlational coefficient The outcome of the calculation of the relationship between two or more observed scores.

Correlational design Any of a variety of nonexperimental research designs in which the primary independent variable of interest is a quantitative variable.

Corroboration The process of evaluating documents against other documents to establish the consistency within the conclusions provided.

Covert Covered up, hidden. Covert data are collected without the subject having knowledge of the collection of the information.

Criterion The yardstick or benchmark used for predicting the accuracy of test scores.

Criterion-related validity Based on the comparison of the tests being used with some known criterion.

Critique An impartial, analytic, and reasonable appraisal of a research report.

Cross-sectional study A study based on data collected at a solitary moment in time with the intent of concluding tendencies over time.

Cross-validation A method for triangulating qualitative data by confirming the results through some other process.

Cumulative Index to Nursing & Allied Health Literature (CINAHL) A database supplying reliable reporting of the literature associated with nursing and allied health.

Database An organized body of related information arranged for speed of access and retrieval.

Data collection The compilation and assembling of information related to concepts and variables in a reputable manner that facilitates answers for PICOT questions, research questions, and hypotheses leading to establishing outcomes.

Data set The collection of information resulting from a research project.

Data triangulation The employment of multiple data sources and data management procedures to validate qualitative data.

Debriefing An interview conducted with the participants following the initial data analysis, during which aspects of the study are exposed, rationales for the employment of deception are explained, and questions that the participants may have about the results are resolved.

Decision making The cognitive practice of realizing a conclusion or choice.

Deductive reasoning The practice of drawing explicit conclusions from broad tenets.

Demographic variable A term that refers to characteristics of the subjects in the study.

Deontology Ethical theory connected with duties and rights, intrinsic nature or "rightness" of an action itself.

Dependent variable The outcome variable that is alleged to be influenced by one or more independent variables; the presumed outcome of the study.

Descriptive design A research study whose foremost intention is providing the truthful depiction of the distinctiveness of persons, situations, or groups and/or an accurate explanation or representation of the condition of a state of affairs or phenomenon.

Descriptive statistics Statistics that concentrate on recounting, summarizing, or explaining.

Dichotomous variable A characteristic that can be measured only in the sense that it is present or not present; often assigned a number for identification purposes, rather than to represent a quantity.

Directional hypothesis A statement that predicts the path or direction that the relationship between variables will take.

Discrete variable A variable that can take on only a finite number of values, usually restricted to whole numbers.

Discursive prose Summary of material provided in a manner organized by themes or identified trend, not as a summary of different reports.

Editorials Statements of the opinions of an owner, manager, or the like. Weight of the evidence is based on the perceived biases associated with the thoughts and statements.

Effect size The expected strength of the relationship between the research variables; used in the calculation of desired sample size through power analysis.

Element The fundamental component that is chosen from the population.

Eligibility criteria The conditions employed by a researcher to indicate the detailed characteristics of the target population that are used to select participants for a study.

Emic term The point of view provided by the individuals directly involved in a situation.

Empiric Established by inspection, experiment, or practice (data and/or results).

Equivalency reliability A measure of reliability that is calculated in the same manner as the consistency and stability coefficients, except, instead of a single variable over two trials, the test is between two forms of a single test.

Error The difference between a factual score and an observed score.

Ethical theories A collection of ideology and philosophy of right behavior; a system of moral principles and ideals.

Ethics The main beliefs, ideology, and guidelines that facilitate the maintenance of an issue that we appreciate and respect.

Ethnocentrism The practice of evaluating individuals from a diverse culture according to the principles of the evaluator's identifiable culture.

Ethnography A type of qualitative research that conscientiously illustrates the customs of a grouping of individuals.

Ethnohistory An investigation into the cultural history of a group of people.

Etic perspective An appreciation for the scientific consideration of reality from an external viewpoint.

Etic term An explanation of the social world under examination from an outsider's viewpoint.

Evaluation Identification of the significance, advantage, or worth of an object being examined.

Evidence Foundation on which beliefs and proofs are established; a pathway to clear and organized proof on a given topic.

Evidence-based practice (EBP) A process of utilizing confirmed evidence (research and quality improvement), decision making, and nursing expertise to guide the delivery of holistic patient care.

Exclusion criteria Characteristics that, if present, would make persons ineligible for participation in a study, even if they meet all of the other inclusion criteria.

Expedited review A method by which a project is quickly appraised by selected members of the full institutional review board.

Experiment A setting in which a researcher impartially scrutinizes a situation that occurs in a rigorously restricted position, with one or more variables being manipulated while others are held steady.

Experimental control In research, the practice of eradicating the degrees of difference resulting from the extraneous variables.

Experimental design Research in which the independent variable is manipulated, a control group is established, and randomized selection of the participants is employed to select who does and does not receive the treatment or intervention.

Experimental group The participants who receive the experimental treatment or intervention.

Expert opinion Information provided by an individual who is viewed as an authority, based upon a set of criteria related to information applicable and/or significant to a designated problem or situation.

External validity The degree to which the analysis outcomes can be generalized to a specific group of persons, settings, times, outcomes, and treatment variations.

Extraneous variable A variable that confuses the association between the independent and dependent variables; for this reason, it needs to be restricted either within the research design or through statistical procedures.

Face validity The degree to which a research tool correctly reflects what it is purposed to measure.

Field notes Annotations recorded by an observer during qualitative research endeavors.

Focus group A small group of people assembled to participate in a moderator-facilitated discussion geared toward the designated topic being researched.

Focus group interview A dialogue with a group of individuals assembled to respond and converse about a prearranged theme.

Forensic science The study of evidence; the process of utilizing data to formulate judgments and decisions.

Formative evaluation   An appraisal conducted to improve the evaluation process.

Framework   The conceptual foundation of a study; sometimes classified as a theoretic framework, for projects centered on a theory, and as a conceptual framework, for projects with a connection to a definite conceptual model.

Generalizability   The extent to which findings from a study can be extended from a sample of a population to the population at large.

Grounded theory   A general methodology for developing new theory that is grounded in data that are systematically gathered and analyzed.

Hawthorne effect   A change in a dependent variable that occurs as a result of the participants' recognition that they are engaged in a study.

Histogram   A diagram that reveals the frequencies and profile resulting from a quantitative variable.

Historic research   Research that uses a practice of methodically investigating past events or mixtures of events to explain what ensued in an earlier period.

Homogeneity   The extent to which items are similar with regard to a select attribute.

Honesty   Integrity, truthfulness, fairness, sincerity.

Human experimentation   Medical testing performed on human beings with the expectation of gaining new knowledge to improve a situation or manage a health-related problem.

Hypothesis   A prediction or educated guess about the relationships among variables; the recognized proclamation of the researcher's prediction of the affiliation that exists among the variables under investigation.

Hypothesis testing   The division of inferential statistics that focuses on how the sample data confirm or reject a null hypothesis.

Ideas   Thoughts, convictions, and/or principles based upon a potential or actual existing foundation, considered to be individual work.

Impact   The consequence or influence resulting from the use of a logic model.

Inclusion criteria   Characteristics that must be met to be considered for participation in a study; also known as eligibility criteria.

Independent variable   The variable in experimental research that is established as the cause or influence on the dependent variable; it may be identified as the manipulated (treatment) variable.

Inductive reasoning   The practice of reasoning from detailed annotations to more common conceptualizations.

Inferential statistics   The category of statistics focused on moving beyond the immediate data and conjecturing the distinctiveness of the populace established by the samples.

Informed consent   The decision of an individual to participate in a research study based on an understanding of the project's purpose, procedures, risks, benefits, alternative procedures, and limits of confidentiality.

Institutional review board (IRB)   A council of individuals representing an institution who assemble to evaluate the ethical considerations related to proposed and ongoing research studies.

Instrument   A tool that a researcher uses to accumulate information.

Integrative reviews   Summarization of prior research studies on a selected topic with a summation provided as a conclusion.

Interclass reliability   The reliability between two measures that are presented in the data as either variables or trials.

Internal validity   The capacity to conclude that a contributory affiliation exists between two or more variables.

Interrater reliability   The extent of agreement or consistency between two or more scorers, judges, or raters (operating independently) for attributes being measured or observed.

Interval scale   Scale of measurement used in statistical analysis that incorporates both order and magnitude within the description but lacks a defined zero point.

Intervention   The experimental treatment or manipulation employed during a research endeavor.

Interview   A data collection technique in which an interviewer poses questions to the interviewee.

Intraclass reliability   A type of reliability that allows a person to develop a reliability coefficient for more than one variable.

In vitro   Requiring the extraction of physiologic materials from a participant in a research study, frequently via a laboratory analysis.

In vivo   Requiring the use of some apparatus to evaluate one or more elements of a participant in a research study.

Journal club   A group that assembles on a regular basis to discuss and appraise research reports for the purpose of judging the possibility of implementing the findings.

Justice   The standard of decent rightness; agreement with truth, fact, or sensible intention.

k   The magnitude of the sampling interval applied in systematic sampling.

Knowing   Four accepted patterns—empirics, aesthetics, ethical, and personal; process of appreciating the information surrounding a topic; allows for the engagement with the topic from various vantage points.

Level of confidence   The likelihood that a confidence interval to be used for a random sample will contain the population characteristics.

Likert scale   A summated rating scale consisting of a series of items to which respondents are requested to indicate their level of agreement.

Literature review   A rigorous examination of research related to a topic of interest that is documented to categorize a research problem or as the beginning of a research use project.

Logic model   A plan that denotes how an intervention produces distinct consequences using four aspects in a linear cycle: inputs, activities, outputs, and outcomes.

Longitudinal design   A study design in which information is accumulated at various times for use in comparisons.

Manipulation An intervention or treatment initiated in an experimental or quasi-experimental study to assess the independent variable's impact on the dependent variable.

Margin of error One-half of the measurement of a confidence interval.

Maturation Any alteration that happens as a result of time that influences the participant's involvement related to the dependent variable.

Mean The mathematical average of a data set.

Measure of central tendency The distinct numeric value deemed generally predictable for the values of a quantitative variable.

Measure of variability A numeric indicator that exhibits information about the extent of variation present.

Median The 50th percentile.

Medical Literature Analysis and Retrieval System Online (MEDLINE) Leading bibliographic database for retrieval of North American biomedical literature.

Medical Subject Heading (MeSH) A glossary for finding the terms that correctly identify or agree with the search terms or concepts in the MEDLINE database; the controlled vocabulary for MEDLINE.

Memoing Chronicling thoughtful observations about information learned from data collected in a research study.

Meta-analysis A process of quantitatively comparing the results from multiple research studies on a selected subject.

Mixed method research (multimethod research) A type of study in which a researcher uses qualitative research methodology for one phase of the study and quantitative research methodology for another phase of the study.

Mode The most frequently occurring number in a data set.

n Designation used to denote the total number of study participants; the sample size.

Naturalistic observation Surveillance conducted in "real-world" surroundings.

NCNR National Center for Nursing Research.

Nesting A collection of comparable ideas and processes related to the management of research projects.

Network sampling The inclusion of participants in a sample as a result of referrals from individuals already in the sample; also called snowball sampling.

NIH National Institutes of Health.

NINR National Institute of Nursing Research.

Nominal scale A level of measurement that applies symbols, such as numbers, to describe, categorize, or recognize people or objects.

Nondirectional hypothesis A statement that predicts a relationship between variables but not the path or direction of that relationship.

Nonequivalent control group A research sampling method where random selection is not used to determine the membership of the control group.

Nonexperimental design A research study in which data are collected without introducing any treatment, and no random assignment of participants to groups occurs.

Nonprobability sampling A sampling strategy that does not include random selection of elements.

Nonsignificant results The outcome of a statistical test demonstrating that the connection between variables could have transpired as a consequence of chance, at the designated level of significance.

Normal distribution A unimodal, symmetric, bell-shaped distribution of the data analysis for a selected variable.

Norms The written and unwritten regulations that denote acceptable behavior.

Novel data New data collected as part of a research study.

Null hypothesis A prediction or educated guess that no relationship exists between the designated variables.

Objectivity The degree to which two researchers working independently would reach comparable findings or conclusions.

Observation Inconspicuous surveillance of people as they engage in everyday activities.

Observed score The actual score seen and/or printed by the instrument or tool.

Obstacle Something that resists, hampers the forward progress of, or reroutes movement in a certain way or path.

Open-ended question A question that permits the respondent to answer without any restrictions or barriers.

Operational definition The characterization of a concept or variable in terms of the operations or procedures by which it is to be measured for a specific research endeavor.

Opinions Attitudes and viewpoints that do not rest on adequate foundations to be viewed as completely without biases, and represent a person's beliefs, judgments, and/or values concerning a designated subject.

Ordinal scale A rank-order level of measurement.

Outcome validity The capacity to generalize concerning assorted, but interrelated, dependent variables.

Outcomes Results that proceed from an accomplishment or achievement; effects; consequences.

Outputs The work or practice of delivering a result.

Overt Accomplished with full knowledge of the subjects under investigation (referring to data collection).

Patient-oriented research Studies carried out with human subjects where a researcher openly interrelates with the participants.

Phenomenology A type of qualitative research in which the researcher endeavors to comprehend how individuals experience a phenomenon.

PICOT The five components of an evidence-based question: patient population of interest, intervention of interest, comparison of interest, outcome of interest, and time.

Pilot study A miniature edition of a study, or trial run, completed prior to the implementation of the full study.

Population The complete group of individuals (or objects) possessing various characteristics to which a researcher wants to generalize the sample results; sometimes referred to as the universe population or target population.

Population-based research Studies incorporating epidemiology, social and behavioral sciences, public health, quality evaluation, and cost-effectiveness.

Power A level at which the likelihood of rejecting the null hypothesis when it is false is set.

Power analysis A statistical calculation of the number of subjects needed to accurately reject a null hypothesis.

Predictive validity A characteristic based on the time between the collection of the alternative method tests to be validated and the criterion measured. It does not limit the researcher to using the Pearson Product Moment (PPM) to develop a validity coefficient, as a linear or logistic regression can also be used.

Primary data Information and/or data collected and/or observed directly from the project.

Primary sources First-hand testimony to facts, findings, or events; reporting of the research results structured by the individual who conducted the study.

Probability sampling Use of a specific sampling strategy using some form of random selection of elements.

Problem statement A declaration of the research problem, occasionally verbalized in the form of a research question.

Purposive sampling A nonprobability sampling process in which the researcher chooses study participants based on personal decisions about which individuals would be most representative of the general population; also identified as judgmental sampling.

Qualitative analysis Examination and investigation using subjective reasoning established on nonquantifiable data.

Qualitative design The analysis of phenomena, characteristically in a comprehensive and holistic manner, through the compilation of abundant narrative notes based on an adaptable research model.

Qualitative research question An inquisitive sentence that poses a query about a selected practice, concern, or phenomenon to be investigated.

Qualitative researcher A researcher who concentrates on investigation or theory creation using qualitative information.

Quality assurance An orderly practice of examining a product or service to determine if it meets precise requirements.

Quality improvement A process utilized to investigate a policy, procedure, or protocol to determine if it addresses an aspect identified through an evidence-based practice process, and works to validate current practice.

Quantitative analysis The numeric representation and manipulation of observations using statistical techniques for the express purpose of describing and explaining the outcomes of research as they pertain to the hypothesis.

Quantitative design   The scrutinizing of a phenomenon that contributes to the collection of meticulous measurement and quantification, while using a painstaking and manipulative strategy.

Quantitative research question   A question that asks about the affiliation that exists between two or more variables.

Quasi-experimental design   An experimental research design in which individuals are not randomly assigned to groups, but rather the researcher manipulates the independent variable and implements specific controls to augment the internal validity of the outcome.

Questionnaire   A self-report data collection tool completed by research participants.

Quota sampling   A nonrandom selection of participants by which the researcher identifies specific properties and/or characteristics that are used to establish the sample and determines sample size for the groups to increase their representativeness.

Random assignment (randomization)   A selection system that creates assignments in a manner that augments the probability that the comparison groups will be equivalent on all extraneous variables.

Random sampling   Selection of a sample such that every member of a population has an equal possibility of being included in the sample.

Random selection   Picking a group of individuals from a population where every member of the population has an equal chance of being included in the sample.

Range   The variation between the uppermost and lowest numbers in a data set.

Ranking   The arranging of responses into ascending or descending sequence.

Ratio scale   A level of measurement that has a true zero position, while also having the characteristics of the nominal (labeling), ordinal (rank ordering), and interval (equal distance) scales.

Receiver operand characteristics   A graphical chart illustrating the functioning of data points.

Reference librarian   An information professional educated and qualified in library and information science, particularly in the area of collection of specialized or technical information or materials.

Reliability   The extent to which a tool measures the attribute it is intended to evaluate; a measure of consistency.

Replication   The premeditated duplication of research procedures in a second examination with the intent of determining whether previous outcomes can be duplicated.

Representative sample   A sample that bears a resemblance to the target population.

Research   A methodical examination that uses regimented techniques to resolve questions or decipher dilemmas.

Research article   Any published manuscript describing the results of a research project.

Research design The inclusive design for addressing a research question that incorporates the outline, plan, or strategy used to enhance the integrity of the study.

Research ethics A series of principles used to guide and aid researchers in determining the most important goals for reconciling contradictory principles.

Research hypothesis A testable statement that predicts the relationship between two or more variables in a population of interest.

Research problem An unfathomable, bewildering, or inconsistent state that can be explored through regimented investigation.

Research process Methodical process of conducting exploration and examination of an identified question.

Research proposal A written text that recapitulates the preceding literature, distinguishes the research topic to be resolved, and stipulates the processes that will be followed to answer the research questions.

Research question A statement of the particular inquiry the researcher desires to resolve through a research endeavor.

Research utilization The application of selected facets of a scientific analysis through a process unconnected to the fundamental research.

Researcher bias An intentional or unintentional manipulation of a study so that it achieves results consistent with what the researcher intends to uncover.

Respect The process of showing honor or appreciation; motivation to demonstrate thoughtfulness or gratitude.

Response rate The proportion of individuals in a sample who participate in a research project.

Retrospective question A question that asks individuals to remember something from a previous time.

Retrospective research The analysis of existing data to address the question to be answered.

Rigor Firmness or precision.

Root cause analysis An approach for recognizing aspects involved in understanding what impacted the development of a harmful outcome in order to detect behaviors and/or actions useful in preventing recurrence of similar harmful outcomes.

Sample A division of a population chosen to participate in a study.

Sample size The number of individuals included in a sample; denoted by n.

Sampling The practice of extracting a designated group from a population.

Sampling bias Misrepresentations that occur when a sample is not representative of the target population from which the group was extracted.

Sampling error The variation between a sample statistic and a population parameter.

Sampling interval The total number within the target population divided by the preferred sample size; denoted by k.

Sampling plan The plan for selection of the study participants proposed prior to the beginning of the study; it specifies the eligibility criteria, the sample selection process, and, in the case of quantitative studies, the number of subjects to be used.

Saturation In qualitative research, the point at which sufficient data have been accumulated for all new data to produce redundant information.

Scientific merit The extent to which an inquiry is methodologically and theoretically complete.

Search engine A web-based tool providing access to needed data. It takes a person to the information and helps to retrieve the information in a format that is accessible visually on screen at an on-site library or in downloadable written/readable format.

Secondary data (secondary analysis) Data initially accumulated by various persons for a purpose other than the present research.

Secondary source Second-hand explanation of proceedings or facts; explanation of a study or studies organized by someone other than the primary researcher.

Sensitivity Frequency that a test will measure a "true" positive results when calculated.

Sentinel event Unanticipated episode resulting in a death or grave physical or psychological injury, or the risk thereof.

Sequential The following of one item after another item.

Sequential research A research process combining cross-sectional and longitudinal projects.

Significance level The boundary used by the researcher to denote the point at which the null hypothesis will be rejected; also known as the alpha level.

Simple hypothesis A statement that specifies the relationship between two variables.

Simple random sampling A population group extracted by a formula in which each member of the population has an equivalent possibility of being chosen.

Snowball sampling A type of sampling in which every research contributor is asked to recommend additional prospective research participants; also referred to as network sampling.

Specificity Determination of the capability of a test to establish a "true" negative result.

Stability The determination of the results from trials and/or test over a set time period which extends greater than 48 hours.

Standard error of measurement A statistic that reflects the fluctuation of the observed score due to the error score.

Statistical Package for the Social Sciences (SPSS) A computer program used for statistical analysis; the initial program was made available in 1968.

Statistical significance An idiom demonstrating that it is improbable that the results achieved in an examination of sample data would have been produced by luck at a particular level of probability.

Stratified random sampling A random selection of study participants from two or more levels of the population.

Subject A person who supplies information in a study. This term is predominantly used in quantitative research studies.

Systematic review A literature review directed by a research question that strives to recognize, evaluate, and integrate relevant research evidence.

Systematic random sampling The selection of research study participants such that each kth individual (or facet) in a sampling frame is selected.

Table of random numbers An inventory of numbers that are generated in a random sequence.

Target population The total population to whom the research outcomes are to be generalized.

Teleology The use of final intention or design as a method of explaining phenomena within an ethical situation.

Test A device used to determine the selected intelligence, talents, behaviors, health status, or cognitive endeavor that is under investigation.

Test–retest reliability A calculation of the uniformity of scores over time.

Theoretical sampling The qualitative research process of selecting new study participants based on emerging findings from previous data collection and analysis; followed until the point of data saturation.

Theory A rationalization that challenges how a phenomenon functions and why it functions as it does; a generalization or series of generalizations employed methodically to clarify certain phenomena.

Time-dimensional design A research tactic employing the investigation into the implications of patterns of change, growth, or trends across time.

Translational research Using both basic and applied research findings to ensure that best practices are incorporated within a population.

Triangulation The application of various methods to accumulate and decipher facts about a phenomenon, and then merge those data to create a precise portrayal of realism.

Trustworthiness An expression used in the appraisal of qualitative data; it is measured based on the decisive factors of credibility, transferability, dependability, and confirmability.

t-test Statistical method used to determine the differences between the means of two groups.

Type I error Discarding a true null hypothesis.

Type II error Failing to discard a false null hypothesis.

Validity The extent to which a research tool measures what it is proposed to measure.

Variable A characteristic of a person or entity that fluctuates.

Vulnerable human beings Distinct groups of individuals whose rights require particular protection because of their inability to grant informed consent or because their state of affairs consigns them to higher-than-average risk of adverse effects from a proposed treatment or intervention.

Index

Note: Page numbers with f and t indicate figures and tables respectively.